THE NINETEENTH-CENTURY NOVEL
A CRITICAL READER

The Nineteenth-Century Novel

The Nineteenth-Century Novel series provides detailed analyses of twelve major realist and non-realist novels, which span the course of the century, together with an indispensable collection of important critical essays. The series seeks to understand the part the novel played in reflecting, dissecting and constructing nineteenth-century culture and concentrates on the rich and diverse experimentation characteristic of the period.

The series comprises:

The Nineteenth-Century Novel: Realisms, edited by Delia da Sousa Correa, London: Routledge in association with The Open University

The Nineteenth-Century Novel: Identities, edited by Dennis Walder, London: Routledge in association with The Open University

The Nineteenth-Century Novel: A Critical Reader, edited by Stephen Regan, London: Routledge in association with The Open University

THE NINETEENTH-CENTURY NOVEL
A CRITICAL READER

edited by

Stephen Regan

London and New York

Published by Routledge
11 New Fetter Lane
London EC4P 4EE

Written and produced by the Open University
Walton Hall
Milton Keynes MK7 6AA

Simultaneously published in the USA and Canada by Routledge
29 West 35th Street
New York, NY 10001

First Published in 2001

Typeset by RefineCatch Limited, Bungay, Suffolk
Printed and bound in Great Britain by TJ International Ltd, Padstow, Cornwall.

A catalogue record for this book is available from the British Library

ISBN 0–415–23828–5

This text forms part of an Open University course AA316 *The Nineteenth-Century Novel*. Details of this and other Open University courses can be obtained from the Course Reservations Centre, PO Box 724, the Open University, Milton Keynes MK7 6ZS, United Kingdom: tel. + 44 (0)1908 653231.

For availability of this or other course components, contact Open University Worldwide Ltd, The Berrill Building, Walton Hall, Milton Keynes MK7 6AA, United Kingdom: tel. + 44 (0)1908 858585, fax + 44 (0)1908 858787, e-mail ouwenq@open.ac.uk

Alternatively, much useful course information can be obtained from the Open University's website: http:www.open.ac.uk

1.1

009766B/aa316book1

CONTENTS

ACKNOWLEDGEMENTS

Every effort has been made to obtain permission to reprint all the extracts included. Persons entitled to fees for any extract reprinted here are invited to apply in writing to the publishers. Permission given by the authors and copyright holders for the following extracts is gratefully acknowledged: Marilyn Butler, extract from *Jane Austen and the War of Ideas* (1975) by permission of Oxford University Press, © Oxford University Press 1975. Marilyn Butler, from the Introduction to *Northanger Abbey* (Penguin Classics 1995) by permission of Penguin Books, © Marilyn Butler 1995. Isobel Armstrong, from *Penguin Critical Studies: Mansfield Park* (Penguin Books 1988) by permission of Penguin Books, © Isobel Armstrong 1988. Claudia L. Johnson, from *Jane Austen: Women, Politics and the Novel* (University of Chicago Press 1988) by permission of the author and University of Chicago Press. Mary Poovey, from *Uneven Developments* (University of Chicago Press 1989) by permission of the author and University of Chicago Press. Robert B. Heilman, 'Charlotte Brontë's "New" Gothic', from *From Austen to Conrad*, ed. R.C. Rathburn and M. Steinmann (University of Minnesota Press 1958) by permission of the author. Gayatri Chakravorty Spivak, '*Jane Eyre*: A Critique of Imperialism', from *Critical Enquiry* 12 (Autumn 1985) by permission of the author. Susan L. Meyer, 'Colonialism and the Figurative Strategy of *Jane Eyre*', from *Victorian Studies* (Winter 1990) by permission of Indiana University Press.

Raymond Williams, by permission of Merryn Williams and the Raymond Williams Estate.

Catherine Waters, 'Ambiguous Intimacy: Brother and Sister Relationships in *Dombey and Son*', from *The Dickensian* 44 (1988) by permission of the author. Suvendrini Perera, 'Wholesale, Retail and for Exportation: Empire and the Family Business in *Dombey and Son*' from *Victorian Studies* 33 (1990) by permission of Indiana University Press. Sally Shuttleworth, from *George Eliot and*

Nineteenth-Century Science (Cambridge University Press 1984) by permission of the author and Cambridge University Press. Gillian Beer, from *Darwin's Plots: Evolutionary Narrative in Darwin, George Eliot and Nineteenth-Century Fiction* (Routledge 1983) by permission of Routledge, Taylor and Francis Books. David Carroll, from *George Eliot and the Conflict of Interpretations* (Cambridge University Press 1992) by permission of the author and Cambridge University Press. Elizabeth Deeds Ermarth, 'George Eliot and the World as Language', from *George Eliot and Europe*, ed. John Rignall (Scholar Press 1997) by permission of the author. Richard C. Carpenter, 'The Mirror and the Sword: Imagery in *Far From the Madding Crowd*', from *Nineteenth Century Fiction* 18, © 1964 by The Regents of the University of California by permission of the author and University of California Press. Judith Bryant Wittenberg, 'Angles of Vision and Questions of Gender in *Far From the Madding Crowd*', from *The Centennial Review* 30 (1986) by permission of the author. Raymond Williams, 'Thomas Hardy', from *The English Novel from Dickens to Lawrence* (Chatto and Windus 1970) by permission of the Random House Archive. Georg Lukács, 'The Zola Centenary', from *Studies in European Realism* (Merlin Press 1950) by permission of Merlin Press. Georg Lukács, 'Narrate or Describe?', from *Writer and Critic*, trans. A. Khan (Merlin Press 1970) by permission of Merlin Press. Henri Mitterand, 'Ideology and Myth: *Germinal* and the Fantasies of Revolt', from *Critical Essays on Émile Zola* (G.K. Hall & Co. 1986) by permission of the Gale Group. Elisabeth Bronfen, from *Over Her Dead Body: Death, Femininity and the Aesthetic* (Manchester University Press, Manchester, UK, 1992) by permission of Manchester University Press. Tony Tanner, 'Fetishism – Castles of Cake, Pellets from the Seraglio, the Damascened Rifle', from *Adultery in the Novel: Contract and Transgression*, pp. 284–91, © 1981 by Johns Hopkins University Press. Jenny Bourne Taylor, from *In the Secret Theatre of Home* (Routledge 1988) by permission of Routledge, Taylor and Francis Books.

D.A. Miller, '*Cage aux Folles*: Sensation and Gender in Wilkie Collins's *The Woman in White*', from *The Nineteenth-Century British Novel*, ed. Jeremy Hawthorn (Arnold 1986) by permission of Arnold. Eugenia C. DeLamotte, from *Perils of the Night: A Feminist Study of Nineteenth-Century Gothic*, © 1990 by Oxford University Press, Inc by permission of Oxford University Press, Inc. Barbara Hardy, from *Henry James: The Later Novels* (Northcote House 1996) by permission of Northcote House. Stephen D. Arata, 'The Occidental Tourist: *Dracula* and the Anxiety of Reverse Colonization', from *Victorian Studies* (Summer 1990) by permission of Indiana University Press. Phyllis A. Roth, 'Suddenly Sexual Women in Bram Stoker's *Dracula*,' from *Literature and Psychology* 27 (1977) by permission of *Literature and Psychology*. Helen Taylor, from *Gender, Race and Region in the Writings of Grace King, Ruth McEnery*

Stuart and Kate Chopin, © 1989 by Louisiana State University Press by permission of Louisiana State University Press. Bert Bender, 'The Teeth of Desire: *The Awakening* and the *Descent of Man*,' from *American Literature* 63.3 (September 1991), © 1991 by Duke University Press. All Rights Reserved. Reprinted with permission of Duke University Press. Elizabeth Ammons, from *Conflicting Stories: American Women Writers at the Turn into the Twentieth Century*, © 1992 by Oxford University Press, Inc by permission of Oxford University Press, Inc.

Anne Goodwyn Jones, from *Tomorrow is Another Day: The Woman Writer in the South 1859–1936*, © 1981 by Louisiana State University Press. Reprinted by permission of Louisiana State University Press. Robert Hampson, 'Conrad and the Idea of Empire', from *L'Époque Conradienne* (1989) by permission of the author and *L'Époque Conradienne*. Edward Said, from *Culture and Imperialism*, © 1993 by Edward W. Said. Reprinted by permission of Alfred A. Knopf, a Division of Random House Inc and the Wylie Agency (UK) Ltd.

PREFACE

This *Critical Reader* has a venerable predecessor: an anthology of writings on the nineteenth-century novel, edited by Arnold Kettle in 1972 and reprinted several times over the decade that followed. Like *The Nineteenth-Century Novel: Critical Essays and Documents*, this volume has been designed with an Open University course in mind. It is worth repeating the prefatory remark of that earlier book: that all anthologies involve a good deal of arbitrariness, but there is something to be said for one in which the selection of items has at least some logic, or even some built-in limitation to it. The current Open University course, 'The Nineteenth-Century Novel,' concentrates on twelve novels published between 1818 and 1902: *Northanger Abbey*, *Jane Eyre*, *Dombey and Son*, *Middlemarch*, *Far from the Madding Crowd*, *Germinal*, *Madame Bovary*, *The Woman in White*, *The Portrait of a Lady*, *Dracula*, *The Awakening* and *Heart of Darkness*.

The aim of this anthology is to make available to Open University students supporting material which is referred to and discussed in the teaching material provided for the course. Other readers of nineteenth-century novels will, I am sure, find much of interest and value in this particular selection of critical readings. An important consideration was to present to readers a variety of critical perspectives, combining some prominent and influential essays from the nineteenth century with some of the most incisive, original and accessible essays from the past few decades, mainly from the 1980s and 1990s. The volume is wide-ranging and eclectic in its selection of theoretical approaches to nineteenth-century fiction, and students will find here representative examples of formalism, Marxism, feminism, psychoanalysis, deconstruction, reader-response criticism, genre criticism and post-colonial theory.

Most Open University course books are the product of sustained collaborative effort, and this one is no exception. I should like to thank my colleagues on 'The Nineteenth-Century Novel' course team for their thoughtful contributions to the book. I owe a great debt of thanks to Julie Dickens, who has worked closely with me on every aspect of the book's production. I am also grateful to Hazel Coleman and Alan Finch, our course editors at the Open University, and to Ruth Bourne, Talia Rodgers, Rosie Waters and Amelia La Fuente at Routledge. For help and advice of various kinds, I wish to thank Sue Asbee, Carolyn Burdett, David Grylls, Sally Ledger, Peter Widdowson and Merryn Williams. The translation from Nietzsche was generously undertaken by Nicolette David and her students in the Department of German at Birkbeck College, University of London: Maren Freudenberg, Marina Radovic, Peter O'Rourke, Russell Sharpe and especially Antonia Brotchie and Michael Trevor.

Stephen Regan

INTRODUCTION

To read a selection of nineteenth-century essays on fiction alongside the critical opinions of a later century is to realise at once the vast and strangely troubling distance between two worlds of intellectual endeavour. Beyond this dramatic and immediate realisation of difference, however, we can begin to discern some surprising continuities and persistent concerns about the nature and purpose of novel writing. It is not just a matter of establishing a marker between 'then' and 'now'. The practice of criticism is so evidently a process: ideas about literature and its social significance are continually being shaped and reshaped, and are always open to debate. Nor is it a matter of observing some simple teleology of criticism, in which the best and most enlightened ideas endure while others wither away. Living in the early years of a new century is no guarantee of wisdom, but it does provide a convenient perspective from which to consider the long and complex reception history of nineteenth-century fiction, and to challenge any easy or settled distinction between 'Victorian' and 'modern' criticism.

The earliest extract in this Reader, from Clara Reeve's *Progress of Romance*, was written in the 1780s. To read it now is to return to a time when 'the novel' still had an air of novelty about it, and when 'realism' was only just beginning to acquire a set of conventions and descriptions. Reeve's series of 'evening conversations' about the practice of writing are largely preoccupied with defining literary forms such as the epic and the romance, and with distinguishing between these kinds of writing and the fictional enterprise that had only recently been termed 'the novel'. If romance is a type of 'heroic fable', the novel is 'a picture of real life and manners; and of the times in which it is written' (p. 14). This definition imparts a now familiar suggestion that the novel is capable of conveying a plausible image of social behaviour and historical events. What constitutes 'a picture', how that picture is composed, and with what degrees of accuracy or invention it 'represents' the world, will continue to be matters of debate. Reeve's interest in typology and genre, in plausibility and representation, and also in questions of morality and censorship, are not simply superseded by later criticism. If later critics acquired a new and more extensive vocabulary for investigating the nature of fiction, they did not altogether abandon the claims and enquiries of their predecessors.

Sir Walter Scott carefully distinguishes between the romance, 'the interests of which turn upon marvellous and uncommon incidents', and the novel, in which 'events are accommodated to the ordinary train of human events, and the modern state of society'. His caveat that there are, of course, 'compositions which it is difficult to assign precisely or exclusively to the one class or the other' (p. 22) seems entirely reasonable according to modern critical standards. Indeed, much of the later critical discussion in this volume, focusing on novels such as *Northanger Abbey*, Jane Eyre and *The Portrait of a Lady*, is concerned precisely with the blending and blurring of fictional modes, and with the persistence of romantic and Gothic elements in nineteenth-century fiction. Very few, if any, of the novels represented here might be said to neglect those essential constituents – the marvellous and the uncommon – which Scott sees as characteristic of romance.

Several essays in Part I of the Reader are concerned with particular novels and novelists, rather than with general statements and definitions. We can see the critical reputations of certain books and authors in the making, with Dickens providing an excellent example. Even though we might now read *Dombey and Son* with purportedly new insights – to do with gender or colonial expansion, for instance – there is nevertheless a sense of freshness and abiding relevance in what critics such as Hippolyte Taine have to say about the elements of grotesquerie, extravagance and pathos in the works of Dickens. We can turn to Henry James, a novelist testing his own critical assumptions in reviews of novels by his contemporaries, and we can find there a set of attitudes and ideas that have persisted in novel criticism for over a century. What James has to say about *Middlemarch* and *Far from the Madding Crowd* continues to exert enormous influence in critical assessment of the work of George Eliot and Thomas Hardy.

Nineteenth-century novel criticism was never narrowly preoccupied with authors and texts. If novels dealt with 'the modern state of society' as Scott claimed, then it followed that criticism, too, had a duty to reflect on social and political realities, and on the adequacy of fictional representations of 'real life'. What emerges very valuably from the essays included here is the extent to which early novel criticism was coterminous with other modes of cultural and political criticism. Nineteenth-century literary criticism is clearly in dialogue with contemporary writings on science, religion, sociology, philosophy and politics, and the range and diversity of its interests are immense. This large intellectual ambit is nowhere better seen than in George Eliot's remarkable essay, 'The Natural History of German Life' (1856). Eliot, like many later critics, gives considerable emphasis to the importance of social class in works of fiction: 'our social novels profess to represent the people as they are, and the unreality of their representations is a grave evil' (p. 29). Her essay argues that art and social policy alike require a special study of 'the people as they are', but this radical conviction is muted by her otherwise conservative, organicist view of social change. The roots of social order must 'remain undisturbed while the process of development is going on' (p. 34). Eliot nevertheless provides a salutary reminder that the sociology of art and literature was not the sinister invention of Marxist critics at Essex University in the 1970s.

George Henry Lewes, with whom Eliot lived for nearly twenty-five years, shows a similar concern for the truthful representation of 'the people': 'Either give us true peasants, or leave them untouched . . . either keep your people silent, or make them speak the idiom of their class' (p. 38). Lewes offers a series of subtle discriminations between Art and Reality, Realism and Idealism, insisting all along that 'Art is a representation of reality' which 'must necessarily be limited by the nature of its medium' (p. 37). His shrewd and discerning remarks about the nature of fiction ought to dispel any casual supposition that nineteenth-century notions of realism were in any sense naive or limited. By 1860, the status of the novel as the dominant literary form of its time was assured, and criticism of the novel had also achieved widespread recognition and popularity. David Masson's *British Novelists and their Styles* (1859) can be regarded as an indication of these trends, being the first full-length critical appraisal of British fiction. At the same time, this growing self-confidence concealed the doubts and uncertainties that continued to trouble writers and critics of fiction alike, especially where the function of realism was concerned. As George Levine argues, nineteenth-century realism was not 'a solidly self-satisfied vision based on a misguided objectivity and faith in representation', but a highly self-conscious attempt to render experiences and events in words (Levine, 1981, p. 20).

While it is clearly important to emphasise some degree of congruence between nineteenth-century and twentieth-century critical opinions, including sophisticated doubts about the very nature of realism, we also need to register some of the seismic shifts that rocked Victorian society in its middle years and profoundly affected its cultural and artistic life. Criticism in the 1860s, especially, shows the powerful impact of new models of scientific enquiry. Darwinian notions of evolution have begun to permeate social and cultural theory, unfixing settled habits of belief, and transformations in philosophy, especially epistemology, have brought about a sharply sceptical spirit in criticism. Walter Pater's ruminations on the modern mind in his 1866 essay on Samuel Taylor Coleridge provide a startling instance of this radically altered disposition: 'To the modern spirit nothing is, or can be rightly known, except relatively and under conditions . . . Hard and abstract moralities are yielding to a more exact estimate of the subtlety and complexity of our life' (p. 49). Pater speaks for so many nineteenth-century novelists – Eliot, Hardy, James and Conrad among them – when he acknowledges 'a world of fine gradations and subtly linked conditions, shifting intricately as we ourselves change' (p. 49).

What Pater recognises as the relative spirit is evident, too, in Friedrich Nietzsche's provocative essay of the same year, 'On Truth and Lying in an Extra-Moral Sense'. Here, truth is but a figure of speech, an illusion we are so accustomed to living with that we have forgotten it is *only* an illusion. Since realism is a convention that changes according to the way in which each culture defines 'reality' and 'truth', it is hardly surprising that the 1860s should have witnessed a severe crisis of representation, and that new, potentially disturbing fictional types, such as the novel of sensation, should have exerted such a strong appeal. The popularity of the novel of sensation (as well as the fear and distrust it prompted) is clearly evinced in the essays by Margaret Oliphant and Henry Mansel, both published in 1862. Oliphant explicitly links the novel of sensation with ideas and values in 'a changed world' (p. 39), though her explanation of its advent has more to do with her fears of democracy (especially in France and America) than with any philosophical scruples. Her recoil from 'shock' and 'violence' in the novel of sensation needs to be understood in relation to the revolutionary tremors throughout Europe in 1848. Pater's relative spirit finds a political corollary in Oliphant's fearful perception that 'everything is legitimate, natural and possible' (p. 42).

E.S. Dallas acknowledges the emergence of the novel of sensation in *The Gay Science* (1866), defining it as a form in which considerations of plot take precedence over those of character, but his main interest is clearly in the mysterious workings of human psychology, in what he calls 'the hidden soul' (p. 55). His stirring account of 'that region of the mind that stretches out of consciousness' (p. 55) provides a fascinating anticipation of Freud. While sharing some of Pater's epistemological concerns, Dallas draws a sharp distinction between the unconscious realm of art and the conscious domain of scientific knowledge.

Dallas is one of the earliest critics to write about 'the art of fiction' (p. 60), a term that is taken up and used repeatedly in the debate initiated by Walter Besant and Henry James in the 1880s. Although disagreements are rife, the terms in which 'the art of fiction' is discussed at this time suggest a growing consensus about the status and prestige of the novel among the other 'fine arts'. Joseph Conrad's vivid account of 'the shape and ring of sentences' (p. 119) is an eloquent testimony to this growing emphasis on the formal properties of fiction. James politely eschews the call from Besant for rules and regulations to govern the art of fiction, yet his own critical practice (including the essays printed here, on Eliot, Hardy and Flaubert) repeatedly draws attention to the primacy of form. Much of the debate in the 1880s and early 1890s is generated by the impact of French naturalism, and the essays by Robert Louis Stevenson and Thomas Hardy in this volume both take a stance against the allegedly excessive attention to detail in the writings of Émile Zola and his associates. Hardy's 1891 essay, 'The Science of Fiction' (an essay that deserves to be better known), is one of the strongest statements against mere 'copyism' in nineteenth-century fiction. Its sentiments appear at times to be firmly anti-realist, though (as Peter Widdowson has pointed out), Hardy's views about the transfiguring potential of art resemble those of Guy de Maupassant: 'The realist, if he is an artist, will seek to give us not a banal photographic representation of life, but a vision that is fuller, more vivid and more compellingly truthful than even reality itself' (quoted in Allott, 1959, pp. 29–30; Widdowson, 1997, p. 420).

The great value of these essays by Conrad, James, Stevenson and Hardy is that they confirm (should we ever need such confirmation) that nineteenth-century novelists were highly self-conscious practitioners, acutely aware of the artificiality of their own stylistic devices and narrative conventions. Well before the impact of modern critical theory, these writers identified and articulated 'the problem of the correspondence between the literary work and the reality which it imitates' (Watt, 1957, p. 11). As Barbara Hardy points out in her essay in Part II, there are good reasons for considering Henry James as the founder of modern criticism of the novel. James provides us with further proof of how difficult it is to distinguish with any certitude between 'late Victorian' and 'early modern' thinking about the art of fiction.

In that difficult transition between the death of the old century and the birth of the new, another formidable and fertile thinker has equal claim on our attention. Sigmund Freud's *Interpretation of Dreams*, by his own admission the great foundational work of his career, was itself a strange transitional phenomenon, first printed in 1899, though dated 1900 by its publisher. It became the biggest non-fiction bestseller of the twentieth century. The book's enduring popularity and fascination have much to do with the fundamental desire to discover meaning in dreams, to give some semblance of narrative coherence to the mind's assorted driftings. As John Forrester has recently suggested, the book retained its appeal, despite attacks on the scientific reputation of psychoanalysis, largely because Freud 'was always an artist . . . mistakenly though calculatingly dressed up as a scientist' (Forrester, 2000, p. 11). *The Interpretation of Dreams* coincided with a widespread critical investigation into the processes of creation. As well as providing a plausible link between dreams and imagination, the book also prompted new thematic and structural developments in literature, painting and film. As Forrester remarks, 'Freud's exploration of the dream-work and its relation to the persistence, vivacity and poignancy of our scattered memories from childhood has been the model for countless artists this century' (Forrester, 2000, p. 12).

Several essays in Part II demonstrate how powerful and persistent Freud's influence has been. Richard C. Carpenter's essay on *Far from the Madding*

Crowd is a good starting-place for readers interested in the application of Freudian psychoanalysis to literary texts. At a rudimentary level, it draws attention to the emotional disturbances caused by repressed desire, and it emphasises the prevalent use of phallic imagery in Hardy's novel. Judith Bryant Wittenberg also turns to psychoanalysis as a way of understanding desire and sexual awakening in Hardy's novel, but she supplements her Freudian reading with an extended analysis of 'the male gaze', drawing resourcefully on a popular dimension of feminist criticism in the 1980s. Freud is powerfully at play in the two essays on *Madame Bovary* by Tony Tanner and Elisabeth Bronfen. Tanner finds significant parallels between Freud's diagnosis of fetishism and Karl Marx's theory of commodification, while Bronfen extends a basic Freudian analysis of repression with the help of the French psychoanalyst, Jacques Lacan. Psychoanalysis also features prominently in an essay on *Dombey and Son* by Catherine Waters, and it provides the basis for Phyllis Roth's discussion of vampirism in her essay on *Dracula*.

For ease of reference, the essays in Part II are organised according to the twelve novels under discussion. There are, however, alternative ways of approaching these essays. As we have seen, particular groups of essays serve to illustrate some of the major theoretical interests in modern criticism of the nineteenth-century novel, including feminism and psychoanalysis. The essays are diverse and eclectic in their methods of analysis and interpretation. Some are staunchly formalist and confine their investigations to issues of style and technique, while others draw extensively on Marxist historicism and cultural materialism, structural linguistics, reader-response criticism and post-colonial theory. Another way of using this volume is to approach the essays chronologically, observing in this particular selection of materials a highly compressed but nevertheless revealing history of novel criticism.

The earliest essays in the second half are the two pieces on Zola by George Lukács, written in 1936 and 1940. While other Marxist critics were turning their attention to the progressive elements in modernist experimentation, Lukács retained a firm belief in the efficacy of social realism and its capacity for rendering a comprehensive vision of social and historical change. For Lukács, the naturalist writer became a passive spectator, too remote from the great struggles of the age and ultimately lacking insight and conviction. The distrust and hostility with which Lukács writes about the naturalist method resurfaces in his later critique of modernist experiment in *The Meaning of Contemporary Realism* (1963). Raymond Williams, writing on Dickens and Hardy in 1970, sedulously avoids that earlier Marxist insistence on social realism and its apprehension of the 'totality' of social relations. Even so, Williams finds in nineteenth-century fiction the unmistakable signs of social upheaval, manifest in new forms of consciousness and experience that novels are capable of registering. At this stage in his career, Williams had not fully formulated the ideas and methods that came to be known as cultural materialism, but his emphasis on class relations and economic disparities in both essays is in keeping with that later development in his work.

Historicist or materialist criticism is well represented here, especially in the essays by Isobel Armstrong, Marilyn Butler and John Lucas, all of which are intent on exploring the politics (including the sexual politics) of nineteenth-century fiction. A different kind of historical enquiry is at work in the essays on *Middlemarch* by Gillian Beer and Sally Shuttleworth. Here, the intention is not so much to interrogate the politics of the text as to establish a set of relations between the work of fiction and the broad intellectual milieu to which it belongs. The method in these essays involves a recognition of the extent to which *Middlemarch* draws upon and contributes to the history of ideas, especially in the realm of nineteenth-century science.

Most of the essays in this volume were written in the 1980s and 1990s, and they show the continuing impact on literary scholarship of new methodologies derived from structural linguistics, especially from the writings of French theorists such as Roland Barthes and Jacques Derrida. The crucial turn from structuralism to post-structuralism can be illustrated through a brief comparison of Henri Mitterand's approach to *Germinal* and Elizabeth Deeds Ermarth's discussion of *Middlemarch*. Mitterand offers a classic structuralist analysis of Zola's novel, seeking out the codes and conventions which govern the organization of the text, but he also shows how this method of exposing the deep underlying structures of a literary work can be fruitfully combined with a Marxist apprehension of its ideological significance. Where structuralist readings of this kind tended to show how literary texts and other cultural artefacts produced an array of meanings, the post-structuralist criticism that emerged from it (and in some ways opposed it) was much more intent on denying the possibility of any stable or coherent meaning in works of literature.

Although the method of deconstruction associated with post-structuralist criticism was widely misunderstood and misapplied, it was strongly identified as being anti-referential or anti-representational, and therefore inimical to realism. Critics hostile to post-structuralism claimed that deconstruction had pushed literary criticism into an intellectual cul-de-sac, where language was ultimately unable to imitate or represent anything other than itself. Realist texts like *Middlemarch* were an obvious target for some of the over-zealous practitioners of deconstruction, and so, too, were those earlier readings of nineteenth-century fiction that had so earnestly emphasised the importance of unity and formal coherence in the great novels of the time. The emphasis now was on the indeterminacy and instability of the text.

One of the consequences of the intense post-structuralist debate about meaning and representation was a spirited defence of realism on the part of critics like George Levine. In *The Realistic Imagination: English Fiction from*

Frankenstein to Lady Chatterley, Levine argues that 'the great novelists of the nineteenth century were never so naïve about narrative conventions or the problems of representation as later realists or modern critics have suggested'. He goes on to claim that while Victorian novelists 'struggled to make contact with the world out there', they were never simply 'deluded into believing that they were in fact offering an unmediated reality' (Levine, 1981, pp. 7–8). Levine's book was important, not least because it helped to redeem nineteenth-century fiction from charges of naïve realism (a simple faith in the correspondence between words and what they purport to describe), and showed instead a high degree of self-consciousness in narrative techniques and conventions.

In a similar vein, Elizabeth Deeds Ermarth argues that George Eliot's fiction contains its own sophisticated doubts about knowledge, truth and representation, in some ways anticipating post-structuralist theory, but also clearly demarcated from it. David Carroll likewise proposes that *Middlemarch*, far from suggesting that meanings can be securely grasped and communicated, is deeply riven with crises of interpretation. What began to emerge in the 1980s and 1990s, then, as these essays testify, was a sense of realism, not as a simple convention to do with imitation or reflection, but as an impulse or process altogether more complex and protean than had earlier been suggested. Some of the most intellectually engaging criticism on nineteenth-century fiction argues strenuously that novels like *Middlemarch*, *Far from the Madding Crowd* and *Dombey and Son* are both responsive to social and historical actualities *and* acutely concerned with their own fictive devices and manoeuvres. Marilyn Butler's essay on *Northanger Abbey* is exemplary in this respect: it shows the extent to which the novel is simultaneously preoccupied with its own artifice *and* intensely curious about prevailing social and economic trends.

A renewed interest in the complexities of realist fiction prompted further work on form and genre, especially on Gothic conventions and the novel of sensation. A fascination with the Gothic can be found in literary criticism considerably earlier than the 1980s (see, for instance, Robert B. Heilman's 1958 essay on Charlotte Brontë's 'new Gothic'), but what occurred in the 1980s and 1990s was a striking proliferation of critical interest in genre, amply represented here by Claudia Johnson on *Northanger Abbey*, Jenny Bourne Taylor and D.A. Miller on *The Woman in White*, and Eugenia C. DeLamotte on *The Portrait of a Lady*. The two essays on *The Woman in White* also draw very impressively on current critical ideas about reception history and reader response. Jenny Bourne Taylor's essay looks at generic conventions and cultural codes in the 1850s, in the context of a rapidly growing and changing readership, while D.A. Miller's essay begins with the unusual suggestion that the meanings generated by *The Woman in White* are intimately connected with the nervous responses of its readers.

Even more pronounced than the recent revival of interest in Gothic writing and the novel of sensation has been the impact of post-colonial theory and minority discourse. There is no better introduction to the study of narrative in relation to the history of empire than Edward Said's comprehensive and lucid *Culture and Imperialism*, from which the essay on Conrad in this volume is extracted. As Said explains in the introduction to the book, his fundamental argument is that 'stories are at the heart of what explorers and novelists say about strange regions of the world; they also become the method colonized people use to assert their own identity and the existence of their own history' (Said, 1993, p. xiii). The power to narrate (or to prevent other, contradictory stories from developing) constitutes for Said one of the crucial connections between culture and imperialism.

Just as there are many different and competing feminist or historicist readings of nineteenth-century novels, so there is no single, definitive post-colonial account of any literary work. The readings included here serve to illustrate the different emphases and alternative viewpoints that might be found in contemporary post-colonial criticism. Gayatri Chakravorty Spivak's insistence on 'the unquestioned idiom of imperialist presuppositions' in *Jane Eyre* (p. 221) can be read alongside Susan L. Meyer's more tentative and speculative account of colonialism in the novel. Similarly, Suvendrini Perera writes about the complicated dynamics of sex, trade and empire in *Dombey and Son*, while Stephen D. Arata claims that Ireland provides a potent source for Bram Stoker's interest in the politics of empire. Anne Goodwyn Jones's sympathetic account of white women's lives in the American South is sharply contrasted with Elizabeth Ammons's uncompromising view of the 'repressed African American context' of Kate Chopin's novel *The Awakening* (p. 484).

The two closing essays are both concerned with Conrad and imperialism. Robert Hampson's essay is unusual in articulating a view of Conrad's politics that depends very much on a prior understanding and assessment of the readership of *Heart of Darkness* and closely related writings in *Blackwood's Magazine* at the end of the nineteenth century. Conrad's narrative is also seen to have significant intertextual connections with other narratives of darkness circulating in late Victorian culture: Henry Stanley's *In Darkest Africa* and William Booth's *In Darkest England*. The essay's contention that Conrad can be seen as both progressive and reactionary, both criticising and reproducing the imperial ideology of his day, is strongly endorsed by Edward Said, though he gets there by a different route.

What Said has to say about Conrad's fiction holds good for other nineteenth-century novelists represented here – Jane Austen, Charlotte Brontë, Charles Dickens, Bram Stoker – all of whom can be seen not just in the narrow terms of their own national affiliations, but as writers whose historical significance has been shaped by colonial enterprises elsewhere in the world. This kind of global analysis is a way of seeing literature as entangled and intertwined with other considerations – social, economic, political – on the broadest historical and geographical terrain. It offers us a challenge, a new beginning, a different narrative.

Works Cited

Allott, Miriam. 1959; reprinted 1973. *Novelists on the Novel*, London: Routledge and Kegan Paul.

Forrester, John. 2000. 'One Man and his Dreams', *Independent on Sunday*, 14 May, 8–12.

Levine, George. 1981. *The Realistic Imagination: English Fiction from Frankenstein to Lady Chatterley*, Chicago and London: University of Chicago Press.

Said, Edward. 1993. *Culture and Imperialism*, London: Chatto and Windus.

Watt, Ian. 1957. *The Rise of the Novel*, Harmondsworth: Penguin.

Widdowson, Peter. 1997. *Thomas Hardy: Selected Poetry and Non-Fictional Prose*, Basingstoke, Macmillan.

PART I

EARLY ESSAYS AND REVIEWS

Clara Reeve, The Progress of Romance (1785)

Clara Reeve (1729–1807) was the author of *The Champion of Virtue: A Gothic Story*, published in 1777 but revised and reissued as *The Old English Baron* in 1778. Her critical interests are amply evident in *The Progress of Romance Through Times, Centuries and Manners* (1785), from which the following extract is taken. The book takes the form of a series of evening conversations among three characters: Euphrasia, Hortensius and Sophronia. Its importance lies in its spirited attempt to distinguish between ancient romance and the modern novel, and to establish criteria of moral value in novel reading.

Preface

While I was collecting materials for this work, I held many conversations with some ingenious friends upon the various subjects, which it offered to be investigated and explained. This circumstance naturally suggested to me the Idea of the dialogue form; in which opposite sentiments would admit of a more full and accurate examination, arguments and objections might be more clearly stated and discussed, than in a regular series of Essays, or even letters, not to mention, that the variety and contrast which naturally arise out of the Dialogue, might enliven a work of rather dry deduction, and render it more entertaining to the reader, and not the less useful or instructive.

Evening VII

Hortensius, Sophronia, Euphrasia.

Hort. We have now, I presume, done with the Romances, and are expecting your investigation of Novels.

Euph. It is now that I begin to be sensible in how arduous an undertaking I have engaged, and to fear I shall leave it unfinished.

Hort. Have no fears, Madam; we shall not suffer you to leave off presently. We expect the completion of the plan you have given us.

Soph. If I judge rightly, the conclusion is yet a great way off.

Euph. This is one of the circumstances that frighten me. If I skim over the subject lightly it will be doing nothing; and if I am too minute I may grow dull and tedious, and tire my hearers.

Hort. You must aim at the medium you recommended to us.

Euph. What Goddess, or what Muse must I invoke to guide me through these vast, unexplored regions of fancy? – regions inhabited by wisdom and folly, – by wit and stupidity, – by religion and profaneness, – by morality and licentiousness. – How shall I separate and distinguish the various and opposite qualities of these strange concomitants? – point out some as the objects of admiration and respect, and others of abhorrence and contempt?

Hort. The subject warms you already, and when that is the case, you will never be heard coldly. – Go on and prosper.

Euph. In this fairy land are many Castles of various Architecture. – Some are built in the air, and have no foundation at all, – others are composed of such heavy materials, that their own weight sinks them into the earth, where they lie buried under their own ruins, and leave not a trace behind, – a third sort are built upon a real and solid foundation, and remain impregnable against all the attacks of Criticism, and perhaps even of time itself.

Soph. So so! – we are indeed got into Fairy-land; it is here that I expect to meet with many of my acquaintance, and I shall challenge them whenever I do.

Euph. I hope that you will assist my labours. – I will drop the metaphor, and tell you that I mean to take notice only of the most eminent works of this kind: – to pass over others slightly and leave the worst in the depths of Oblivion.

The word *Novel* in all languages signifies something new. It was first used to distinguish these works from Romance, though they have lately been confounded together and are frequently mistaken for each other.

Soph. But how will you draw the line of distinction, so as to separate them effectually, and prevent future mistakes?

Euph. I will attempt this distinction, and I presume if it is properly done it will be followed, – If not, you are but where you were before. The Romance is an heroic fable, which treats of fabulous persons and things. – The Novel is a picture of real life and manners, and of the times in which it is written. The Romance in lofty and elevated language, describes what never happened nor is likely to happen. – The Novel gives a familiar relation of such things, as pass every day before our eyes, such as may happen to our friend, or to ourselves; and the perfection of it, is to represent every scene, in so easy and natural a manner, and to make them appear so probable, as to deceive us into a persuasion (at least while we are reading) that all is real, until we are affected by the joys or distresses, of the persons in the story, as if they were our own.

Evening X
Hortensius, Sophronia, Euphrasia.

Euph. You are truly welcome my friends. – I receive you in my library, because we shall want to have recourse to our books.

Hort. Make me your Librarian, or employ me in some way as your assistant.

Euph. I make use of your permission, pray take down the *Monthly Review* for the year 1761 – and look for *Sidney Biddulph.*

Soph. This looks like doing business; – but pray do not transfer your task to the Reviewers.

Euph. Never fear, there will still remain employment enough for me.

Hort. I have it here – 'In the work before us, the Author seems to have designed to draw tears from the reader by distressing innocence and virtue as much as possible. – Now though we are not ignorant that this may be a true picture of human life in some instances; yet we are of opinion that such representations are by no means calculated to encourage or promote virtue.'

Euph. Stop there if you please, I do not want the whole Article. I have in my notes an extract from the *Critical Review*, which will be a proper contrast to the other.

'The design of this work is to prove that neither prudence, foresight, nor even the best disposition the human heart is capable of, are of themselves sufficient to defend us from the inevitable evils to which human nature is liable. – Whether this inference is favourable to the encouragement of virtue, we could not stop to enquire: we were so interested in the distress of *Sidney Biddulph*, and so absorbed in the events of her life, that in short, every arrow of Criticism was unpointed. – Instead of thinking these evils were allotted to her, we perceive that they arose from a want of knowledge of the world, from too easy credulity, and from unsuspecting innocence. – We can only wish that few of our readers may want her example to inspire and direct them.' – You have heard the evidence on both sides and now I ask *your* opinion *Sophronia?*

Soph. I had rather you had given your own, but as you desire it I will. – This book is a great favorite of mine, the Story is admirably told, and the language is so easy and natural, that every thing seems real in it, and we sorrow as for a well known and beloved friend; in my opinion it well deserves the encomium the Critical Reviewers have given it.

Hort. It is worthy of observation, that laying aside the dictatorial style of Censors, they speak of it, as if it was a true history. – 'Instead of thinking these evils were *allotted* to her, we perceive that they *arose* from want of knowledge of the world, &c.' – I cannot help smiling at it.

Euph. Your observation is *deep* as well as *pleasant*, perhaps there is not a better Criterion of the merit of a book, than our losing sight of the Author.

Hort. You have really converted my remark into solid value, and I readily agree to your criterion.

Soph. And so do I. – But I am mistaken if *Euphrasia* had not a further meaning in applying to me for my opinion of this book. – I am fond of melancholy stories, and she prefers those that end happily, she meant to oblige me to declare my sentiments, and afterwards give her own; and then ask you to decide upon them.

Euph. I find you know my meaning by my gaping. – I do really think that books of a gloomy tendency do much harm in this country, and especially to young minds; – they should be shown the truth through the medium of chearfulness, and led to expect encouragement in the practice of the social duties, and rewards for virtuous actions. – If they should be unfortunate, they will see the reverse of the medal soon enough.

Hort. But will not the expectations of nothing but peace and happiness, disqualify them to sustain the reverse?

Euph. I should think not. – The mind that is always ruminating upon the evils of life, will be apt to cast every object into shade.

Soph. Authors of the first eminence have written upon both principles, and if your doctrine was to be followed, we should have no Tragedies, and no pathetic stories. – What says *Hortensius?*

Hort. There is much to be said on both sides; I do not presume to decide upon the subject. – But for myself, I subscribe to *Euphrasia*'s opinion, that virtue stands in need of every encouragement, considering the many trials we must encounter in her constant warfare. – That youth should be led to expect the rewards of virtue in the present life, without losing sight of a better expectation hereafter: and this will be a powerful antidote against the unavoidable evils of life. – Virtue should always be represented in the most beautiful and amiable light, capable of attracting the hearts of her votaries, and of rewarding every sacrifice they can make to her: – but in truth there are too many moralists (and I might add divines,) who represent her in so austere and disgusting a manner, as to discourage and frighten her pupils away from her presence.

Evening XII

Hortensius, Sophronia, Euphrasia

Euph. – Hortensius you shall say all that you can against Novels, – I will reply to your censures, and *Sophronia* shall be Moderator between us.

Hort. I shall not spare them, notwithstanding the ill success I have had whenever I have been your opponent.

Euph. Nor shall I contradict you, unless when your censure is too general and indiscriminate, on works of Genius, taste, and morality.

Soph. It is no easy task to separate and select them, for they are found altogether, good, bad, and indifferent, in the Chaos of a circulating Library.

Euph. A Circulating Library is indeed a great evil, – young people are allowed to subscribe to them, and to read indiscriminately all they contain; and thus both food and poison are conveyed to the young mind together.

Hort. I should suppose that if books of the worst kind were excluded; still there would be enough to lay a foundation of idleness and folly – A person used to this kind of reading will be disgusted with every thing serious or solid, as a weakened and depraved stomach rejects plain and wholesome food.

Soph. There is truth and justice in your observation, – but how to prevent it?

Hort. There are yet more and greater evils behind. – The seeds of vice and folly are sown in the heart, – the passions are awakened, – false expectations are raised. – A young woman is taught to expect adventures and intrigues, – she expects to be addressed in the style of these books, with the language of flattery and adulation. – If a plain man addresses her in rational terms and pays her the greatest of compliments, – that of desiring to spend his life with her, – that is not sufficient, her vanity is disappointed, she expects to meet a Hero in Romance.

Euph. No *Hortensius*, – not a Hero in Romance, but a fine Gentleman in a Novel: – you will not make the distinction.

Hort. I ask your pardon, I agreed to the distinction and therefore ought to observe it.

Euph. I would not have interrupted you on this punctilio; but let us walk into the house, and pursue the subject in the Library.

Hort. Now you are armed with your extracts, you think yourself invulnerable.

Euph. I will not attempt to contradict you, unless I have good reason for it. – I beg you to proceed with your remarks.

Hort. From this kind of reading, young people fancy themselves capable of judging of men and manners, and that they are knowing, while involved in the profoundest ignorance. They believe themselves wiser than their parents and guardians, whom they treat with contempt and ridicule: – Thus armed with ignorance, conceit, and folly, they plunge into the world and its dissipations, and who can wonder if they become its victims? – For such as the foundation is, such will be the superstructure.

Euph. All this is undoubtedly true, but at the same time would you exclude all works of fiction from the young reader? – In this case you would deprive him of the pleasure and improvement he might receive from works of genius, taste and morality.

Hort. Yes, I would serve them as the Priest did *Don Quixote*'s library, burn the good ones for being found in bad company.

Euph. That is being very severe, especially if you consider how far your execution would extend. – If you would prohibit reading *all* works of fiction, what will become of your favourites the great Ancients, as well as the most ingenious and enlightened modern writers?

Soph. Surely this is carrying the prohibition too far, and though it may sound well in Theory, it would be utterly impracticable.

Hort. I do not deny that. – There are many things to be wished, that are not to be hoped. I see no way to cure this vice of the times, but by extirpating the cause of it.

Euph. Pray *Hortensius*, is all this severity in behalf of our sex or your own?

Hort. Of both. – Yet yours are most concerned in my remonstrance for they read more of these books than ours, and consequently are most hurt by them.

Euph. You will then become a Knight errant, to combat with the windmills, which your imagination represents as Giants: while in the mean time you leave a side unguarded.

Hort. And you have found it out. – Pray tell me without metaphors, your meaning in plain English?

Euph. It seems to me that you are unreasonably severe upon these books, which you suppose to be appropriated to our sex, (which however is not the case): – not considering how many books of worse tendency, are put into the hands of the youth of your own, without scruple.

Hort. Indeed! – how will you bring proofs of that assertion?

Euph. I will not go far for them. I will fetch them from the School books, that generally make a part of the education of young men. – They are taught the History – the Mythology – the morals – of the great Ancients, whom you and all learned men revere. – But with these, they learn also – their Idolatry – their follies – their vices – and every thing that is shocking to virtuous manners. – *Lucretius* teaches them that *fear* first made Gods – that men grew out of the earth like trees, and that the indulgence of the passions and appetites, is the truest wisdom. – *Juvenal* and *Persius* describe such scenes, as I may venture to affirm that Romance and Novel writers of any credit would blush at: – and *Virgil* – the modest and delicate *Virgil*, informs them of many things, they had better be ignorant of. – As a woman I cannot give this argument its full weight. – But a hint is sufficient, – and I presume you will not deny the truth of my affection.

Hort. I am astonished – admonished – and convinced! – I cannot deny the truth of what you have advanced, I confess that a reformation is indeed wanting in the mode of Education of the youth of our sex.

Soph. Of both sexes you may say. – We will not condemn yours and justify our own. – You are convinced, and *Euphrasia* will use her victory generously I am certain.

Euph. You judge rightly. – I do not presume to condemn indiscriminately, the books used in the education of youth; but surely they might be better selected, and some omitted, without any disadvantage. – I fear there is little prospect of such a general reformation as *Hortensius* generously wishes for. If any method can be found to alleviate these evils, it must be lenient – gradual – and practicable. – Let us then try to find out some expedient, with respect to those kind of books, which are our proper subject.

As this kind of reading is so common, and so much in every body's power, it is the more incumbent on parents and guardians to give young people a good taste for reading, and above all to lay the foundation of good principles from their very infancy; to make them read what is really good, and by forming their taste teach them to despise paltry books of every kind. – When they come to maturity of reason, they will scorn to run over a circulating Library, but will naturally aspire to read the best books of all kinds.

Soph. In most cases it would supersede the evil we complain of: but for the middling and lower ranks of people, I apprehend this would not hinder either children or servants from reading Novels.

Euph. The best way to do this is to find them constant employment. In every rank and situation, people may superintend the education of their children, and '*train them up in the way they should go*.' There is no duty enjoined but what is practicable. – I am afraid the negligence of parents, is too often the cause of a wrong bias in their children, – or else their false indulgence, which is equally prejudicial to them.

With all these precautions in view, I would select such books as were proper to be put into the hands of youth; and with the same circumspection I would carry them to the Theaters, to satisfy the curiosity of youth, and prevent their taking these amusements clandestinely, for how in an age like this, cou'd I flatter myself I cou'd prevent them?

Soph. This is indeed the medium between the two extremes, and I think *Hortensius* can make no objection to it.

Hort. I can only say that were I a father, I would suffer no such books to come into my house.

Euph. Then your children would borrow them of their young friends, – indeed *Hortensius* your prohibition would be to no purpose.

Hort. Then I thank God I am not in a situation to want to use it!

Euph. You do not consider that there are some works of this kind to which you have given your plaudit, and others, which I have shewn you were written as an antidote to the bad effects of them tho' under the disguise and name of Novels.

Hort. Well, that is true, and I will allow that when the principles are fixed, and the character formed, they may be read with safety, but that there are very few of them proper for youth to read: and as there are upon a moderate calculation ten of the wrong sort to one of the right, it is ten to one that a child meets with the former . . .

Soph. It is now that I may enter upon my office of Moderator. – *Hortensius* would prohibit the reading all Novels in order to exclude the bad ones. – *Euphrasia* would make a separation in favour of works of Genius, taste, and morality; she would recommend such methods of preventing the mischiefs arising from novel reading, as are moderate, prudent, and above all *practicable*. –

The objections to bad books of this species, are equally applicable to all other kinds of writing, – indecent novels, indecent plays, essays, memories, dialogues are equally to be exploded: but it does not follow that all these kinds of writing are to be extirpated, because some are bad. – By the same kind of reasoning we might plead for the prohibition of all kinds of writing; for excellent and unexceptionable works of every species, may be contrasted with vicious and immoral ones. All these objections amount to no more than that bad books are bad things; – but shall we therefore prohibit reading?

Hort. You have spoken to some purpose. – I know that mine is an *Utopian* scheme; and I acknowledge that *Euphrasia*'s is practicable, if parents and guardians would give due attention to it.

Euph. Then we are agreed at last, – Selection is to be strongly recommended, and good books to be carefully chosen by all that are concerned in the education of youth. – In order to make this work of ours of some public utility, I would recommend some that may properly be given to children even from their infancy, and as they grow up towards maturity: – that is to say, if my friends think it worthy to be offered to the public.

Hort. Why, if you will do it in your own name I have no objection, – but I should not choose that mine should appear in print.

Euph. I will so disguise it that you shall not know yourself, and *Sophronia* likewise shall appear in Masquerade.

Soph. I leave it entirely to you to dispose of me, in whatever way you think most proper for your service.

Hort. I am thinking, that from your part in our past conversations, any person who did not know you well, would conclude that your principal, if not only study, had been Romances and Novels.

Euph. I am under no concern on that account, it is not of any consequence how much or how little one knows, but the use one makes of the knowledge one has acquired. – If like the industrious bee I have cull'd from various flowers my share of Honey, and stored it in the common Hive, I shall have performed the duties of a good citizen of the Republic of letters, and I shall not have lived in vain.

Hort. You are entitled to this approbation from your intention, – and further –

Euph. No further I beseech you. If you pay me any compliments, I shall be obliged to expunge them from my copy. – If my work deserves public approbation, I trust it will meet with it.

Soph. I am concerned that you should have limited yourself to a year, for I have wished you to speak of some books of later date.

Euph. As Novels I cannot, but only as books deserving public honours, on the score of public utility. – As such I have a desire to mention the works of the Countess of *Genlis*. – *The Theatre of Education* for young people, and excellent work. – And her other Publications, *Theodore and Adelaide*, and the *Tales of the Castle*, are a school for Parents, Guardians, and Preceptors. – I had rather be the Author of such books as these, than be reckoned the first wit of the Age.

Soph. You have done them justice, but there are some Novels of merit within the last ten years.

Euph. The public will do them justice, and time will shew, whether they owed their success to intrisic merit, or to the caprice of fashion. I will not be drawn in to say any thing more of them.

Hort. We will not urge you any further, – you have fully executed the plan you laid down, and we leave the conclusion to you.

Euph. Here then I conclude, and thank you for your assistance, and the patience with which you have attended me in my progress. As soon as I have made out my list of books, I will return your visit *Hortensius*, and desire your opinion upon it.

Hort. I shall hope for that pleasure soon. – I now take my leave wishing you the best reward of your labours, Fame and Profit!

Soph. I join heartily in the same wish.

Euph. Every kind of happiness attend you my good friends! – For what remains, I shall (without asking the aid of puffing, or the influence of the tide of fashion,) leave the decision to an impartial and discerning public.

The Author of the *Progress of Romance*, does not presume to direct such Parents and Guardians in the choice of books for youth, as are qualified to select them; but only to offer to those, who have not thought much upon the subject themselves, and those who commit the charge of education to others; a list of such books as may be put into the hands of children with safety, and also with advantage. This list is confined to books in our own language, and is intended chiefly for the female sex. It is certainly the duty of every Mother, to consider seriously, the consequences of suffering children to read all the books that fall in their way indiscriminately. It is also a very bad and too frequent practice, to give them books above their years and understandings, by the reading of which they seem to the partial parent to acquire a prematurity of knowledge; while in reality, they are far more ignorant, than those who advance slowly and surely, – whose understandings are gradually cultivated, without being over loaded, – and whose reason is assisted gently and carefully, till it attains its full maturity.

Walter Scott, On Romance (1824)

Sir Walter Scott (1771–1832) was a prolific poet and novelist, whose reputation soared throughout the nineteenth century. Although his popularity has waned, his writings are still generally regarded as a major source of inspiration behind the Romantic movement, and novels such as *Waverley* (1814) and *Rob Roy* (1817) still occupy an important place in Scottish cultural history. Scott was also a shrewd and discerning critic who helped to shape opinion on the writing of history and fiction. The extract that follows is taken from his 'Essay on Romance', published in 1824 and reprinted in volume six of his *Miscellaneous Prose Works* (1882).

Dr. Johnson has defined Romance in its primary sense, to be 'a military fable of the middle ages; a tale of wild adventures in love and chivalry.' But although this definition expresses correctly the ordinary idea of the word, it is not sufficiently comprehensive to answer our present purpose. A composition may be a legitimate romance, yet neither refer to love nor chivalry – to war nor to the middle ages. The 'wild adventures' are almost the only absolutely essential ingredient in Johnson's definition. We would be rather inclined to describe a *Romance* as 'a fictious narrative in prose or verse; the interest of which turns upon marvellous and uncommon incidents;' thus being opposed to the kindred term *Novel*, which Johnson has described as 'a smooth tale, generally of love'; but which we would rather define as 'a fictitious narrative, differing from the Romance, because the events are accommodated to the ordinary train of human events, and the modern state of society.' Assuming these definitions, it is evident, from the nature of the distinction adopted, that there may exist compositions which it is difficult to assign precisely or exclusively to the one class or the other; and which, in fact, partake of the nature of both. But, generally speaking, the distinction will be found broad enough to answer all general and useful purposes . . .

The *epic* poem and the *romance of chivalry* transport us to the world of wonders, where supernatural agents are mixed with human characters, where the human characters themselves are prodigies, and where events are produced by causes widely and manifestly different from those which regulate the course of human affairs. With such a world we do not think of comparing our actual situation; to such characters we do not presume to assimilate ourselves or our neighbours; from such a concatenation of marvels we draw no conclusions with regard to our expectations in real life. But real life is the very thing which *novels* affect to imitate; and the young and inexperienced will sometimes be too ready to conceive that the picture is true, in those respects at least in which they wish it to be so. Hence both their temper, conduct, and happiness may be materially injured. For novels are often *romantic*, not indeed by the relation of what is obviously miraculous or impossible, but by deviating, though perhaps insensibly, beyond the bounds of probability or consistency.

Hippolyte Taine, Charles Dickens: son talent et ses œuvres (1856)

Hippolyte Taine (1828–1893) was a professor of art and aesthetics at the École des Beaux Arts and a leading critic of literature and painting in nineteenth-century France. He believed very firmly that a writer's sensibility was determined by heredity, environment and historical circumstance. Although his essay on Dickens was highly controversial, it can be seen to anticipate and prepare the ground for many of the recurring concerns in later critical studies, especially in its preoccupation with the quality of excess in Dickens's imagination. The extract that follows is taken from an essay that first appeared in the *Revue des deux Mondes* in 1856 and was reprinted in Taine's *Histoire de la Littérature anglaise* (1863–4).

The imagination of Dickens is like that of monomaniacs. To plunge oneself into an idea, to be absorbed by it, to see nothing else, to repeat it under a hundred forms, to enlarge it, to carry it, thus enlarged, to the eye of the spectator, to dazzle and overwhelm him with it, to stamp it upon him so firmly and deeply that he can never again tear it from his memory, – these are the great features of this imagination and style. In this, *David Copperfield* is a masterpiece. Never did objects remain more visible and present to the memory of a reader than those which he describes. The old house, the parlour, the kitchen, Peggotty's boat, and above all the school play-ground, are interiors whose relief, energy, and precision are unequalled. Dickens has the passion and patience of the painters of his nation; he reckons his details one by one, notes the various hues of the old tree-trunks; sees the dilapidated cask, the greenish and broken flagstones, the chinks of the damp walls; he distinguishes the strange smells which rise from them; marks the size of the mildewed spots, reads the names of the scholars carved on the door, and dwells on the form of the letters. And this minute description has nothing cold about it: if it is thus detailed, it is because the contemplation was intense: it proves its passion by its exactness. We felt this passion without accounting for it; suddenly we find it at the end of a page; the boldness of the style renders it visible, and the violence of the phrase attests the violence of the impression. Excessive metaphors bring before the mind grotesque fancies. We feel ourselves beset by extravagant visions. Mr Mell takes his flute, and blows on it, says Copperfield, 'until I almost thought he would gradually blow his whole being into the large hole at the top, and ooze away at the keys'

[*Copperfield*, ch. v]. Tom Pinch, disabused at last, discovers that his master Pecksniff is a hypocritical rogue. He 'had so long been used to steep the Pecksniff of his fancy in his tea, and spread him out upon his toast, and take him as a relish with his beer, that he made but a poor breakfast on the first morning after his expulsion' [*Chuzzlewit*, ch. xxxvi]. We think of Hoffmann's fantastic tales; we are arrested by a fixed idea, and our head begins to ache. These eccentricities are in the style of sickness rather than of health.

Therefore Dickens is admirable in depicting hallucinations. We see that he feels himself those of his characters, that he is engrossed by their ideas, that he enters into their madness. As an Englishman and a moralist, he has described remorse frequently. Perhaps it may be said that he makes a scarecrow of it, and that an artist is wrong to transform himself into an assistant of the policeman and the preacher.

. . . Dickens does not perceive great things; this is the second feature of his imagination. Enthusiasm seizes him in connection with everything, especially in connection with vulgar objects, a curiosity shop, a sign-post, a town-crier. He has vigour, he does not attain beauty. His instrument produces vibrating, but not harmonious sounds. If he is describing a house, he will draw it with geometrical clearness; he will put all its colours in relief, discover a face and thought in the shutters and the spouts; he will make a sort of human being out of the house, grimacing and forcible, which attracts our attention, and which we shall never forget; but he will not see the grandeur of the long monumental lines, the calm majesty of the broad shadows boldly divided by the white plaster; the cheerfulness of the light which covers them, and becomes palpable in the black niches in which it dives as though to rest and to sleep. If he is painting a landscape, he will perceive the haws which dot with their red fruit the leafless hedges, the thin vapour steaming from a distant stream, the motions of an insect in the grass; but the deep poetry which the author of *Valentine* and *André* [George Sand] would have felt, will escape him. He will be lost, like the painters of his country, in the minute and impassioned observation of small things; he will have no love of beautiful forms and fine colours. He will not perceive that the blue and the red, the straight line and the curve, are enough to compose vast concerts, which amidst so many various expressions maintain a grand serenity, and open up in the depths of the soul a spring of health and happiness. Happiness is lacking in him; his inspiration is a feverish rapture, which does not select its objects, which animates promiscuously the ugly, the vulgar, the ridiculous, and which communicating to his creations an indescribable jerkiness and violence, deprives them of the delight and harmony which in other hands they might have retained . . .

This sensibility can hardly have more than two issues – laughter and tears.

There are others, but they are only reached by lofty eloquence; they are the path to sublimity, and we have seen that for Dickens this path is cut off. Yet there is no writer who knows better how to touch and melt; he makes us weep, absolutely shed tears; before reading him we did not know there was so much pity in the heart. The grief of a child, who wishes to be loved by his father, and whom his father does not love; the despairing love and slow death of a poor half-imbecile young man: all these pictures of secret grief leave an ineffaceable impression. The tears which he sheds are genuine, and compassion is their only source. Balzac, George Sand, Stendhal have also recorded human miseries; is it possible to write without recording them? But they do not seek them out, they hit upon them; they do not dream of displaying them to us; they were going elsewhere, and met them on their way. They love art better than men . . .

This same writer is the most railing, the most comic, the most jocose of English authors. And it is moreover a singular gaiety! It is the only kind which would harmonise with this impassioned sensibility. There is a laughter akin to tears. Satire is the sister of elegy: if the second pleads for the oppressed, the first combats the oppressors. Feeling painfully all the wrongs that are committed, and the vices that are practised, Dickens avenges himself by ridicule. He does not paint, he punishes. Nothing could be more damaging than those long chapters of sustained irony, in which the sarcasm is pressed, line after line, more sanguinary and piercing in the chosen adversary . . . In reality, Dickens is gloomy, like Hogarth; but, like Hogarth, he makes us burst with laughter by the buffoonery of his invention and the violence of his caricatures. He pushes his characters to absurdity with unwonted boldness. Pecksniff hits off moral phrases and sentimental actions in so grotesque a manner, that they make him extravagant. Never were heard such monstrous oratorical displays. Sheridan had already painted an English hypocrite, Joseph Surface; but he differs from Pecksniff as much as a portrait of the eighteenth century differs from a cartoon of *Punch*. Dickens makes hypocrisy so deformed and monstrous, that his hypocrite ceases to resemble a man; we would call him one of those fantastic figures whose nose is greater than his body. This exaggerated comicality springs from excess of imagination . . .

Take away the grotesque characters, who are only introduced to fill up and to excite laughter, and you will find that all Dickens' characters belong to two classes – people who have feelings and emotions, and people who have none. He contrasts the souls which nature creates with those which society deforms. One of his last novels, *Hard Times*, is an abstract of all the rest. He there exalts instinct above reason, intuition of heart above positive knowledge; he attacks education built on statistics, figures, and facts: overwhelms the positive and mercantile spirit with misfortune and ridicule; and campaigns against the pride, hardheartedness and selfishness of the businessman and the aristocrat;

falls foul of manufacturing towns, combats the pride, harshness, selfishness of the merchant towns of smoke and mud, which fetter the body in an artificial atmosphere, and the mind in a factitious existence. He seeks out poor artisans, mountebanks, a foundling, and crushes beneath their common sense, generosity, delicacy, courage, and gentleness, the false science, false happiness, and false virtue of the rich and powerful who despise them. He satirises oppressive society; mourns over oppressed nature; and his elegiac genius, like his satirical genius, finds ready to his hand in the English world around him, the sphere which it needs for its development . . .

Let us look at some different personages. In contrast with these bad and factitious characters, produced by national institutions, we find good creatures such as nature made them; and first, children.

We have none in French literature. Racine's little Joas could only exist in a piece composed for the ladies' college of Saint Cyr; the little child speaks like a prince's son, with noble and acquired phrases, as if repeating his catechism. Now-a-days these portraits are only seen in France in New-year's books, written as models for good children. Dickens painted his with special gratification; he did not think of edifying the public, and he has charmed it. All his children are of extreme sensibility; they love much, and they crave to be loved. To understand this gratification of the painter, and this choice of characters, we must think of their physical type. English children have a colour so fresh, a complexion so delicate, a skin so transparent, eyes so blue and pure, that they are like beautiful flowers. No wonder if a novelist loves them . . .

The working-classes are like children, dependent, not very cultivated, akin to nature, and liable to oppression. And so Dickens extols them . . .

In reality, the novels of Dickens can all be reduced to one phrase, to wit: Be good, and love; there is genuine joy only in the emotions of the heart; sensibility is the whole man. Leave science to the wise, pride to the nobles, luxury to the rich; have compassion on humble wretchedness; the smallest and most despised being may in himself be worth as much as thousands of the powerful and the proud. Take care not to bruise the delicate souls which flourish in all conditions, under all costumes, in all ages. Believe that humanity, pity, forgiveness, are the finest things in man; believe that intimacy, expansion, tenderness, tears, are the sweetest things in the world. To live is nothing; to be powerful, learned, illustrious, is little; to be useful is not enough. He alone has lived and is a man who has wept at the remembrance of a kind action which he himself has performed or received . . .

George Eliot, The Natural History of German Life (1856)

George Eliot was the pseudonym of Mary Anne (or Marian) Evans (1819–1880). Although primarily a novelist, she was also an accomplished translator and critic.

'The Natural History of German Life' reveals her strong interests in German culture and in prevailing sociological methods at an early stage in her career. The essay, which first appeared in the *Westminster Review* in 1856, was a review of two books by the eminent German historian, W.H. Von Riehl: *Die Bürgerliche Gesellschaft* [*Bourgeois Society*] (1855) and *Land und Leute* [*Land and People*] (1856). The essay is a seminal document in George Eliot studies, both for its concern with the accurate representation of 'the people' and for its views about the laws of history and the organic development of social structures.

It is an interesting branch of psychological observation to note the images that are habitually associated with abstract or collective terms – what may be called the picture-writing of the mind, which it carries on concurrently with the more subtle symbolism of language. Perhaps the fixity or variety of these associated images would furnish a tolerably fair test of the amount of concrete knowledge and experience which a given word represents, in the minds of two persons who use it with equal familiarity. The word *railways*, for example, will probably call up, in the mind of a man who is not highly locomotive, the image either of a 'Bradshaw,' or of the station with which he is most familiar, or of an indefinite length of tram-road; he will alternate between these three images, which represent his stock of concrete acquaintance with railways. But suppose a man to have had successively the experience of a 'navvy,' an engineer, a traveller, a railway director and shareholder, and a landed proprietor in treaty with a railway company, and it is probable that the range of images which would by turns present themselves to his mind at the mention of the *word* 'railways,' would include all the essential facts in the existence and relations of the *thing*. Now it is possible for the first-mentioned personage to entertain very expanded views as to the multiplication of railways in the abstract, and their ultimate function in civilization. He may talk of a vast net-work of railways stretching over the globe, of future 'lines' in Madagascar, and elegant refreshment-rooms in the Sandwich Islands, with none the less glibness because his distinct conceptions on the subject do not extend beyond his one station and his indefinite length of tram-road. But it is evident that if we want a railway to be made, or its affairs to be managed, this man of wide views and narrow observation will not serve our purpose.

Probably, if we could ascertain the images called up by the terms 'the people,' 'the masses,' 'the proletariat,' 'the peasantry,' by many who theorize on those bodies with eloquence, or who legislate for them without eloquence, we should find that they indicate almost as small an amount of concrete knowledge – that they are as far from completely representing the complex facts summed up in the collective term, as the railway images of our non-locomotive gentleman. How little the real characteristics of the working-classes are known to those who are outside them, how little their natural history has been studied is sufficiently disclosed by our Art as well as by our political and social theories. Where, in our picture exhibitions, shall we find a group of true peasantry? What English artist even attempts to rival in truthfulness such studies of popular life as the pictures of Teniers or the ragged boys of Murillo? Even one of the greatest painters of the pre-eminently realistic school, while, in his picture of 'The Hireling Shepherd,' he gave us a landscape of marvellous truthfulness, placed a pair of peasants in the foreground who were not much more real than the idyllic swains and damsels of our chimney ornaments. Only a total absence of acquaintance and sympathy with our peasantry, could give a moment's popularity to such a picture as 'Cross Purposes,' where we have a peasant girl who looks as if she knew L. E. L.'s poems by heart, and English rustics, whose costume seems to indicate that they are meant for ploughmen, with exotic features that remind us of a handsome *primo tenore*. Rather than such cockney sentimentality as this, as an education for the taste and sympathies, we prefer the most crapulous group of boors that Teniers eye painted. But even those among our painters who aim at giving the rustic type of features, who are far above the effeminate feebleness of the 'Keepsake' style, treat their subjects under the influence of traditions and prepossessions rather than of direct observation. The notion that peasants are joyous, that the typical moment to represent a man in a smock-frock is when he is cracking a joke and showing a row of sound teeth, that cottage matrons are usually buxom, and village children necessarily rosy and merry, are prejudices difficult to dislodge from the artistic mind, which looks for its subjects into literature instead of life. The painter is still under the influence of idyllic literature, which has always expressed the imagination of the cultivated and town-bred, rather than the truth of rustic life. Idyllic ploughmen are jocund when they drive their team afield; idyllic shepherds make bashful love under hawthorn bushes; idyllic villagers dance in the chequered shade and refresh themselves, not immoderately, with spicy nut-brown ale. But no one who has seen much of actual ploughmen thinks them jocund; no one who is well acquainted with the English peasantry can pronounce them merry. The slow gaze, in which no sense of beauty beams, no humour twinkles, – the slow utterance, and the heavy slouching walk, remind one rather of that melancholy animal the camel, than of the sturdy countryman, with striped stockings, red waistcoat, and hat aside, who represents the traditional English peasant. Observe a company of haymakers. When you see them at a distance, tossing up the forkfuls of hay in the golden light, while the wagon creeps slowly with its increasing burthen over the meadow, and the bright green space which tells of work done gets larger and larger, you pronounce the scene "smiling," and you think these companions in labour must be as bright and cheerful as the picture to which they give animation. Approach nearer, and you will certainly find that haymaking time is a time for joking, especially if there are women among the labourers; but the coarse laugh that bursts out every now and then, and expresses the triumphant taunt, is as far as possible from your conception of idyllic merriment. That delicious effervescence of the mind which we call fun, has no equivalent for the northern peasant, except tipsy revelry; the only realm of fancy and imagination for the English clown exists at the bottom of the third quart pot.

The conventional countryman of the stage, who picks up pocket-books and never looks into them, and who is too simple even to know that honesty has its opposite, represents the still lingering mistake, that an unintelligible dialect is a guarantee for ingenuousness, and that slouching shoulders indicate an upright disposition. It is quite true that a thresher is likely to be innocent of any adroit arithmetical cheating, but he is not the less likely to carry home his master's corn in his shoes and pocket; a reaper is not given to writing begging-letters, but he is quite capable of cajolling the dairymaid into filling his small-beer bottle with ale. The selfish instincts are not subdued by the sight of buttercups, nor is integrity in the least established by that classic rural occupation, sheep-washing. To make men moral, something more is requisite than to turn them out to grass.

Opera peasants, whose unreality excites Mr. Ruskin's indignation, are surely too frank an idealization to be misleading; and since popular chorus is one of the most effective elements of the opera, we can hardly object to lyric rustics in elegant laced bodices and picturesque motley, unless we are prepared to advocate a chorus of colliers in their pit costume, or a ballet of charwomen and stocking-weavers. But our social novels profess to represent the people as they are, and the unreality of their representations is a grave evil. The greatest benefit we owe to the artist, whether painter, poet, or novelist, is the extension of our sympathies. Appeals founded on generalizations and statistics require a sympathy ready-made, a moral sentiment already in activity; but a picture of human life such as a great artist can give, surprises even the trivial and the selfish into that attention to what is apart from themselves, which may be called the raw material of moral sentiment. When Scott takes us into Luckie Mucklebackit's cottage, or tells the story of 'The Two Drovers,' – when Wordsworth sings to us the reverie of 'Poor Susan,' – when Kingsley shows us Alton Locke gazing yearningly over the gate which leads from the highway into the first wood he ever saw, – when Hornung paints a group of chimney-sweepers, – more is done towards linking the higher classes with the lower, towards obliterating the vulgarity of exclusiveness, than by hundreds of sermons and philosophical dissertations. Art is the nearest thing to life; it is a mode of amplifying experience and extending our contact with our fellow-men beyond the bounds of our personal lot. All the more sacred is the task of the artist when he undertakes to paint the life of the People.

Falsification here is far more pernicious than in the more artificial aspects of life. It is not so very serious that we should have false ideas about evanescent fashions – about the manners and conversation of beaux and duchesses; but it *is* serious that our sympathy with the perennial joys and struggles, the toil, the tragedy, and the humour in the life of our more heavily-laden fellow-men, should be perverted, and turned towards a false object instead of the true one.

This perversion is not the less fatal because the misrepresentation which gives rise to it has what the artist considers a moral end. The thing for mankind to know is, not what are the motives and influences which the moralist thinks *ought* to act on the labourer or the artisan, but what are the motives and influences which *do* act on him. We want to be taught to feel, not for the heroic artisan or the sentimental peasant, but for the peasant in all his coarse apathy, and the artisan in all his suspicious selfishness.

We have one great novelist who is gifted with the utmost power of rendering the external traits of our town population; and if he could give us their psychological character – their conceptions of life, and their emotions – with the same truth as their idiom and manners, his books would be the greatest contribution. Art has ever made to the awakening of social sympathies. But while he can copy Mrs. Plornish's colloquial style with the delicate accuracy of a sun-picture, while there is the same startling inspiration in his description of the gestures and phrases of 'Boots,' as in the speeches of Shakspeare's mobs or numskulls, he scarcely ever passes from the humorous and external to the emotional and tragic, without becoming as transcendent in his unreality as he was a moment before in his artistic truthfulness. But for the precious salt of his humour, which compels him to reproduce external traits that serve, in some degree, as a corrective to his frequently false psychology, his preternaturally virtuous poor children and artisans, his melodramatic boatmen and courtezans, would be as noxious as Eugène Sue's idealized proletaires in encouraging the miserable fallacy that high morality and refined sentiment can grow out of harsh social relations, ignorance, and want; or that the working-classes are in a condition to enter at once into a millennial state of *altruism*, wherein everyone is caring for everyone else, and no one for himself.

If we need a true conception of the popular character to guide our sympathies rightly, we need it equally to check our theories, and direct us in their application. The tendency created by the splendid conquests of modern generalization, to believe that all social questions are merged in economical science, and that the relations of men to their neighbours may be settled by algebraic equations, – the dream that the uncultured classes are prepared for a condition which appeals principally to their moral sensibilities, – the aristocratic dilettantism which attempts to restore the 'good old times' by a sort of idyllic masquerading, and to grow feudal fidelity and veneration as we grow prize turnips, by an artificial system of culture, – none of these diverging mistakes can co-exist with a real knowledge of the People, with a thorough study of their habits, their ideas, their motives. The landholder, the clergyman, the mill-owner, the mining-agent, have each an opportunity for making precious observations on different sections of the working-classes, but unfortunately their experience is too often not registered at all, or its results are too scattered to be available as a source of information and stimulus to the public mind generally. If any man of sufficient moral and intellectual breadth, whose observations would not be vitiated by a foregone conclusion, or by a professional point of view, would devote himself to studying the natural history of our social classes, especially of the small shopkeepers, artisans, and peasantry, – the degree in which they are influenced by local conditions, their maxims and habits, the points of view from which they regard their religious teachers, and the degree in which they are influenced by religious doctrines, the interaction of the various classes on each other, and what are the tendencies in their position towards disintegration or towards development, – and if, after all this study, he would give us the result of his observations in a book well nourished with specific facts, his work would be a valuable aid to the social and political reformer.

What we are desiring for ourselves has been in some degree done for the Germans by Riehl . . . and we wish to make these books known to our readers, not only for the sake of the interesting matter they contain and the important reflections they suggest, but also as a model for some future or actual student of our own people. By way of introducing Riehl to those who are unacquainted with his writings, we will give a rapid sketch from his picture of the German Peasantry, and perhaps this indication of the mode in which he treats a particular branch of his subject may prepare them to follow us with more interest when we enter on the general purpose and contents of his works.

In England, at present, when we speak of the peasantry, we mean scarcely more than the class of farm-servants and farm-labourers; and it is only in the most primitive districts, as in Wales, for example, that farmers are included under the term. In order to appreciate what Riehl says of the German peasantry, we must remember what the tenant-farmers and small proprietors were in England half a century ago, when the master helped to milk his own cows, and the daughters got up at one o'clock in the morning to brew, – when the family dined in the kitchen with the servants, and sat with them round the kitchen fire in the evening. In those days, the quarried parlour was innocent of a carpet, and its only specimens of art were a framed sampler and the best tea-board; the daughters even of substantial farmers had often no greater accomplishment in writing and spelling than they could procure at a dame-school; and, instead of carrying on sentimental correspondence, they were spinning their future table-linen, and looking after every saving in butter and eggs that might enable them to add to the little stock of plate and china which they were laying in against their marriage. In our own day, setting aside the superior order of farmers, whose style of living and mental culture are often equal to that of the professional class in provincial towns, we can hardly enter the least imposing farm-house without finding a bad piano in the 'drawing-room,' and some old annuals, disposed with a symmetrical imitation of negligence, on the table; though the daughters may still drop their *h's*, their vowels are studiously narrow; and it is only in very primitive regions that they will consent to sit in a covered vehicle without springs, which was once thought an advance in luxury on the pillion . . .

The German novelists who undertake to give pictures of peasant-life, fall into the same mistake as our English novelists; they transfer their own feelings to ploughmen and woodcutters, and give them both joys and sorrows of which they know nothing. The peasant never questions the obligation of family-ties – he questions *no custom*, – but tender affection, as it exists amongst the refined part of mankind, is almost as foreign to him as white hands and filbert-shaped nails. That the aged father who has given up his property to his children on condition of their maintaining him for the remainder of his life, is very far from meeting with delicate attentions, is indicated by the proverb current among the peasantry – 'Don't take your clothes off before you go to bed.' Among rustic moral tales and parables, not one is more universal than the story of the ungrateful children, who made their grey-headed father, dependent on them for a maintenance, eat at a wooden trough, because he shook the food out of his trembling hands. Then these same ungrateful children observed one day that their own little boy was making a tiny wooden trough; and when they asked him what it was for, he answered – that his father and mother might eat out of it, when he was a man and had to keep them.

Marriage is a very prudential affair, especially among the peasants who have the largest share of property. Politic marriages are as common among them as among princes; and when a peasant-heiress in Westphalia marries, her husband adopts her name, and places his own after it with the prefix *geborner* (*née*). The girls marry young, and the rapidity with which they get old and ugly is one among the many proofs that the early years of marriage are fuller of hardships than of conjugal tenderness. 'When our writers of village stories,' says Riehl, 'transferred their own emotional life to the peasant, they obliterated what is precisely his most predominant characteristic, namely, that with him general custom holds the place of individual feeling.'

We pay for greater emotional susceptibility too often by nervous diseases of which the peasant knows nothing. To him headache is the least of physical evils, because he thinks headwork the easiest and least indispensable of all labour. Happily, many of the younger sons in peasant families, by going to seek their living in the towns, carry their hardy nervous system to amalgamate with the over-wrought nerves of our town population, and refresh them with a little rude vigour. And a return to the habits of peasant life is the best remedy for many moral as well as physical diseases induced by perverted civilization . . .

Our readers will perhaps already have gathered from the foregoing portrait of the German peasant, that Riehl is not a man who looks at objects through the spectacles either of the doctrinaire or the dreamer; and they will be ready to believe what he tells us in his Preface, namely that years ago he began his wanderings over the hills and plains of Germany for the sake of obtaining in immediate intercourse with the people that completion of his historical, political and economical studies which he was unable to find in books. He began his investigations with no party prepossessions, and his present views were evolved entirely from his own gradually amassed observations. He was first of all, a pedestrian, and only in the second place a political author. The views at which he has arrived by this inductive process, he sums up in the term – *social-political-conservatism*; but his conservatism is, we conceive, of a thoroughly philosophical kind. He sees in European society *incarnate history*, and any attempt to disengage it from its historical elements must, he believes, be simply destructive of social vitality.[1] What has grown up historically can only die out historically, by the gradual operation of necessary laws. The external conditions which society has inherited from the past are but the manifestation of inherited internal conditions in the human beings who compose it; the internal conditions and the external are related to each other as the organism and its medium, and development can take place only by the gradual consentaneous development of both. Take the familiar example of attempts to abolish titles, which have been about as effective as the process of cutting off poppy-heads in a corn-field. *Jedem Menschen*, says Riehl, *ist sein Zopf angeboren, warum soll denn der sociale Sprachgebrauch nicht auch seinen Zopf haben?* – which we may render – 'as long as snobbism runs in the blood, why should it not run in our speech?' As a necessary preliminary to a purely rational society, you must obtain purely rational men, free from the sweet and bitter prejudices of hereditary affection and antipathy, which is as easy as to get running streams without springs, or the leafy shade of the forest without the secular growth of trunk and branch.

The historical conditions of society may be compared with those of language. It must be admitted that the language of cultivated nations is in anything but a rational state; the great sections of the civilized world are only approximately intelligible to each other, and even that, only at the cost of long study; one word stands for many things, and many words for one thing; the subtle shades of meaning, and still subtler echoes of association, make language an instrument which scarcely anything short of genius can wield with definiteness and certainty. Suppose, then, that the effort which has been again and again made to construct a universal language on a rational basis has at length succeeded, and that you have a language which has no uncertainty, no whims of idiom, no cumbrous forms, no fitful shimmer of many-hued significance, no hoary archaisms 'familiar with forgotten years' – a patent de-odorized and non-resonant language, which effects the purpose of communication as perfectly and rapidly as algebraic signs. Your language may be a perfect medium of expression to science, but will never express *life*, which is a great deal more than science. With the anomalies and inconveniences of historical language, you will have parted with its music and its passion, with its vital qualities as an expression of individual character, with its subtle capabilities of wit, with everything that gives it power over the imagination; and the next step in simplification will be the invention of a talking watch, which will achieve the utmost facility and dispatch in the communication of ideas by a graduated adjustment of ticks, to be represented in writing by a corresponding arrangement of dots. A melancholy 'language of the future!' The sensory and motor nerves that run in the same sheath, are scarcely bound together by a more necessary and delicate union than that which binds men's affections, imagination, wit, and humour, with the subtle ramifications of historical language. Language must be left to grow in precision, completeness, and unity, as minds grow in clearness, comprehensiveness, and sympathy. And there is an analogous relation between the moral tendencies of men and the social conditions they have inherited. The nature of European men has its roots intertwined with the past, and can only be developed by allowing those roots to remain undisturbed while the process of development is going on, until that perfect ripeness of the seed which carries with it a life independent of the root. This vital connexion with the past is much more vividly felt on the Continent than in England, where we have to recall it by an effort of memory and reflection; for though our English life is in its core intensely traditional, Protestantism and commerce have modernized the face of the land and the aspects of society in a far greater degree than in any continental country:—

> 'Abroad,' says Ruskin, 'a building of the eighth or tenth century stands ruinous in the open street, the children play round it, the peasants heap their corn in it, the buildings of yesterday nestle about it, and fit their new stones in its rents, and tremble in sympathy as it trembles. No one wonders at it, or thinks of it as separate, and of another time; we feel the ancient world to be a real thing, and one with the new; antiquity is no dream; it is rather the children playing about the old stones that are the dream. But all is continuous; and the words "from generation to generation," understandable here.'

This conception of European society as incarnate history, is the fundamental idea of Riehl's books. After the notable failure of revolutionary attempts conducted from the point of view of abstract democratic and socialistic theories, after the practical demonstration of the evils resulting from a bureaucratic system which governs by an undiscriminating, dead mechanism, Riehl wishes to urge on the consideration of his countrymen, a social policy founded on the special study of the people as they are – on the natural history of the various social ranks. He thinks it wise to pause a little from theorizing, and see what is the material actually present for theory to work upon. It is the glory of the Socialists – in contrast with the democratic doctrinaires who have been too much occupied with the general idea of 'the people' to inquire particularly into the actual life of the people – that they have thrown themselves with enthusiastic zeal into the study at least of one social group, namely, the factory operatives; and here lies the secret of their partial success. But unfortunately, they have made this special study of a single fragment of society the basis of a theory which quietly substitutes for the small group of Parisian proletaires or English factory workers, the society of all Europe – nay, of the whole world. And in this way they have lost the best fruit of their investigations. For, says Riehl, the more deeply we penetrate into the knowledge of society in its details, the more thoroughly we shall be convinced that *a universal social policy has no validity except on paper*, and can never be carried into successful practice. The conditions of German society are altogether different from those of French, of English, or of Italian society; and to apply the same social theory to these nations indiscriminately, is about as wise a procedure as Triptolemus Yellowley's application of the agricultural directions in Virgil's 'Georgics' to his farm in the Shetland Isles.

It is the clear and strong light in which Riehl places this important position, that in our opinion constitutes the suggestive value of his books for foreign as well as German readers. It has not been sufficiently insisted on, that in the various branches of Social Science there is an advance from the general to the special, from the simple to the complex, analogous with that which is found in the series of the sciences, from Mathematics to Biology. To the laws of quantity comprised in Mathematics and Physics are superadded, in Chemistry, laws of quality; to these again are added, in Biology, laws of life; and lastly, the conditions of life in general, branch out into its special conditions, or Natural History, on the one hand, and into its abnormal conditions, or Pathology, on the other. And in this series or ramification of the sciences, the more general science will not suffice to solve the problems of the more special. Chemistry embraces phenomena which are not explicable by Physics; Biology embraces phenomena which are not explicable by Chemistry; and no biological generalization will enable us to predict the infinite specialities produced by the complexity of vital conditions. So Social Science, while it has departments which in their fundamental generality correspond to mathematics and physics, namely, those grand and simple generalizations which trace out the inevitable march of the human race as a whole, and, as a ramification of these, the laws of economical science, has also, in the departments of government and jurisprudence, which embrace the conditions of social life in all their complexity, what may be called its Biology, carrying us on to innumerable special phenomena which outline the sphere of science, and belong to Natural History. And just as the most thorough acquaintance with physics, or chemistry, or general physiology will not enable you at once to establish the balance of life in your private vivarium, so that your particular society of zoophytes, molluscs, and echinoderms may feel themselves, as the Germans say, at ease in their skin; so the most complete equipment of theory will not enable a statesman or a political and social reformer to adjust his measures wisely, in the absence of a special acquaintance with the section of society for which he legislates, with the peculiar characteristics of the nation, the province, the class whose well being he has to consult. In other words, a wise social policy must be based not simply on abstract social science, but on the Natural History of social bodies . . .

[B]efore quitting these admirable volumes, let us say, lest our inevitable omissions should have left room for a different conclusion, that Riehl's conservatism is not in the least tinged with the partisanship of a class, with a poetic fanaticism for the past, or with the prejudice of a mind incapable of discerning the grander evolution of things to which all social forms are but temporarily subservient. It is the conservatism of a clear-eyed, practical, but withal large-minded man – a little caustic, perhaps, now and then in his epigrams on democratic doctrinaires who have their nostrum for all political and social diseases, and on communistic theories which he regards as 'the despair of the individual in his own manhood, reduced to a system,' but nevertheless able and willing to do justice to the elements of fact and reason in every shade of opinion and every form of effort. He is as far as possible from the folly of supposing that the sun will go backward on the dial, because we put the hands of our clock backward; he only contends against the opposite folly of decreeing that it shall be mid-day, while in fact the sun is only just touching the mountain-tops, and all along the valley men are stumbling in the twilight.

George Henry Lewes, Realism in Art: Recent German Fiction (1858)

George Henry Lewes (1817–1878) was one of the most formidable intellectuals of his time, whose writings encompassed literary criticism, biography, philosophy and science, as well as creative endeavours in fiction and drama. Among his notable publications were *A Biographical History of Philosophy* (1845), *The Life and Works of Goethe* (1855), and *Studies of Animal Life* (1862). The essay from which this extract is taken was first printed in the *Westminster Review* in 1858. It shows the strong interest that Lewes took in contemporary debates about the meaning and function of realism, and it reveals the literary and artistic interests that he shared with George Eliot, with whom he lived from 1854 until his death.

[German] libraries swarm with works having but the faintest possible relation to any form of human life, and the strongest infusion of what is considered the 'ideal element.' The hero is never a merchant, a lawyer, an artisan – *Gott bewahre!*[1] He must have a pale face and a thoughtful brow; he must be either a genius or a Herr Baron. The favourite hero is a poet, or an artist, often a young nobleman who has the artistic nature; but always a man of genius; because prose can be found at every street-corner, and art must elevate the public by 'beautifying' life.

This notion of the function of Art is widely spread. It has its advocates in all countries, for it is the natural refuge of incompetence, to which men fly, impelled by the secret sense of their inability to portray Reality so as to make it interesting. A distinction is drawn between Art and Reality, and an antithesis established between Realism and Idealism which would never have gained acceptance had not men in general lost sight of the fact that Art is a Representation of Reality – a Representation which, inasmuch as it is not the thing itself, but only represents it, must necessarily be limited by the nature of its medium; the canvas of the painter, the marble of the sculptor, the chords of the musician, and the language of the writer, each bring with them peculiar laws; but while thus limited, while thus regulated by the necessities imposed on it by each medium of expression, Art always aims at the representation of Reality, *i.e.* of Truth; and no departure from truth is permissible, except such as inevitably lies in the nature of the medium itself. Realism is thus the basis of all Art, and its antithesis is not Idealism, but *Falsism.* When our painters represent peasants with regular features and irreproachable linen; when their milkmaids have the air of Keepsake beauties, whose costume is picturesque, and never old or dirty; when Hodge is made to speak refined sentiments in unexceptionable English, and children utter long speeches of religious and poetic enthusiasm; when the conversation of the parlour and drawing-room is a succession of philosophical remarks, expressed with great clearness and logic, an attempt is made to idealize, but the result is simple falsification and bad art. To misrepresent the forms of ordinary life is no less an offence than to misrepresent the forms of ideal life: a pug-nosed Apollo, or Jupiter in a great-coat, would not be more truly shocking to an artistic mind than are those senseless falsifications of nature into which incompetence is led under the pretence of 'beautifying' nature. Either give us true peasants, or leave them untouched; either paint no drapery at all, or paint it with the utmost fidelity; either keep your people silent, or make them speak the idiom of their class.

Raphael's marvellous picture, the 'Madonna di San Sisto,' presents us with a perfect epitome of illustration. In the figures of the Pope and St. Barbara we have a real man and woman, one of them a portrait, and the other not elevated above sweet womanhood. Below, we have the two exquisite angel children, intensely childlike, yet something *more*, something which renders their wings congruous with our conception of them. In the never-to-be-forgotten divine babe, we have at once the intensest realism of presentation, with the highest idealism of conception: the attitude is at once grand, easy, and natural; the face is that of a child, but the child is divine: in those eyes, and on that brow, there is an indefinable something[2] which, greater than the expression of the angels' [sic], grander than that of pope or saint, is, to all who see it, a perfect *truth*; we feel that humanity in its highest conceivable form is before us, and that to transcend such a form would be to lose sight of the *human* nature there represented. In the virgin mother, again, we have a real woman, such as the *campagna* of Rome will furnish every day, yet with eyes subdued to a consciousness of her divine mission. Here is a picture which from the first has enchained the hearts of men, which is assuredly in the highest sense real – a real man, a real woman, real angel-children, and a real Divine Child; the last a striking contrast to the ineffectual attempts of other painters to spiritualize and idealize the babe – attempts which represent no babe at all . . .

We may now come to an understanding on the significance of the phrase Idealism in Art. Suppose two men equally gifted with the perceptive powers and technical skill necessary to the accurate representation of a village group, but the one to be gifted, over and above these qualities, with an emotional sensibility which leads him to sympathize intensely with the emotions playing amid that village group. Both will delight in the forms of external nature, both will lovingly depict the scene and scenery; but the second will not be satisfied therewith: his sympathy will lead him to express something of the emotional life of the group; the mother in his picture will not only hold her child in a graceful attitude, she will look at it with a mother's tenderness; the lovers will be tender; the old people venerable. Without once departing from strict reality, he will have thrown a sentiment into his group which every spectator will recognise as poetry. Is he not more *real* than a Teniers, who, admirable in externals, had little or no sympathy with the internal life, which, however, is as real as the other? But observe, the sentiment must be real, truly expressed as a sentiment, and as the sentiment of the very people represented; the tenderness of *Hodge* must not be that of *Romeo* . . .

In like manner the novelist . . . expresses his mind in his novels, and according as his emotional sympathy is keen and active, according to his poetic disposition, will the choice and treatment of his subject be poetical:

but it must always be real – true. If he select the incidents and characters of ordinary life, he must be rigidly bound down to accuracy in the presentation. He is at liberty to avoid such subjects, if he thinks them prosaic and uninteresting (which will mean that he does not feel their poetry and interest), but having chosen, he is not at liberty to falsify, under pretence of beautifying them; every departure from truth in motive, idiom, or probability, is, to that extent, a defect.

Margaret Oliphant, Sensation Novels (1862)

Margaret Oliphant (1828–1897) was a prolific novelist, biographer and critic, the author of over 100 books and a frequent contributor to *Blackwood's Magazine*, in which this essay first appeared. Her *Autobiography* (1899) records the struggle of a professional woman writer to provide for her own and her brother's family. Her essay on sensation novels is remarkable for its perceptive account of 'a new beginning in fiction' and for its explanation of the social and political circumstances precipitating this new style of writing.

Ten years ago the world in general had come to a singular crisis in its existence. The age was lost in self-admiration. We had done so many things that nobody could have expected a century before – we were on the way to do so many more, if common report was to be trusted. We were about inaugurating the reign of universal peace in a world too deeply connected by links of universal interest ever to commit the folly of war again – we had invented everything that was most unlikely, and had nothing before us but to go on perfecting our inventions, and, securing all the powers of nature in harness, to do all manner of peaceable work for us like the giants in the children's story. What a wonderful difference in ten years! Instead of linking peaceful hands, and vowing to study war no more, we have turned Industry away from her vaunted work of putting a girdle round the world, and set her to forge thunderbolts in volcanic din and passion. In that momentous interval great wars have begun and ended, and fighting has come into fashion throughout the palpitating earth. We who once did, and made, and declared ourselves masters of all things, have relapsed into the natural size of humanity before the great events which have given a new character to the age. Though we return with characteristic obstinacy and iteration to the grand display of wealth and skill which in 1851 was a Festival of Peace, we repeat the celebration with very different thoughts. It is a changed world in which we are now standing. If no distant sound of guns echoes across seas and continents upon our ears as we wander under the South Kensington domes, the lack of the familiar sound will be rather disappointing than satisfactory. That distant roar has come to form a thrilling accompaniment to the safe life we lead at home. On the other side of the Atlantic, a race *blasée* and lost in universal *ennui* has bethought itself of the grandest expedient for procuring a new sensation; and albeit we follow at a humble distance, we too begin to feel the need of a supply of new shocks and wonders. Those fell Merrimacs and Monitors, stealing forth with a certain devilish invulnerability and composure upon the human ships and men to be made fire and carnage of, are excitement too high pitched for comfort; but it is only natural that art and literature should, in an age which has turned to be one of events, attempt a kindred depth of effect and shock of incident. In the little reflected worlds of the novel and the drama the stimulant has acted strongly, and the result in both has been a significant and remarkable quickening of public interest. Shakespeare, even in the excitement of a new interpretation, has not crowded the waning playhouse, as has the sensation drama with its mock catastrophes; and Sir Walter himself never deprived his readers of their lawful rest to a greater extent with one novel than Mr Wilkie Collins has succeeded in doing with his 'Woman in White.' We will not attempt to decide whether the distance between the two novelists is less than that which separates the skirts of Shakespeare's regal mantle from the loftiest stretch of Mr Bourcicault. But it is a fact that the well-known old stories of readers sitting up all night over a novel had begun to grow faint in the public recollection. Domestic histories, however virtuous and charming, do not often attain that result – nor, indeed, would an occurrence so irregular and destructive of all domestic proprieties be at all a fitting homage to the virtuous chronicles which have lately furnished the larger part of our light literature. Now a new fashion has been set to English novel-writers. Whether it can be followed extensively, or whether it would be well if that were possible, are very distinct questions; but it cannot be denied that a most striking and original effort, sufficiently individual to be capable of originating a new school in fiction, has been made, and that the universal verdict has crowned it with success.

Mr Wilkie Collins is not the first man who has produced a sensation novel. By fierce expedients of crime and violence, by *diablerie* of divers kinds, and by the wild devices of a romance which smiled at probabilities, the thing has been done before now. The higher class of American fiction, as represented by Hawthorne, attempts little else. In that strange hybrid between French excitement and New England homeliness, we recognise the influence of a social system which has paralysed all the wholesome wonders and nobler mysteries of human existence. Hectic rebellion against nature – frantic attempts by any kind of black art or mad psychology to get some grandeur and sacredness restored to life – or if not sacredness and grandeur, at least horror and mystery, there being nothing better in earth or heaven; Mesmerism possibly for a make-shift, or Socialism, if perhaps it might be more worth while to turn ploughmen and milkmaids than ladies and gentlemen; or, if none of these would do, best to undermine life altogether, and find what creeping honours might be underground; here a Scarlet Letter and impish child of shame, there a snake-girl, horrible junction of reptile and woman. The result is no doubt a class of books abounding in sensation; but the effect is invariably attained by violent and illegitimate means, as fantastic in themselves as they are contradictory to actual life. The Master of English fiction, Sir E. B. Lytton, has accomplished the same end, by magic and supernaturalism, as in the wild and beautiful romance of 'Zanoni.' We will not attempt to discuss his last wonderful effort of this class, which is a species by itself and to be judged only by special rules, which space debars us from considering. Of all the productions of the supernatural school, there is none more perfect in its power of sensation, or more entirely effective in its working out, than the short story of the 'Haunted House,' most thrilling of ghostly tales; but we cannot enter upon this school of fiction, which is distinct from our present subject. Mr Dickens rarely writes a book without an attempt at a similar effect by means of some utterly fantastic creation, set before his readers with all that detail of circumstance in which he is so successful. Amid all these predecessors in the field, Mr Wilkie Collins takes up an entirely original position. Not so much as a single occult agency is employed in the structure of his tale. Its power arises from no overstraining of nature: – the artist shows no love of mystery for mystery's sake; he wastes neither wickedness nor passion. His plot is astute and deeply-laid, but never weird or ghastly; he shows no desire to tinge the daylight with any morbid shadows. His effects are produced by common human acts, performed by recognisable human agents, whose motives are never inscrutable, and whose line of conduct is always more or less consistent. The moderation and reserve which he exhibits; his avoidance of extremes; his determination, in conducting the mysterious struggle, to trust to the reasonable resources of the combatants, who have consciously set all upon the stake for which they play, but whom he assists with no weapons save those of quick wit, craft, courage, patience and villany – tools common to all men – make the lights and shadows of the picture doubly effective. The more we perceive the perfectly legitimate nature of the means used to produce the sensation, the more striking does that sensation become. The machinery of miracle, on the contrary, is troublesome and expensive, and never satisfactory; a miraculous issue ought to come out of it to justify the miraculous means; and miraculous issues are at war with all the economy of nature, not to say that they are difficult of invention and hard to get credit for. A writer who boldly takes in hand the common mechanism of life, and by means of persons who might all be living in society for anything we can tell to the contrary, thrills us into wonder, terror, and breathless interest, with positive personal shocks of surprise and excitement, has accomplished a far greater success than he who effects the same result through supernatural agencies, or by means of the fantastic creations of lawless genius or violent horrors of crime. When we are to see a murder visibly done before our eyes, the performers must be feeble indeed if some shudder of natural feeling does not give force to their exertions; and the same thing is still more emphatically the case when the spiritual and invisible powers, to which we all more or less do secret and unwilling homage, are actors in the drama. The distinguishing feature of Mr Wilkie Collins' success is, that he ignores all these arbitrary sensations, and has boldly undertaken to produce effects as startling by the simplest expedients of life. It is this which gives to his book the qualities of a new beginning in fiction. There is neither murder, nor seduction, nor despair – neither startling eccentrics nor fantastic monsters in this remarkable story. A much more delicate and subtle power inspires its nation. We cannot object to the means by which he startles and thrills his readers; everything is legitimate, natural, and possible; all the exaggerations of excitement are carefully eschewed, and there is almost as little that is objectionable in this highly-wrought sensation-novel, as if it had been a domestic history of the most gentle and unexciting kind.

Except, indeed, in one point. The sympathies of the reader on whom the 'Woman in White' lays her spell, are, it is impossible to deny, devoted to the arch-villain of the story. The charm of the book, so far as character counts in its effect, is Fosco. He is a new type of the perennial enemy of goodness. But there is no resisting the charm of his good-nature, his wit, his foibles, his personal individuality. To put such a man so diabolically in the wrong seems a mistake somehow – though it is evident that an innocent man could never have been invested with such a combination of gifts. No villain of the century, so far as we are aware, comes within a hundred miles of him: he is more real, more genuine, more *Italian* even, in his fatness and size, in his love of pets and poetry, than the whole array of conventional Italian villains, elegant and subtle, whom we are accustomed to meet in literature. Fosco from his first entrance is master of the scene – his noiseless movements, his villanous bland philosophies, his enjoyment of life, his fine waistcoats – every detail about him is necessary to his perfection. Not Riccabocca himself, noble impersonation of national character as he is, is more complete or individual. The manner in which he despises and overawes and controls the violent and weak Sir Percival – the absolute but flattering way he exercises over his wife, the way in which he pervades the whole surrounding atmosphere with his deep 'ringing voice,' his snatches of song, his caresses to his pets – is quite masterly. The reader shares in the unwilling liking to which, at his first appearance, he beguiles Marian Halcombe; but the reader, notwithstanding the fullest proof of Fosco's villany, does not give him up, and take to hating him, as Marian does. The fact is, that he is by a very long way the most interesting personage in the book, and that it is with a certain sensation of sympathetic triumph that we watch him drive away in safety at last, after the final scene with Hartright, in which his own victorious force and cleverness turn discomfiture and confession into a brilliant climax of self-disclosure. So far from any vindictive desire to punish his ill-doing, we cannot understand how Hartright, or any other man, finds it in his heart to execute justice upon so hearty, genial, and exhilarating a companion. In short, when it turns out that Laura is not dead, and that the woman in white was not assisted to die, Count Fosco becomes rather an ill-used personage than otherwise. He has not done a single superfluous bit of villany – he has conducted himself throughout with a certain cheerful consideration for the feelings of his victims. He is so undaunted and undauntable save for a single moment – always master of the position, even when he retreats and gives in – that it is impossible to treat him as his crimes deserve. He is intended to be an impersonation of evil, a representative of every diabolical wile: but Fosco is not detestable; on the contrary, he is more interesting, and seizes on our sympathies more warmly than any other character in the book.

This, in the interests of art, it is necessary to protest against. The Foscos of ordinary life are not likely, we admit to take encouragement from Mr Wilkie Collins; but if this gentleman has many followers in fiction, it is a matter of certainty that the disciples will exaggerate the faults of their leader, and choose his least pleasant peculiarities for special study. Already it is a not uncommon result of fictitious writings, to make the worse appear the better cause. We have just laid down a clever novel, called 'East Lynne,' which some inscrutable breath of popular liking has blown into momentary celebrity. It is occupied with the story of a woman who permitted herself, in passion and folly, to be seduced from her husband. From first to last it is she alone in whom the reader feels any interest. Her virtuous rival we should like to bundle to the door and be rid of, anyhow. The Magdalen herself, who is only moderately interesting while she is good, becomes, as soon as she is a Magdalen, doubly a heroine. It is evident that nohow, except by her wickedness and sufferings, could she have gained so strong a hold upon our sympathies. This is dangerous and foolish work, as well as false, both to Art and Nature. Nothing can be more wrong and fatal than to represent the flames of vice as a purifying fiery ordeal, through which the penitent is to come elevated and sublimed. The error of Mr Wilkie Collins is of a different kind, but it is perhaps even more dangerous. Fosco in suffering would be Fosco in collapse, totally unmanned and uninteresting. It is the perfect ease, comfort, and light-heartedness of the man – what virtuous people would call his 'simple tastes,' his thorough enjoyment of life, and all the pleasant things within reach – his charming vanity and amiableness, as well as his force, strength and promptitude, that recommend him to our regard. Whatever the reason may be, few good men are permitted in books to enjoy their existence as this fat villain is permitted to enjoy his. He spreads himself out in the sun with a perfect pleasure and satisfaction, which it is exhilarating to behold. His crimes never give him an apparent twinge; his own complacent consciousness of the perfect cleverness with which they are carried out, confounds all compunctions. He is so smilingly aware of the successful evil he has done, and unaware of the guilt of it, that it seems heartless to take so innocent and genial a soul to task for his peccadilloes. Such is the great and radical drawback of the most notable of sensation novels. Fosco is, unquestionably, destined to be repented to infinitude, as no successful work can apparently exist in this imitative age without creating a shoal of copyists; and with every fresh imitation the picture will take more and more objectionable shades. The violent stimulant of serial publication – of *weekly* publication, with its necessity for frequent and rapid recurrence of piquant situation and startling incident – is the thing of all others most likely to develop the germ, and bring it to fuller and darker bearing. What Mr Wilkie Collins has done with delicate care and laborious reticence, his followers will attempt without any such discretion. We have already had specimens, as many as are desirable, of what the detective policeman can do for the enlivenment of literature: and it is into the hands of the literary Detective that this school of storytelling must inevitably fall at last. He is not a collaborateur whom we welcome with any pleasure into the republic of letters. His appearance is neither favourable to taste nor morals. It is only in rare cases, even in real life, that bystanders side with those conspirators of justice; and in fiction it is almost a necessity that the criminal who is tracked through coil after coil of evidence should become interesting, as we see him thrust into a corner by his remorseless pursuers. The rise of a Sensation School of art in any department is a thing to be watched with jealous eyes; but nowhere is it so dangerous as in fiction, where the artist cannot resort to a daring physical plunge, as on the stage, or to a blaze of palpable colour, as in the picture-gallery, but must take the passions and emotions of life to make his effects withal. We will not deny that the principle may be used with high and pure results, or that we should have little fault to find with it were it always employed with as much skill and self-control as in the 'Woman in White;' but that is an unreasonable hope; and it seems but too likely that Mr Wilkie Collins, in his remarkable novel, has given a new impulse to a kind of literature which must, more or less, find its inspiration in crime, and, more or less, make the criminal its hero.

Henry Mansel, Sensation Novels (1863)

Henry Longueville Mansel (1820–1871) was Professor of Ecclesiastical History at Oxford University. His critical views are representative of a mid-nineteenth-century conservative (High Church and High Tory) response to popular fiction. His essay on

'Sensation Novels', which first appeared in the *Quarterly Review* in 1862, is interesting for its analysis of a new kind of fiction which acts upon the nerves and fosters a diseased outlook. This new 'class of literature' is seen to mould the habits and attitudes of a particular readership, insidiously undermining traditional moral and religious values. Mansel blames periodicals, circulating libraries and railway bookstalls for having promoted the sales and circulation of a corrupt and morbid literature.

'I don't like preaching to the nerves instead of the judgement,' was the remark of a shrewd observer of human nature, in relation to a certain class of popular sermons. A class of literature has grown up around us, usurping in many respects, intentionally or unintentionally, a portion of the preacher's office, playing no inconsiderable part in moulding the minds and forming the habits and tastes of its generation; and doing so principally, we had almost said exclusively, by 'preaching to the nerves.' It would almost seem as if the paradox of Cabanis, *les nerfs, voilà tout l'homme*,[1] had been banished from the realm of philosophy only to claim a wider empire in the domain of fiction – at least if we may judge by the very large class of writers who seem to acknowledge no other element in human nature to which they can appeal. Excitement, and excitement alone, seems to be the great end at which they aim – an end which must be accomplished at any cost by some means or other, 'si possis, recte; si non, quocumque modo.'[2] And as excitement, even when harmless in kind, cannot be continually produced without becoming morbid in degree, works of this class manifest themselves as belonging, some more, some less, but all to some extent, to the morbid phenomena of literature – indications of a wide-spread corruption, of which they are in part both the effect and the cause; called into existence to supply the cravings of a diseased appetite, and contributing themselves to foster the disease, and to stimulate the want which they supply . . .

Various causes have been at work to produce this phenomenon of our literature. Three principal ones may be named as having had a large share in it – periodicals, circulating libraries, and railway bookstalls. A periodical, from its very nature, must contain many articles of an ephemeral interest, and of the character of goods made to order. The material part of it is a fixed quantity, determined by rigid boundaries of space and time; and on this Procrustean bed the spiritual part must needs be stretched to fit. A given number of sheets of print, containing so many lines per sheet, must be produced weekly or monthly, and the diviner element must accommodate itself to these conditions. A periodical, moreover, belongs to the class of works which most men borrow, and do not buy, and in which, therefore, they take only a transitory interest. Few men will burden their shelves with a series of volumes which have no coherence in their parts, and no limit in their number, whose articles of personal interest may be as one halfpennyworth of bread to an intolerable quantity of sack,[3] and which have no other termination to their issue than the point at which they cease to be profitable. Under these circumstances, no small stimulus is given to the production of tales of the marketable stamp, which, after appearing piecemeal in weekly or monthly instalments, generally enter upon a second stage of their insect-life in the form of a handsome reprint under the auspices of the circulating library.

This last-named institution is the oldest of the three . . . From the days of the 'Minerva Press' (that synonym for the dullest specimens of the light reading of our grandmothers)[4] to those of the thousand and one tales of the current season, the circulating library has been the chief hot-bed for forcing a crop of writers without talent and readers without discrimination. It is to literature what a *magasin de modes* is to dress, giving us the latest fashion, and little more . . . Subscription, as compared with purchase, produces no doubt a great increase in the quantity of books procurable, but with a corresponding deterioration in the quality. The buyer of books is generally careful to select what for his own purposes is worth buying; the subscriber is often content to take the good the gods provide him,[5] glancing lazily down the library catalogue, and picking out some title which promises amusement or excitement. . . .

The railway stall, like the circulating library, consists partly of books written expressly for its use, partly of reprints in a new phase of their existence – a phase internally that of the grub, with small print and cheap paper, externally that of the butterfly, with a tawdry cover, ornamented with a highly-coloured picture, hung out like a signboard, to give promise of the entertainment to be had within. The picture, like the book, is generally of the sensation kind, announcing some exciting scene to follow. A pale young lady in a white dress, with a dagger in her hand, evidently prepared for some desperate struggle, or a Red Indian in his war-paint; or, if the plot turns on smooth instead of violent villany, a priest persuading a dying man to sign a paper; or a disappointed heir burning a will; or a treacherous lover telling his flattering tale to some deluded maid or wife. The exigencies of railway travelling do not allow much time for examining the merits of a book before purchasing it; and keepers of bookstalls, as well as of refreshment-rooms, find an advantage in offering their customers something hot and strong, something that may catch the eye of the hurried passenger, and promise temporary excitement to relieve the dulness of a journey.

These circumstances of production naturally have their effect on the quality of the articles produced. Written to meet an ephemeral demand, aspiring only to an ephemeral existence, it is natural that they should have recourse to rapid and ephemeral methods of awakening the interest of their readers, striving to act as the dram or the dose, rather than as the solid food, because the effect is more immediately perceptible. And as the perpetual cravings of the dramdrinker or the valetudinarian for the spirits or physic are hardly intelligible to the man of sound health and regular appetites, so, to one called from more wholesome studies to survey the wide field of sensational literature, it is difficult to realise the idea which its multifarious contents necessarily suggest, that these books must form the staple mental food of a very large class of readers . . .

The sensation novel, be it mere trash or something worse, is usually a tale of our own times. Proximity is, indeed, one great element of sensation. It is necessary to be near a mine to be blown up by its explosion; and a tale which aims at electrifying the nerves of the reader is never thoroughly effective unless the scene be laid in our own days and among the people we are in the habit of meeting. We read with little emotion, though it comes in the form of history, Livy's narrative of the secret poisonings carried on by nearly two hundred Roman ladies; we feel but a feeble interest in an authentic record of the crimes of a Borgia or a Brinvilliers; but we are thrilled with horror, even in fiction, by the thought that such things may be going on around us and among us. The man who shook our hand with a hearty English grasp half an hour ago – the woman whose beauty and grace were the charm of last night, and whose gentle words sent us home better pleased with the world and with ourselves – how exciting to think that under these pleasing outsides may be concealed some demon in human shape, a Count Fosco or a Lady Audley! He may have assumed all that heartiness to conceal some dark plot against our life or honour, or against the life and honour of one yet dearer: she may have left that gay scene to muffle herself in a thick veil and steal to a midnight meeting with some villanous accomplice. He may have a mysterious female, immured in a solitary tower or a private lunatic asylum, destined to come forth hereafter to menace the name and position of the excellent lady whom the world acknowledges as his wife: she may have a husband lying dead at the bottom of a well, and a fatherless child nobody knows where. All this is no doubt very exciting; but even excitement may be purchased too dearly; and we may be permitted to doubt whether the pleasure of a nervous shock is worth the cost of so much morbid anatomy if the picture be true, or so much slanderous misrepresentation if it be false.

Walter Pater, The Modern Mind (1866)

Walter Horatio Pater (1839–1894) was one of the most subtle and influential thinkers of his time. His elegant, poetic prose was greatly admired and emulated by his contemporaries. An unusual art critic and aesthetic philosopher, Pater habitually drew the attention of his readers to the qualities of beauty and strangeness in the art and literature that he chose to write about. As a fellow of Brasenose College, Oxford, from 1864 onwards, he was well placed to influence a generation of writers and painters that included Algernon Charles Swinburne,

Dante Gabriel Rossetti, Oscar Wilde, Gerard Manley Hopkins and W.B. Yeats. His novel *Marius the Epicurean* was published in 1885, but it was his *Studies in the History of the Renaissance* (1873), later revised and republished as *The Renaissance* (1877), that made the greatest impact and came to be seen as a founding text for the Aesthetic Movement. The extract that follows is taken from an essay on Coleridge that first appeared in the *Westminster Review* in 1866 and was later reprinted in *Appreciations* (1889). The essay is remarkable for its frankness and acuity in describing the characteristic tendencies of modern thought.

Forms of intellectual and spiritual culture sometimes exercise their subtlest and most artful charm when life is already passing from them. Searching and irresistible as are the changes of the human spirit on its way to perfection, there is yet so much elasticity of temper that what must pass away sooner or later is not disengaged all at once, even from the highest order of minds. Nature, which by one law of development evolves ideas, hypotheses, modes of inward life, and represses them in turn, has in this way provided that the earlier growth should propel its fibres into the later, and so transmit the whole of its forces in an unbroken continuity of life. Then comes the spectacle of the reserve of the elder generation exquisitely refined by the antagonism of the new. That current of new life chastens them while they contend against it. Weaker minds fail to perceive the change: the clearest minds abandon themselves to it. To feel the change everywhere, yet not abandon oneself to it, is a situation of difficulty and contention. Communicating, in this way, to the passing stage of culture, the charm of what is chastened, high-strung, athletic, they yet detach the highest minds from the past, by pressing home its difficulties and finally proving it impossible. Such has been the charm of many leaders of lost causes in philosophy and in religion. It is the special charm of Coleridge, in connexion with those older methods of philosophic inquiry, over which the empirical philosophy of our day has triumphed.

Modern thought is distinguished from ancient by its cultivation of the 'relative' spirit in place of the 'absolute'. Ancient philosophy sought to arrest every object in an eternal outline, to fix thought in a necessary formula, and the varieties of life in a classification by 'kinds,' or *genera*. To the modern spirit nothing is, or can be rightly known, except relatively and under conditions. The philosophical conception of the relative has been developed in modern times through the influence of the sciences of observation. Those sciences reveal types of life evanescing into each other by inexpressible refinements of change. Things pass into their opposites by accumulation of undefinable quantities. The growth of those sciences consists in a continual analysis of facts of rough and general observation into groups of facts more precise and minute. The faculty for truth is recognised as a power of distinguishing and fixing delicate and fugitive detail. The moral world is ever in contact with the physical, and the relative spirit has invaded moral philosophy from the ground of the inductive sciences. There it has started a new analysis of the relations of body and mind, good and evil, freedom and necessity. Hard and abstract moralities are yielding to a more exact estimate of the subtlety and complexity of our life. Always, as an organism increases in perfection, the conditions of its life become more complex. Man is the most complex of the products of nature. Character merges into temperament: the nervous system refines itself into intellect. Man's physical organism is played upon not only by the physical conditions about it, but by remote laws of inheritance, the vibration of long-past acts reaching him in the midst of the new order of things in which he lives. When we have estimated these conditions he is still not yet simple and isolated; for the mind of the race, the character of the age, sway him this way or that through the medium of language and current ideas. It seems as if the most opposite statements about him were alike true: he is so receptive, all the influences of nature and of society ceaselessly playing upon him, so that every hour in his life is unique, changed altogether by a stray word, or glance, or touch. It is the truth of these relations that experience gives us, not the truth of eternal outlines ascertained once for all, but a world of fine gradations and subtly linked conditions, shifting intricately as we ourselves change – and bids us, by a constant clearing of the organs of observation and perfecting of analysis, to make what we can of these. To the intellect, the critical spirit, just these subtleties of effect are more precious than anything else. What is lost in precision of form is gained in intricacy of expression. It is no vague scholastic abstraction that will satisfy the speculative instinct in our modern minds. Who would change the colour or curve of a rose-leaf for that *οὐσία ἀχρώματος, ἀσχημάτιστος, ἀναφής* – that colourless, formless, intangible, being – Plato put so high? For the true illustration of the speculative temper is not the Hindoo mystic, lost to sense, understanding, individuality, but one such as Goethe, to whom every moment of life brought its contribution of experimental, individual knowledge; by whom no touch of the world of form, colour, and passion was disregarded.

Friedrich Nietzsche, On Truth and Lying in an Extra-Moral Sense (1865)

The writings of Friedrich Wilhelm Nietzsche (1844–1900) have had a profound impact on philosophy, literature and critical theory since the late nineteenth century. Novelists and poets such as D.H. Lawrence and W.B. Yeats have been influenced by Nietzsche, and his powerful presence continues to be felt in the writings of theorists such as Jacques Derrida and Jean-François Lyotard. Among Nietzsche's best-known works are *The Birth of Tragedy* (1872), *Beyond Good and Evil* (1886), and *The Will to Power* (1901). The essay that follows is an early and little-known composition, but one that carries immense significance in relation to contemporary debates about perception, truth and knowledge.

The intellect as a means of preserving the individual develops its greatest strength in dissimulation, for this is the means by which weaker, less robust individuals preserve themselves when as such it would be futile to fight for their existence with horns or sharp predatory teeth. In Man this art of dissimulation reaches its peak: here deception, flattery, lies and deceit, the talking behind someone's back, the representing, the living in borrowed glory, the wearing of masks, the euphemistic convention, the playing out of roles for others and for oneself, in short the perpetual fluttering around that *one* flame of vanity is so much the rule and the law, that almost nothing is more inconceivable than that human beings could ever be subject to a pure and honourable drive towards Truth. They are steeped in illusion and dream images, their eye slides only over the surface of things and sees 'Forms'; their way of feeling leads nowhere into Truth, but contents itself with receiving stimuli and at the same time playing a game of tag on the back of things. Thus Man, through a lifetime of nights of dreams allows himself to be deceived, without his moral feeling seeking in any way to hinder this: and yet it is said there are those who through sheer strength of will have overcome the habit of snoring. What does Man really know about himself? Yes, were he just once to glimpse himself wholly, laid out, as if in an illuminated glass case . . .

In so far as the individual wants to preserve himself against other individuals, in the natural state of things he uses intellect for the most part only as disguise: since, however, at the same time, Man wishes, out of boredom and necessity, to exist as part of society and as one of the herd, he needs a peace agreement and endeavours that at least the greatest *bellum omnium contra omnes* should vanish from his world. This peace agreement brings something with it which looks like the first step towards attaining this elusive drive for Truth. Namely, that is established which from now on is to be taken as 'Truth', that is, an evenly valid and binding description of things is invented, and the legislation of language also yields the first laws of Truth: since here for the first time the contrast emerges between Truth and Lie. The liar uses valid descriptions, words, to make the unreal appear real; he says for instance: 'I am rich', whereas for his state, plain 'poor' would be the right description. He abuses firm conventions through any kind of exchange or even turning names back to front. If he does this in a selfish and even damaging way, society will not trust him anymore and will therefore exclude him. Men flee from betrayal less than from injury through betrayal; in the same way, they hate not so much deception as the bad, hostile consequences of certain kinds of deception. In a similarly restricted sense Man wants only Truth, he desires the pleasant, life preserving consequences of Truth, is indifferent to its pure recognition without consequence, and even inclined to be hostile to damaging and destructive Truths. And furthermore: how does it stand with the conventions of language? Are they perhaps products of knowledge, of the sense of Truth, do things and descriptions match one another? Is language the adequate expression of all realities?

Only through forgetfulness can Man begin to believe, wrongly, that he possesses a 'Truth' as I have described it. If he will not content himself with Truth in the form of tautology, i.e. with empty shells, he will always be trading Truths for illusions. What is a word? The re-imaging of a nerve stimulus in sounds. The leap from the nerve stimulus to a cause beyond us is, however, already the result of a wrong and unjustified application of the basic principle. How could we, if Truth alone were crucial in the genesis of language, if just the perspective of certainty were decisive to description, how could we say: the stone is hard: as though 'hard' were already otherwise known to us and were not just a purely subjective stimulus! We divide things into genders, we characterise the tree as masculine, the plant as feminine: what arbitrary transpositions! How far beyond from the canon of certainty! We speak of a snake, the definition implies only that which writhes and could just as well apply to a worm. What arbitrary partitions, what one-sided preferences, now this, now that quality of a thing. The various languages, put side by side, show that with words it is neither a question of Truth nor of adequate expression: otherwise there would be fewer languages. The 'thing-in-itself' (which would be pure Truth without consequences) is wholly inconceivable to the shaper of language and absolutely not worth striving for. He describes only the relations of things to human beings and expresses them with the help of the sharpest metaphors. A nerve stimulus first transposed into an image! First metaphor. The image reshaped into a sound! Second metaphor . . .

Let us think in particular of the forming of concepts. Every word becomes a concept immediately in that it does not serve simply as a memory for the single, utterly original experience to which it owes its creation, but must apply at the same time to countless other cases, more or less similar and thus strictly speaking never identical, and hence to entirely different cases. Every concept evolves through likening the unlike. As surely as one leaf is never quite like another, so the concept of a leaf is formed by the random fall of these individual differences, by forgetting how they differ and awakens the idea that in nature there might be, apart from leaves, something that is 'leaf', a prototype, from which all leaves are woven, drawn, measured, dyed, crimped and painted, but by unskilled hands so that no single one turns out as correct and reliable as a true copy of the original . . .

What, then, is Truth? – a moveable hoard of metaphors, metonymies, anthropomorphisms, in short a sum of human relations which, poetically and rhetorically intensified, transposed, adorned and after long use comes to be seen by people as firm, canonical and binding. Truths are illusions, whereby we have forgotten that they are such, metaphors that have become worn out and have lost their force of meaning, coins that have lost their picture and are now considered as mere metal, no longer as coins.

We still do not know from where the drive for truth comes, for until now we have only heard of the duty that a society imposes in order to exist: being truthful, that is to say, using the usual metaphors, thus expressed in moral terms; lying from commitment following an established convention, lying with the herd in a style binding for all. Now of course Man forgets that this is how it stands with him, he lies unknowingly in the given manner, and according to a hundred years of habit, and arrives through just this *unknowing*, through just this forgetting, at a feeling of Truth. With the feeling of being committed to characterising one thing as red, another as cold and a third as dumb, a moral response relating to Truth is awakened: by his opposition to the liar whom nobody trusts, whom all exclude, Man is reassured of that in Truth which is venerable, trustworthy and useful. He places his actions as a '*reasoning*' being under the domination of abstractions, he no longer suffers being torn away by sudden impressions and perceptions. He generalises all these impressions first to more colourless, cooler concepts, on which to harness the vehicle of his life and actions. Everything that raises Man above the animals depends on this ability to sweep these metaphors of perception into a schema, thus to dissolve an image into a concept.

Within the realm of these schemata, something is possible which the vividness of first impressions would never permit, a pyramidal order built up of rank and caste, to create a new world of laws, privileges, subordinations and delimitations which now stands against that other vivid perceptual world of first impressions as more solid, more general, familiar and human and thus the more regulatory and imperative. Whilst every metaphor of perception is individual and without parallel and thus knows how to evade all categorisation, the great structure of concepts displays the rigid regularity of a Roman columbarium and exhales in its logic that severity and coolness that is proper to mathematics. No one who feels the breath of this coolness would readily believe that the concept itself, bony and eight-cornered like a die and like others interchangeable, is only left over as the *residue of a metaphor*, and that the illusion of artistic transposition of nerve stimulus into images is, if not the mother, then the grandmother of each and every concept. Within this conceptual game of dice, 'Truth' means using each die as it is marked, counting its eyes exactly, creating proper rubrics and never offending against the orders of caste and the protocols of class and status . . .

It is only through forgetting that primitive world of metaphor, only through the hardening and rigidifying of a natural mass of images streaming in a molten flow from the primeval wealth of human imagination, only through the unconquerable belief that *this* sun, *this* window, *this* table is a Truth in itself, only through forgetting himself as a subject, as an *artistic, creative* subject, that Man lives in some peace, security and consequence: could he leave the prison walls of this belief for only a moment, his self-assurance would instantly be gone. It even costs him effort to admit to himself that an insect or a bird perceives an entirely different world than does a human being, and that the question which of the two perceptions of the world is the more correct, is a meaningless one, since this can only be assessed with the yardstick of '*correct perception*', which means with a yardstick that is *not present.* Above all, however, it seems to me, 'correct perception' – that would mean the adequate expression of an object in the subject – is an impossibility, an un-thing full of contradictions, for between two utterly different spheres, as between subject and object, there is no causality, no correctness, no expression but at most only an *aesthetic* relation, meaning a hinting transposition, a stammered translation into a completely foreign language which requires a mediating sphere, a mediating energy freely poetic and freely creative. The word 'appearance' is a seductive one, for which reason I avoid it wherever possible, for it is not true that the essence of things appears in the empirical world. A painter who lacks hands and who would like to express in song the image floating before him, will always betray more in this exchange of spheres than the empirical world betrays of the essence of things. Even the relation between a nerve-stimulus and the image it creates is not in itself a necessary one: though if the same image is generated a million times over and passed down through many generations of men it will eventually appear to the whole of mankind as an invariable response to the same occasion and thus finally acquire the same meaning for people as if it were the single necessary image, and as if that relation between the original nerve-stimulus and the image created were a close causal one: as when a constantly recurring dream becomes experienced as reality and judged as such. The hardening and rigidifying of a metaphor is, however, no guarantee for the necessity and exclusive justification of that metaphor . . .

That drive to construct metaphors, that basic drive of human beings, which one cannot discount for an instant because in so doing one would discount humanity itself is, despite the fact that a uniform and rigid new world is built as an imprisoning fortress out of the concepts which are its ephemeral products, nevertheless not compelled and scarcely constrained. Man seeks out for himself a new realm for his actions and a different river bed and he finds it in myth and above all in art. He constantly shifts and changes the rubrics and the cells of concepts by setting up new transpositions, metaphors and metonymies; he constantly shows the desire to reshape the existing world of the waking man, to make it as colourfully irregular, as inconsequent and incoherent, as attractive and always new, as is the world of dreams. Indeed, it is only through the rigid and regular web of concepts that the waking man can be clear that he is awake, and he will come to believe that he is dreaming should this web of concepts be torn apart by art. Pascal was right when he maintained that should we dream the same dream every night, it would matter to us as much as the things we see every day. 'If a craftsman could be sure of dreaming for twelve hours every night that he was a king, I believe,' says Pascal, 'that he would be as happy as the king who dreamt for twelve hours every night that he was a craftsman.' The waking day of a people who respond to myth, as the ancient Greeks did, is in fact, through the constantly acting wonder that myth engenders, more like a dream than is the day of the scientifically sobered thinker. If every tree is able to speak as a nymph, and a god in the likeness of a bull able to carry off young women, if the goddess Athene herself is suddenly to be seen driving with a fine span of horses in the company of Peisistratos through the markets of Athens – and the honest citizen of Athens believed this – then anything is possible at any moment as in a dream, and the whole of Nature swarms about Man, as if she were nothing more than the Masquerade of the Gods, whose amusement it was to take on any shape, to the deception of Mankind.

E.S. Dallas, The Gay Science (1866)

Eneas Sweetland Dallas (1828–1879) was a journalist, literary critic and aesthetic philosopher, best known for his *Poetics: An Essay on Poetry* (1852) and *The Gay Science* (1866), from which the following extracts are taken. As these extracts make clear, Dallas is essentially concerned with distinguishing between the object of science, which is knowledge ('a perfect grasp of all the facts which lie within the sphere of consciousness') and the object of art, which is pleasure ('a sensible possession or enjoyment of the world beyond consciousness'), but his writings also dwell on the moral value of art and reveal a strong interest in the novel of sensation and its sexual politics. The term 'Gay Science', as Dallas explains, is adopted from 'El Gai Saber', allegedly used by the troubadour poets to describe their vocation.

The Hidden Soul

I have now at some length, though after all we have but skimmed along the ground, gone over nearly all the heads of evidence that betoken the existence of a large mental activity – a vast world of thought, out of consciousness. I have tried to show with all clearness the fact of its existence, the magnitude of its area and the potency of its effects. In the dark recesses of memory, in unbidden suggestions, in trains of thought unwittingly pursued, in multiplied waves and currents all at once flashing and rushing, in dreams that cannot be laid, in the nightly rising of the somnambulist, in the clairvoyance of passion, in the force of instinct, in the obscure, but certain, intuitions of the spiritual life, we have glimpses of a great tide of life ebbing and flowing, rippling and rolling and beating about where we cannot see it; and we come to a view of humanity not very different from that which Prospero, though in melancholy mood, propounded when he said:

We are such stuff
As dreams are made of; and our little life
Is rounded with a sleep.

We are all more or less familiar with this doctrine as it is put forward by divines. 'The truth is,' says Henry More, 'man's soul in this drunken, drowsy condition she is in, has fallen asleep in the body, and, like one in a dream, talks to the bed-posts, embraces her pillow instead of her friend, falls down before statues instead of adoring the eternal and invisible God, prays to stocks and stones instead of speaking to Him that by his word created all things.' Such expressions as these however have about them the looseness of parable; and one can accept Prospero's lines almost literally. For what is it? Our little life is rounded with a sleep; our conscious existence is a little spot of light, rounded or begirt with a haze of slumber – not a dead but a living slumber, dimly-lighted and like a visible darkness, but full of dreams and irrepressible activity, an unknown and indefinable, but real and enjoyable mode of life – a Hidden Soul.

See, then, the point at which we have now arrived, and let us look about us before we go further. It has been shown that our minds lead a double life – one life in consciousness, another and a vaster life beyond it. Never mind for the present how much I have failed in the attempt to map with accuracy the geography of that region of the mind which stretches out of consciousness, if the existence of such a tract be recognised. We have a conscious and voluntary life; we have at the same time, of not less potency, an unconscious and involuntary life; and my argument is that the unknown, automatic power which in common parlance we call imagination is but another name for one of these lives – the unknown and automatic life of the mind with all its powers. Our conscious life we know so well that we have been able to divide it into parts, calling this part memory, that reason, and that other, feeling; but of the unconscious life we know so little that we lump it under the one name of imagination, and suppose imagination to be a division of the mind co-ordinate with memory, reason, or feeling. I should hope that by the mere description of the hidden life I may have, to some extent, succeeded in making this thesis good – or may at least have established a presumption in its favour. The completion of the proof however will rest upon the next chapter, in which it ought to be shown that the free play of thought, the spontaneous action of the mind, generates whatever we understand as the creation of fantasy. This chapter has been all analysis; the next should be synthetic. Hitherto we have regarded the existence of the hidden soul only as a fact; now it has to be shown that imagination is nothing else. I could not help giving, in the course of this chapter, a few indications of the proof. Now the proof may be demanded in all due form.

The Secrecy of Art

We ought now to proceed at once to the consideration of pleasure. I began by showing that pleasure is the end of art. I brought forward a cloud of witnesses to prove that this has always been acknowledged. And after showing that all these witnesses, in their several ways, define and limit the pleasure which art seeks, we discovered that the English school of critics has, more than any other, the habit of insisting on a limitation to it, which is more full of meaning as a principle in art than all else that has been advanced by the various schools of criticism. That the pleasure of art is the pleasure of imagination is the one grand doctrine of English criticism, and the most pregnant doctrine of all criticism. But it was difficult to find out what imagination really is; and therefore the last three chapters were allotted to an inquiry into the nature of it. The result at which we have arrived is that imagination is but another name for that unconscious action of the mind which may be called the Hidden Soul. And with this understanding, we ought now to proceed to the scrutiny of pleasure. I will, however, ask the reader to halt for a few minutes, that I may point out how this understanding as to the nature of imagination bears on the definition with which we started – that pleasure is the end of art. Few are willing to acknowledge pleasure as the end of art. I took some pains to defend pleasure in this connection as a fit object of pursuit, and if I have not satisfied every mind, I hope now to do so by the increased light which the analysis of imagination will have thrown upon the subject.

We started with the common doctrine, that art is the opposite of science, and that, as the object of science is knowledge, so that of art is pleasure. But if the reader has apprehended what I have tried to convey to him as to the existence within us of two great worlds of thought – a double life, the one known or knowable, the other unknown and for the most part unknowable, he will be prepared, if not to accept, yet to understand this further conception of the difference between science and art that the field of science is the known and the knowable, while the field of art is the unknown and the unknowable. It is a strange paradox that the mind should be described as possessing and compassing the unknown. But my whole argument has been working up to this point, and, I trust, rendering it credible – that the mind may possess and be possessed by thoughts of which nevertheless it is ignorant.

Now, because such a statement as this will appear to be a paradox to those who have not considered it; also, because to say that the field of art is the unknown, is like saying that the object of art is a negation, it is fit that in ordinary speech we should avoid such phrases, and be content with the less paradoxical expression – that the object of art is pleasure. The object of science, we say, is knowledge – a perfect grasp of all the facts which lie within the sphere of consciousness. The object of art is pleasure – a sensible possession or enjoyment of the world beyond consciousness. We do not know that world, yet we feel it – feel it chiefly in pleasure, but sometimes in pain, which is the shadow of pleasure. It is a vast world we have seen; of not less importance to us than the world of knowledge. It is in the hidden sphere of thought, even more than in the open one, that we live, and move, and have our being; and it is in this sense that the idea of art is always a secret. We hear much of the existence of such a secret, and people are apt to say – If a secret exist, and if the artist convey it in his art, why does he not plainly tell us what it is? But here at once we fall into contradictions, for as all language refers to the known, the moment we begin to apply it to the unknown, it fails. Until the existence of an unknown hidden life within us be thoroughly well accepted, not only felt, but also to some extent understood, there will always be an esoteric mode of stating the doctrine, which is not for the multitude.

The Ethics of Art

. . . The frequent condemnation of art is, I say, but a part of this general law by which, at some time or other, we malign our own joys, and almost always despise the joys of our neighbours. The discontent of the human heart and its egotism are two main characteristics that have an enormous but unacknowledged influence on our estimate of pleasure, indeed, on all our moral judgments. Pleasure is the most conceited thing on earth: nothing like our own choice morsel. Ozanam, the mathematician, said it was for the Sorbonne to discuss, for the Pope to decide, and for the mathematician to go to heaven in a perpendicular line. If Plato turned the poets out of his republic, he made the philosophers kings in it. This is the egotism of pleasure; as in Bacon's objection to poetry that it is the pleasure of a lie, we see chiefly the discontent of it. The prevalence of such facts leads us straight to the conclusion, that the mere statement of dislike to art, and the mere assertion of its moral wrong, must – aloof from intelligible reasoning – go for nought. It is but part of a widespread asceticism, which clings like a parasite to the sense of enjoyment, always irritates it, and sometimes sucks it dry. We may reject assertion, therefore, and insist on dealing only with facts and arguments.

Now, in pushing any inquiry into the moral influence of art, I suppose it is almost needless to begin by explaining that here there is no question as to the direct lesson which art *professes* to teach, if it make any profession at all. Its worth is not to be measured by the lower – that is, the more palpable order of utilities. Bartholin declared that ailments, chiefly the falling sickness, were curable by rhymes; Dr. Serenus Sammonicus offered to cure a quartan ague by laying the fourth book of the Iliad under the patient's head; Virgil was once believed to be an excellent fortune-teller. The moral usefulness which we expect from art bears no sort of resemblance to these physical utilities. Any one who will look for conscious moral aim in art, will find it nearly purposeless. The troubadour gave to his calling the name of El Gai Saber, the gay science. To conclude, however, that nobleness of tendency may not flourish under gaiety of mien, is to imitate the poor satyr, puzzled to understand how a man could blow hot and cold with one and the same mouth. The avowed object of the poet is pleasure, and he seems to have his eye set only on present enjoyment, but it is like a rower, that looks one way and pulls another. Shenstone paints the village schoolmistress as disguised in looks profound. On the contrary, it was a reproach to the greatest of all teachers that he was a wine-bibber and a friend of sinners. The artist has still less the air of a teacher, and if he puts on the air of one, it sometimes happens that his influence is directly the reverse of his precepts.

Take the novelist, Richardson, for example, as he appears in his earliest work, which Fielding could not refrain from satirising. No book has ever been written in which there is such a parade of morality as in *Pamela*: nevertheless, it is a mischievous work that makes one sympathise with the disgust which it excited in Fielding. There is no end to the morals which it professes to instil – morals for husbands, morals for wives, morals for parents, morals for children, morals for masters, morals for servants. Ostensibly we are taught to admire the strength of virtue, and to note the reward of victory; but to understand the virtue, we are introduced to all the arts of the deceiver. There is a continual handling of pitch, in order to see how well it can be washed off: there is a continual drinking of poison, in order to show the potency of the antidote. The girl resists the seducer; but the pleasure of the story consists in entering into all the details of the struggle, and seeing how the squire takes liberties with the maid. When our senses have been duly tickled by these glowing descriptions, our consciences are soothed by a thick varnish of moral reflections and warnings that are entirely out of place. Notwithstanding its great show of virtue, such an exhibition seems to have a much more immoral tendency than the frank sinfulness of Fielding's works. 'Here is my hero,' says Fielding, 'full of wickedness and good heart: come and read of his doings.' 'Here is my heroine, full of virtue,' says Richardson: 'come and read of all her goodness.' But the descriptions of both are equally indelicate. It may be safely taken for granted that the force of Richardson's preachings goes for very little in comparison with the force of his pictures.

In justice, however, to so great a writer as Richardson, I should take particular care to state that these strictures apply only to his earliest work. In all his novels there is a parade of moral laws, but that parade is not offensive and hollow in the later ones. Notwithstanding the tediousness of its commencement, it is not risking much to say that *Clarissa Harlowe* is the finest novel in the English language. No one thinks of Richardson, with all his weak vanity, as a great genius; yet we have to recognise the existence of this curious phenomenon that, as a grig like Boswell produced our best piece of biography, so a squat, homely burgess, who fed his mind on 'says he' and 'says she,' produced what is still our best novel. It is not Richardson, however, that we have now to do with. The point I wish to bring out is this, that it is not moral sermons which constitute the moral force of a novel: it is example.

The Ethical Current

Not only does Thackeray insist upon a theory of character which implies in the sense of the poet the withering of the individual; we see precisely the same tendency in the school of fiction, which is the right opposite of his – what is called the sensation school. In that school the first consideration is given to the plot; and the characters must succumb to the exigencies of the plot. This is so clearly necessary that at length it has become a matter of course to find in a sensation novel a fine display of idiocy. There is always, in a sensation novel, one, or it may be two, half-witted creatures. The utility of these crazy beings is beyond belief. The things they see which nobody thought they would see, and remember which nobody thought they would remember, are even more remarkable than the things which, do what their friends will, they cannot be made to comprehend, and cannot be counted upon to repeat. Now, this species of novel is very much sneered at by persons of supposed enlightenment, and certainly it is more satisfactory to the pride of human nature to write and to read a novel of character. But I am not sure that, viewed in the abstract, such a work is either more true or more philosophical than the species of fiction in which the plot is of most importance. Suppose we attempt to state in abstract terms the difference between the two kinds of fiction.

Both profess to give us pictures of life, and both have to do with certain characters going through certain actions. The difference between the two lies solely in the relation of the characters portrayed to the actions described. In the novel of character man appears moulding circumstances to his will, directing the action for himself, supreme over incident and plot. In the opposite class of novel man is represented as made and ruled by circumstance; he is the victim of change and the puppet of intrigue. Is either of these views of life wholly true or wholly false? We may like the one better than the other. We may like to see men generally represented as possessed of decided character, masters of their destiny, and superior to circumstance; but is this view of life a whit more true than that which pictures the mass of men as endowed with faint characters, and as tossed hither and thither by the accidents of life, which we sometimes call fate and sometimes fortune? The art of fiction, which makes character succumb to the exigencies of plot, is just as defensible as that which breaks down incident before the weight of character. In point of fact, however, most novelists attempt to mix up the two extreme views of life, though they cannot help leaning to the one side or to the other; and the chief weakness of the plotting novels, as they are now written, is, that while they represent circumstances and incident as all-important, and characters amid the current of events as corks upon the waves, they generally introduce one character who, in violent contrast to all the others, is superior to the plot, plans the events, guides the storm, and holds the winds in the hollow of his hand. It is quite wonderful to see what one picked character can do in these stories in comparison with the others, who can do nothing. He predominates over the plot, and the plot predominates over all else. The violence of this contrast is an artistic error; but the views themselves which are thus contrasted are not necessarily false. To show man as the sport of circumstance may be a depressing view of human nature; but it is not fair to regard it as immoral nor to denounce it as utterly untrue. And whether it be true or false, still, as a popular view of life, it is one of the facts which we have to regard, when we consider either the Laureate's view, that the individual withers, or Archdeacon Hare's view, that this is an age of superficial character . . .

We continue to travel on the same line of rails, if now we give a few moments' attention to another characteristic of current literature – the feminine influence that pervades it. Women are of much account in it, and women produce a large share of it. Of late, indeed, the women have been having it all their own way in the realm of fiction. There was a time when the chief characters in fiction were men, and when to find a female portrait well drawn, especially if she was intended to rank as a heroine, was a rare exception. How colourless, for example, are most of Sir Walter Scott's heroines, when compared with the men in whom he delights. Now all the more important characters seem to be women. Our novelists have suddenly discovered that feminine character is an unworked mine of wealth, and they give us jewels of women in many a casket. This is all the more natural, seeing that most of our novelists just now seem to belong to the fair sex. But their masculine rivals follow in the same track. Nor is this tendency evident only in prose fiction. Look at Mr. Tennyson. A great poet is supposed to be the most perfect representative of his age, and the greater part of the Laureate's poetry may be described as a 'dream of fair women.' For one man he paints half a dozen women, and we remember the women better than the men. We remember the Princess and all her train; we remember Enid, Elaine, Vivien, Guinevere, Dora, Lilian, Isabel, the Gardener's Daughter, Maud, Godiva, the May Queen, Mariana, Lady Clara, and many more. How many men of the Laureate's drawing can we get against such a splendid array of women?

It must be allowed that this feminine tendency in our literature is not all for good. But the evil which belongs to it is not what one would expect. Woman embodies our highest ideas of purity and refinement. Cornelius Agrippa argues for the superiority of women over men, because Adam signifies earth, but Eve life. And in the thinking of the mediæval times we are often reminded that Adam was formed out of the dust of the earth, but Eve out of the living flesh; that Adam was created no one knows where, but that Eve was born in the garden of Eden. And now, when the influence of women is being poured into our literature, we expect to feel within it an evident access of refinement. We find the very opposite. The first object of the novelist is to get personages in whom we can be interested; the next is to put them in action. But when women are the chief characters, how are you to set them in motion? The life of women cannot well be described as a life of action. When women are thus put forward to lead the action of a plot, they must be urged into a false position. To get vigorous action they are described as rushing into crime, and doing masculine deeds. Thus they come forward in the worst light, and the novelist finds that to make an effect he has to give up his heroine to bigamy, to murder, to child-bearing by stealth in the Tyrol, and to all sorts of adventures which can only signify her fall. The very prominence of the position which women occupy in recent fiction leads by a natural process to their appearing in a light which is not good. This is what is called sensation. It is not wrong to make a sensation; but if the novelist depends for his sensation upon the action of a woman, the chances are that he will attain his end by unnatural means.

Walter Besant, The Art of Fiction (1884)

Sir Walter Besant (1836–1901) was a novelist and historian, perhaps best known for his two novels exposing the miserable conditions of working-class life in the East End of London: *All Sorts and Conditions of Men* (1882) and *Children of Gibeon* (1886). His philanthropic activities included the founding of 'The People's Palace' (a venue for theatre) on the Mile End Road. He also founded the Society of Authors to secure better legal protection for writers and worked to secure improved international copyright agreements. His Royal Institution lecture, 'The Art of Fiction', in which he acknowledged fiction as one of the fine arts and established its general 'laws', persuaded Henry James to write his famous reply with the same title.

I desire, this evening, to consider Fiction as one of the Fine Arts. In order to do this, and before doing it, I have first to advance certain propositions. They are not new, they are not likely to be disputed, and yet they have never been so generally received as to form part, so to speak, of the national mind. These propositions are three, though the last two directly spring from the first. They are:–

1. That Fiction is an Art in every way worthy to be called the sister and the equal of the Arts of Painting, Sculpture, Music, and Poetry; that is to say, her field is as boundless, her possibilities as vast, her excellences as worthy of admiration, as may be claimed for any of her sister Arts.

2. That it is an Art which, like them, is governed and directed by general laws; and that these laws may be laid down and taught with as much precision and exactness as the laws of harmony, perspective, and proportion.

3. That, like the other Fine Arts, Fiction is so far removed from the mere mechanical arts, that no laws or rules whatever can teach it to those who have not already been endowed with the natural and necessary gifts.

These are the three propositions which I have to discuss. It follows as a corollary and evident deduction, that, these propositions once admitted, those who follow and profess the Art of Fiction must be recognised as artists, in the strictest sense of the word, just as much as those who have delighted and elevated mankind by music and painting; and that the great Masters of Fiction must be placed on the same level as the great Masters in the other Arts. In other words, I mean that where the highest point, or what seems the highest point, possible in this Art is touched, the man who has reached it is one of the world's greatest men.

I cannot suppose that there are any in this room who would refuse to admit these propositions; on the contrary, they will seem to most here self-evident; yet the application of theory to practice, of principle to persons, may be more difficult. For instance, so boundless is the admiration for great Masters such as Raphael or Mozart, that if one were to propose that Thackeray should be placed beside them, on the same level, and as an equal, there would be felt by most a certain shock. I am not suggesting that the art of Thackeray is to be compared with that of Raphael, or that there is any similarity in the work of the two men; I only say that, Fiction being one Art, and Painting another and a sister Art, those who attain the highest possible distinction in either are equal.

Let us, however, go outside this room, among the multitudes by whom a novelist has never been considered an artist at all. To them the claim that a great novelist should be considered to occupy the same level as a great musician, a great painter, or a great poet, would appear at first a thing ludicrous and even painful. Consider for a moment how the world at large regards the novelist. He is, in their eyes, a person who tells stories, just as they used to regard the actor as a man who tumbled on the stage to make the audience laugh, and a musician as a man who fiddled to make the people dance. This is the old way of thinking, and most people think first as they have been taught to think; and next, as they see others think. It is, therefore, quite easy to understand why the art of novel-writing has always been, by the general mass, undervalued. First, while the leaders in every other branch of Art, in every department of Science, and in every kind of profession, receive their share of the ordinary national distinctions, no one over hears of honours being bestowed upon novelists. Neither Thackeray nor Dickens was ever, so far as I know, offered a Peerage; neither King, Queen, nor Prince in any country throughout the whole world takes the least notice of them. I do not say they would be any the better for this kind of recognition, but its absence clearly proves, to those who take their opinions from others, that they are not a class at all worthy of special honour. Then, again, in the modern craze which exists for every kind of art – so that we meet everywhere, in every household, amateur actors, painters, etchers, sculptors, modellers, musicians and singers, all of them serious and earnest in their aims – amateur novelists alone regard their Art as one which is learned by intuition. Thirdly, novelists are not associated as are painters; they hold no annual exhibitions, dinners, or conversazioni; they put no letters after their name; they have no President or Academy; and they do not themselves seem desirous of being treated as followers of a special Art. I do not say that they are wrong, or that much would be gained for Art if all the novelists of England were invited to Court and created into a Royal Academy. But I do say that for these three reasons it is easy to understand how the world at large does not even suspect that the writing of novels is one of the Fine Arts, and why they regard the story-teller with a sort of contempt. It is, I acknowledge, a kindly contempt – even an affectionate contempt; it is the contempt which the practical man feels for the dreamer, the strong man for the weak, the man who can do for the man who can only look on and talk.

. . . I would wish, in short, that from the very beginning their minds should be fully possessed with the knowledge that Fiction is an Art, and, like all other Arts, that it is governed by certain laws, methods, and rules, which it is their first business to learn.

It is then, first and before all, a real Art. It is the oldest, because it was known and practised long before Painting and her sisters were in existence or even thought of; it is older than any of the Muses from whose company she who tells stories has hitherto been excluded; it is the most widely spread, because in no race of men under the sun is it unknown, even though the stories may be always the same, and handed down from generation to generation in the same form; it is the most religious of all the Arts, because in every age until the present the lives, exploits and sufferings of gods, goddesses, saints and heroes have been the favourite theme; it has always been the most popular, because it requires neither culture, education, nor natural genius to understand and listen to a story; it is the most moral, because the world has always been taught whatever little morality it possesses by way of story, fable, apologue, parable, and allegory. It commands the widest influence, because it can be carried easily and everywhere, into regions where pictures are never seen and music is never heard; it is the greatest teaching power, because its lessons are most readily apprehended and understood. All this, which might have been said thousands of years ago, may be said to-day with even greater force and truth. That world which exists not, but is an invention or an imitation – that world in which the shadows and shapes of men move about before our eyes as real as if they were actually living and speaking among us, is like a great theatre accessible to all of every sort, on whose stage are enacted, at our own sweet will, whenever we please to command them, the most beautiful plays: it is, as every theatre should be, the school in which manners are learned: here the majority of reading mankind learn nearly all that they know of life and manners, of philosophy and art; even of science and religion. The modern novel converts abstract ideas into living models; it gives ideas, it strengthens faith, it preaches a higher morality than is seen in the actual world; it commands the emotions of pity, admiration, and terror; it creates and keeps alive the sense of sympathy; it is the universal teacher; it is the only book which the great mass of reading mankind ever do read; it is the only way in which people can learn what other men and women are like; it redeems their lives from dulness, puts thoughts, desires, knowledge, and even ambitions into their hearts: it teaches them to talk, and enriches their speech with epigrams, anecdotes and illustrations. It is an unfailing source of delight to millions, happily not too critical. Why, out of all the books taken down from the shelves of the public libraries, four-fifths are novels, and of all these that are bought nine-tenths are novels. Compared with this tremendous engine of popular influence, what are all the other Arts put together? Can we not alter the old maxim, and say with truth, Let him who pleases make the laws if I may write the novels?

As for the field with which this Art of Fiction occupies itself, it is, if you please, nothing less than the whole of Humanity. The novelist studies men and women; he is concerned with their actions and their thoughts, their errors and their follies, their greatness and their meanness; the countless forms of beauty and constantly varying moods to be seen among them; the forces which act upon them; the passions, prejudices, hopes and fears which pull them this way and that. He has to do, above all, and before all, with men and women. No one, for instance, among novelists, can be called a landscape painter, or a painter of sea-pieces, or a painter of fruit and flowers, save only in strict subordination to the group of characters with whom he is dealing. Landscape, sea, sky, and air, are merely accessories introduced in order to set off and bring into greater prominence the figures on the stage. The very first rule in Fiction is that the human interest must absolutely absorb everything else.

. . . It is, therefore, the especial characteristic of this Art, that, since it deals exclusively with men and women, it not only requires of its followers, but also creates in readers, that sentiment which is destined to be a most mighty engine in deepening and widening the civilization of the world. We call it Sympathy, but it means a great deal more than was formerly understood by the word . . . The modern Sympathy includes not only the power to pity the sufferings of others, but also that of understanding their very souls; it is the reverence for man, the respect for his personality, the recognition of his individuality, and the enormous value of the one man, the perception of one man's relation to another, his duties and responsibilities. Through the strength of this newly-born faculty, and aided by the guidance of a great artist, we are enabled to discern the real indestructible man beneath the rags and filth of a common castaway, and the possibilities of the meanest gutter child that steals in the streets for its daily bread. Surely that is a wonderful Art which endows the people – all the people – with this power of vision and of feeling. Painting has not done it, and could never do it; Painting has done more for nature than for humanity. Sculpture could not do it, because it deals with situation and form, rather than action. Music cannot do it, because Music (if I understand rightly) appeals especially to the individual concerning himself and his own aspirations. Poetry alone is the rival of Fiction, and in this respect it takes a lower place, not because Poetry fails to teach and interpret, but because Fiction is, and must always be, more popular.

. . . Humanity is so vast a field, that to one who goes about watching men and women, and does not sit at home and evolve figures out of inner consciousness, there is not and can never be any end or limit to the freshness and interest of these figures. It is the work of the artist to select the figures, to suppress, to copy, to group, and to work up the incidents which each one offers. The daily life of the world is not dramatic – it is monotonous; the novelist makes it dramatic by his silences, his suppressions, and his exaggerations. No one, for example, in fiction behaves quite in the same way as in real life; as on the stage, if an actor unfolds and reads a letter, the simple action is done with an exaggeration of gesture which calls attention to the thing and to its importance, so in romance, while nothing should be allowed which does not carry on the story, so everything as it occurs must be accentuated and yet deprived of needless accessory details. The gestures of the characters at an important juncture, their looks, their voices, may all be noted if they help to impress the situation. Even the weather, the wind and the rain, with some writers, have been made to emphasize a mood or a passion of a heroine. To know how to use these aids artistically is to the novelist exactly what to the actor is the right presentation of a letter, the handing of a chair, even the removal of a glove.

A third characteristic of Fiction, which should alone be sufficient to give it a place among the noblest forms of Art, is that, like Poetry, Painting, and Music, it becomes a vehicle, not only for the best thoughts of the writer, but also for those of the reader, so that a novelist may write truthfully and faithfully, but simply, and yet be understood in a far fuller and nobler sense than was present to his own mind. This power is the very highest gift of the poet. He has a vision and sees a thing clearly, yet perhaps afar off; another who reads him is enabled to get the same vision, to see the same thing, yet closer and more distinctly. For a lower intellect thus to lead and instruct a higher is surely a very great gift, and granted only to the highest forms of Art. And this it is which Fiction of the best kind does for its readers. It is, however, only another way of saying that Truth in Fiction produces effects similar to those produced by Truth in every other Art.

So far, then, I have showed that this Art of Fiction is the most ancient of all Arts, and the most popular; that its field is the whole of humanity; that it creates and develops that sympathy which is a kind of second sight; that, like all other Arts, its function is to select, to suppress, and to arrange; that it suggests as well as narrates. More might be said – a great deal more – but enough has been said to show that in these, the leading characteristics of any Art, Fiction is on exactly the same level as her sisters. Let me only add that in this Art, as in the others, there is, and will be always, whatever has been done already, something new to discover, something new to express, something new to describe. Surgeons dissect the body, and account for every bone and every nerve, so that the body of one man, considered as a collection of bones and nerves, is so far exactly like the body of another man. But the mind of man cannot be so exhausted: it yields discoveries to every patient student; it is absolutely inexhaustible; it is to every one a fresh and virgin field: and the most successful investigator leaves regions and tracts for his successor as vast as those he has himself gone over. Perhaps, after all, the greatest Psychologist is not the metaphysician but the novelist . . .

Again, the modern English novel, whatever form it takes, almost always starts with a conscious moral purpose. When it does not, so much are we accustomed to expect it, that one feels as if there has been a debasement of the Art. It is, fortunately, not possible in this country for any man to defile and defame humanity and still be called an artist; the development of modern sympathy, the growing reverence for the individual, the over-widening love of things beautiful and the appreciation of lives made beautiful by devotion and self-denial, the sense of personal responsibility among the English-speaking races, the deep-seated religion of our people, even in a time of doubt, are all forces which act strongly upon the artist as well as upon his readers, and lend to his work, whether he will or not, a moral purpose so clearly marked that it has become practically a law of English Fiction. We must acknowledge that this is a truly admirable thing, and a great cause for congratulation. At the same time, one may be permitted to think that the preaching novel is the least desirable of any, and to be unfeignedly rejoiced that the old religious novel, written in the interests of High Church or Low Church or any other Church, has gone out of fashion.

Next, just as in Painting and Sculpture, not only are fidelity, truth, and harmony to be observed in Fiction, but also beauty of workmanship. It is almost impossible to estimate too highly the value of careful workmanship, that is, of style. Every one, without exception, of the great Masters in Fiction, has recognised this truth. You will hardly find a single page in any of them which is not carefully and even elaborately worked up. I think there is no point on which critics of novels should place greater importance than this, because it is one which young novelists are so very liable to ignore. There ought not to be in a novel, any more than in a poem, a single sentence carelessly worded, a single phrase which has not been considered. Consider, if you please, any one of the great scenes in Fiction – how much of the effect is due to the style, the balanced sentences, the very words used by the narrator! This, however, is only one more point of similarity between Fiction and the sister Arts. There is, I know, the danger of attaching too much attention to style at the expense of situation, and so falling a prey to priggishness, fashions, and mannerisms of the day. It is certainly a danger; at the same time, it sometimes seems, when one reads the slipshod, careless English which is often thought good enough for story-telling, that it is almost impossible to overrate the value of style. There is comfort in the thought that no reputation worth having can be made without attending to style, and that there is no style, however rugged, which cannot be made beautiful by attention and pains . . .

In fact, every scene, however unimportant, should be completely and carefully finished. There should be no unfinished places, no sign anywhere of weariness or haste – in fact, no scamping. The writer must so love his work as to dwell tenderly on every age and be literally unable to send forth a single page of it without the finishing touches. We all of us remember that kind of novel in which every scene has the appearance of being hurried and scamped.

To sum up these few preliminary and general laws. The Art of Fiction requires first of all the power of description, truth and fidelity, observation, selection, clearness of conception and of outline, dramatic grouping, directness of purpose, a profound belief on the part of the story-teller in the reality of his story, and beauty of workmanship. It is, moreover, an Art which requires of those who follow it seriously that they must be unceasingly occupied in studying the ways of mankind, the social laws, the religions, philosophies, tendencies, thoughts, prejudices, superstitions of men and women. They must consider as many of the forces which act upon classes and upon individuals as they can discover; they should be always trying to put themselves into the place of another; they must be as inquisitive and as watchful as a detective, as suspicious as a criminal lawyer, as eager for knowledge as a physicist, and withal fully possessed of that spirit to which nothing appears mean, nothing contemptible, nothing unworthy of study, which belongs to human nature.

I repeat that I submit some of these laws as perhaps self-evident. If that is so, many novels which are daily submitted to the reviewer are written in wilful neglect and disobedience of them. But they are not really self-evident; those who aspire to be artists in Fiction almost invariably begin without any understanding at all of these laws. Hence the lamentable early failures, the waste of good material, and the low level of Art with which both the novel-writer and the novel-reader are too often contented. I am certain that if these laws were better known and more generally studied, a very large proportion of the bad works of which our critics complain would not be produced at all. And I am in great hopes that one effect of the establishment of the newly founded Society of Authors will be to keep young writers of fiction from rushing too hastily into print, to help them to the right understanding of their Art and its principles, and to guide them into true practice of their principles while they are still young, their imaginations strong, and their personal experiences as yet not wasted in foolish failures.

Henry James, The Art of Fiction (1884)

Henry James (1843–1916) was born in the United States, but became a British subject in 1915. This transatlantic experience, coupled with an education in Paris, Geneva and other European cities, underlies the strongly cosmopolitan sensibility of both his fiction and criticism. James continues to be widely praised as a critic, especially for his subtle appreciation of formal and stylistic devices in novel writing (see, for instance, Barbara Hardy's essay on James in Part II of this volume). 'The Art of Fiction' appeared in *Longman's Magazine* in September 1884 and responded explicitly to some of the concerns raised in Walter Besant's lecture of the same title. The references to Besant's lecture are amiable and good-humoured. While James wholeheartedly approves of Besant's recognition of fiction as one of the fine arts, he considers Besant's rules and regulations to be narrowly prescriptive and insists that there should be 'no limit' to the novelist's experiments, discoveries and achievements.

I should not have affixed so comprehensive a title to these few remarks, necessarily wanting in any completeness, upon a subject the full consideration of which would carry us far, did I not seem to discover a pretext for my temerity in the interesting pamphlet lately published under this name by Mr. Walter Besant. Mr. Besant's lecture at the Royal Institution – the original form of his pamphlet – appears to indicate that many persons are interested in the art of fiction and are not indifferent to such remarks as those who practise it may attempt to make about it. I am therefore anxious not to lose the benefit of this favourable association, and to edge in a few words under cover of the attention which Mr. Besant is sure to have excited. There is something very encouraging in his having put into form certain of his ideas on the mystery of story-telling.

It is a proof of life and curiosity – curiosity on the part of the brotherhood of novelists, as well as on the part of their readers. Only a short time ago it might have been supposed that the English novel was not what the French call *discutable*. It had no air of having a theory, a conviction, a consciousness of itself behind it – of being the expression of an artistic faith, the result of choice and comparison. I do not say it was necessarily the worse for that; it would take much more courage than I possess to intimate that the form of the novel, as Dickens and Thackeray (for instance) saw it, had any taint of incompleteness. It was, however, *naïf* (if I may help myself out with another French word); and, evidently, if it is destined to suffer in any way for having lost its *naïveté*, it has now an idea of making sure of the corresponding advantages. During the period I have alluded to there was a comfortable, good-humoured feeling abroad that a novel is a novel, as a pudding is a pudding, and that this was the end of it. But within a year or two, for some reason or other, there have been signs of returning animation – the era of discussion would appear to have been to a certain extent opened. Art lives upon discussion, upon experiment, upon curiosity, upon variety of attempt, upon the exchange of views and the comparison of standpoints; and there is a presumption that those times when no one has anything particular to say about it, and has no reason to give for practice or preference, though they may be times of genius, are not times of development, are times, possibly even, a little, of dulness. The successful application of any art is a delightful spectacle, but the theory, too, is interesting; and though there is a great deal of the latter without the former, I suspect there has never been a genuine success that has not had a latent core of conviction. Discussion, suggestion, formulation, these things are fertilizing when they are frank and sincere. Mr. Besant has set an excellent example in saying what he thinks, for his part, about the way in which fiction should be written, as well as about the way in which it should be published; for his view of the 'art,' carried on into an appendix, covers that too. Other labourers in the same field will doubtless take up the argument, they will give it the light of their experience, and the effect will surely be to make our interest in the novel a little more what it had for some time threatened to fail to be – a serious, active, inquiring interest, under protection of which this delightful study may, in moments of confidence, venture to say a little more what it thinks of itself.

It must take itself seriously for the public to take it so. The old superstition about fiction being 'wicked' has doubtless died out in England; but the spirit of it lingers in a certain oblique regard directed toward any story which does not more or less admit that it is only a joke. Even the most jocular novel feels in some degree the weight of the proscription that was formerly directed against literary levity; the jocularity does not always succeed in passing for gravity. It is still expected, though perhaps people are ashamed to say it, that a production which is after all only a 'make believe' (for what else is a 'story?') shall be in some degree apologetic – shall renounce the pretension of attempting really to compete with life. This, of course, any sensible wide-awake story declines to do, for it quickly perceives that the tolerance granted to it on such a condition is only an attempt to stifle it, disguised in the form of generosity. The old Evangelical hostility to the novel, which was as explicit as it was narrow, and which regarded it as little less favourable to our immortal part than a stage-play, was in reality far less insulting. The only reason for the existence of a novel is that it *does* compete with life. When it ceases to compete as the canvas of the painter competes, it will have arrived at a very strange pass. It is not expected of the picture that it will make itself humble in order to be forgiven; and the analogy between the art of the painter and the art of the novelist is, so far as I am able to see, complete. Their inspiration is the same, their process (allowing for the different quality of the vehicle) is the same, their success is the same. They may learn from each other, they may explain and sustain each other. Their cause is the same, and the honour of one is the honour of another. Peculiarities of manner, of execution, that correspond on either side, exist in each of them and contribute to their development. The Mahometans think a picture an unholy thing, but it is a long time since any Christian did, and it is therefore the more odd that in the Christian mind the traces (dissimulated though they may be) of a suspicion of the sister art should linger to this day. The only effectual way to lay it to rest is to emphasize the analogy to which I just alluded – to insist on the fact that as the picture is reality, so the novel is history. That is the only general description (which does it justice) that we may give of the novel. But history also is allowed to compete with life, as I say; it is not, any more than painting, expected to apologize. The subject-matter of fiction is stored up likewise in documents and records, and if it will not give itself away, as they say in California, it must speak with assurance, with the tone of the historian. Certain accomplished novelists have a habit of giving themselves away which must often bring tears to the eyes of people who take their fiction seriously. I was lately struck, in reading over many pages of Anthony Trollope, with his want of discretion in this particular. In a digression, a parenthesis or an aside, he concedes to the reader that he and this trusting friend are only 'making believe.' He admits that the events he narrates have not really happened, and that he can give his narrative any turn the reader may like best. Such a betrayal of a sacred office seems to me, I confess, a terrible crime; it is what I mean by the attitude of apology, and it shocks me every whit as much in Trollope as it would have shocked me in Gibbon or Macaulay. It implies that the novelist is less occupied in looking for the truth than the historian, and in doing so it deprives him at a stroke of all his standing-room. To represent and illustrate the past, the actions of men, is the task of either writer, and the only difference that I can see is, in proportion as he succeeds, to the honour of the novelist, consisting as it does in his having more difficulty in collecting his evidence, which is so far from being purely literary. It seems to me to give him a great character, the fact that he has at once so much in common with the philosopher and the painter; this double analogy is a magnificent heritage.

It is of all this evidently that Mr. Besant is full when he insists upon the fact that fiction is one of the *fine* arts, deserving in its turn of all the honours and emoluments that have hitherto been reserved for the successful profession of music, poetry, painting, architecture. It is impossible to insist too much on so important a truth, and the place that Mr. Besant demands for the work of the novelist may be represented, a trifle less abstractly, by saying that he demands not only that it shall be reputed artistic, but that it shall be reputed very artistic indeed. It is excellent that he should have struck this note, for his doing so indicates that there was need of it, that his proposition may be to many people a novelty. One rubs one's eyes at the thought; but the rest of Mr. Besant's essay confirms the revelation. I suspect, in truth, that it would be possible to confirm it still further, and that one would not be far wrong in saying that in addition to the people to whom it has never occurred that a novel ought to be artistic, there are a great many others who, if this principle were urged upon them, would be filled with an indefinable mistrust. They would find it difficult to explain their repugnance, but it would operate strongly to put them on their guard. 'Art,' in our Protestant communities, where so many things have got so strangely twisted about, is supposed, in certain circles, to have some vaguely injurious effect upon those who make it an important consideration, who let it weigh in the balance. It is assumed to be opposed in some mysterious manner to morality, to amusement, to instruction. When it is embodied in the work of the painter (the sculptor is another affair!) you know what it is; it stands there before you, in the honesty of pink and green and a gilt frame; you can see the worst of it at a glance, and you can be on your guard. But when it is introduced into literature it becomes more insidious – there is danger of its hurting you before you know it. Literature should be either instructive or amusing, and there is in many minds an impression that these artistic preoccupations, the search for form, contribute to neither end, interfere indeed with both. They are too frivolous to be edifying, and too serious to be diverting; and they are, moreover, priggish and paradoxical and superfluous. That, I think, represents the manner in which the latent thought of many people who read novels as an exercise in skipping would explain itself if it were to become articulate. They would argue, of course, that a novel ought to be 'good,' but they would interpret this term in a fashion of their own, which, indeed, would vary considerably from one critic to another. One would say that being good means representing virtuous and aspiring characters, placed in prominent positions; another would say that it depends for a 'happy ending' on a distribution at the last of prizes, pensions, husbands, wives, babies, millions, appended paragraphs and cheerful remarks. Another still would say that it means being full of incident and movement, so that we shall wish to jump ahead, to see who was the mysterious stranger, and if the stolen will was ever found, and shall not be distracted from this pleasure by any tiresome analysis or 'description.' But they would all agree that the 'artistic' idea would spoil some of their fun. One would hold it accountable for all the description, another would see it revealed in the absence of sympathy. Its hostility to a happy ending would be evident, and it might even, in some cases, render any ending at all impossible. The 'ending' of a novel is, for many persons, like that of a good dinner, a course of dessert and ices, and the artist in fiction is regarded as a sort of meddlesome doctor who forbids agreeable aftertastes. It is therefore true that this conception of Mr. Besant's, of the novel as a superior form, encounters not only a negative but a positive indifference. It matters little that, as a work of art, it should really be as little or as much concerned to supply happy endings, sympathetic characters, and an objective tone, as if it were a work of mechanics; the association of ideas, however incongruous, might easily be too much for it if an eloquent voice were not sometimes raised to call attention to the fact that it is at once as free and as serious a branch of literature as any other.

Certainly, this might sometimes be doubted in presence of the enormous number of works of fiction that appeal to the credulity of our generation, for it might easily seem that there could be no great substance in a commodity so quickly and easily produced. It must be admitted that good novels are somewhat compromised by bad ones, and that the field, at large, suffers discredit from overcrowding. I think, however, that this injury is only superficial, and that the superabundance of written fiction proves nothing against the principle itself. It has been vulgarised, like all other kinds of literature, like everything else, to-day, and it has proved more than some kinds accessible to vulgarisation. But there is as much difference as there ever was between a good novel and a bad one: the bad is swept, with all the daubed canvases and spoiled marble, into some unvisited limbo or infinite rubbish-yard, beneath the back-windows of the world, and the good subsists and emits its light and stimulates our desire for perfection. As I shall take the liberty of making but a single criticism of Mr. Besant, whose tone is so full of the love of his art, I may as well have done with it at once. He seems to me to mistake in attempting to say so definitely beforehand what sort of an affair the good novel will be. To indicate the danger of such an error as that has been the purpose of these few pages; to suggest that certain traditions on the subject, applied *a priori*, have already had much to answer for, and that the good health of an art which undertakes so immediately to reproduce life must demand that it be perfectly free. It lives upon exercise, and the very meaning of exercise is freedom. The only obligation to which in advance we may hold a novel without incurring the accusation of being arbitrary, is that it be interesting. That general responsibility rests upon it, but it is the only one I can think of. The ways in which it is at liberty to accomplish this result (of interesting us) strike me as innumerable and such as can only suffer from being marked out, or fenced in, by prescription. They are as various as the temperament of man, and they are successful in proportion as they reveal a particular mind, different from others. A novel is in its broadest definition a personal impression of life; that, to begin with, constitutes its value, which is greater or less according to the intensity of the impression. But there will be no intensity at all, and therefore no value, unless there is freedom to feel and say. The tracing of a line to be followed, of a tone to be taken, of a form to be filled out, is a limitation of that freedom and a suppression of the very thing that we are most curious about. The form, it seems to me, is to be appreciated after the fact; then the author's choice has been made, his standard has been indicated; then we can follow lines and directions and compare tones. Then, in a word, we can enjoy one of the most charming of pleasures, we can estimate quality, we can apply the test of execution. The execution belongs to the author alone; it is what is most personal to him, and we measure him by that. The advantage, the luxury, as well as the torment and responsibility of the novelist, is that there is no limit to what he may attempt as an executant – no limit to his possible experiments, efforts, discoveries, successes. Here it is especially that he works, step by step, like his brother of the brush, of whom we may always say that he has painted his picture in a manner best known to himself. His manner is his secret, not necessarily a deliberate one. He cannot disclose it, as a general thing, if he would; he would be at a loss to teach it to others. I say this with a due recollection of having insisted on the community of method of the artist who paints a picture and the artist who writes a novel. The painter *is* able to teach the rudiments of his practice, and it is possible, from the study of good work (granted the aptitude), both to learn how to paint and to learn how to write. Yet it remains true, without injury to the *rapprochement*, that the literary artist would be obliged to say to his pupil much more than the other, 'Ah, well, you must do it as you can!' It is a question of degree, a matter of delicacy. If there are exact sciences there are also exact arts, and the grammar of painting is so much more definite that it makes the difference.

I ought to add, however, that if Mr. Besant says at the beginning of his essay that the 'laws of fiction may be laid down and taught with as much precision and exactness as the laws of harmony, perspective, and proportion,' he mitigates what might appear to be an over-statement by applying his remark to 'general' laws, and by expressing most of these rules in a manner with which it would certainly be unaccommodating to disagree. That the novelist must write from his experience, that his 'characters must be real and such as might be met with in actual life;' that 'a young lady brought up in a quiet country village should avoid descriptions of garrison life,' and 'a writer whose friends and personal experiences belong to the lower middle-class should carefully avoid introducing his characters into Society;' that one should enter one's notes in a common-place book; that one's figures should be clear in outline; that making them clear by some trick of speech or of carriage is a bad method, and 'describing them at length' is a worse one; that English Fiction should have a 'conscious moral purpose;' that 'it is almost impossible to estimate too highly the value of careful workmanship – that is, of style;' that 'the most important point of all is the story,' that 'the story is everything' – these are principles with most of which it is surely impossible not to sympathise. That remark about the lower middle-class writer and his knowing his place is perhaps rather chilling; but for the rest, I should find it difficult to dissent from any one of these recommendations. At the same time I should find it difficult positively to assent to them, with the exception, perhaps, of the injunction as to entering one's notes in a common-place book. They scarcely seem to me to have the quality that Mr. Besant attributes to the rules of the novelist – the 'precision and exactness' of 'the laws of harmony, perspective, and proportion.' They are suggestive, they are even inspiring, but they are not exact, though they are doubtless as much so as the case admits of; which is a proof of that liberty of interpretation for which I just contended. For the value of these different injunctions – so beautiful and so vague – is wholly in the meaning one attaches to them. The characters, the situation, which strike one as real will be those that touch and interest one most, but the measure of reality is very difficult to fix. The reality of Don Quixote or of Mr. Micawber is a very delicate shade; it is a reality so coloured by the author's vision that, vivid as it may be, one would hesitate to propose it as a model; one would expose one's self to some very embarrassing questions on the part of a pupil. It goes without saying that you will not write a good novel unless you possess the sense of reality; but it will be difficult to give you a recipe for calling that sense into being. Humanity is immense and reality has a myriad forms; the most one can affirm is that some of the flowers of fiction have the odour of it, and others have not; as for telling you in advance how your nosegay should be composed, that is another affair. It is equally excellent and inconclusive to say that one must write from experience; to our suppositious aspirant such a declaration might savour of mockery. What kind of experience is intended, and where does it begin and end? Experience is never limited and it is never complete; it is an immense sensibility, a kind of huge spider-web, of the finest silken threads, suspended in the chamber of consciousness and catching every air-borne particle in its tissue. It is the very atmosphere of the mind; and when the mind is imaginative – much more when it happens to be that of a man of genius – it takes to itself the faintest hints of life, it converts the very pulses of the air into revelations. The young lady living in a village has only to be a damsel upon whom nothing is lost to make it quite unfair (as it seems to me) to declare to her that she shall have nothing to say about the military. Greater miracles have been seen than that, imagination assisting, she should speak the truth about some of these gentlemen. I remember an English novelist, a woman of genius, telling me that she was much commended for the impression she had managed to give in one of her tales of the nature and way of life of the French Protestant youth. She had been asked where she learned so much about this recondite being, she had been congratulated on her peculiar opportunities. These opportunities consisted in her having once, in Paris, as she ascended a staircase, passed an open door where, in the household of a *pasteur*, some of the young Protestants were seated at table round a finished meal. The glimpse made a picture; it lasted only a moment, but that moment was experience. She had got her impression, and she evolved her type. She knew what youth was, and what Protestantism; she also had the advantage of having seen what it was to be French; so that she converted these ideas into a concrete image and produced a reality. Above all, however, she was blessed with the faculty which when you give it an inch takes an ell, and which for the artist is a much greater source of strength than any accident of residence or of place in the social scale. The power to guess the unseen from the seen, to trace the implication of things, to judge the whole piece by the pattern, the condition of feeling life, in general, so completely that you are well on your way to knowing any particular corner of it – this cluster of gifts may almost be said to constitute experience, and they occur in country and in town, and in the most differing stages of education. If experience consists of impressions, it may be said that impressions *are* experience, just as (have we not seen it?) they are the very air we breathe. Therefore, if I should certainly say to a novice, 'Write from experience, and experience only,' I should feel that this was a rather tantalising monition if I were not careful immediately to add, 'Try to be one of the people on whom nothing is lost!'

I am far from intending by this to minimise the importance of exactness – of truth of detail. One can speak best from one's own taste, and I may therefore venture to say that the air of reality (solidity of specification) seems to me to be the supreme virtue of a novel – the merit in which all its other merits (including that conscious moral purpose of which Mr. Besant speaks) helplessly and submissively depend. If it be not there, they are all as nothing, and if these be there, they owe their effect to the success with which the author has produced the illusion of life. The cultivation of this success, the study of this exquisite process, form, to my taste, the beginning and the end of the art of the novelist. They are his inspiration, his despair, his reward, his torment, his delight. It is here, in very truth, that he competes with life; it is here that he competes with his brother the painter, in *his* attempt to render the look of things, the look that conveys their meaning, to catch the colour, the relief, the expression, the surface, the substance of the human spectacle. It is in regard to this that Mr. Besant is well inspired when he bids him take notes. He cannot possibly take too many, he cannot possibly take enough. All life solicits him, and to 'render' the simplest surface, to produce the most momentary illusion, is a very complicated business. His case would be easier, and the rule would be more exact, if Mr. Besant had been able to tell him what notes to take. But this I fear he can never learn in any hand-book; it is the business of his life. He has to take a great many in order to select a few, he has to work them up as he can, and even the guides and philosophers who might have most to say to him must leave him alone when it comes to the application of precepts, as we leave the painter in communion with his palette. That his characters 'must be clear in outline,' as Mr. Besant says – he feels that down to his boots; but how he shall make them so is a secret between his good angel and himself. It would be absurdly simple if he could be taught that a great deal of 'description' would make them so, or that, on the contrary, the absence of description and the cultivation of dialogue, or the absence of dialogue and the multiplication of 'incident,' would rescue him from his difficulties. Nothing, for instance, is more possible than that he be of a turn of mind for which this odd, literal opposition of description and dialogue, incident and description, has little meaning and light. People often talk of these things as if they had a kind of internecine distinctness, instead of melting into each other at every breath and being intimately associated parts of one general effort of expression. I cannot imagine composition existing in a series of blocks, nor conceive, in any novel worth discussing at all, of a passage of description that is not in its intention narrative, a passage of dialogue that is not in its intention descriptive, a touch of truth of any sort that does not partake of the nature of incident, and an incident that derives its interest from any other source than the general and only source of the success of a work of art – that of being illustrative. A novel is a living thing, all one and continuous, like every other organism, and in proportion as it lives will it be found, I think, that in each of the parts there is something of each of the other parts. The critic who over the close texture of a finished work will pretend to trace a geography of items will mark some frontiers as artificial, I fear, as any that have been known to history. There is an old-fashioned distinction between the novel of character and the novel of incident, which must have cost many a smile to the intending romancer who was keen about his work. It appears to me as little to the point as the equally celebrated distinction between the novel and the romance – to answer as little to any reality. There are bad novels and good novels, as there are bad pictures and good pictures; but that is the only distinction in which I see any meaning, and I can as little imagine speaking of a novel of character as I can imagine speaking of a picture of character. When one says picture, one says of character, when one says novel, one says of incident, and the terms may be transposed. What is character but the determination of incident? What is incident but the illustration of character? What is a picture or a novel that is *not* of character? What else do we seek in it and find in it? It is an incident for a woman to stand up with her hand resting on a table and look out at you in a certain way; or if it be not an incident, I think it will be hard to say what it is. At the same time it is an expression of character. If you say you don't see it (character in *that* – *allons donc!*) this is exactly what the artist who has reasons of his own for thinking he *does* see it undertakes to show you. When a young man makes up his mind that he has not faith enough, after all, to enter the Church, as he intended, that is an incident, though you may not hurry to the end of the chapter to see whether perhaps he doesn't change once more. I do not say that these are extraordinary or startling incidents. I do not pretend to estimate the degree of interest proceeding from them, for this will depend upon the skill of the painter. It sounds almost puerile to say that some incidents are intrinsically much more important than others, and I need not take this precaution after having professed my sympathy for the major ones in remarking that the only classification of the novel that I can understand is into the interesting and the uninteresting.

The novel and the romance, the novel of incident and that of character – these separations appear to me to have been made by critics and readers for their own convenience, and to help them out of some of their difficulties, but to have little reality or interest for the producer, from whose point of view it is, of course, that we are attempting to consider the art of fiction. The case is the same with another shadowy category, which Mr. Besant apparently is disposed to set up – that of the 'modern English novel;' unless, indeed, it be that in this matter he has fallen into an accidental confusion of standpoints. It is not quite clear whether he intends the remarks in which he alludes to it to be didactic or historical. It is as difficult to suppose a person intending to write a modern English, as to suppose him writing an ancient English, novel; that is a label which begs the question. One writes the novel, one paints the picture, of one's language and of one's time, and calling it modern English will not, alas! make the difficult task any easier. No more, unfortunately, will calling this or that work of one's fellow artist a romance – unless it be, of course, simply for the pleasantness of the thing, as, for instance, when Hawthorne gave this heading to his story of Blithedale. The French, who have brought the theory of fiction to remarkable completeness, have but one word for the novel, and have not attempted smaller things in it, that I can see, for that. I can think of no obligation to which the 'romancer' would not be held equally with the novelist; the standard of execution is equally high for each. Of course it is of execution that we are talking – that being the only point of a novel that is open to contention. This is perhaps too often lost sight of, only to produce interminable confusions and cross-purposes. We must grant the artist his subject, his idea, what the French call his *donnée*; our criticism is applied only to what he makes of it. Naturally I do not mean that we are bound to like it or find it interesting: in case we do not our course is perfectly simple – to let it alone. We may believe that of a certain idea even the most sincere novelist can make nothing at all, and the event may perfectly justify our belief; but the failure will have been a failure to execute, and it is in the execution that the fatal weakness is recorded. If we pretend to respect the artist at all we must allow him his freedom of choice, in the face, in particular cases, of innumerable presumptions that the choice will not fructify. Art derives a considerable part of its beneficial exercise from flying in the face of presumptions, and some of the most interesting experiments of which it is capable are hidden in the bosom of common things. Gustave Flaubert has written a story about the devotion of a servant-girl to a parrot, and the production, highly finished as it is, cannot on the whole be called a success. We are perfectly free to find it flat, but I think it might have been interesting; and I, for my part, am extremely glad he should have written it; it is a contribution to our knowledge of what can be done – or what cannot. Ivan Turgénieff has written a tale about a deaf and dumb serf and a lap-dog, and the thing is touching, loving, a little masterpiece. He struck the note of life where Gustave Flaubert missed it – he flew in the face of a presumption and achieved a victory.

Henry James, Novels by Eliot, Hardy and Flaubert (1873, 1874, 1914)

These three reviews are indicative of the immense authority and confidence that James exercised as a literary critic in the later nineteenth century. Together, they provide a measure of the formal and stylistic excellence that James sought in fiction writing, but they also reveal deep-seated prejudices about the 'proper' scope of fiction. The lofty, patrician tone that some modern readers have found objectionable is amply evident in the essay on Hardy. The review of *Middlemarch* appeared in *Galaxy* in March 1873. James's ambivalent response is neatly summed up in his memorable statement: '*Middlemarch* is a treasure-house of details, but it is an indifferent whole'. The review of *Far from the Madding Crowd*, published in the *Nation* in 1874, further demonstrates James's devaluation of novels that failed to match his own uncompromising standards of formal perfection. Ironically, George Eliot is used as the stick with which to beat Hardy for his inferior art. The essay on *Madame Bovary*, from *Notes on Novelists* (1914), praises the formal perfection of Flaubert's novel, but regrets that Emma Bovary is too 'small' a character to bear the weight of Flaubert's immense imaginative endeavour.

Middlemarch

Middlemarch is at once one of the strongest and one of the weakest of English novels. Its predecessors as they appeared might have been described in the same terms; *Romola* is especially a rare masterpiece, but the least *entraînant* of masterpieces. *Romola* sins by excess of analysis; there is too much description and too little drama; too much reflection (all certainly of a highly imaginative sort) and too little creation. Movement lingers in the story, and with it attention stands still in the reader. The error in *Middlemarch* is not precisely of a similar kind, but it is equally detrimental to the total aspect of the work. We can well remember how keenly we wondered, while its earlier chapters unfolded themselves, what turn in the way of form the story would take – that of an organized, moulded, balanced composition, gratifying the reader with a sense of design and construction, or a mere chain of episodes, broken into accidental lengths and unconscious of the influence of a plan. We expected the actual result, but for the sake of English imaginative literature which, in this line, is rarely in need of examples, we hoped for the other. If it had come we should have had the pleasure of reading, what certainly would have seemed to us in the immediate glow of attention, the first of English novels. But that pleasure has still to hover between prospect and retrospect. *Middlemarch* is a treasure-house of details, but it is an indifferent whole.

Our objection may seem shallow and pedantic, and may even be represented as a complaint that we have had the less given us rather than the more. Certainly the greatest minds have the defects of their qualities, and as George Eliot's mind is preëminently contemplative and analytic, nothing is more natural than that her manner should be discursive and expansive. 'Concentration' would doubtless have deprived us of many of the best things in the book – of Peter Featherstone's grotesquely expectant legatees, of Lydgate's medical rivals, and of Mary Garth's delightful family. The author's purpose was to be a generous rural historian, and this very redundancy of touch, born of abundant reminiscence, is one of the greatest charms of her work. It is as if her memory was crowded with antique figures, to whom for very tenderness she must grant an appearance. Her novel is a picture – vast, swarming, deep-colored, crowded with episodes, with vivid images, with lurking master-strokes, with brilliant passages of expression; and as such we may freely accept it and enjoy it. It is not compact, doubtless; but when was a panorama compact? And yet, nominally, *Middlemarch* has a definite subject – the subject indicated in the eloquent preface. An ardent young girl was to have been the central figure, a young girl framed for a larger moral life than circumstance often affords, yearning for a motive for sustained spiritual effort and only wasting her ardor and soiling her wings against the meanness of opportunity. The author, in other words, proposed to depict the career of an obscure St. Theresa. Her success has been great, in spite of serious drawbacks. Dorothea Brooke is a genuine creation, and a most remarkable one when we consider the delicate material in which she is wrought. George Eliot's men are generally so much better than the usual trowsered offspring of the female fancy, that their merits have perhaps overshadowed those of her women. Yet her heroines have always been of an exquisite quality, and Dorothea is only that perfect flower of conception of which her predecessors were the less unfolded blossoms. An indefinable moral elevation is the sign of these admirable creatures; and of the representation of this quality in its superior degrees the author seems to have in English fiction a monopoly. To render the expression of a soul requires a cunning hand; but we seem to look straight into the unfathomable eyes of the beautiful spirit of Dorothea Brooke. She exhales a sort of aroma of spiritual sweetness, and we believe in her as in a woman we might providentially meet some fine day when we should find ourselves doubting of the immortality of the soul. By what unerring mechanism this effect is produced – whether by fine strokes or broad ones, by description or by narration, we can hardly say; it is certainly the great achievement of the book. Dorothea's career is, however, but an episode, and though doubtless in intention, not distinctly enough in fact, the central one. The history of Lydgate's *ménage*, which shares honors with it, seems rather to the reader to carry off the lion's share. This is certainly a very interesting story, but on the whole it yields in dignity to the record of Dorothea's unresonant woes. The 'love-problem,' as the author calls it, of Mary Garth, is placed on a rather higher level than the reader willingly grants it. To the end we care less about Fred Vincy than appears to be expected of us. In so far as the writer's design has been to reproduce the total sum of life in an English village forty years ago, this commonplace young gentleman, with his somewhat meager tribulations and his rather neutral egotism, has his proper place in the picture; but the author narrates his fortunes with a fulness of detail which the reader often finds irritating. The reader indeed is sometimes tempted to complain of a tendency which we are at loss exactly to express – a tendency to make light of the serious elements of the story and to sacrifice them to the more trivial ones. Is it an unconscious instinct or is it a deliberate plan? With its abundant and massive ingredients *Middlemarch* ought somehow to have depicted a weightier drama. Dorothea was altogether too superb a heroine to be wasted; yet she plays a narrower part than the imagination of the reader demands. She is of more consequence than the action of which she is the nominal centre. She marries enthusiastically a man whom she fancies a great thinker, and who turns out to be but an arid pedant. Here, indeed, is a disappointment with much of the dignity of tragedy; but the situation seems to us never to expand to its full capacity. It is analyzed with extraordinary penetration, but one may say of it, as of most of the situations in the book, that it is treated with too much refinement and too little breadth. It revolves too constantly on the same pivot; it abounds in fine shades, but it lacks, we think, the great dramatic *chiaroscuro*. Mr. Casaubon, Dorothea's husband (of whom more anon) embittered, on his side, by matrimonial disappointment, takes refuge in vain jealousy of his wife's relations with an interesting young cousin of his own and registers this sentiment in a codicil to his will, making the forfeiture of his property the penalty of his widow's marriage with this gentleman. Mr. Casaubon's death befalls about the middle of the story, and from this point to the close our interest in Dorothea is restricted to the question, will she or will she not marry Will Ladislaw? The question is relatively trivial and the implied struggle slightly factitious. The author has depicted the struggle with a sort of elaborate solemnity which in the interviews related in the last two books tends to become almost ludicrously excessive.

The dramatic current stagnates; it runs between hero and heroine almost a game of hair-splitting. Our dissatisfaction here is provoked in a great measure by the insubstantial character of the hero. The figure of Will Ladislaw is a beautiful attempt, with many finely-completed points; but on the whole it seems to us a failure. It is the only eminent failure in the book, and its defects are therefore the more striking. It lacks sharpness of outline and depth of color; we have not found ourselves believing in Ladislaw as we believe in Dorothea, in Mary Garth, in Rosamond, in Lydgate, in Mr. Brooke and Mr. Casaubon. He is meant, indeed, to be a light creature (with a large capacity for gravity, for he finally gets into Parliament), and a light creature certainly should not be heavily drawn. The author, who is evidently very fond of him, has found for him here and there some charming and eloquent touches; but in spite of these he remains vague and impalpable to the end. He is, we may say, the one figure which a masculine intellect of the same power as George Eliot's would not have conceived with the same complacency; he is, in short, roughly speaking, a woman's man. It strikes us as an oddity in the author's scheme that she should have chosen just this figure of Ladislaw as the creature in whom Dorothea was to find her spiritual compensations. He is really, after all, not the ideal foil to Mr. Casaubon which her soul must have imperiously demanded, and if the author of the 'Key to all Mythologies' sinned by lack of ardor, Ladislaw too has not the concentrated fervor essential in the man chosen by so nobly strenuous a heroine. The impression once given that he is a *dilettante* is never properly removed, and there is slender poetic justice in Dorothea's marrying a *dilettante*. We are doubtless less content with Ladislaw, on account of the noble, almost sculptural, relief of the neighboring figure of Lydgate, the real hero of the story. It is an illustration of the generous scale of the author's picture and of the conscious power of imagination that she has given us a hero and heroine of broadly distinct interests – erected, as it were, two suns in her firmament, each with its independent solar system.

Lydgate is so richly successful a figure that we have regretted strongly at moments, for immediate interest's sake, that the current of his fortunes should not mingle more freely with the occasionally thin-flowing stream of Dorothea's. Toward the close, these two fine characters are brought into momentary contact so effectively as to suggest a wealth of dramatic possibility between them; but if this train had been followed we should have lost Rosamond Vincy – a rare psychological study. Lydgate is a really complete portrait of a *man*, which seems to us high praise. It is striking evidence of the altogether superior quality of George Eliot's imagination that, though elaborately represented, Lydgate should be treated so little from what we may roughly (and we trust without offence) call the sexual point of view. Perception charged with feeling has constantly guided the author's hand, and yet her strokes remain as firm, her curves as free, her whole manner as serenely impersonal, as if, on a small scale, she were emulating the creative wisdom itself. Several English romancers – notably Fielding, Thackeray, and Charles Reade – have won great praise for their figures of women: but they owe it, in reversed conditions, to a meaner sort of art, it seems to us, than George Eliot has used in the case of Lydgate; to an indefinable appeal to masculine prejudice – to a sort of titillation of the masculine sense of difference. George Eliot's manner is more philosophic – more broadly intelligent, and yet her result is as concrete, or, if you please, as picturesque. We have no space to dwell on Lydgate's character; we can but repeat that he is a vividly consistent, manly figure – powerful, ambitious, sagacious, with the maximum rather than the minimum of egotism, strenuous, generous, fallible, and altogether human. A work of the liberal scope of *Middlemarch* contains a multitude of artistic intentions, some of the finest of which become clear only in the meditative after-taste of perusal. This is the case with the balanced contrast between the two histories of Lydgate and Dorothea. Each is a tale of matrimonial infelicity, but the conditions in each are so different and the circumstances so broadly opposed that the mind passes from one to the other with that supreme sense of the vastness and variety of human life, under aspects apparently similar, which it belongs only to the greatest novels to produce. The most perfectly successful passages in the book are perhaps those painful fireside scenes between Lydgate and his miserable little wife. The author's rare psychological penetration is lavished upon this veritably mulish domestic flower. There is nothing more powerfully real than these scenes in all English fiction, and nothing certainly more *intelligent*. Their impressiveness and (as regards Lydgate) their pathos, is deepened by the constantly low key in which they are pitched. It is a tragedy based on unpaid butcher's bills, and the urgent need for small economies. The author has desired to be strictly real and to adhere to the facts of the common lot, and she has given us a powerful version of that typical human drama, the struggles of an ambitious soul with sordid disappointments and vulgar embarrassments. As to her catastrophe we hesitate to pronounce (for Lydgate's ultimate assent to his wife's worldly programme is nothing less than a catastrophe). We almost believe that some terrific explosion would have been more probable than his twenty years of smothered aspiration. Rosamond deserves almost to rank with Tito in *Romola* as a study of a gracefully vicious, or at least of a practically baleful nature. There is one point, however, of which we question the consistency. The author insists on her instincts of coquetry, which seems to us a discordant note. They would have made her better or worse – more generous or more reckless; in either case more manageable. As it is, Rosamond represents, in a measure, the fatality of British decorum.

In reading, we have marked innumerable passages for quotation and comment; but we lack space and the work is so ample that half a dozen extracts would be an ineffective illustration. There would be a great deal to say on the broad array of secondary figures, Mr. Casaubon, Mr. Brooke, Mr. Bulstrode, Mr. Farebrother, Caleb Garth, Mrs. Cadwallader, Celia Brooke. Mr. Casaubon is an excellent invention; as a dusky *repoussoir* to the luminous figure of his wife he could not have been better imagined. There is indeed something very noble in the way in which the author has apprehended his character. To depict hollow pretentiousness and mouldy egotism with so little of narrow sarcasm and so much of philosophic sympathy, is to be a rare moralist as well as a rare story-teller. The whole portrait of Mr. Casaubon has an admirably sustained greyness of tone in which the shadows are never carried to the vulgar black of coarser artists. Every stroke contributes to the unwholesome, helplessly sinister expression. Here and there perhaps (as in his habitual diction), there is a hint of exaggeration; but we confess we like fancy to be fanciful. Mr. Brooke and Mr. Garth are in their different lines supremely genial creations; they are drawn with the touch of a Dickens chastened and intellectualized. Mrs. Cadwallader is, in another walk of life, a match for Mrs. Poyser, and Celia Brooke is as pretty a fool as any of Miss Austen's. Mr. Farebrother and his delightful 'womankind' belong to a large group of figures begotten of the superabundance of the author's creative instinct. At times they seem to encumber the stage and to produce a rather ponderous mass of dialogue; but they add to the reader's impression of having walked in the Middlemarch lanes and listened to the Middlemarch accent. To but one of these accessory episodes – that of Mr. Bulstrode, with its multiplex ramifications – do we take exception. It has a slightly artificial cast, a melodramatic tinge, unfriendly to the richly natural coloring of the whole. Bulstrode himself – with the history of whose troubled conscience the author has taken great pains – is, to our sense, too diffusely treated; he never grasps the reader's attention. But the touch of genius is never idle or vain. The obscure figure of Bulstrode's comely wife emerges at the needful moment, under a few light strokes, into the happiest reality.

All these people, solid and vivid in their varying degrees, are members of a deeply human little world, the full reflection of whose antique image is the great merit of these volumes. How bravely rounded a little world the author has made it – with how dense an atmosphere of interests and passions and loves and enmities and strivings and failings, and how motley a group of great folk and small, all after their kind, she has filled it, the reader must learn for himself. No writer seems to us to have drawn from a richer stock of those long-cherished memories which one's later philosophy makes doubly tender. There are few figures in the book which do not seem to have grown mellow in the author's mind. English readers may fancy they enjoy the 'atmosphere' of *Middlemarch*; but we maintain that to relish its inner essence we must – for reasons too numerous to detail – be an American. The author has commissioned herself to be real, her native tendency being that of an idealist, and the intellectual result is a very fertilizing mixture. The constant presence of thought, of generalizing instinct, of *brain*, in a word, behind her observation, gives the latter its great value and her whole manner its high superiority. It denotes a mind in which imagination is illumined by faculties rarely found in fellowship with it. In this respect – in that broad reach of vision which would make the worthy historian of solemn fact as well as wanton fiction – George Eliot seems to us among English romancers to stand alone. Fielding approaches her, but to our mind, she surpasses Fielding. Fielding was didactic – the author of *Middlemarch* is really philosophic. These great qualities imply corresponding perils. The first is the loss of simplicity. George Eliot lost hers some time since; it lies buried (in a splendid mausoleum) in *Romola*. Many of the discursive portions of *Middlemarch* are, as we may say, too clever by half. The author wishes to say too many things, and to say them too well; to recommend herself to a scientific audience. Her style, rich and flexible as it is, is apt to betray her on these transcendental flights; we find, in our copy, a dozen passages marked 'obscure.' *Silas Marner* has a delightful tinge of Goldsmith – we may almost call it; *Middlemarch* is too often an echo of Messrs. Darwin and Huxley. In spite of these faults – which it seems graceless to indicate with this crude rapidity – it remains a very splendid performance. It sets a limit, we think, to the development of the old-fashioned English novel. Its diffuseness, on which we have touched, makes it too copious a dose of pure fiction. If we write novels so, how shall we write History? But it is nevertheless a contribution of the first importance to the rich imaginative department of our literature.

Far from the Madding Crowd

Mr Hardy's novel came into the world under brilliant auspices – such as the declaration by the London *Spectator* that either George Eliot had written it or George Eliot had found her match. One could make out in a manner what the *Spectator* meant. To guess, one has only to open *Far from the Madding Crowd* at random:

> Mr Jan Coggan, who had passed the cup to Henery, was a crimson man with a spacious countenance and a private glimmer in his eye, whose name had appeared on the marriage register of Weatherbury and neighbouring parishes as best-man and chief witness in countless unions of the previous twenty years; he also very frequently filled the post of head godfather in baptisms of the subtly jovial kind.

That is a very fair imitation of George Eliot's humorous manner. Here is a specimen of her serious one: 'He fancied he had felt himself in the penumbra of a very deep sadness when touching that slight and fragile creature. But wisdom lies in moderating mere impressions, and Gabriel endeavoured to think little of this.' But the *Spectator*'s theory had an even broader base, and we may profitably quote a passage which perhaps constituted one of its solidest blocks. The author of *Silas Marner* has won no small part of her fame by her remarkable faculty as a reporter of ale-house and kitchen-fire conversations among simple-minded rustics. Mr Hardy has also made a great effort in this direction [and] has evidently read to good purpose the low-life chapters in George Eliot's novels; he has caught very happily her trick of seeming to humour benignantly her queer people and look down at them from the heights of analytic omniscience. But we have quoted the episode because it seems to us an excellent example of the cleverness which is only cleverness, of the difference between original and imitative talent – the disparity, which it is almost unpardonable not to perceive, between first-rate talent and those inferior grades which range from second-rate downward, and as to which confusion is a more venial offence. Mr Hardy puts his figures through a variety of comical movements; he fills their mouths with quaint turns of speech; he baptizes them with odd names ('Joseph Poorgrass' for a bashful, easily-snubbed Dissenter is excellent); he pulls the wires, in short, and produces a vast deal of sound and commotion; and his novel, at a cursory glance, has a rather promising air of life and warmth. But by critics who prefer a grain of substance to a pound of shadow it will, we think, be pronounced a decidedly delusive performance; it has a fatal lack of magic. We have found it hard to read, but its shortcomings are easier to summarize than to encounter in order. Mr Hardy's novel is very long, but his subject is very short and simple, and the work has been distended to its rather formidable dimensions by the infusion of a large amount of conversational and descriptive padding and the use of an ingeniously verbose and redundant style. It is inordinately diffuse, and, as a piece of narrative, singularly inartistic. The author has little sense of proportion, and almost none of composition. We learn about Bathsheba and Gabriel, Farmer Boldwood and Sergeant Troy, what we can rather than what we should; for Mr Hardy's inexhaustible faculty for spinning smart dialogue makes him forget that dialogue in a story is after all but episode, and that a novelist is after all but a historian, thoroughly possessed of certain facts, and bound in some way or other to impart them. To tell a story almost exclusively by reporting people's talks is the most difficult art in the world, and really leads, logically, to a severe economy in the use of rejoinder and repartee, and not to a lavish expenditure of them. *Far from the Madding Crowd* gives us an uncomfortable sense of being a simple 'tale', pulled and stretched to make the conventional three volumes; and the author, in his long-sustained appeal to one's attention, reminds us of a person fishing with an enormous net, of which the meshes should be thrice too wide.

We are happily not subject, in this (as to minor matters) much emancipated land, to the tyranny of the three volumes; but we confess that we are nevertheless being rapidly urged to a conviction that (since it is in the nature of fashions to revolve and recur) the day has come round again for some of the antique restrictions as to literary form. The three unities, in Aristotle's day, were inexorably imposed on Greek tragedy; why shouldn't we have something of the same sort for English fiction in the day of Mr Hardy? Almost all novels are greatly too long, and the being too long becomes with each elapsing year a more serious offence. Mr Hardy begins with a detailed description of his hero's smile, and proceeds thence to give a voluminous account of his large silver watch. Gabriel Oak's smile and his watch were doubtless respectable and important phenomena; but everything is relative, and daily becoming more so; and we confess that, as a hint of the pace at which the author proposed to proceed, his treatment of these facts produced upon us a deterring and depressing effect. If novels were the only books written, novels written on this scale would be all very well; but as they compete, in the esteem of sensible people, with a great many other books, and a great many other objects of interest of all kinds, we are inclined to think that, in the long run, they will be defeated in the struggle for existence unless they lighten their baggage very considerably and do battle in a more scientific equipment. Therefore, we really imagine that a few arbitrary rules – a kind of depleting process – might have a wholesome effect. It might be enjoined, for instance, that no 'tale' should exceed fifty pages and no novel two hundred; that a plot should have but such and such a number of ramifications; that no ramification should have more than a certain number of persons; that no person should utter more than a given number of words; and that no description of an inanimate object, should consist of more than a fixed number of lines. We should not incline to advocate this oppressive legislation as a comfortable or ideal finality for the romancer's art, but we think it might be excellent as a transitory discipline or drill. Necessity is the mother of invention, and writers with a powerful tendency to expatiation might in this temporary strait-jacket be induced to transfer their attention rather more severely from quantity to quality. The use of the strait-jacket would have cut down Mr Hardy's novel to half its actual length and, as he is a clever man, have made the abbreviated work very ingeniously pregnant. We should have had a more occasional taste of all the barn-yard worthies – Joseph Poorgrass, Laban Tall, Matthew Moon, and the rest – and the vagaries of Miss Bathsheba would have had a more sensible consistency. Our restrictions would have been generous, however, and we should not have proscribed such a fine passage as this:

> Then there came a third flash. Manoeuvres of the most extraordinary kind were going on in the vast firmamental hollows overhead. The lightning now was the colour of silver, and gleamed in the heavens like a mailed army. Rumbles became rattles. Gabriel, from his elevated position, could see over the landscape for at least half a dozen miles in front. Every hedge, bush, and tree was distinct as in a line engraving. In a paddock in the same direction was a herd of heifers, and the forms of these were visible at this moment in the act of galloping about in the wildest and maddest confusion, flinging their heels and tails high into the air, their heads to earth. A poplar in the immediate foreground was like an ink-stroke on burnished tin. Then the picture vanished, leaving a darkness so intense that Gabriel worked entirely by feeling with his hands.

Mr Hardy describes nature with a great deal of felicity, and is evidently very much at home among rural phenomena. The most genuine thing in his book, to our sense, is a certain aroma of the meadows and lanes – a natural relish for harvesting and sheep-washings. He has laid his scene in an agricultural county, and his characters are children of the soil – unsophisticated country-folk. Bathsheba Everdene is a rural heiress, left alone in the world, in possession of a substantial farm. Gabriel Oak is her shepherd, Farmer Boldwood is her neighbour, and Sergeant Troy is a loose young soldier who comes a-courting her. They are all in love with her, and the young lady is a flirt, and encourages them all. Finally she marries the Sergeant, who has just seduced her maid-servant. The maid-servant dies in the workhouse, the Sergeant repents, leaves his wife, and is given up for drowned. But he reappears and is shot by Farmer Boldwood, who delivers himself up to justice. Bathsheba then marries Gabriel Oak, who has loved and waited in silence, and is, in our opinion, much too good for her. The chief purpose of the book is, we suppose, to represent Gabriel's dumb, devoted passion, his biding his time, his rendering unsuspected services to the woman who has scorned him, his integrity and simplicity and sturdy patience. In all this the tale is very fairly successful, and Gabriel has a certain vividness of expression. But we cannot say that we either understand or like Bathsheba. She is a young lady of the inconsequential, wilful, mettlesome type which has lately become so much the fashion for heroines, and of which Mr Charles Reade is in a manner the inventor – the type which aims at giving one a very intimate sense of a young lady's *womanishness*. But Mr Hardy's embodiment of it seems to us to lack reality; he puts her through the Charles Reade paces, but she remains alternately vague and coarse, and seems always artificial. This is Mr Hardy's trouble; he rarely gets beyond ambitious artifice – the mechanical stimulation of heat and depth and wisdom that are absent. Farmer Boldwood is a shadow, and Sergeant Troy an elaborate stage-figure. Everything human in the book strikes us as factitious and insubstantial; the only things we believe in are the sheep and the dogs. But, as we say, Mr Hardy has gone astray very cleverly, and his superficial novel is a really curious imitation of something better.

Madame Bovary

Flaubert's imagination was great and splendid; in spite of which, strangely enough, his masterpiece is not his most imaginative work. *Madame Bovary*, beyond question, holds that first place, and *Madame Bovary* is concerned with the career of a country doctor's wife in a petty Norman town. The elements of the picture are of the fewest, the situation of the heroine almost of the meanest, the material for interest, considering the interest yielded, of the most unpromising; but these facts only throw into relief one of those incalculable incidents that attend the proceedings of genius. *Madame Bovary* was doomed by circumstances and causes – the freshness of comparative youth and good faith on the author's part being perhaps the chief – definitely to take its position, even though its subject was fundamentally a negation of the remote, the splendid and the strange, the stuff of his fondest and most cultivated dreams. It would have seemed very nearly to exclude the free play of the imagination, and the way this faculty on the author's part nevertheless presides is one of those accidents, manœuvres, inspirations, we hardly know what to call them, by which masterpieces grow. He of course knew more or less what he was doing for his book in making Emma Bovary a victim of the imaginative habit, but he must have been far from designing or measuring the total effect which renders the work so general, so complete an expression of himself. His separate idiosyncrasies, his irritated sensibility to the life about him, with the power to catch it in the fact and hold it hard, and his hunger for style and history and poetry, for the rich and the rare, great reverberations, great adumbrations, are here represented together as they are not in his later writings. There is nothing of the near, of the directly observed, though there may be much of the directly perceived and the minutely detailed, either in *Salammbo* or in *Saint Anthony*, and little enough of the extravagance of illusion in that indefinable last word of restrained evocation and cold execution the *Sentimental Education*. M. Faguet has of course excellently noted this – that the fortune and felicity of the book were assured by the stroke that made the central figure an embodiment of helpless romanticism. Flaubert himself but narrowly escaped being such an embodiment after all, and he is thus able to express the romantic mind with extraordinary truth. As to the rest of the matter he had the luck of having been in possession from the first, having begun so early to nurse and work up his plan that, familiarity and the native air, the native soil, aiding, he had finally made out to the last lurking shade the small sordid sunny dusty village picture, its emptiness constituted and peopled. It is in the background and the accessories that the real, the real of his theme, abides; and the romantic, the romantic of his theme, accordingly occupies the front. Emma Bovary's poor adventures are a tragedy for the very reason that in a world unsuspecting, unassisting, unconsoling, she has herself to distil the rich and the rare. Ignorant, unguided, undiverted, ridden by the very nature and mixture of her consciousness, she makes of the business an inordinate failure, a failure which in its turn makes for Flaubert the most pointed, the most *told* of anecdotes.

There are many things to say about *Madame Bovary*, but an old admirer of the book would be but half-hearted – so far as they represent reserves or puzzlements – were he not to note first of all the circumstances by which it is most endeared to him. To remember it from far back is to have been present all along at a process of singular interest to a literary mind, a case indeed full of comfort and cheer. The finest of Flaubert's novels is today, on the French shelf of fiction, one of the first of the classics; it has attained that position, slowly but steadily, before our eyes; and we seem so to follow the evolution of the fate of a classic. We see how the thing takes place; which we rarely can, for we mostly miss either the beginning or the end, especially in the case of a consecration as complete as this. The consecrations of the past are too far behind and those of the future too far in front. That the production before us *should* have come in for the heavenly crown may be a fact to offer English and American readers a mystifying side; but it is exactly our ground and a part moreover of the total interest. The author of these remarks remembers, as with a sense of the way such things happen, that when a very young person in Paris he took up from the parental table the latest number of the periodical in which Flaubert's then duly unrecognized masterpiece was in course of publication. The moment is not historic, but it was to become in the light of history, as may be said, so unforgettable that every small feature of it yet again lives for him: it rests there like the backward end of the span. The cover of the old Revue de Paris was yellow, if I mistake not, like that of the new, and *Madame Bovary: Mœurs de Province*, on the inside of it, was already, on the spot, as a title, mysteriously arresting, inscrutably charged. I was ignorant of what had preceded and was not to know till much later what followed; but present to me still is the act of standing there before the fire, my back against the low beplushed and begarnished French chimney-piece and taking in what I might of that instalment, taking it in with so surprised an interest, and perhaps as well such a stir of faint foreknowledge, that the sunny little salon, the autumn day, the window ajar and the cheerful outside clatter of the Rue Montaigne are all now for me more or less in the story and the story more or less in them. The story, however, was at that moment having a difficult life; its fortune was all to make; its merit was so far from suspected that, as Maxime Du Camp – though verily with no excess of contrition – relates, its cloth of gold barely escaped the editorial shears. This, with much more, contributes for us to the course of things to come. The book, on its appearance as a volume, proved a shock to the high propriety of the guardians of public morals under the second Empire, and Flaubert was prosecuted as author of a work indecent to scandal. The prosecution in the event fell to the ground, but I should perhaps have mentioned this agitation as one of the very few, of any public order, in his short list. *The Candidate* fell at the Vaudeville Theatre, several years later, with a violence indicated by its withdrawal after a performance of but two nights, the first of these marked by a deafening uproar; only if the comedy was not to recover from this accident the misprised lustre of the novel was entirely to reassert itself. It is strange enough at present – so far have we travelled since then – that *Madame Bovary* should in so comparatively recent a past have been to that extent a cause of reprobation; and suggestive above all, in such connections, as to the large unconsciousness of superior minds. The desire of the superior mind of the day – that is the governmental, official, legal – to distinguish a book with such a destiny before it is a case conceivable, but conception breaks down before its design of making the distinction purely invidious. We can imagine its knowing so little, however face to face with the object, what it had got hold of; but for it to have been so urged on by a blind inward spring to publish to posterity the extent of its ignorance, that would have been beyond imagination, beyond everything but pity.

And yet it is not after all that the place the book has taken is so overwhelmingly explained by its inherent dignity; for here comes in the curiosity of the matter. Here comes in especially its fund of admonition for alien readers. The dignity of its substance is the dignity of Madame Bovary herself as a vessel of experience – a question as to which, unmistakably, I judge, we can only depart from the consensus of French critical opinion. M. Faguet for example commends the character of the heroine as one of the most living and discriminated figures of women in all literature, praises it as a field for the display of the romantic spirit that leaves nothing to be desired. Subject to an observation I shall presently make and that bears heavily in general, I think, on Flaubert as a painter of life, subject to this restriction he is right; which is a proof that a work of art may be markedly open to objection and at the same time be rare in its kind, and that when it is perfect to this point nothing else particularly matters. *Madame Bovary* has a perfection that not only stamps it, but that makes it stand almost alone; it holds itself with such a supreme unapproachable assurance as both excites and defies judgment. For it deals not in the least, as to unapproachability, with things exalted or refined; it only confers on its sufficiently vulgar elements of exhibition a final unsurpassable form. The form is in *itself* as interesting, as active, as much of the essence of the subject as the idea, and yet so close is its fit and so inseparable its life that we catch it at no moment on any errand of its own. That verily is to *be* interesting – all round; that is to be genuine and whole. The work is a classic because the thing, such as it is, is ideally *done*, and because it shows that in such doing eternal beauty may dwell. A pretty young woman who lives, socially and morally speaking, in a hole, and who is ignorant, foolish, flimsy, unhappy, takes a pair of lovers by whom she is successively deserted; in the midst of the bewilderment of which, giving up her husband and her child, letting everything go, she sinks deeper into duplicity, debt, despair, and arrives on the spot, on the small scene itself of her poor depravities, at a pitiful tragic end. In especial she does these things while remaining absorbed in romantic intention and vision, and she remains absorbed in romantic intention and vision while fairly rolling in the dust. That is the triumph of the book as the triumph stands, that Emma interests us by the nature of her consciousness and the play of her mind, thanks to the reality and beauty with which those sources are invested. It is not only that they represent *her* state; they are so true, so observed and felt, and especially so shown, that they represent the state, actual or potential, of all persons like her, persons romantically determined. Then her setting, the medium in which she struggles, becomes in its way as important, becomes eminent with the eminence of art; the tiny world in which she revolves, the contracted cage in which she flutters, is hung out in space for her, and her companions in captivity there are as true as herself.

I have said enough to show what I mean by Flaubert's having in this picture expressed something of his intimate self, given his heroine something of his own imagination: a point precisely that brings me back to the restriction at which I just now hinted, in which M. Faguet fails to indulge and yet which is immediate for the alien reader. Our complaint is that Emma Bovary, in spite of the nature of her consciousness and in spite of her reflecting so much that of her creator, is really too small an affair. This, critically speaking, is in view both of the value and the fortune of her history, a wonderful circumstance. She associates herself with Frédéric Moreau in the *Education* to suggest for us a question that can be answered, I hold, only to Flaubert's detriment. Emma taken alone would possibly not so directly press it, but in her company the hero of our author's second study of the 'real' drives it home. Why did Flaubert choose, as special conduits of the life he proposed to depict, such inferior and in the case of Frédéric such abject human specimens? I insist only in respect to the latter, the perfection of Madame Bovary scarce leaving one much warrant for wishing anything other. Even here, however, the general scale and size of Emma, who is small even of her sort, should be a warning to hyperbole. If I say that in the matter of Frédéric at all events the answer is inevitably detrimental I mean that it weighs heavily on our author's general credit. He wished in each case to make a picture of experience – middling experience, it is true – and of the world close to him; but if he imagined nothing better for his purpose than such a heroine and such a hero, both such limited reflectors and registers, we are forced to believe it to have been by a defect of his mind. And that sign of weakness remains even if it be objected that the images in question were addressed to his purpose better than others would have been; the purpose itself then shows as inferior. The *Sentimental Education* is a strange, an indescribable work, about which there would be many more things to say than I have space for, and all of them of the deepest interest. It is moreover, to simplify my statement, very much less satisfying a thing, less pleasing whether in its unity or its variety, than its specific predecessor. But take it as we will, for a success or a failure – M. Faguet indeed ranks it, by the measure of its quantity of intention, a failure, and I on the whole agree with him – the personage offered us as bearing the weight of the drama, and in whom we are invited to that extent to interest ourselves, leaves us mainly wondering what our entertainer could have been thinking of. He takes Frédéric Moreau on the threshold of life and conducts him to the extreme of maturity without apparently suspecting for a moment either our wonder or our protest – 'Why, why *him*?' Frédéric is positively too poor for his part, too scant for his charge; and we feel with a kind of embarrassment, certainly with a kind of compassion, that it is somehow the business of a protagonist to prevent in his designer an excessive waste of faith. When I speak of the faith in Emma Bovary as proportionately wasted I reflect on M. Faguet's judgment that she is from the point of view of deep interest richly or at least roundedly representative. Representative of what? He makes us ask even while granting all the grounds of misery and tragedy involved. The plea for her is the plea made for all the figures that live without evaporation under the painter's hand – that they are not only particular persons but types of their kind, and as valid in one light as in the other. It is Emma's 'kind' that I question for this responsibility, even if it be inquired of me why I then fail to question that of Charles Bovary, in its perfection, or that of the inimitable, the immortal Homais. If we express Emma's deficiency as the poverty of her consciousness for the typical function, it is certainly not, one must admit, that she is surpassed in this respect either by her platitudinous husband or by his friend the pretentious apothecary. The difference is none the less somehow in the fact that they are respectively studies but of their character and office, which function in each expresses adequately *all* they are. It may be, I concede, because Emma is the only woman in the book that she is taken by M. Faguet as *femininely* typical, typical in the larger illustrative way, whereas the others pass with him for images specifically conditioned. Emma is this same for myself, I plead; she is conditioned to such an excess of the specific, and the specific in her case leaves out so many even of the commoner elements of conceivable life in a woman when we are invited to see that life as pathetic, as dramatic agitation, that we challenge both the author's and the critic's scale of importances. The book is a picture of the middling as much as they like, but does Emma attain even to *that*? Hers is a narrow middling even for a little imaginative person whose 'social' significance is small. It is greater on the whole than her capacity of consciousness, taking this all round; and so, in a word, we feel her less illustrational than she might have been not only if the world had offered her more points of contact, but if she had had more of these to give it.

Robert Louis Stevenson, A Humble Remonstrance (1884)

Robert Louis Stevenson (1850–1894) is remembered for his novels, among them *Treasure Island* (1883), *The Strange Case of Dr Jekyll and Mr Hyde* (1886), *Kidnapped* (1886) and *Catriona* (1893), but he was also an ardent writer of children's literature, travel stories and literary essays. 'A Humble Remonstrance' appeared in *Longman's Magazine* and carried on the debate initiated by Walter Besant and Henry James (with whom Stevenson formed a lasting friendship). Stevenson strongly disputes the idea that art can ever 'compete' with life and challenges those theories of fiction based on scrupulous imitation or exact transcription of 'life'. Where James offers an elevated account of what 'art may aspire to at its highest', Stevenson offers a more practical (and 'humble') account of 'what it must be on the lowest terms'.

We have recently enjoyed a quite peculiar pleasure: hearing, in some detail, the opinions about the art they practise of Mr. Walter Besant and Mr. Henry James; two men certainly of very different calibre: Mr. James so precise of outline, so cunning of fence, so scrupulous of finish, and Mr. Besant so genial, so friendly, with so persuasive and humorous a vein of whim: Mr. James the very type of the deliberate artist, Mr. Besant the impersonation of good nature. That such doctors should differ will excite no great surprise; but one point in which they seem to agree fills me, I confess, with wonder. For they are both content to talk about the 'art of fiction;' and Mr. Besant, waxing exceedingly bold, goes on to oppose this so-called 'art of fiction' to the 'art of poetry.' By the art of poetry he can mean nothing but the art of verse, an art of handicraft, and only comparable with the art of prose. For that heat and height of sane emotion which we agree to call by the name of poetry, is but a libertine and vagrant quality; present, at times, in any art, more often absent from them all; too seldom present in the prose novel, too frequently absent from the ode and epic. Fiction is in the same case; it is no substantive art, but an element which enters largely into all the arts but architecture. Homer, Wordsworth, Phidias, Hogarth, and Salvini, all deal in fiction; and yet I do not suppose that either Hogarth or Salvini, to mention but these two, entered in any degree into the scope of Mr. Besant's interesting lecture or Mr. James's charming essay. The art of fiction, then, regarded as a definition, is both too ample and too scanty. Let me suggest another; let me suggest that what both Mr. James and Mr. Besant had in view was neither more nor less than the art of narrative.

But Mr. Besant is anxious to speak solely of 'the modern English novel,' the stay and bread-winner of Mr. Mudie; and in the author of the most pleasing novel on that roll, 'All Sorts and Conditions of Men,' the desire is natural enough. I can conceive, then, that he would hasten to propose two additions, and read thus: the art of *fictitious* narrative *in prose*.

Now the fact of the existence of the modern English novel is not to be denied; materially, with its three volumes, leaded type, and gilded lettering, it is easily distinguishable from other forms of literature; but to talk at all fruitfully of any branch of art, it is needful to build our definitions on some more fundamental ground than binding. Why, then, are we to add 'in prose'?

The 'Odyssey' appears to me among the best of romances; the 'Lady of the Lake' to stand high in the second order; and Chaucer's tales and prologues to contain more of the matter and art of the modern English novel than the whole treasury of Mr. Mudie. Whether a narrative be written in blank verse or the Spenserian stanza, in the long period of Gibbon or the chipped phrase of Charles Reade, the principles of the art of narrative must be equally observed. The choice of a noble and swelling style in prose affects the problem of narration in the same way, if not to the same degree, as the choice of measured verse; for both imply a closer synthesis of events, a higher key of dialogue, and a more picked and stately strain of words . . . [B]y what discrimination are you to open your doors to the 'Pilgrim's Progress' and close them on the 'Faery Queen'? To bring things closer home, I will here propound to Mr. Besant a conundrum. A narrative called 'Paradise Lost' was written in English verse by one John Milton; what was it then? It was next translated by Chateaubriand into French prose; and what was it then? Lastly, the French translation was, by some inspired compatriot of George Gilfillan (and of mine), turned bodily into an English novel; and, in the name of clearness, what was it then?

But, once more, why should we add 'fictitious'? The reason why is obvious. The reason why not, if something more recondite, does not want for weight. The art of narrative, in fact, is the same, whether it is applied to the selection and illustration of a real series of events or of an imaginary series. Boswell's 'Life of Johnson' (a work of cunning and inimitable art) owes its success to the same technical manœuvres as (let us say) 'Tom Jones': the clear conception of certain characters of man, the choice and presentation of certain incidents out of a great number that offered, and the invention (yes, invention) and preservation of a certain key in dialogue. In which these things are done with the more art – in which with the greater air of nature – readers will differently judge. Boswell's is, indeed, a very special case, and almost a generic; but it is not only in Boswell, it is in every biography with any salt of life, it is in every history where events and men, rather than ideas, are presented – in Tacitus, in Carlyle, in Michelet, in Macaulay – that the novelist will find many of his own methods most conspicuously and adroitly handled. He will find besides that he, who is free – who has the right to invent or steal a missing incident, who has the right, more precious still, of wholesale omission – is frequently defeated, and, with all his advantages, leaves a less strong impression of reality and passion. Mr. James utters his mind with a becoming fervour on the sanctity of truth to the novelist; on a more careful examination truth will seem a word of very debatable propriety, not only for the labours of the novelist, but for those of the historian. No art – to use the daring phrase of Mr. James – can successfully 'compete with life'; and the art that does so is condemned to perish *montibus aviis*. Life goes before us, infinite in complication; attended by the most various and surprising meteors; appealing at once to the eye, to the ear, to the mind – the seat of wonder, to the touch – so thrillingly delicate, and to the belly – so imperious when starved. It combines and employs in its manifestation the method and material, not of one art only, but of all the arts. Music is but an arbitrary trifling with a few of life's majestic chords; painting is but a shadow of its gorgeous pageantry of light and colour; literature does but drily indicate that wealth of incident, of moral obligation, of virtue, vice, action, rapture, and agony, with which it teems. To 'compete with life,' whose sun we cannot look upon, whose passions and diseases waste and slay us – to compete with the flavour of wine, the beauty of the dawn, the scorching of fire, the bitterness of death and separation – here is, indeed, a projected escalade of heaven; here are, indeed, labours for a Hercules in a dress coat, armed with a pen and a dictionary to depict the passions, armed with a tube of superior flake-white to paint the portrait of the insufferable sun. No art is true in this sense: none can 'compete with life': not even history, built indeed of indisputable facts, but these facts robbed of their vivacity and sting; so that even when we read of the sack of a city or the fall of an empire, we are surprised, and justly commend the author's talent, if our pulse be quickened. And mark, for a last differentia, that this quickening of the pulse is, in almost every case, purely agreeable; that these phantom reproductions of experience, even at their most acute, convey decided pleasure; while experience itself, in the cockpit of life, can torture and slay.

What, then, is the object, what the method, of an art, and what the source of its power? The whole secret is that no art does 'compete with life.' Man's one method, whether he reasons or creates, is to half-shut his eyes against the dazzle and confusion of reality. The arts, like arithmetic and geometry, turn away their eyes from the gross, coloured, and mobile nature at our feet, and regard instead a certain figmentary abstraction. Geometry will tell us of a circle, a thing never seen in nature; asked about a green circle or an iron circle, it lays its hand upon its mouth. So with the arts. Painting, ruefully comparing sunshine and flake-white, gives up truth of colour, as it had already given up relief and movement; and instead of vying with nature, arranges a scheme of harmonious tints. Literature, above all in its most typical mood, the mood of narrative, similarly flees the direct challenge and pursues instead an independent and creative aim. So far as it imitates at all, it imitates not life but speech: not the facts of human destiny, but the emphasis and the suppressions with which the human actor tells of them. The real art that dealt with life directly was that of the first men who told their stories round the savage camp-fire. Our art is occupied, and bound to be occupied, not so much in making stories true as in making them typical; not so much in capturing the lineaments of each fact, as in marshalling all of them towards a common end. For the welter of impressions, all forcible but all discrete, which life presents, it substitutes a certain artificial series of impressions, all indeed most feebly represented, but all aiming at the same effect, all eloquent of the same idea, all chiming together like consonant notes in music or like the graduated tints in a good picture. From all its chapters, from all its pages, from all its sentences, the well-written novel echoes and re-echoes its one creative and controlling thought; to this must every incident and character contribute; the style must have been pitched in unison with this; and if there is anywhere a word that looks another way, the book would be stronger, clearer, and (I had almost said) fuller without it. Life is monstrous, infinite, illogical, abrupt, and poignant; a work of art, in comparison, is neat, finite, self-contained, rational, flowing, and emasculate. Life imposes by brute energy, like inarticulate thunder; art catches the ear, among the far louder noises of experience, like an air artificially made by a discrete musician. A proposition of geometry does not compete with life; and a proposition of geometry is a fair and luminous parallel for a work of art. Both are reasonable, both untrue to the crude fact; both inhere in nature, neither represents it. The novel which is a work of art exists, not by its resemblances to life, which are forced and material, as a shoe must still consist of leather, but by its immeasurable difference from life, which is designed and significant, and is both the method and the meaning of the work.

The life of man is not the subject of novels, but the inexhaustible magazine from which subjects are to be selected; the name of these is legion; and with each new subject – for here again I must differ by the whole width of heaven from Mr. James – the true artist will vary his method and change the point of attack. That which was in one case an excellence, will become a defect in another; what was the making of one book, will in the next be impertinent or dull. First each novel, and then each class of novels, exists by and for itself. I will take, for instance, three main classes, which are fairly distinct: first, the novel of adventure, which appeals to certain almost sensual and quite illogical tendencies in man; second, the novel of character, which appeals to our intellectual appreciation of man's foibles and mingled and inconstant motives; and third, the dramatic novel, which deals with the same stuff as the serious theatre, and appeals to our emotional nature and moral judgment.

And first for the novel of adventure. Mr. James refers, with singular generosity of praise, to a little book about a quest for hidden treasure; but he lets fall, by the way, some rather startling words. In this book he misses what be calls the 'immense luxury' of being able to quarrel with his author. The luxury, to most of us, is to lay by our judgment, to be submerged by the tale as by a billow, and only to awake, and begin to distinguish and find fault, when the piece is over and the volume laid aside. Still more remarkable is Mr. James's reason. He cannot criticise the author, as he goes, 'because,' says he, comparing it with another work, '*I have been a child, but I have never been on a quest for buried treasure.*' Here is, indeed, a wilful paradox; for if he has never been on a quest for buried treasure, it can be demonstrated that he has never been a child. There never was a child (unless Master James) but has hunted gold, and been a pirate, and a military commander, and a bandit of the mountains; but has fought, and suffered shipwreck and prison, and imbrued its little hands in gore, and gallantly retrieved the lost battle, and triumphantly protected innocence and beauty. Elsewhere in his essay Mr. James has protested with excellent reason against too narrow a conception of experience; for the born artist, he contends, the 'faintest hints of life' are converted into revelations; and it will be found true, I believe, in a majority of cases, that the artist writes with more gusto and effect of those things which he has only wished to do, than of those which he has done. Desire is a wonderful telescope, and Pisgah the best observatory. Now, while it is true that neither Mr. James nor the author of the work in question has ever, in the fleshly sense, gone questing after gold, it is probable that both have ardently desired and fondly imagined the details of such a life in youthful day-dreams; and the author, counting upon that, and well aware (cunning and low-minded man!) that this class of interest, having been frequently treated, finds a readily accessible and beaten road to the sympathies of the reader, addressed himself throughout to the building up and circumstantiation of this boyish dream. Character to the boy is a sealed book; for him, a pirate is a beard in wide trousers and literally bristling with pistols. The author, for the sake of circumstantiation and because he was himself more or less grown up, admitted character, within certain limits, into his design; but only within certain limits. Had the same puppets figured in a scheme of another sort, they had been drawn to very different purpose; for in this elementary novel of adventure, the characters need to be presented with but one class of qualities – the warlike and formidable. So as they appear insidious in deceit and fatal in the combat, they have served their end. Danger is the matter with which this class of novel deals; fear, the passion with which it idly trifles; and the characters are portrayed only so far as they realise the sense of danger and provoke the sympathy of fear. To add more traits, to be too clever, to start the hare of moral or intellectual interest while we are running the fox of material interest, is not to enrich but to stultify your tale. The stupid reader will only be offended, and the clever reader lose the scent.

The novel of character has this difference from all others: that it requires no coherency of plot, and for this reason, as in the case of 'Gil Blas,' it is sometimes called the novel of adventure. It turns on the humours of the persons represented; these are, to be sure, embodied in incidents, but the incidents themselves, being tributary, need not march in a progression; and the characters may be statically shown. As they enter, so they may go out; they must be consistent, but they need not grow. Here Mr. James will recognise the note of much of his own work: he treats, for the most part, the statics of character, studying it at rest or only gently moved; and, with his usual delicate and just artistic instinct, he avoids those stronger passions which would deform the attitudes he loves to study, and change his sitters from the humourists of ordinary life to the brute forces and bare types of more emotional moments. In his recent 'Author of "Beltraffio,"' so just in conception, so nimble and neat in workmanship, strong passion is indeed employed; but observe that it is not displayed. Even in the heroine the working of the passion is suppressed; and the great struggle, the true tragedy, the *scène-à-faire*, passes unseen behind the panels of a locked door. The delectable invention of the young visitor is introduced, consciously or not, to this end: that Mr. James, true to his method, might avoid the scene of passion. I trust no reader will suppose me guilty of undervaluing this little masterpiece. I mean merely that it belongs to one marked class of novel, and that it would have been very differently conceived and treated had it belonged to that other marked class, of which I now proceed to speak.

I take pleasure in calling the dramatic novel by that name, because it enables me to point out by the way a strange and peculiarly English misconception. It is sometimes supposed that the drama consists of incident. It consists of passion, which gives the actor his opportunity; and that passion must progressively increase, or the actor, as the piece proceeded, would be unable to carry the audience from a lower to a higher pitch of interest and emotion. A good serious play must therefore be founded on one of the passionate *cruces* of life, where duty and inclination come nobly to the grapple; and the same is true of what I call, for that reason, the dramatic novel . . . In this kind of novel the closed door of the 'Author of "Beltraffio"' must be broken open; passion must appear upon the scene and utter its last word; passion is the be-all and the end-all, the plot and the solution, the protagonist and the *deus ex machinâ* in one. The characters may come anyhow upon the stage: we do not care; the point is, that, before they leave it, they shall become transfigured and raised out of themselves by passion. It may be part of the design to draw them with detail; to depict a full-length character, and then behold it melt and change in the furnace of emotion. But there is no obligation of the sort; nice portraiture is not required; and we are content to accept mere abstract types, so they be strongly and sincerely moved . . .

And here I can imagine Mr. James, with his lucid sense, to intervene. To much of what I have said he would apparently demur; in much he would, somewhat impatiently, acquiesce. It may be true; but it is not what he desired to say or to hear said. He spoke of the finished picture and its worth when done; I, of the brushes, the palette, and the north light. He uttered his views in the tone and for the ear of good society; I, with the emphasis and technicalities of the obtrusive student. But the point, I may reply, is not merely to amuse the public, but to offer helpful advice to the young writer. And the young writer will not so much be helped by genial pictures of what an art may aspire to at its highest, as by a true idea of what it must be on the lowest terms. The best that we can say to him is this: Let him choose a motive, whether of character or passion; carefully construct his plot so that every incident is an illustration of the motive and every property employed shall bear to it a near relation of congruity or contrast; avoid a sub-plot, unless, as sometimes in Shakespeare, the sub-plot be a reversion or complement of the main intrigue; suffer not his style to flag below the level of the argument; pitch the key of conversation, not with any thought of how men talk in parlours, but with a single eye to the degree of passion he may be called on to express; and allow neither himself in the narrative nor any character in the course of the dialogue, to utter one sentence that is not part and parcel of the business of the story or the discussion of the problem involved. Let him not regret if this shortens his book; it will be better so; for to add irrelevant matter is not to lengthen but to bury. Let him not mind if he miss a thousand qualities, so that he keeps unflaggingly in pursuit of the one he has chosen. Let him not care particularly if he miss the tone of conversation, the pungent material detail of the day's manners, the reproduction of the atmosphere and the environment. These elements are not essential: a novel may be excellent, and yet have none of them; a passion or a character is so much the better depicted as it rises clearer from material circumstance. In this age of the particular, let him remember the ages of the abstract, the great books of the past, the brave men that lived before Shakespeare and before Balzac. And as the root of the whole matter, let him bear in mind that his novel is not a transcript of life, to be judged by its exactitude; but a simplification of some side or point of life, to stand or fall by its significant simplicity. For although, in great men, working upon great motives, what we observe and admire is often their complexity, yet underneath appearances the truth remains unchanged: that simplification was their method, and that simplicity is their excellence.

Thomas Hardy, The Science of Fiction (1891)

Thomas Hardy (1840–1928) continues to be revered as a poet and a novelist, despite persistent condescension in critical studies of his work. With the exception of 'The Dorsetshire Labourer' (1883), Hardy's essays have been largely ignored, though Peter Widdowson's excellent annotated edition of *Selected Poetry and Non-Fictional Prose* (Basingstoke: Macmillan, 1997) should help to remedy this neglect. 'The Science of Fiction' was first published in the *New Review* in April 1891, as the final part of a symposium involving Walter Besant and Paul Bourget (a French novelist and acquaintance of Henry James). Hardy offers a lucid and forthright account of the shortcomings of excessive realism or 'copyism' (his main target is the naturalism of Émile Zola). Henry James's impression of Hardy as a clumsy and naive provincial writer is immediately displaced by this essay's complex and comprehensive grasp of theoretical debates about realism.

Since Art is science with an addition, since some science underlies all Art, there is seemingly no paradox in the use of such a phrase as 'the Science of Fiction.' One concludes it to mean that comprehensive and accurate knowledge of realities which must be sought for, or intuitively possessed, to some extent, before anything deserving the name of an artistic performance in narrative can be produced.

The particulars of this science are the generals of almost all others. The materials of Fiction being human nature and circumstances, the science thereof may be dignified by calling it the codified law of things as they really are. No single pen can treat exhaustively of this. The Science of Fiction is contained in that large work, the cyclopædia of life.

In no proper sense can the term 'science' be applied to other than this fundamental matter. It can have no part or share in the construction of a story, however recent speculations may have favoured such an application. We may assume with certainty that directly the constructive stage is entered upon, Art – high or low – begins to exist.

The most devoted apostle of realism, the sheerest naturalist, cannot escape, any more than the withered old gossip over her fire, the exercise of Art in his labour or pleasure of telling a tale. Not until he becomes an automatic reproducer of all impressions whatsoever can he be called purely scientific, or even a manufacturer on scientific principles. If in the exercise of his reason he select or omit, with an eye to being more truthful than truth (the just aim of Art), he transforms himself into a technicist at a move.

As this theory of the need for the exercise of the Dædalian faculty for selection and cunning manipulation has been disputed, it may be worth while to examine the contrary proposition. That it should ever have been maintained by such a romancer as M. Zola, in his work on the *Roman Expérimental*, seems to reveal an obtuseness to the disproof conveyed in his own novels which, in a French writer, is singular indeed. To be sure that author – whose powers in story-telling, rightfully and wrongfully exercised, may be partly owing to the fact that he is not a critic – does in a measure concede something in the qualified counsel that the novel should keep as close to reality *as it can*; a remark which may be interpreted with infinite latitude, and would no doubt have been cheerfully accepted by Dumas père or Mrs. Radcliffe. It implies discriminative choice; and if we grant that we grant all. But to maintain in theory what he abandons in practice, to subscribe to rules and to work by instinct, is a proceeding not confined to the author of *Germinal* and *La Faute de l'Abbé Mouret*.

The reasons that make against such conformation of story-writing to scientific processes have been set forth so many times in examining the theories of the realist, that it is not necessary to recapitulate them here. Admitting the desirability, the impossibility of reproducing in its entirety the phantasmagoria of experience with infinite and atomic truth, without shadow, relevancy, or subordination, is not the least of them. The fallacy appears to owe its origin to the just perception that with our widened knowledge of the universe and its forces, and man's position therein, narrative, to be artistically convincing, must adjust itself to the new alignment, as would also artistic works in form and colour, if further spectacles in their sphere could be presented. Nothing but the illusion of truth can permanently please, and when the old illusions begin to be penetrated, a more natural magic has to be supplied.

Creativeness in its full and ancient sense – the making a thing or situation out of nothing that ever was before – is apparently ceasing to satisfy a world which no longer believes in the abnormal – ceasing at least to satisfy the vancouriers of taste; and creative fancy has accordingly to give more and more place to realism, that is, to an artificiality distilled from the fruits of closest observation.

This is the meaning deducible from the work of the realists, however stringently they themselves may define realism in terms. Realism is an unfortunate, an ambiguous word, which has been taken up by literary society like a view-halloo, and has been assumed in some places to mean copyism, and in others pruriency, and has led to two classes of delineators being included in one condemnation.

Just as bad a word is one used to express a consequence of this development, namely 'brutality,' a term which, first applied by French critics, has since spread over the English school like the other. It aptly hits off the immediate impression of the thing meant; but it has the disadvantage of defining impartiality as a passion, and a plan as a caprice. It certainly is very far from truly expressing the aims and methods of conscientious and well-intentioned authors who, notwithstanding their excesses, errors, and rickety theories, attempt to narrate the *vérité vraie*.

To return for a moment to the theories of the scientific realists. Every friend to the novel should and must be in sympathy with their error, even while distinctly perceiving it. Though not true, it is well found. To advance realism as complete copyism, to call the idle trade of story-telling a science, is the hyperbolic flight of an admirable enthusiasm, the exaggerated cry of an honest reaction from the false, in which the truth has been impetuously approached and overleapt in fault of lighted on.

Possibly, if we only wait, the third something, akin to perfection, will exhibit itself on its due pedestal. How that third something may be induced to hasten its presence, who shall say? Hardly the English critic.

But this appertains to the Art of novel-writing, and is outside the immediate subject. To return to the 'science.' . . . Yet what is the use? Its very comprehensiveness renders the attempt to dwell upon it a futility. Being an observative responsiveness to everything within the cycle of the suns that has to do with actual life, it is easier to say what it is not than to categorise its *summa genera*. It is not, for example, the paying of a great regard to adventitious externals to the neglect of vital qualities, not a precision about the outside of the platter and an obtuseness to the contents. An accomplished lady once confessed to the writer that she could never be in a room two minutes without knowing every article of furniture it contained and every detail in the attire of the inmates, and, when she left, remembering every remark. Here was a person, one might feel for the moment, who could prime herself to an unlimited extent and at the briefest notice in the scientific data of fiction; one who, assuming her to have some slight artistic power, was a born novelist. To explain why such a keen eye to the superficial does not imply a sensitiveness to the intrinsic is a psychological matter beyond the scope of these notes; but that a blindness to material particulars often accompanies a quick perception of the more ethereal characteristics of humanity, experience continually shows.

A sight for the finer qualities of existence, an ear for the 'still sad music of humanity,' are not to be acquired by the outer senses alone, close as their powers in photography may be. What cannot be discerned by eye and ear, what may be apprehended only by the mental tactility that comes from a sympathetic appreciativeness of life in all its manifestations, this is the gift which renders its possessor a more accurate delineator of human nature than many another with twice his powers and means of external observation, but without that sympathy. To see in half and quarter views the whole picture, to catch from a few bars the whole tune, is the intuitive power that supplies the would-be story-writer with the scientific bases for his pursuit. He may not count the dishes at a feast, or accurately estimate the value of the jewels in a lady's diadem; but through the smoke of those dishes, and the rays from these jewels, he sees written on the wall:—

We are such stuff
As dreams are made of, and our little life
Is rounded with a sleep.

Thus, as aforesaid, an attempt to set forth the Science of Fiction in calculable pages is futility; it is to write a whole library of human philosophy, with instructions how to feel.

Once in a crowd a listener heard a needy and illiterate woman saying of another poor and haggard woman who had lost her little son years before: 'You can see the ghost of that child in her face even now.'

That speaker was one who, though she could probably neither read nor write, had the true means towards the 'Science' of Fiction innate within her; a power of observation informed by a living heart. Had she been trained in the technicalities, she might have fashioned her view of mortality with good effect; a reflection which leads to a conjecture that, perhaps, true novelists, like poets, are born, not made.

Émile Zola, The Experimental Novel (1893)

Émile Zola (1840–1902), more than any other writer, is strongly identified with the theory and practice of literary naturalism. His Rougon-Macquart series of novels (subtitled *Histoire naturelle et sociale d'une famille sous le Second Empire*) is concerned explicitly with the influences of heredity and environment that formed a major part of the naturalist interest in what constitutes 'character'. 'The Experimental Novel' is one of the great manifestos of nineteenth-century naturalism. It takes its bearings from the pioneering scientific work of Claude Bernard in his 'Introduction to the Study of Experimental Medicine'. Although the parallels Zola establishes between the work of the experimental scientist and the work of the naturalist writer are not always easy to follow, the central conviction is clear: the novelist is both an observer and an experimenter. Countering claims that naturalism is narrowly factual or documentary, Zola asserts that the naturalist writer only begins with observed facts: he must see, but also understand and invent.

In my literary essays I have often spoken of the application of the experimental method to the novel and to the drama. The return to nature, the naturalistic evolution which marks the century, drives little by little all the manifestation of human intelligence into the same scientific path. Only the idea of a literature governed by science is doubtless a surprise, until explained with precision and understood. It seems to me necessary, then, to say briefly and to the point what I understand by the experimental novel.

I really only need to adapt, for the experimental method has been established with strength and marvelous clearness by Claude Bernard in his 'Introduction à l'Etude de la Medecine Expérimentale'. This work, by a savant whose authority is unquestioned, will serve me as a solid foundation. I shall here find the whole question treated, and I shall restrict myself to irrefutable arguments and to giving the quotations which may seem necessary to me. This will then be but a compiling of texts, as I intend on all points to intrench myself behind Claude Bernard. It will often be but necessary for me to replace the word 'doctor' by the word 'novelist', to make my meaning clear and to give it the rigidity of a scientific truth.

What determined my choice, and made me choose 'L'Introduction' as my basis, was the fact that medicine, in the eyes of a great number of people, is still an art, as is the novel. Claude Bernard all his life was searching and battling to put medicine in a scientific path. In his struggle we see the first feeble attempts of a science to disengage itself little by little from empiricism,[1] and to gain a foothold in the realm of truth, by means of the experimental method. Claude Bernard demonstrates that this method, followed in the study of inanimate bodies in chemistry and in physics, should be also used in the study of living bodies, in physiology and medicine. I am going to try and prove for my part that if the experimental method leads to the knowledge of physical life, it should also lead to the knowledge of the passionate and intellectual life. It is but a question of degree in the same path which runs from chemistry to physiology, then from physiology to anthropology and to sociology. The experimental novel is the goal.

To be more clear, I think it would be better to give a brief *résumé* of 'L'Introduction' before I commence. The applications which I shall make of the texts will be better understood if the plan of the work and the matters treated are explained.

Claude Bernard, after having declared that medicine enters the scientific path, with physiology as its foundation, and by means of the experimental method, first explains the differences which exist between the sciences of observation and the sciences of experiment. He concludes, finally, that experiment is but provoked observation. All experimental reasoning is based on doubt, for the experimentalist should have no preconceived idea, in the face of nature, and should always retain his liberty of thought. He simply accepts the phenomena which are produced, when they are proved.

In the second part he reaches his true subject and shows that the spontaneity of living bodies is not opposed to the employment of experiment. The difference is simply that an inanimate body possesses merely the ordinary, external environment, while the essence of the higher organism is set in an internal and perfected environment endowed with constant physico-chemical properties exactly like the external environment; hence there is an absolute determinism in the existing conditions of natural phenomena; for the living as for the inanimate bodies. He calls determinism the cause which determines the appearance of these phenomena. This nearest cause, as it is called, is nothing more than the physical and material condition of the existence or manifestation of the phenomena. The end of all experimental method, the boundary of all scientific research, is then identical for living and for inanimate bodies; it consists in finding the relations which unite a phenomenon of any kind to its nearest cause, or, in other words, in determining the conditions necessary for the manifestation of this phenomenon. Experimental science has no necessity to worry itself about the 'why' of things; it simply explains the 'how'.

After having explained the experimental considerations common to living beings and to inanimate, Claude Bernard passes to the experimental considerations which belong specially to living beings. The great and only difference is this, that there is presented to our consideration, in the organism of living beings, a harmonious group of phenomena. He then treats of practical experiments on living beings, of vivisection, of the preparatory anatomical conditions, of the choice of animals, of the use of calculation in the study of phenomena, and lastly of the physiologist's laboratory.

Finally, in the last part of 'L'Introduction', he gives some examples of physiological experimental investigations in support of the ideas which he has formulated. He then furnishes some examples of experimental criticism in physiology. In the end he indicates the philosophical obstacles which the experimental doctor encounters. He puts in the first rank the false application of physiology to medicine, the scientific ignorance as well as certain illusions of the medical mind. Further, he concludes by saying that empirical medicine and experimental medicine, not being incompatible, ought, on the contrary, to be inseparable one from the other. His last sentence is that experimental medicine adheres to no medical doctrine nor any philosophical system.

This is, very broadly, the skeleton of 'L'Introduction' stripped of its flesh. I hope that this rapid *exposé* will be sufficient to fill up the gaps which my manner of proceeding is bound to produce; for naturally, I shall cite from the work only such passages as are necessary to define and comment upon the experimental novel. I repeat that I use this treatise merely as a solid foundation on which to build, but a foundation very rich in arguments and proofs of all kinds. Experimental medicine, which but lisps as yet, can alone give us an exact idea of experimental literature, which, being still unhatched, is not even lisping.

I

The first question which presents itself is this: Is experiment possible in literature, in which up to the present time observation alone has been employed?

Claude Bernard discusses observation and experiment at great length. There exists, in the first place, a very clear line of demarcation, as follows: 'The name of "observer" is given to him who applies the simple or complex process of investigation in the study of phenomena which he does not vary, and which he gathers, consequently, as nature offers them to him; the name of "experimentalist" is given to him who employs the simple and complex process of investigation to vary or modify, for an end of some kind, the natural phenomena, and to make them appear under circumstances and conditions in which they are not presented by nature.' For instance, astronomy is a science of observation, because you cannot conceive of an astronomer acting upon the stars; while chemistry is an experimental science, as the chemist acts upon nature and modifies it. This, according to Claude Bernard, is the only true and important distinction which separates the observer from the experimentalist.

I cannot follow him in his discussion of the different definitions given up to the present time. As I have said before, he finishes by coming to the conclusion that experiment is but provoked observation. I repeat his words: 'In the experimental method the search after facts, that is to say, investigation, is always accompanied by a reason, so that ordinarily the experimentalist makes an experiment to confirm and verify the value of an experimental idea. In this case you can say that experiment is an observation instigated for the purpose of verification.'

To determine how much observation and experimenting there can be in the naturalistic novel, I only need to quote the following passages:

> The observer relates purely and simply the phenomena which he has under his eyes . . . He should be the photographer of phenomena, his observation should be an exact representation of nature . . . He listens to nature and he writes under its dictation. But once the fact is ascertained and the phenomenon observed, an idea or hypothesis comes into his mind, reason intervenes, and the experimentalist comes forward to interpret the phenomenon. The experimentalist is a man who, in pursuance of a more or less probable, but anticipated, explanation of observed phenomena, institutes an experiment in such a way that, according to all probability, it will furnish a result which will serve to confirm the hypothesis or preconceived idea. The moment that the result of the experiment manifests itself, the experimentalist finds himself face to face with a true observation which he has called forth, and which he must ascertain, as all observation, without any preconceived idea. The experimentalist should then disappear, or rather transform himself instantly into the observer, and it is not until after he has ascertained the absolute results of the experiment, like that of an ordinary observation, that his mind comes back to reasoning, comparing, and judging whether the experimental hypothesis is verified or invalidated by these same results.

The mechanism is all there. It is a little complicated, it is true, and Claude Bernard is led on to say: 'When all this passes into the brain of a savant who has given himself up to the study of a science as complicated as medicine still is, then there is such an entanglement between the result of observation and what belongs to experiment that it will be impossible and, besides, useless to try to analyze, in their inextricable *mélange*, each of these terms.' In one word, it might be said that observation 'indicates' and that experiment 'teaches'.

Now, to return to the novel, we can easily see that the novelist is equally an observer and an experimentalist. The observer in him gives the facts as he has observed them, suggests the point of departure, displays the solid earth on which his characters are to tread and the phenomena to develop. Then the experimentalist appears and introduces an experiment, that is to say, sets his characters going in a certain story so as to show that the succession of facts will be such as the requirements of the determinism of the phenomena under examination call for. Here it is nearly always an experiment '*pour voir*', as Claude Bernard calls it. The novelist starts out in search of a truth. I will take as an example the character of the Baron Hulot, in *Cousine Bette*, by Balzac. The general fact observed by Balzac is the ravages that the amorous temperament of a man makes in his home, in his family, and in society. As soon as he has chosen his subject he starts from known facts; then he makes his experiment, and exposes Hulot to a series of trials, placing him amid certain surroundings in order to exhibit how the complicated machinery of his passions works. It is then evident that there is not only observation there, but that there is also experiment; as Balzac does not remain satisfied with photographing the facts collected by him, but interferes in a direct way to place his character in certain conditions, and of these he remains the master. The problem is to know what such a passion, acting in such a surrounding and under such circumstances, would produce from the point of view of an individual and of society; and an experimental novel, *Cousine Bette*, for example, is simply the report of the experiment that the novelist conducts before the eyes of the public. In fact, the whole operation consists in taking facts in nature, then in studying the mechanism of these facts, acting upon them, by the modification of circumstances and surroundings, without deviating from the laws of nature. Finally, you possess knowledge of the man, scientific knowledge of him, in both his individual and social relations.

Doubtless we are still far from certainties in chemistry and even physiology. Nor do we know any more the reagents which decompose the passions, rendering them susceptible of analysis. Often, in this essay, I shall recall in similar fashion this fact, that the experimental novel is still younger than experimental medicine, and the latter is but just born. But I do not intend to exhibit the acquired results, I simply desire to clearly expose a method. If the experimental novelist is still groping in the most obscure and complex of all the sciences, this does not prevent this science from existing. It is undeniable that the naturalistic novel, such as we understand it to-day, is a real experiment that a novelist makes on man by the help of observation.

Besides, this opinion is not only mine, it is Claude Bernard's as well. He says in one place: 'In practical life men but make experiments on one another.' And again, in a more conclusive way, he expresses the whole theory of the experimental novel: 'When we reason on our own acts we have a certain guide, for we are conscious of what we think and how we feel. But if we wish to judge of the acts of another man, and know the motives which make him act, that is altogether a different thing. Without doubt we have before our eyes the movements of this man and his different acts, which are, we are sure, the modes of expression of his sensibility and his will. Further, we even admit that there is a necessary connection between the acts and their cause; but what is this cause? We do not feel it, we are not conscious of it, as we are when it acts in ourselves; we are therefore obliged to interpret it, and to guess at it, from the movements which we see and the words which we hear. We are obliged to check off this man's actions one by the other; we consider how he acted in such a circumstance, and, in a word, we have recourse to the experimental method.' All that I have spoken of further back is summed up in this last phrase, which is written by a savant.

I shall still call your attention to another illustration of Claude Bernard, which struck me as very forcible: 'The experimentalist is the examining magistrate of nature.' We novelists are the examining magistrates of men and their passions.

But see what splendid clearness breaks forth when this conception of the application of the experimental method to the novel is adequately grasped and is carried out with all the scientific rigor which the matter permits to-day. A contemptible reproach which they heap upon us naturalistic writers is the desire to be solely photographers. We have in vain declared that we admit the necessity of an artist's possessing an individual temperament and a personal expression; they continue to reply to us with these imbecile arguments, about the impossibility of being strictly true, about the necessity of arranging facts to produce a work of art of any kind. Well, with the application of the experimental method to the novel that quarrel dies out. The idea of experiment carries with it the idea of modification. We start, indeed, from the true facts, which are our indestructible basis; but to show the mechanism of these facts it is necessary for us to produce and direct the phenomena; this is our share of invention, here is the genius in the book. Thus without having recourse to the questions of form and of style, which I shall examine later, I maintain even at this point that we must modify nature, without departing from nature, when we employ the experimental method in our novels. If we bear in mind this definition, that 'observation indicates and experiment teaches', we can even now claim for our books this great lesson of experiment.

The writer's office, far from being lessened, grows singularly from this point of view. An experiment, even the most simple, is always based on an idea, itself born of an observation. As Claude Bernard says: 'The experimental idea is not arbitrary, nor purely imaginary; it ought always to have a support in some observed reality, that is to say, in nature.' It is on this idea and on doubt that he bases all the method. 'The appearance of the experimental idea,' he says further on, 'is entirely spontaneous and its nature absolutely individual, depending upon the mind in which it originates; it is a particular sentiment, a *quid proprium*, which constitutes the originality, the invention, and the genius of each one.' Further, he makes doubt the great scientific lever. 'The doubter is the true savant; he doubts only himself and his interpretations; he believes in science; he even admits in the experimental sciences a criterion or a positive principle, the determinism of phenomena, which is absolute in living beings as in inanimate bodies.' Thus, instead of confining the novelist within narrow bounds, the experimental method gives full sway to his intelligence as a thinker, and to his genius as a creator. He must see, understand, and invent. Some observed fact makes the idea start up of trying an experiment, of writing a novel, in order to attain to a complete knowledge of the truth. Then when, after careful consideration, he has decided upon the plan of his experiment, he will judge the results at each step with the freedom of mind of a man who accepts only facts conformable to the determination of phenomena. He sets out from doubt to reach positive knowledge; and he will not cease to doubt until the mechanism of the passion, taken to pieces and set up again by him, acts according to the fixed laws of nature. There is no greater, no more magnificent work for the human mind. We shall see, further on, the miseries of the scholastics, of the makers of systems, and those theorizing about the ideal, compared with the triumph of the experimentalists.

I sum up this first part by repeating that the naturalistic novelists observe and experiment, and that all their work is the offspring of the doubt which seizes them in the presence of truths little known and phenomena unexplained, until an experimental idea rudely awakens their genius some day, and urges them to make an experiment, to analyze facts, and to master them.

II

. . . Now, science enters into the domain of us novelists, who are to-day the analyzers of man, in his individual and social relations. We are continuing, by our observations and experiments, the work of the physiologist, who has continued that of the physicist and the chemist. We are making use, in a certain way, of scientific psychology to complete scientific physiology; and to finish the series we have only to bring into our studies of nature and man the decisive tool of the experimental method. In one word, we should operate on the characters, the passions, on the human and social data, in the same way that the chemist and the physicist operate on inanimate beings, and as the physiologist operates on living beings. Determinism dominates everything. It is scientific investigation, it is experimental reasoning, which combats one by one the hypotheses of the idealists, and which replaces purely imaginary novels by novels of observation and experiment.

I certainly do not intend at this point to formulate laws. In the actual condition of the science of man the obscurity and confusion are still too great to risk the slightest synthesis. All that can be said is that there is an absolute determinism for all human phenomena. From that on investigation is a duty. We have the method; we should go forward, even if a whole lifetime of effort ends but in the conquest of a small particle of the truth. Look at physiology: Claude Bernard made grand discoveries, and he died protesting that he knew nothing, or nearly nothing. In each page he confesses the difficulties of his task. 'In the phenomenal relations,' he says, 'such as nature offers them to us, there always reigns a complexity more or less great. In this respect the complexity of mineral phenomena is much less great than that of living phenomena; that is why the sciences restricted to inanimate bodies have been able to formulate themselves more quickly. In living beings the phenomena are of enormous complexity, and the greater mobility of living organisms renders them more difficult to grasp and to define.' What can be said, then, of the difficulties to be encountered by the experimental novel, which adds to physiology its studies upon the most delicate and complex organs, which deals with the highest manifestations of man as an individual and a social member? Evidently analysis becomes more complicated here. Therefore, if the physiologist is but drawing up his principles to-day, it is natural that the experimental novelist should be only taking his first steps: We foresee it as a sure consequence of the scientific evolution of the century; but it is impossible to base it on certain laws. Since Claude Bernard speaks of 'the restricted and precarious truths of biological science', we can freely admit that the truths of the science of man, from the standpoint of his intellectual and passionate mechanism, are more restricted and precarious still. We are lisping yet, we are the last comers, but that should be only one incentive the more to push us forward to more exact studies; now that we possess the tool, the experimental method, our goal is very plain – to know the determinism of phenomena and to make ourselves master of these phenomena.

Without daring, as I say, to formulate laws, I consider that the question of heredity has a great influence in the intellectual and passionate manifestations of man. I also attach considerable importance to the surroundings. I ought to touch upon Darwin's theories; but this is only a general study of the experimental method as applied to the novel, and I should lose myself were I to enter into details. I will only say a word on the subject of surroundings. We have just seen the great importance given by Claude Bernard to the study of those inter-organic conditions which must be taken into account if we wish to find the determinism of phenomena in living beings. Well, then! In the study of a family, of a group of living beings, I think that the social condition is of equal importance. Some day the physiologist will explain to us the mechanism of the thoughts and the passions; we shall know how the individual machinery of each man works; how he thinks, how he loves, how he goes from reason to passion and folly; but these phenomena, resulting as they do from the mechanism of the organs, acting under the influence of an interior condition, are not produced in isolation or in the bare void. Man is not alone; he lives in society, in a social condition; and consequently, for us novelists, this social condition unceasingly modifies the phenomena. Indeed our great study is just there, in the reciprocal effect of society on the individual and the individual on society. For the physiologist, the exterior and interior conditions are purely chemical and physical, and this aids him in finding the laws which govern them easily. We are not yet able to prove that the social condition is also physical and chemical. It is that certainly, or rather it is the variable product of a group of living beings, who themselves are absolutely submissive to the physical and chemical laws which govern alike living beings and inanimate. From this we shall see that we can act upon the social conditions, in acting upon the phenomena of which we have made ourselves master in man. And this is what constitutes the experimental novel; to possess a knowledge of the mechanism of the phenomena inherent in man, to show the machinery of his intellectual and sensory manifestations, under the influences of heredity and environment, such as physiology shall give them to us, and then finally to exhibit man living in social conditions produced by himself, which he modifies daily, and in the heart of which he himself experiences a continual transformation. Thus, then, we lean on physiology; we take man from the hands of the physiologist solely, in order to continue the solution of the problem, and to solve scientifically the question of how men behave when they are in society.

These general ideas will be sufficient to guide us to-day. Later on, when science is farther advanced, when the experimental novel has brought forth decisive results, some critic will explain more precisely what I have but indicated to-day.

. . . I have reached this point: the experimental novel is a consequence of the scientific evolution of the century; it continues and completes physiology, which itself leans for support on chemistry and medicine; it substitutes for the study of the abstract and the metaphysical man the study of the natural man, governed by physical and chemical laws, and modified by the influences of his surroundings; it is in one word the literature of our scientific age, as the classical and romantic literature corresponded to a scholastic and theological age. Now I will pass to the great question of the application of all this, and of its justification.

III

The object of the experimental method in physiology and in medicine is to study phenomena in order to become their master. Claude Bernard in each page of 'L'Introduction' comes back to this idea. He declares: 'All natural philosophy is summed up in this: To know the laws which govern phenomena. The experimental problem reduces itself to this: To foresee and direct phenomena.' Farther on he gives an example: 'It will not satisfy the experimental doctor, though it may the merely empirical one, to know that quinine cures fever; the essential thing is to know what fever is, and to understand the mechanism by which quinine cures. All this is of the greatest importance to the experimental doctor; for as soon as he knows it positively, the fact that quinine cures fever will no longer be an isolated and empirical fact, but a scientific fact. This fact will be connected then with the conditions which bind it to other phenomena, and we shall be thus led to the knowledge of the laws of the organism, and to the possibility of regulating their manifestations.' A striking example can be quoted in the case of scabies. 'To-day the cause of this disease is known and determined experimentally; the whole subject has become scientific, and empiricism has disappeared. A cure is surely and without exception effected when you place yourself in the conditions known by experiment to produce this end.'

This, then, is the end, this is the purpose in physiology and in experimental medicine: to make one's self master of life in order to be able to direct it. Let us suppose that science advances and that the conquest of the unknown is finally completed; the scientific age which Claude Bernard saw in his dreams will then be realized. When that time comes the doctor will be the master of maladies; he will cure without fail; his influence upon the human body will conduce to the welfare and strength of the species. We shall enter upon a century in which man, grown more powerful, will make use of nature and will utilize its laws to produce upon the earth the greatest possible amount of justice and freedom. There is no nobler, higher, nor grander end. Here is our rôle as intelligent beings: to penetrate to the wherefore of things, to become superior to these things, and to reduce them to a condition of subservient machinery.

Well, this dream of the physiologist and the experimental doctor is also that of the novelist, who employs the experimental method in his study of man as a simple individual and as a social animal. Their object is ours; we also desire to master certain phenomena of an intellectual and personal order, to be able to direct them. We are, in a word, experimental moralists, showing by experiment in what way a passion acts in a certain social condition. The day in which we gain control of the mechanism of this passion we can treat it and reduce it, or at least make it as inoffensive as possible. And in this consists the practical utility and high morality of our naturalistic works, which experiment on man, and which dissect piece by piece this human machinery in order to set it going through the influence of the environment. When things have advanced further, when we are in possession of the different laws, it will only be necessary to work upon the individuals and the surroundings if we wish to find the best social condition. In this way we shall construct a practical sociology, and our work will be a help to political and economical sciences. I do not know, I repeat, of a more noble work, nor of a grander application. To be the master of good and evil, to regulate life, to regulate society, to solve in time all the problems of socialism, above all, to give justice a solid foundation by solving through experiment the questions of criminality – is not this being the most useful and the most moral workers in the human workshop?

Let us compare, for one instant, the work of the idealistic novelist to ours; and here this word idealistic refers to writers who cast aside observation and experiment, and base their works on the supernatural and the irrational, who admit, in a word, the power of mysterious forces outside of the determinism of the phenomena. Claude Bernard shall reply to this for me: 'What distinguishes experimental reasoning from scholastic is the fecundity of the one and the sterility of the other. It is precisely the scholastic, who believes he has absolute certitude, who attains to no results. This is easily understood, since by his belief in an absolute principle he puts himself outside of nature, in which everything is relative. It is, on the contrary, the experimenter, who is always in doubt, who does not think he possesses absolute certainty about anything, who succeeds in mastering the phenomena which surround him, and in increasing his power over nature.' By and by I shall return to this question of the ideal, which is in truth but the question of indeterminism. Claude Bernard says truly: 'The intellectual conquest of man consists in diminishing and driving back indeterminism, and so, gradually, by the aid of the experimental method, gaining ground for determinism.' We experimental novelists have the same task; our work is to go from the known to the unknown, to make ourselves masters of nature; while the idealistic novelists deliberately remain in the unknown, through all sorts of religious and philosophical prejudices, under the astounding pretense that the unknown is nobler and more beautiful than the known. If our work, often cruel, if our terrible pictures needed justification, I should find, indeed, with Claude Bernard this argument conclusive: 'You will never reach really fruitful and luminous generalizations on the phenomena of life until you have experimented yourself and stirred up in the hospital, the amphitheater, and the laboratory the fetid or palpitating sources of life. If it were necessary for me to give a comparison which would explain my sentiments on the science of life, I should say that it is a superb salon, flooded with light, which you can only reach by passing through a long and nauseating kitchen.' . . .

Hence, in our novels, when we experiment on a dangerous wound which poisons society, we proceed in the same way as the experimentalist doctor; we try to find the simple initial cause in order to reach the complex causes of which the action is the result. Go back once more to the example of Baron Hulot in *Cousine Bette*. See the final result, the dénouement of the novel: an entire family is destroyed, all sorts of secondary dramas are produced, under the action of Hulot's amorous temperament. It is there, in this temperament, that the initial cause is found. One member, Hulot, becomes rotten, and immediately all around him are tainted, the social circulus is interrupted, the health of that society is compromised. What emphasis Balzac lays on the character of Baron Hulot; with what scrupulous care he analyzes him! The experiment deals with him chiefly, because its object is to master the symptoms of this passion in order to govern it. Suppose that Hulot is cured, or at least restrained and rendered inoffensive, immediately the drama ceases to have any longer any *raison d'être*; the equilibrium, or more truly the health, of the social body is again established. Thus the naturalistic novelists are really experimental moralists.

And I reach thus the great reproach with which they think to crush the naturalistic novelists, by treating them as fatalists. How many times have they wished to prove to us that as soon as we did not accept free will, that as soon as man was no more to us than a living machine, acting under the influence of heredity and surroundings, we should fall into gross fatalism, we should debase humanity to the rank of a troop marching under the baton of destiny. It is necessary to define our terms; we are not fatalists, we are determinists, which is not at all the same thing. Claude Bernard explains the two terms very plainly: 'We have given the name of determinism to the nearest or determining cause of phenomena. We never act upon the essence of phenomena in nature, but only on their determinism, and by this very fact, that we act upon it, determinism differs from fatalism, upon which we could not act at all. Fatalism assumes that the appearance of any phenomenon is necessary apart from its conditions, while determinism is just the conditions essential for the appearance of any phenomenon, and such appearance is never forced. Once the search for the determinism of phenomena is placed as a fundamental principle of the experimental method, there is no longer either materialism, or spiritualism, or inanimate matter, or living matter; there remain but phenomena of which it is necessary to determine the conditions, that is to say, the circumstances which play, by their proximity to these phenomena, the rôle of nearest cause.' This is decisive. All we do is to apply this method in our novels, and we are the determinists who experimentally try to determine the condition of the phenomena, without departing in our investigations from the laws of nature. As Claude Bernard very truly says, the moment that we can act, and that we do act, on the determining cause of phenomena – by modifying their surroundings, for example – we cease to be fatalists.

Here you have, then, the moral purpose of the experimental novelist clearly defined. I have often said that we do not have to draw a conclusion from our works; and this means that our works carry their conclusion with them. An experimentalist has no need to conclude, because, in truth, experiment concludes for him. A hundred times, if necessary, he will repeat the experiment before the public; he will explain it; but he need neither become indignant nor approve of it personally; such is the truth, such is the way phenomena work; it is for society to produce or not to produce these phenomena, according as the result is useful or dangerous. You cannot imagine, as I have said elsewhere, a savant being provoked with azote because azote is dangerous to life; he suppresses azote when it is harmful, and not otherwise. As our power is not the same as that of a savant, as we are experimentalists without being practitioners, we ought to content ourselves with searching out the determinism of social phenomena, and leaving to legislators and to men of affairs the care of controlling sooner or later these phenomena in such a way as to develop the good and reject the bad, from the point of view of their utility to man.

In our rôle as experimental moralists we show the mechanism of the useful and the useless, we disengage the determinism of the human and social phenomena so that, in their turn, the legislators can one day dominate and control these phenomena. In a word, we are working with the whole country toward that great object, the conquest of nature and the increase of man's power a hundredfold. Compare with ours the work of the idealistic writers, who rely upon the irrational and the supernatural, and whose every flight upward is followed by a deeper fall into metaphysical chaos. We are the ones who possess strength and morality.

IV

. . . Though I have frequently written the same words and given the same advice, I will repeat them here: 'The experimental method alone can bring the novel out of the atmosphere of lies and errors in which it is plunged. All my literary life has been controlled by this conviction. I am deaf to the voices of the critics who demand that I shall formulate the laws of heredity and the influence of surroundings in my characters; those who make these discouraging objections and denials but speak from slothfulness of mind, from an infatuation for tradition, from an attachment more or less conscious to philosophical and religious beliefs. The experimental direction which the novel is taking to-day is a definite one. And it is no longer the ephemeral influence of a personal system of any kind, it is the result of the scientific evolution, of the study of man himself. My convictions in this respect are so strong that I endeavor to impress them clearly upon the minds of the young writers who read my works; for I think it necessary, above all things else, to inspire them with the scientific spirit, and to initiate them into the ideas and the tendencies of modern science.' . . .

. . . The conclusion to which I wish to come is this: If I were to define the experimental novel I should not say, as Claude Bernard says, that a literary work lies entirely in the personal feeling, for the reason that in my opinion the personal feeling is but the first impulse. Later nature, being there, makes itself felt, or at least that part of nature of which science has given us the secret, and about which we have no longer any right to romance. The experimental novelist is therefore the one who accepts proven facts, who points out in man and in society the mechanism of the phenomena over which science is mistress, and who does not interpose his personal sentiments, except in the phenomena whose determination is not yet settled, and who tries to test, as much as he can, this personal sentiment, this idea *a priori*, by observation and experiment.

I cannot understand how our naturalistic literature can mean anything else. I have only spoken of the experimental novel, but I am fairly convinced that the same method, after having triumphed in history and in criticism, will triumph everywhere, on the stage and in poetry even. It is an inevitable evolution. Literature, in spite of all that can be said, does not depend merely upon the author; it is influenced by the nature it depicts and by the man whom it studies. Now if the savants change their ideas of nature, if they find the true mechanism of life, they force us to follow them, to precede them even, so as to play our rôle in the new hypotheses. The metaphysical man is dead; our whole territory is transformed by the advent of the physiological man. No doubt 'Achilles' Anger', 'Dido's Love', will last forever on account of their beauty: but to-day we feel the necessity of analyzing anger and love, of discovering exactly how such passions work in the human being. This view of the matter is a new one; we have become experimentalists instead of philosophers. In short, everything is summed up in this great fact: the experimental method in letters, as in the sciences, is in the way to explain the natural phenomena, both individual and social, of which the metaphysics, until now, has given only irrational and supernatural explanations.

Joseph Conrad, Preface to *The Nigger of the Narcissus* (1897)

Jozef Teodor Konrad Korzeniowski (1857–1924) was born of Polish parents in the Ukraine, and from an early age was acquainted with exile and displacement. In 1874 he went to Marseilles and began a twenty-year career as a sailor. The title of this essay refers to a ship, the *Narcissus*, on which he sailed from Bombay to Dunkirk in 1884. His novella, *The Nigger of the 'Narcissus'* (1897), was written after the publication of his first novel, *Almayer's Folly* (1895), but preceded his best-known works, such as *Lord Jim* (1900), *Heart of Darkness* (1902), *Nostromo* (1904), and *The Secret Agent* (1907). Conrad's 'Preface' is the most revealing statement he wrote about the creative process of writing fiction. Like Walter Besant and Henry James, Conrad stresses the art of fiction, invoking parallels with painting, sculpture and music. The essay shows the influence of Walter Pater's aesthetic ideals, as well as the impact of French impressionism and symbolism in the 1890s, but Conrad's recognition of the novelist's 'invincible conviction of solidarity that knits together the loneliness of innumerable hearts' is distinctively his own. Ian Watt provides a detailed and illuminating exegesis of the 'Preface' in the Norton Critical Edition of *The Nigger of the 'Narcissus'*, ed. Robert Kimbrough (New York: Norton, 1979), pp. 151–67.

A work that aspires, however humbly, to the condition of art should carry its justification in every line. And art itself may be defined as a single-minded attempt to render the highest kind of justice to the visible universe, by bringing to light the truth, manifold and one, underlying its every aspect. It is an attempt to find in its forms, in its colours, in its light, in its shadows, in the aspects of matter and in the facts of life, what of each is fundamental, what is enduring and essential – their one illuminating and convincing quality – the very truth of their existence. The artist, then, like the thinker or the scientist, seeks the truth and makes his appeal. Impressed by the aspect of the world the thinker plunges into ideas, the scientist into facts – whence, presently emerging, they make their appeal to those qualities of our being that fit us best for the hazardous enterprise of living. They speak authoritatively to our common sense, to our intelligence, to our desire of peace, or to our desire of unrest; not seldom to our prejudices, sometimes to our fears, often to our egoism – but always to our credulity. And their words are heard with reverence, for their concern is with weighty matters; with the cultivation of our minds and the proper care of our bodies; with the attainment of our ambitions; with the perfection of the means and the glorification of our precious aims.

It is otherwise with the artist.

Confronted by the same enigmatical spectacle the artist descends within himself, and in that lonely region of stress and strife, if he be deserving and fortunate, he finds the terms of his appeal. His appeal is made to our less obvious capacities; to that part of our nature which, because of the warlike conditions of existence, is necessarily kept out of sight within the more resisting and hard qualities – like the vulnerable body within a steel armour. His appeal is less loud, more profound, less distinct, more stirring – and sooner forgotten. Yet its effect endures for ever. The changing wisdom of successive generations discards ideas, questions facts, demolishes theories.

But the artist appeals to that part of our being which is not dependent on wisdom; to that in us which is a gift and not an acquisition – and, therefore, more permanently enduring. He speaks to our capacity for delight and wonder, to the sense of mystery surrounding our lives; to our sense of pity, and beauty, and pain; to the latent feeling of fellowship with all creation; and to the subtle but invincible conviction of solidarity that knits together the loneliness of innumerable hearts: to that solidarity in dreams, in joy, in sorrow, in aspirations, in illusions, in hope, in fear, which binds men to each other, which binds together all humanity – the dead to the living, and the living to the unborn.

It is only some such train of thought, or rather of feeling, that can in a measure explain the aim of the attempt made in the tale which follows, to present an unrestful episode in the obscure lives of a few individuals out of all the disregarded multitude of the bewildered, the simple, and the voiceless. For, if there is any part of truth in the belief confessed above, it becomes evident that there is not a place of splendour or a dark corner of the earth that does not deserve, if only a passing glance of wonder and pity. The motive, then, may be held to justify the matter of the work; but this preface, which is simply an avowal of endeavour, cannot end here – for the avowal is not yet complete.

Fiction – if it at all aspires to be art – appeals to temperament. And in truth it must be, like painting, like music, like all art, the appeal of one temperament to all the other innumerable temperaments whose subtle and resistless power endows passing events with their true meaning, and creates the moral, the emotional atmosphere of the place and time. Such an appeal, to be effective, must be an impression conveyed through the senses; and, in fact, it cannot be made in any other way, because temperament, whether individual or collective, is not amenable to persuasion. All art, therefore, appeals primarily to the senses, and the artistic aim when expressing itself in written words must also make its appeal through the senses, if its high desire is to reach the secret spring of responsive emotions. It must strenuously aspire to the plasticity of sculpture, to the colour of painting, and to the magic suggestiveness of music – which is the art of arts. And it is only through complete, unswerving devotion to the perfect blending of form and substance; it is only through an unremitting, never-discouraged care for the shape and ring of sentences, that an approach can be made to plasticity, to colour; and the light of magic suggestiveness may be brought to play for an evanescent instant over the commonplace surface of words: of the old, old words, worn thin, defaced by ages of careless usage.

The sincere endeavour to accomplish that creative task, to go as far on that road as his strength will carry him, to go undeterred by faltering, weariness, or reproach, is the only valid justification for the worker in prose. And if his conscience is clear, his answer to those who, in the fulness of a wisdom which looks for immediate profit, demand specifically to be edified, consoled, amused; who demand to be promptly improved, or encouraged, or frightened, or shocked, or charmed, must run thus: My task which I am trying to achieve is, by the power of the written word, to make you hear, to make you feel – it is, before all, to make you *see*! That – and no more: and it is everything! If I succeed, you shall find there according to your deserts: encouragement, consolation, fear, charm – all you demand; and, perhaps, also that glimpse of truth for which you have forgotten to ask.

To snatch in a moment of courage, from the remorseless rush of time, a passing phase of life, is only the beginning of the task. The task approached in tenderness and faith is to hold up unquestioningly, without choice and without fear, the rescued fragment before all eyes and in the light of a sincere mood. It is to show its vibration, its colour, its form; and through its movement, its form, and its colour, reveal the substance of its truth – disclose its inspiring secret: the stress and passion within the core of each convincing moment. In a single-minded attempt of that kind, if one be deserving and fortunate, one may perchance attain to such clearness of sincerity that at last the presented vision of regret or pity, of terror or mirth, shall awaken in the hearts of the beholders that feeling of unavoidable solidarity; of the solidarity in mysterious origin, in toil, in joy, in hope, in uncertain fate – which binds men to each other and all mankind to the visible world.

It is evident that he who, rightly or wrongly, holds by the convictions expressed above cannot be faithful to any one of the temporary formulas of his craft. The enduring part of them – the truth which each only imperfectly veils – should abide with him as the most precious of his possessions, but they all: Realism, Romanticism, Naturalism; even the unofficial sentimentalism (which, like the poor, is exceedingly difficult to get rid of); all these gods must, after a short period of fellowship, abandon him – even on the very threshold of the temple – to the stammerings of his conscience and to the outspoken consciousness of the difficulties of his work. In that uneasy solitude the cry of Art for Art itself, loses the exciting ring of its apparent immorality. It sounds far off. It has ceased to be a cry, and is heard only as a whisper, often incomprehensible, but at times, and faintly, encouraging.

Sometimes, stretched at ease in the shade of a roadside tree, we watch the motions of a labourer in a distant field, and, after a time, begin to wonder languidly as to what the fellow may be at. We watch the movements of his body, the waving of his arms; we see him bend down, stand up, hesitate, begin again. It may add to the charm of an idle hour to be told the purpose of his exertions. If we know he is trying to lift a stone, to dig a ditch, to uproot a stump, we look with a more real interest at his efforts; we are disposed to condone the jar of his agitation upon the restfulness of the landscape; and even, if in a brotherly frame of mind, we may bring ourselves to forgive his failure. We understood his object, and, after all, the fellow has tried, and perhaps he had not the strength – and perhaps he had not the knowledge. We forgive, go on our way – and forget.

And so it is with the workman of art. Art is long and life is short, and success is very far off. And thus, doubtful of strength to travel so far, we talk a little about the aim – the aim of art, which, like life itself, is inspiring, difficult – obscured by mists. It is not in the clear logic of a triumphant conclusion; it is not in the unveiling of one of those heartless secrets which are called the Laws of Nature. It is not less great, but only more difficult!

To arrest, for the space of a breath, the hands busy about the work of the earth, and compel men entranced by the sight of distant goals to glance for a moment at the surrounding vision of form and colour, of sunshine and shadows; to make them pause for a look, for a sigh, for a smile – such is the aim, difficult and evanescent, and reserved only for a very few to achieve. But sometimes, by the deserving and the fortunate, even that task is accomplished. And when it is accomplished – behold! all the truth of life is there: a moment of vision, a sigh, a smile – and the return to an eternal rest.

Sigmund Freud, The Interpretation of Dreams (1899)

Sigmund Freud (1856–1939) was the founder of psychoanalysis. From Vienna, his home until 1938, when the Nazi invasion of Austria forced him into exile in London, he pioneered therapeutic techniques for uncovering the unconscious repression of childhood emotions. His early work concentrated on nervous diseases, hysteria and infantile sexuality. *The Interpretation of Dreams* was his first great work, and very much the defining book of his long and prodigious career. It was, by his own reckoning, the book that contained his most valuable discoveries. Although dated 1900 by its publisher, the book was in fact printed in November 1899. *The Interpretation of Dreams* provides the most helpful introduction to Freud's theory of the unconscious and its mysterious workings. Together with the closely related *Psychopathology of Everyday Life* (1901), the book assembles evidence of various degrees of neurotic behaviour in all human beings and establishes the basis for Freud's later work on understanding the psyche. Psychoanalysis has provided a model for literary critics interested in exploring the 'unconscious' elements of the text. Modern criticism has long been fascinated by the ways in which certain nineteenth-century novels, including *Jane Eyre*, *Far from the Madding Crowd*, *The Portrait of a Lady*, *Dracula* and *Heart of Darkness*, anticipate and confirm Freud's psychoanalytical investigations.

The relationships of our typical dreams to fairy-tales and other poetic materials are certainly neither isolated nor accidental. The poet is normally the instrument of the transformation process, but on occasion the keen poet's eye has understood it analytically and pursued it backwards, tracing the poem back to the dream. A friend has drawn my attention to the following passage from G. Keller's *Green Henry*: 'It is not my wish, my dear Lee, that you should ever learn from experience the exquisitely piquant truth in Odysseus' situation when he appears naked and covered with mud before Nausicaa and her companions! Do you want to know what is going on in it? Some time, when you are separated from your homeland and all you hold dear, roaming in foreign lands, and when you have seen much and experienced much, when you are acquainted with grief and sorrow, are wretched and deserted, then at night you are sure to dream that you are drawing near your homeland. You will see it shining, radiant in the loveliest colours. Fair and gracious figures come to meet you. Then you suddenly discover that you are walking in rags, naked and covered in dust. A nameless shame and fear take hold of you. You try to cover yourself, to hide, and you wake bathed in sweat. As long as mankind has existed, this has been the dream of the sorrowful, storm-tossed man, and thus it is that Homer has taken that situation from the depths of man's eternal nature.'

The depths of mankind's eternal nature, which the poet invariably counts on arousing in his listeners, are made of those motions of our inner life rooted in that time of our childhood which later becomes prehistoric. From behind the irreproachable wishes of the homeless man which are suitable for consciousness, infantile wishes break out which have become impermissible, and that is why the dream externalized in the legend of Nausicaa invariably turns into an anxiety-dream.

My own dream of running up the stairs, which turned soon afterwards into being rooted to the spot, is also an exhibition-dream, as it shows the essential elements of its kind. So it should be traceable back to childhood experiences, and knowledge of these should enlighten us as to how far the maidservant's behaviour towards me, her objection that I dirtied the carpet, helps her to the position she has in the dream. In fact I can supply the desired explanation. In a psychoanalysis one learns to reinterpret closeness in time as closeness in subject-matter. Two ideas, apparently unconnected, following immediately upon each other, belong to a unity which is to be inferred, just as an 'a' and a 'b' which I write down one after the other have to be spoken as a syllable, 'ab'. Likewise in relating elements to one another in dreams. The dream of the stairs referred to is taken from a series of dreams, and I am familiar with the interpretation of the other items in it. This dream, surrounded by the others, must belong in the same context. Now at the basis of the other dreams around it there was the memory of a nursemaid who looked after me from some date when I was still being breastfed until I was two-and-a-half years old. According to information I recently gathered from my mother, she was old and ugly, but very intelligent and competent. From what I may conclude from my dreams, she did not always treat me with the most loving care, and had harsh words for me if I failed to respond satisfactorily to her upbringing in cleanliness. So, in taking it on herself to continue this work of education, the maidservant earns the right to be treated as an incarnation of the prehistoric old nurse in my dream. We may assume that, despite her ill-treatment, the child was fond of this tutelary figure.

Another group of dreams which may be called typical are those in which a dear relative, a parent, or brother or sister, a child, and so on, has died. We must immediately distinguish two classes of these dreams: those where the dreamer remains untouched by sorrow, so that on waking he wonders at his lack of feeling; and the others, in which the dreamer feels profound grief at the death, indeed, expressing it even by weeping passionately in his sleep.

The dreams of the first group we may put aside. They have no claim to be regarded as typical. On analysis we find that they mean something different from what they contain, that they are intended to conceal some other wish. Take the dream of the aunt who sees her sister's only son before her in his coffin. That does not mean that she wishes her little nephew were dead but, as we learned, it means the wish to see a certain much-loved person again after a long parting, the same person she had once seen again after a similar long interval at the dead body of another nephew. This wish, which is the true content of the dream, offers no occasion for grief, and that is why no grief is felt in the dream either. We note here that the affect contained in the dream does not belong to the manifest but to the latent dream-content, and that the emotional content of the dream has remained free of the distortion that affected its representational content.

The case of dreams where the death of a dear relative is represented is different when emotions of sorrow are also felt. These mean what their content says: the wish that the person concerned might die. And as I may expect that all my readers' feelings and those of everyone who has had a dream of this kind will baulk at my interpretation, I must attempt to prove it on the broadest of foundations.

We have already explained one dream which taught us that the wishes that are represented as fulfilled in our dreams are not always current wishes. They can also be wishes that are past, over and done, overlaid or repressed, but which we are still obliged to credit with a kind of continued existence only because they surface again in our dreams. They are not dead as we conceive the dead, but are like the shades in the *Odyssey* who wake to a kind of life once they have drunk blood. That dream of the dead child in the box is concerned with a wish that was active fifteen years before and frankly admitted to be from that time. It is perhaps not unimportant for the theory of dreams if I add that at the basis even of this dream there lies a memory from earliest childhood. As a little girl – it cannot be said for certain when – the dreamer had heard that during the pregnancy of which she was the product her mother had fallen into a deep depression and with all her heart had wished the child in her womb dead. Now an adult and pregnant herself, she was only following her mother's example.

If anyone has a dream filled with grief that their mother or father, brother or sister has died, I never take this dream for evidence that the dreamer wishes them dead *now*. The theory of dreams does not make so great a demand; it is content to conclude that – some time in childhood – he *has* wished them dead. But I am afraid this qualification will still do little to pacify my critics; they may dispute just as energetically the possibility that they ever had such a thought, just as they feel sure that they do not nurse such wishes at the present time. That is why I have to restore a part of the lost inner life of childhood, according to the evidence that the present still has to show.

Let us first look at the relationship children have to their brothers and sisters. I do not know why we assume that it must be a loving one, for there are insistent examples of hostility between adult siblings in everyone's experience, and we are so often able to establish that these quarrels began in childhood or have always existed. But very many adults too, who are very close to their siblings today and support them, lived in a state of scarcely interrupted enmity with them during childhood. The older child has mistreated the younger, told tales about him, stolen his toys; the younger, in helpless rage at the older, admires him, envies him, and fears him, or turns his first conscious stirrings for freedom and justice against the oppressor. The parents say the children don't get on well, and cannot find the reason for it. It is not difficult to see that even the character of a good child is different from what would be desirable in an adult. Children are absolutely self-centred, they feel their needs intensely and aim quite ruthlessly at their satisfaction, particularly at the expense of their rivals, other children, and above all their brothers and sisters. But that does not make us call the child 'wicked'; we call him 'naughty'; he is not responsible for his bad deeds, neither in our judgement nor before the law. And rightly so. For we may expect that within the lifespan we ascribe to children, stirrings of altruism and a sense of morality will awaken, and that, as Meynert puts it, a secondary ego will overlay the primary and inhibit it. Morality probably will not develop at the same time in every child; also, the length of the amoral childhood period is different in different individuals. If this morality fails to develop, it pleases us to speak of 'degeneration', though obviously it is a matter of hampered development. Where the primary character has already been overlaid by later development, it can still come to the surface again at least partially, if the subject falls ill with hysteria. The similarity of what we call the hysterical character with that of a naughty child is really quite striking. Obsessional neurosis, by contrast, corresponds to an excessive morality, reinforcing the burden on the primary character as this begins to stir again.

Thus many people who love their brothers and sisters today, and would feel bereft at their death, carry ill wishes towards them in their unconscious from long ago, which can be realized in dreams. But it is particularly interesting to observe small children of up to three years old or a little more in their behaviour towards their younger siblings. Until now, the child was the one and only. Now he is told that the stork has brought a new baby. The child inspects the new arrival and declares firmly: 'The stork can take it away again.' It is my entirely serious opinion that the child has the measure of the disadvantage it has to expect from the stranger. I was told by a lady close to me, who gets on very well today with her sister, four years her junior, that when she heard the news of the new arrival, she answered with the reservation: 'But I won't give her my red cap.' Even if the child did not reach this insight until later, the arousal of her hostility would still date from that moment. I know of a case in which a little girl not yet three years old attempted to strangle the baby in its cradle, sensing that no good would come of its further presence. Children of about this age are capable of jealousy, intensely and unmistakably. Or it can happen that the baby really does disappear quite soon, and once again the child is the centre of all the tenderness in the house. But then a new one arrives, sent by the stork. Is it not quite reasonable that our darling should generate within him the wish that his new competitor might meet with the same fate as the earlier one, so that things go as well again for him as they did before and in the interim? Of course, in normal circumstances this behaviour of the child to the later infant is a simple function of the difference in their ages. If the interval in age is greater, motherly instincts towards the helpless newborn baby will already begin to stir in the older girl.

Feelings of hostility towards siblings must be far more frequent in childhood than the imperceptive adult may observe.

In the case of my own children, who followed quickly on one another, I missed the opportunity to make observations of this kind. I am catching up on them now with my little nephew, whose sole reign was disturbed after fifteen months by the appearance of a rival. True, I am told that the young man behaves very chivalrously towards his little sister, kisses her hand, and strokes her. But I am becoming convinced that even before he is two years old he is using his ability to talk to criticize a creature who does, after all, appear superfluous in his eyes. Whenever the talk turns to her, he joins in the conversation and exclaims with displeasure: 'Too little, too little.' In recent months, weaned away from this contemptuous attitude by his excellent development, he has found different grounds for his admonition that she does not deserve so much attention. He reminds us on every occasion that offers:

'She hasn't got any teeth.' We all recall the story of the eldest daughter of another sister: six years old at the time, for half an hour she kept asking all her aunts to reassure her: 'Lucie can't understand that yet, can she?' Lucie was her rival, two-and-a-half years her junior.

I have come upon the dream of a sibling's death appropriate to this intensified hostility in every one of my women patients, for example. I found only one exception, which could easily be interpreted as proving the rule. Once during a consultation I was explaining this state of affairs to a lady whose symptoms seemed worth considering under this aspect. To my astonishment she responded that she never had dreams of this kind. Another dream occurred to her which ostensibly had nothing to do with it. It was a dream she first had when she was four years old, as the youngest child at the time, and had then dreamed many times. *A flock of children, all her brothers, sisters, and cousins, were romping in a meadow. Suddenly they grew wings, flew up in the air, and were gone.* She had no idea what the dream meant. It will not be hard for us to recognize it as a dream of the death of all her brothers and sisters in its original form, very little affected by the censorship. I will venture to replace it with the following analysis. At the death of one of the flock – in this case the children of two brothers were brought up together as brothers and sisters – our little mourner, not yet four years old, will have asked a wise grown-up: 'What happens to children when they are dead?' The answer will have been: 'Then they grow wings and become little angels.' In the dream, in accordance with this explanation, all the brothers and sisters have wings like angels and – and this is the main thing – they fly away. Our little angel-maker is left alone – think of it! – the only one left after such a great flock! The children romping in a meadow and then flying away from it is surely an unmistakable reference to butterflies, as if the child were drawn by the same combination of ideas as moved the ancients to picture the psyche with butterflies' wings.

Now perhaps someone will interject: 'Granted the hostile impulse of children towards their siblings, but how could a tender infant disposition reach such heights of wickedness as to wish its rivals or sturdier playfellows dead, as if every offence were only to be expiated by the death penalty?' Anyone who says this is not taking into account the child's idea of 'being dead', which has only the word and very little else in common with ours. The child knows nothing of the horrors of decomposition, of freezing in the cold grave, of the terror of endless Nothingness which the adult's imagination cannot bear to contemplate, as all the myths of the world to come bear witness. The fear of death is unknown to the child; that is why he will play with the terrible word and threaten another: 'If you do that again, you'll die, like Franz!' – which makes his poor mother shudder, for she may be unable to forget that the greater part of mankind born on this earth will not outlive the years of childhood. Even at the age of eight, back from a visit to the Science Museum, a child can say to his mother: 'Mama, I love you so much; when you die I'll have you stuffed and set you up here in this room so that I can see you for ever and ever!' That is how little the child's idea of being dead resembles ours.

To the child, who is, after all, spared the scenes of suffering before death, being dead is much the same as 'being away', no longer disturbing the survivors. The child does not distinguish how this absence comes about, whether on account of a journey, an estrangement, or death. If in the prehistoric years his nurse is sent away and his mother dies a while later, the two events as they are uncovered in the course of analysis overlay each other in his memory. That the child does not miss them very intensely in their absence is something many a mother has learned to her sorrow on returning home after a summer trip of several weeks, when, in response to her enquiries she has to hear: 'The children haven't asked after their mama, not once.' But if she really has made the journey to 'That undiscovered country from whose bourne / No traveller returns', the children will seem to have forgotten her at first and they will begin to remember her only *in retrospect*.

So if the child has motives for wishing another child away, there is nothing to stop him giving this wish the form of wanting him dead, and the psychical reaction to the wishful dream of death is evidence that, despite all the differences in content, the child's wish is nevertheless somehow the same as the consonant wish in the adult.

But if this wish for his brothers or sisters to die is explained by the child's self-centredness, which makes him see them as rivals, how are we to explain his death-wish towards his parents, who are for the child the givers of love and fulfillers of his needs, and whose preservation he should wish for simply from selfish motives?

We are led to a solution of this difficulty by our experience that dreams of a parent's death most frequently concern the parent who shares the same sex as the dreamer, so that a man mostly dreams of his father's death, a woman of her mother's. I cannot set this up as the rule, but the predominance of the pattern I have indicated is so distinct that it requires to be explained by a factor of general significance. Put crudely, it is as though a sexual preference were established very early, as though the boy saw a rival for love in his father, and the girl in her mother, and removing them could only be of benefit to the child.

Before this idea is rejected as monstrous, let us take a good look at the real relationships between parents and children. We have to distinguish what the cultural demand to honour our parents requires of this relationship from what daily observation tells us is the case. There is more than one occasion for hostility hidden in the relationship between parents and children; the conditions for creating wishes which will not pass the censorship are present in abundance. Let us dwell first on the relation of father and son. It is my opinion that the sanctity we have accorded the Ten Commandments blunts our perception of reality. Perhaps we do not dare to notice that the greater part of mankind put themselves above obeying the Fourth Commandment. At the lowest levels of human society as much as at the highest, parental respect habitually yields to other interests. The dark tidings that reach us in myth and legend from the primeval days of human society give us some idea of the power of the father and the ruthlessness with which he wielded it that is most disagreeable. Cronos devours his children, rather as the boar devours the mother-sow's farrow, and Zeus castrates his father and takes his place as ruler. The more absolute the father's rule in the ancient family, the more the son as rightful successor is forced into the position of enemy, and the greater his impatience to come to power himself through the death of the father. Even in our middle-class families, by refusing his son his independence and the wherewithal to support it, the father is helping to develop the natural seeds of enmity in him. The physician is often enough in a position to notice that in his grief at the loss of his father, the son cannot suppress his satisfaction at gaining his freedom at last. The father habitually keeps a rigid grip on the remnants of the dreadfully antiquated *potestas patris familias* in our society today, and every writer is sure of making an impact if, like Ibsen, he pushes the ancient battle between father and son to the foreground in his plot. The occasions for conflict between daughter and mother arise when the daughter grows up and sees her mother as her wardress while she herself desires her sexual freedom; on the other hand, as her daughter blossoms the mother is reminded that the time has come for her to give up her own claims to sexuality.

All these relationships are plain for everyone to see. But they do not take us any further in our aim to explain the dreams of a parent's death in persons whose honour for their father and mother has long been something sacrosanct. Moreover, our previous discussions have prepared us to expect that the death-wish towards the parents will derive from earliest childhood.

This assumption is confirmed by our analyses in the case of psychoneurotics with a certainty that excludes any doubt. We learn from them that sexual wishes in the child – insofar as they can be called that at such an early stage – develop very early, and that the girl's first affection is for her father, and the boy's first infant desire is for his mother. Thus the father becomes an intrusive rival for the boy, as the mother does for the girl, and we have already explained in the case of siblings how little the child needs for this feeling to lead to a death-wish. As a rule their sexual choice is already determined by the parents' preferences. A natural inclination sees to it that the husband will spoil his little daughter, the wife take her son's part, while both of them – as long as the magic of sex does not upset their judgement – will be strict in their influence on the little ones' upbringing. The child is quite aware of the preference and rebels against the parent who opposes it. To be loved by the grown-ups means for him not only the satisfaction of a particular need, but also that he will get his way in all other respects too. Thus the child follows his or her own sexual impulses and at the same time perpetuates what the parents initiated by choosing between them along the same lines as they did . . .

In my experience, which is already very extensive, parents play the main parts in the inner life of all children who later become psychoneurotics. Being in love with the one parent and hating the other belong to the indispensable stock of psychical impulses being formed at that time which are so important for the later neurosis. But I do not believe that in this respect psychoneurotics are to be sharply distinguished from other children of Adam with a normal development in their capacity to create something absolutely new and theirs alone. It is far more likely – and this is supported by occasional observations of normal children – that with these loving and hostile wishes towards their parents too, psychoneurotics are only revealing to us, by magnifying it, what goes on less clearly and less intensely in the inner life of most children. In support of this insight the ancient world has provided us with a legend whose far-reaching and universal power can only be understood if we grant a similar universality to the assumption from child-psychology we have just been discussing.

I refer to the legend of King Oedipus and the drama of that name by Sophocles. Oedipus, son of Laius, King of Thebes, and Jocasta, is abandoned as an infant because an oracle had proclaimed to his father that his son yet unborn would be his murderer. He is rescued and grows up as a king's son at a foreign court, until he himself consults the oracle about his origins, and receives the counsel that he should flee his home city, because he would perforce become his father's murderer and his mother's spouse. On the road from his supposed home city he encounters King Laius and kills him in a sudden quarrel. Then he arrives before Thebes, where he solves the riddle of the Sphinx as she bars his way, and in gratitude he is chosen by the Thebans to be their king and presented with Jocasta's hand in marriage. He reigns long in peace and dignity, and begets two sons and two daughters with his – unbeknown – mother, until a plague breaks out, occasioning fresh questioning of the oracle by the Thebans. At this point Sophocles' tragedy begins. The messengers bring word that the plague will end when the murderer of Laius is driven from the land. But where is he?

> . . . Where shall we hope to uncover
> The faded traces of that far-distant crime?

The action of the play consists now in the gradually intensified and skilfully delayed revelation – comparable to the work of a psychoanalysis – that

Oedipus himself is Laius' murderer, but also that he is the son of the murdered king and Jocasta. Shattered by the abomination he has in his ignorance committed, Oedipus blinds himself and leaves his homeland. The oracle is fulfilled.

Oedipus the King is what we call a tragedy of fate; its tragic effect is supposed to depend on the contrast between the all-powerful will of the gods and the vain struggles of men threatened by disaster. What the deeply moved spectator is meant to learn from the tragedy is submission to the will of the divinity and insight into his own powerlessness. Consequently, modern dramatists have tried to achieve a similar tragic effect by weaving the same contrast into a plot of their own invention. But the spectators have looked on unmoved as, despite all the efforts of innocent humans, some curse or oracle is fulfilled. The later tragedies of fate have failed in their effect.

If *Oedipus the King* is able to move modern man no less deeply than the Greeks who were Sophocles' contemporaries, the solution can only be that the effect of Greek tragedy does not depend on the contrast between fate and human will, but is to be sought in the distinctive nature of the subject-matter exemplifying this contrast. There must be a voice within us that is ready to acknowledge the compelling force of fate in *Oedipus*, while we are able to reject as arbitrary such disposals as are to be found in *Die Almfran* or other tragedies of fate. And a factor of this kind is indeed contained in the story of King Oedipus. His fate moves us only because it could have been our own as well, because at our birth the oracle pronounced the same curse upon us as it did on him. It was perhaps ordained that we should all of us turn our first sexual impulses towards our mother, our first hatred and violent wishes against our father. Our dreams convince us of it. King Oedipus, who killed his father Laius and married his mother Jocasta, is only the fulfilment of our childhood wish. But, more fortunate than he, we have since succeeded, at least insofar as we have not become psychoneurotics, in detaching our sexual impulses from our mothers and forgetting our jealousy of our fathers. We recoil from the figure who has fulfilled that ancient childhood wish with the entire sum of repression which these wishes have since undergone within us. As the poet brings Oedipus' guilt to light in the course of his investigation, he compels us to recognize our own inner life, where those impulses, though suppressed, are still present. The contrast with which the chorus takes its leave:

> . . . behold: this was Oedipus,
> Greatest of men; he held the key to the deepest mysteries;
> Was envied by all his fellow-men for his great prosperity;
> Behold, what a full tide of misfortune swept over his head . . .

This admonition refers to us too and our pride, who have grown so wise and powerful in our own estimation since our childish years. Like Oedipus we live in ignorance of those wishes, offensive to morality and forced upon us by Nature, and once they have been revealed, there is little doubt we would all rather turn our gaze away from the scenes of our childhood.

There is an unmistakable indication in the text of Sophocles' tragedy itself that the legend of Oedipus sprang from that ancient dream material which contains the painful disturbance of our relations with our parents by the first stirrings of our sexuality. Jocasta consoles Oedipus at a stage where he has not yet learned the truth, but is troubled by the memory of what the oracle proclaimed. She refers to a dream which many indeed do dream, but without – or so she thinks – its having any significance:

> Nor need this mother-marrying frighten you;
> Many a man has dreamt as much. Such things
> Must be forgotten, if life is to be endured.

The dream of having sexual intercourse with the mother is dreamed by many today as it was then, and they recount it with indignation and amazement. It is clearly the key to the tragedy and the complement to the dream of the father's death. The Oedipus story is the imagination's reaction to these two typical dreams, and just as the dreams of the adult are filled with feelings of revulsion, the legend too is bound to include the horror and self-punishment in its content. Its further revision derives from a misleading secondary revision of the subject-matter, which seeks to make use of it for theological ends. (The attempt to reconcile divine omnipotence with human responsibility, of course, is bound to be defeated by this material, as by any other.)[1]

I cannot leave the typical dreams of the death of dear relatives without adding some words to elucidate their general significance for the theory of dreams. These dreams present the very unusual instance of a dream-thought formed by a repressed wish escaping any censorship and entering the dream unaltered. There must be quite special conditions to make this fate possible. I think these dreams are encouraged by the following two factors. First, we cannot think of a wish more remote from us than this one; we believe that to wish *that* 'would not occur to us in our wildest dreams', and that is why the dream-censorship has no weapons against this monstrous thing, rather as Solon's laws were unable to decree any punishment for parricide. Secondly, however, it is just here that a remnant of the day very frequently comes halfway to meet the suppressed and unsuspected wish in the shape of a *care and concern* for the life of the dear person. The only way this concern can enter the dream and leave its mark is by making use of the congruent wish; but the wish is able to mark itself with the care and concern which has come to life during the day. If we take the view that all this happens more simply, that we are only continuing at night and in our dreams what we are concerned about by day, then we are just cutting off these dreams of the death of someone dear from their explanation, and holding on unnecessarily to an easily soluble puzzle.

PART II

MODERN CRITICISM

1

JANE AUSTEN, *NORTHANGER ABBEY*

In the opening essay on *Northanger Abbey*, Marilyn Butler begins by looking at Jane Austen's early writings, especially the novel *Susan* (later retitled *Catharine*). She claims that *Northanger Abbey* draws on techniques and thematic interests evident in the juvenilia, especially the idea of the naive, inexperienced heroine who stands on the threshold of life, precariously discriminating between true and false impressions. This essay, extracted from *Jane Austen and the War of Ideas*, argues that although the early fiction is slow to portray the inner life of its characters with sufficient confidence, it nevertheless handles dialogue impressively. It goes on to claim that Austen inherits a set of conservative, anti-Jacobin sentiments from earlier writers, and that her great achievement is in the subtle technical ability with which she recasts the material of the conservative novel to give it a convincing and consistent fictional world.

The second essay by Marilyn Butler is her introduction to the Penguin edition of *Northanger Abbey*. Here, she makes strong claims for *Northanger Abbey* as an ambitious, experimental novel, progressively concerned with its own fictive status and intellectually curious about the nature of artistic representation. Reading books is, in itself, a pervasive theme in the novel: a pleasurable pastime, a form of social bonding, but also a preparation for ways of reading and decoding the world. The essay adopts a trenchant historicist perspective, closely relating a distinctive preoccupation with reading to the growing commodity culture of the late eighteenth and early nineteenth centuries. Character and motive in *Northanger Abbey* are seen to be affected by the acquisition of goods and by the social markers of income and taste: 'Everyone in Austen's Bath becomes involved in the display or reading of signs'.

Isobel Armstrong's essay, extracted from her critical study of *Mansfield Park*, takes a strongly dissenting view of the popular idea that Jane Austen's novels are essentially conservative. In this respect, her critical approach differs considerably from that of Marilyn Butler, though both critics are profoundly concerned with the historical and political significance of Austen's work. She proposes that the 'conservative' Jane Austen is the product of a critical tradition that has persistently interpreted the novels in terms of their 'narrow' social and emotional range, and she argues that there are elements in the text that have too often been ignored or overlooked. The extreme subtlety of language in the novels masks the uneasiness and wariness with which they apprehend political and moral dilemmas. Far from being conservative, the novels open up space for a radical critique of the social and political formation from which they emerge.

Claudia L. Johnson's essay, from *Women, Politics and the Novel*, approaches the sexual politics of *Northanger Abbey* through its affiliation with Gothic fiction. It argues that *Northanger Abbey* (often seen as a parody of Gothic fiction) does not refute, but rather clarifies and reclaims, Gothic conventions in a way that keeps alive the political ramifications of the genre. In particular, Johnson points to a pervasive distrust of patriarchy in Gothic writing, usually figured in the character of the tyrannical father. In *Northanger Abbey*, General Tilney is not only a repressive father, but a 'self-professed defender of national security'. Part of Catherine's education is in learning to distrust paternal figures and to recognize her own 'power of refusal'.

Marilyn Butler, The Juvenilia and *Northanger Abbey* (1975)

If Jane Austen was no more than sixteen when she wrote this, it is something of a *tour de force*; and what makes it more remarkable is that the resourceful use of language supports other appropriate narrative techniques. Catherine's situation is well prepared in the opening pages of exposition. We are shown that she is especially vulnerable because she is solitary: her childhood friends, the Wynnes, have gone away, and she is left in the company of her aunt, Mrs. Percival, who is fussy and prosaic. Catherine likes to indulge her sentimental regret for the Wynnes alone in her 'Bower', a romantic spot which, as the sub-title indicates, was to have been given special symbolic significance. Mrs. Percival, a prototype perhaps for Mrs. Jennings or Miss Bates, objects to her habit of going there, but for valetudinarian reasons which at the moment Catherine finds it easy to dismiss. The real threat offered by the Bower was clearly to have been to her moral health, for it encourages her in a dangerously solipsistic reverie; and it is there, appropriately, that Edward Stanley appeals to her emotions by seizing her hand. It is clear even from these short beginnings that the story was to have encompassed both the natural evolution of Catherine's error, and its moral implications, so that in conception and, primitively, in technique, it belongs to the series that culminates with *Emma*.

The first of Jane Austen's novels to be completed for publication, *Northanger Abbey*[1] makes use of all the same important features. A naïve, inexperienced heroine stands at the threshold of life and needs to discriminate between true friends and false. The evidence she is given are words and the system of value they express; so that the reader, cleverer or at least more cleverly directed than Catherine, is able to make the correct discriminations for herself as the action unfolds. In one important respect the second Catherine is a coarser conception than the first, for she has been crossed with the burlesque heroine of the 'female quixote' variety, so that many of her intellectual errors are grosser and far more improbable. Yet although *Northanger Abbey* is often remembered for its sequence at the abbey, when Catherine is led by her reading of (presumably) Mrs. Radcliffe's *Romance of the Forest*[2] into fantastic imaginings, the central impulse of *Northanger Abbey*, and its serious achievement, has nothing to do with burlesque. Like *Catharine*, it uses the literary conversation not for the sake of the subject, but in order to give an appropriate morally objective ground against which character can be judged.

Catherine Morland has five important conversations about the Gothic novel: with Isabella Thorpe (vol. 1, ch. 6); with John Thorpe (1, 7); with Eleanor and Henry Tilney (1, 15); with Henry Tilney, in his phaeton on the way to Northanger Abbey (2, 5); and with Henry Tilney again, when he uncovers her suspicions of his father, the General (2, 9). In all of these conversations, as in *Catharine*, the reader is not asked to criticize certain novels, nor the habit of novel-reading,[3] but rather to consider the habits of mind which the different speakers reveal. For example, when Isabella and Catherine first discuss horrid novels together, in chapter six of the first volume, Isabella's knowledge proves superficial: she is dependent on her friend Miss Andrews for all her information, and Miss Andrews knows what is current, but not *Sir Charles Grandison*. From this conversation it emerges that Isabella's mind is not held by novels, for it continually runs after young men, whereas Catherine's comments are characterized by extreme, if naïve, interest. 'I do not pretend to say that I was not very much pleased with him [Henry Tilney]; but while I have *Udolpho* to read, I feel as if nobody could make me miserable' (2, 14). Again, when Catherine raises the subject 'which had long been uppermost in her thoughts' with John Thorpe, it is to discover that despite his assurance he does not know *Udolpho* is by Mrs. Radcliffe, and that he has got less than halfway in the first volume of the five-volume *Camilla*. On the other hand, the characteristic of the Tilneys which emerges when Catherine raises the subject with them is informed interest. 'I have read all Mrs. Radcliffe's works,' says Henry, 'and most of them with great pleasure' (1, 14). The mild qualification is important, for the proper attitude of the person who reads is a discriminating exactness – the quality Henry shows when he challenges Catherine's word 'nice', and Eleanor when she emends it to 'interesting' (1, 14).

After discussing novels the Tilneys move on to the subject of history, just as the earlier Catharine of the juvenilia did. Both topics, together with the Tilneys' choice of landscape, enable Jane Austen to illustrate character at a light and amusing level without imputing triviality. Choice of these as subjects for conversation already implies a certain degree of thoughtfulness and rationality – unlike John Thorpe's topics of horses, curricles, drink, and money, and Isabella's of 'dress, balls, flirtations and quizzes' (1, 4). Thus far at least the conversations about Gothic novels in *Northanger Abbey* belong to the overall strategy of the novel, which is concerned first to reveal the character of the heroine, second to contrast the minds of her two sets of friends, the Thorpes and the Tilneys.

The clarity of Jane Austen's conception appears to waver in the second volume. Henry's teasing conversation with Catherine during their drive to the abbey is, as earlier dialogues were not, a series of observations directed *at* the Gothic mode. What Henry invents is a burlesque Gothic story, compounded of various clichés – ancient housekeeper, isolated chamber, secret passage, instruments of torture, hidden manuscripts, and extinguished candle – though it should also be noticed, since it is typical of the discriminating reader in the period, that he puts as much stress upon verbal blunders as upon extravagances of plot. He imagines Catherine surmounting an '*unconquerable*' horror of the bed, and discovering a secret door through 'a division in the tapestry so artfully constructed as to defy the minutest inspection' (2, 5). Henry's lively and critical approach to his Gothic material is thus contrasted with Catherine's selection of precisely the wrong aspect to comment on. 'Oh! Mr. Tilney, how frightful! – This is just like a book! – But it cannot really happen to me. I am sure your housekeeper is not really Dorothy' (2, 5).

The memory of Henry's intelligent detachment in this conversation lingers as an unspoken commentary on Catherine's series of interior monologues at Northanger – while she searches her room, or lies terror-stricken in bed, or concocts wild fantasies concerning the General and the death of Mrs. Tilney. Typically, it is in the 'objective' form of dialogue, where we are equally detached from both parties, and not in subjective thought-processes, that we hear, reliably, the note of rationality. And it is through another speech from Henry that Catherine is brought at last to an understanding of the 'real' world of long-lasting social and religious institutions:

> 'What have you been judging from? Remember the country and the age in which we live. Remember that we are English, that we are Christians. Consult your own understanding, your own sense of the probable, your own observation of what is passing around you – Does our education prepare us for such atrocities? Do our laws connive at them? Could they be perpetrated without being known, in a country like this, where social and literary intercourse is on such a footing; where every man is

surrounded by a neighborhood of voluntary spies, and where roads and newspapers lay everything open? Dearest Miss Morland, what ideas have you been admitting?' (2, 9).

There is clearly a difference in Jane Austen's use of dialogue in the first volume and in the second. In the first, it is the reader alone who is enlightened, by comparable dialogues between Catherine and the Thorpes, and Catherine and the Tilneys. During the same period the heroine neither learns to discriminate between her two groups of friends, nor to be discriminating about them. Although Henry Tilney has been setting her a good example for virtually a full volume, Catherine returns from her walk with him and Eleanor nearly as unenlightened as when she set out:

> It was no effort to Catherine to believe that Henry Tilney could never be wrong. His manner might sometimes surprize, but his meaning must always be just: – and what she did not understand, she was almost as ready to admire, as what she did (1, 14).

In the second volume the impact on Catherine of Henry's remarks and, negatively, of Isabella's letters, is far greater. Aided no doubt by prosaic external evidence at the Abbey, she is brought sharply to a sense of reality:

> The visions of romance were over. Catherine was completely awakened. Henry's address, short as it had been, had more thoroughly opened her eyes to the extravagance of her late fancies than all their several disappointments had done. Most grievously was she humbled. Most bitterly did she cry (2, 10).

When she becomes more tranquil, Catherine continues soberly to recognize that 'it had been all a voluntary, self-created delusion, each trifling circumstance receiving importance from an imagination resolved on alarm, and everything forced to bend to one purpose by a mind which, before she entered the Abbey, had been craving to be frightened' (2, 10). This, then, is the typical moment of *éclaircissement* towards which all the Austen actions tend, the moment when a key character abandons her error and humbly submits to objective reality.

During the period of *Northanger Abbey's* evolution, before its near-appearance as *Susan* in 1803, Maria Edgeworth was experimenting with similar devices. *Belinda* has precisely the same stylized arrangement of characters, according to their contrasting philosophies of life, and perhaps an even more fully developed sense of the relationship between verbal style and quality of mind. What is very different in *Northanger Abbey*, however, different even from Maria Edgeworth's rather undistinguished execution in *Angelina*, is Jane Austen's reluctance to commit herself to her heroine's consciousness. It is not merely Catherine's emotional distress after she discovers her errors that receives hurried treatment; her actual mental processes are also summarily dealt with. From the consistent *naïveté* of her earlier thinking to her final state of enlightenment is a long step, but Jane Austen is not really concerned to examine it. Ultimately this is because, unlike Maria Edgeworth, she does not value the personal process of learning to reason as an end in itself. What is required of Catherine is rather a suspension of a particular kind of mental activity, her habit of romantic invention; at the moment Jane Austen is not concerned to define positively what kind of regular mental process it is that will keep Catherine sensible. For the naturalistic treatment of an individual's inner history which was promised in the first *Catharine*, here we have to make do with facetious stylization, and allusion to a ready-made inner world acquired from reading other people's books. We are shown that Catherine has learnt a significant general rule, that human nature is worse than she first thought: for, apart from her aberration over the General, she has successively overrated the Thorpes, Frederick Tilney, and perhaps even Henry, with all the sentimentalist's optimism about human nature. The reader is asked to take it on trust that henceforth she will apply more caution, more scepticism, more concern for the objective evidence. Of the actual change in her habits of mind that would make such a revolution possible he sees little or nothing.

Jane Austen was slower to handle the inner life confidently than to deploy dialogue: her next novel with a similar format, *Pride and Prejudice*, also fails to give Elizabeth's train of thought with the same clarity and brilliance with which it presents the dialogue. Yet *Northanger Abbey* is consistent and ingenious in dramatizing the author's point of view, like all Jane Austen's novels to employ a fallible heroine. It establishes the antiphonal role of dialogue and free indirect speech which is to be so important in Jane Austen's career. It deploys characters around the heroine with the kind of antithetical precision that is typical of Mrs. West, but much more amusingly and naturally. Even if Catherine's mind is a somewhat implausible blank, the arrangement of the two pairs of brothers and sisters, the Tilneys and the Thorpes, virtually forces the reader into a series of ethical comparisons between them on the author's terms. However strong his training and his inclination to involve himself uncritically in the heroine's emotions, he is manipulated into undertaking an unfamiliar kind of intellectual activity. Stylistically the novel induces him to value sincerity and accuracy, rather than those emotions which are harder to account for or specify. Formally it requires him to use his judgment and not his feeling.

At the same time *Northanger Abbey* is very much a novel, which is to say that it succeeds in creating and maintaining an autonomous fictional world. The story is not a parody of a novel story, but actually, like *Pride and Prejudice*, employs the common novelist's fantasy of the poor girl who meets, and after a series of vicissitudes marries, the rich young man. Catherine may not be a 'heroine' in the idealized mode of sentimental fiction, but she is a very good heroine at the level which matters. She invites and keeps our sympathy, and she makes us feel that what happens to her matters to us. No wonder, indeed, that in the famous passage in chapter five Jane Austen ironically refuses to condemn the novel: for *Northanger Abbey* is quite as much a novel as *Udolpho* is.

It is perhaps because Catherine is so pleasing, even when she blunders, that some recent critics have felt that Jane Austen ends *Northanger Abbey* by reversing its whole moral tendency; that she turns her irony on the good sense advocated by Henry Tilney, and at least in part vindicates Catherine's intuition. The central piece of evidence cited is that the General, Montoni-like, turns Catherine out of Northanger Abbey, and thus proves to be a villain after all. But an act of rudeness is not villainy. It is not even, to use Andrew Wright's term, 'violence'.[4] It arises from the ill-tempered pique of a snobbish man who has just discovered that Catherine is a person of no social recount. There is plenty of evidence throughout the novel that Henry and Eleanor are aware of their father's bad temper, as well as of his snobbery and formality: Eleanor's instant obedience on all occasions, for example, suggests that she has learnt to fear the General's anger. His treatment of Catherine comes nearer to confirming their view of him than hers, although it is perhaps not fully in keeping with either.[5]

Again, after Catherine returns home her romantic feelings are opposed to Mrs. Morland's worthy moralizing, and here at least Jane Austen appears to be on Catherine's side: 'There was a great deal of good sense in all this; but there are some situations of the human mind in which good sense has very little power; and Catherine's feelings contradicted almost every position her mother advanced' (2, 15).

But it is only by taking this observation out of context that we can read into it a serious meaning which relates to the whole book. The nice little vignette of Catherine's relations with her mother after her return home is surely yet another literary borrowing, this time from Fanny Burney's *Camilla*. Camilla's parents think that Camilla has been spoilt by high life, when really she is pining for the loss of her lover, Edgar Mandlebert; and Mrs. Morland is mistaken in just the same way. Had she really tried to cure a case of true love by fetching down a volume of *The Mirror* (containing 'a very clever Essay . . . about young girls that have been spoilt for home by great acquaintance' (2, 14), the incident might indeed suggest that Jane Austen was after all merely balancing the merits of feeling and sense. In fact Mrs. Morland's error is no more than a joke designed to reintroduce the hero in the lightest and least emotional manner possible.

Northanger Abbey is a novel, and it works as a novel, while at the same time it subjects the conventional matter of the merely subjective novel to consistently critical handling. Ideologically it is a very clear statement of the anti-Jacobin position; though, compared with other anti-Jacobin novels, it is distinctive for the virtuosity with which it handles familiar clichés of the type. Very pleasing, for example, is the cleverly oblique presentation of the subject under attack.

Most anti-Jacobin novels include characters who profess the new ideology, and are never tired of canvassing it in conversation. In *Northanger Abbey* there is no overtly partisan talk at all. ('By an easy transition [Henry] . . . shortly found himself arrived at politics; and from politics, it was an easy step to silence' (2, 14) But in *Northanger Abbey* Jane Austen develops, perhaps from the prototypes the Stanleys in *Catharine*, her version of the revolutionary character, the man or woman who by acting on a system of selfishness, threatens friends of more orthodox principles; and ultimately, through cold-blooded cynicism in relation to the key social institution of marriage, threatens human happiness at a very fundamental level. Isabella Thorpe, worldly, opportunist, bent on self-gratification, is one of a series of dangerous women created by Jane Austen. Lucy Steele, Lady Susan, Mary Crawford, all like Isabella pursue the modern creed of self, and as such are Jane Austen's reinterpretation of a standard figure of the period, the desirable, amoral woman whose activities threaten manners and morals. Moreover, already in *Northanger Abbey* the opportunists find allies where they should properly be most vigorously opposed – among those who uphold only the forms, and not the essence, of orthodoxy. The pompous but mercenary General is as much implicated as John Thorpe in the pursuit of Catherine's mythical fortune. In the same vein, Henry and Mary Crawford meet no resistance, but encouragement, when they threaten to introduce anarchy into Mr. Rushworth's ancestral estate (*Mansfield Park*). And William Walter Elliott finds an easy dupe, even an ally, in the empty figure-head he despises, Sir Walter (*Persuasion*).

That Jane Austen is perfectly clear what she is doing can be demonstrated by identifying the same cluster of themes and characters in *Sense and Sensibility*. Inheriting a set of conservative dogmas, and some impossibly theatrical characters – notably the revolutionary villain – already in her first two full-length novels she produces a more natural equivalent, on a scale appropriate to comedy. Her villains are not only better art than her rivals; they are also better propaganda. The tendency among the routine anti-Jacobins was to create Satanic demon–villains who were dangerously close in the temper of the times to being heroes. Jane Austen's intelligence, like Burke's, is more subtle. Her selfish characters are consistently smaller and meaner than their orthodox opponents, the heroines; they are restricted within the bounds of their own being, and their hearts and minds are impoverished. Jane Austen's achievement, the feat of the subtlest technician among the English novelists, is to rethink the material of the conservative novel in terms that are at once naturalistic and intellectually consistent.

Marilyn Butler, Introduction to *Northanger Abbey* (1995)

Writing, 1798–1817

Northanger Abbey was the first of Austen's novels to be completed for publication, though she had previously made a start on *Sense and Sensibility* and *Pride and Prejudice*. According to Cassandra Austen's Memorandum, *Susan* (as it was first called) 'was written about the years [17]98 & 99'. Austen at that time was twenty-three or twenty-four, and still lived in her childhood home, the Rectory in the small village of Steventon, Hampshire.[1]

The greater part of the novel is set in the resort city of Bath, which Jane Austen visited in November 1797, when she stayed with a wealthy aunt and uncle, the Leigh-Perrots, and May 1799, when she stayed at Queen Square with her wealthiest brother, Edward (Austen) Knight. She moved there to live with her parents in 1801, at 4 Sidney Terrace, following her father's retirement as rector of Stevenson in favour of his eldest son James. Her experience of the tourist's and visitor's Bath visibly enriches the first twenty of the novel's thirty chapters, which are set in the public rooms, the nearby streets and the walks and drives within easy reach.

Jane Austen's Advertisement, written in 1816 to precede what became *Northanger Abbey*, says it was 'finished in 1803, and intended for immediate publication', wording which indicates that some work at least was done on the manuscript at the last moment. In the spring of 1803 the London firm of Richard Crosby and Co. paid ten pounds for the novel to an employee of Austen's brother Henry; they advertised it for publication, but failed to publish it, without explaining why. Six years later Jane Austen, writing under the pseudonym of Mrs Ashton Dennis, wrote Crosby a tough letter asking for an explanation, and offering another copy of the novel if the first was lost; she threatened that if he did not cooperate she would approach another publisher. Crosby replied that in such a case he would take legal proceedings against the rival publisher. The best he would offer was to return the manuscript 'for the same as we paid for it'.[2]

By now Austen had been through two years of financial uncertainty and wandering, following the death of her father in 1805. In 1809 she was settling into her last home, with her mother and sister; a small, pleasant village house belonging to her brother Edward Knight in the Hampshire village of Chawton, close to the small town of Alton, and at a fork of main roads linking

London to Winchester and Portsmouth. In spite of her first disappointing experience of publishers, Austen was at last in a position to contemplate novel-writing in earnest: hence, presumably, the attempt to publish or recover *Susan*. But in fact she did not pay to retrieve the manuscript at this time; instead she wrote *Sense and Sensibility* (1811) and then *Pride and Prejudice* (1813). It was not until she had published *Emma* in December 1815 that, again employing Henry, she bought back *Susan*, and then, in 1816, took steps that showed she meant to publish it. All that we know of these for certain is that she implemented a change in her heroine's name, and consequently a change of title, to *Catharine*, and that she wrote her brief Advertisement.

From the autumn of 1816 Austen became seriously ill with the kidney disease that led to her death on 18 July 1817. On 13 March 1817 she wrote to her niece Fanny Knight, 'Miss Catherine is put on the Shelve for the present, and I do not know that she will ever come out.' Retitled *Northanger Abbey*, and preceded by a significant, influential Notice by her brother Henry, the novel was brought out posthumously in late December 1817 (given as 1818 on the title-page), as the first two of a four-volume set with *Persuasion*. Neither novel had undergone the author's final revision; nor, obviously, had she seen proofs.

Austen had all along kept her own copy of *Susan*, as she shows in her letter of 1809, when she offers Crosby a second copy. She could have worked on it at any time after 1803, but would hardly have wanted to while Crosby owned the copyright. Buying back the manuscript was a legal necessity but also a needless expense, in her years of real poverty after her father's death, and indeed until the success of her other novels made her confident of finding a publisher for her first venture. But if these are fairly cogent reasons why she probably did not revise it before the beginning of 1816, did she ever find the time and inclination after that?

Almost alone among Austen's established critics, Brian Southam has made the case that she did make substantial changes, probably in 1816, after she finished *Persuasion* in July. He points to the well-developed satirical portrait of General Tilney as a consumer, which he thinks shares concerns general to the postwar period from 1816. Among Jane Austen's other works, the closest thematically is in Southam's view the fragment *Sanditon*, on which she worked January–March 1817.[3] Yet we know that Austen was already seriously ill that autumn. Moreover, a case can also be made for the fashionableness of consumerism as a theme, in fiction as well as general social commentary, both before 1800, and in 1809. It was surely the very fact that parts of the novel continued to touch a fashionable nerve that led to Austen's renewed interest at different points of her career – only to discover, equally inevitably, that other parts had dated. While not stating that the novel she now offers is identical with the one submitted as *Susan* in 1803, Austen's Advertisement of

1816 confesses that she has not updated it in a way that apparently she, as well as many of her readers, might have thought desirable; so that its representation of society would have seemed fully current. (She had after all just sketched, in *Persuasion*, a very different portrait of fashionable Bath, one where the wealthy and titled entertain one another in private.) If she was unable to make those practical, and commercial, changes, is there any reason to suppose she made improvements of a more subtle literary kind?

Most of Austen's critics and editors in fact take a view opposed to Southam's, that relatively little new work was done on *Northanger Abbey* after 1803. Most of them believe that it contains very few references to public events, though that is certainly a view that needs revising. Another proposition seems to hold much better; references that can be dated belong to the period pre-1803. James King, the real-life master of ceremonies of the Lower Rooms, who in vol. I, chapter 3, introduces Henry Tilney to Catherine, moved to the Upper Rooms in 1805. The riots in St George's Fields of which Eleanor Tilney thinks when, on the walk to Beechen Cliff, Catherine speaks of horrid news from London, appears to be a reference to the worst disturbances in the metropolis in living memory, the Gordon riots of 1780. Sir Benjamin Thompson, Count von Rumford (1753–1814), made his name in 1796 as inventor of the state-of-the-art 'stove', actually an efficient fireplace, which General Tilney has recently installed in his drawing-room. Rumford's long article on how to make an economical, heat-projecting but smokeless fireplace appears in vol. I of his *Essays Political, Economic and Philosophical* (London, Cadell, 1796), but the more extensive modifications to the cooking facilities in General Tilney's kitchen depend on an essay, 'The Management of Fire and the Economy of Fuel' (3rd edition, 1797, vol. 2, pp. 1–196).

The promotion of the Rumford stove is as public and more datable (because unique) than any riot. It is also more typical of *Northanger Abbey*, where external events tend to be media events: Austen consciously refers to knowledge she assumes she shares with readers because it has been well covered in recent newspapers and reviews. *Northanger Abbey* also has far more literary allusions of a more bookish kind than any other Austen novel, and the dates of the works cited are powerful evidence for the case that *Northanger Abbey* is essentially a work of the late 1790s. Apart from two references to works by Edgeworth of 1800 and 1801, each certain allusion to another text dates before 1800. The Gothic novels listed by Isabella at Bath (1, 3) as being currently the rage belong to the years 1794–9. The novels most closely used in the text (i.e. those Austen had presumably read) include a number of works of the 1780s, some even earlier. The three Gothic novels which are virtually quoted, all by Ann Radcliffe, were published between 1790 and 1794. Other leading cultural themes – the picturesque, gardening, estate management, the modernization of ancient buildings – are equally characteristic of the

1790s, and will perhaps appear specific to that decade, when some of the detail is more closely examined.

Northanger Abbey and books: 1. The world of romance

If critics have toyed with complicated theories of revisions, insertions, the possible merger of two parodies (of Bath novels and of Gothic novels), it is because they suspect the book does not hang together as it stands. While leading nineteenth-century admirers of Austen mostly warmed to *Northanger Abbey*, their successors often complain it moves jerkily between the social comedy of the Bath scenes and the Gothic burlesque of the shorter sequence at Northanger Abbey. Or they protest that burlesque has no place in a novel elsewhere trying to be naturalistic. By being in patches self-consciously literary, or so the consensus runs, *Northanger Abbey* belongs with the juvenilia Austen wrote in her precocious adolescence in the early 1790s, rather than with the sustained naturalistic masterpieces generated in her maturity, *Mansfield Park, Emma* and *Persuasion*.

Like Fanny Price of *Mansfield Park*, Catherine Morland of *Northanger Abbey* is first described as a child. The changing coherence of Fanny's thoughts, as she enters the adult world for the first time, is one of the remarkable technical feats of Austen's later, maturer writing. It takes Catherine almost the length of the novel to grow up, a fact signalled by her discontinuous, rather unreflective inner life. Again, comparison with Emma and with Anne Elliot of *Persuasion* (heroines decidedly grown up when we first meet them) can make *Northanger Abbey* itself seem immature, like its heroine. But criticism of Austen's six novels has dwelt too narrowly on the heroines, as if each one functions comparably as the vessel of the reader's consciousness and a reliable guide to the novel's world. Such a notion bears hardest on *Northanger Abbey*, in many respects the most individual of the six.

Any critical tendency which denigrates the Mozartian elegance and *élan* of *Pride and Prejudice* ought to seem suspect. *Northanger Abbey*, playful, youthful and warm, is nearer than the others to *Pride and Prejudice* in its reliance on dialogue, but it is odder, more experimental, far more challenging in respect of their medium, the novel. It is, in fact, time to acknowledge *Northanger Abbey* for what it is: an ambitious, innovative piece of work, quizzically intellectual about fiction itself.

Austen's training as a writer was first a training as a reader, as one of seven children brought up in the country by parents who enjoyed acting and reading aloud. Novel-reading was not for the Austens a private activity, but social and communal; the occasion for reader participation, commentary, contested interpretation. *Northanger Abbey*, so carefully grounded as a story in its heroine's parsonage childhood, is also quintessentially concerned with novel-reading, and other reading too, of serious non-fiction, guidebooks, even newspapers (Bath had three, all weeklies). Just as Austen's characters have different reading prehistories, so do her readers. But she anticipates that we come with a considerable fund of common knowledge, as we embark on this most social and referential of her novels.

What is the experiment being conducted here? Austen plays a game, with her reader as a partner: you must be a novel-reader to play, or you will not pick up the clues; you must be a general reader to score well. For all its good humour, *Northanger Abbey* can be disconcerting, since from its first paragraph it moves to characterize the naïve romantic private reader as a beginner; it flatters and shames her into becoming more ambitious. In this educative process Catherine the heroine shows the way. Foregrounding her unusual contract with us, Austen launches on the novel by way of a quick checklist of the fictional conventions she supposes us used to: heroines' exceptional beauty; the difficulties they are likely to meet; the failures of the standard guardian figures, parents, chaperones, and marriageable men. While reading *Northanger Abbey* we must bear in mind the many books and stories we have read before.

The result eventually is an anatomy of the heroine-centred, woman-targeted novel of the day, in some of its variant forms. *Northanger Abbey* is uniquely self-conscious among Austen's novels about what it is, a popular mode of representing the world. Its selfconsciousness makes it a true performance of the sophisticated 1790s, the decade when the words 'ideology' and 'ideologue' were coined, and words such as 'discourse' and 'culture' took on their modern meanings. It also anticipates our own *fin de siècle* fascination with endlessly remaking what has been made before.

The so-called romantic revolution was preoccupied with genre: it took its name from its revival of an old genre, used to challenge or oust more recent ones. Romance, ballad, and sonnet, all of them archaic forms, reappeared in the last quarter of the eighteenth century, at the expense of the forms neoclassical taste had privileged, epic, tragedy, satire and history. Within the novel, an impulse towards a dizzy proliferation of plots, or the fragmentation of plot, was more apparent throughout the century than any move to conform to classical unities. Pleasure in many plots, or in the playful frustration of the plot, competed with an opposite tendency, to tell a simple powerful story out of a common stock of folkloric or mythic stories. Towards the close of the century, a sub-genre which purported to revive old stories and beliefs established itself as the Gothic novel; a sophisticated format, based on the conversation, or the Socratic philosophical dialogue, enjoyed intellectual prestige but for obvious reasons never became equally popular.[4] Both traditions are used in *Northanger Abbey*, that compulsive reflector of novels as they are.

The thinking fiction reader of 1800 was likely to know the classic eighteenth-century defence of the novel, Johnson's celebrated discussion in *The Rambler* (no. 4). Austen must have warmed to its eloquent praise of the manner of Richardson and his followers (but not Fielding) for their accurate observation of character, naturalistic mixing of virtues and weaknesses, and moral, educative intention. 'The purpose of these writings is not only to show mankind, but to . . . teach the means of avoiding the snares which are laid by Treachery for Innocence.' But in one typically robust paragraph Johnson has fun at the expense of ignorant novel-readers; it is equally Austenian slyly to pick out a paragraph potentially so embarrassing to herself and the like-minded circle she addresses. This has surely been a starting-point for Austen's plot and for the character of a heroine who is herself an avid reader. 'These books are written', says Johnson,

> chiefly to the young, the ignorant, and the idle, to whom they serve as lectures of conduct, and introductions into life. They are the entertainment of minds unfurnished with ideas, and therefore easily susceptible of impressions; not fixed by principles, and therefore easily following the current of fancy; not informed by experience, and consequently open to every false suggestion and partial account.[5]

Sure enough, Catherine somewhere exhibits each of these defects. To a sophisticated reader of novels and about novels, she plays the archetypal simple reader, a hostile caricature of oneself. In much the same way, she acts like the giddy girls rebuked in another *Rambler* essay, no. 97, which was apparently contributed by Richardson (and which Austen herself cites as Richardson's, in a rare footnote she supplies in 1, 3). Catherine does just what she should not, by falling in love with her man without waiting for him to make the first move, and neglecting domestic business 'for routs, drums, balls, assemblies, and such like markets for women'.[6] But if Catherine can at moments even seem so foolish that we distance ourselves from her, this state of affairs rarely lasts long. Even Johnson would probably have felt that her honest, unwavering attraction to Henry, and her equally honest pleasure in (most) balls and assemblies, make this warm, spontaneous character one of the admirable people actually recommended in *Rambler* no. 4 as the best and most moral of all examples to set before impressionable readers.

Fifteen years after Johnson's death, his severity about the potential danger of romance was being sturdily challenged, by proponents of what was by 1799 the high tide of an overwhelming romance revival. After Thomas Warton's *History of English Literature to 1603* (1774–81) and Clara Reeve's philosophical dialogue *The Progress of Romance* (1785), the reputation of the novel became enhanced by its claim of descent from medieval and classical romance, and thus a history going back to the Greeks. Reeve's argument peters out disappointingly, but as set up it makes the rousing feminist case that women have their own ancient literary genres, implying women's presence from the outset, as creators and audience, in cultural traditions based on primitive pre-literate forms.

Joanna Baillie, in her sixty-page Introductory Discourse to her *Plays on the Passions* (1798), and William Godwin, in a long-unpublished essay, 'Of History and Romance' (*c.* 1797), follow Reeve in capitalizing on the association of both romance and novel with women writers and readers, rather than apologizing for it. They argue that epic and formal history are, by contrast, the superseded genres of archaic, militaristic cultures. The modern reader is typically a domesticated person – and thus, it is hinted, a woman. She will prefer historical novels, centred on people, to the history of external events (Godwin), and domestic drama, based on the passions generated by personal relationships, to high tragedy or epic (Baillie).[7] To use the generic word preferred by Reeve, Godwin and Baillie, the modern age is seeing the return of romance, but in a sophisticated rather than a regressive form, for which writers of both sexes may take credit.

Not that Catherine, resistant to most books, knows anything of that current debate. Walking with the Tilneys round Beechen Cliff (1, 14), she makes engagingly teenage complaints against the tedium of history. Yet Catherine unaware becomes a participant in the still-running philosophical dialogue instigated by Reeve and carried on in the later 1790s in prestigious reviews, articles and books.

The conversation at Beechen Cliff reads very differently, then, according to who is reading. Austen challenges us to pick up her text's play of allusion; anyone who does not, but reads the scene at the level of the beginner Catherine, has lost a layer of ironic comedy, and a key cross-reference to current claims for women's place in culture as *readers and creators of genres of their own*. If that case goes by default, it becomes natural to assume, as most critics do, that Henry prevails over Catherine in the Beechen Cliff conversation – merely because he champions 'grown-up' history. On the contrary: the first round goes to Eleanor, Catherine's knowledgeable ally, for defending the use of fiction (that is of invented speeches and trains of thought) by some older historians. This is a more skilled, informed debating point than Austen's mock-solemn defence of the novel in 1, 5, and it catches Henry where he is vulnerable – for he has already conceded ground to fictional history at its most extravagantly fictitious, by acknowledging how much he enjoys the historical novels of Ann Radcliffe.

But though 'female' romance scores first, Henry successfully counter-attacks from the masculinist side when the sensible, well-read Eleanor believes she hears Catherine announcing shocking news from London. In fact Catherine is uncritically repeating real publicity material issued by the down-market Minerva Press to promote its new fiction list.[8] The muddle created by the women gives Henry the opening he needs as a debater to ridicule Eleanor, while sparing Catherine – and, just as notably, leaving intact the claims of romance. Genres are systems, each with its own rules; a reader has to take responsibility for knowing which genre she is in. The mistake prepares us for Catherine's potentially damaging confusion of the same categories when, after arriving at Northanger, she takes General Tilney for the villain of a novel; but it also makes it human and forgivable.

In *Northanger Abbey*, living in the world involves reading, of people, behaviour, dress and conversation as well as of books. Reading takes in more and more genres; there is so much to learn that everyone proceeds by trial, and at least some error. Women are not more stupid than men, the debate on Beechen Cliff seems to show, but anyone young has further to go, and needs to progress to knowledge where it is to be found, in a variety of forms. For issues of economics and social justice – which Henry connects with the making and unmaking of landscapes – Catherine proves herself unready: 'by an easy transition . . . to forests, the inclosure of them, waste lands, crown lands and government, he shortly found himself arrived at politics; and from politics, it was an easy step to silence.'[9] Henry, who has appointed himself Catherine's opener of doors, gently shuts this one for now.

The conversation at Beechen Cliff establishes the novel's central trio of principal characters, two women and a man (an echo perhaps of Reeve's *Progress of Romance*, a dialogue featuring just such a trio). Superseding Catherine's earlier conversations with Henry alone, the trio format, engaging her with both Tilneys, on the whole prevails in volume 2. Meanwhile, somewhere on the road to Clifton, in a curricle for two, James Morland and Isabella Thorpe are becoming engaged – a 'false climax' to the novel, which will itself supply conversational topics to the central trio in the second volume. Typically for Austen, outings are used to focus relationships. On Beechen Cliff an underlying harmony emerges between the three characters concerned, matched in the novel only by the pleasurable excursion to Woodston towards the end of volume 2. But the other group's excursion to Clifton turns out an ill-planned, uncomfortable outing, we find at second hand from the younger Thorpe sisters, a foretaste of the way the union between James and Isabella will turn out.

On Beechen Cliff, in natural-seeming conversation, characters exchange important principles, priorities which reveal their value-systems and philosophies of life. Largely thanks to the Tilneys (and no thanks to her first mentor Isabella) Catherine finds not one world but many worlds opening to her through books. Henry develops and brings to a close the main theme of his courtship to date, which is to explore the world through play. Understanding comes from seeing how many different games there are. Genres are for adults what games are for children (and adults too), special systems which provisionally reduce reality to order, and make conclusions possible. Henry shows Catherine, who at this point only half hears him, that the mind orders the world through genres, lives in them, and plays between them.

Northanger Abbey and books: 2. Three other women novelists

Northanger Abbey presents reading as at once a trivial pursuit, a form of social bonding, the quest for pleasure and satisfaction, and a trainee's preparation in reading the world. The pervasiveness of the theme of reading, from the first paragraph to the last, queries the frequent claim that the novel fails to hang together; yet it does not dispense with it entirely, since Austen cross-refers to very different kinds of novel. Strictly speaking, the Bath scenes, comprehensively built on plot motifs from the heroine-centred Richard-sonian type of novel, rely on other well-known novels as literally and unmistakably as the scenes at Northanger. From the first two chapters, throughout the Bath visit, it becomes clear that the model Austen most wants her reader to keep in mind is that of Richardson's important successor, Frances Burney; to some extent her *Evelina* (1778), which is set partly in Bath, or *Cecilia* (1782), where the hero belongs to a snobbish aristocratic family, but far more pervasively *Camilla* (1796), a novel to which Austen subscribed before publication.

Catherine's family circumstances, as the elder daughter of a caring but hard-pressed clergyman and his capable, unsentimental wife, duplicates Camilla's. Just as Camilla is entrusted to the care of her worthy but foolish, inattentive uncle Sir Hugh Tyrold, who inadvertently causes many of her difficulties, so Catherine is sent off with the silly Mrs Allen, who allows her to fall into the clutches of the Thorpes. Camilla was to have been Sir Hugh's heir, and throughout the novel this possibility surfaces again, to make trouble for her; echoing that distinctive complication, Catherine's rumoured expectations from the Allens drive the plot of *Northanger Abbey*.

Reminders of these literary precedents come frequently. Austen pauses in 1, 2, to give a full description of Mrs Allen, 'that the reader may be able to judge, in what manner her actions will hereafter tend to promote the general distress of the work'. John Thorpe is not merely a vulgar 'rattle' in the style of Mr Dubster in *Camilla*, and a burlesque version of the Richardsonian villain who abducts the heroine in a carriage: he himself brings up the topic of *Camilla* (1, 6), when he boastfully refuses to read it. Any reader who has read it spots not only John Thorpe's shortcomings as a critic of Burney's novel, but his habit of acting as if he lived in it. Meanwhile Catherine too in some senses *is* Camilla – young, inexperienced, impetuous, charming and fundamentally virtuous.[10] Henry Tilney, as the lover who is also a mentor, has the role, if not the humourless personality, of Burney's Edgar Mandelbert. Isabella, beautiful, ignorant and rapacious, is cleverer than Camilla's spoilt cousin, the beauty Indiana, but similar in her role of unsympathetic foil to the amiable heroine. The many parallels, extending to the daily incidents – which are typically spoilt excursions – constantly undercut Austen's claims to naturalness. Again, the well-read reader experiences a different *Northanger Abbey* from the reader who cannot read down to the layer in the text that repeats *Camilla*.

It would be too crude to suggest Austen *requires* us to have read any single book, even her own favourite *Camilla* or her heroine's current preoccupation, *The Mysteries of Udolpho*. For most purposes it is enough to notice the variety of roles novels play in the text simply by their shadowy presence. Talk about books stands for sociability, even friendship, so often based on shared interests and pursuits: two very different styles of friendship are revealed on Beechen Cliff and by Isabella when she hands on Miss Andrews's library book list in the sixth chapter. All the same, wholly new aspects of *Northanger Abbey* unfold if readers have an impression of the world of eighteenth-century novels – their leading characters, for example, and the outline of their plots. The novels listed in 1, 5 (Burney's *Cecilia*, 1782, and *Camilla*, 1796, and Edgeworth's *Belinda*, 1801), are all stories featuring the dangerous entry into the adult world of an inexperienced, vulnerable heroine. So for that matter is Richardson's *Sir Charles Grandison* (1753), dismissed by Isabella in 1, 6. The same plot, with its stereotyped dangers amplified and psychologized, occurs in Radcliffe's historical romances *The Sicilian Romance* (1790), *Romance of the Forest* (1791) and *Mysteries of Udolpho* (1794); Henry skillfully weaves together key episodes from all three in the parody of Gothic with which he entertains Catherine on their drive to Northanger. In other words, the main conventions of Gothic writing cannot be cleanly detached from those of the more natural-seeming Richardson–Burney tradition. By pooling the contemporary novel's sub-genres together to make her own continuous plot, Austen draws attention to a family similarity and a common stock of motifs found widely dispersed in time. Ultimately, indeed, *Northanger Abbey* depends for its own interest, suspense and colour on being itself a romance. Catherine shares her adventures with the Jack who climbs the Beanstalk, Sindbad the Sailor, the wayfaring Constance, and the *ingénue* bride in Bluebeard's Castle.[11]

Though Austen is on her most dignified behaviour when praising her four chosen novels in 1, 5 – not even Radcliffe gets admitted into this élite company – she also has non-canonical and quite modest sources. Edgeworth's elegant and innovative children's tales in the collection called *The Parent's Assistant* (1796, enlarged second edition 1800) owe something to French fables and Arabian tales, while also offering young English readers a crash course in small-business capitalism. It is these tales, not the more elaborate *Belinda*, which come close to the Austen of *Northanger Abbey* in style, setting and handling of character.

Equally, it may be from these tales rather than from Hannah More and the conduct-book tradition of the 1800s that Austen draws her striking pre-occupation with the world of goods.[12] Edgeworth's classic volumes of children's fiction are rightly placed by Austen among the literary breakthroughs of the 1790s because of their clever adaptation to the social realities of a commercial, entrepreneurial age. Here small marketable things assume a high degree of visibility, and their value is carefully explored. Pretty shells or stones fetch a price as wall or grotto decoration, and thus help save the family finances in a story called 'Lazy Lawrence'. Elsewhere the value of such desirable, collectible objects is negative: in 'The Bracelets', presents are seen as cheap ways of buying popularity; in 'The Purple Jar', Rosalind buys a useless flask of coloured water from a chemist's window, when what she needed was a pair of shoes. The Edgeworthian child living in the city is a consumer of luxury goods; her village child typically belongs to a family cultivating expensive fruit or flowers to sell to Bristol suburbanites on weekend carriage jaunts. Sparkling, up-to-date, economically knowledgeable, Edgeworth's children's fiction analyses the mainsprings of the late-century consumer boom and at the same time naturalizes it in humble daily life.

Austen presents things in *Northanger Abbey* in a revised version of Edgeworth's new evaluative vocabulary. Edgeworth on the whole celebrates the entrepreneurial spirit as more egalitarian and generally beneficial than a hierarchical order. She also qualifies her approval, for instance by pushing hard on questions of value, exploring the specific function of exchanges and gifts, and identifying things which for one reason or another cost too much. By contrast Austen rarely values commodities: instead she uses things in *Northanger Abbey* to mark out character and motive within a traditional, moralized register of feeling. Later in Austen's career this relatively predictable approach allows surprisingly fine shades of characterization, through the exact comic matching of possession and possessor. In *Emma*, Harriet's stub of pencil and Mr Woodhouse's smooth, thin water-gruel speak volumes about their two possessors, whereas in *Northanger Abbey* Mrs Allen, Isabella and even Catherine are all capable of fretting, without much differentiation, over their headpieces.

But, though Austen afterwards learnt to pinpoint her characters' possessions more exactly, the novelist's subtle shift of attention from people to their goods had more significance than this. *Northanger Abbey* displays artefacts, a proto-anthropological technique, because their accumulation of itself conveys a prosperous society bent on pleasure and acquisition. The shops and assembly-rooms of Bath, the house and gardens of Northanger, are equally consumerist treasure houses, full of colourful, shifting signs which are the markers of income and taste. The minor characters who represent 'the World' in this novel display objects as signs to others of their own wealth, status and taste. Even the stupid Mrs Allen is keen-eyed about the lace on the pelisse of her old schoolfriend Mrs Thorpe, since it establishes the difference of their incomes. Austen is no neutral observer of this reflection, still less does she fall in with the modernizing, entrepreneurial spirit. At times her detachment makes her analytical, at other times she becomes judgemental. Mrs Allen damns herself in the reader's eyes by using anything so trivial as lace and muslin as her yardstick of quality.

We tend to accept Austen's moralism, and to be convinced when she contrasts commodity value unfavourably with mental, moral and polite qualities without a visible price-tag: good sense, taste, honest feeling and the ability to speak in sentences and paragraphs. All the same it is the appearance of the commodities, and their sophisticated treatment, that is deeply interesting in the novels of Austen and her contemporaries, and seems to mark a periodic shift in representational style. Everyone in Austen's Bath becomes involved in the display or reading of signs. Austen involves herself, by allowing the worth of so many of her characters to be quantified for us by things they have bought. Her foregrounding of artefacts advertises the novel as another commodity, a product of the commercial publisher-bookseller and stable-mate of the advertisement-led popular press.

In her first version of *Northanger Abbey* Austen seems to acknowledge the emergence of a new style, by alluding in her title to the longest, most adult and most thoughtful of Edgeworth's tales for children, 'Simple Susan' (1800). The heroine of this novella, Susan Price, aged about thirteen, succeeds in rescuing her family from a financial crisis, when her father is about to be drafted into the army and her mother is seriously ill. The girl first earns money by baking and taking in washing; when that is not enough, she reluctantly sells the pet lamb her mother gave her to the village butcher, after which it will be served up at the new squire's Sunday table. Susan in effect grows up in the course of the tale by learning different ways of valuing the lamb, and also how 'to shift for herself' in an adult world containing predators. So does the first of the characters Austen presumably named after her, the young, inexperienced, familial Susan who eventually became the Catherine of *Northanger Abbey*. So do those other Austen good daughters, Fanny and Susan Price of *Mansfield Park*.

It has become an accepted scholarly fact that Austen changed the name of her novel from *Susan* because an anonymous novel of that name appeared in 1809.[13] Having already decided she must change the name if she ever published the novel, she was free to make use of it elsewhere, in *Mansfield Park*. But the eventual *Northanger Abbey* sustains a loss. To have signalled through the title *Susan* the presence of Edgeworth, a notable new voice in 1801–2, would have brought out decisively Austen's claim to be joining a new sophisticated group of woman novelists.

Of all the literary cross-references in *Northanger Abbey*, those of the visit to the abbey itself are the most sustained and complex. By going to the abbey Catherine for a chapter or two takes the reader with her into the setting and plot of a Radcliffean novel of terror, mystery and self-induced illusion. Even the Bath scenes momentarily anticipate the superstitious, surreal effects Radcliffe uses in her Gothic plotting. Henry inexplicably goes away and returns; Mrs Allen wishes and wishes for a friend in Bath, and as in a fairy tale her wish is ironically fulfilled, by the appearance of false friends, the Thorpes. Then, on the journey towards Northanger, Henry rehearses in a full-dress way what might be expected to happen there: he distils key sequences from three Radcliffe novels, *A Sicilian Romance* (1790), *The Romance of the Forest* (1791) and *The Mysteries of Udolpho* (1794), to produce a skillful reduction, delightful to the omnivorous Gothic reader, of the external props Radcliffe introduces into her most characteristic situation – the exploration, by night, of a vast and ancient building.

From the mid nineteenth century until late in the twentieth century, Romantic Gothic was often decried, both as pasteboard, gimcrack architecture and as a sensational sub-genre of fiction deliberately aimed at a semi-educated readership. In fact William Lane's Minerva Press (founded 1790), which published the *Horrid Mysteries* on Isabella's library list (1, 6), was indeed launched specifically to appeal to lower-middle-class females.[14] Radcliffe's principal Gothic novels were by no means put by contemporaries into the same category. Austen acknowledged, as did Scott, Coleridge, Godwin, Byron and Shelley, that Radcliffe has opened up a profoundly imaginative, intellectually ambitious fictional genre. True, Radcliffe bases her action and setting on conventions established by Horace Walpole in *The Castle of Otranto* (1764), and developed by several successors, which typically centre on the figure of a cruel tyrant, and use his vast prison-like fortress as the setting for his crimes. But she also moves far beyond routine, mechanical deployment of Walpole's devices, and shifts the emphasis in significant ways. She diverts the reader's attention from the compelling but stagey villain to the heightened, paranoid consciousness of his female victim, that is from event to the reception and interpretation of event. This degree of internalization lessens or at least complicates what is in Walpole and in Radcliffe's challenger Matthew Gregory Lewis a somewhat obvious political allegory, whereby the feudal baron stands for domination and political injustice in the family and in the state.

Henry Tilney, that skilled reader, extracts certain sequences in Radcliffe novels which crystallize her manner: essentialist and psychologically acute. The Radcliffe heroine is isolated and surrounded by strangers, enemies or equivocal friends. Her parents are dead, possibly dead, or not certainly known – the last, an equally powerful, more suggestive indicator of her alienation. At the nodal point or points in her story she comes to a building which may provide a seeming refuge by day but becomes a threatening, haunted maze by night: 'a mystery seems to hang over these chambers, which it is still, perhaps, my lot to develope'.[15] Always at midnight, in fear of discovery by the other people of the house, in fear of ghosts and whatever else she may find, she unlocks hidden doorways, feels her way down dark passages, and finds the equivocal keys to the past – a familiar-looking portrait, a blood-stained dagger, a scroll of paper or a chest big enough to hold a human skeleton.

When the Radcliffe heroine resolves to explore the hidden nocturnal world she simultaneously tries her courage and reveals her immaturity. Terror of the dark belongs to her childhood self, which she has barely left behind. By mastering fear and opting for rationality she chooses the world as it is, a state of civilization committed to order and reason. Though Chesterfield gibes at women as 'children of a larger growth', Radcliffe shows her heroines emerging from dependency and irrational fear to self-reliance; by implication, qualifying themselves for a modern daylight society on the same terms of citizenship as men. Adeline and Emily take charge of their own destinies, and in so doing put behind them the injustice, superstition and abject dependence of history's medieval shadowland. Radcliffe's plot concerning an individual woman's rite of passage to maturity can also be read, then, as a historical and civic allegory. The values of Protestant self-reliance have replaced, but not everywhere, or not within everyone, the values of the old aristocratic, Catholic world order.

Much of the best modern criticism of Radcliffe has shown, excitingly, how modern she seems. She teaches her successors, Austen included, how to give the reader access to a heroine's consciousness. Yet more sophisticated is Radcliffe's stunning use of spatial imagery, an architecture of extremes: from coffin-like passages and cells to vast halls, or (in *A Sicilian Romance*) a broken stairwell, reminiscent of Piranesi's fantastic drawings of a Roman prison, *I Carceri*, in which neither the roof nor the ground is visible. For post-Freudians, the settings suggest the landscape of the Unconscious, while the plots of parental violence, guilt and suffering re-enact the repressed traumas of infancy. This imagery speaks across time of women's fear of sexually active men, whether strangers, lovers or fathers.[16]

That modern sympathetic version of Radcliffe is thought-provoking when we now read her novels; but though Austen responded imaginatively to her contemporary, she never understood her by quite this light. She indicates otherwise in her three imitations, arguably parodies, in *Northanger Abbey*: one by Catherine, when she first imagines her forthcoming visit to Northanger Abbey (2, 2); Henry Tilney's, on the journey from Bath (2, 5); and Catherine's actual attempts at exploration (2, 7 and 2, 8). These episodes add up to a much more extensive treatment of Radcliffe than Austen's scattered references in the first volume to many novels; their length and textual fidelity bring Radcliffe's voice into two or three chapters of *Northanger Abbey*, an invasion of the text unparalleled elsewhere in her oeuvre. But Austen's representation of her fellow novelist is calculatedly selective. There is no architectural fantasy of the house's hidden other regions; instead Catherine is forced to endure the General's itemized tour, informative in the language of an auctioneer, and too exhaustive to leave room for unvisited wings or cellars. There was a mother – Eleanor's, not Catherine's – and she is dead; but her last days, and the recurrent stomach trouble that killed her, again rule out the idea that her husband poisoned her. Catherine does not imagine a sexual motive for the General's supposed crime, though the Radcliffe heroine lives in fear of rape, and lust is always at the root of evil in the violent, primitive and passionate Radcliffean past. Austen never allows the dark shadows of the past to encroach on the present, either in a political form, as despotism, or psychologically, in the return of a tragic or traumatized subconscious. Her omissions flatten Radcliffe's extraordinary spatial perspective, and the temporal one too: General and the late Mrs Tilney inhabited the same daylit commodious world as the modern generation.

Austen does, however, encourage readers to merge Radcliffe's symbolic plot with her own – though with striking substitutions. Eleanor, at least, repeats the Gothic stereotype of young womanhood. Passive and pensive, isolated and repressed, she endures from an unfeeling father daily constraints not far from imprisonment, and has never got over the loss of her mother. But once her foolish Radcliffean hypothesis is dismissed, Catherine is free to tackle Eleanor's unhappiness in a more appropriate and natural manner, by intuiting her grief and her need to talk. Her sister-like friendship with Eleanor, a delicately drawn, subtly emotional but unsexual relationship, in fact comes to share the central narrative space with Henry's courtship of Catherine. In conversation with Eleanor and Henry, she even unravels *some* truths about sexuality via the novel's secondary plots, Isabella's flirtations with James Morland and Frederick Tilney. Again, the secondhand, indirect narration of Isabella's amours occupies the room that Radcliffe gives in her closing chapters to intense fantasies of older women's forbidden and insatiable sexuality.

If Radcliffe is taken as the third of Austen's three important mentors, together with Burney and Edgeworth, she is, like the others, at once source, involuntary collaborator and target of an extensive, coherent rewriting. The literary relationship which emerges between Austen and Radcliffe is by no means obvious, at least to modern readers, who often take Austen for the champion of modernity. In fact the Protestant Radcliffe approaches the Catholic past critically; by contrast, Austen, though wedded to an exact modern setting, has also inherited the Tory leaning, more Catholic than Reformed, lightly asserted in her juvenile *History of England*. *Northanger Abbey* itself will imply she respects village England and its unwritten customs as a source of law and the constitution, the church and the clergy back to monastic times for their social commitment. Ironically, then, it is Austen of these two who is 'ancient' in her sympathies.

Three characters and the heroine

Perhaps the least questioned generalization about Austen is that readers see the world of each novel through its heroine's eyes. But if the character and actions of Susan/Catherine derive wholly or partly from other heroines, and we notice that, we can hardly immerse ourselves innocently in her adventures. In any case, Catherine's judgements, though not her feelings, are often immediately exposed as unreliable. At least three other characters in the novel convey more usable and certainly more knowing information about their world. These are, in ascending order of importance, General Tilney, Isabella Thorpe and Henry Tilney.

The first two look at first sight typologically very simple. Compared with later, more naturalistically conceived Austen minor characters, their speeches are relatively flat and unoriginal. But the General and Isabella also perform quite elaborate functions which are not part of naturalistic characterization. Austen in this novel urges her readers to become unusually active as interpreters, and unusually aware of artifice, intrigue and plotting. The General and Isabella are notable deceivers, whose machinations in the end prove responsible for almost everything that happens. They are so active, between them, that we may not notice the actual scarcity of minor characters, even in a novel where the crowds are dense enough to threaten Mrs Allen's muslin and headpiece. Partly thanks to their links with Radcliffe's world, they also hint at ranges of villainy her other novels avoid: male cruelty and oppression, female lust, treachery and corruption.

The General is, by profession, family role and temperament, a disciplinarian who believes in his right to rule. He intervenes in national and county affairs, runs his estate, has chosen his sons' professions and is currently deciding who his younger children should marry. When he is present, these grown children cannot freely dispose of their day, since his word is law on mealtimes, exercise times and journey times. His 'type' is that of the despot or, in late-eighteenth-century fiction, the aristocrat. His predecessors include Count Manfred, in Horace Walpole's *Castle of Otranto* (1764) and Dorriforth, the Catholic priest, peer, severe husband and father, in Elizabeth Inchbald's radical fable, *A Simple Story* (1791).

The apprentice novel-reader Catherine can currently think of only one model for the General: Montoni, the orphaned heroine's uncle-by-marriage and self-appointed guardian in Ann Radcliffe's *Mysteries of Udolpho* (1794). Identifying the two, she suspects the General, as Emily suspects Montoni, of doing away with his wife. Catherine is wrong, as was Emily: both are presented as hysterics, and Radcliffe disapproves of irrationality as much as Austen. But if innocent on this score, the General and Montoni stand for unpleasant behaviour commoner than wife murder in the modern world. A meticulous catalogue of his possessions and some oblique but exact dialogues supply the evidence for other charges to level at the General. In fact, as any well-read person would certainly recognize, he is one of the spendthrift wealthy landowners consistently criticized and satirized in eighteenth-century writing from Pope's *Moral Essays* down to a huge body of books, tracts and didactic poems on the uses and abuses of land in Austen's own day, the 1780s and 1790s.

To take a single analogy, a notorious and extreme case in Austen's lifetime. In 1763 Joseph Damer, soon to be created first Baron Milton, a member of a family enriched by moneylending, bought a fine estate in Dorset. It included a huge, ancient and largely intact abbey church and the ruins of the abbey itself, which adjoined the market town of Milton Abbas. Milton employed Capability Brown to devise a scheme for the park which involved the removal of much of the town, and the re-siting of its grammar school ten miles away. In the early 1770s he brought in the architect Sir William Chambers to design an exotic mansion in the oriental style, abutting the abbey church, which was transformed and in the process 'beautified' as an outsize chapel. As drawings done for Lord Milton 'Before' and 'After' confirm, the siting of the large new house required the destruction of most of the remains of the abbey. By the early 1790s the new-built house was attracting tourists, including Fanny Burney, who admired it.

But a more copious literature of complaint was by then available. A local scholar, the Revd George Bingham, published a memoir on the grammar school's late master, who had also written a history of Dorset, *Biographical Anecdotes of the Rev John Hutchins MA* (1785). The book exposed some of the stratagems Milton had used to get rid of the school, and condemned him as a selfish petty tyrant, indifferent to the interests of his tenants and the local people. Bingham was, significantly, a friend of the jurist William Blackstone, whose *Commentaries on the Laws of England* (1765–9) was in certain respects a consensual work. Blackstone sets out what is since Locke the basic reality of modern English society, the right to the secure ownership of property, conceived above all as property in land. But he also accepts older forms of right, when he argues that the English constitution and law is *customary*: it acknowledges local unwritten practices. This caveat had implications for the many late-eighteenth-century landowners who sought to enclose land or, in reorganizing the use of land in the name of efficiency, to abolish the customary rights of poor people in pasturing, gleaning or wood-gathering. It is relevant to the cases of Lord Milton and General Tilney that Blackstone famously compares common law, incorporating custom, to a venerable building (an image evoking Gothic abbeys and castles) which should be conserved not on aesthetic but on moral and social grounds.[17]

General Tilney is one of Austen's distasteful improvers; the Rushworths of Sotherton in *Mansfield Park* are others. Both families have enjoyed their estates, significantly, from the time of the destruction of the monasteries in Tudor times, when monastic lands were distributed among families in royal favour. In both these novels touching on improvement Austen leads her heroine towards marriage with a clergyman, thus prompting readers to feel the contrast between the selfish hedonism of wealthy families, in Tudor times or the present, and the original use of the land to serve religion and the poor. The clergyman had a traditional role in this debate, especially in more conservative, nostalgic views of tradition, as the champion of the poor. Austen has in short a historical view of social norms and obligations, and of legitimate and illegitimate practices in land management and by extension in marketing or milling too. Taken together, this web of mutual obligations, incorporating paternalistic protections, constitutes what E. P. Thompson has called 'the moral economy of the poor'.[18]

The clashes of the poor with the rich in the 1790s were not always over the enclosure or reorganization of land. In 1795 a bad harvest produced a scarcity which was exacerbated by farmers and merchants, who withheld corn in order to drive up the price of bread. Large farmers and corn merchants grew visibly richer, while the poor grew poorer or starved. Incidents both local and national which highlighted the conflict of interest between community and capitalist were regularly reported in the press, and the constitutional issue brought out. The Lord Chief Justice, Lord Kenyon, for example, instructed a Shropshire Grand Jury in 1795, and repeated the same view in another case in 1800, that it was an indictable offence 'at common law, coeval with the constitution', to 'forestall', that is withhold grain in order to drive up the price.[19] Austen must have been especially interested by Gilpin's essay of 1791 on the economic history of the New Forest, in his and her native Hampshire, which depicts 'forest law' as bad law from its inception, because populated, cultivated land was appropriated to make a huge royal hunting-ground for the Norman kings, and savage penalties exacted, unknown to Anglo-Saxon monarchs, when the laws were breached. 'Forest law indeed was one of the greatest incroachments that ever was made upon the natural rights of mankind; and . . . one of the greatest insults of tyranny.[20]

In the most famous controversy over 'improvements' of the decade, Uvedale Price and Richard Payne Knight, two landowners from Hereford (neighbouring country to General Tilney's Gloucestershire) attacked between 1794 and 1797 the purely aesthetic theories of Humphry Repton, the most fashionable landscape gardener of the day. Price in particular demanded instead that landowners should present their estates as the natural environment of human activity, and improvements as changes that brought benefits to tenants and agricultural workers rather than solely the landowner.[21]

The General is plainly an improver of Austen's time, not Pope's. As the vandal of the abbey ruins, he has continued what his father began. He even updates Lord Milton, in being more concerned with what is virtually a new technology, market gardening, than with landscaping a park. All the more topically, he exhibits the unacceptable face of contemporary capitalism: his ultra-efficiency benefits no one but himself. Tenants and smallholders are nowhere to be seen: the gardeners work as employees within the General's walls, their former status ironically remembered by Austen's wording. 'The walls seemed countless in number, endless in length; a village of hot-houses seemed to arise among them, and a whole parish to be at work within the inclosure' (2, 7). The General grows exotic fruits in order to dine on them out of season, and modernizes his rooms in order to excite the envy of his guests. He has a showman's pride in the dinner-service and Rumfordized cooking facilities which advertise not only his disposable wealth but his technological know-how: this, like the showmanship, places him among that section of the wealthy landlord class that has most thoroughly imbibed the ideology of capitalism. For all his family pride, then, and the venerable sound of his address, the General is in the grip of the modernizing fever, and has lost all claim to be the good old squire of Tory and folk mythology.

Iconographically the rich, selfish aristocrat had often made a contrasting pair with the poor but benign and paternalist country clergyman. Goldsmith gives a classic example of each: in the poem 'The Deserted Village' (1770), the landowner has cleansed a once-human landscape in order to create a 'natural', non-human park; in *The Vicar of Wakefield* (1766), the clergyman hero is the kindly father of a large family and pastor of his flock. Echoing that pattern, the General's younger son Henry has been set up as vicar of an outlying parish, Woodston, which the General also owns: Henry's lifestyle, which has been that of Catherine's childhood, and will be her future, implies a Goldsmithian rejection of the General's example. But Woodston too has been subtly updated by Austen, to make the traditionalist point in a modern form. By now thoroughly tired of the General, Catherine longs to escape his pompous abbey and its army of underemployed, anonymous servants for Woodston. The first things she sees on arrival are the signs of commercial, working activity in the 'populous' village from which the parsonage is only 'tolerably disengaged'. Fully aware from the General's comments that villages should be small, quaintly dilapidated and set in hilly country, 'Catherine was ashamed to say how pretty she thought it . . . in her heart she preferred it to any place she had ever been at', little chandler's shops and all (2, 11). Catherine's character and upbringing incline her to the localized, communitarian perspective, and shield her from the campaign to gentrify the parsonage, to which the General is about to try to recruit her.

From the early 1960s – before the arrival of feminist criticism – it became almost obligatory for critics of *Northanger Abbey* to insist that Catherine has it fundamentally right earlier, when she identifies the General as another Montoni. Feminist critics took up the point from the 1970s, tempted by their interest in Gothic fiction as a form that symbolizes male power and female subordination. Austen draws on that polarity, yet is by no means content with it. Readers who insist on sharing Catherine's Gothic obsession do what she does only for a while – they fail to pick up the social and natural explanations being provided of the General's motives and misdeeds.

As the novel's busiest character, Isabella Thorpe comes near to dominating the Bath scenes, and does far more than anyone else to typify Bath society for us. If Catherine's character comes out of conduct literature and novels, Isabella's comes from novels and even guidebooks promoting Bath, the habitat in which she flourishes. As the best-known of these guidebooks enthuses,

> The young, the old, the grave, the gay, the infirm, and the healthy, all resort to this vortex of amusement. Ceremony beyond the essential rules of politeness is totally exploded; everyone mixes in the Rooms upon an equality . . . The constant rambling about of the younger part of the company is very enlivening and cheerful.[22]

Isabella indeed rambles, in this republic of pleasure-seekers. Her confident mobility, signalled in 'the graceful spirit of her walk' (1, 4), is what Catherine first admires in her, and what she may even begin to imitate, if there is any truth in the General's compliment that Catherine's own walk has 'elasticity' (1, 13). Isabella criss-crosses the town, always within the fashionable town centre in which the chairmen ply their trade, a circle which has a radius of 500 yards from the Pump Room. Once her brother John produces his curricle, however, she restlessly wants to take jaunts out of town in every direction. Isabella seizes every chance offered her by the formal constitutions of the two assembly rooms, the rules of which proclaim that the subscribers to the Upper and Lower Rooms and the concerts are their own legislators. She determines the right places to strut, observe, make assignations. She is also the self-appointed Mistress of Ceremonies of the quartet of young Morlands and Thorpes, which she rules by whim and dictat, and (if Mr Allen is right) in disregard of the proprieties.

From their first meeting, Isabella dictates to Catherine their conversational agenda – 'dress, balls, flirtations and quizzes' – from the vantage point of being 'four years older than Miss Morland, and at least four years better informed' (1, 4). She knows where to be seen, when and under what sign. At most this is a new hat – a purple turban, perhaps – and more typically it is an illusion of newness worked with netting or ribbon, for where Mrs Allen can afford to change her dress day by day, Isabella has to achieve stylishness through cheap accessories. The fact that she *manages* arises from her and of course Austen's grasp of the semiotics by which membership of a style-conscious group is claimed. A modern journalistic slogan on style evidently already worked in Austen's Bath, 'You see what I like. You see what I am worth.' But Austen seems too eager to rub in the literal cheapness of Isabella's devices: she dictates to Catherine from her pocketbook (1, 4). Game adventuress Isabella appears rewritten by Thackeray as Becky Sharp, a more sympathetic climber up Society's greasy pole.

Though she instantly turns Catherine into a fan of Mrs Radcliffe, Isabella is not much of a reader herself. Books serve as one of her conversational gambits, like horses and sports for her brother John. The list of 'ten or twelve' recent shockers (in fact only seven) that she dictates to Catherine from her pocketbook (1, 6) came secondhand from her friend Miss Andrews. Like Catherine's enthusiastic description of a new book on Beechen Cliff, this must derive literally from the publicity material of William Lane's Minerva Press, the publisher of six of the seven novels. If so, Miss Andrews and her friends probably expected to read them in one of the network of Minerva-only libraries Lane set up, often in small shops, across the country.[23] In a manner typical of modern consumer culture, Isabella spreads the news about the latest commodities, and about where they are to be had at less than the full price. Conversely, if a book is not current but nearly half a century old, like Richardson's *Sir Charles Grandison*, she will not talk of it or read it at all. Her news items are really news flashes, short enough for the advertising, personal and gossip columns of a newspaper: what is in a shop window, or playing at the theatre, or who is contemplating adultery with whom. For the doctor, chemist and social critic Thomas Beddoes, the feverish search for novelty typified in the younger Thorpes is a symptom and source of the nervous illnesses he finds endemic in modern society.[24] Austen does not encourage generalizations of quite so pessimistic a kind. But Isabella's praise of novels in 1, 6, does something to counter and ironize the celebration of novels Austen gives us in 1, 5.

Though the Thorpes are seldom remembered affectionately among the vintage Austen characters, the novel could hardly function without at least Isabella. She is an anti-heroine who provides far more incident, intrigue and thick, anthropological description than the heroine can. Her restlessness and ear for news demonstrate how Bath itself works and, since we endlessly see and hear her, seem to draw us in. But this puts the reader on the spot: if Isabella is as vulgar as she seems, we ought not, strictly speaking, to be keeping her company, still less parading with her along the Crescent or chasing unknown young men down Milsom Street. Isabella implicates the reader in improper, reckless or vulgar actions, and we collude in her knowingness. Though we love Catherine with our hearts, our heads give us access to Isabella.

All three of the key characters whom Catherine has difficulty in decoding are presented to us as to some degree mysterious: we are asked to think twice about the General and Henry Tilney, and even the seemingly transparent Isabella. Certainly characters in the novel fail to agree about her. Mrs Thorpe, Catherine and James Morland admire her, and John Thorpe, insolent to his mother and younger sisters, treats her with circumspection. Mr Allen on the other hand queries her behaviour in riding around with James in a curricle; and the younger Tilneys, though constrained by Catherine's innocence in what they can say, are united in their disapproval. They feel sure Frederick would never think of her as a wife, or that if he did their father would not accept her as a daughter-in-law. This is partly the judgement of polite people on a vulgar person. Yet in giving her the prime responsibility for the flirtation with her brother they see her as a moral agent, which is surely nearer our understanding than Catherine's assumption that she is Frederick's passive victim.

Since we have no access to Isabella's consciousness, we have no reliable information about her feelings other than what her actions suggest. In an unusually serious, sustained conversation she has with Catherine in 2, 3, Isabella speculates about Catherine's feelings for John Thorpe, and in doing so gives what could be a pretty accurate account of her own state of mind: 'A little harmless flirtation or so will occur, and one is often drawn on to give more encouragement than one wishes to stand by . . . What one means one day, you know, one may not mean the next' (2, 3).

Might she have been 'in love' with Frederick, at least for a day or so, in the feverish fashion of a novelty-chasing society? Or has she merely calculated the great difference in income between the eldest sons of an obscure country clergyman and a leading Gloucestershire landowner? If it's hard to feel sorry for Isabella when she loses both men, it's not clear that she didn't suffer, just a little. But the plot of *Northanger Abbey* resembles the plot of *Emma*; each is a detective story without a detective. A reader going back over the clues can build up a case against Isabella which is blacker than anything quite said of her.

Is it only events that seem to conspire against the innocent heroine? For many years Isabella, eldest of the fatherless Thorpe children, must have been hearing the name of one of her mother's few prosperous friends, Mrs Allen of

Fullerton. It is surely no coincidence that when John Thorpe meets at Oxford a fellow student, James Morland, who comes from Fullerton, he is encouraged to bring him home that very Christmas vacation. During his week with the Thorpes at Putney, James is easily fascinated by Isabella. Soon she has got him to talk about his family, and the Allens, and his sister Catherine's imminent visit to Bath with the Allens. Isabella's first stratagem is to lead a family party, of her mother and sisters, to Bath. Otherwise John and James would not be arriving in Bath to see Isabella – rather than Catherine, as Catherine supposes. Isabella has her own engagement in mind from the outset, and presumably John's, or he would not be cooperating; but the eventually disposable fortune of the childless Allens may well be a target she has in view for herself and James, even if John Thorpe believes it is coming to him. She takes care to walk home with Catherine on the day of their meeting, and in the 'eight or nine days' before the arrival of John and James she is in the company of Catherine and Mrs Allen each day.

Harder than her mother and more purposeful than John, Isabella is, according to this reading, the conspirator who at Bath controls the threads of the plot. Soon she fills the timetable of her whole circle. Her effective management of Catherine not only forces Catherine constantly into John's company, whether indoors or out, but interrupts Catherine's friendship with the Tilneys. The latter return to Bath on the same day as John and James reach it, and during the next few days Henry finds his efforts to make contact with Catherine frustrated. It is in the full knowledge of Catherine's confessed interest in Henry that the Thorpes entangle her in a web of engagements: Isabella emerges in this interpretation a female Iago or Iachimo, who comes close to wrecking Catherine's happiness as well as her brother's.

Within the novel, Isabella's game is readable only by Henry; for if she is temporarily Mistress of Ceremonies, he is always the Master of Games. His scenes with Catherine are often themselves games. But at their sudden first scene together in the third chapter, he could almost be the magician Comus, luring her to play:

> . . . forming his features into a set smile, and affectedly softening his voice . . . 'Have you been long in Bath, madam?'
>
> 'About a week, sir', replied Catherine, trying not to laugh.

She feeds him the answers he wants, being quick enough and young enough to pick up games by instinct. He is the first person she meets who knows Bath, and he is checking her knowledge of its weekly timetable – which, as a quick learner, she already knows.[25] Henry in fact complements Isabella as a guide to Bath: where she moves round it, to see, be seen, meet people she means to use, Henry celebrates resort life for offering a model of varied, regulated pleasure, where no activity becomes wearisome because by then it is giving way to another. Embedded in the guidebook passage which is appropriate to Isabella, since it dwells on the Bath crowd's freedom and mobility, is a sentence which Henry's conversation seems to echo: 'the entertainments are so wisely regulated that although there is never a cessation of them, neither is there a lassitude from bad hours or from an excess of dissipation'.

When Henry asserts that Catherine keeps a diary, and invents entries for it, she challenges him. Once he has strayed into speaking her lines for her he begins to spoil a game first invented for them both: she instinctively stops playing, resuming her natural voice, to warn him that even the inventor of the rules has no power over another player once play has begun. A girl who has been playing games with other children for years is naturally a quicker, more independent player than Mrs Allen, whom Henry easily manoeuvres into playing herself in a comic sketch of his devising. When after his ten-day absence from Bath Henry next dances with Catherine, he picks up where they left off, by remarking that dancing is an emblematic or play version of marriage (1, 10); 'We have entered into a contract of mutual agreeableness for the space of an evening.' In that case, as the knowing reader (but not Catherine) might also notice, it is also emblematic of society, in which citizens and rulers have tacitly made a contract entailing mutual obligations.

Henry's epigram also proves meaningful for the novel as a whole, for other Austen novels and for novels as an art form. As a theorist of ordered activities such as games-playing and art, he is more of a philosopher than any other character Austen invented. Catherine follows him best on play and on books, the pleasures she knows; far less well when he touches on public-sphere contracts and obligations, within a community and society outside the parameters of the family. At that first meeting Catherine fears his theorizing is beyond her, but from the beginning this is only half true. After denying that dancing is like marriage, she in fact adopts his principle of the contract, faithfully kept, as a working rule of conduct for herself. The Bath scenes of their courtship are already true dialogues, anticipating the sparring love scenes of *Pride and Prejudice*, and implying that Catherine is equipped for a partnership on the terms of equality games require.

The dialogues at Northanger have shifted in register, however, to become gentler and more serious. In the famous scene in which Catherine betrays to Henry that she supposes his father to be a murderer (2, 9), his rebuke to her is a warning that she must address herself to the community in which she lives. 'Consult . . . your own observation of what is passing around you – Does our education prepare us for such atrocities? Do our laws connive at them?' More than the imposed constraint of the law, the 'well-connectedness' of polite society and its mechanisms of cultural exchange make her heated fantasies improbable: 'Could they be perpetrated without being known, in a country like this, where social and literary intercourse is on such a footing; where every man is surrounded by a neighbourhood of voluntary spies, and where roads and newspapers lay every thing open?'

Politeness is a social ideal; it is the principle Henry opposes in Bath to Isabella's self-seeking and talent for spreading disorder and ill-will. Community, a more traditional concept, is Henry's implied answer in the Northanger chapters to his father's self-serving programme of conspicuous consumption. In his shorthand reference to modern social and literary intercourse – 'roads and newspapers' – Henry pulls together the novel's very different milieux in a single metaphor for our urban/suburban interconnectedness.

The fact that Henry at twenty-four or twenty-five talks to seventeen-year-old Catherine like her big brother, and that he sets about educating her, has alienated some recent critics, who have found him patronizing or worse, a bully.[26] Plainly Austen as she builds up this relationship interleaves scenes of play with scenes of instruction: in this respect Henry resembles one of those new-style progressive educators popularized by Thomas Day and the Barbauld and Edgeworth families. Many late-eighteenth-century parents were keen to educate younger children in particular at home: manuals specially written for them showed how lessons could be delivered as family conversations, affectionate and to a point child-led.[27] Thus Henry plays down mere facts and instead indicates ground-rules by surprising propositions – a dance is just like a marriage – that invite a child to test them. Catherine learns informally from Henry, by skips and jumps, and does not notice herself doing it. By comparison, other novelists who allowed the hero to instruct the heroine showed far less lightness of touch. Harriet Byron has to take in interminable lectures from Sir Charles Grandison; Burney slyly satirizes but also repeats Grandison with her Edgar Mandelbert, censorious fiancé to Camilla.

Henry is a very different games-player from Isabella (and her sportsman brother John), a very different mentor from his father General Tilney. Yet it is becoming common to lump the novel's three self-appointed male guardians together, as though, perhaps following a lead set in Burney's *Cecilia* and *Camilla*, Austen shows 'Man' or patriarchy combining to manipulate and coerce Catherine. Rather than seeming aligned with his father and Thorpe (both, like Frederick Tilney, men's men), Henry is a mysterious, almost allegorical figure, who stands for androgynous ideas, youthful play, the comic spirit, romance. Literally, he is named after Austen's favourite brother, four years older than herself. But at a deeper level, the fictional Henry doubles for Jane Austen, twice over: by being much her age (twenty-four) at the time of writing, several years senior to the adolescent Catherine; by representing, in his inventiveness and playfulness, the voice and creative role of the author.

Catherine has to be known as other characters get to know her, in her conversations. Though always having to cope with her seniors, she acquits herself firmly from the start. She stands up to bullying by Isabella, John and her brother James over their proposed expedition to Clifton, and shrewdly sees through John Thorpe. Because we are more used to admiring the thoughts of other heroines, we may overlook how much detail we learn about Catherine, through this novel's underrated, brilliant dialogues. She is exceptionally patient and good-humoured with Mrs Allen, for instance, a good child on her best behaviour; but then at the end of the book, delivered back at last to her own family, tired, out of sorts and uncooperative, in a believable resumption of her adolescent behaviour when at home.

As a seventeen-year-old, she seems drawn from life: not too good to be true, and certainly not too wise to be true. The reader, alongside the Tilneys, watches her get wiser. She is always capable of saying a good thing – which is either to the point, or refreshingly honest, or naïve but disarmingly loyal to her parents and brothers and sisters. Each of her conversations with Henry proves her capable of resisting him. She does this most tellingly when Henry seems to be trying to tell her that Frederick's exploitation of women does not matter, as long as they are women like Isabella. Her constrained remark, that it is understandable Henry should side with a brother, for once speaks volumes more than its surface meaning. She is learning to deploy a double meaning, the characteristic of adult speech, and also to trust her judgement as well as his.

Alone with Eleanor, Catherine is 'natural' in another way. Their few scenes together belong to some elegant tale of pathos and sentiment that celebrates the values of the heart over those of the head. When Henry questions Catherine about her view of his mother's death, she is loyally anxious to clear Eleanor of any blame. Insofar as the novel is about believable people – and the Morlands and Tilneys do seem believable – it climaxes not with Catherine's stereotypical blunder, to invent a murder that never happened, but with the scene on the last Sunday morning at Northanger, when Eleanor gets up to see Catherine off, and each makes the other a gift of value. Eleanor lends Catherine the money she will need to get home. Catherine, at first too offended with the General to say she will write, changes her mind when she notices how much Eleanor needs her letters. They have become instinctive sisters.

If other characters' responses condition our knowledge of Catherine and her story, so does the one set-piece excursion that deserves the name of a pleasure-party – the day at Woodston. Like the outing to Sotherton in *Mansfield Park*, or the parties in *Emma* at Box Hill and Donwell Abbey, this scene highlights the key characters and their motivations with dramatic brio, in contrast to the even day-by-day narration of the previous three-week sequence. Occurring between Northanger Abbey, the great house from which

Catherine is about to be ejected, and Fullerton, the shabby vicarage to which she will soon return, it shows the near-identity of values between Henry and Catherine, but also complicates the climax by elaborately establishing the material value of Catherine's future married home.

The General here outdoes himself in villainy, by echoing Satan's temptation of Christ in the wilderness in the language he knows best, that of a salesman of real estate. But he is also classically ridiculous, in urging Catherine to spend yet more of his money on altering the drawing-room, though to add a bow window conflicts with the best taste. He agrees, in an extravagant deferral to her judgement, to retain the labourer's cottage in the centre of the view which he previously meant to sweep away. Like her approval of the village at the parsonage gates, her intervention in favour of the cottage shows us that Catherine's feelings and values are closing with Henry's. Significantly, it is she who now decides what she thinks; in this scene, which quietly brings marriage into view, Henry barely speaks. The General talks for him, so that even Catherine at last understands his drift – the imminent appearance of marriage contracts. To escape him she takes flight into the open air, and finds relief in a childish occupation, 'a charming game of play with the puppies in the yard'.

Within a week, the General has packed Catherine off home – on a Sunday, moreover, a breach of decorum, especially for a clergyman's daughter, which sets the seal on his insult to her family. But the too-recent memory of the happy day at Woodston is yet another instance of the General's comic bad luck as a strategist. Henry is able to juxtapose his father's cynical efforts to bribe Catherine with Catherine's unforced at-home-ness in a 'well-connected' parsonage and parish, rather than a grandly spurious abbey.

Woodston Parsonage is for the modern reader intensely realizable, not historically, as a Goldsmithian pastoral idyll, but as an ideal home Catherine has drawn, along with a husband, in a very lucky lottery. But first readers must have felt the same satisfaction. Of all the consumerist pleasures, among the most solid and communicable are those that belong to setting up house, room by furnishable room. Just as Elizabeth's tour of Pemberley, Darcy's house and estate in Derbyshire, gives readers of *Pride and Prejudice* a deeply gratifying foretaste of her future wealth, comfort and status, so Catherine's day at Woodston lets us imagine what is in store for her, a comfortable family existence in what the General calls, not one hopes with too much hype, one of the best small parsonages in the country. It is ironic, that the most criticized character in the novel, the greedy, accumulating General, should have lured us all, even as we are told he is not luring Catherine, with the smaller property he has on offer.

The Austen narrative method, even in this uniquely decentred form, has delivered not only the classic, universally condoned reward of romance for the romantic – a journey's end in lovers' meeting. It has also given the wedding an up-to-date inflection, timely around 1800, and after nearly two centuries as fresh as ever. Austen's compact with her readers is never puritanical. Traditional stories end with satisfied desire; surprisingly often this encompasses the desire for goods. Happiness comes in *Northanger Abbey* as a sitting-room with a window down to the floor, and a view of apple trees.

Isobel Armstrong, 'Conservative' Jane Austen? – Some Views (1988)

The following note on critical views of Jane Austen is not intended to survey her reputation exhaustively. That has been very effectively done recently by B. C. Southam in his Critical Heritage volumes. This last section of my study is intended to ask some questions about the ways in which Jane Austen has been discussed and to strike a cautionary note. First of all, why has her work so long been regarded as that of an essentially conservative writer? Why has this been assumed and celebrated, with some significant exceptions, right up to the 1970s? Why, subsequently, has this view been modified?

The most famous discussion of Jane Austen as a writer working within narrow social limits and expectations is undoubtedly that of Charlotte Brontë. In 1848 she wrote to G. H. Lewes in the following terms:

> An accurate daguerrotyped portrait of a commonplace face; a carefully fenced, highly cultivated garden, with neat borders and delicate flowers; but no glance of a bright vivid physiognomy, no open country, no fresh air; no blue hill, no bonny beck. I should hardly like to live with her ladies and gentlemen, in their elegant but confined houses.

Charlotte Brontë was writing of *Pride and Prejudice*, but her strictures are possibly more relevant to a reading of *Mansfield Park* if one works within the terms she uses. She was thinking, of course, of the lack of intensity and passion in Jane Austen's work as well as its restricted social field, but her description implies conservatism in both the general and political senses of the word. Many nineteenth-century readers agreed with her. Either, like Carlyle, they thought of her work as mere 'dish-washings' (a remark of 1850 quoted by Francis Espinasse in his *Literary Recollections*, 1893) and described it in terms of 'dull stories without incidents, full of level conversation, and concerned with characters of middle life' (article in *Christian Remembrancer*, 1853), or they celebrated what they saw as a meticulously realist painting of the society of English country gentlemen 'as it was, in all its features' (Goldwin Smith in *The Nation*, 1870) and delighted in the fidelity of her art to known social experience.

Those who considered Jane Austen more daring and inventive than these descriptions suggest made an interesting move. They compared her with Shakespeare, implying a range, depth and insight far beyond that of most poets as well as of most novelists. Tennyson, rather unexpectedly, was one such critic, and is said to have rushed to the spot in Lyme Regis where one of the characters in *Persuasion*, Louisa, fell down some steps. But the sense of a novelist writing of and from within a closed society continued well into the twentieth century. Her recognition of the limits and realities of social life, it was assumed, gave her a supreme moral insight into the nature of permanent human problems in society and provided a basis for judgement and ethical discrimination which transcended her particular historical situation. Lord David Cecil represents this view most typically in the twentieth century: 'her graceful unpretentious philosophy, founded as it is on an unwavering recognition of fact, directed by an unerring perception of moral quality, is as impressive as those of the most majestic novelists,' he wrote in his Leslie Stephen Lecture on Jane Austen in 1935. He said that he would go to Jane Austen for moral advice and would be very perturbed if she were to disagree with him. Cecil belongs to the cult of Jane Austen (often nicknamed 'Janeites'), people who read Jane Austen as if every detail of her novels belongs not to the world of fiction but to their experience, people who believe that because they are at home in her world, she would be at home in theirs.

One can begin to see the basis of the conservative reading of Jane Austen. It is a moral reading and a class-based reading which are intertwined. Those, like Charlotte Brontë, who disliked her work linked the restricted social world of the novels to emotional and moral narrowness. Those who responded positively to her work assumed that the restricted class base of the novels was so natural to Jane Austen and so completely assimilated that it was virtually naturalized and provided a basis of stability and security from which the most scrupulous observation and moral judgement could operate. Since she herself appeared to ignore the major historical and political movements of her time (though I hope I have managed to dispel that impression), we ourselves could be justified in ignoring them too and lift Jane Austen's work out of history into the realm of moral universals.

An alternative form of the same strategy is to praise, as Virginia Woolf did, 'her greatness as an artist'. Writing in *The Times Literary Supplement* in 1913 she described the 'conservative spirit' of Jane Austen in terms of the finesse and subtlety of aesthetic form: 'More than any other novelist she fills every inch of her canvas with observation, fashions every sentence into meaning, stuffs up every chink and cranny of the fabric until each novel is a little living world, from which you cannot break off a scene or even a sentence without bleeding some of its life.' Here it is the organic unity and completeness of Jane Austen's world which is being praised as much as its ethical sensitivity. Virginia Woolf's criteria of wholeness and intricacy later led her to compare

Jane Austen's art with that of Henry James and Proust (*Athenaeum*, 15 December 1923). James had earlier praised Jane Austen in the same terms, arguing that even the 'dropped stitches' of her imagination produced 'little glimpses of steady vision, little master-strokes of imagination' (an essay of 1905, reprinted in *The House of Fiction*). The academic descendant of these views is the classic study by Mary Lascelles, *Jane Austen and Her Art* (1939). In this kind of study there is a move towards formalism rather than morality, but the effect can often be the same: in both approaches the history and politics crossed by the novels (and crossing them) begins to disappear.

One exceptional nineteenth-century critic, Richard Simpson, writing in *The North British Review* (1870), speaks in terms very different from those of his nineteenth-century contemporaries, and, it must be said, in terms often very different from twentieth-century writers. This is a particularly notable achievement when one remembers that the influential *Memoir* of Jane Austen published in 1870 by her nephew, J. E. Austen-Leigh, which presented a sentimental and conventional picture of Jane Austen, was the occasion of his review. Simpson writes of Jane Austen's intelligence, her irony, her 'critical spirit . . . at the foundation of her artistic faculty'. He represents a minority tradition which surfaces again in the work of Reginald Farrer, who asked for an 'objective' reading of the novels ('Jane Austen', *Quarterly Review*, July 1917), in D. W. Harding's 'Regulated Hatred' (*Scrutiny*, 1940) and in W. H. Auden's poem 'Letter to Lord Byron' in *Letters from Iceland* (1937), which describes Jane Austen's revelation of 'The economic basis of society' so 'frankly and with such sobriety'.

If we are not to assume eclectically that these are all different 'approaches', all equally valid and each representing the different ideological positions of different readers, it is necessary to inquire a little further into these differing readings. It is interesting to note that the harsher, satirical Jane Austen emerges in criticism at times of national stress, war or danger. Simpson was writing in a decade which saw renewed conflict in Europe and further demands for political reform at home. Farrer was writing during the First World War, Harding in the Second and Auden just before. This may be to displace critical relativism from writers to a moment in history, but it does suggest that moments of cultural stress or lack of cohesion open up the conservative readings of Jane Austen to inspection and disclose elements in the texts which have been ignored or have remained unnoticed. Perhaps one could say that they hardly existed until they were named. The radical readings certainly draw attention to the fact that every reading of a text is a construction. But even if we see that readings are called out by particular historical moments and particular positions, it is not necessary to return to the eclectic position that anything is valid, anything goes.

To begin with, if a text discloses a reading different from a conventional one, that may be because there are areas of unease, unsolved problems and contradictions working in the writing which enable quite contradictory readings to occur. Most readings tidy up and foreclose on uncertainties. The more insistent the closure, the less convincing the reading. Both conservative and radical readings can do this. On the other hand, it is another kind of closure simply to say that a text is fundamentally contradictory and leave it at that, another form of mastery. There is no right reading, but what one can do is to try and determine where the unsolved elements of the text occur, what is left in play, where they are derived from and how they are configured in the text. For instance, if one is aware of the religious and radical discourses simultaneously debating the nature of qualities such as patience, delicacy and gentleness in the decades preceding the writing of *Mansfield Park*, it should be possible to see not only that there is considerable conflict about these in the novel but that they are also being subjected to a subtle critique which also has its uncertainties. This is evident from a reading of the text alone; to go outside it helps to clarify the problems further. The same is true of the degree of play and unease round the idea of representation and the idea of service. It is arguable that such a cluster of anxieties are, as it were, Tory anxieties. One could certainly point outside the novel to statements by Jane Austen about these issues which are pretty uncompromising. But it is, as I have already said, possible to make a radical critique without being a radical, and if it is preferable to see this as a conservative critique, then the limits and anxieties of that confrontation are just as important as any other. What we find ourselves doing is attending to the network of connections within the text and to its language and to the relations of that with the languages of other texts. We find ourselves asking questions rather than providing answers. My own reading of the novel convinces me that areas of the text are confused – one would point to the worries around *Henry VIII* – just as other areas of it are deeply subversive – and here one would point to the sexual politics of the novel. Another area of uncertainty is around the ultimate elimination of the Crawfords. There will always be contested areas in complex texts and that is why readings will always be contested. By clarifying the way in which problems are configured and exposed, however, one provides grounds for rational debate. Such debate cannot take place if we assume that any position is valid or that changing critical views are simply the result of changing critical fashion. One will be much more sharply aware of the ideological reading, just as one will be more sharply aware of the ideology of the text and its problems, if one explores the unease at work in a piece of writing.

Readings of *Mansfield Park* in the twentieth century have tended to try and decide what the novel is about in order to erase the critic's puzzlement and the uncertainty which arises from the difficult gravitas of the text. Lionel Trilling's classic essay on *Mansfield Park* is troubled on many points: he is worried about the passivity and delicacy of Fanny; he is worried about the scandal of the play and the almost Victorian prudery which its presentation evokes; he is worried about the sobriety of the ending and the rather gloomy rectitude which dismisses the energy of the Crawfords. This essay, reprinted in *The Opposing Self* (1955), tends to close off areas of conflict by assuming that the text unequivocally opts for particular conclusions rather than exploring a set of problems. Thus uneasiness is located not in the novel but in the mind of the critic, who is worried by what he interprets as Jane Austen's closed solutions. Trilling believes that the reassertion of the values of stability and Christian integrity embodied in the marriage of Edmund and Fanny leads to a deliberate acceptance of a world in which the play of energy and vitality is repressed in favour of the ethical life of sacrifice and passivity. The disapproval of the play is a part of that cutting-off of energy. He explains the resistance to acting as a resistance to the deceit of representation deeply felt in European culture, particularly where there was, as in *Mansfield Park*, a strong ethical code. The ending chooses low-pulsed rectitude as against the thrusting Crawford vitalities. It is clear that he is trying to empathize with a value system which deeply perturbs him. Where he can, he retrieves from the novel a liberal Jane Austen oddly like himself.

Other criticisms of *Mansfield Park* have not attempted the imaginative effort of getting inside what they interpret as its values and ideology but have simply assumed that its values are narrow and antipathetic. Farrer attacked the hypocrisy of the ending, which celebrated the marriage of a prig and a passive girl materially rewarded for being morally right: the novel 'is vitiated throughout by a radical dishonesty'. Kingsley Amis mounted a full-scale attack on *Mansfield Park* in an aggressive essay written in 1957, 'What Became of Jane Austen?'. Like Farrer, who described Fanny as 'the female prig-pharisee', Amis attacks Fanny for lacking 'self-knowledge, generosity and humility'. Edmund's 'notions and feelings are vitiated by a narrow and unreflecting pomposity, Fanny's are made odious by a self-regard utterly unredeemed by any humour.'

But Trilling's act of empathy and Amis's aggression both assume that the novel closes on fixed positions. Neither assume internal inquiry, critique, openness, unease or anxiety. Neither assume a text in dialogue with itself. Both concentrate overwhelmingly on the actions of characters as indicators of the ideological position of the author, in spite of the sophistication with which they discuss the text.

My own belief is that a radical reading of *Mansfield Park*, that most serious and troubled of Jane Austen's works, is possible when one stops reading decisions of character as decisions of the author and sees the text as an exploration of the constitution of a great middle-class family, its repressions, tyrannies, tragedies and compromises – perhaps the marriage of Edmund and

Fanny is the greatest compromise. Recently, the work of novelists writing in the same period as Jane Austen has been reprinted. Often they deal with the same themes (Susan Ferrier's *Marriage*, for instance) and yet these energetic and intelligent novelists (Maria Edgeworth, Charlotte Lennox, Mary Brunton, for instance) go nothing like so far in critical analysis as Jane Austen. This is one indication of her capacity for critique.

The reading of Jane Austen which challenges the conservative view has emerged concurrently with accounts of the text and the act of reading which explore the possibility of seeing the text in terms of critique. In very different ways Marxism and deconstruction enable this kind of reading. That is why it might be more useful for the new reader of Jane Austen to look at Barthes's *S/Z* (1974) or Bakhtin's *The Dialogic Imagination* (1981), or some contemporary works on narratology, such as Peter Brook's *Reading for the Plot* (1984), rather than particular studies of her texts. Such theoretical work provides a suggestive and speculative context in which to think about her work.

The study of Jane Austen will always breed problems because one is dealing with a writer who starts with conservative problems and contemplates radical solutions. Hence Rebecca West's remark, in an extraordinarily penetrating Preface to a new edition of *Northanger Abbey* in 1932, 'For the feminism of Jane Austen . . . was very marked. It was, I think, quite conscious', which has remained unnoticed for many years. We stand at a very interesting point in Jane Austen criticism, when rereadings in the light of new forms of thought in the subject are likely to emerge. Jane Austen has recently been well served by historians (Marilyn Butler's *Jane Austen and the War of Ideas*, 1975, re-established the political and intellectual context of the novels), but a great deal more work on the complexities of the politics of the novels is required. Much more feminist history and sustained and careful studies of Jane Austen's language are required. There are signs that this is happening: Elaine Jordan has written seriously of *Lovers' Vows* and Mary Evans has explored the politics of the novels in *Jane Austen and the State* (1987). A computerized study of the language of the novels charts the areas of unease and critical investigation with some subtlety (J. F. Burrows, *Computation into Criticism*, 1987).

Interestingly, Marilyn Butler's *Jane Austen and the War of Ideas*, which argues emphatically for Jane Austen as a conservative writer – Professor Butler describes the first part of *Mansfield Park* in particular as 'a skilful dramatization of the conservative case' – was published in the same year, 1975, as Barbara Hardy's *A Reading of Jane Austen*, which argues a very different case. Professor Hardy cannot read Jane Austen as a conservative and presents her as a novelist who 'criticizes society through the drama of complex and particular types and groups'. Her reading is particularly sensitive to language: she remarks, for instance, on the 'ironic and moral' significance of the 'four inserted words' which open *Mansfield Park* and the description of Sir Thomas's marriage. Maria Ward 'had the good luck to captivate' Sir Thomas Bertram. It is such extreme subtlety of language which makes the conservative reading problematical by sharply calling attention to the 'luck' of class and money. Her enthralling chapter 'Properties and Possessions' likewise shows how the novels conduct a probing critique of the way people relate to property.

Recently Marilyn Butler has returned to the case for the conservative reading, prefacing the paperback edition of her book (1987) with a new and substantial introduction. She reviews her book of 1975, which was an important moment in Jane Austen criticism, self-critically but unapologetically in the light of a comprehensive review of the decade or so of criticism since, which has seen the rapid growth of very different kinds of theoretical criticism – feminist criticism, post-structuralist criticism, deconstruction, psychoanalysis and Marxism. She argues that, as a historical critic, it is still proper for her to maintain her 'conservative' analysis of 1975. Since she is a critic of very considerable standing who commands attention, it is worth going into her discussion. She criticizes feminist accounts of Jane Austen as a 'subversive' as essentially lacking in historical understanding. Even such impressive works as Elaine Showalter's *A Literature of their Own* (1977) and Susan Gubar and Sandra Gilbert's *Madwoman in the Attic* (1979) are, she feels, naïve about a woman's tradition and unscholarly in their readings of the past – or in their failure to read it. 'Only accurate, comprehensive, particularized historical criticism, distanced from immediate classroom pressures, willing to take minor work, published and unpublished, male and female, as evidence, will enable us fully to reconstruct the context in which women writers wrote' (p. xlv).

But there are more theoretical questions at stake here than Professor Butler suggests, for what exactly constitutes 'history' is a deeply problematical matter. Isn't 'historical criticism' as much one of the ideological 'classroom pressures' as feminism is? And isn't the dream of the ultimate and total reconstruction of a historical context a scholar's fantasy? Marilyn Butler writes as if there is only one 'history' to which we can finally return in all its purity. But there are many histories, and all, as Hegel realized when he said that history depends on the categories brought to it by the historian, will be organized through the conceptualization of history brought to it with the writer of history. We do not have to fall into a facile relativism to see this. Professor Butler foregrounds some kinds of history in her book at the expense of others, but this is inevitable, and the selectiveness gives point to her argument.

No criticism can do without the conceptualizating of history, but scholars should be warned against the hubris of believing that 'their' historical methodology is the only one which will lead to a 'correct' reading. There are many histories: that of language, women, colonial discourse, for example. And they are often histories of representation and the struggle for representation. Franco Moretti, for instance, has recently seen Jane Austen's work (he discusses *Pride and Prejudice* rather than *Mansfield Park*) in relation to the history of the bourgeois *bildungsroman* of the nineteenth century, in which there is a tension between individual self-development and social normalization, an opposition created by the contradictions of bourgeois values. His 'history' leads to a very different kind of reading of Jane Austen's texts than that pursued by Professor Butler. It is the history of a class morality and aesthetic (*The Way of the World: The* Bildungsroman *in European Culture*, 1987).

But even if one feels one has arrived at the 'right' way of thinking history (and the question is a complex one), there is still a problematical gap between this and the text, which is paradoxically both a part of the 'history' it is in dialogue with and separate from it by the fact of being a fiction. The 'right' history doesn't necessarily guarantee the 'right' reading. For instance, Marilyn Butler sees *Lovers' Vows* as an ideologically questioning intrusion into the novel, which ultimately closes ranks against it and reaffirms conservative values. David Musselwhite, in his *Partings Welded Together: Politics and Desire in the Nineteenth Century Novel* (1987), also sees the response to *Lovers' Vows* as a conservative one, but his reading is entirely different and is, moreover, based on a very different definition of 'conservatism' itself. He argues that the incorporation of the seemingly disruptive *Lovers' Vows* into the novel is a middle-class strategy of appropriation which takes over radical politics and normalizes and tames it.

The terms 'history' and 'conservative', then, turn out to be problematic. A reader of *Mansfield Park* and its contested readings – 'conservative', 'subversive' – has to be a disciplined and meticulous reader of the texts surrounding the novel and the novel itself in order to mediate between opposing interpretations. I believe, however, that it is possible to mediate between these opposing interpretations. To do so involves not so much a historical but a theoretical move. It is possible to recognize the conservative provenance of a writer while understanding the fiction in terms of radical critique. The 'conservative' concern of Southey for the poor, for instance, becomes in the text of *Mansfield Park* a sharper and more complex matter, a questioning of privilege rather more uneasy than that of Southey. The question of what constitutes a historical reading opens up immense problems which cannot be fully discussed here, but one can ask a rather different question of a text: does it open up a space for a radical reading? Some texts do, some do not. In the very anxieties in the text about its own conservative reading, I see the possibilities for radical critique. They are not imposed on it. Marilyn Butler, a critic for whom the greatest respect is appropriate, closes on the conservative reading. It is possible to propose that the conservative reading generates its radical opposition and that this can be seen at many points in the text and above all in the language of the novel. At any rate, this is what my reading has attempted to do.

Within the next decade, perhaps, Jane Austen studies will be taken into new areas. *Mansfield Park*, with its difficult gravitas and sombre perceptions, remains paradoxically the most breathtaking and daring of Jane Austen's novels and will always be a challenge to the critic.

Claudia L. Johnson, Jane Austen: Women, Politics and the Novel: *Northanger Abbey* (1988)

When Jane Austen began to compose her full-scale parody *Northanger Abbey* sometime in the mid-1790s, the Gothic novel had already been thoroughly imbued with political implications.[1] As Ronald Paulson has put it, 'By the time *The Mysteries of Udolpho* appeared (1794), the castle, prison, tyrant, and sensitive young girl could no longer be presented naively; they had all been familiarized and sophisticated by the events in France.'[2] Paulson's short catalogue of Gothic images would seem implicitly to serve the progressive agenda to protect the powerless and the feminine from the abuses of a decaying but still powerful patriarchy, and some progressive novelists, such as Eliza Fenwick in *Secresy, or, The Ruin on the Rock* (1795) or Wollstonecraft in *The Wrongs of Woman*, *or Maria*, did employ the form or much of its imagery for precisely such purposes. Charlotte Smith, of course, combined politics and Gothicism most regularly, as in *The Old Manor House* (1793) and *Marchmont* (1796). In the overtly polemical *Desmond*, in fact, her own heroine calls attention to how Gothic 'excesses' figure forth realities which young girls ought to know about. Coming to Gothic fiction only after her unhappy marriage, she reports how she now devoured

> the mawkish pages that told of damsels, most exquisitely beautiful, confined by a cruel father, and escaping to a heroic lover, while a wicked Lord laid in wait to tear her from him, and carried her off to some remote castle – Those delighted me most that ended miserably . . . Had the imagination of a young person been liable to be much affected by these sorts of histories, mine would, probably, have taken a romantic turn, and at eighteen, when I was married, I should have hestitated whether I should obey my friends [sic] directions, or have waited till the hero appeared . . . But, far from doing so, I was, you see, 'obedient – very obedient . . .'[3]

Would that Geraldine *had* had the benefit of Gothic fiction to show her how to be disobedient and teach her what to suspect from her protectors. The distresses she reads about, alas, are now her own: her family commanded her unsuitable marriage for money, her husband is plotting to sell her to a rich duke, her treacherous family, entrapping her with words like 'duty' and 'obedience,' is now confining her because they suspect that her 'hero' – the progressive Desmond – will rescue her. To Smith, as to other reform-minded novelists, the Gothic was not a grotesque, but in some ways a fairly unmediated representation of the world 'as it is,' if not as 'it ought to be.'

But in Radcliffean Gothic, the focus of Austen's parody, the political valence of Gothicism is not so clear, and this despite the conservatism of Radcliffe herself. True, *The Mysteries of Udolpho* affirms a Burkean strain of paternalism by reiterating negative object lessons in the need for regulating violently subversive passional energies, lessons which apply equally to Emily, Valencourt, and Montoni.[4] But when one shows how father-surrogates like Montoni wield legal and religious authority over women in order to force marriages and thereby consolidate their own wealth, one is describing what patriarchal society daily permits as a matter of course, not what is an aberration from its softening and humanizing influences. The cozy La Vallée, presided over by the benevolent father St. Aubert, and the isolated Udolpho, ruled by the brooding and avaricious Montoni, can be seen not as polar opposites, then, but as mirror images, for considered from the outside, protectors of order and agents of tyranny can look alarmingly alike. Struck by the same double message in turn-of-the-century architecture, Mark Girouard relates the Gothic revival in English country houses specifically to the 'spectre of the French Revolution' and subsequent reassertion of authority: 'Country houses could project a disconcerting double image – relaxed and delightful to those who had the entrée, arrogant and forbidding to those who did not.'[5]

Radcliffe's novels present the double image Girouard elucidates, for they provide a Burkean rationale for repression, as well as describe the grounds for rebelling against it. In *The Italian* (1797) especially, stock characters, images, and situations veer almost entirely out of control, and a conservative agenda is maintained only by pacing the action of the novel so rapidly as to hinder reflection on politically sensitive issues intrinsic to the material – such as the extent of familial authority, the tension between private affections and public obligations, and the moral authority of the church and its representatives. The movement of the novel as a whole is to cover up. We needn't be alarmed at the ease with which fathers *could* murder daughters, because Schedoni turns out not to be Ellena's father after all; we needn't worry about the lengths to which aristocratic families go to prevent their sons from marrying beneath them, because Ellena turns out to be nobly born; we needn't protest the corruption of religious institutions, for the officers of the Inquisition, after a few perfunctorily gruesome threats of torture, finally acquit themselves as responsible ministers of truth and justice. As if unwilling herself to follow through with the potentially radical implications of her material, Radcliffe opens creaking doors to dark and dreadful passages only to slam them shut in our faces.

It has seemed to many readers that Austen's parody in *Northanger Abbey* debunks Gothic conventions out of an allegiance to the commonsense world of the ordinary, where life is sane and dependable, if not always pleasant.[6] But by showing that the Gothic is in fact the inside out of the ordinary, that the abbey does indeed present a disconcerting double image, particularly forbidding and arrogant to one who, like Catherine Morland, does not have an entrée, *Northanger Abbey* does not refute, but rather clarifies and reclaims, Gothic conventions in distinctly political ways. Austen's parody here, as in the juvenilia, 'makes strange' a fictional style in order better to determine what it really accomplishes, and in the process it does not ridicule Gothic novels nearly as much as their readers. Clearly the danger for a reader like Henry Tilney, too often mistaken for an authorial surrogate, is to dismiss Gothic novels as a 'good read' – as a set of stock situations and responses to them which need not trouble us with a moment's serious reflection after we have put the book down. He is, in fact, a perfect reader for Radcliffe's particularly evasive brand of escapist thrills about the horrors that occur in safely remote Catholic countries. By contrast, the danger for a reader like Catherine is to mistake Gothic exaggerations for unmediated representation, to fail to recognize their conventional trappings. Thus while Henry categorically denies the Gothic any legitimately mimetic provenance, Catherine imagines that no more or less than the literal imprisonment and murder of an unhappy wife is the only crime a bad man can be charged with. By making the distrust of patriarchy which Gothic fiction fosters itself the subject for outright discussion, Austen obliges us first to see the import of conventions which we, like Henry perhaps, dismiss as merely formal, and then to acknowledge, as Henry never does, that the 'alarms of romance' are a canvas onto which the 'anxieties of common life' (2, 10) can be projected in illuminating, rather than distorting, ways. Austen may dismiss 'alarms' concerning stock Gothic *machinery* – storms, cabinets, curtains, manuscripts – with blithe amusement, but alarms concerning the central Gothic *figure*, the tyrannical father, she concludes, are commensurate to the threat they actually pose.

In turning her powers of parody to a saliently politicized form, Austen raised the stakes on her work. Imperious aristocrats, frowning castles, dark dungeons, and torture chambers were safe enough before 1790, and sometimes in the juvenile sketches, such as 'Henry and Eliza' and 'Evelyn,' they surface in uproariously telescoped fashion. But once social stability was virtually equated with paternal authority, Gothic material was potent stuff, and in *Northanger Abbey* Austen does not shy away from it. If anything, she emphasizes the political subtext of Gothic conventions: her villain, General Tilney, is not only a repressive father, but also a self-professed defender of national security. To Catherine, the General seems most like Montoni – that is, 'dead to every sense of humanity' – when he, 'with downcast eyes and contracted brow,' paces the drawing room gloomily, pondering political 'pamphlets' and the 'affairs of the nation' (2, 8). By depicting the villain as an officious English gentleman, publically respected on the local as well as national level, and 'accustomed on every ordinary occasion to give the law in his family' (2, 15), *Northanger Abbey*, to use Johnsonian terms, 'approximates the remote and familiarizes the wonderful' in Gothic fiction, and in the process brings it into complete conjunction with the novel of manners. This conjunction is reinforced by the two-part format of the novel. The world which Catherine is entering for the first time comprises Bath and Northanger Abbey, both of which are menacing and 'strange' – Catherine's recurrent expression – to one whose 'real power,' as Eleanor Tilney says of herself, 'is nothing' (2, 13).

Just as conspicuously as *Mansfield Park, Northanger Abbey* concerns itself explicitly with the prerogatives of those who have what Eleanor calls 'real power' and the constraints of those who do not. Henry Tilney is far from believing that women in general, much less Catherine or his own sister, have no 'real power.' To him, women's power – in marriage, in country dances, in daily life generally – is limited, but very real: '[M]an has the advantage of choice, woman only the power of refusal' (1, 10). Henry's aphorism describes the conditions of female propriety as they had been traditionally conceived, and as they were reasserted throughout the 1790s by conservative advocates of female modesty. Women, by such accounts, are not initiators of their own choices, but rather are receivers of men's. If the 'power of refusal' seems detrimental or frustrating in its negativity, it is still better than nothing, for it does not leave women without any control of their destinies: women may not be permitted to pursue what they want, but they may resist what they do not want. But in Austen's novels, as in so much eighteenth-century fiction about women, women's power of refusal is severely compromised. Many Austenian men – from Collins to Crawford to Wentworth – cannot take 'no' for an answer.

In *Northanger Abbey*, bullying of various sorts is rampant, and Tilney's confidence in the feminine power of refusal is put to the test. Indeed Catherine's own friends have no scruples about lying in order to force her to comply with them rather than keep her own engagement with the Tilneys, and when caught in his lie, John Thorpe, with the apparent concurrence of Catherine's brother, 'only laughed, smacked his whip . . . and drove on,' overbearing her refusal: 'angry and vexed as she was, having no power of getting away, [Catherine] was obliged to give up the point and submit'

(1, 11). When mere lying and abduction are not apropos, James and the Thorpes join forces to compel Catherine to surrender her power of refusal. Together, they 'demand' her agreement; they refuse her 'refusal;' they 'attack' her with reproach and supplication; and they resort to emotional manipulation ('I shall think you quite unkind, if you still refuse'), fraternal bullying ('Catherine, you must go'), and eventually even to physical compulsion ('Isabella . . . caught hold of one hand; Thorpe of the other' (1, 13). So little is Catherine's brother inclined to respect woman's 'only' power, refusal, that he defines, if not feminine, then at least sisterly virtue as a sweet-tempered yielding of her will altogether to his: 'I did not think you had been so obstinate . . . you were not used to be so hard to persuade; you once were the kindest, best-tempered of my sisters' (1, 13). The moral and physical coercion of powerless females which figures so predominantly in Gothic fiction is here transposed to the daytime world of drawing room manners, where it can be shown for the everyday occurrence it is, but no less 'strange' for all that.

Against the selfishness of James Morland and the bluster of John Thorpe, Henry Tilney stands out, not in opposition, but if anything in clearer relief, for his unquestioning confidence in his focality and in the breadth of his understanding prompts him to preempt not only the female's power of refusal but indeed even her power of speech in analogous ways, without doubting the propriety of his doing so. Brothers are treated with great respect in Austenian criticism, certainly with much more than they deserve if *Northanger Abbey* and *The Watsons* are considered with due weight. Because it is assumed that Austen's feelings for her brothers – about which we actually know rather little – were fond and grateful to the point of adoration, the sceptical treatment brother figures receive in her fiction has been little examined. Between Thorpe's remark that his younger sisters 'both looked very ugly' (1, 7) and Tilney's reference to Eleanor as 'my stupid sister' (1, 14), there is little difference, for in each case, the cool possession of privilege entitles them to disparaging banter, not the less corrosive for being entirely in the normal course of things. On most occasions, however, Tilney's bullying is more polished. A self-proclaimed expert on matters feminine, from epistolary style to muslin, Tilney simply believes that he knows women's minds better than they do, and he dismisses any 'no' to the contrary as unreal. On the first day he meets Catherine, for example, he tells her exactly what she ought to write in her journal the next morning – the entry he proposes, needless to say, is devoted entirely to the praise of himself. Female speech is never entirely repressed in Austen's fiction, but instead is dictated so as to mirror or otherwise reassure masculine desire. But when Catherine protests, 'But, perhaps, I keep no journal,' Henry, flippantly but no less decisively does not take her 'no' for an answer: 'Perhaps you are not sitting in this room, and I am not sitting by you. These are points in which a doubt is equally possible' (1, 3).

That, it would appear, is that, if for no other reason than that Henry himself has said so. But – for all we know to the contrary – Catherine does *not* keep a journal, and this will not be the first time that Henry, believing, as he says here, that reality itself is sooner doubted than the infallibility of his own inscriptions, will with magisterial complacence lay down the law. The effect for a woman like Catherine, 'fearful of hazarding an opinion' of her own 'in opposition to that of a self-assured man' (1, 7), is silencing, even when she knows she is right. Catherine would no more dream of opposing Henry here than she would the General himself when he announces that even his heir must have a profession, for as Austen makes clear, silence is exactly what he wishes: 'The imposing effect of this last argument was equal to his wishes. The silence of the lady [Catherine] proved it to be unanswerable' (2, 7).

Henry too, then, takes away the feminine power of refusal, simply by turning a deaf ear to it. In this respect, he is more graceful, but he is not essentially different from the General, who asks Eleanor questions only to answer them himself, or from John Thorpe, who declares that his horses are unruly when they are manifestly tame. The characteristic masculine activity in *Northanger Abbey* is measurement, a fiatlike fixing of boundaries – of mileage, of time, of money, and in Henry's case, of words. Although these boundaries turn out to be no less the projection of hopes and fears than are the overtly fanciful stuff of Gothic novels, they are decreed as unanswerable facts, and the self-assurance of their promulgators enforces credence and silences dissent. Because Henry dictates the parameters of words, the kind of control he exercises extends to thought itself, the capacity for which he describes in explicitly sexual terms. Appearing to consider his respect for 'the understanding of women' a somewhat unwarranted concession, Henry quips, 'nature has given them so much [understanding], that they never find it necessary to use more than half' (1, 14). A great stickler for words, he bristles at any loosening of strict definition – such as relaxing the terms 'nice' and 'amazement' – and he is in the habit of 'overpowering' offenders with 'Johnson and Blair' (1, 14) when their usage transgresses prescribed boundaries. But when Catherine and Eleanor get entangled in their famous malentendu concerning 'something very shocking indeed, [that] will soon come out in London' (1, 14), linguistic looseness has served them where Henry's correctness could not. To Catherine, of course, what is shocking, horrible, dreadful, and murderous can only be a new Gothic novel; to Eleanor it can only be a mob uprising of three thousand. Henry regards the interchangeability of this vocabulary as proof of a feminine carelessness of thought and language which is regrettable, laughable, and endearing at the same time, and he enlightens them by vaunting his manliness and his lucidity: 'I will prove myself a man, no less by the generosity of my soul than the clearness of my head' (1, 14).

Henry may be bantering again, but politically speaking the linguistic and intellectual superiority he boasts is no joke. During the 1790s in particular, privileged classes felt their hegemony on language, and with that power, seriously challenged by radical social critics – some of them women, and many of the men self-educated – from below, and as one scholar has recently demonstrated, conservatives met this challenge by asserting that the superiority of their language rendered them alone fit for participation in public life. Tilney's esteemed Dr. Johnson played a posthumous role in this process, for those 'aspects of Johnson's style that embodied hegemonic assessments of language' were 'developed and imitated' as proper models.[7] With the authority of Johnson and Blair behind him, then, Henry is empowered to consider feminine discourse – conversation or Gothic novels – as either mistaken or absurd, and in any case requiring his arbitration. The course of the novel attests, however, that the misunderstanding between Catherine and Eleanor is plausible and even insightful: political unrest and Gothic fiction are well served by a common vocabulary of 'horror' because they are both unruly responses to repression. Such, however, is not how Henry reads Gothic novels, nor how he, in effect, teaches Catherine to read them. Indeed, the reason Catherine assents to ludicrously dark surmises about the cabinet is not that her imagination is inflamed with *Radcliffean* excesses, but rather that she trusts *Henry*'s authority as a sensible man, and does not suspect that he, like John Thorpe but with much more charm, would impose on her credulity in order to amuse himself. 'How could she have so imposed on herself,' Catherine wonders. But soon she places the blame where it belongs: 'And it was in a great measure his own doing, for had not the cabinet appeared so exactly to agree with his description of her adventures, she should never have felt the smallest curiosity about it' (2, 7). This exercise of power by 'the knowing over the ignorant' is, as Judith Wilt has argued, 'pure Gothic,' and it is structured into the system of female education and manners.[8] In 'justice to men,' the narrator slyly avers that sensible men prefer female 'ignorance' to female 'imbecility' – let alone to the 'misfortune' of knowledge – precisely because it administers to their 'vanity' of superior knowledge (1, 14). Catherine's tendency to equate the verbs 'to torment' and 'to instruct' seems less confused given the humiliating upshot of her lesson in the Gothic at Henry's hands.

But Henry, as we have seen, does not know everything. And what he does not know about Gothic fiction in particular is explicitly related to his political outlook. Even though Austen spares us Tilney's 'short disquisition on the state of the nation' (1, 14) – delivered in part to bring Catherine to 'silence' – she does not hesitate to caricature his conservative tendency to be pollyannaish about the status quo. Catherine is a 'hopeful scholar' not only in landscape theory but also in Gothic novels, and her sensitivity to the lessons they afford far surpasses the capacity of her tutor, because her powerlessness and dependency give her a different perspective on the status quo. Gothic novels teach the deferent and self-deprecating Catherine to do what no one and nothing else does: to distrust paternal figures and to feel that her power of refusal is continuously under siege. While still in Bath, Catherine does not feel completely secure with the attentiveness of Mr. Allen's protection; she feels impelled 'to resist such high authority' (1, 9) as her brother's on the subject of John Thorpe's powers of pleasing ladies; and though she finds it almost impossible to doubt General Tilney's perfect gentility, she cannot ignore the pall he casts on his household. Further, Gothic novels teach Catherine about distrust and concealment, about cruel secrets hidden beneath formidable and imposing surfaces. Before she goes to Northanger, she expects to find 'some awful memorials of an injured and ill-fated nun' (2, 2), and what she eventually turns up there about the injured and ill-fated Mrs. Tilney is not that wide of the mark. If these were to be the 'lessons' inculcated to flighty young girls, it is small wonder conservatives should feel that they should be expunged. Writing as late as 1813, the high Tory Eaton Stannard Barrett considered Gothic fiction still dangerous enough to warrant savage burlesquing in his own novel *The Heroine*. His anti-heroine's first and most heinous offense is to take Gothic novels seriously enough to doubt her good father's paternity, and with that to resist his authority. From such delusions, it is only a short step to the three volumes of utter dementia that finally land her in a lunatic asylum. As the sensible Mr. Stuart patiently explains to her at the end, novels like *Coelebs* and *The Vicar of Wakefield* 'may be read without injury,' but Gothic novels 'present us with incidents and characters which we can never meet in the world,' and are thus 'intoxicating stimulants.'[9]

Such of course is precisely the lesson Henry would impress upon Catherine, and it is a lesson he himself believes. When Henry Tilney learns that Catherine has suspected his father of murder, he is stupefied by a 'horror' which he has 'hardly words to—' (2, 9). Evidently, Johnson and Blair do not supply Henry with words adequate to what Gothic novels describe all the time, and the reason the manly and 'clear-headed' Henry never read Gothic fiction sensitively enough to realize this is that it insists on a doubleness which he finds semantically, as well as politically, imponderable. Because he considers England as a uniquely civilized nation, where church, education, laws, neighborhoods, roads, and newspapers make heartless husbands and their crimes rare, improbable, almost unknown, the Gothic 'horror' Catherine intuits is as preposterous and even as subversive as the earlier malentendu about the 'shocking' news from London. But Gothic fiction represents a world which is far more menacing and ambiguous, where figureheads of political and domestic order silence dissent, where a father can be a British subject, a Christian, a respectable citizen, *and* a ruthless and mean-spirited tyrant at the same time, one who, moreover, in some legitimate sense of the term can 'kill' his wife slowly by quelling her voice and vitality. When General Tilney sacrifices decency to avarice and banishes the now reluctant Gothic heroine into the night, he proves that 'human nature, at least in the midland countries of England' *can* in fact be looked for in 'Mrs. Radcliffe's works' and those of 'all her imitators' (2, 10). We are never informed of Henry Tilney's reflections on this occasion, and have no reason to suppose him cognizant of the need to revise his lecture to Catherine and to acknowledge the accuracy of her suspicions. But by the end of the novel, Catherine at least is capable of reaching this conclusion on her own: 'in suspecting General Tilney of either murdering or shutting up his wife, she had scarcely sinned against his character, or magnified his cruelty' (2, 15).

Given the political ambience of British fiction during the 1790s, it is not surprising that of all Austen's novels, *Northanger Abbey*, arguably her earliest, should be the most densely packed with topical details of a political character – enclosure, riots, hothouses, pamphlets, and even antitreason laws authorizing the activities of 'voluntary spies' (2, 9).[10] The political contemporaneity of *Northanger Abbey* does not stop with these allusions and with its critical treatment of paternal authority, but indeed extends to another, related theme: the status of promises. The obligation to abide by promises is an important moral rule in the history of political thought, especially since it underlies the contract theory of Locke as well as older natural law theories. At the end of the century, however, the very idea of promises had been radically criticized by Godwin as one of many possible kinds of socially mediating agencies of human decision and practice which cramp the judgment of the individual subject. Debates about the value and violability of promises figure prominently in turn-of-the-century fiction. In anti-Jacobin novels, pernicious or merely benighted characters philosophize as they break their words and betray their trusts left and right . . .

Since social stability depends in large part on keeping one's word, it is not surprising that Godwin's critique of promises and trusts proved upsetting to conservative readers. But for reform-minded novelists, keeping promises is more likely to promote cynical and sterile legalism than social cohesiveness. Stopping well this side of Godwin's radical critique of promises, they expose how the sanctity of promises is something for underlings always to observe and for perfidious overlords to omit whenever it suits their interests . . . In *Northanger Abbey* Austen dramatizes the implications of promise breaking and keeping as a function of the power of the characters concerned.

Breaking engagements and words of honor of all sorts is the predominant activity in *Northanger Abbey*. Instances may vary in intensity, but they all amount to the same thing: Isabella's 'engagement' to marry James Morland; Catherine's 'engagement' to walk with the Tilneys; Henry's 'promise' to wait and read *The Mysteries of Udolpho* with his sister; General Tilney's pompously worded assurance 'to make Northanger Abbey not wholly disagreeable' (2, 2) to Catherine, to name only a few. The issue of promise breaking, of course, predates the social criticism of the 1790s, and can thus illustrate the polarization that took place as the reaction wore on. Richardson's Grandison can criticize fashionable lying on generally accepted grounds, but in the 1790s, the topic is marked as radical. An eighteenth-century reader would have recognized as a breach of trust General Tilney's order to deny Catherine at the door when he and his daughter were really at home . . . It is no accident that manners in Bath seem as 'strange' to Catherine as the behavior in Gothic fiction, for in both nothing is predictable and no one can be depended upon, least of all the figures one has been taught to trust. When the deceived Catherine meditates on 'broken promises and broken arches; phaetons and false hangings, Tilneys and trap-doors' (1, 11), her associations betray a seepage of the Gothic into the quotidian that begins to localize her anxieties. Henry, as we have seen, discredits Gothic novels because he believes that English 'law' itself, as well as the pressure of 'social and literary intercourse' (2, 9), enforces decency. But in depicting a strange world of broken promises and betrayed trusts, Catherine's Gothic novels and *Northanger Abbey* alike denude familiar institutions and figures of their amiable facades in order to depict the menacing aspect they can show to the marginalized.

Henry Tilney explicitly raises the issue of promises, and his famous conceit jocularly likening marriage to a country dance is striking for the anxiety it persistently evinces about infidelity:

> We have entered into a contract of mutual agreeableness for the space of an evening, and all our agreeableness belongs solely to each other for that time. Nobody can fasten themselves on the notice of one, without injuring the rights of the other. I consider a country-dance as an emblem of marriage. Fidelity and complaisance are the principal duties of both; and those men who do not chuse to dance or marry themselves, have no business with the partners or wives of their neighbours . . . (1, 10)

Frederick Tilney's subsequent interference with the dancing, as well as marital plans, of Isabella Thorpe and James Morland engages the serious subjects Tilney flippantly raises here. Given the centrality of illicit sexuality to the fiction of the time, Henry's disquisition rings with special significance, especially since it is always attempting to forestall the threat of faithlessness. In comparison to that of her contemporaries, Austen's fiction is exceedingly discreet. Though she never excludes the illicit entirely, she displaces it onto the periphery of her plots. But from there it exercises considerable influence. Henry's speech is the closest Austen gets to commentary on the subject of fidelity until *Mansfield Park*, and even there the topic is integrated into the dramatic fabric of the plot, rather than isolated and discussed as an abstract issue, as it is here. To Catherine, of course, Henry's comparison is absurd, since an engagement to dance merely binds people 'for half an hour,' while '[p]eople that marry can never part' (1, 9). Catherine feels this difference acutely, and her failure to appreciate Henry's humor is another instance of the wisdom she unwittingly articulates throughout the novel. After all, the deceased Mrs. Tilney and her Gothic avatar, the 'injured and ill-fated nun' (2, 2) whose memorials Catherine expects to find at Northanger, both epitomize the lot of females immured in remote abbeys who would not have the power to leave even if they were not bound by indissoluble vows. To be sure, Austen is emphatically not recommending the passage of divorce laws, as had novelists such as Imlay, Godwin and Holcroft. But neither does she here or anywhere else in her fiction overlook the desolation experienced by those who have more than enough 'cause for wishing that [they] had bestowed themselves elsewhere' (1, 10).

Few characters in *Northanger Abbey* have kept promises as faithfully as Mrs. Tilney, not even Henry who, as we have seen, is not above imposing on Catherine's credulity for the sake of a joke. Henry finds the formulation 'faithful promise' ludicrous. The self-appointed monitor of Catherine's language, he rather atypically sputters at some length about its redundancy: 'Promised so faithfully! – A faithful promise! – That puzzles me. – I have heard of a faithful performance. But a faithful promise – the fidelity of promising!' (2, 9). Henry naturally disapproves of the phrase because in one very important matter at least he is so eminently faithful: at the end of the novel, Henry feels himself so 'bound as much in honour as in affection to Miss Morland,' that nothing the angry General does can 'shake his [Henry's] fidelity,' and nothing can justify the General's 'unworthy retraction of a tacit consent' (2, 14). A faithful subject in a civilized land, Henry, despite what the ingenuous Catherine considers his satirical turn, is too sanguine to acknowledge the aptness of the phrase in a world where almost all promises are not faithful. Isabella Thorpe, of course, is the most conspicuous promise breaker in the novel: 'Isabella had promised and promised again' (2, 10) to write, Catherine exclaims, as yet unaware that Isabella's promises – of friendship or love – routinely give way to interest. But Isabella's faithlessness is so foregrounded that it is possible to overlook how it functions to implicate promise breakers like the General and others who, because they possess power, breach trust with impunity. Conservative novels, such as *A Gossip's Story*, counterbalance the moral instability of selfish and flighty females with the sobriety and responsibility of firm father figures, and thus provide a benign rationale for paternal repression. But in *Northanger Abbey* these two tropic figures are mutually illuminating, for in every respect except the position of authority, General Tilney and Isabella Thorpe are similar characters who cause disorder because they never mean what they say.

Already thinking about dropping James Morland in favor of Frederick Tilney, Isabella remarks, 'What one means one day, you know, one may not mean the next. Circumstances change, opinions alter' (2, 3). The mutability Isabella describes does release people from some engagements. After Catherine is apprised of Isabella's duplicity, she admits, 'I cannot still love her' (2, 10), without appearing to realize how her behavior here exemplifies the pertinence of Isabella's earlier observation on the justness of dissolving certain promises. But Isabella's faithlessness, like the General's, results, not from a change of heart, but from a choice of policy favoring wealth. Just as Isabella chooses Frederick Tilney solely because he, as the General states, 'will perhaps inherit as considerable a landed property as any private man in the county' (2, 7), General Tilney courts Catherine solely because he believes her to be heiress to Mr. Allen's large estate. Thus the two figures who most belittle the advantages of wealth also, to Catherine's bewilderment, pursue it the most greedily and unscrupulously. In Isabella's case, of course, this means, as Eleanor Tilney puts it, 'violating an engagement voluntarily entered into with another man' (2, 10). In the General's case, this means, in effect, stealing Catherine from another man who had at the time 'pretty well resolved upon marrying Catherine himself' (2, 15).

The self-interest which prompts Isabella to deploy her charms in order to secure Captain Tilney is surely no more dishonorable than that which prompts the General 'to spare no pains in weakening [Thorpe's] boasted interest and ruining his dearest hopes' (2, 15). In very important respects it is less so, for the General's superior position obligates him to consider the care of dependents, let alone invited guests, more conscientiously. Unlike Captain Tilney, Catherine is an unsuspecting party to brute self-interest, and as a woman is wholly dependent upon the good will and guidance of superiors. As it turns out, however, Catherine's trust that the General 'could not propose any thing improper for her' (2, 5) is sorely misplaced. Having strong-armed Catherine into Northanger Abbey, 'courting [her] from the protection of real friends' (2, 13) and encouraging her sense of 'false security' (2, 13), he just as authoritatively thrusts her out, without any qualms about violated trust, and without 'allowing her even the appearance of choice' (2, 13). While the pledges made to dependents ought to be observed with, if anything, greater attention, General Tilney appears to believe that they do not matter and can therefore be flouted without inviting the embarrassments of social reproach which Henry believes, in Burkean fashion, restrain the insolent from abusiveness. Indifferent to the 'patriarchal hospitality' which a conservative novelist like West associated with men of his position, the General banishes Catherine from his house precisely *because* he considers her beneath the imperatives of common civility: 'to turn her from the house seemed the best, though to his feelings an inadequate proof of his resentment towards herself, and his contempt of her family' (2, 15). To depict the respectable country gentleman not as one who binds himself benevolently and responsibly to inferiors, but who on the contrary behaves as though his social superiority absolved him from responsibility to inferiors, is to cross over into the territory of radical novelists, whose fictions expose petty tyrants of General Tilney's ilk. Not until *Persuasion* would Austen again arraign a figure of his stature so decisively.

For Isabella, the matter stands quite differently. Merely mercenary herself, she is outmatched by Frederick Tilney. A permutation of the Gothic villain, he appears on the scene with no other purpose than to gratify his vanity of dominion by breaking a pre-existing engagement. Backing away from the depiction of the violation of vows within marriage, Austen nevertheless imputes to a representative of the ruling class – an oldest son, heir, and guardian of national security – an activity which conservative novelists impute to the minions of Robespierre. If Henry's earlier speech on marriage and country dances is a reliable guide, then Isabella does not bear sole responsibility for the jilting of James Morland. At that time Henry, annoyed by Thorpe's ostensible civilities to Catherine, argues, 'He has no business to withdraw the attention of my partner from me . . . our agreeableness belongs solely to each other, and nobody can fasten themselves on the notice of one, without injuring the rights of the other' (1, 10). Remembering this, Catherine questions Henry closely about his brother's brazen interference and until the end of the novel finds it impossible to believe that Captain Tilney would connive at breaking others' promises and knowingly injure 'the rights' of her brother. Whatever her own inattention, Isabella believes that Frederick Tilney is attached to her: 'he would take no denial' (1, 1), and in this novel refusing the denials of women is a very common activity, no matter how pleasing Isabella may have found it in the present case. Because Captain Tilney not only 'fastens' himself on her attention, but pledges an intention to marry where none exists – in Catherine's words he 'only made believe to do so for mischief's sake' (2, 12) – Isabella's breach of promise to Morland looks less self-willed. If she has acted only to secure her own interest, she in turn has been acted upon by Frederick only to destroy James's. Ever the defender of the status quo, Henry does not consider Frederick's trespasses to bespeak any remarkable fault. But when he imputes the whole affair to Isabella's heartlessness, the unconvinced Catherine replies with a scepticism that marks the beginning of her detachment from Tilney's judgment and her awareness of its partiality: 'It is very right that you should stand by your brother' (2, 12).

As garrulous and high-spirited as it is, *Northanger Abbey* is an alarming novel to the extent that it, in its own unassuming and matter-of-fact way, domesticates the Gothic and brings its apparent excesses into the drawing rooms of 'the midland countries of England' (2, 10). With the exception of Isabella, who is herself betrayed, the agents of betrayal are figures from whom Catherine has every right to expect just the opposite. James Morland, hardly a sage or exemplary figure, is not only an eldest son, but is also destined for the Church, as Austen repeats; and yet he considers promises of so little importance that he countenances and even participates in abusive attempts to compel his sister to break her engagements. More formidable personnages – General Tilney and his son – with insolent abandon flout agreements basic to civility. Depicting guardians of national, domestic, and even religious authority as socially destabilizing figures, *Northanger Abbey* has indeed appropriated the Gothic, in a distinctively progressive way. Catherine, unencumbered by the elaborate properties that tie the hands of Gothic heroines, is free to make blunt declarations and to ask embarrassing questions that expose the duplicity and the deficiency of those on whom innocence such as her own ought to rely. Whether she is thanking her brother for coming to Bath to visit her, asking Henry what Captain Tilney could mean by flirting with an engaged woman, or trying to reconcile the General's claims of liberality with his anticipated objections to Isabella's poverty, she is discovering – unwittingly perhaps, but with stunning accuracy – the betrayals of paternal figures and the discourse they wield. It is no accident, then, that Austen can back gracefully out of the impasse to which she brings Catherine at the end only by resorting to an authorially underscored *surplus* of the conventions she parodies. Alluding to the 'tell-tale compression of the pages before them' which can only signal that 'we are all hastening together to perfect felicity' (2, 16), and declining to describe Eleanor's new-found husband because 'the most charming young man in the world is instantly before the imagination of us all' (2, 16), Austen turns Radcliffean conclusions, which labor to undo disturbing and subversive implications, back on themselves: the General's 'cruelty,' we are assured, was actually 'rather conducive' (2, 16) to the felicity of Henry and Catherine, since it provided them with the occasion to get to know each other. But carrying over the practice of her juvenilia into her mature work, Austen draws attention to the artificiality, rather than the *vraisemblance*, of her conclusion, and implies in the process that the damage wrought by the likes of General Tilney is in fact not resolvable into the 'perfect felicity' of fiction, and that the convention of the happy ending conceals our all-too-legitimate cause for alarm.

A fitting sequel to the juvenilia, *Northanger Abbey* considers the authority of men and books, women's books in particular, and suggests how the latter can illuminate and even resist the former. Having been 'ashamed of liking Udolpho' (1, 14) herself, Catherine regards novels as a preeminently feminine genre which men are right to pooh-pooh as they do: 'gentlemen,' she explains, 'read better books' (1, 14). Henry pounces with a characteristically conclusory retort: 'The person, be it gentleman or lady, who has not pleasure in a good novel, must be intolerably stupid' (1, 14). Here, as elsewhere, Henry's position is more glib than acute, because Austen herself claims a value for fiction that goes well beyond the pleasure of suspense which Henry appears to think is the only thing Gothic novels have to offer: 'when I had once begun [*The Mysteries of Udolpho*], I could not lay down again' (1, 14). But *Northanger Abbey* is a dauntlessly self-affirming novel, which Austen undertakes to place alongside *Cecilia*, *Camilla*, and *Belinda* as likewise displaying 'the greatest powers of the mind' and 'the most thorough knowledge of human nature' (1, 5).

Of course *Northanger Abbey* stands beside *The Italian* and *The Mysteries of Udolpho* as well, since parodies are acknowledgments of respect, as well as acts of criticism. Austen's display of human nature in *Northanger Abbey* is necessarily coupled with Radcliffe's, and is executed by showing the justification for Gothic conventions, not by dismissing them. Continuously sensitizing us to the mediating properties of Gothic conventions, Austen provides the readers of her own as well as Radcliffe's novels with the distance necessary to see the dark and despotic side of the familiar and to experience it as 'strange' rather than as proper and inevitable. *Northanger Abbey* accomplishes its social criticism, then, not only by what it says, but also by how it says it, for Austen creates an audience not only able but also inclined to read their novels and their societies with critical detachment.

2

CHARLOTTE BRONTË, *JANE EYRE*

Mary Poovey's essay on the ambiguous role of the governess in nineteenth-century culture provides a crucial interpretative context for *Jane Eyre*. She argues that the figure who epitomized the Victorian domestic ideal was also the figure who threatened to destroy it, and she draws attention to the various ways in which the governess was seen as potentially threatening to middle-class family stability. If the governess was meant to provide an image of moral propriety within the home, she was also treated with suspicion as a sexually available single woman; and while she resembled the middle-class mother in the work she performed, she was like a working-class woman in terms of the wages she received. These ambiguities help to explain why the governess was often associated with social outcasts such as the lunatic and the fallen woman.

Robert B. Heilman's essay looks at the various uses of Gothic conventions in *Jane Eyre*. He draws attention to those instances when the Gothic is invoked but 'characteristically undercut': when Gothic images and motifs are treated with humour and irony, for instance. His argument, however, is that *Jane Eyre* does not so much dispense with Gothic traits as reinvent them. The novel finds new ways of putting Gothic devices to work, drawing resourcefully on the 'intensification of feeling' and the apprehension of 'extra-rational' force traditionally associated with Gothic writing. Heilman praises *Jane Eyre* for its radical revision of the Gothic mode and regards this as one of the distinguishing elements in Charlotte Brontë's novels.

In '*Jane Eyre*: A Critique of Imperialism', Gayatri Chakravorty Spivak argues that imperialism is a crucial part of cultural representation, in which literature plays a formidable role. In explaining how literary texts are informed by and help to articulate cultural values, she draws on a potent mix of theoretical approaches. Her insistence on reading texts as sites of struggle owes something to Michel Foucault's work on discourse and power, while her concern with the colonial politics of so-called 'canonical' texts is similar to that of Edward Said. The sharp, provocative line of argument, however, is distinctively her own, as is her relentless probing of the instabilities and contradictions in particular literary works. In the case of *Jane Eyre* she finds a certain unevenness or lack of consonance between the novel's incipient feminism and its relatively unenlightened view of racial difference. For Jane, a measure of progress and emancipation is afforded by her acceptance and legal entitlement within the nuclear family, but Bertha Mason remains an indeterminate figure, half animal, half human, outside the letter of the law. If *Jane Eyre* embraces nineteenth-century feminist individualism, it also carries within it 'the unquestioned idiom of imperialist presuppositions'.

Susan L. Meyer finds Spivak's reading of *Jane Eyre* problematic in its analysis of the workings of imperialist ideology and its relation to feminism. In 'Colonialism and the Figurative Strategy of *Jane Eyre*', she argues that the historical alliance between the ideology of male domination and the ideology of colonial domination is sensitively acknowledged in the novel. Although the novel suppresses the damning history of slavery and racist oppression, it nevertheless betrays a restless anxiety about colonialism and racial difference, and also shows a degree of self-consciousness about its own complicity in colonial politics. While Spivak points to the 'unquestioned' imperialist assumptions at work in *Jane Eyre*, Meyer draws attention to its deep disquietude.

Mary Poovey, The Anathematized Race: The Governess and *Jane Eyre* (1989)

The governess was a familiar figure to midcentury middle-class Victorians, just as she is now to readers of Victorian novels.[1] Even before Becky Sharp and Jane Eyre gave names to the psychological type of the governess, her 'plight' was the subject of numerous 1830s novels; by the 1840s, the governess had become a subject of concern to periodical essayists as well. In part, the attention the governess received in the 1840s was a response to the annual reports of the Governesses' Benevolent Institution, the charity founded in 1841 and reorganized in 1843.[2] But the activities of the GBI were also responses to a widespread perception that governesses were a problem of – and for – all members of the middle class. For many women, the problem was immediate and concrete; after all, as one editor of the *English Woman's Journal* remarked in 1858, every middle-class woman knows at least one governess, either because she has been taught by one or because she has 'some relative or cherished friend . . . actually engaged in teaching, or having formerly been so engaged.'[3] For most men, the governess represented a more abstract – but no less pressing – problem. As a competitor for work in an unregulated and increasingly overcrowded profession, the governess epitomized the toll capitalist market relations could exact from society's less fortunate members.

Modern historians do not generally dispute that governesses suffered increasing economic and social hardships after the 1830s. The bank failures of that decade combined with the discrepancy between the numbers of marriageable women and men and the late marriage age to drive more middle-class spinsters, widows, and daughters of respectable bankrupts into work outside the home. At the same time that the economic pressure to work increased, the range of activities considered socially acceptable for middle-class women decreased; whereas in the 1790s, middle-class women had worked as jailors, plumbers, butchers, farmers, seedsmen, tailors, and saddlers, by the 1840s and 1850s, dressmaking, millinery, and teaching far outstripped all other occupational activities.[4] Of these occupations, private teaching was widely considered the most genteel, largely because the governess's work was so similar to that of the female norm, the middle-class mother. The overcrowding these conditions produced within the teaching profession drove salaries down and competition for places up; at the same time, employers could and often did demand an increasingly wide range of services from would-be governesses, ranging from childcare for the very youngest children to instruction in French, music, and paper-flower-making for older daughters.

Despite these very real hardships, however, modern historians also point out that, given the relatively small number of women affected by the governess's woes, the attention this figure received in the 1840s and 1850s was disproportionate to the problem.[5] The 1851 Census lists 25,000 governesses, for example, but at the same time there were 750,000 female domestic servants, whose working conditions and wages were often more debilitating but markedly less lamented than the distress of the governess. In this chapter, I address some of the reasons why the governess received so much attention during these decades. I argue that the social stress the governess suffered aroused so much concern when it did at least partly because the economic and political turmoil of the 'hungry forties' drove members of the middle class to demand some barrier against the erosion of middle-class assumptions and values; because of the place they occupied in the middle-class ideology, women, and governesses in particular, were invoked as the bulwarks against this erosion.[6] The governess is also significant for my analysis of the ideological work of gender because of the proximity she bears to two of the most important Victorian representations of woman: the figure who epitomized the domestic ideal, and the figure who threatened to destroy it. Because the governess was like the middle-class mother in the work she performed, but like both a working-class woman and man in the wages she received, the very figure who theoretically should have defended the naturalness of separate spheres threatened to collapse the difference between them. Moreover, that discussions of the governesses' plight had dovetailed, by the mid-1850s, with feminist campaigns to improve both employment opportunities for women and women's education reveals the critical role representations of the governess played, not, as conservatives desired, in defending the domestic ideal, but in capitalizing on the contradiction it contained.

The periodical essayists of the 1840s justified the attention they devoted to the distressed governess by emphasizing the central role she played in reproducing the domestic ideal. As a teacher and example for young children, they argued, the governess was charged with inculcating domestic virtues and, especially in the case of young girls, with teaching the 'accomplishments' that would attract a good husband without allowing the sexual component of these accomplishments to get the upper hand. The governess was therefore expected to preside over the contradiction written into the domestic ideal – in the sense both that she was meant to police the emergence of undue assertiveness or sexuality in her maturing charges and that she was expected not to display willfulness or desires herself.[7] Theoretically, the governess's position neutralized whatever temptation she, as a young woman herself, might have presented to her male associates; to gentlemen she was a 'tabooed woman,' and to male servants she was as unapproachable as any other middle-class lady.[8]

If the governess was asked to stabilize the contradiction inherent in the middle-class domestic ideal by embodying and superintending morality, then she was also expected to fix another, related boundary: that between 'well-bred, well-educated and perfect gentlewomen,' on the one hand, and, on the other, the 'low-born, ignorant, and vulgar' women of the working class.[9] The assumption implicit in these conjunctions, as in the middle-class preference for governesses from their own class, was that only 'well-bred' women were morally reliable. In this reading of contemporary affairs, the unfortunate circumstances that bankrupted some middle-class fathers were critical to the reproduction of the domestic ideal, for only such disasters could yield suitable teachers for the next generation of middle-class wives.

One reason the governess was a figure of such concern to her middle-class contemporaries, then, was simply that she was a middle-class woman in a period when women were considered so critical to social stability. Especially in the 'hungry forties,' women became both the focus of working-class men's worries about competition for scarce jobs and the solution advanced by middle-class men for the social and political discontent hard times fostered. If only women would remain in the home, men of all classes argued, work would be available to men who needed it and both the family wage and morality would be restored. The assumptions implicit in this argument are those I have already discussed: that morality is bred and nurtured in the home as an effect of maternal instinct, and that if lower-class women were to emulate middle-class wives in their deference, thrift, and discipline, the homes of rich and poor alike would become what they ought to be – havens from the debilitating competition of the market.

A second reason the governess was singled out for special attention was that she did not seem to be fulfilling this critical social task. In fact, contemporaries openly worried that the governess was not the bulwark against immorality and class erosion but the conduit through which working-class habits would infiltrate the middle-class home. One source of this anxiety was the widespread belief that more tradesmen's daughters were entering the ranks of governess, therefore heralding the 'degradation of a body so important to the moral interest of the community.'[10] Against such 'degradation,' middle-class commentators proposed a range of defenses, including most of the solutions formulated to end the governesses' plight.[11] Whatever their practical value, all of the suggested remedies functioned to defend the class barrier that was also assumed to mark a moral division; even the Governesses' Benevolent Institution reinforced the distinction between ladies 'with character' and other women by providing the former with a separate residence and source of charity.[12]

A second source of the anxiety about governesses surfaces in discussions of the hardships of their situation. As these hardships were most vividly imagined, they were not primarily physical or economic but emotional; the threat they posed was to the governess's self-control and, even more ominously, to her sexual neutrality. This danger surfaces most explicitly in fictional representations of the governess, and I pursue it in a moment in relation to one of the period's most famous governess novels, Charlotte Brontë's *Jane Eyre*.[13] In periodical essays about the governess, allusions to her sexual susceptibility are more indirect, but precisely because of this indirection, they direct our attention to the governess's place in the complex system of associations in which the domestic ideal was also embedded. Two of the figures to which the governess was repeatedly linked begin to suggest why her sexlessness seemed so important – and so unreliable – to her contemporaries. These figures are the lunatic and the fallen woman.

The connection contemporaries made between the governess and the lunatic was, in the first instance, causal. According to both the author of the 1844 'Hints on the Modern Governess System' and Lady Eastlake's 1847 review of the GBI's annual report, governesses accounted for the single largest category of women in lunatic asylums.[14] Lady Eastlake attributes this unfortunate fact to the 'wounded vanity' a governess suffers, but the author of 'Hints' connects this 'wound' more specifically to sexual repression. Citing 'an ordinary case,' this author describes a young girl trained for her governess position in 'one of those schools which are usually mere gymnasia for accomplishments and elegant manners.' There her 'animal spirits' are indulged, and her youthful 'elasticity' becomes a 'craving for pleasures.' Once she leaves the school, however, and takes up her governessing work, this 'craving' is subject to the frustration and denial her position demands.

> She must live daily amidst the trials of a home without its blessings; she must bear about on her heart the sins she witnesses and the responsibilities that crush her; without any consent of her will, she is made the *confidante* of many family secrets; she must live in a familial circle as if her eyes did not perceive the tokens of bitterness; she must appear not to hear sharp sayings and *mal-a-propos* speeches; kindly words of courtesy must be always on her lips; she must be ever on her guard; let her relax her self-restraint for one moment, and who shall say what mischief and misery might ensue to all from one heedless expression of hers?[15]

If the allusion to some mischievous 'expression' hints at the governess's latent feelings, this author will not elaborate the nature of these feelings; instead, the writer turns to the 'nervous irritability, dejection, [and] loss of energy' that result from repressing them (*FM* 575). The 'twisted coil of passion and levity,' the author concludes, 'may be moved into sobriety by the help of forbearance and long-suffering,' but too often the very girls who have sprung up 'like plants in a hot-house,' fade before their 'bloom' is gone. 'It is no exaggeration to say that hundreds snap yearly from the stalk, or prolong a withered, sickly life, till they, too, sink, and are carried out to die miserably in the by-ways of the world' (*FM* 575, 574).

The image of the short-lived or barren plant elaborates the causal connection between the governess and the lunatic by metaphorically tying both to a vitality stunted, silenced, driven mad by denial and restraint. This vitality may not be explicitly represented as sexuality here, but its sexual content *is* present in the images to which this last phrase alludes. The representation of the governess 'carried out to die miserably in the by-ways of the world' metonymically links the governess to the victim of another kind of work that was also represented as 'white slavery' at midcentury – the distressed needlewoman 'forced to take to the streets.'[16] The association between the two figures is further reinforced by the fact that the governess and the needlewoman were two of the three figures that symbolized working women for the early and mid-Victorian public; the third was the factory girl.[17] Significantly, both of the working-class members of this trio were specifically linked by middle-class male commentators to the danger of unregulated female sexuality. Henry Mayhew's determination to expose (and, by extension, control) the 'prostitution' he identified among needlewomen in 1849 expresses the same concern to curtail female promiscuity that Lord Ashley voiced in the 1844 parliamentary debate about factory conditions.[18] For both Mayhew and Lord Ashley, the relevant issue was any extramarital sexuality, not just sex for hire; Mayhew's interviews make it clear that for him any woman who lived or had sexual relations with a man outside of marriage was a prostitute.

That representations of the governess in the 1840s brought to her contemporaries' minds not just the middle-class ideal she was meant to reproduce, but the sexualized and often working-class women against whom she was expected to defend, reveals the mid-Victorian fear that the governess could not protect middle-class values because she could not be trusted to regulate her own sexuality. The lunatic's sexuality might have been rhetorically contained by the kind of medical categories I have already discussed, after all, but the prostitute's sexual aggression was undisguised; to introduce either such sexuality or such aggression into the middle-class home would have been tantamount to fomenting revolution, especially in a period in which both were imaginatively linked to the discontent expressed by disgruntled members of the working class and by the 'strong-minded women' who were just beginning to demand reform. The conjunction of economic, moral, and political anxieties that could be mobilized by the image of an army of aggressive, impoverished governesses emerges in the warning advanced by the author of 'Hints': if someone does not remedy the current injustices, this writer worries, 'the miseries of the governess may even swell that sickening clamour about the "rights of women" which would never have been raised had women been true to themselves' (*FM* 573).

This author's wishful plea that women be 'true to themselves' explicitly enjoins middle-class employers and employees to unite in defense of the domestic ideal that the governesses' distress threatens to disturb. Implicitly, however, the plea for women to unite has more subversive implications because it calls attention to the fact that middle-class women have something in common, which is epitomized in the governesses' plight. This more controversial reading of the governesses' situation was made explicit in 1847 by Elizabeth Rigby, later Lady Eastlake, in her review of *Vanity Fair*, *Jane Eyre*, and the 1847 report of the Governesses' Benevolent Institution. Like many other essayists, Lady Eastlake's express concern was the fate of governesses who could no longer find work, for, as she phrases it, their situation more 'painfully expresses the peculiar tyranny of our present state of civilization' than any other social ill.[19] The governess was so affecting to Lady Eastlake, as to many male commentators, because she epitomized the helplessness unfortunate individuals experienced, not just from ordinary poverty but from the volatile fluctuations of the modern, industrializing economy; the toll these fluctuations exacted had become starkly visible in the depression of the 1840s, and contemporaries feared such hardship lay behind working-class discontent. But to Lady Eastlake, the governess was a special kind of victim, for, unlike lower-class men, she was born to neither discomfort nor labor. 'The case of the governess,' she explains, 'is so much the harder than that of any other class of the community, in that they are not only quite as liable to all the vicissitudes of life, but are absolutely supplied by them.' What was distressing to Lady Eastlake in this fact was that the governess's plight could be any middle-class woman's fate. Lady Eastlake recognized, however reluctantly, that the governess revealed the price of all middle-class women's dependence on men: 'Take a lady, in every meaning of the word, born and bred, and let her father pass through the gazette, and she wants nothing more to suit our highest *beau ideal* of a guide and instructress to our children. We need the imprudencies, extravagancies, mistakes, or crimes of a certain number of fathers, to sow that seed from which we reap the harvest of governesses' (*QR* 176).

Such a recognition could have led Lady Eastlake to identify fully with the 'lady' whose imprudent, extravagant, or criminal father has squandered her security; it could have led her, as it did women like Barbara Bodichon, to urge women to unite against the dependence that tied them to their fathers' luck and business sense. Instead, however, Lady Eastlake explicitly rejects such a conclusion; she defends against her identification with the governess by simply asserting the necessity of women's dependence, which she bases on the natural difference between men's work and the 'precious' work of women. 'Workmen may rebel,' Lady Eastlake writes, 'and tradesmen may combine, not to let you have their labour or their wares under a certain rate; but the governess has no refuge – no escape; she is a needy *lady*, whose services are of too precious a kind to have any stated market value, and is therefore left to the mercy, or what they call the *means*, of the family that engages her' (*QR* 179).

In the law that places the governess's 'precious' work above market value but beneath a fair wage, Lady Eastlake sees that moral superintendence is simultaneously devalued and exploited. Still, she insists that things must be this way: after all, the difference between work whose value can be judged and work that is too 'precious' to be subjected to market evaluation is what saves ladies from being like men. But if the difference between working men and leisured ladies is obvious to Lady Eastlake, the definition of ladies becomes problematic when one must establish some difference *among* them. The problem, as she formulates it, is that the difference among ladies is difficult to see because it is not based on some natural distinction. The difference among ladies, she complains,

> is not one which will take care of itself, as in the case of a servant. If she [the governess] sits at table she does not shock you – if she opens her mouth she does not distress you – her appearance and manners are likely to be as good as your own – her education rather better; there is nothing upon the face of the thing to stamp her as having been called to a different state of life from that in which it has pleased God to place you; and therefore the distinction has to be kept up by a fictitious

> barrier which presses with cruel weight upon the mental strength or constitutional vanity of a woman. (*QR* 177)

Because neither sex nor class 'stamp[s]' the governess as different from the lady who employs her, Lady Eastlake is once more drawn toward identifying with her. Yet even though she realizes the barrier between them is 'fictitious' and 'cruel,' Lady Eastlake will not lower it for a moment. Instead, she turns away again, this time decisively, by appealing to another kind of nature – 'the inherent constitution of English habits, feelings, and prejudices': 'We shall ever prefer to place those immediately about our children who have been born and bred with somewhat of the same refinement as ourselves. We must ever keep them in a sort of isolation, for it is the only means for maintaining that distance which the reserve of English manners and the decorum of English families exact' (*QR* 178).

Lady Eastlake's appeal to 'the inherent constitution' of the English is meant to resolve the paradox whereby two persons who are by class and sex the same must be treated differently. Her invocation of national character therefore extends the work we have already seen this concept perform. Like the discussions of Dickens I have already examined, Lady Eastlake's appeal to the unassailable authority of national character generalizes middle-class 'reserve' and 'decorum' to all 'English families.' Beyond this, however, it also rationalizes a difference among members of the middle class that is otherwise unaccountable: the difference of circumstances or luck.

Lady Eastlake's discussion of governesses follows her reviews of two recently published governess novels, *Vanity Fair* and *Jane Eyre*.[20] The substance of these reviews highlights both the conservatism and the potential subversiveness of Eastlake's position. In general, Lady Eastlake approves of Thackeray's novel, despite the immorality of Becky Sharp, but she declares the heroine of *Jane Eyre* to be 'vulgar-minded,' a woman 'whom we should not care for as an acquaintance, whom we should not seek as a friend, whom we should not desire for a relation, and whom we should scrupulously avoid for a governess' (*QR* 176, 174). Eastlake formulates her objections in religious language, but she focuses specifically on the threat this heroine poses to the barrier she will soon admit is 'fictitious' – the barrier between one wellborn (if penniless) lady and another. 'It is true Jane does right,' Lady Eastlake begrudgingly admits, in discussing Jane's decision to leave Rochester,

> and [she] exerts great moral strength, but it is the strength of a mere heathen mind which is a law unto itself . . . Jane Eyre is proud, and therefore she is ungrateful too. It pleased God to make her an orphan, friendless, and penniless – yet she thanks nobody, and least of all Him,

> for the food and raiment, the friends, companions, and instructors of her helpless youth . . . The doctrine of humility is not more foreign to her mind than it is repudiated by her heart. It is by her own talents, virtues, and courage that she is made to attain the summit of human happiness, and, as far as Jane Eyre's own statement is concerned, no one would think that she owed anything either to God above or to man below. (*QR* 173)

As Lady Eastlake continues, her religious argument explicitly becomes a warning against the political upheavals threatened by working-class discontent. What has happened here is that the difference of circumstance that Lady Eastlake acknowledges to be a matter of chance has become a matter of class, which is a difference she assumes to be authoritative because it is appointed by God. 'Altogether the auto-biography of Jane Eyre is pre-eminently an anti-Christian composition,' she asserts.

> There is throughout it a murmuring against the comforts of the rich and against the privations of the poor, which, as far as each individual is concerned, is a murmuring against God's appointment . . . There is a proud and perpetual assertion of the rights of man . . . a pervading tone of ungodly discontent which is at once the most prominent and the most subtle evil which the law and the pulpit, which all civilized society in fact has at the present day to contend with. We do not hesitate to say that the tone of mind and thought which has overthrown authority and violated every code human and divine abroad, and fostered Chartism and rebellion at home, is the same which has also written Jane Eyre. (*QR* 173–74).

If this objection targets the class issues contemporaries associated with the governess, then Lady Eastlake's other complaint about *Jane Eyre* centers on the second anxiety this figure aroused. The protagonist's 'language and manners . . . offend you in every particular,' she asserts, especially when Rochester 'pours into [Jane's] ears disgraceful tales of his past life, connected with the birth of little Adele,' and the governess 'listens as if it were nothing new, and certainly nothing distasteful' (*QR* 167, 164). What offends Lady Eastlake here is the 'perpetual disparity between the account [Jane Eyre] herself gives of the effect she produces, and the means shown us by which she brings that about' – the gap between Jane's professed innocence and the sexual knowledge the author insinuates in the language and action of the novel. What this implies is that the author of the novel knows more about sexual matters than the character admits and that the novel is 'vulgar' because it makes the hypocrisy of women's professed innocence legible.

Despite Lady Eastlake's strenuous complaint about *Jane Eyre*'s 'gross vulgarity' – or, rather, precisely because of this complaint – she draws out the similarities rather than the differences between herself and the author of the novel. If Lady Eastlake sees sexuality in Jane's 'restlessness,' after all, there is little to distinguish her from the writer who created this sexuality in the first place. Just as Lady Eastlake inadvertently exposes her likeness to the governess, then, so she betrays her resemblance to the author she disdains. If we turn for a moment to Brontë's novel, we can begin to identify some of the implications of this similarity and some of the reasons discussions of the governesses' plight sparked other controversies that eventually challenged the domestic ideal.

Jane Eyre may be neither a lunatic nor a fallen woman, but when she refuses Rochester's proposal in chapter 27 that she become his mistress, her language specifically calls to mind the figures to whom the governess was so frequently linked by her contemporaries. Despite her passion, Jane says, she is not 'mad,' like a lunatic; her principles are 'worth' more than the pleasure that becoming Rochester's mistress would yield.[21] The two women metaphorically invoked here are also dramatized literally in the two characters that precede Jane Eyre as Rochester's lovers – the lunatic Bertha and the mistress Céline Varens. But if the juxtaposition of these characters calls attention to the problematic sexuality that connects them, the way Brontë works through Jane's position as governess seems to sever the links among them. Read one way, Brontë's novel repeats such conservative resolutions of the governesses' plight as Lady Eastlake's, for Jane's departure from Rochester's house dismisses the sexual and class instabilities the governess introduces, in a way that makes Jane the guardian of sexual and class order rather than its weakest point. When considered in terms of the entire novel, however, Brontë's treatment of the governess problem does not seem so conservative. In introducing the possibility that women may be fundamentally alike, Brontë raises in a more systematically critical way the subversive suggestions adumbrated by Lady Eastlake.

The issues of sexual susceptibility and social incongruity that contemporaries associated with the governess are inextricably bound up with each other in Jane's situation at Thornfield Hall: Jane is vulnerable to Rochester's advances because, as his employee, she lacks both social peers and the means to defend herself against her attractive, aggressive employer. But Brontë symbolically neutralizes both of these problems by revising the origin, the terms, and the conditions of Jane's employment. While Jane seeks employment because she has no one to support her, Brontë makes it clear that, in this case, the social incongruity that others might attribute to her position as governess precedes Jane's taking up this work. It is, in part, a family matter; Jane is 'less than a servant,' as her cousin John Reed sneers, because she is an orphan and a dependent ward (ch. 2). In part, Jane's 'heterogeneity' comes from her personality; she is called 'a discord' and 'a noxious thing,' and she thinks that her temperament makes her deserve these names (ch. 2).

The effect of making Jane's dependence a function of family and personality is to individualize her problems so as to detach them from her position as governess. Brontë further downplays the importance of Jane's position by idealizing her work. Not only is there no mother to satisfy at Thornfield and initially no company from which Jane is excluded, but Adele is a tractable, if untaught, child, and Jane's actual duties are barely characterized at all. Beside the physical and psychological deprivations so extensively detailed in the Lowood section of the novel, in fact, what Jane terms her 'new servitude' seems luxurious; the only hardship she suffers as a governess is an unsatisfied craving for something she cannot name – something that is represented as romantic love.

When Rochester finally appears at Thornfield, Brontë completes what seems to be a dismissal of Jane's employment by subsuming the economic necessity that drove Jane to work into the narrative of an elaborate courtship. Rochester's temperamental 'peculiarities,' for which Mrs. Fairfax has prepared us, lead him to forget Jane's salary at one point, to double, then halve it, at another. By the time Blanche Ingram and her companions ridicule the 'anathematized race' of governesses in front of Jane, Brontë has already elevated her heroine above this 'race' by subordinating her poverty to her personality and to the place it has earned her in Rochester's affections. 'Your station,' Rochester exclaims, 'is in my heart.' The individualistic and psychological vocabulary Rochester uses here pervades Brontë's characterization of their relationship: 'You are my sympathy,' Rochester cries to Jane at one point (ch. 27); 'I have something in my brain and heart,' Jane tells the reader, 'that assimilates me mentally to him' (ch. 17).

When Rochester proposes marriage to Jane, the problems of sexual susceptibility and class incongruity that intersect in the governess's role ought theoretically to be solved. In this context, Mrs. Fairfax's warning that 'gentlemen in [Rochester's] station are not accustomed to marry their governesses' (ch. 24), Blanche Ingram's admonitory example of the governess dismissed for falling in love and Jane's insistence that she still be treated as a 'plain, Quakerish governess' (ch. 24) all underscore the alternative logic behind Jane's situation – a logic that eroticizes economics so that class and financial difficulties are overcome by the irresistible (and inexplicable) 'sympathy' of romantic love. But the very issues that foregrounding personality and love should lay to rest come back to haunt the novel in the most fully psychologized episodes of *Jane Eyre*: Jane's dreams of children.[22]

According to Jane's exposition in chapter 21, emotional affinity, or 'sympathy,' is a sign of a mysterious but undeniable kinship: 'the unity of the source to which each traces his origin'. But Jane's discussion of sympathy here focuses not on the bond of kinship, which she claims to be explaining, but on some *disturbance* within a family relationship. Specifically, Jane is recalling her old nursemaid Bessie telling her that 'to dream of children was a sure sign of trouble, either to oneself or to one's kin' (ch. 21). Jane then reveals that Bessie's superstition has come back to her because every night for a week she has dreamed of an infant, 'which I sometimes hushed in my arms, sometimes dandled on my knee, sometimes watched playing with daisies on a lawn . . . It was a wailing child this night, and a laughing one the next: now it nestled close to me, and now it ran from me' (ch. 21). This revelation is immediately followed by Jane's discovering that the obvious 'trouble' presaged by her dream is at her childhood home, Gateshead: John has gambled the Reed family into debt and is now dead, probably by his own hand, and Mrs. Reed, broken in spirit and health, lies near death asking for Jane.

The implications of this 'trouble' surface when this reference is read against the other episodes adjacent to the dream. Jane's journey to Gateshead follows two scenes in which Rochester wantonly taunts Jane with his power: in chapter 20 he teases her that he will marry Blanche Ingram, and in chapter 21 he refuses to pay her her wages, thereby underscoring her emotional and financial dependence. Once at Gateshead, Jane discovers that Mrs. Reed has also been dreaming of a child – of Jane Eyre, in fact, that 'mad,' 'fiend'-like child who was so much 'trouble' that Mrs. Reed has withheld for three years the knowledge that Jane has other kin and that her uncle, John Eyre, wants to support her (ch. 21). Mrs. Reed's malice has thereby prolonged Jane's economic dependence while depriving her of the kinship for which she has yearned. Jane explicitly denies feeling any 'vengeance . . . rage . . . [or] aversion' toward Mrs. Reed, but her very denial calls attention to the rage she expressed when she was similarly helpless at Lowood. Foregrounding the structural similarities among the scenes conveys the impression that John Reed's suicide and the stroke that soon kills Mrs. Reed are displaced expressions of Jane's anger at them for the dependence and humiliation they have inflicted on her. These symbolic murders, which the character denies, can also be seen as displacements of the rage at the other figure who now stands in the same relation of superiority to Jane as the Reeds once did: Rochester. That both the character and the plot of the novel deny this anger, however, leads us to the other 'trouble' adjacent to this dream of a child: Bertha's attack on her brother, Richard Mason.

As soon as Mason enters the narrative, he is rhetorically linked to Rochester: he appears when and where Rochester was expected to appear, and in her description of him Jane compares him explicitly to Rochester (ch. 28). Like the sequence I have just examined, Mason's arrival punctuates a series of painful reminders of Jane's dependence and marginality; he interrupts the engagement party (when Jane, obsessed with watching Rochester and Blanche, specifically denies that she is jealous, and his arrival is immediately followed by the gypsy scene, in which Rochester so completely invades Jane's thoughts that she wonders 'what unseen spirit' has taken up residence in her heart (ch. 19). When the gypsy reveals that s/he is Rochester, Jane voices more rage toward her 'master' than at any other time: 'It is scarcely fair, sir,' Jane says; 'it was not right' (ch. 19). Jane's hurt is soon repaid, however, even if what happens is not acknowledged as revenge. Jane suddenly, and with a marked carelessness, remembers Mason's presence. The effect on Rochester is dramatic. Leaning on Jane as he once did before (and will do again), Rochester 'staggers' and exclaims, 'Jane, I've got a blow – I've got a blow, Jane!' (ch. 19). The 'blow' Jane's announcement delivers is then graphically acted out when Bertha, who is Jane's surrogate by virtue of her relation to Rochester, attacks Mason, whose textual connection to Rochester has already been established. As before, anger and violence are transferred from one set of characters to another, revenge is displaced from Jane's character, and agency is dispersed into the text.

The text – not as agent but as effect – turns out to be precisely what is at stake in these series, for in each of them Rochester's most serious transgression has been to usurp Jane's control over what is, after all, primarily her story. In the gypsy scene he has told her what she feels, in words as 'familiar . . . as the speech of my own tongue' (ch. 19), and in the scene immediately following Bertha's assault on Mason, he has usurped her authority even more, first commanding her not to speak (ch. 20), then asking her to imagine herself 'no longer a girl . . . but a wild boy' – to imagine she is Rochester, in other words, while he tells *his* story to her as if she were telling her own story to herself (ch. 20). The precarious independence Jane earned by leaving Gateshead has been figured in the ability to tell (if not direct) her own story; thus, the measure of autonomy gained by translating Jane's economic dependence into a story of love is undercut by Rochester's imperious demand that she listen to him tell his story and hers, that she be dependent – seen and not heard, as women (particularly governesses) should be.

Jane's second reference to dreaming of children extends and elaborates his pattern of enforced dependence and indirect revenge. Once more, Jane's narration of the dream is temporally displaced from the moment of her dreaming. When she does disclose to Rochester and the reader what frightened her, Jane also reveals that when Bertha awakened her, Jane had twice been dreaming of a child. In the first dream, 'some barrier' divided her and Rochester. 'I was following the windings of an unknown road,' Jane explains; 'total obscurity environed me; rain pelted me; I was burdened with the charge of a little child . . . My movements were fettered, and my voice still died away inarticulate; while you, I felt, withdrew farther and farther every moment' (ch. 25). In the next dream, of Thornfield Hall in ruins, the child still encumbers Jane. 'Wrapped up in a shawl,' she says,

> I still carried the unknown little child: I might not lay it down anywhere, however tired were my arms – however much its weight impeded my progress, I must retain it. I heard the gallop of a horse . . . I was sure it was you; and you were departing for many years, and for a distant country. I climbed the thin wall with frantic, perilous haste . . . The stones rolled from under my feet, the ivy branches I grasped gave way, the child clung round my neck in terror, and almost strangled me . . . I saw you like a speck on a white track, lessening every moment . . . The wall crumbled; I was shaken; the child rolled from my knee, I lost my balance, fell, and woke. (ch. 25)

To this 'preface' Jane then appends the story of the 'trouble' that followed: Bertha's rending Jane's wedding veil. This is immediately followed by the much more devastating 'trouble' of Mason's denunciation in the church, Rochester's revelation that he is already married, and the obliteration of Jane's hopes to formalize her 'kinship' with Rochester.

Alone in her bedroom, Jane surveys her ruined love – which she likens to 'a suffering child in a cold cradle'; once more she denies that she is angry at Rochester ('I would not ascribe vice to him; I would not say he had betrayed me,' ch. 26), but even more explicitly than before, the plot suggests that the person who has hurt Jane is now indirectly suffering the effects of the rage that follows from such hurt: Jane's letter to John Eyre, after all, led her uncle to expose to Mason her planned marriage, and Jane's desire for some independence from Rochester led her to write her uncle in the first place. In this instance, of course, Jane initially suffers as much as – if not more than – Rochester does: not only is she subjected to the humiliating offer of his adulterous love, but she also forces herself to leave Thornfield and she almost dies as a consequence. Jane's suffering, however, turns out to be only the first stage in her gradual recovery of kinship, independence, money, and enough mastery to write both her story and Rochester's. By contrast, Rochester is further reduced by the novel's subsequent action; when he is blinded and maimed in the fire Bertha sets, the pattern of displaced anger is complete again.[23]

Why does dreaming of children signify 'trouble' in these sequences, and why does the trouble take this form? When Jane dreams of children, some disaster follows that is a displaced expression of the anger against kin that the character denies. In the sense that narrative effect is split off from psychological cause, *Jane Eyre* becomes at these moments what we might call a hysterical text, in which the body of the text symptomatically acts out what cannot make its way into the psychologically realistic narrative. Because there was no permissible plot in the nineteenth century for a woman's anger, whenever Brontë explores this form of self-assertion the text splinters hysterically, provoked by and provoking images of dependence and frustration.

Dreaming of children, then, is metanymically linked to a rage that remains implicit at the level of character but materializes at the level of plot. And *this* signifies 'trouble' both because the children that appear in these dreams metaphorically represent the dependence that defined women's place in bourgeois ideology (and that was epitomized in the governess) *and* because the disjunction that characterizes these narrative episodes shows that hysteria is produced as the condition in which a lady's impermissible emotions are expressed. What Jane's dreams of children reveal, then, in their content, their placement, and their form, is that the helplessness enforced by the governess's dependent position – along with the frustration, self-denial, and maddened, thwarted rage that accompanies it – marks every middle-class woman's life because she is not allowed to express (or possess) the emotions that her dependence provokes. The structural paradigm underlying the governess's sexual vulnerability and her social incongruity – her lunacy and her class ambiguity – is dependence, and this is the position all middle-class women share.

From one perspective, Brontë neutralizes the effects of this revelation and downplays its subversive implications. By making Jane leave Thornfield, Brontë seems to reformulate her dilemma, making it once more an individual, moral, emotional problem and not a function of social position or occupation. As soon as Jane stops being a governess, she is 'free' to earn her happiness according to the paradoxical terms of the domestic ideal: even the skeptical Lady Eastlake conceded that the self-denial Jane expresses in renouncing Rochester's love and nearly starving on the heath gives her a right to earthly happiness. When Jane discovers she has both money and kin, then, the dependence epitomized by the governess's position seems no longer to be an issue – a point made clear by the end to which Jane puts her newfound wealth: she liberates Diana and Mary from having to be governesses and so frees them to a woman's 'natural' fate – marriage.

From another perspective, however, Brontë's 'resolution' of the governess's dilemma can be seen to underscore – not dismiss – the problem of women's dependence. That only the coincidence of a rich uncle's death can confer on a single woman autonomy and power, after all, suggests just how intractable her dependence really was in the 1840s. Brontë also calls attention to the pervasiveness of this dependence in the very episode in which Jane ceases to be a governess, the episode at Whitcross. As soon as Jane is not a governess, her irreducable likeness to other women returns with stark clarity – and in the very form that relieving Jane of her economic dependence should theoretically have displaced: the sexual vulnerability and class uncertainty epitomized in the lunatic and the fallen woman. 'Absolutely destitute,' 'objectless and lost,' Jane is mistaken for an 'eccentric sort of lady,' a thief, and a figure too 'sinister' to be named: 'you are not what you ought to be,' sneers the Rivers' wary servant (ch. 28).

The return of these other women at the very moment at which Jane is least of all a governess functions to reinscribe the similarity between the governess and these sexualized women. At the same time, it lets us glimpse both why it was so important for contemporaries like Lady Eastlake to insist that the governess was different from other women and why it was so difficult to defend this assertion. For the fact that the associations return even though Jane is *not* a governess suggests the instability of the boundary that all the nonfiction accounts of the governess simultaneously took for granted and fiercely upheld: the boundary between such aberrant women as lunatic, prostitute, and governess and the 'normal' woman – the woman who is a wife and mother . . .

Brontë's novel reveals that the figure from whom the mother had to be distinguished was not just the lower-class prostitute but the middle-class governess as well, for the governess was both what a woman who should be a mother might actually become and the woman who had to be paid for doing what the mother should want to do for free. If the fallen woman was the middle-class mother's opposite, the middle-class governess was her next-of-kin, the figure who ought to ensure that a boundary existed between classes of women but who could not, precisely because her sexuality made her like the women from whom she ought to differ.[24]

This is the ideological economy whose instabilities Brontë exposes when she 'resolves' the problem of the governess by having Jane marry Rochester. Jane's marriage imperils this symbolic economy in two ways. In the first place, despite her explicit disavowal of kinship, Jane has effectively been inscribed in a series that includes not just a lunatic and a mistress, but also a veritable united nations of women. In telling Jane about these other lovers, Rochester's design is to insist on difference, to draw an absolute distinction between some kinds of women, who cannot be legitimate wives, and Jane, who can. This distinction is reinforced by both racism and nationalist prejudice: that Bertha is West Indian 'explains' her madness, just as Céline's French birth 'accounts for' her moral laxity. But Jane immediately sees that if she assents to Rochester's proposal, she will become simply 'the successor of these poor girls' (ch. 27). She sees, in other words, the likeness that Rochester denies: *any* woman who is not a wife is automatically like a governess in being dependent, like a fallen woman in being 'kept.'

Emphasizing the likeness among women is subversive not merely because doing so highlights all women's dependence – although this is, of course, part of the point. Beyond this, the fact that the likeness Brontë stresses is not women's selflessness or self-control but some internal difference suggests that the contradiction repressed by the domestic ideal is precisely what makes a woman womanly. This internal difference is figured variously as madness and as sexuality. Jane's own descriptions of herself show her growing from the 'insanity' of childhood rebellion to the 'restlessness' of unspecified desire: 'I desired more,' she says, ' . . . than I possessed' (ch. 12). In the passage in chapter 12 in which Jane describes this 'restlessness,' she compares it specifically to the 'ferment' that feeds 'political rebellions' and she opposes it explicitly to the self-denial that caring for children requires. This passage returns us once more to Jane's dreams of children, for the manifest content of the majority of those dreams reveals how carrying a child burdens the dreamer, impeding her efforts to reach her lover or voice her frustrated love. 'Anybody may blame me who likes,' Jane says of the 'cool language' with which she describes her feelings for Adele, but caring for the child is not enough; 'I believed in the existence of other and more vivid kinds of goodness, and what I believed in I wished to behold' (ch. 12). Even when Jane has her own child at the end of the novel, her only reference to him subordinates maternal love to the sexual passion that Rochester's eyes have consistently represented.[25]

Positioning Jane within a series of women and characterizing her as 'restless' and passionate transform the difference among women . . . into a difference within all women – the 'difference' of sexual desire. This similarity thus subverts the putative difference between the governess and the lunatic or mistress, just as it obliterates the difference between the governess and the wife. Having Jane marry Rochester – transforming the governess into a wife – extends the series of aberrant women to include the figure who ought to be exempt from this series, who ought to be the norm. The point is that, as the boundary between these two groups of women, the governess belongs to both sides of the opposition: in her, the very possibility of an opposition collapses.

The second sense in which Jane's marriage is subversive follows directly from this relocation of difference. If all women are alike in being 'restless,' then they are also like – not different from – men. Charlotte Brontë makes this point explicitly in chapter 12, in the passage I have been quoting. 'Women are supposed to be very calm generally,' Jane notes, 'but women feel just as men feel; they need exercise for their faculties, and a field for their efforts as much as their brothers do; they suffer from too rigid a restraint, too absolute a stagnation, precisely as men would suffer; and it is . . . thoughtless to condemn them, or laugh at them, if they seek to do more or learn more than custom has pronounced necessary for their sex' (ch. 12). The implications of this statement may not be drawn out consistently in this novel, but merely to assert that the most salient difference was located within every individual and not between men and women was to raise the possibilities that women's dependence was customary, not natural, that their sphere was kept separate only by artificial means, and that women, like men, could grow through work outside the home. Even though Jane marries Rochester, then, she does so as an expression of her desire, not as the self-sacrifice St. John advocates; the image with which she represents her marriage fuses man and woman instead of respecting their separate bodies, much less their separate spheres. 'Ever more absolutely bone of his bone and flesh of his flesh,' Jane represents herself as taking the law of coverture to its logical extreme.

What Lady Eastlake objected to in *Jane Eyre* is exactly this subversive tendency. But despite her objection, Eastlake's intermittent – and irrepressible – recognition that the governess's plight is, theoretically at least, that of every middle-class woman repeats Brontë's subversive move. Moreover, Eastlake's charge that the 'crimes of fathers' sow the crop of governesses figures men as the villains behind women's dependence even more specifically than Brontë was willing to do.[26] This charge – that men are responsible for the fetters women wear – also appears in the bitter myth recounted in 'Hints on the Modern Governess System.' ''Twas a stroke of policy in those rantypole barons of old,' the author writes, 'to make their lady-loves idols, and curb their wives with silken idleness. Woman was raised on a pinnacle to keep her in safety. Our chivalrous northern knights had a religious horror of the Paynim harems. They never heard of Chinese shoes in those days, so they devised a new chain for the weaker sex. They made feminine labour disgraceful' (*FM* 576). The implicit accusation here is that women had to be idolized and immobilized for some men to think them safe from other men's rapacious sexual desire and from their own susceptibility. Just as some medical men attempted to regulate medical practice so as to control fears about sexuality, so our 'chivalrous northern knights' curtail women's honorable labor to protect men from the appetite they represent as uncontrollable and destructive.

Neither Lady Eastlake nor the author of 'Hints on the Modern Governess System' developed this indictment of men into an extended argument; instead, they continued to see the problem in terms of a natural difference between the sexes and the inevitability of women's dependence. So fixed did these writers imagine women's dependence to be, in fact, that the only solution they could devise was to defer their criticism of men, to make women responsible for remedying the trouble they identified: Lady Eastlake yokes her plea that upper-class employers pay their governesses higher wages to an argument that middle-class women – not to mention those in lesser ranks – resume their maternal duties; the author of 'Hints' explicitly states that 'the modern governess system is a case between woman and woman. Before one sex demands its due from the other, let it be just to itself' (*FM* 573).

Robert B. Heilman, Charlotte Brontë's 'New' Gothic (1958)

. . . From childhood terrors to all those mysteriously threatening sights, sounds, and injurious acts that reveal the presence of some malevolent force and that anticipate the holocaust at Thornfield, the traditional Gothic in *Jane Eyre* has often been noted, and as often disparaged. It need not be argued that Charlotte Brontë did not reach the heights while using hand-me-down devices, though a tendency to work through the conventions of fictional art was a strong element in her make-up. This is true of all her novels, but it is no more true than her counter-tendency to modify, most interestingly, these conventions. In both *Villette* and *Jane Eyre* Gothic is used but characteristically is undercut.

Jane Eyre hears a 'tragic . . . preternatural . . . laugh,' but this is at 'high noon' and there is 'no circumstance of ghostliness'; Grace Poole, the supposed laugher, is a plain person, than whom no 'apparition less romantic or less ghostly could . . . be conceived'; Brontë apologizes ironically to the 'romantic reader' for telling 'the plain truth' that Grace generally bears a 'pot of porter.' Brontë almost habitually revises 'old Gothic,' the relatively crude mechanisms of fear, with an infusion of the anti-Gothic. When Mrs. Rochester first tried to destroy Rochester by fire, Jane 'baptized' Rochester's bed and heard Rochester 'fulminating strange anathemas at finding himself lying in a pool of water.' The introduction of comedy as a palliative of straight Gothic occurs on a large scale when almost seventy-five pages are given to the visit of the Ingram-Eshton party to mysterious Thornfield; here Brontë, as often in her novels, falls into the manner of the Jane Austen whom she despised. When Mrs. Rochester breaks loose again and attacks Mason, the presence of guests lets Brontë play the nocturnal alarum for at least a touch of comedy: Rochester orders the frantic women not to 'pull me down or strangle me'; and 'the two dowagers, in vast white wrappers, were bearing down on him like ships in full sail.'

The symbolic also modifies the Gothic, for it demands of the reader a more mature and complicated response than the relatively simple thrill or momentary intensity of feeling sought by primitive Gothic. When mad Mrs. Rochester, seen only as 'the foul German spectre – the Vampyre,' spreads terror at night, that is one thing; when, with the malicious insight that is the paradox of her madness, she tears the wedding veil in two and thus symbolically destroys the planned marriage, that is another thing, far less elementary as art. The midnight blaze that ruins Thornfield becomes more than a shock when it is seen also as the fire of purgation; the grim, almost roadless forest surrounding Ferndean is more than a harrowing stage-set when it is also felt as a symbol of Rochester's closed-in life.

The point is that in various ways Brontë manages to make the patently Gothic more than a stereotype. But more important is that she instinctively finds new ways to achieve the ends served by old Gothic – the discovery and release of new patterns of feeling, the intensification of feeling. Though only partly unconventional, Jane is nevertheless so portrayed as to evoke new feelings rather than merely exercise old ones. As a girl she is lonely, 'passionate,' 'strange,' 'like nobody there'; she feels superior, rejects poverty, talks back precociously, tells truths bluntly, enjoys 'the strangest sense of freedom,' tastes 'vengeance'; she experiences a nervous shock which is said to have a lifelong effect, and the doctor says 'nerves not in a good state'; she can be 'reckless and feverish,' 'bitter and truculent'; at Thornfield she is restless, given to 'bright visions,' letting 'imagination' picture an existence full of 'life, fire, feeling.' Thus Brontë leads away from standardized characterization toward new levels of human reality, and hence from stock responses toward a new kind of passionate engagement.

Brontë moves toward depth in various ways that have an immediate impact like that of Gothic. Jane's strange, fearful symbolic dreams are not mere thrillers but reflect the tensions of the engagement period, the stress of the wedding-day debate with Rochester, and the longing for Rochester after she has left him. The final Thornfield dream, with its vivid image of a hand coming through a cloud in place of the expected moon, is in the surrealistic vein that appears most sharply in the extraordinary pictures that Jane draws at Thornfield: here Brontë is plumbing the psyche, not inventing a weird *décor*. Likewise in the telepathy scene, which Brontë, unlike Defoe in dealing with a similar episode, does her utmost to actualize: 'The feeling was not like an electric shock; but it was quite as sharp, as strange, as startling: . . . that inward sensation . . . with all its unspeakable strangeness . . . like an inspiration . . . wondrous shock of feeling . . . ' In her flair for the surreal, in her plunging into feeling that is without status in the ordinary world of the novel, Brontë discovers a new dimension of Gothic.

She does this most thoroughly in her portrayal of characters and of the relations between them. If in Rochester we see only an Angrian-Byronic hero and a Brontë wish-fulfillment figure (the two identifications which to some readers seem entirely to place him), we miss what is more significant, the exploration of personality that opens up new areas of feeling in intersexual relationships. Beyond the 'grim,' the 'harsh,' the eccentric, the almost histrionically cynical that superficially distinguish Rochester from conventional heroes, there is something almost Lawrentian: Rochester is 'neither tall nor graceful'; his eyes can be 'dark, irate, and piercing'; his strong features 'took my feelings from my own power and fettered them in his.'

Without using the vocabulary common to us, Brontë is presenting maleness and physicality, to which Jane responds directly. She is 'assimilated' to him by 'something in my brain and heart, in my blood and nerves'; she 'must love' and 'could not unlove' him; the thought of parting from him is 'agony.' Rochester's oblique amatory maneuvers become almost punitive in the Walter-to-Griselda style and once reduce her to sobbing 'convulsively'; at times the love-game borders on a power-game. Jane, who prefers 'rudeness' to 'flattery,' is an instinctive evoker of passion: she learns 'the pleasure of vexing and soothing him by turns' and pursues a 'system' of working him up 'to considerable irritation' and coolly leaving him; when, as a result, his caresses become grimaces, pinches, and tweaks, she records that, sometimes at least, she 'decidedly preferred these fierce favours.' She reports, 'I crushed his hand . . . red with the passionate pressure'; she 'could not . . . see God for his creature,' and in her devotion Rochester senses 'an earnest, religious energy.'

Brontë's remolding of stock feeling reaches a height when she sympathetically portrays Rochester's efforts to make Jane his mistress; here the stereotyped seducer becomes a kind of lost nobleman of passion, and of specifically physical passion: 'Every atom of your flesh is as dear to me as my own . . . ' The intensity of the pressure which he puts upon her is matched, not by the fear and revulsion of the popular heroine, but by a responsiveness which she barely masters: 'The crisis was perilous; but not without its charm . . . ' She is 'tortured by a sense of remorse at thus hurting his feelings'; at the moment of decision 'a hand of fiery iron grasped my vitals . . . blackness, burning . . . my intolerable duty'; she leaves in 'despair'; and after she has left, 'I longed to be his; I panted to return . . . ' – and for the victory of principle 'I abhorred myself . . . I was hateful in my own eyes.' This extraordinary openness to feeling, this escape from the bondage of the trite, continues in the Rivers relationship, which is a structural parallel to the Rochester affair: as in Rochester the old sex villain is seen in a new perspective, so in Rivers the clerical hero is radically refashioned; and Jane's almost accepting a would-be husband is given the aesthetic status of a regrettable yielding to a seducer. Without a remarkable liberation from conventional feeling Brontë could not fathom the complexity of Rivers – the earnest and dutiful clergyman distraught by a profound inner turmoil of conflicting 'drives': sexuality, restlessness, hardness, pride, ambition ('fever in his vitals,' 'inexorable as death'); the hypnotic, almost inhuman potency of his influence on Jane, who feels 'a freezing spell,' 'an awful charm,' an 'iron shroud'; the relentlessness, almost the unscrupulousness, of his wooing, the resultant fierce struggle (like that with Rochester), Jane's brilliantly perceptive accusation, '. . . you almost hate me . . . you would kill me. You are killing me now'; and yet her mysterious near-surrender: 'I was tempted to cease struggling with him – to rush down the torrent of his will into the gulf of his existence, and there lose my own.'

Aside from partial sterilization of banal Gothic by dry factuality and humor, Brontë goes on to make a much more important – indeed, a radical – revision of the mode: in *Jane Eyre* and in the other novels, as we shall see, that discovery of passion, that rehabilitation of the extra-rational, which is the historical office of Gothic, is no longer oriented in marvelous circumstance but moves deeply into the lesser known realities of human life. This change I describe as the change from 'old Gothic' to 'new Gothic.'. The kind of appeal is the same; the fictional method is utterly different.

. . . Gothic is variously defined. In a recent book review Leslie Fiedler implies that Gothic is shoddy mystery-mongering, whereas F. Cudworth Flint defines the Gothic tradition, which he considers 'nearly central in American literature,' as 'a literary exploration of the avenues to death.' For Montague Summers, on the other hand, Gothic was the essence of romanticism, and romanticism was the literary expression of supernaturalism. Both these latter definitions, though they are impractically inclusive, have suggestive value. For originally Gothic was one of a number of aesthetic developments which served to breach the 'classical' and 'rational' order of life and to make possible a kind of response, and a response to a kind of thing, that among the knowing had long been taboo. In the novel it was the function of Gothic to open horizons beyond social patterns, rational decisions, and institutionally approved emotions; in a word, to enlarge the sense of reality and its impact on the human being. It became then a great liberator of feeling. It acknowledged the nonrational – in the world of things and events, occasionally in the realm of the transcendental, ultimately and most persistently in the depths of the human being. (Richardson might have started this, but his sense of inner forces was so overlaid by the moralistic that his followers all ran after him only when he ran the wrong way.) The first Gothic writers took the easy way: the excitement of mysterious scene and happening, which I call old Gothic. Of this Charlotte Brontë made some direct use, while at the same time tending toward humorous modifications (anti-Gothic); but what really counts is its indirect usefulness to her: it released her from the patterns of the novel of society and therefore permitted the flowering of her real talent – the talent for finding and giving dramatic form to impulses and feelings which, because of their depth or mysteriousness or intensity or ambiguity, or of their ignoring or transcending everyday norms of propriety or reason, increase wonderfully the sense of reality in the novel. To note the emergence of this 'new Gothic' in Charlotte Brontë is not, I think, to pursue an old mode into dusty corners but rather to identify historically the distinguishing, and distinguished, element in her work.

Gayatri Chakravorty Spivak, *Jane Eyre*: A Critique of Imperialism (1985)

It should not be possible to read nineteenth-century British literature without remembering that imperialism, understood as England's social mission, was a crucial part of the cultural representation of England to the English. The role of literature in the production of cultural representation should not be ignored. These two obvious 'facts' continue to be disregarded in the reading of nineteenth-century British literature. This itself attests to the continuing success of the imperialist project, displaced and dispersed into more modern forms.

If these 'facts' were remembered, not only in the study of British literature but in the study of the literatures of the European colonizing cultures of the great age of imperialism, we would produce a narrative, in literary history, of the 'worlding' of what is now called 'the Third World.' To consider the Third World as distant cultures, exploited but with rich intact literary heritages waiting to be recovered, interpreted, and curricularized in English translation fosters the emergence of 'the Third World' as a signifier that allows us to forget that 'worlding,' even as it expands the empire of the literary discipline.[1]

It seems particularly unfortunate when the emergent perspective of feminist criticism reproduces the axioms of imperialism. A basically isolationist admiration for the literature of the female subject in Europe and Anglo-America establishes the high feminist norm. It is supported and operated by an information-retrieval approach to 'Third World' literature which often employs a deliberately 'nontheoretical' methodology with self-conscious rectitude.

In this essay, I will attempt to examine the operation of the 'worlding' of what is today 'the Third world' by what has become a cult text of feminism: *Jane Eyre.* I plot the novel's reach and grasp, and locate its structural motors . . .

I need hardly mention that the object of my investigation is the printed book, not its 'author.' To make such a distinction is, of course, to ignore the lessons of deconstruction. A deconstructive critical approach would loosen the binding of the book, undo the opposition between verbal text and the biography of the named subject 'Charlotte Brontë,' and see the two as each other's 'scene of writing.' In such a reading, the life that writes itself as 'my life' is as much a production in psychosocial space (other names can be found) as the book that is written by the holder of that named life – a book that is then consigned to what *is* most often recognized as genuinely 'social': the world of publication and distribution.[2] To touch Brontë's 'life' in such a way, however, would be too risky here. We must rather strategically take shelter in an essentialism which, not wishing to lose the important advantages won by U.S. mainstream feminism, will continue to honor the suspect binary oppositions – book and author, individual and history – and start with an assurance of the following sort: my readings here do not seek to undermine the excellence of the individual artist. If even minimally successful, the readings will incite a degree of rage against the imperialist narrativization of history, that it should produce so abject a script for her. I provide these assurances to allow myself some room to situate feminist individualism in its historical determination rather than simply to canonize it as feminism as such.

Sympathetic U.S. feminists have remarked that I do not do justice to Jane Eyre's subjectivity. A word of explanation is perhaps in order. The broad strokes of my presuppositions are that what is at stake, for feminist individualism in the age of imperialism, is precisely the making of human beings, the constitution and 'interpellation' of the subject not only as individual but as 'individualist.'[3] This stake is represented on two registers: childbearing and soul making. The first is domestic-society-through-sexual-reproduction cathected as 'companionate love'; the second is the imperialist project cathected as civil-society-through-social-mission. As the female individualist, not-quite/not-male, articulates herself in shifting relationship to what is at stake, the 'native female' as such (*within* discourse, as a signifier) is excluded from any share in this emerging norm.[4] If we read this account from an isolationist perspective in a 'metropolitan' context, we see nothing there but the psychobiography of the militant female subject. In a reading such as mine, in contrast, the effort is to wrench oneself away from the mesmerizing focus of the 'subject-constitution' of the female individualist . . .

Elizabeth Fox-Genovese, in an article on history and women's history, shows us how to define the historical moment of feminism in the West in terms of female access to individualism.[5] The battle for female individualism plays itself out within the larger theater of the establishment of meritocratic individualism, indexed in the aesthetic field by the ideology of 'the creative imagination.' Fox-Genovese's presupposition will guide us into the beautifully orchestrated opening of *Jane Eyre*.

It is a scene of the marginalization and privatization of the protagonist: 'There was no possibility of taking a walk that day . . . Out-door exercise was now out of the question. I was glad of it,' Brontë writes (ch. 1). The movement continues as Jane breaks the rules of the appropriate topography of withdrawal. The family at the center withdraws into the sanctioned architectural space of the withdrawing room or drawing room; Jane inserts herself – 'I slipped in' – into the margin – 'A small breakfastroom *adjoined* the drawing room' (ch. 1; my emphasis).

The manipulation of the domestic inscription of space within the upwardly mobilizing currents of the eighteenth- and nineteenth-century bourgeoisie in England and France is well known. It seems fitting that the place to which Jane withdraws is not only not the withdrawing room but also not the dining room, the sanctioned place of family meals. Nor is it the library, the appropriate place for reading. The breakfast room 'contained a book-case' (ch. 1). As Rudolph Ackerman wrote in his *Repository* (1823), one of the many manuals of taste in circulation in nineteenth-century England, these low bookcases and stands were designed to 'contain all the books that may be desired for a sitting-room without reference to the library.'[6] Even in this already triply off-center place, 'having drawn the red moreen curtain nearly close, I [Jane] was shrined in double retirement' (ch. 1).

Here in Jane's self-marginalized uniqueness, the reader becomes her accomplice: the reader and Jane are united – both are reading. Yet Jane still preserves her odd privilege, for she continues never quite doing the proper thing in its proper place. She cares little for reading what is *meant* to be read: the 'letter-press.' *She* reads the pictures. The power of this singular hermeneutics is precisely that it can make the outside inside. 'At intervals, while turning over the leaves of my book, I studied the aspect of that winter afternoon.' Under 'the clear panes of glass,' the rain no longer penetrates, 'the drear November day' is rather a one-dimensional 'aspect' to be 'studied,' not decoded like the 'letter-press' but, like pictures, deciphered by the unique creative imagination of the marginal individualist (ch. 1).

Before following the track of this unique imagination, let us consider the suggestion that the progress of *Jane Eyre* can be charted through a sequential arrangement of the family/counter-family dyad. In the novel, we encounter, first, the Reeds as the legal family and Jane, the late Mr. Reed's sister's daughter, as the representative of a near incestuous counter-family; second, the Brocklehursts, who run the school Jane is sent to, as the legal family and Jane, Miss Temple, and Helen Burns as a counter-family that falls short because it is only a community of women; third, Rochester and the mad Mrs. Rochester as the legal family and Jane and Rochester as the illicit counter-family. Other items may be added to the thematic chain in this sequence: Rochester and Céline Varens as structurally functional counter-family; Rochester and Blanche Ingram as dissimulation of legality – and so on. It is during this sequence that Jane is moved from the counter-family to the family-in-law. In the next sequence, it is Jane who restores full family status to the as-yet-incomplete community of siblings, the Riverses. The final sequence of the book is a *community of families*, with Jane, Rochester, and their children at the center.

In terms of the narrative energy of the novel, how is Jane moved from the place of the counter-family to the family-in-law? It is the active ideology of imperialism that provides the discursive field.

(My working definition of 'discursive field' must assume the existence of discrete 'systems of signs' at hand in the socius, each based on a specific axiomatics. I am identifying these systems as discursive fields. 'Imperialism as social mission' generates the possibility of one such axiomatics. How the individual artist taps the discursive field at hand with a sure touch, if not with transhistorical clairvoyance, in order to make the narrative structure move I hope to demonstrate through the following example. It is crucial that we extend our analysis of this example beyond the minimal diagnosis of 'racism.')

Let us consider the figure of Bertha Mason, a figure produced by the axiomatics of imperialism. Through Bertha Mason, the white Jamaican Creole, Brontë renders the human/animal frontier as acceptably indeterminate, so that a good greater than the letter of the Law can be broached. Here is the celebrated passage, given in the voice of Jane:

> In the deep shade, at the further end of the room, a figure ran backwards and forwards. What it was, whether beast or human being, one could not . . . tell: it grovelled, seemingly, on all fours; it snatched and growled like some strange wild animal: but it was covered with clothing, and a quantity of dark, grizzled hair, wild as a mane, hid its head and face. (ch. 26)

In a matching passage, given in the voice of Rochester speaking *to* Jane, Brontë presents the imperative for a shift beyond the Law as divine injunction rather than human motive. In the terms of my essay, we might say that this is the register not of mere marriage or sexual reproduction but of Europe and its not-yet-human Other, of soul making. The field of imperial conquest is here inscribed as Hell:

> One night I had been awakened by her yells . . . it was a fiery West Indian night . . .
>
> 'This life,' said I at last, 'is hell! – this is the air – those are the sounds of the bottomless pit! *I have a right* to deliver myself from it if I can . . . Let me break away, and go home to God!' . . .
>
> A wind fresh from Europe blew over the ocean and rushed through the open casement: the storm broke, streamed, thundered, blazed, and the air grew pure . . . It was true Wisdom that consoled me in that hour, and showed me the right path . . .
>
> The sweet wind from Europe was still whispering in the refreshed leaves, and the Atlantic was thundering in glorious liberty . . .
>
> 'Go,' said Hope, 'and live again in Europe . . . You have done all that God and Humanity require of you.' (ch. 27, my emphasis)

It is the unquestioned ideology of imperialist axiomatics, then, that conditions Jane's move from the counter-family set to the set of the family-in-law. Marxist critics such as Terry Eagleton have seen this only in terms of the ambiguous *class* position of the governess.[7] Sandra Gilbert and Susan Gubar, on the other hand, have seen Bertha Mason only in psychological terms, as Jane's dark double.[8]

I will not enter the critical debates that offer themselves here. Instead, I will develop the suggestion that nineteenth-century feminist individualism could conceive of a 'greater' project than access to the closed circle of the nuclear family. This is the project of soul making beyond 'mere' sexual reproduction. Here the native 'subject' is not almost an animal but rather the object of what might be termed the terrorism of the categorical imperative.

I am using 'Kant' in this essay as a metonym for the most flexible ethical moment in the European eighteenth century. Kant words the categorical imperative, conceived as the universal moral law given by pure reason, in this way: 'In all creation everything one chooses and over which one has any power, may be used *merely as means*; man alone, and with him every rational creature, is an *end in himself*.' It is thus a moving displacement of Christian ethics from religion to philosophy. As Kant writes: 'With this agrees very well the possibility of such a command as: *Love God above everything, and thy neighbor as thyself*. For as a command it requires respect for a law which *commands love* and does not leave it to our own arbitrary choice to make this our principle.'[9]

The 'categorical' in Kant cannot be adequately represented in determinately grounded action. The dangerous transformative power of philosophy, however, is that its formal subtlety can be travestied in the service of the state. Such a travesty in the case of the categorical imperative can justify the imperialist project by producing the following formula: *make* the heathen into a human so that he can be treated as an end in himself.[10] This project is presented as a sort of tangent in *Jane Eyre*, a tangent that escapes the closed circle of the *narrative* conclusion. The tangent narrative is the story of St. John Rivers, who is granted the important task of concluding the *text*.

At the novel's end, the *allegorical* language of Christian psychobiography – rather than the textually constituted and seemingly *private* grammar of the creative imagination which we noted in the novel's opening – marks the inaccessibility of the imperialist project as such to the nascent 'feminist' scenario. The concluding passage of *Jane Eyre* places St. John Rivers within the fold of *Pilgrim's Progress*. Eagleton pays no attention to this but accepts the novel's ideological lexicon, which establishes St. John Rivers' heroism by identifying a life in Calcutta with an unquestioning choice of death. Gilbert and Gubar, by calling *Jane Eyre* 'Plain Jane's progress,' see the novel as simply replacing the male protagonist with the female. They do not notice the distance between sexual reproduction and soul making, both actualized by the unquestioned idiom of imperialist presuppositions evident in the last part of *Jane Eyre*:

> Firm, faithful, and devoted, full of energy, and zeal, and truth, [St. John Rivers] labours for his race . . . His is the sternness of the warrior Greatheart, who guards his pilgrim convoy from the onslaught of Apollyon . . . His is the ambition of the high master-spirit[s] . . . who stand without fault before the throne of God; who share the last mighty victories of the Lamb; who are called, and chosen, and faithful. (ch. 38)

Earlier in the novel, St. John Rivers himself justifies the project: 'My vocation? My great work? . . . My hopes of being numbered in the band who have merged all ambitions in the glorious one of bettering their race – of carrying knowledge into the realms of ignorance – of substituting peace for war – freedom for bondage – religion for superstition – the hope of heaven for the fear of hell?' (ch. 32). Imperialism and its territorial and subject-constituting project are a violent deconstruction of these oppositions.

When Jean Rhys, born on the Caribbean island of Dominica, read *Jane Eyre* as a child, she was moved by Bertha Mason: 'I thought I'd try to write her a life.'[11] *Wide Sargasso Sea*, the slim novel published in 1965, at the end of Rhys' long career, is that 'life.'

I have suggested that Bertha's function in *Jane Eyre* is to render indeterminate the boundary between human and animal and thereby to weaken her entitlement under the spirit if not the letter of the Law. When Rhys rewrites the scene in *Jane Eyre* where Jane hears 'a snarling, snatching sound, almost like a dog quarrelling' and then encounters a bleeding Richard Mason (ch. 20), she keeps Bertha's humanity, indeed her sanity as critic of imperialism, intact. Grace Poole, another character originally in *Jane Eyre*, describes the incident to Bertha in *Wide Sargasso Sea*: 'So you don't remember that you attacked this gentleman with a knife? . . . I didn't hear all he said except "I cannot interfere legally between yourself and your husband". It was when he said "legally" that you flew at him' (*WSS*, p. 150). In Rhys' retelling, it is the dissimulation that Bertha discerns in the word 'legally' – not an innate bestiality – that prompts her violent *re*action.

In the figure of Antoinette, whom in *Wide Sargasso Sea* Rochester violently renames Bertha, Rhys suggests that so intimate a thing as personal and human identity might be determined by the politics of imperialism. Antoinette, as a white Creole child growing up at the time of emancipation in Jamaica, is caught between the English imperialist and the black native. In recounting Antoinette's development, Rhys reinscribes some thematic of Narcissus.

There are, noticeably, many images of mirroring in the text. I will quote one from the first section. In this passage, Tia is the little black servant girl who is Antoinette's close companion: 'We had eaten the same food, slept side by side, bathed in the same river. As I ran, I thought, I will live with Tia and I will be like her . . . When I was close I saw the jagged stone in her hand but I did not see her throw it . . . We stared at each other, blood on my face, tears on hers. It was as if I saw myself. Like in a looking glass' (*WSS*, p. 38).

A progressive sequence of dreams reinforces this mirror imagery. In its second occurrence, the dream is partially set in a *hortus conclusus*, or 'enclosed garden' – Rhys uses the phrase (*WSS*, p. 50) – a Romance rewriting of the Narcissus topos as the place of encounter with Love.[12] In the enclosed garden, Antoinette encounters not Love but a strange threatening voice that says merely 'in here,' inviting her into a prison which masquerades as the legalization of love (*WSS*, p. 50).

In Ovid's *Metamorphoses*, Narcissus' madness is disclosed when he recognizes his Other as his self: 'Iste ego sum.'[13] Rhys makes Antoinette see her *self* as her Other, Brontë's Bertha. In the last section of *Wide Sargasso Sea*, Antoinette acts out *Jane Eyre*'s conclusion and recognizes herself as the so-called ghost in Thornfield Hall: 'I went into the hall again with the tall candle in my hand. It was then that I saw her – the ghost. The woman with streaming hair. She was surrounded by a gilt frame but I knew her' (*WSS*, p. 154). The gilt frame encloses a mirror: as Narcissus' pool reflects the selfed Other, so this 'pool' reflects the Othered self. Here the dream sequence ends, with an invocation of none other than Tia, the Other that could not be selfed, because the fracture of imperialism rather than the Ovidian pool intervened. (I will return to this difficult point.) 'That was the third time I had my dream, and it ended . . . I called "Tia" and jumped and woke' (*WSS*, p. 155). It is now, at the very end of the book, that Antoinette/Bertha can say: 'Now at last I know why I was brought here and what I have to do' (*WSS*, pp. 155–56). We can read this as her having been brought into the England of Brontë's novel: 'This cardboard house' – a book between cardboard covers – 'where I walk at night is not England' (*WSS*, p. 148). In this fictive England, she must play out her role, act out the transformation of her 'self' into that fictive Other, set fire to the house and kill herself, so that Jane Eyre can become the feminist individualist heroine of British fiction. I must read this as an allegory of the general epistemic violence of imperialism, the construction of a self-immolating colonial subject for the glorification of the social mission of the colonizer. At least Rhys sees to it that the woman from the colonies is not sacrificed as an insane animal for her sister's consolidation.

Critics have remarked that *Wide Sargasso Sea* treats the Rochester character with understanding and sympathy.[14] Indeed, he narrates the entire middle section of the book. Rhys makes it clear that he is a victim of the patriarchal inheritance law of entailment rather than of a father's natural preference for the firstborn: in *Wide Sargasso Sea*, Rochester's situation is clearly that of a younger son dispatched to the colonies to buy an heiress. If in the case of Antoinette and her identity, Rhys utilizes the thematics of Narcissus, in the case of Rochester and his patrimony, she touches on the thematics of Oedipus. (In this she has her finger on our 'historical moment.' If, in the nineteenth century, subject-constitution is represented as childbearing and soul making, in the twentieth century psychoanalysis allows the West to plot the itinerary of the subject from Narcissus [the 'imaginary'] to Oedipus [the 'symbolic']. This subject, however, is the normative male subject. In Rhys' reinscription of these themes, divided between the female and the male protagonist, feminism and a critique of imperialism become complicit.)

In place of the 'wind from Europe' scene, Rhys substitutes the scenario of a suppressed letter to a father, a letter which would be the 'correct' explanation of the tragedy of the book.[15] 'I thought about the letter which should have been written to England a week ago. Dear Father . . . ' (*WSS*, p. 57). This is the first instance: the letter not written. Shortly afterward:

> Dear Father. The thirty thousand pounds have been paid to me without question or condition. No provision made for her (that must be seen to) . . . I will never be a disgrace to you or to my dear brother the son you love. No begging letters, no mean requests. None of the furtive shabby manoeuvres of a younger son. I have sold my soul or you have sold it, and after all is it such a bad bargain? The girl is thought to be beautiful, she is beautiful. And yet . . . (*WSS*, p. 59).

This is the second instance: the letter not sent. The formal letter is uninteresting; I will quote only a part of it:

> Dear Father, we have arrived from Jamaica after an uncomfortable few days. This little estate in the Windward Islands is part of the family property and Antoinette is much attached to it . . . All is well and has gone according to your plans and wishes. I dealt of course with Richard Mason . . . He seemed to become attached to me and trusted me completely. This place is very beautiful but my illness has left me too exhausted to appreciate it fully. I will write again in a few days' time. (*WSS*, p. 63).

And so on.

Rhys' version of the Oedipal exchange is ironic, not a closed circle. We cannot know if the letter actually reaches its destination. 'I wondered how they got their letters posted,' the Rochester figure muses. 'I folded mine and put it into a drawer of the desk . . . There are blanks in my mind that cannot be filled up' (*WSS*, p. 64). It is as if the text presses us to note the analogy between letter and mind.

Rhys denies to Brontë's Rochester the one thing that is supposed to be secured in the Oedipal relay: the Name of the Father, or the patronymic. In *Wide Sargasso Sea*, the character corresponding to Rochester has no name. His writing of the final version of the letter to his father is supervised, in fact, by an image of the *loss* of the patronymic: 'There was a crude bookshelf made of three shingles strung together over the desk and I looked at the books, Byron's poems, novels by Sir Walter Scott, *Confessions of an Opium Eater* . . . and on the last shelf, *Life and Letters of* . . . The rest was eaten away' (*WSS*, p. 63).

Wide Sargasso Sea marks with uncanny clarity the limits of its own discourse in Christophine, Antoinette's black nurse. We may perhaps surmise the distance between *Jane Eyre* and *Wide Sargasso Sea* by remarking that Christophine's unfinished story is the tangent to the latter narrative, as St. John Rivers' story is to the former. Christophine is not a native of Jamaica; she is from Martinique. Taxonomically, she belongs to the category of the good servant rather than that of the pure native. But within these borders, Rhys creates a powerfully suggestive figure.

Christophine is the first interpreter and named speaking subject in the text. 'The Jamaican ladies had never approved of my mother, "because she pretty like pretty self" Christophine said,' we read in the book's opening paragraph (*WSS*, p. 15). I have taught this book five times, once in France, once to students who had worked on the book with the well-known Caribbean novelist Wilson Harris, and once at a prestigious institute where the majority of the students were faculty from other universities. It is part of the political argument I am making that all these students blithely stepped over this paragraph without asking or knowing what Christophine's patois, so-called incorrect English, might mean.

Christophine is, of course, a commodified person. '"She was your father's wedding present to me"' explains Antoinette's mother, '"one of his presents"' (*WSS*, p. 18). Yet Rhys assigns her some crucial functions in the text. It is Christophine who judges that black ritual practices are culture-specific and cannot be used by whites as cheap remedies for social evils, such as Rochester's lack of love for Antoinette. Most important, it is Christophine alone whom Rhys allows to offer a hard analysis of Rochester's actions, to challenge him in a face-to-face encounter. The entire extended passage is worthy of comment. I quote a brief extract:

> 'She is Creole girl, and she have the sun in her. Tell the truth now. She don't come to your house in this place England they tell me about, she

> don't come to your beautiful house to beg you to marry with her. No, it's you come all the long way to her house – it's you beg her to marry. And she love you and she give you all she have. Now you say you don't love her and you break her up. What you do with her money, eh?' [And then Rochester, the white man, comments silently to himself] Her voice was still quiet but with a hiss in it when she said 'money.' (*WSS*, p. 130)

Her analysis is powerful enough for the white man to be afraid: 'I no longer felt dazed, tired, half hypnotized, but alert and wary, ready to defend myself' (*WSS*, p. 130).

Rhys does not, however, romanticize individual heroics on the part of the oppressed. When the Man refers to the forces of Law and Order, Christophine recognizes their power. This exposure of civil inequality is emphasized by the fact that, just before the Man's successful threat, Christophine had invoked the emancipation of slaves in Jamaica by proclaiming: 'No chain gang, no tread machine, no dark jail either. This is free country and I am free woman' (*WSS*, p. 131).

Susan L. Meyer, Colonialism and the Figurative Strategy of *Jane Eyre* (1990)

In her childhood and adolescence in the late 1820s and '30s, Charlotte Brontë wrote hundreds of pages of fiction set in an imaginary British colony in Africa. Her stories demonstrate some knowledge of African history and of the recent history of British colonialism in Africa: she makes reference to the Ashanti Wars of the 1820s, uses the names of some actual Ashanti leaders, and locates her colony near Fernando Po, which a writer for *Blackwood's Magazine* had been advocating as an apt spot for British colonization.[1] Other aspects of Brontë's juvenile stories suggest her knowledge of events in the British West Indies as well. Specific tortures used by West Indian planters on rebellious slaves appear in Brontë's early fiction, enacted on both black and white characters, and her most important black character, Quashia Quamina, who leads periodic revolutions against her white colonists, bears the surname of the slave who led the Demerara uprising of 1823 in British Guiana – as well as a first name derived from the racist epithet 'Quashee.'

Colonialism is also present – and used figuratively – in each of Brontë's major novels. In both *Shirley* (1849) and *Villette* (1853) the men with whom the heroines are in love either leave or threaten to leave Europe for places of European colonization, and both men imagine their relationships with colonized people as standing in for their relationships with white women. In *Shirley*, Louis Moore proposes to go to North America and live with the Indians, and immediately suggests that he will take one of the 'sordid savages,' rather than Shirley, as his wife.[2] At the end of *Villette* M. Paul departs for the French West Indian colony of Guadeloupe, to look after an estate there instead of marrying Lucy . . . In *The Professor* (1846), white women's resistance to male domination is more overtly figured as 'black.' The novel begins as an unreceived letter, whose intended recipient has disappeared into 'a government appointment in one of the colonies.'[3] . . . Even in the two existing chapters of Brontë's final and unfinished novel *Emma* (1853), race relations seem to be about to play an important figurative role: the heroine's suddenly apparent blackness suggests her social disenfranchisement due to her gender, age, and social class . . .

Brontë uses references to colonized races to represent various social situations in British society: female subordination in sexual relationships, female insurrection and rage against male domination, and the oppressive class position of the female without family ties and a middle-class income. She does so with a mixture of both sympathy for the oppressed and commonplace racism: Matilda's patronymic is a racial slur, yet the situation which provokes Mr. Ellin's harsh racism also evokes the reader's sympathy for Matilda. Lucy Snowe's strength of character is one of her most admirable traits – and yet to represent it Brontë invokes the Eurocentric idea of colonized savages. The figurative use of race relations in Brontë's fiction reveals a conflict between sympathy for the oppressed and racism, one that becomes most apparent in *Jane Eyre* (1847).

1

The figurative use of race is so important to *Jane Eyre* that, much as it begins to be in *Emma*, the figure is enacted on the level of character. In representing an actual Jamaican black woman, Brontë finds herself confronting the non-figurative reality of British race relations. And Brontë's figurative use of blackness in part arises from the history of British colonialism: the function of racial 'otherness' in the novel is to signify a generalized oppression. But Brontë makes class and gender oppression the overt significance of racial 'otherness,' displacing the historical reasons why colonized races would suggest oppression, at some level of consciousness, to nineteenth-century British readers. What begins then as an implicit critique of British domination and an identification with the oppressed collapses into merely an appropriation of the metaphor of 'slavery.' But the novel's closure fails, in interesting ways, to screen out entirely the history of British colonial oppression.

This complex figurative use of race explains much of the difficulty of understanding the politics of *Jane Eyre*. In an important reading of the significance of colonialism in this novel, Gayatri Chakravorty Spivak argues that 'the unquestioned ideology of imperialist axiomatics' informs Brontë's narrative and enables the individualistic social progress of the character Jane which has been celebrated by 'U.S. mainstream feminists.' Her reading describes Bertha as a 'white Jamaican Creole' who can nonetheless be seen in the novel as a 'native "subject,"' indeterminately placed between human and animal and consequently excluded from the individualistic humanity which the novel's feminism claims for Jane.[4] While I agree with Spivak's broad critique of an individualistic strain of feminism, I find her reading problematic in its analysis of the workings of imperialist ideology and its relation to feminism, both in general and in *Jane Eyre*.

Spivak describes Bertha as at once a white woman and a colonized 'native,' that is, as what she terms, with little definition, a 'native "subject."' She is thus able to designate Bertha as either native or white in order to criticize both Brontë's *Jane Eyre* and Jean Rhys's *Wide Sargasso Sea* as manifestations of exclusive feminist individualism. *Jane Eyre*, she argues, gives the white Jane individuality at the expense of the 'native' Bertha; *Wide Sargasso Sea*, on the other hand, she contends, retells the story of *Jane Eyre* from Bertha's perspective and thus merely 'rewrites a canonical English text within the European novelistic tradition in the interest of the white Creole rather than the native' (p. 253). Bertha is either native or not native in the interests of Spivak's critique. Thus it is by sleight of hand that Spivak shows feminism to be inevitably complicitous with imperialism.

My own proposition is that the historical alliance between the ideology of male domination and the ideology of colonial domination which informs the metaphors of so many texts of the European colonial period in fact resulted in a very different relation between imperialism and the developing resistance of nineteenth-century British women to the gender hierarchy, *Jane Eyre* was written in response to the same ideological context which led Anthony Trollope, in his short story 'Miss Sarah Jack of Spanish Town, Jamaica,' to describe the fiancée of a post-emancipation West Indian planter with this resonant analogy: 'Poor Maurice had often been nearly broken-hearted in his endeavours to manage his freed black labourers, but even that was easier than managing such as Marian Leslie.'[5] In *Jane Eyre*, Brontë responds to the seemingly inevitable analogy in nineteenth-century British texts that compares white women with blacks in order to degrade both groups and assert the need for white male control. Brontë uses the analogy in *Jane Eyre* for her own purposes, to signify not shared inferiority but shared oppression. This figurative strategy induces some sympathy with blacks as those who are also oppressed, but does not preclude racism. Yet while for the most part the novel suppresses the damning history of slavery and racist oppression, its ending betrays an anxiety that colonialism and the oppression of other races constitute a 'stain' upon English history and that the novel's own appropriation of the racial 'other' for figurative ends bears a disturbing resemblance to that history. Thus while the perspective the novel finally takes towards imperialism is Eurocentric and conservative, I find in *Jane Eyre* not Spivak's 'unquestioned ideology' of imperialism, but an ideology of imperialism which is questioned – and then reaffirmed – in interesting and illuminating ways.

An interpretation of the significance of the British empire in *Jane Eyre* must begin by making sense of Bertha Mason Rochester, the mad, drunken West Indian wife whom Rochester keeps locked up on the third floor of his ancestral mansion. Bertha functions in the novel as the central locus of Brontë's anxieties about oppression, anxieties that motivate the plot and drive it to its conclusion. The conclusion then settles these anxieties partly by eliminating the character who seems to embody them. Yet Bertha only comes into the novel after about a third of its action has taken place. As she emerges, anxieties which have been located elsewhere, notably in the character of Jane herself, become absorbed and centralized in the figure of Bertha, thus preparing the way for her final annihilation.

I read Bertha's odd ambiguity of race – an ambiguity which is marked within the text itself, rather than one which needs to be mapped onto it – as directly related to her function as a representative of dangers which threaten the world of the novel. She is the heiress to a West Indian fortune, the daughter of a father who is a West Indian planter and merchant, and the sister of the yellow-skinned yet socially white Mr. Mason. She is also a woman whom the younger son of an aristocratic British family would consider marrying, and so she is clearly imagined as white – or as passing as white – in the novel's retrospective narrative. And critics of the novel have consistently assumed that Bertha is a white woman, basing the assumption on this part of the narrative, although Bertha has often been described as a 'swarthy' or 'dark' white woman.[6] But when she actually emerges in the course of the action, the narrative associates her with blacks, particularly with the black Jamaican antislavery rebels, the Maroons. In the form in which she becomes visible in the novel, Bertha has *become* black as she is constructed by the narrative, much as Matilda Fitzgibbon becomes black in *Emma*.

Even in Rochester's account of the time before their marriage, when Bertha Mason was 'a fine woman, in the style of Blanche Ingram: tall, dark, and majestic,' there are hints, as there are in the early descriptions of Matilda Fitzgibbon, of the ambiguity of her race. Immediately after Rochester describes Bertha as 'tall, dark, and majestic,' he continues: 'her family wished to secure me because I was of a good race' (ch. 27). In the context of a colony where blacks outnumbered whites by twelve to one, where it was a routine and accepted practice for white planters to force female slaves to become their 'concubines,' and where whites were consequently uneasily aware of the large population of mulattoes, Rochester's phrase accrues a significance beyond its immediate reference to his old family name. In this context the phrase suggests that Bertha herself may not be of as 'good' a race as he.[7] Bertha is the daughter, as Richard Mason oddly and apparently unnecessarily declares in his official attestation to her marriage with Rochester, 'of Jonas Mason, merchant, and of Antoinetta Mason, his wife, a Creole' (ch. 26).

The ambiguity of Bertha's race is marked by this designation of her mother as a 'Creole.' The word 'creole' was used in the nineteenth century to refer to both blacks and whites born in the West Indies, a usage which caused some confusion: for instance, in its definition of the word the *OED* cites a nineteenth-century history of the U.S. in which the author writes: 'There are creole whites, creole negroes, creole horses, &c.; and creole whites, are, of all persons, the most anxious to be deemed of pure white blood.'[8] When Rochester exclaims of Bertha that 'she came of a mad family; idiots and maniacs through three generations! Her mother, the Creole, was both a madwoman and a drunkard!' he locates both madness and drunkenness in his wife's maternal line, which is again emphatically and ambiguously labelled 'Creole.' By doing so, he associates that line with two of the most common stereotypes associated with blacks in the nineteenth century.[9]

As Bertha emerges as a character in the novel, her blackness is made more explicit, despite Rochester's wish to convince Jane, and perhaps temporarily himself, that 'the swelled black face' and 'exaggerated stature' of the woman she has seen are 'figments of imagination, results of nightmare' (Ch. 25). But when Jane describes to Rochester the face she has seen reflected in the mirror, the *topoi* of racial 'otherness' are very evident: she tells him that the face was

> 'Fearful and ghastly to me – oh sir, I never saw a face like it! It was a discoloured face – it was a savage face. I wish I could forget the roll of the red eyes and the fearful blackened inflation of the lineaments!'
>
> 'Ghosts are usually pale, Jane.'
>
> 'This, sir, was purple: the lips were swelled and dark; the brows furrowed: the black eyebrows widely raised over bloodshot eyes.' (ch. 25)

The emphasis on Bertha's coloring in this passage – she is emphatically not 'pale' but, 'discoloured,' 'purple,' 'blackened' – the reference to rolling eyes and to 'swelled,' 'dark' lips all insistently and stereotypically mark Bertha as non-white. Jane's use of the word 'savage' underlines the implication of her description of Bertha's features, and the redness which she sees in Bertha's rolling eyes suggests the drunkenness which, following the common racist convention, Brontë has associated with blacks since her childhood. As Bertha's 'lurid visage flame[s] over Jane' while she lies in bed, causing her to lose consciousness, the ambiguously dark blood Bertha has inherited from her maternal line becomes fully evident in a way that recalls a passage from Brontë's African juvenilia. In this passage in her *Roe Head Journal* the revolutionary Quashia has triumphed in an uprising against the white British colonists, and having occupied the palace built by the colonists, revels drunkenly, in symbolic violation, on the 'silken couch' of the white queen.[10] Like the rebellious Quashia, the Jamaican Bertha-become-black is the novel's incarnation of the desire for revenge on the part of the colonized races, and Brontë's fiction suggests that such a desire for revenge is not unwarranted. The association of Bertha with fire recalls Jane's earlier question to herself: 'What crime was this, that lived incarnate in this sequestered mansion, and could neither be expelled nor subdued by the owner? – what mystery, that broke out, now in fire and now in blood, at the deadest hours of the night?' (ch. 20). The language of this passage strongly evokes that used to describe slave uprisings in the British West Indies, where slaves used fires both to destroy property and to signal to each other than an uprising was taking place. White colonists of course responded to slave insurrections with great anxiety, like that expressed by one writer for *Blackwood's*, in October 1823, in response to the news of the Demerara slave uprising: 'Give them [the abolitionists] an opportunity of making a few grand flowery speeches about liberty, and they will read, without one shudder, the narrative of a whole colony bathed in blood and fire, over their chocolate the next morning.'[11]

Brontë finished writing *Jane Eyre* in 1846, eight years after the full emancipation of the British West Indian slaves in 1838. But the novel itself is definitely set before emancipation. Q.D. Leavis has shown that it may not be possible to pinpoint the closing moment of the novel further than within a range of twenty-seven years, between 1819 and 1846.[12] When Jane says, at the end of her autobiography, 'I have now been married ten years,' the date is at the latest 1846 when Brontë finished writing the novel; thus Jane's marriage with Rochester probably takes place in 1836 at the latest. The year before their marriage, Rochester tells Jane that he has kept Bertha locked for ten years in his third-story room ('she has now for ten years made [it] a wild beast's den – a goblin's cell,' as he puts it (ch. 28). At the latest, then, Rochester first locked Bertha in that room in 1825, and since he lived with her before that for four years, they were probably married in 1821. Brontë doubtless meant to leave the precise date of the novel ambiguous – she marks the year of Rochester's and Bertha's wedding with a dash in Richard Mason's attestation to their marriage – but it is clear that even at the latest possible dates, events in the novel occur well before emancipation, which was declared in 1834 but only fulfilled in 1838. Brontë may have meant for the events of the novel to occur in the 1820s and '30s, as I have suggested above, during the years in which, due to the economic decline of the British sugar colonies in the West Indies, planters imposed increasing hardship on the slaves and increasingly feared their revolt. When Bertha escapes from her ten years' imprisonment to attempt periodically to stab and burn her oppressors, and as Rochester says, to hang her 'black and scarlet visage over the nest of my dove' (ch. 27), she is symbolically enacting precisely the sort of revolt feared by the British colonists in Jamaica.

But why would Brontë write a novel suggesting the possibility of a slave uprising in 1846, after the emancipation of the British (though not the U.S. or French) slaves had already taken place? Indeed, in 1846 it was evident that the British West Indian colonies were failing rapidly, and the focus of British colonial attention was shifting to India. While the novel's use of colonialism is most overtly figurative, nonetheless it in part does engage colonialism on a non-figurative level. The story of Bertha, however finally unsympathetic to her as a human being, nonetheless does indict British colonialism in the West Indies and the 'stained' wealth that came from its oppressive rule. When Jane wonders 'what crime . . . live[s] incarnate' in Rochester's luxurious mansion 'which [can] neither be expelled nor subdued by the owner' (ch. 19), the novel suggests that the black-visaged Bertha, imprisoned out of sight in a luxurious British mansion, does indeed 'incarnate' a historical crime. Rochester himself describes Thornfield as a 'tent of Achan' (ch. 27), alluding to Joshua 7, in which Achan takes spoils wrongfully from another people and buries it under his tent, thus bringing down a curse upon all the children of Israel. The third floor of the mansion, where Bertha is imprisoned, Jane thinks, is 'a shrine of memory' to which 'furniture once appropriated to the lower apartments had from time to time been removed . . . as fashions changed' (ch. 11). The symbolically resonant language Brontë uses as Jane tours the house suggests that Thornfield, and particularly its third floor, incarnates the history of the English ruling class as represented by the Rochesters, whom Mrs. Fairfax, acting simultaneously as family historian and guide to the house – that is, guide to the 'house' of Rochester in both senses – acknowledges to have been 'rather a violent than a quiet race in their time.' The atmosphere of the third floor of this 'house' is heavy with the repressed history of crimes committed by a 'violent race,' crimes which have been removed from sight as fashions changed. History keeps erupting into the language of this passage, as it does a few sentences later when Jane, climbing out onto the roof of the hall, finds herself on a level with the black rooks who live there, just above Bertha's head, and who are here referred to, with an eerie – and racist – resonance, as 'the crow colony'. Jane's response to this place dense with history – she is intrigued but 'by no means covet[s] a night's repose on one of those wide and heavy beds' (ch. 19) – suggests her awareness of the oppressive atmosphere of colonial history and her uneasiness lest she, by lying in the bed of the Rochesters, should get caught up in it.

Brontë's description of the room where Bertha has been locked up for ten years – without a window, with only one lamp hung from a symbolic chain – also reveals her awareness that the black-visaged Bertha, like Quashia Quamina, has ample reason to take revenge on a 'violent race.' In these moments in *Jane Eyre* Brontë subtly suggests that the history locked up in the English 'shrine of memory' is one of 'crime incarnate' in Bertha. But the 'slavery' which Bertha's coloring and imprisonment suggest has a more deliberate figurative function. The numerous parallels that Brontë draws between Bertha and other characters in the novel suggest that her most important narrative function is to embody these parallels, to give them a vivid and concrete form.

The 'slave' uprisings that Bertha's nocturnal violence evokes also have a figurative significance. As in her juvenilia and, less prominently, in her other major novels, Brontë uses slavery in *Jane Eyre* as a figure for economic oppression, a figure that the presence of Bertha illustrates and makes literal. Among recent critics who have described issues of social class as central to the politics of *Jane Eyre*, Terry Eagleton finds the novel the most conservative. He sees in *Jane Eyre*, as in all Brontë's novels, a struggle between individualistic bourgeois values and conservative aristocratic values. Eagleton reads Brontë's novels as 'myths' that work toward balancing these values, in part through conservative endings in which the protagonists 'negotiate passionate self-fulfillment on terms which preserve the social and moral conventions intact' by taking positions within the social system that has oppressed them earlier in the novel.[13]

Both Carol Ohmann and Igor Webb see a more radical thrust in *Jane Eyre*, in part because they both consider issues of gender to be as central to the novel as issues of class.[14] Ohmann argues that Brontë is concerned with gender and class 'deprivation' in *Jane Eyre*, and that, caught between her conservatism and her radicalism, she offers a solution only on an individual level. But, Ohmann concludes, 'in the very rendering of Jane Eyre's longing for fulfillment, Brontë conveys a moral imperative with broadly social implications,' although the novel does not follow these out (p. 762). Webb sees Jane as the carrier of a 'revolutionary individualism' through whom the novel struggles against inequality of gender and class. He too sees the novel as able to achieve revolutionary equality only on an individual level: 'the full transformation of society seems daunting, and the novel retreats into its overgrown paradise. This paradise serves at once as a criticism of that other, public world and as an announcement of the deep dispiriting gulf between active self-fulfillment and social possibility' (p. 86). With Ohmann and Webb, I find a more radical impulse in *Jane Eyre* than does Eagleton, and I agree with their emphasis on the novel's dual struggle against class and gender inequality. Yet I find Brontë's struggle against class inequality both more social and more limited than Ohmann and Webb do. *Jane Eyre* does suggest the need for a broader redistribution of wealth, but it also limits the recipients of this newly equalized wealth to a specific group, the lower-middle class. The novel's position on economic redistribution is worked out through the central figurative elements of racial 'otherness,' colonialism, and slavery.

As in her early African tales, Brontë does not use slavery as an analogy for the lot of the working class but for that of the lower-middle class, for those who are forced into 'governessing slavery' as Rochester puts it (ch. 24). Jane's governessing at Thornfield becomes like slavery to her only when Rochester arrives with his ruling-class friends and she experiences the dehumanizing regard of her class superiors. Before this, those around Jane treat her as a social equal. Mrs. Fairfax helps Jane remove her bonnet and shawl when she first arrives, and Adèle is too young and also of too dubious an origin to treat her governess with superiority. Brontë specifically constructs the atmosphere between the three of them – though significantly not between the three of them and the servants – as a utopian retreat from a world dominated by class hierarchy. Mrs. Fairfax distinctly marks the exclusion of the working class from this classless utopia when she tells Jane, just after expressing her delight that Jane has come to be her 'companion': 'you know in winter times one feels dreary quite alone, in the best quarters. I say alone – Leah is a nice girl to be sure, and John and his wife are very decent people; but then you see they are only servants, and one can't converse with them on terms of equality; one must keep them at a due distance for fear of losing one's authority' (ch. 11). Some awareness of the costs even of having a class lower than one's own, a problem with which the novel is in general very little concerned, comes through in this passage.

For the most part, however, *Jane Eyre* pays scant attention to the working class. Instead it draws parallels between slavery and Jane's social position as one of the disempowered lower-middle class. Both Jane and the narrator draw these analogies, not in response to the work Jane has to perform but in response to the humiliating attitudes of her class superiors. As a child when she first bursts out at John Reed, she cries: 'You are like a murderer – you are like a slave-driver – you are like the Roman emperors!' and the adult Jane explains to the reader, 'I had drawn parallels in silence, which I never thought thus to have declared aloud' (ch. 1). Jane as narrator not only accepts the child's simile but makes it into a more emphatic metaphor when she continues, 'I was conscious that a moment's mutiny had already rendered me liable to strange penalties, and, like any *other* rebel slave, I felt resolved, in my desperation, to go all lengths' (ch. 2, my emphasis). Later, when Jane has been placed by Brocklehurst on the stool, she thinks of herself as 'a slave or victim' (ch. 7). The novel itself draws a parallel between slavery and Jane's social position as a child through the character Bertha. Jane's sudden explosion of fury against her treatment at Gateshead occurs in her tenth year there: Mrs. Reed complains to the adult Jane, 'to this day I find it impossible to understand: how for nine years you could be patient and quiescent under any treatment, and in the tenth break out all fire and violence' (ch. 21). Jane brings herself to 'mutiny' and becomes a 'rebel slave' in her tenth year, like Bertha who after ten years in her third floor room 'br[eaks] out, now in fire and now in blood' (ch. 20).

The imagery of social class slavery recurs in Jane's adulthood in the context of her awareness of the economic inequality between her and Rochester. She comments after their engagement that receiving his valuable gifts makes her feel like a degraded slave, and when he boasts that he will cover her head with a priceless veil, she protests that if he does she will feel 'like an ape in a harlequin's jacket' (ch. 24). Given the racist nineteenth-century association of blacks with apes, the apparition of Bertha's black face under the embroidered veil incarnates Jane's analogies.

This central passage, in which Jane glimpses Bertha's black face under the wedding veil, reflected in her own mirror, and then watches Bertha tear the veil in half, epitomizes the other form of slavery that Bertha both embodies for Jane and then enables her to avoid. Several feminist critics have commented on this passage, interpreting Bertha as either the surrogate or the double who expresses Jane's rage against the restraints of gender. Sandra Gilbert and Susan Gubar particularly elaborate on this pattern in the novel, describing Bertha as Jane's 'dark double,' the untamed, animal-like embodiment of Jane's flaming anger.[15] What I would add is an emphasis on the darkness of the double, on the way in which, by creating the 'savage' Jamaican Bertha as Jane's 'dark double,' Brontë uses the emotional force of the ideas of slavery and of explosive race relations following emancipation in the colonies to represent the tensions of the gender hierarchy in England.

The imagery of slavery is both pervasive and closely tied to colonial actualities. When Rochester tells Jane, as he narrates the story of his life, 'hiring a mistress is the next worse thing to buying a slave: both are often by nature, and always by position, inferior: and to live familiarly with inferiors is degrading' (ch. 27), his words take on a startling resonance in the context of the story he has just told. Rochester acquired a West Indian fortune by marrying a Jamaican wife and subsequently lived in Jamaica for four years. A wealthy white man living in Jamaica before emancipation would undoubtedly have had slaves to wait upon him, and his Jamaican fortune would of course have been the product of slave labor, so when Rochester discusses what it is like to buy and live with slaves he knows what he is talking about. When he compares his relationships with women to keeping slaves, then, the parallel is given a shocking vividness by his own history as a slave master. Rochester draws this parallel just after the reader, with Jane, has seen his wife's 'black and scarlet' face emerging from her prison, an event that makes clear that it is not only Rochester's mistresses who are his 'slaves.' When Jane takes warning then from Rochester's analogy, Brontë suggests that Jane is learning more than that she would not be wise to become Rochester's lover without legal sanction.

3

Jane Eyre associates dark-skinned peoples with oppression by drawing parallels between the black slaves, in particular, and those oppressed by the hierarchies of social class and gender in Britain. So far the narrative function of the dark-featured Bertha and of the novel's allusions to colonialism and slavery has a certain fidelity to history, although as the association between blacks and apes reveals (to take only one example), these analogies are not free from racism. In addition, this use of the slave as a metaphor focuses attention not so much on the oppression of blacks as on the situation of oppressed whites in Britain. Nonetheless, the analogies at least implicitly acknowledge the oppressive situation of the non-white races subjected to the British empire. But oddly, the allusions to dark skin and to empire arise in precisely the opposite context in the novel as well, most strikingly in the descriptions of Blanche Ingram.

The haughty Blanche, with her 'dark and imperious' eye (ch. 18), whose behavior makes Jane so painfully aware of her own social inferiority, seems mainly to illustrate class oppression. Yet when Mrs. Fairfax describes Blanche to Jane, she emphasizes her darkness: 'she was dressed in pure white,' Mrs. Fairfax relates, she had an 'olive complexion, dark and clear,' 'hair raven-black . . . and in front the longest, the glossiest curls I ever saw' (ch. 16). When Jane first sees Blanche, she too emphasizes her darkness – 'Miss Ingram was dark as a Spaniard,' Jane notes – adding that Blanche has the 'low brow' which, like dark skin, was a mark of racial inferiority according to nineteenth-century race-science. Rochester directly associates Blanche with Africa: he might be speaking of Bertha when he tells Jane, with unnecessary nastiness, that his apparent fiancée is 'a real strapper . . . big, brown, and buxom; with hair just such as the ladies of Carthage must have had' (ch. 20).

These references to Blanche's darkness, and to her other similarities to 'inferior,' dark races, only make sense in the context of the odd phrase, 'dark and imperious.' The use of the word 'imperious' to describe Blanche's ruling-class sense of superiority evokes the contact between the British and their dark-skinned imperial subjects. In that contact, it was not the dark people who were 'imperious,' that is, in the position of haughty imperial power, but the British themselves. By associating the qualities of darkness and imperiousness in Blanche, Brontë suggests that imperialism brings out both these undesirable qualities in Europeans – that the British have been sullied, 'darkened,' and made 'imperious' or oppressive by contact with the racial 'other,' and that such contact makes them arrogant oppressors both abroad, and, like Blanche, at home in England.[16] Blanche's white dresses, her mother's pet name for her ('my lily-flower,' ch. 17), and the meaning of her name all emphasize the ironic incongruity between what she tries to be and what she is: rather than embodying ideal white European femininity, this aristocratic Englishwoman is besmirched by the contagious darkness and oppressiveness of British colonialism.

The association of the class oppressor with 'dark races' is hinted at in the descriptions of the Reeds as well as the Ingrams. John Reed reviles his mother for 'her dark skin, similar to his own' (ch. 2), and Jane compares John to a Roman emperor. John grows into a young man with 'such thick lips' (ch. 10), while Mrs. Reed's face in her last illness becomes, like Bertha's, 'disfigured and discoloured' (ch. 22). Lady Ingram, who derides governesses in front of Jane, and who within Jane's hearing announces that she sees in Jane's physiognomy 'all the faults of her class' (ch. 17) also has features like Bertha's: her face is 'inflated and darkened' – with pride (ch. 7). Like John Reed, Lady Ingram has 'Roman features,' and she too is associated with the British empire. She has, Jane says, 'a shawl turban of some gold-wrought Indian fabric [which] invested her (I suppose she thought) with a truly imperial dignity' (ch. 17). The novel draws unflattering parallels between the British empire, evoked by Lady Ingram's Indian shawl, and the Roman empire, whose emperors, the young Jane has said, are murderers and slave drivers. Both the class oppressiveness of these wealthy Britons and their dark features arise, in the novel's symbolic framework, from their association with empire.

With this odd twist, racial 'otherness' becomes also the signifier of the oppressor. By using dark-skinned peoples to signify not only the oppressed but also the oppressor, Brontë dramatically empties the signifier of dark skin in her novel of any of its meaning in historical reality and makes it merely expressive of 'otherness.' By assigning these two contradictory meanings to the signifier 'non-white,' the novel follows this logic: oppression in any of its manifestations is 'other' to the English world of the novel, thus racial 'otherness' signifies oppression. This is the most fundamentally dishonest move in the novel's figurative strategy, the one that reveals the greatest indifference to the humanity of those subject to British colonialism. The passages that associate English oppressors with 'dark races' are the most evasive about British participation in slavery and empire. The novel's anti-colonial politics, it becomes clear, are conservative. The opposition to colonialism arises not out of concern for the well-being of the 'dark races' subject to British colonization – the African slaves in the West Indian colonies, the Indians whose economy was being destroyed under British rule – but primarily out of concern for the British who were, as the novel's figurative structure represents it, being contaminated by their contact with the intrinsic despotism and oppressiveness of dark-skinned people.

The novel also associates the gender oppressor with darkness, primarily through Rochester. Rochester's darkness and the symbolic reason for it emerge in the central charade passage. The first two scenes Rochester enacts are thinly disguised episodes from his own life. In the first, which enacts the word 'bride,' Rochester weds a tall, 'strapping,' dark woman. The second scene enacts the word 'well' by representing the meeting of Eliezer with his intended bride, whom, as is the case with Rochester, Eliezer has been directed to wed by his father. The final scene, enacting the word 'Bridewell,' both suggests the imprisonment attendant upon making such a marriage and symbolizes the effects of Rochester's contact with dark-skinned people in search of fortune. In this scene Rochester is himself fettered like a slave and his face is 'begrimed' by a darkness that has rubbed off onto him. That his contact with the colonies is the source of his situation is suggested both by the preceding scenes and by the description of his coat which looks 'as if it had been almost torn from his back in a scuffle' (ch. 18) like the one he has with Bertha not long afterward.

Rochester's darkness is emphasized when his 'begriming' past is alluded to and when he asserts the potentially oppressive power of his position in the gender hierarchy. During the period of Rochester's and Jane's betrothal, Brontë continues to use the imagery of slavery to represent Jane's lesser power in the relationship. But she veers away from making a direct parallel with the British enslavement of Africans by associating Rochester's dominating masculine power over Jane with that not of a British but of an Eastern slave master. This part of the novel is rich in images of Turkish and Persian despots, sultans who reward their favorite slaves with jewels, Indian wives forced to die in 'suttee,' and women enslaved in Eastern harems. The reality of British participation in slavery arises at one point in this part of the narrative – Rochester echoes the abolitionists' slogan when he tells Jane that she is too restrained with 'a man and a brother' (ch. 14) – but the novel persistently displaces the blame for slavery onto the 'dark races' themselves, only alluding to slavery directly as a practice of dark-skinned people. At one point, for example, the novel uses strong and shocking imagery of slavery to describe the position of wives, but despite references to such aspects of British slavery as slave markets, fetters, and mutiny, the scenario invoked represents not British colonial domination but the despotic, oppressive customs of non-whites. Rochester has just compared himself to 'the Grand Turk,' declaring that he prefers his 'one little English girl' to the Turk's 'whole seraglio' (ch. 24), to which Jane responds with spirit:

> 'I'll not stand you an inch in the stead of a seraglio . . . If you have a fancy for anything in that line, away with you, sir, to the bazaars of Stanboul, without delay, and lay out in extensive slave-purchases some of that spare cash you seem so at a loss to spend satisfactorily here.'
>
> 'And what will you do, Janet, while I am bargaining for so many tons of flesh and such an assortment of black eyes?'
>
> 'I'll be preparing myself to go out as a missionary to preach liberty to them that are enslaved – your harem inmates amongst the rest . . . I'll stir up mutiny; and you, three-tailed bashaw as you are, sir, shall in a trice find yourself fettered amongst our hands; nor will I, for one, cut your bonds till you have signed a charter, the most liberal that despot ever yet conferred.' (ch. 24)

By associating Rochester's position at the top of the oppressive gender hierarchy, like Jane's position at the bottom, with dark-skinned peoples, the novel represses the history of British colonial oppression and, in particular, British enslavement of Africans, by marking all aspects of oppression 'other' – non-British, non-white, the result of a besmirching contact with 'dark races.' Even when Rochester directly asserts his power over Jane, speaking of 'attach[ing her] to a chain' (ch. 24), the novel compares him to a sultan, rather than to a white-skinned British slave master. All aspects of oppression in this conservative twist in the novel's figurative strategy become something the British are in danger of being sullied by, something foreign and 'other' to them.

In opposition to this danger – the danger of becoming 'begrimed' by the oppression which the novel associates with the dark-skinned – Brontë poses an alternative directly out of middle-class domestic ideology: keeping a clean house.[17] Clean and unclean, healthy and unhealthy environments form a central symbolic structure in the novel. In *Shirley*, Caroline's illness is anticipated by a passage about the arrival of 'the yellow taint of pestilence, covering white Western isles with the poisoned exhalations of the East, dimming the lattices of English homes with the breath of Indian plague' (p. 421). Similarly, in *Jane Eyre* Brontë consistently associates unhealthy, contagious environments with racial 'otherness' and with oppression, that 'poisoned exhalation of the East.' When Rochester decides to leave Jamaica where he has taken a dark wife as a 'slave,' participated in slavery, and become 'blackened,' the novel poses the opposition between oppressive Jamaica and pure England in terms of atmosphere. As Rochester recounts it:

> 'it was a fiery West Indian night; one of the description that frequently precede the hurricances of those climates. Being unable to sleep in bed, I got up and opened the window. The air was like sulphur streams – I could find no refreshment anywhere. Mosquitoes came buzzing in and hummed sullenly around the room . . . the moon was setting in the waves, broad and red, like a hot cannon-ball – she threw her last bloody glance over a world quivering with the ferment of tempest. I was physically influenced by the atmosphere. . . . I meant to shoot myself . . .
>
> 'A wind fresh from Europe blew over the ocean and rushed through the open casement: the storm broke, streamed, thundered, blazed, and the air grew pure. I then framed and fixed a resolution.' (ch. 27)

Under the influence of 'the sweet wind from Europe,' Rochester resolves to return to England, to 'be clean' in his own sight (ch. 27) by leaving the site of colonial oppression.

In a very similar passage Jane associates oppression and freedom with healthy and unhealthy environments. After she has fled Thornfield and settled at Morton, she reprimands herself for repining: 'Whether it is better,' Jane asks, 'to be a slave in a fool's paradise at Marseilles – fevered with delusive bliss one hour – suffocated with the bitterest tears of remorse and shame the next – or to be a village schoolmistress, free and honest, in a breezy mountain nook in the healthy heart of England?' (ch. 31). Jane here imagines the gender and class slavery she would endure as Rochester's mistress as a feverish, suffocating, southern atmosphere.[18]

The damp pestilential fog of Lowood School is one of the novel's most drastically unhealthy environments; the atmosphere at this orphan institution where Jane thinks of herself as 'a slave or victim' is the direct result of class oppression. After so many students die of the typhus fever fostered by the unhealthy environment, 'several wealthy and benevolent individuals in the county' transform it into a less oppressive institution by the act of cleaning; a new building is erected in a healthier location, and 'brackish fetid water' (ch. 10) is no longer used in preparation of the children's food.

Creating a clean, healthy, middle-class environment stands as the novel's symbolic alternative to an involvement in oppression. As Rochester is engaging in his most manipulative attempt to assure himself of Jane's love, by bringing home an apparent rival, he also orders that his house be cleaned. A great fuss is made over cleaning the house Jane had innocently thought to be already 'beautifully clean and well arranged' (ch. 17). But what Rochester most needs to have cleaned out of his house as he is trying to attain an Englishwoman's love is the black-faced wife in his attic who represents his sullying colonial past, his 'marriage' to the colonies. So despite all the cleaning – 'such scrubbing,' Jane says, 'such brushing, such washing of paint and beating of carpets, such taking down and putting up of pictures, such polishing of mirrors and lustres, such lighting of fires in bedrooms, such airing of sheets and feather-beds on hearths, I never beheld, either before or since' (ch. 17) – the presence remains in Thornfield that makes Rochester call it 'a great plague-house' (ch. 15). All that he can do with the 'plague' in his house is to hire a woman to 'clean' her away into a remote locked room. And as a reminder of this 'plague,' Grace Poole periodically emerges, amidst all the cleaning, from the third story, 'damping' Jane's cheerfulness and causing her 'dark' conjectures, in order, as both the most expert cleaner and as the signifier of the great 'stain' in the house, to give advice to the other servants: 'just to say a word, perhaps . . . about the proper way to polish a grate, or clean a marble mantlepiece, or take stains from papered walls' (ch. 17).

The other great cleaning activity in the novel occurs as Jane decides to 'clean down' Moor House (ch. 34), and it marks a more successful attempt at washing away oppression than the one at Thornfield. Jane cleans the house to celebrate the egalitarian distribution of her newly acquired legacy, which will enable her to live there happily with her new-found family. Brontë writes of Jane's 'equal' division of her fortune, using the rhetoric of a revolution against class oppression, although symbolically it represents a redistribution of wealth in favor of only a limited group of people, the lower-middle class. When St. John Rivers tells Jane that he, Diana, and Mary will be her brother and sisters without this sacrifice of her 'just rights,' she responds, in a tone of passionate conviction Brontë obviously endorses: '"Brother? Yes; at the distance of a thousand leagues! Sisters? Yes; slaving amongst strangers! I wealthy – gorged with gold I never earned and do not merit! You, penniless! Famous equality and fraternization! Close union! Intimate attachment!"' (ch. 33). This sort of redistribution of wealth, Brontë suggests, giving Jane the language of the French revolution – '*Liberté! Egalité! Fraternité!*' – will right the wrongs of the lower-middle class, and clean from it the mark of blackness which represents oppression. Its women will no longer have to 'slave' among strangers like blacks; its men will no longer have to venture into the distant, dangerous environment of the 'dark races' in the colonies. With Jane, Brontë redefines the claims of 'brotherhood,' as her plot redistributes wealth: truly acknowledged 'fraternity,' the novel suggests, requires distributing wealth equally, not letting a brother or sister remain a penniless 'slave.'

But to only a limited group among those who might ask 'Am I not a man and a brother?' does the novel answer 'Yes.' The plot of *Jane Eyre* works toward a redistribution of power and wealth, equalization and an end to oppression just as Jane herself does, but its utopia remains partial; its 'revolution' improves only the lot of the middle class, closing out both the working class and those from whom the figure of 'slavery' has been appropriated in the first place. As Jane phrases her 'revolution,' it is one which specifically depends on erasing the mark of racial 'otherness.'

To signify her utopian end to economic injustice, Jane creates a clean, healthy environment, free of plague: her aim, she tells St. John, is 'to *clean down* (do you comprehend the full force of the expression?) to *clean down* Moor House from chamber to cellar' (ch. 34). Jane works literally to 'set her own house in order,' creating a clean, healthy, egalitarian, middle-class, domestic environment as the alternative to oppression. This environment is not, however, to the taste of St. John, who wants to force Jane into an inegalitarian marriage and to take her to the unhealthy atmosphere of British India (both of which she says would kill her), to help him preach his rather different values of hierarchy and domination to dark-skinned people. Jane recognizes this difference in mentality and their incompatibility when St. John fails to appreciate her house-cleaning: 'this parlour is not his sphere,' she realizes, 'the Himalayan ridge, or Caffre bush, even the plague-cursed Guinea Coast swamp, would suit him better' (ch. 34).

Instead of deciding that it is her vocation to enter this new environment of plague, 'dark races,' and hierarchical oppression, Jane feels 'called' to return to a house which, being larger and more stained by oppression, will be more difficult to 'clean down' – Rochester's Thornfield. But of course when she gets there she finds that this 'plague-house' has already been 'cleaned down.' Brontë's plot participates in the same activity as Jane – cleaning, purifying, trying to create a world free of oppression. And the plot works precisely in the terms of the rhetoric of Jane's 'revolution.' It redistributes wealth and equalizes gender power, and it does so by cleaning away Bertha, the staining dark woman who has represented oppression.

In the ending of the novel, Brontë creates the world she can imagine free of the forms of oppression the novel most passionately protests against: gender oppression and the economic oppression of the lower-middle class. In the novel's utopian closure lies much of the revolutionary energy that made its contemporary readers anxious: the novel enacts Brontë's conception of a gender and middle-class revolution. The mutilation of Rochester (which interestingly has made critics of the novel far more uneasy than the killing of Bertha) and the loss of his property in Thornfield redistributes power between him and the newly-propertied Jane. Jane tells her former 'master' emphatically that she is now both independent and rich: 'I am,' she says, 'my own mistress' (ch. 37). And in the last chapter Jane explicitly describes their marriage as egalitarian, unlike most: 'I hold myself supremely blest beyond what language can express: because I am my husband's life as fully as he is mine' (ch. 38). The closure of the novel also severely punishes Rochester for his acquisition of colonial wealth. Fulfilling Rochester's own allusion to the accursed wealth wrongfully stolen by Achan, Brontë's ending enacts a purification like that of Achan, who is 'stoned with stones and burned with fire' (Joshua 7: 25) for bringing the 'accursed thing' into the camp of Israel. Unlike Achan, Rochester survives, but his 'tent of Achan' – his luxurious, oppressive, 'plague-house' – is destroyed and his misbegotten wealth exorcised from the novel.

But this revolution against gender oppression and the economic oppression of the middle class, and even this purifying away of ill-gotten colonial wealth, is made possible by another sort of oppression and suppression. The revolution behind Jane's revolution is that of the black woman who signifies both the oppressed and the oppressor. Bertha institutes the great act of cleaning in the novel, which burns away Rochester's oppressive colonial wealth and diminishes the power of his gender, but then she herself is cleaned away by it – burned and as it were purified from the novel. Brontë creates the racial 'other' as the incarnate signifier of oppression, and then makes this sign, by the explosive instability of the situation it embodies, destroy itself.

Jane Eyre ends with a glimpse of the purified, more egalitarian world created by this figurative sacrifice of the racial 'other,' Brontë's complex working-out of culturally available metaphors. But the novel does not end as peacefully as we might expect after this holocaust of the sign of racial 'otherness' and oppression. The ending betrays Brontë's uneasiness about her own figurative tactics, about the way in which her use of racial difference as a signifier involves a brutal silencing, an erasing of the humanity of the actual people inside the bodies marked 'other.'

This uneasiness becomes evident in the way the spectre of the racial 'other' remains to haunt the ending of the novel, although evaporated into the form of the 'insalubrious' mist which hovers over Ferndean, where Jane and Rochester settle after the 'cleaning down' of Thornfield (ch. 37). The dank and unhealthy atmosphere of Ferndean disrupts the utopian elements of the ending, indicating that the world of the novel is still not fully purified of oppression. And the oppression which that mist must signify, now that it no longer refers to class or gender oppression, is that original oppression which on one level the novel has tried so hard to displace and repress: the oppression of various dark-skinned peoples by the British.

The atmosphere of Ferndean recalls the fact that, even if Rochester's tainted colonial wealth has been burned away, the wealth Jane is able to bring him, enabling her to meet him on equal terms – and the wealth she earlier distributes in such a scrupulously egalitarian and 'revolutionary' spirit – has a colonial source. It comes from her uncle in Madeira, who is an agent for a Jamaican wine manufacturer, Bertha's brother. And the location of Jane's uncle John in Madeira, off Morocco, on the East Africa coast, where Richard Mason stops on his way home from England, also evokes, through Mason's itinerary, the triangular route of the British slave traders, and suggests that John Eyre's wealth is implicated in the slave trade. The details of the scene in which Brontë has Jane acquire her fortune mark Jane's economic and literary complicity in colonialism as well. St. John announces Jane's accession to fortune by pulling the letter out of a 'morocco pocket-book', and he is able to identify Jane as the heiress because she has written her name, on a white sheet of paper, in 'Indian Ink' (ch. 33).

In this way the novel connects the act of writing with colonialism. Specifically writing 'Jane Eyre,' creating one's own triumphant identity as a woman no longer oppressed by class or gender – or writing *Jane Eyre*, the fiction of a redistribution of wealth and power between men and women – depends on a colonial 'ink.' Whether advertently or not, Brontë acknowledges that dependence in the conclusion of *Jane Eyre*. Like colonial exploitation itself, bringing home the spoils of other countries to become commodities, such as Indian ink,[19] the use of the racial 'other' as a metaphor for class and gender struggles in England commodifies colonial subjects as they exist in historical actuality and transforms them into East or West 'Indian ink,' ink with which to write a novel about ending oppression in England.

The eruption of the words 'Indian ink' into the novel suggests, at some level, Brontë's uneasiness about the East Indian colonialism to which England was turning in 1848, as well as about the West Indian colonies which were by then clearly becoming unprofitable after the abolition of slavery. St. John, the East Indian missionary who is given the last words in the novel, writes them as he is dying – killed off by the 'insalubrious' atmosphere of oppression in British India, as Rochester just misses dying when his West Indian plague-house collapses on him. Brontë's anxiety about British colonialism is everywhere apparent in the ending of *Jane Eyre*. The novel is finally unable to rest easily in its figurative strategy and its conservative anticolonial politics: its opposition to a 'contaminating' and self-destructive contact with the colonies, and its advocacy of a middle-class domesticity freed from some of the most blatant forms of gender and class oppression. *Jane Eyre* is thus a fascinating example of the associations – and dissociations – between a resistance to the ideology of male domination and a resistance to the ideology of colonial domination.

The critique of colonialism which the novel promises to make through its analogy between forms of oppression finally collapses into a mere uneasiness about the effects of empire on domestic social relations in England. That disquietude is the only remnant of Brontë's potentially radical revision of the analogy between white women and colonized races, and it is the only incomplete element in the ideological closure of the novel. The insalubrious mist which suggests British colonial contact with the racial 'other,' diffused throughout the ending of the novel, betrays Brontë's lingering anxiety about British colonialism and about her own literary treatment of the racial 'other,' about the way in which, through oppressive figurative tactics, she has tried to make the world of her novel 'clean.'

3

CHARLES DICKENS, *DOMBEY AND SON*

In his Introduction to *Dombey and Son* (from the Penguin edition of 1970), Raymond Williams sees the novel coinciding with a critical phase of social and political upheaval in the 1840s: the extended development of the Industrial Revolution, the accelerated transition to an urban society, and the bitter struggle for democratic rights. The decade is regarded by Williams as both disturbed and creative, by turns transforming, liberating and threatening in its impact on people's lives. Williams's critical method is fuelled by a determination to understand how this new and complex experience shapes human consciousness. His reading of the novel concentrates on Dickens's 'way of seeing the world': his depiction of the city and the railway, the nature of his moral analysis and his engagement with issues of social class. Williams pays tribute to Dickens as 'a great radical novelist', who not only depicted the new social and economic forces of his time with remarkable insight, but also drew resourcefully on popular culture, making it the basis of his radical critique. The essay was published at the same time as Williams's Cambridge lectures in *The English Novel from Dickens to Lawrence* and should be read alongside the chapter on Dickens in that book.

Catherine Waters concentrates on the intensity and complexity of the brother–sister relationships in *Dombey and Son*. She points to the tension between the idealisation of the sibling bond and the troubling sexual suggestiveness and potential solipsism that it seems to involve. The relationship between Paul and Florence, in particular, is seen as profoundly ambiguous: neither blatantly incestuous nor purely innocent. The essay is valuable for its more general remarks about the presentation of sexuality in the novel, especially its analysis of the ways in which sexual feelings coexist with Victorian ideals of femininity and domesticity.

Suvendrini Perera's essay considers *Dombey and Son* both as a parable of mercantile capitalism and as a narrative deeply implicated in the economic interests of the Empire. Two aspects of Perera's essay are worth stressing: the connections it sees in the novel between mercantile capital and early voyages of exploration, and the tension, also evident in the novel, between old-style monopolistic mercantilism and the rapid growth of free trade. There is also an intriguing gender dimension to Perera's essay, to do with the appeal of 'romance' and 'adventure' in sea-faring voyages. The argument, then, is subtle and multi-faceted: it draws attention to the complex interplay of sex, trade and empire, not always apparent beneath the novel's ostensible concern with 'family'.

Raymond Williams, Introduction to *Dombey and Son* (1970)

1

It can seem superfluous to introduce Dickens. Before all English writers, Dickens introduces himself. His approach to his readers is the approach of the presenter: direct and self-conscious; telling his story rather than letting it appear to tell itself. In this, as in so much else, Dickens belongs to a popular tradition: going straight to an audience. The impersonality of other traditions – the learned and the polite – has been widely used in fiction. For certain ways of seeing, and for certain kinds of story, it is admirable and indeed inevitable. But in Dickens's way of seeing his world, direct address and presentation are radically necessary. It is not only a question of tradition or influence; it is part of his deepest creative and moral intention. And it is then profoundly important that we should see this great novelist, at a particular crisis of English society, at once drawing and composing a unique strength from the popular culture and the popular traditions of his time.

Dombey and Son first appeared in book form in 1848. It was a year of outstanding importance in English and European history. It was also an exceptional period in the development of the English novel. Within some twenty months not only *Dombey and Son* but *Vanity Fair*, *Wuthering Heights*, *Jane Eyre*, *Mary Barton*, *Tancred* and *The Tenant of Wildfell Hall* were first published. There has been no higher point in the whole history of English fiction. Several times before, there had been major individual novelists. Now, as it were suddenly, there was a generation.

Of course we see this more easily, looking back. We can see the 1840s as the decisive period in which the consciousness of a new phase of civilization was being formed and expressed. The radical transformation of life in Britain, by the extended development of the first industrial revolution, by the transition from a predominantly rural to a predominantly urban society, and by the consequent political struggles for representative democracy and for and against the emergence of an organized working class, was then in its most disturbed and creative phase. It was a decade which produced, in addition to the new generation of novelists, the direct and influential social criticism of

Carlyle and Engels, the great articulation of consciousness of Chartism and the struggle for the Ten Hours Bill, and, in the dominant line, the effective organization of the institutions of a new urban culture: in the popular press, in theatres and music-halls, in public parks, museums and libraries, in cheap books and their distribution. Many of the novels of the decade express these changes directly, as they express also the major economic and social changes: the struggle against poverty, the campaigns for public health and urban planning, the transforming extension of the railways.

But all these are the separable items of an active and connected history. What comes through most decisively in the novels is the effect on consciousness of this transforming, liberating and threatening time. If we take only the major achievements in fiction, we find a diversity of method but, more critically, a willing confidence in experiment: a creation of forms to express whole new experiences. And what we must then say, with the advantage of being able to look back and to distinguish the most creative achievements, is that for expressing this transformation and crisis, in its widest social reality, the methods of Dickens, proceeding directly from the issues and manners of the widest popular life, were the most decisive contribution and discovery. Emily Brontë created a supreme form of that opposition between the passion of primary relationships and the intertia of conventional relationships which was to go on being experienced throughout this disturbed civilization. Charlotte Brontë, less significantly but more influentially, created the novel of that form of isolated feeling and desire which became, in later periods, the powerful and extensive fiction of special pleading on behalf of a separated individual. So much that was new was being created and struggled with that it is right, initially, to put the emphasis on a generation. But then as we see the generation, and its relations with its world, we see Dickens as its largest and most central spirit: at once exposed and confident over the widest possible range of experience. His incompleteness, his failures, can of course be readily discerned, but we have to put the main stress on what he achieved, out of a disturbance so great that it seemed to threaten chaos.

This stress on his creative power, evident as much in the new forms of his novels as in the more widely recognized particular achievements of situation, character and language, needs now to be very firmly made, since from the generation following that of the 1840s, a very different and very strong kind of novel emerged: a kind of novel which, as it happens, contradicts that of Dickens in almost every criterion of success. That new kind of novel, associated above all in England with the name of George Eliot, belongs to a period which, though no less disturbed than the 1830s and 1840s, was nevertheless a time in which certain agreed bearings, certain unities of tone and concern, certain confidences of scale, had been at least temporarily achieved. It is a period we can describe as that of the liberal novel, in a positive sense. It achieves a balance, a point of view, between individual character and social context – those liberal descriptions – which is, in its turn, one of the great creative achievements. In the end this balance broke down yet again: from the last decades of the nineteenth century new disturbances, a new sense of a transforming and disintegrating world, exerted pressures which again, and very decisively, altered the methods of fiction. In the twentieth century, in a culture and in a fiction again necessarily experimental, the innovating and at once idiosyncratic and popular genius of Dickens could again be understood.

But the size, the confidence, the calm of that intervening period had had its profound critical effects. Understanding of the novel, as a literary form, had been based on that magnificent but temporary and somewhat narrow achievement. Certain criteria of seriousness – the slow building of rounded characters, the intricacy of developing relationships, a certain tact in analysis and indication matched by the sobriety and subtlety of the novelist's direct language – had become decisively established. Roundness, intricacy, tact: whether operating as real modes of insight or as critical counters, these qualities not only defined what were undoubtedly major novels, from George Eliot to Henry James, but defined, or seemed to define, what was wrong, what was inadequate, what was merely popular in Dickens. From that disability, of viewing one great kind of English novel through the critical sense of another great but radically different kind, we are only now, and with difficulty, beginning to recover.

In fact it is the contrast – the profound contrast – between Dickens and George Eliot that is the beginning of any important critical understanding of the English nineteenth-century novel. Yet this essential contrast is still not clearly seen; or rather it is not seen as a choice between two possible roads – a choice which is not yet complete, in continuing literature and experience. George Eliot's strength came, in the main, from the learned, the educated, even the polite world: with some inevitable difficulty, since much of her deepest feeling was rooted in everyday and customary life and effort. That extension of her world of concern, and yet its control, or attempted control, by an educated idiom and manner of composition, is the measure of her relation to and her distance from Jane Austen. And it is not surprising that most critics, belonging themselves to that learned and educated world, have adopted her achievement as a general standard for English fiction: overriding the historical and social pressures which in reality provoked the choice, the distance, between the two main roads.

It is indeed easy to respond to that major and indispensable achievement of George Eliot and her successors. But when, from its habits, the reader – the critic – turns to Dickens, he is all too likely to forget the fundamental choice; the division of two great roads. He may then find himself looking in Dickens for things he believes to be essential in any important novel: not for presented character, but for revealed character; not for direct moral address, but for enacted and in a way tacit significance; not for the language of display and persuasion, but for the quieter language of description, analysis and comprehension; not for the products of the year and the day but for the imperceptible processes of the minutes. And if, nevertheless, such a reader likes Dickens, and finds the essential response happening in spite of his preconceptions, he may well fall back on the popular tradition, as a reference, an explanation, an explaining away.

But this is the cart before the horse. Dickens was not a splendid exception in the novel: a great entertainer and persuader, a writer of marvellous energy, who somehow found himself, paradoxically, inside the quieter world. He was, from the beginning, another kind of novelist, another kind of creator, in another and essentially different historical period and outlook. The popular tradition – in the theatre, in newspapers, in songs and spoken stories – is indeed where he starts from, but not as a liability; as one major way, a majority way, of responding to a very particular and rapidly changing world. It is not the old folk tradition of a pre-industrial society; it is that tradition altered, extended, sharpened, by the experience of industrial life and of cities; a popular culture, part of what it both expresses and opposes. Dickens began from this because it was, by experience, his own way of seeing his world. He was not separated, for advantage and disadvantage, from that crowded, noisy, miscellaneous life. He did not see it from another experience and through another idiom; he belonged to it, found his way in it, wrote his penny-a-line with the others. But then the important thing is that by an extraordinary effort of creative development he made it available to literature, in very original ways. Just as George Eliot's kind of novel developed, in relation to earlier novels, from the polite essay, the learned character, the sustained and documented history – all of them bearing on the narrative of personal experience – so Dickens's kind, again related to earlier novels, developed from the popular theatre, the newspapers, the public platform and the pulpit, and the stories and songs of the taverns.

These were two social worlds, though of course in reality they overlapped. Each has its strengths and its weaknesses in approaching different kinds of experience. To tell this full story (which is indeed not yet complete) would take us out into much wider fields. But we can see, when we read Dickens, that the popular tradition, which has been so much neglected, gives its life not only to continuations of itself – a crowded, many-voiced, anonymous world of jokes, stories, rumours, songs, shouts, banners, greetings, idioms, addresses. It gives its life also, through its highly original use by this remarkable writer, to a very novel form of sustained imaginative creation – to a unique and necessary way of seeing and responding to what was then an unprecedented world; to the crowded, noisy, miscellaneous world of the nineteenth-century city, and of the industrial-capitalist civilization of which the city, and above all the metropolis, was the principal embodiment. And what is new in this kind of novel is not only this new kind of life – so markedly different from the more obviously knowable and traditional communities of the village and the country town which gave form to an alternative fiction. It is also, and necessarily, a new way of seeing and valuing: above all, a new way of seeing the qualities that make for and against life and goodness. It is a way of seeing, deeply rooted in the popular tradition, in which general vices such as pride, general virtues such as innocence, are known at once in traditional terms – as abstractions as much as individual traits – and yet at the same time are seen as being created, in all their generality, by the pressures, the relationships, the governing character of a history and a society.

2

Thus it is easy to see and to say that *Dombey and Son* is a novel about pride. But we have to go on and make a more difficult distinction. There is a kind of moral analysis in which society is a background against which the drama of personal virtues and vices is enacted. There is another kind – increasingly important in the development of nineteenth-century literature – in which society is the creator of virtues and vices; its active relationships and institutions at once generating and controlling, or failing to control, what in the earlier mode of analysis could be seen as faults of the soul.

And then the important thing to realize about *Dombey and Son* is that Dickens uses, and relies on, both these kinds. In a way it is true to say that *Dombey and Son* is the novel in which he makes a decisive transition from the first to the second, in his essential organization. But compared with some of his later works, and especially with *Little Dorrit*, *Our Mutual Friend* and *Great Expectations*, *Dombey and Son* still often relies, in an isolated way, on the more traditional way of seeing error and failure.

> 'I have dreamed,' said Edith in a low voice, 'of a pride that is all powerless for good, all powerful for evil; of a pride that has been galled and goaded, through many shameful years, and has never recoiled except upon itself; a pride that has debased its owner with the consciousness of deep humiliation, and never helped its owner boldly to resent it or avoid it, or to say, "This shall not be!" a pride that, rightly guided, might have led perhaps to better things, but which, misdirected and perverted, like all else belonging to the same possessor, has been self-contempt, mere hardihood and ruin.' . . . (ch. 43)

In the same spirit, there is a traditional invocation, to wake from error, in the description of Florence going into her father's room:

> Awake, unkind father! Awake now, sullen man! The time is flitting by; the hour is coming with an angry tread. Awake!
> Awake, doomed man, while she is near! The time is flitting by; the hour is coming with an angry tread; its foot is in the house. Awake! (ch. 43)

But this is not the only way in which this destructive pride is seen. House has two meanings: the family home and the firm. And the outlook of the firm – a social institution, trading in the confident spirit of its time – is seen, from the beginning, as a creator of this destructively indifferent pride. Here, characteristically, Dickens does not plead, emotionally, but sets down, ironically:

> The earth was made for Dombey and Son to trade in, and the sun and moon were made to give them light. Rivers and seas were formed to float their ships; rainbows gave them promise of fair weather; winds blew for or against their enterprises; stars and planets circled in their orbits, to preserve inviolate a system of which they were the centre. Common abbreviations took new meanings in his eyes, and had sole reference to them. A.D. had no concern with anno Domini, but stood for anno Dombei – and Son. (ch. 1)

It could not be better or more clearly said. It is a familiar Dickens joke, but a joke about something central and disturbing. Later, we find him reflecting, directly, on the question of the sources of a destructive pride:

> Was Mr Dombey's master-vice, that ruled him so inexorably, an unnatural characteristic? It might be worth while sometimes, to inquire what Nature is, and how men work to change her, and whether, in the enforced distortions so produced, it is not natural to be unnatural. Coop any son or daughter of our mighty mother within narrow range, and bind the prisoner to one idea, and foster it by servile worship of it on the part of the few timid or designing people standing round, and what is Nature to the willing captive who has never risen up upon the wings of a free mind – drooping and useless soon – to see her in her comprehensive truth! . . . (ch. 47)

It is interesting to see where this question has led Dickens. Beginning with Dombey's 'master-vice', and its traditional reference to 'Nature', he has gone on to describe a process in which men work to change nature, and produce 'enforced distortions'. And then the argument slips, imperceptibly, to the strongest social feeling he then had: his horror in seeing the diseased slums of the city, produced by indifference and neglect.

But it is even more interesting to see how his argument continues. These 'odious sights' are all too visible, even if 'dainty delicacy' refuses to believe them. But something else is at work, which is not visible in these ways; which requires an active effort of the imagination and sympathy; a creative, even a magical intervention:

> Those who study the physical sciences, and bring them to bear upon the health of Man, tell us that if the noxious particles that rise from vitiated air were palpable to the sight, we should see them lowering in a dense black cloud above such haunts, and rolling slowly on to corrupt the better portions of a town. But if the moral pestilence that rises with them, and, in the eternal laws of outraged Nature, is inseparable from them, could be made discernible too, how terrible the revelation! Then should we see depravity, impiety, drunkenness, theft, murder, and a long train of nameless sins against the natural affections and repulsions of mankind, overhanging the devoted spots, and creeping on, to blight the innocent and spread contagion among the pure. Then should we see how the same poisoned fountains that flow into our hospitals and lazarhouses, inundate the jails, and make the convict-ships swim deep, and roll across the seas, and overrun vast continents with crime. Then should we stand appalled to know, that where we generate disease to strike our children down and entail itself on unborn generations, there also we breed, by the same certain process, infancy that knows no innocence, youth without modesty or shame, maturity that is mature in nothing but in suffering and guilt, blasted old age that is a scandal on the form we bear. Unnatural humanity! When we shall gather grapes from thorns, and figs from thistles; when fields of grain shall spring up from the offal in the bye-ways of our wicked cities, and roses bloom in the fat churchyards that they cherish; then we may look for natural humanity, and find it growing from such seed . . . (ch. 47)

This very different invocation is remarkable. It is not the appeal to an individual man to wake from his error, before it is too late. It is an appeal to a society to wake from error, but it is also something more: an invocation of a particular creative spirit; a way of seeing this otherwise unseen reality. The image of the 'dense black cloud' overhanging the city, though unseen by its inhabitants, is strikingly powerful. It is, in related forms, an image to which Dickens often returns. But what is new is the idea of intervention: the 'good spirit' who will 'take the house-tops off'. In *A Christmas Carol* Dickens had used just such spirits; the idea comes aptly to his mind, from traditional sources. But what is now happening, in a stage beyond magic, is a way for the novelist himself to see his own role. It is in this making plain what others cannot or will not see; in this making of connections between fragmentary and divided experiences; in this creation, from social chaos, of 'one common end, to make the world a better place', that Dickens, essentially, sees himself and his work. In *Dombey and Son* he is still often in detail uncertain, but he has defined his intention, and is beginning to find ways of realizing it. This can fairly be called the achievement, in the novel, of a new dimension of social consciousness.

It is usual, of course, when Dickens is writing like this, to dismiss it as preaching, moralizing or even rant. But seen from the tradition in which he is working, and which he is so notably extending, this is a trivial reaction; a self-protection by tone, a 'dainty delicacy'. For it must not be taken for granted that this is a generalized way of seeing, with the implication of generalizing weakness. It is not generalizing but general: a way of seeing beyond isolated errors and vices, to their breeding-ground in society. It is indeed one of the classic moments in which a particular moral and philosophical tradition is challenged and transcended by another, in an experience which is the great creative achievement of the nineteenth century: a way of learning to see general social causes behind and beyond individual failures and weaknesses. What is seen, and challenged, is a system that breeds misery: now passionately when in the beginning ironically: 'to preserve inviolate a system of which [the enterprises of Dombey and Son] were the centre.' But what is also challenged is a systematic distortion, in ways of seeing the world: not only an isolated indifference – that individual characteristic – but a settled indifference, in those 'who have never looked out upon the world of human life around them, to a knowledge of their own relation to it'. This, again classically, is seen as an alienation, an 'enforced distortion'. To fail in just this consciousness of our relation to society, to this 'world of human life', is to breed sickness in its turn; not only the known sickness, of the neglected and rotting slums into which other human beings have been forced, but an invisible sickness, that rots the hearts and minds of the socially and physically confident and secure: 'a perversion of nature in their own contracted sympathies and estimates; as great, and yet as natural in its development when once begun, as the lowest degradation known'.

Pride, from being an isolable quality, a traditional vice, is now seen also as something created by a particular social world, and by the habits of heart and mind which such a world teaches and sustains.

3

One controlling element of this social world is the city. Dickens was the first English novelist to explore the modern city – in its form as the metropolis – as a social fact and as a human landscape. It is a complicated exploration, over a wide range of feeling. He can respond, warmly, to the miscellaneous bustle and colour of this mobile commercial life.

> Mr Dombey's offices were in a court where there was an old established stall of choice fruit at the corner; where perambulating merchants, of both sexes, offered for sale at any time between the hours of ten and five, slippers, pocket-books, sponges, dogs' collars, and Windsor soap, and sometimes a pointer or an oil-painting.
>
> The pointer always came that way, with a view to the Stock Exchange, where a sporting taste (originating generally in bets of new hats) is much in vogue. (ch. 13)

It is characteristic that when Mr Dombey arrives, none of these passing commodities is offered to him. His kind of trade, reflected in his house – his 'Home-Department' – has established itself in colder, more settled, more remote ways; and then another aspect of the city is evident:

> Mr Dombey's house was a large one, on the shady side of a tall, dark, dreadfully genteel street in the region between Portland Place and Bryanstone Square. It was a corner house, with great wide areas containing cellars frowned upon by barred windows, and leered at by crooked-eyed doors leading to dustbins. It was a house of dismal state, with a circular back to it, containing a whole suite of drawing-rooms looking upon a gravelled yard, where two gaunt trees, with blackened trunks and branches, rattled rather than rustled, their leaves were so smoke-dried. The summer sun was never on the street, but in the morning about breakfast-time, when it came with the water-carts and the old-clothes men, and the people with geraniums, and the umbrella-mender, and the man who trilled the little bell of the Dutch clock as he went along. It was soon gone again to return no more that day; and the bands of music and the straggling Punch's shows going after it, left it a prey to the most dismal of organs, and white mice; with now and then a porcupine, to vary the entertainments; until the butlers whose families were dining out, began to stand at the house-doors in the twilight, and the lamplighter made his nightly failure in attempting to brighten up the street with gas. (ch. 3)

The contrast between the dismal establishment and the strolling variety of the streets is very clearly made. The description of the house introduces us, also, to a method which Dickens was remarkably to develop, and which is one of his most original ways of seeing the city as a human fact. A stage can be reached, in the development of a city, in which its most evident inhabitants are buildings; or, to put it another way, in which its human features, often compressed or distorted, are most visible in the shapes and aspects of its physical architecture. Blake, in his poem 'London', and Wordsworth, in the great seventh book, 'Residence in London', of the *Prelude*, had foreshadowed this way of seeing the human qualities of the city; no longer in individual features, but in a collective face, the physical features of houses and streets. Dickens uses this mode of description more extensively later, especially in *Little Dorrit*. But there is a good example, here, of a kind of writing which is also a way of seeing, in which the characteristics of houses and of people are consciously exchanged: the one described in terms of the other, 'cellars frowned upon by barred windows, and leered at by crooked-eyed doors'. This transposition of detail can then be extended, again with some traditional support, to a way of seeing the city as a destructive animal, a monster, utterly beyond the individual human scale:

> She often looked with compassion, at such a time, upon the stragglers who came wandering into London, by the great highway hard by, and who, footsore and weary, and gazing fearfully at the huge town before them, as if foreboding that their misery there would be but as a drop of water in the sea, or as a grain of sea-sand on the shore, went shrinking on, cowering before the angry weather, and looking as if the very elements rejected them. Day after day, such travellers crept past, but always, as she thought, in one direction – always towards the town. Swallowed up in one phase or other of its immensity, towards which they seemed impelled by a desperate fascination, they never returned. Food for the hospitals, the churchyards, the prisons, the river, fever, madness, vice, and death, – they passed on to the monster, roaring in the distance, and were lost. (ch. 33)

That is one way of seeing it: the rhetorical, totalizing view from outside. But Dickens moves with still greater certainty into the streets themselves: into that experience of the streets – the crowd of strangers – which most of us now have got used to but which again, in Blake and Wordsworth, was felt as strange and threatening. Dickens recreates and extends this experience, when Florence runs away from her father's dark house:

> Florence saw surprise and curiosity in the faces flitting past her; saw

> long shadows coming back upon the pavement; and heard voices that were strange to her asking her where she went, and what the matter was; and though these frightened her the more at first, and made her hurry on the faster, they did her the good service of recalling her in some degree to herself, and reminding her of the necessity of greater composure.
>
> Where to go? Still somewhere, anywhere! still going on; but where! She thought of the only other time she had been lost in the wild wilderness of London – though not lost as now – and went that way. (ch. 48)

It is seen in very particular ways: an everyday business, not frightening in itself, but amounting in its combined effect to a 'wild wilderness', a place as difficult to relate to as her 'shut-up house'. But another note is struck: a physical effect which is also a social fact, sharply seen: the same social fact against which Dickens's effort at recognition and kindness is consistently made 'the rising clash and roar of the day's struggle'. The only companion she finds is her dog, and she goes on with him:

> With this last adherent, Florence hurried away in the advancing morning, and the strengthening sunshine, to the City. The roar soon grew more loud, the passengers more numerous, the shops more busy, until she was carried onward in a stream of life setting that way, and flowing, indifferently, past marts and mansions, prisons, churches, market-places, wealth, poverty, good, and evil, like the broad river side by side with it, awakened from its dreams of rushes, willows, and green moss, and rolling on, turbid and troubled, among the works and cares of men, to the deep sea. (ch. 48)

What is emphatic here is not only the noise, the everyday business; not only the miscellaneity – 'prisons, churches', but through all this, the indifference, in an unwilled general sense, 'a stream of life setting that way, and flowing, indifferently'. It is again not a matter of particular acts or characters. It is a general phenomenon – a stream, a way of life . . .

This is again an advance in consciousness, as it is very clearly a gain – now absorbed – in fictional method. For the connection between Mr Dombey's 'master-vice' and the city which has been built to his and its specifications is not one of background but of spirit. The human life and colour which passes briefly and fitfully through a city it does not own, a city that seen from the distance is a devouring monster but that life is struggling all the time to repossess or at least to survive in – this loving and creative human spirit is what the indifference of Dombey, the indifference of his system, centred only on its own activities and priorities, almost but never quite crushes: in a man, in a family, in the streets and buildings of a city.

4

What does it do, in detail, to people; this pride of class and wealth; this indifference of trade; this reduction of human connections to their convenience for business? This is the great opening moment in *Dombey and Son*: the birth of a child in a house; a birth at once transformed, deformed, by a different sense of human ends: 'The House will once again, Mrs Dombey,' said Mr Dombey, 'be not only in name but in fact Dombey and Son; . . . Dom-bey and Son!' But the human agent of this foundation dies; the mother dies. The child, the future partner, needs human care, another mother. But human milk can be bought from a 'hired serving-woman'. Mrs Toodle, the wife of a railway-worker, with several children of her own, is assigned this function (the relationship is built into the language). Mr Dombey interviews her with her husband (ch. 2) . . .

In what is called his mode of caricature, Dickens is here profoundly expressing a practical alienation: a cold using of others, at the very sources of life, as 'a mere matter of bargain and sale, hiring and letting'. It is characteristic that Dombey deprives his agent – the woman who is giving his own child milk – of her ordinary identity, her name, which he replaces indifferently, within his own scheme of things. This is the pressure, all the time, on ordinary people: to fit in with the needs of those who can hire them; to suppress, for the time being, their particular life. This cold using of others is even recommended, as here by Miss Tox, as a way of teaching a higher kind of life: service could be seen as a kind of cultural advantage to the servant. But this, once again, is a question of identity: an attempt to supersede the particular person, and substitute what is taken as a higher style. What is then deeply encouraging, as always in Dickens, is that this last alienation is resisted:

> 'Lor, you'll be so smart,' said Miss Tox, 'that your husband won't know you; will you, Sir?'
>
> 'I should know her,' said Toodle, gruffly, 'anyhows and anywheres.'
>
> Toodle was evidently not to be bought over. (ch. 2)

And it is not only that he will not be bought. It is that he retains, as a matter of course (so much so that it can be done as a joke, a misunderstanding of Miss Tox's conventional but still patronizing phrase) a kind of human recognition, of human knowledge, which is deeper and more decisive than the recognition-signals of wagework and fashion. It is this spark of recognition, of life-recognition, which Dickens is always trying to fan into a flame, against a conventional, calculating and sombre society.

5

In an alternative kind of fiction, this development of living feelings, against a deadening environment, would be a matter of intricate growth, through slowly developing relationships. The decisive interactions would arise from a soberly rendered everyday world: avoiding too explicit declaration or too arranged confrontation: a steady plausibility of human character and event. But Dickens's method is not of this kind. His presentation is direct and explicit, as in a dramatic or theatrical form. People declare themselves, not by involuntary revelation, but consciously, openly, drawing attention to their position. Characters appear and reappear, with their defining descriptions clearly displayed, and with their mode of speech – that crucially defining characteristic – essentially unaltered as the action proceeds. There is a sense in which what would in other novels be called conversations between characters are always, in Dickens, public encounters from certain fixed positions. In the same sense, what happens in Dickens, as the action proceeds, is not so much relationship as collision. The fixed positions clash, in certain arranged encounters. And this is always the point about a Dickens plot, which from an alternative tradition can be described so readily as contrived, melodramatic, dependent on mere coincidences. That is an external and mechanical judgement. The logic of the plot is precisely the arrangement of encounters – the more open and dramatic the better – between the fixed and declared human positions. What comes through and is meant to come through is a declared morality, which the action demonstrates.

It is of course easy to relate this to elements in the popular tradition: of preaching, caricature, propaganda, the morality novel and pamphlet and play. But it is at just this point that we see not only the influence on Dickens, but his mode of creative transformation. For what he had seized, imaginatively, was the strength of this mode for the dramatization of the particular crisis of his time. He is responding to a society which in its scale and complexity is very far from transparent, which is indeed in some decisive ways opaque – even deliberately opaque – as he sees it in the image of the dark but invisible cloud above the city. The steady empiricism, the known and felt life of the other kind of novel was in danger here of being merely helpless, or of withdrawing, as later happened, to a more selected and more easily knowable world. Dickens's genius shows in nothing more clearly than in his insistence on methods which can 'take the housetops off'; which can make open, and explicit, a full social and personal position which in detail, and moment by moment, might be very difficult to see; and beyond even this, to be able to dramatize, as if they were characters, those social forces which are wholly real, in a collective action, but which may never clearly appear in any isolated or individual moments.

His way of seeing characters, in their brief fixed appearances, defined by certain phrases, is a way of seeing that belongs to the streets: to faces and gestures briefly seen, phrases briefly and tellingly heard, in the crowded passage of men and women in the city. It is not the slowly known, slowly learned personality, the steadily emerging relationships, of a smaller, more continuous, more knowable community. Yet it is a human community nevertheless: pursuing definite purposes, experiencing definite consequences; connected and interacting in the very complexity and opacity of its multiple relationships. The world of the Dickens novel, in its unique and crowded form, is above all an imaginative response to the fact of the city, where men and women appear to be pursuing individual courses but where what they do, in its known and unknown effects, creates an effective common life within which all the individual lives are eventually held and shaped. It might have been possible to create this life from a few known and selected individuals, a few clear and emerging relationships, outwards to a more general reality. But Dickens's method, which as a response to the city has never been surpassed, was an insistence, first, on the defining types of this life, and then on their open interaction. The source of the strength of *Dombey and Son* is its juxtaposition of the most primary relationships – the family and the house – with the social forms of family and house in a city determined by a trading civilization. The most immediate human values, the love and kindness on which he always insisted, are then directly counterpoised to the most general reality; the crowded and apparently indifferent human landscape within which people try to find their way and their happiness. This presentation is, as I have said, his deepest creative and moral intention: creative because, through those particular methods, he can portray an unprecedented – crowded and rushing – human and social organization; moral, because he assumes from the beginning that he is free to intervene – to demonstrate, by any available device, the facts of this organization, the bearing of the facts, and the ways in which, by exhortation or by manipulation of the action, they can be deliberately altered.

This last kind of intervention is central to Dickens. It is again a quality that the alternative tradition is quick to condemn. But without it Dickens would not have wanted to write. There is in fact a difference, in *Dombey and Son*, from some of the later novels. Most of his early interventions are in the form of an arranged change of heart: a learning from collision, as the pieces of life are picked up:

> Mr Dombey is a white-haired gentleman, whose face bears heavy marks of care and suffering; but they are traces of a storm that has passed on for ever, and left a clear evening in its track. Ambitious projects trouble him no more. His only pride is in his daughter and her husband. (ch. 62)

This kind of change he always held to. Everything that was important to him would have been lost if he had not. But just as there were two ways of seeing a moral quality like pride – as a personal characteristic and as a social creation – so there are two ways, eventually, of seeing this deep kind of change: as a personal transformation, or as an alteration and amendment of the institutions which teach and confirm and deny. Dickens, though he repeatedly argued for this larger kind of change, was only rarely able, even in his kind of actions, to bring it about; to show it actually happening. In his later novels, he more commonly ends with a frank juxtaposition of innocence and complicity; the unbreakable strength of goodness and yet the persistent force of an existing and destructive way of life. In *Dombey and Son* his vision is not yet so sombre. It is characteristic of him that after 1850, when most of the society became more settled, more confident, more optimistic of reasonable change, Dickens became harsher, more disturbed and questioning, more uncertain of any foreseeable outcome. But in *Dombey and Son*, given the necessary learning from experience, the firm itself can be re-established:

> a foundation going on, upon which . . . an Edifice . . . is gradually rising, perhaps to equal, perhaps excel, that of which he was once the head, and the small beginnings of which . . . escaped his memory. Thus . . . from his daughter, after all, another Dombey and Son will ascend . . . triumphant. (ch. 62)

It is almost a terrible irony, but it is in tune with the whole of that willingly re-created illusion which is here Dickens's actual intervention: 'Mr Gills's money has begun to turn itself, and . . . it is turning over and over pretty briskly.' Kindness and capitalism – a small firm, humbly remembering its origins – are made compatible after all. The pride of the system is cured in a personal change.

It was to be different later, but the point, here, is the intervention: the willed and moral intervention. It is part of Dickens's way of seeing the world, in its fixed appearances and collisions, that he believes he can alter it by writing: here by a simple, an innocent goodwill.

6

One last point remains to be stressed, as a mark of the power of Dickens's creation. I have said that he was able, by his general method, to grasp certain social forces almost as if they were characters: as in the later examples of the Circumlocution Office, of Bleeding Heart Yard, of Expectations, of Shares. The House of Dombey and Son is already a creation of this type, but there is also another, of a simple and early kind, where it is not so much the observation as the operation that is original. To see the railways as the agents of change was not particularly difficult. Their physical presence was obvious, in this decisive period of expansion. But what is remarkable is that Dickens uses their power both as traditional dramatic force – as in the death of Carker (ch. 55) – and as a knowable social agency: his characteristic combination of traditional and extended literary methods. His description of the disintegration of an old social world by this new kind of activity is striking enough.

> The first shock of a great earthquake had, just at that period, rent the whole neighbourhood to its centre. Traces of its course were visible on every side. Houses were knocked down; streets broken through and stopped; deep pits and trenches dug in the ground; enormous heaps of earth and clay thrown up; buildings that were undermined and shaking, propped by great beams of wood. Here, a chaos of carts, overthrown and jumbled together, lay topsy-turvy at the bottom of a steep unnatural hill; there, confused treasures of iron soaked and rusted in something that had accidentally become a pond (ch. 6) . . .

But the decisive insight is the later description, in which the society is shown as reorganized, reorganizing itself, around this new force and method:

> The miserable waste ground, where the refuse-matter had been heaped of yore, was swallowed up and gone; and in its frowsy stead were tiers of warehouses, crammed with rich goods and costly merchandise. The old by-streets now swarmed with passengers and vehicles of every kind; the new streets that had stopped disheartened in the mud and waggon-ruts, formed towns within themselves, originating wholesome comforts and conveniences belonging to themselves, and never tried nor thought of until they sprung into existence. Bridges that had led to nothing, led to villas, gardens, churches, healthy public walks. The carcasses of houses, and beginnings of new thoroughfares, had started off upon the line at steam's own speed, and shot away into the country in a monster train . . . (ch. 15)

The complexity of this feeling is a true complexity of insight. All the pride of power – the new power of the industrial revolution – is felt in the language: the circulation by railway is the 'life's blood'.

But there is also the sense of this power overriding all other human habits and purposes: that sense which is confirmed, later, in

> the power that forced itself upon its iron way – its own – defiant of all paths and roads, piercing through the heart of every obstacle, and dragging living creatures of all classes, ages and degrees behind it. (ch. 20)

It is at once the 'life's blood' and 'the triumphant monster, Death'. In this dramatic enactment, Dickens is responding to the real contradiction – the power for life or death; for disintegration, order and false order – of the new social and economic forces of his time. His concern, always, is to keep human recognition and human kindness alive, through these unprecedented strains, and within this unrecognizably altered landscape. And as we see this unique correspondence between his methods and his intentions, those profoundly related creative and moral impulses, we put the final stress not on what he was unable to see, on insights and ideas he was unable or unwilling to reach; but on the remarkable emergence, at that critical moment, of a great radical novelist; a writer who shared and drew life from a popular tradition, and who succeeded in transforming and extending it, into a living, enduring and questioning radical culture.

Catherine Waters, Ambiguous Intimacy: Brother and Sister Relationships in *Dombey and Son* (1988)

Sisters were important figures for Dickens in both his fiction and his life. Michael Slater, discussing Dickens's relationship with his sister, Fanny, and its supposed portrayal in *The Haunted Man*, comments,

> This image of a brother and sister living together in a sort of sexless marriage, supporting each other against the world, is a persistent one in Dickens's fiction, beginning with Nicholas and Kate Nickleby (Ruth and Tom Pinch in *Martin Chuzzlewit* are another example).[1]

While brother–sister menages are certainly a recurrent feature in the fiction of Dickens, they do not exhibit the uniformity which this remark might suggest. Tom and Ruth Pinch, for example, who gleefully set up house like a pair of newlyweds, contrast markedly in characterisation and function with the faded and care-worn John and Harriet Carker in *Dombey and Son*. While the bond between Tom and Ruth is made a source of comedy in the narrative because of its self-consciously absurd approximation to the stereotype of wedded bliss, the tie between John and Harriet provides a sober parallel for the relationships between Florence and Paul, and Florence and Walter in the novel. The insularity of their domestic life together reflects upon the inwardness of the 'two' sibling relationships involving Florence. *Dombey and Son* not only offers a 'particularly interesting' analysis of the father–daughter relation (as Lydia Zwinger has recently shown),[2] but also provides an important illustration of the complexity of Dickens's vision of the brother–sister relationship, revealing a tension between the idealisation of this bond, and the demonstration of its sexual ambiguity and solipsism.

Three brother–sister relationships are explored in *Dombey and Son*: those between Mr Dombey and Mrs Chick, John and Harriet Carker, and Florence and Paul. Mr Dombey and Mrs Chick share a bond that is commercial and social, rather than emotional and personal. The sisterly 'devotion' shown by Louisa consists of subtle obsequiousness, overt flattery and mock self-depreciation. She consistently provides a carefully staged performance, and her pretence is continually underlined and satirised in the novel. Louisa's 'juvenile manner'[3] of dress links her with the Mrs Skewtons, Volumnia Dedlocks and Lady Tippinses of Dickensian fiction, whose physical artificiality, masking decrepitude, is accompanied by a more or less appalling emotional immaturity. The skill with which she appeals to her brother's pride is shown in her emphatic praise of little Paul's 'Dombeyism' in chapter 1. Mr Dombey is flattered not only by her reiterated description of the baby as 'a perfect Dombey', but by the 'feminine weakness' Louisa so insistently 'betrays' in her response:

> My dear Paul, it's very weak and silly of me, I know, to be so trembly and shakey from head to foot; but I am so very queer that I must ask you for a glass of wine and a morsel of that cake. I thought I should have fallen out of the staircase window as I came down from seeing dear Fanny, and that tiddy ickle sing.

The self-consciousness apparent in Louisa's emphatic agitation undercuts her claims to have lost control of her feelings.[4] She describes the visible features of her performance, as if she were determined to incorporate the stage directions into her dialogue, and the redundancy stresses her calculation and pretence. Louisa invokes the Victorian stereotype of women as hysterical creatures whose emotional susceptibility manifests itself in tears and swoons. Her purpose is to flatter the masculinity of her brother, and she is all too successful.

Just as Mr Dombey is said by the narrator to have 'pitied himself through [Paul]', so Louisa effectively appeals to her brother through her admiration for his son. Referring to Louisa's discussion of the pin-cushion made by Miss Tox to welcome the new baby, the narrator notes,

> Even the sort of recognition of Dombey and Son, conveyed in the foregoing conversation, was so palatable to him, that his sister, Mrs Chick – though he affected to consider her a weak good-natured person – had perhaps more influence over him than anybody else.

The nature of this 'influence' is ambiguous. While indicating at one level her ability to establish Miss Tox in her brother's regard, and her role in directing Paul's nursing, baptism and education, it also signifies her part of the development of Mr Dombey's key traits: his extraordinary pride and narcissism. In chapter 40, the narrator observes of his implacable nature, 'deference and concession swell its evil qualities, and are the food it grows upon'. Louisa parallels Mr Carker and Major Bagstock in her obsequious behaviour towards her brother; and insofar as her stance conforms with the Victorian ideal of sisterly subservience, the more blatant servility of the two male sycophants emphasises the pernicious implications of the ideal. Louisa is not so adept a flatterer as Carker or Bagstock however, failing occasionally to comprehend her brother's opinion before voicing her imitation of it.

Mr Dombey's extreme narcissism is demonstrated in his preoccupation with the 'Little Dombey', his namesake, Paul. He tells Mrs Chick,

> Paul and myself will be able, when the time comes, to hold our own – the House, in other words, will be able to hold its own, and maintain its own, and hand down its own of itself.

His highly reflexive and almost masturbatory grammar describes a process of parthenogenesis. Mrs Chick both acknowledges and encourages her brother's narcissism by continually invoking him as a standard for his own behaviour. In expressing agreement with her brother in chapter 5, Louisa effusively declares,

> Very true, my dear Paul, . . . and spoken like yourself. I might have expected nothing else from you. I might have known that such would have been your opinion.

Mr Dombey constitutes both tenor and vehicle in her simile here. Again, in chapter 29, she announces her satisfaction in knowing that her brother 'is so true to himself, and to his name of Dombey; although, of course [she says] I always knew he would be'. She concludes her explanation to Miss Tox with the comment,

> Therefore, of course my brother Paul has done what was to be expected of him, and what anybody might have foreseen he would do, if he entered the marriage state again.

The circularity and tautology of Mrs Chick's description pander to the inordinate self-absorption of her brother, who is implicitly held to defy comparison with anyone else but himself. The confusion with which she interweaves instances of foresight and hindsight to affirm Mr Dombey's fulfilment of the expectation he himself arouses, is a similar concession to his narcissism.

Mrs Chick's preoccupation with her brother Paul, and with the affairs of his household, is reflected in the consignment of her husband to a conspicuously peripheral position in the novel. He is almost mute beneath Louisa's avalanche of words, and his significance is inversely proportionate to the omnipotence of his brother-in-law. Her own children – George and Frederick – are merely afforded passing mentions in the novel, their mother apparently preferring to devote herself, with the help of Miss Tox, to the daily superintendence of her brother's son. Given the precedence of the sibling tie and its concomitant aunt's status in the life of Mrs Chick, her interest in the prospect of a new Mrs Dombey is not surprising.

According to the narrator, the two objections held by Louisa towards her sister-in-law Fanny, were 'her having married her brother – in itself a species of audacity – and her having, in the course of events, given birth to a girl instead of a boy'. Louisa's complaints display an absurd mixture of pride and self-interest. While alert to the financial benefits likely to profit the sister of a wealthy, bachelor brother, she must also be seen to share Mr Dombey's paternal ambitions. The most expedient course available to Louisa after Fanny's death is to furnish her brother with a wife of her own choosing, and as her most faithful acolyte, and one who is unlikely to produce children of her own, Miss Tox is the best candidate. When Mr Dombey unexpectedly selects a wife for himself, she is forced to abandon this 'tack' and to squash the romantic expectations she has awakened in the breast of Miss Tox.

The design apparent in the execution of Louisa's retreat in chapter 29, again demonstrates her hypocrisy and self-interest. The mingling of 'a little stateliness' with her demeanour, her resort to 'the art of coughing', her refusal to look at Miss Tox and the evasiveness with which she broaches the subject of Mr Dombey's forthcoming marriage, all illustrate her prevarication, and contrast comically with the unfortunate simplicity of her 'friend'. Louisa's resentment at her brother's independent choice of a wife is made evident in the juxtaposition of her histrionic self-depreciation, with her vociferously proclaimed satisfaction at his decision. Her 'concluding' assurance – 'I much prefer it, as it is' – is belied by her preceding and succeeding emphasis upon

Mr Dombey's disregard for her advice. According to the narrator, '[She] continued to hold forth, as if in defiance of somebody':

> 'If my brother Paul had consulted with me, which he sometimes does – or rather, sometimes used to do; for he will naturally do that no more now, and this is a circumstance which I regard as a relief from responsibility,' said Mrs Chick, hysterically, 'for I thank Heaven I am not jealous –' here Mrs Chick again shed tears: 'if my brother Paul had come to me, and had said, "Louisa, what kind of qualities would you advise me to look out for, in a wife?" I should certainly have answered, "Paul, you must have family, you must have beauty, you must have dignity, you must have connexion." Those are the words I should have used.'

The conspicuous interposition of the narrator's reporting and explanatory clauses within Louisa's speech emphasises the theatricality of her behaviour. The pretentiousness that characterises her discourse with Mr Dombey is ironically foregrounded here as she regretfully rehearses the part she had been denied the opportunity to play. However, her indignation at being ousted from her brother's confidence is somewhat mollified by the apparent eligibility of Edith Grainger, and she comforts herself with a sharpened sense of her brother's social superiority. She condemns Miss Tox with a cry of outrage in which the assumption of her own innocence is undercut by the excessiveness of her protest: 'That you might . . . dare to aspire to contemplate the possibility of his uniting himself to *you* . . . '. In defining her sense of self-importance here, Louisa refers to herself as 'the sister of my brother – and as the sister-in-law of my brother's wife – and as a connexion by marriage of my brother's wife's mother – may I be permitted to add, as a Dombey?' and the extraordinary tautology indicates both her perception of herself as a 'relative creature' and her tenacious regard for the sibling, rather than the conjugal, tie. As Louise Yelin comments, Mrs Chick here 'affects an appropriate pose . . . in order to trade on her relationship with Dombey'[5] – a commercial response which itself attests to the kinship identity being claimed.

Louisa Chick's exploitation of the brother–sister relationship contrasts markedly with the behaviour of the other adult sister in *Dombey and Son*, Harriet Carker. Harriet is sister to John and James Carker, but lives with the former, having 'chosen' to follow and devote herself to this ruined brother when his attempt at embezzlement is discovered. She has sacrificed her youth, her beauty and the prospect of a husband to accompany John in his removal to the 'blighted country' on the outskirts of London. As a result of this loyalty, she is disowned by James. The mutual exile of the two siblings represents a type of ironic expulsion from an unlikely Paradise, in which Harriet shares the consequences of her brother's Fall, and functions as his 'redeeming spirit' and 'solitary angel' (ch. 33). Indeed the language used to describe the sister is characterised by biblical allusion. She is invested with the status of an unacknowledged saint whose face is said to shine 'like a light' upon her brother's heart, and in her apparently sanctifying power, she is identified with Florence. However, her relationship with John is not void of tension, as her 'comforting' presence is also a reminder to him of his crime:

> The cordial face she lifted up to his to kiss him, was his home, his life, his universe, and yet it was a portion of his punishment and grief; for in the cloud he saw upon it – though serene and calm as any radiant cloud at sunset – and in the constancy and devotion of her life, and in the sacrifice she made of ease, enjoyment, and hope, he saw the bitter fruits of his old crime, for ever ripe and fresh. (ch. 33)

The irony of this situation is reflected in Florence's relationship with her father, for the very intensity of her love for him strengthens his aversion for her. Women, it seems, can never determine the effects of their influence.

In their 'poor small house, barely and sparely furnished, but very clean' (ch. 33), John and Harriet are brought together in a domestic arrangement that is more like the menage of a husband and wife, than a brother-sister relationship. Harriet embodies many of the ideals associated with the dutiful Victorian middle-class wife. She occupies herself in providing an attractive home for her brother, secluded from the noisy affairs of the public workplace. The provision of this domestic haven involves an unremitting round of lovingly performed household tasks, including the attempt to decorate the bower by training 'homely flowers' about the porch and the garden. The middle-class housewife was responsible for the learning and practice of 'Domestic Economy': as Mrs Beeton insists, 'Frugality and Economy are Home Virtues without which no household can prosper'.[6] Accordingly, when her domestic chores were completed, the narrator says, Harriet

> counted her little stock of money, with an anxious face, and went out thoughtfully to buy some necessaries for their table, planning and contriving, as she went, how to save. (ch. 33)

She greets and farewells her brother at the doorway to their home as he journeys to and from his workplace in the city, and spends the remainder of her day 'musing and working by turns' (ch. 33) in anticipation of her brother's homecoming. But Harriet is not only wife-like in her provisions for the bodily comfort of her brother: she also enters into that community of mind with him, recommended as one of a woman's first duties to her husband. As Harriet Martineau observes, a woman

> is to be the participator in his happiness, the consoler of his sorrows, the support of his weakness, and his friend under all circumstances.[7]

When John describes his fondness for the supposedly drowned Walter Gay, Harriet expresses a wish that she had seen or known the boy. Her brother gently dismisses the wish, and Harriet's response identifies her wifely position:

> 'Is not your sorrow mine? And if I had, perhaps you would feel that I was a better companion to you in speaking about him, than I may seem now.'
> 'My dearest sister! Is there anything within the range of rejoicing or regret, in which I am not sure of your companionship?'
> 'I hope you think not, John, for surely there is nothing!'
> 'How could you be better to me, or nearer to me then, than you are in this, or anything?' said her brother.
> 'I feel that you did know him, Harriet, and that you shared my feelings towards him.' (ch. 33)

In her relationship with John, Harriet is portrayed as the 'chosen companion of his joys and sorrows' (to borrow Mrs Ellis's phrase[8]), and thus as a quasi-wife. When Harriet finally marries the 'hazel-eyed' old bachelor, Mr Morfin, her brother, the 'grey-haired Junior', goes to live with them in a parodic *ménage à trois*, the brother filling the place conventionally occupied by the lover.

Harriet's selfless and constant devotion to her brother John parallels Florence's love for Paul in the novel. But whereas the former is a woman who stoically embraces the immediate prospect of spinsterhood, the latter is a child wounded by parental disfavour. Mr Dombey's disregard of Florence and pride in Paul have a decisive impact upon the relationship between the sister and brother. Florence's exclusion from her father's interest and affection is made more prominent by his overwhelming concern for Paul, and she is harnessed in the household worship of the small idol.

Thus, while shared play between opposite-sex siblings was encouraged by the Victorian advice-manuals as a means of reinforcing sexual differentiation, Florence is enlisted to sport and play before, rather than with, her brother, in order to amuse and enliven him:

> 'Now Florence child!' said her aunt, briskly, 'what are you doing, love? Show yourself to him. Engage his attention, my dear!'

The significance of Florence's situation lies not only in the preclusion of spontaneity involved – play, like creativity, cannot be willed[9] – but in the way she is pressed into her baby brother's service.

This exploitation is emphasised in the well-known letter Dickens wrote to Forster expressing his intentions with regard to *Dombey and Son*. He comments that Paul's

> love and confidence are all bestowed upon his sister, whom Mr Dombey has used – and so has the boy himself too, for that matter – as a mere convenience and handle to him.[10]

Paul's use of Florence is unlike his father's, consisting of his demands upon her as a surrogate mother – a source of untiring emotional and physical nurturance. But Florence also functions as a repository for the values and experiences of childhood denied to her brother, curing the precociousness induced by Mr Dombey's impatient ambition. Her appearance is shown to awaken Paul from his 'old fashioned' moods. Responding to Paul's demand, in chapter 8, Florence arrives to attend him to bed:

> The child immediately started up with sudden readiness and animation, and raised towards his father in bidding him goodnight, a countenance so much brighter, so much younger, and so much more child-like altogether, that Mr Dombey, while he felt greatly reassured by the change, was quite amazed at it.

However, from Mr Dombey's point of view, Paul's relationship with Florence represents a particularly repugnant obstacle in his son's 'steeple-chase towards manhood'. Despite his attempts to diminish the bond between them, the siblings' mutual emotional privation as motherless children increases their attachment to a degree of intensity that has led critics to postulate the existence of an incestuous relationship here. Mark Spilka argues that

> Paul Dombey's affection for his sister is bathetic and incestuous; or as Freud might say, it is bathetic *because* it is incestuous, because it is rooted in Dickens's own incestuous longing for his sister Fanny and for the child-like Mary Hogarth.[11]

Similarly, Russell M. Goldfarb asserts that 'in the foreground of *Dombey and Son* there is a complicated incestuous relationship'.[12] Judith Schelly dismisses Goldfarb's view as an 'oversimplification' and claims that

> Dickens's attitude toward sibling intimacy becomes comprehensible only in terms of the Levi-Straussian model which sees the desire for incest as a nostalgia for a presocial Eden . . . Dickens freely borrows the language of erotic love, but only because he regards the affection of Paul and Florence as a refuge from adult degradation.[13]

But the relationship between Paul and Florence is shown, I think, to be neither blatantly incestuous nor nostalgically pre-lapsarian. Its nature is more ambiguous.

Florence's love for her brother is indeed ardent and desperate, and is first manifested in her cry to the nurse in chapter 5, 'Oh, pray, pray, let me lie by my brother to-night, for I believe he's fond of me!'. Paul's affection for his sister grows equally intense, as his nurse comically insinuates in describing the mysterious power of her niece, Betsey Jane: 'She took fancies to people; whimsical fancies, some of them; others, affections that one might expect to see – only stronger than common. They all died'. (ch. 8)

Mrs Wickam concludes by warning Miss Berry, ' . . . be thankful that Master Paul is not too fond of you'.

At school, Paul's extraordinarily close affection for his sister is manifested in his exclusive preference for her company. Being wheeled down to the seashore each day by Old Glubb, Paul becomes distressed by the presence of other children:

> 'Go away, if you please,' he would say to any child who came to bear him company. 'Thank you, but I don't want you.' (ch. 8)

His comment to Florence, 'We don't want any others, do we? Kiss me, Floy!', implicitly assumes the reciprocal intensity of her attachment. Demonstrating a childish but masculine confidence in his possession of Florence, Paul tells Mrs Pipchin,

> 'I mean . . . to put my money all together in one Bank, never try to get any more, go away into the country with my darling Florence, have a beautiful garden, fields, and woods, and live there with her all my life.' (ch. 14)

This idealized scenario resembles the dreamy future anticipated by another brother and sister: Tom and Maggie Tulliver in Book First, chapter 5, of *The Mill on the Floss*. The futility of Paul's plan is emphasised by his impending death. Moreover, the insubstantiality of this stereotypic vision of a blissful, life-long sibling union is ironically exposed by the disillusioning situation of the colourless John and Harriet Carker.

As Paul's health becomes more precarious during his term at the Academy of Doctor Blimber, he looks towards Florence's attendance at the end-of-term party as his one 'great theme'. When she arrives for the event, Paul is so enraptured by her beauty as she kneels to kiss him, he can 'hardly make up his mind to let her go again, or take away her bright and loving eyes from his face'. According to the invitations sent by Doctor and Mrs Blimber, the 'hour' of the party is 'half-past seven o'clock' and 'the object [is] Quadrilles'; however, Paul and Florence are shown to be less interested in the dancing than in each other. The narrator notes that

> Nobody stood before [Paul] . . . when they observed that he liked to see Florence dancing, but they left the space in front quite clear, so that he might follow her with his eyes. (ch. 14)

The engrossing link between brother and sister, between onlooker and participator, conspicuously cuts across the conventional, marriage-like pairing which characterises dancing, and dramatically emphasises the primacy of the sibling tie. The intensity of this tie culminates in the final embrace of brother and sister at Paul's death, where, as Spilka comments, 'there is almost a consummation between them':[14]

> Sister and brother wound their arms around each other, and the golden light came streaming in, and fell upon them, locked together.
> 'How fast the river runs, between its green banks and the rushes, Floy! But it's very near the sea. I hear the waves! They always said so!' (ch. 16)

The final water union of Florence and Paul resembles the 'reunion' of Maggie and Tom Tulliver in the flooded River Floss – an embrace of death which also has ambiguous sexual implications. However, Florence and Paul are still children, and their desperate meeting is informed by a desire to be reunited with their lost mother. Paul identifies Florence with his mother here, just as Florence's sleeping embrace of her baby brother in chapter 5 allows her to dream of her mother's 'loving arms again wound round her.'[15] Florence's status as a surrogate mother thus compounds the incestuous aura surrounding her relationship with Paul. The incongruity between her identity as mother and sister, between her maternity and celibacy, characterises her sexuality as curiously parthenogenetic, and thereby contributes to the suggestions of inwardness and inbreeding also apparent in Mr Dombey's narcissistic relation to his son.

Florence's union with Walter Gay sustains the incestuous aura that surrounds her relationship with Paul. Referring to her brother, she tells Walter,

> 'he liked you very much, and said before he died that he was fond of you, and said "Remember Walter!" and if you'll be a brother to me Walter, now that he is gone and I have none on earth, I'll be your sister all my life, and think of you like one wherever we may be!' (ch. 19)

Florence's memory of Paul's death significantly distorts the 'reality' presented in chapter 16. Paul's dying injunction, 'Remember Walter', is made to his father, and involves no reference to Florence. Yet his sister applies the admonition to herself. It is not Paul who 'seems to suggest that his relationship to Florence might be transferred to Walter Gay';[16] rather, Florence herself casts Walter as a new brother, despite his evident and longheld desire to be somewhat more than this.

Since the only emotionally fulfilling heterosexual relationship available to Florence has been her tie with Paul (through which she has defined herself), her response to Walter is psychologically consistent. After he sails for the West Indies he is believed to be drowned at sea, just as Paul's discovery of what the waves were always saying marks his death, and so the parallel is strengthened. Florence's relationship with Walter demonstrates the way in which the brother-sister tie continues to shape her experience even after Paul's death. She merges her memory of Paul with her memory of Walter to the point where her eventual marriage no longer involves even a spiritual choice between brother and lover.

Florence's grief at Paul's death is intense and private. After the first bout of unrestrained tears, she gradually begins to occupy herself again. But her singing is described as being 'more like the mournful recollection of what she had done at his request on that last night, than the reality repeated', and her handiwork is taken up 'as if it had been sentient and had known him' (ch. 18). Her preoccupation with the dead Paul becomes increasingly morbid as it persists. While Mr Dombey is buying himself a new wife at Leamington, and his house in London is being refurbished to receive her, Florence indulges in 'the softer memories connected with the dull old house' (ch. 28). Concluding her visit to Sir Barnet and Lady Skettles, she rejoices in the immanence of her dead brother:

> How long it seemed since she had wandered through the silent rooms: since she had last crept, softly and afraid, into those her father occupied: since she had felt the solemn but yet soothing influence of the beloved dead in every action of her daily life! This new farewell reminded her, besides, of her parting with poor Walter: of his looks and words that night: and of the gracious blending she had noticed in him, of tenderness for those he left behind, with courage and high spirit. His little history was associated with the old house too, and gave it a new claim and hold upon her heart. (ch. 28)

When Florence returns from her father's wedding, she reassumes her 'old simple mourning for dear Paul' and again links her memory of him with her memory of Walter as she cries beside Diogenes:

> Florence cannot see {Diogenes} plainly, in a little time, for there is a mist between her eyes and him, and her dead brother and dead mother shine in it like angels. Walter, too, poor wandering ship-wrecked boy, oh, where is he! (ch. 31)

Florence's morbid absorption in the memory of Paul is undercut in chapter 41 by the description of 'New Voices in the Waves' to which she remains deaf. Florence visits Brighton again, and finds 'a tender melancholy pleasure' in sitting pensively and hearing 'in the wild low murmur of the sea, his little story told again, his very words repeated'. The masculine personal pronouns here are supplied without a referent in any preceding sentence, and yet their usage is unambiguous. That such grammatical specification is unnecessary is a reflection of Paul's omnipresence. However, accompanying Florence is Mr Toots, who comically 'dotes upon' her, just as she dotes upon her image of Paul, and in addition to a 'requiem of little Dombey', he hears 'praise of Florence' in the waves. Doctor Blimber hears the sea say '"Gentlemen, we will now resume our studies"', while Mr Feeder B.A.,

> plainly hears the waves informing him, as he loiters along, that Doctor Blimber will give up the business; and he feels a soft romantic pleasure in looking at the outside of the house, and thinking that the Doctor will first paint it, and put it into thorough repair.

These more mundane messages highlight the idealizing imagination with which Florence remembers her brother. What the waves always say is shown to be determined by the preoccupations of the hearer. The waves themselves do not possess any inherent spiritual significance, but occupy a sanctified place in Florence's memory because of their association with Paul.

Florence's identification of Walter with Paul is intensified when she flees to the shop of Solomon Gills. Captain Cuttle teases her with laments for the 'drowned' Walter and thereby activates an equivalent longing for Paul:

> 'Ah! If I had him for my brother now!' cried Florence.
> 'Don't! don't take on, my pretty!' said the Captain, 'awast, to obleege me! He *was* your nat'ral born friend like, warn't he Pet?'
> Florence had no words to answer with. She only said, 'Oh dear, dear Paul! oh Walter!' (ch. 49)

Even when Walter miraculously reappears, Florence's regard for him is governed by her attachment to Paul:

> She had no thought of him but as a brother, a brother rescued from the grave; a shipwrecked brother saved and at her side; and rushed into his arms. In all the world, he seemed to be her hope, her comfort, refuge, natural protector. 'Take care of Walter, I was fond of Walter!' The dear remembrance of the plaintive voice that said so, rushed upon her soul, like music in the night. 'Oh welcome home, dear Walter! Welcome to this stricken breast!' She felt the words, although she could not utter them, and held him in her pure embrace. (ch. 49)

It is not Walter himself, but the remembrance of Paul with whom he is associated, that has the greatest impact upon Florence. The memory of Paul's voice affects her with a lover-like ecstasy, as it rushes 'upon her soul like music in the night'. Walter is again thwarted in his desire to be more than a quasi-brother to Florence. Indeed, part of Walter's insipidness in the novel stems from the way in which he is eclipsed, or absorbed, by the lingering memory of Paul. The effusive sentimentality characterising the reunion of Florence and Walter and their subsequent discourse, is comically undercut by his repeated, but frustratingly ineffectual attempts to dissolve the quasi-brother-sister relationship she so tenaciously adheres to. Walter declares his devotion:

> 'If anything could make me happier in being allowed to see and speak to you, would it not be the discovery that I had any means on earth of doing you a moment's service! Where would I not go, what would I not do, for your sake!' She smiled, and called him brother. (ch. 49)

Florence's engagement predictably leads her to redefine herself in relation to Walter. In response to his question, 'Are you nothing?', she answers, 'Nothing but your wife' and explains,

> 'I am nothing any more, that is not you. I have no earthly hope any more, that is not you. I have nothing dear to me any more, that is not you.' (ch. 56)

The melodramatic fervour of this declaration is comically undercut by the bathetic reaction of Mr Toots, who rushes out of the room here and every time he finds he 'cannot endure the contemplation of Lieutenant Walters's bliss' (ch. 56). But Florence's perception of herself as an adjunct of Walter significantly echoes her childhood devotion to Paul. When Florence is abducted by Good Mrs Browne, and later found by Walter, she identifies herself to him as 'my little brother's only sister', her use of the third person emphasising the extraordinary extent to which she defines herself as a 'relative creature'. As

Louise Yelin notes, her self-denial here contrasts with the way in which Mrs Chick self-consciously exploits her role as Mrs Dombey's sister in chapter 29. Florence's equivalent dependence upon Paul and Walter for her self-definition, highlights not only the lack of identity from which she suffers as a Victorian woman, but the correspondence between her roles as sister and wife. Even in her future husband's embrace, Florence continues to think of Paul as she 'weep[s] with happiness' within the 'refuge' Walter provides: 'The more she clung to it, the more the dear dead child was in her thoughts' (ch. 56). Moreover, Walter is fully aware of Florence's overriding preoccupation with Paul. As they depart on their sea voyage, he anticipates the meditations of his new bride:

> 'As I hear the sea,' says Florence, 'and sit watching it, it brings so many days into my mind. It makes me think so much—'
> 'Of Paul, my love. I know it does.'
> Of Paul and Walter. (ch. 57)

Paul's shadowy presence within the lives of Florence and Walter effectively completes a type of posthumous *ménage à trois*, that parallels the Carker, Carker and Morfin trio.

The formation of such familial trios as part of the denouement ostensibly establishes the *ménage à trois* of brother, sister and husband as an ideal in the novel. However, the suggestions of insularity and inbreeding which surround such households undercut their idealisation. The incestuous climate of the household sustained by the ministrations of Florence surpasses that apparent in the domestic establishment of Harriet Carker Morfin. Florence's menage comprises not a brother, sister and husband, but a brother, sister and quasi-brother. Moreover, she and Walter give birth to a second generation sister and brother who are named, of course, Florence and Paul. An extraordinary narcissism characterises this family in which the first generation sister and brother are reproduced in a second generation through a connubial union between a quasi-brother and sister. While Mr Dombey's preoccupation with the values of the masculine, public sphere is condemned in the novel, the private sphere of kinship, love and domesticity, cultivated by Florence at the other extreme, is shown to be sequestered, cloying and thus also limited. Florence and Walter effectively parody the Victorian cult of domesticity – the 'vision that perceived the family as both enfolding its members and excluding the outside world'[17] – in their excessive inwardness and isolation. Florence's journey to the church with Walter on their wedding day is marked by the same absorption in an 'old enchanted dream of life' (ch. 28), that characterised her behaviour after the loss of Paul:

> Not even in that childish walk of long ago, were they so far removed from all the world about them as today. The childish feet of long ago, did not tread such enchanted ground as theirs do now . . . But through the light, and through the shade, they go on lovingly together, lost to everything around; thinking of no other riches, and no prouder home, than they have now in one another. (ch. 57)

The suggestions of self-absorption and withdrawal which colour their union render it an equivocal ideal.

In *Dombey and Son*, the sibling bond between Florence and Paul is shown to shape and determine the conjugal tie between Florence and Walter, thereby demonstrating the primacy of the brother-sister relationship in their lives. Relevant to the analysis of such intense Victorian sibling bonds, is the controversy which surrounded the 'Marriage with a Deceased Wife's Sister Bill'. This Bill proposed the exemption of a wife's sister from the list of fixed degrees of consanguinity and affinity within which the marriage was prohibited. It was first introduced into parliament in 1842 (*Dombey and Son* was published in parts from October 1846 until April 1848), and after decades of heated debate, was finally passed in 1907. As Nancy F. Anderson demonstrates, contention over the Bill throughout the Victorian period was closely related to a growing concern over incest in nineteenth-century culture:

> the heated insistence on maintaining sexless purity between in-laws suggests . . . transferred anxiety about emotional intimacy between siblings.[18]

The atypical character of the two *ménages à trois* depicted in *Dombey and Son* enables Dickens to displace the controversy associated with the more usual household grouping of husband, wife and wife's sister. However, the correspondence between Florence's identity as a wife and a quasi-sister in her marriage to Walter provides a significant commentary upon one of the objections raised against the Bill in 1865. According to Anderson, as part of the argument that passage of the Bill would lead to removal of restrictions on marriages within other prohibited degrees, William Adam, the Liberal Party whip in Gladstone's first ministry, insisted that

> consanguineous marriages 'confuse the reciprocal duties of domestic life, and thereby retard the formation of moral character and prevent real moral progress.' If, for example, a son married his mother, there could not be 'pure filial reverence and pure maternal affection.' To the offspring, the father would also be the brother, and 'the authority of the father and the equality of the brother are lost and annulled.'[19]

The relationships between Florence and Walter, and between Harriet and John Carker, are both marked by an equivalence in the woman's identity as wife and sister. Yet this potentially schizophrenic situation causes no serious trauma for the characters involved. The confusion of incompatible roles and duties, feared by William Adam, is not realised in these relationships. This 'unproblematic' conflation of the double identities assumed by Florence and Harriet thus has fundamental implications for the presentation of sexuality in *Dombey and Son*. It either represents a way of sublimating the conjugal tie, or emphasises the resonant emotional incestuousness of the extraordinarily intense sibling relationships portrayed in the novel. The simultaneous availability of these alternative implications finally constitutes the novel's ambiguous vision of the brother-sister bond. The significance of this vision for nineteenth-century fiction lies in Dickens's identification and exploration of the way in which the sexual feeling underlying intense fraternal relationships emerges from the Victorian ideals of femininity and domesticity.

Suvendrini Perera, Wholesale, Retail and for Exportation: Empire and the Family Business in *Dombey and Son* (1990)

> Commissioners: What articles of trade are best suited to your people, or what would you like brought to your country?
> Obi: Cowies, cloth, muskets, powder, handkerchiefs, coral, beads, hats – anything from the white man's country will please.
> Commissioners: You are the King of this country, as our Queen is the sovereign of Great Britain; but she does not wish to trade with you; she only desires that her subjects may trade fairly with yours . . . The Queen of England's subjects would be glad to trade for raw cotton, indigo, ivory, gums, camwood. Now have your people these things to offer in return for English trade goods?
> Obi: Yes.[1]

This unequal exchange performs, through several filters of official interpretation, the recognizable dynamics of colonial trade. Obi's interlocutors represent one of the best-known trade delegations of the early Victorian period, the Niger Expedition, a joint project of the Colonial Office and the Admiralty with the cooperation of abolitionist and missionary interests. The Expedition's aims were, in its own words, 'to assist in the abolition of the Slave Trade, and further the innocent trade of her Majesty's subjects'; or in the words of Dickens's 1848 review of the Expedition's authorized *Narrative*, to bring about 'the abolition, in great part, of the Slave Trade, by means of treaties with native chiefs, to whom were to be explained the immense advantages of general unrestricted commerce with Great Britain in lieu thereof' (p. 46).

The ceremonial dialogue of trade negotiation does not obscure the power relations implicit in this missionary armada, designed as it was to 'awaken' Africans 'to a proper sense of their own degradation' ('Niger,' p. 47). As Eric Williams and others have suggested, abolitionist blockades and trade expeditions in fact prepared the way for the full-scale colonization of Africa, subverting local economies by the introduction of British goods and accumulating valuable information during these exploratory forays.[2] Both Dickens and the official *Narrative* represent the free trade of empire, or 'general unrestricted commerce with Great Britain,' as 'innocent' in contrast to the un-English monopoly in slaves attributed to Obi (p. 46). Dickens's essay, seven years after the event, however, turns out to be not a defence of the abolitionist premises of the Expedition, but a violent repudiation of 'the heated visions of philanthropists for the railroad Christianisation of Africa, and the abolition of the Slave Trade' (p. 62). By this time, indeed, the Niger Expedition had become a byword of costly failure. Bad planning, unsuitable climate, and African covert resistance (in Dickens's terms, 'their climate, their falsehood, and deceit') had ended in scores of deaths among the English crew, and the abandoning of the whole project (p. 46). Dickens's 1848 essay, I want to suggest, becomes more than a simple review of the Expedition's *Narrative*; it is a means of commenting on the recent direction of colonial and trade policy, and indirectly on the wider issues of free trade and empire, domestic ethics and foreign policy, and, most significantly, the source of moral authority over these issues at home.

This debate over moral authority was profoundly shaped by contemporary representations of woman's influence. Judith Newton and others have shown that a domestic sphere of soft, conciliatory feminine influence was a particularly mid-Victorian creation, formulated in response to the growing social and economic power of the middle classes.[3] Although Bernard Semmel has demonstrated that 'the essentially mercantilist assumptions and objectives embodied in . . . "classic" . . . Imperialism were far from absent in the thinking [that] erected the system of free trade in the last half of the eighteenth and in the first half of the nineteenth centuries,' the doctrine of free trade has usually been cast as inherently anti-imperialist.[4] A key aspect of the mid-Victorian debate over colonial policy was the ostensible pacifism of free trade, often perceived as a softening or feminization of a more assertive expansionism. In the Niger essay, Dickens attributes the misguided humanitarianism of the Expedition to 'the weird old women who go about, and exceedingly roundabout, on the Exeter Hall Platform.'[5] *Bleak House* (1853) firmly locates feminine moral authority in Esther's housewifely skills, whereas Mrs. Jellyby's exercise of 'telescopic philanthropy' in the Borrioboola Gha project, another experimental settlement on the Niger, leads directly to household mismanagement and anarchy. The usurpation of the masculine platforms of economy and colonial policy by 'weird old women' (both politicized women and men feminized by humanitarianism) thus simultaneously perverts the ideology of gendered spheres of influence and guarantees disaster at home and abroad.

I

The text I want to situate in relation to this discourse of empire, trade, and feminine moral authority is not *Bleak House*, however, but *Dombey and Son*, a novel usually discussed for its treatment of the local effects of mid-Victorian capitalism. As the repressed second half of the title makes clear, *Dealings with the Firm of Dombey and Son, Wholesale, Retail and for Exportation* is Dickens's parable of mercantile capitalism; it is also inherently and immediately a narrative predicated on an economy of empire. The passage situating the House of Dombey against the key institutions of metropolitan power maps this fundamental connection:

> Though the offices of Dombey and Son were within the liberties of the City of London . . . yet were there hints of adventurous and romantic story to be obtained in some of the adjacent objects . . . The Royal Exchange was close at hand; the Bank of England, with its vaults of gold and silver 'down among the dead men' underground, was their magnificent neighbour. Just around the corner stood the rich East India House, teeming with suggestions of precious stuffs and stones, tigers, elephants, howdahs, hookahs, umbrellas, palm trees, palanquins, and gorgeous princes of a brown complexion . . . with their slippers very much turned up at the toes. Anywhere in the immediate vicinity there might be seen pictures of ships speeding away full sail to all parts of the world; outfitting warehouses ready to pack off anybody anywhere, fully equipped in half an hour; and little timber midshipmen in obsolete naval uniforms, eternally employed outside the shop doors of nautical Instrument-makers. (ch. 4).

Empire not only supplies the obvious link between the separated 'money world' and 'water world' previous critics have discerned in the novel; it activates capitalist expansion, generating ships, outfitting warehouses and scientific instruments.[6] The financial institutions of the Bank, the Royal Exchange, and the House of Dombey combine the power of an empire represented by neighbouring East India House, translating the stuff of oriental romance directly into the substance of metropolitan wealth and converting the interior of the Bank of England to subterranean coffers of piratical gold.[7] Dickens's cartography locates the novel's opposing forces, the House of Dombey and the Wooden Midshipman's shop, the one signifying money and destructive pride, the other romance and childlike love, on the meeting ground of the East India Docks. But how is the textual promise of 'romantic and adventurous story' here separable from the grim moral of capitalist expansion interrogated in Dombey's career? The doctrine of empire represented in East India House encompasses the spirit of romance and adventure that enraptures Walter Gay and his quixotic naval guardians, Uncle Sol and Captain Cuttle. At the same time, empire is the incontrovertible image of Dombey's solipsism: 'The earth was made for Dombey and Son to trade in, and the sun and moon were made to give them light. Rivers and seas were formed to float their ships . . . winds blew for or against their enterprises; stars and planets circled in their orbits, to preserve inviolate a system of which they were the centre' (ch. 1) . . .

In his *Ideology of Adventure*, Michael Nerlich discusses the collaboration of merchant capital and state force in early voyages of exploration, and points out that 'the Crown, merchant adventurers, and explorer or conqueror adventures' all combined in the appropriation of England's earliest colonies.[8] The fundamental connection between mercantile capital and colonial enterprise is encapsulated in the twin meanings of 'adventure': 'both the exploration with its risks and the (risky) business venture.'[9] By the mid-nineteenth century, the growth of industrial capital and the hunt for foreign markets had brought the older mercantile monopolies into conflict with the new orthodoxy of free trade. That classic monopolist enterprise, the East India Company, would be dismantled in 1858, signifying, Ramkrishna Mukherjee has shown, the movement of capital from its overtly expansionist mercantile phase to the free trade strategies of triumphant industrialism.[10] In [*Dombey and Son*] the tensions between old-style monopolistic mercantilism and free trade are reflected in the separation of the hitherto linked concepts of capital, colonization, and adventure: the 'hints of adventurous and romantic story' are transferred, apparently unquestioned, to the colonial margins, while the operations of mercantile capital are measured mainly in their social and human cost to the metropolis (ch. 4). Most often, this cost is measured in its impact on family and sexual relations, with a trading institution figured as The House, and domestic subjects – women and children – commodified within the mercantile economy.

Such a displacement of mercantilism's impact might account for a tendency to structure the novel as a series of binary oppositions: feminine/masculine, nature/progress, love/capitalism.[11] In *Dombey and Son*, this polarization, based on the conflict between Florence and Dombey, is often characterized by a symbolism of the sea as natural, fluid, and cyclical, as opposed to the unyielding industrial realities of man-made progress. In Nina Auerbach's reading, for example, the ocean becomes a privileged symbol of the feminine:

> Florence's realm, the sea, exists independent of the mechanized products of civilization. It is natural and eternal: Paul's dying vision relates it . . . to the River of Life, flowing through Paradise. Like the ebb and flow of the female cycle . . . its rhythms are involuntary and unconscious, related to the flow of emotion and dream; lacking a destination to shape its movements, it has all the interminable attraction of a world without end. Unlike the railroad's shriek, its voice is quiet and its language private . . . The mindlessness of its repeated motions reminds us of Florence's incessant returns to the unyielding breast of her father until it melts for her . . . Her kinship with the sea is appropriate to her role as vessel of woman's influence.
>
> (Auerbach, p. 117)

But the sea and Florence's femininity are less eternal and immutable in their operations than they are socially and ideologically constituted agents. In Newton's essay on the formulation of a mid-Victorian ideal of womanhood, 'the awful inevitability of Florence' reveals 'the hold of the ideology of woman's influence' on Dickens as well as on Dombey; a hold Newton demystifies in her nuanced materialist analysis (p. 133). Similarly, the ocean in *Dombey and Son* can be read as an eternal reservoir of natural 'femininity' only if we exclude its more evident operation as a means of global traffic and imperial wealth, making it as much an agent of trade and capital as is the metropolis, disrupted and fragmented by an eruption of railroads.[12] Colonial voyages are undertaken by all the sympathetic characters of the novel, to named destinations, for the performance of specific tasks necessary to the profitable maintenance of empire. Walter and Florence embark on a trading voyage to a China forcibly opened to England's opium trade; Dombey sends Walter aboard the prophetically named 'Son and Heir' to act as a junior clerk in his factory in Barbados; Uncle Sol uses his scientific skills to work his way as a seaman from Demerara to China in search of his missing nephew.[13]

I suggest, then, that gender and trade are organized rather as linked operations of a mercantile economy, with Florence's unrelenting and seemingly *immutable 'femininity'* as much a construct of that economy as Dombey's financial thuggery.[14] Instead of an oppositional structure of masculine/feminine and railroad/ocean, *Dombey and Son* can be seen as a complex interchange between the key categories of capital and adventure, or 'romance,' each enmeshed in the overarching ideology of empire. Crucial to my argument is the interplay between the continually evolving discourses that constituted and managed both gender and empire. The *Narrative* of the Niger Expedition, Dickens's critique of it, and *Dombey and Son* all employ a vocabulary of private and public, domestic and foreign, to participate in a discourse of trade and empire which simultaneously addresses the 'local' issues of home, family, and 'woman's influence.'

II

> Commissioners: Is there any road from Aboh to Benin?
> Obi: Yes.
> Commissioners: They must all be open to the English.
> Obi: Yes.
> Commissioners: All the roads in England are open alike to all foreigners . . . Will Obi let the English build, cultivate, buy and sell without annoyance?
> Obi: Certainly.
> Commissioners: If your people do wrong to them, will you punish them?
> Obi: They shall be judged, and if guilty, punished.
> Commissioners: When the English do wrong, Obi must send word to an English officer . . . You must not punish white people.
> Obi: I assent to this. (*He now became restless and impatient*).
>
> ('Niger,' p. 53; Dickens's emphasis)

In 1833, Harriet Martineau published a fierce attack on the East India Company's practices in Ceylon in her 'Cinnamon and Pearls,' a tale devoted to proving that 'the evil spirit of monopoly' had perverted the true ends of colonization.[15] *Dombey and Son* is much more ambiguous in its treatment of the honourable Company, yet details of the free trade controversy trouble Dickens's text as Paul's dancing master is obsessed by a particular mystery: 'what you were to do with your raw materials, when they came into your ports in return for your drain of gold . . . Sir Barnet Skettles had much to say . . . but it did not appear to solve the question, for Mr Baps retorted, Yes, but supposing Russia stepped in with her tallows; which struck Sir Barnet almost dumb, for he could . . . only say, Why, then you must fall back up on your cottons, he supposed.'[16]

Despite the supposed pacifism of free-trade ideology, 'the free trade era,' as Richard Pares has asserted, 'was the great age of colonization and colonial trade' (qtd. in Semmel, p. 8). English foreign policy worked to ensure that more and more trade passages were 'open to the English.' The First Opium War of 1840, when Chinese ports were besieged to force the free passage of English narcotics, was the logical conclusion of an aggressive free trade policy, while in India a series of 'annexations' along the northwestern frontier were found necessary as a protection against Russia, the rising trade rival so dreaded by Mr. Baps.[17] Compared to these military incursions, and the overt expansionism of earlier and later stages in English history, the Niger Expedition reflects the minority and losing impulse of the period, the 'sentiments of cosmopolitanism, internationalism, humanitarianism and pacifism,' which ultimately served to reinforce the interests of an intensified and more violent imperialism (Semmel, p. 2).

. . . Dickens's severe criticism of the Niger Expedition and the expansionist and adventurous vision of imperial trade interrogated in *Dombey and Son* can be read, in this context, as complementary contributions to the free-trade debates of the period. Viewed in this light, the personal transactions most often seen as the primary concern of *Dombey and Son* reflect the workings of these debates over trade and empire, adventure and quietism, and their impact on the issues of home, family, and woman's influence.

If empire mirrors Dombey's solipsism, Dombey himself is the embodiment of old-style mercantilism: 'a pecuniary Duke of York,' a merchant prince 'paramount in the greatest city in the universe,' with 'a name . . . that is known and honoured in the British possessions abroad' (chs 21, 10). Partners with lesser stakes in the imperial connection also people *Dombey and Son*, ranging from the 'black cook in a black caboose' serving on Walter's ship, to the ferocious little Bill Blitherstone, one of a long line of unfortunate children returned 'home' from India to acquire a metropolitan education (ch. 19). Blitherstone is the means of the Dombeys' introduction to Major Bagstock, a soldier of 'Imperial complexion' who 'did all sorts of things . . . with every description of firearm . . . in the East and West Indies' (chs 20, 10). The Major, fulsome in his admiration of Dombey's immense colonial holdings, is accompanied by 'a dark servant . . . Miss Tox was quite content to classify as a "native" without connecting him with any geographical idea whatever' (chs 10, 7). An inhabitant of the anonymous outlands of empire, 'the Native,' 'currently believed to be a prince in his own country,' is himself nameless, answering to 'any vituperative epithet' Bagstock might choose for him (ch. 20). Nor is 'the Native' ever heard to speak; his only function in the text is to serve the Major and receive his gratuitous abuse.[18] In Bagstock and his attendant, Dickens revives an extinct species of literary tradition, the bygone nabobs and absentee landlords recalled by Disraeli in *Sybil*: 'the West Indies exhausted, and Hindostan plundered, the breeds died away, and now exist only in our English comedies from Wycherly and Congreve to Cumberland and Morton.'[19]

But if Dickens's types appear anachronistic in detail, they are true to the contemporary realities of imperial power. In spite of its satiric treatment, the relationship between the ridiculous Bagstock and his cipher of a servant enacts the certainties of imperial mastery. The 'ideological presuppositions' underlying a text are revealed, Mineke Schipper points out, by the questions 'who has *no* right to speak?' 'who does *not* act?' and, most significant here, 'whose view is *not* expressed?'[20] The power relations governing *Dombey and Son* are laid bare in the text's assumption of 'the Native's' unrepresentability in human terms; in its confidence that 'the Native's' predicament is comic, and *can* only be represented humorously. This utter negation of the colonial subject is summed up in a striking image of dispossession as the Major appropriates even the shade of 'the Native's' body: 'The afternoon being sunny and hot, he ordered the Native and the light baggage to the front, and walked in the shadow of that expatriated prince.'[21]

Bagstock's attendant serves a second function in the accumulation-ridden society of *Dombey and Son*. Raymond Williams has commented on the problem of representing colonial wealth in literature: Jane Austen's 'eye for a house, for timber, for the details of improvement, is quick, accurate, monetary. Yet money of other kinds, from the trading houses, from the colonial plantations, has no visual equivalent; it has to be converted to these signs of order to be recognised at all.'[22] While 'improvement,' in all its moral and material connotations, is an indicator of colonial success in novels like *Mansfield Park* and *Persuasion*, a different aesthetic tradition relies on the artifacts and objects of empire as a convenient means of reproducing colonial wealth and power. This practice, derived from portraiture and commercial art, frequently employed dark-skinned servants either as emblems of their masters' status or as icons of commercial prosperity.[23] In his reading of Hogarth's family group, *The Wollastons*, David Dabydeen points out that the dark servant, 'a blob of black paint, a shadowy figure with no personality or expression,' is represented in the portrait only as a 'token of their affluence and colonial business interests, not . . . in his own right: among the sitters are a daughter of a Bank of England Director, a Portugal Merchant and Director of the Royal Exchange Assurance, and a future South Sea Company Director and Governor of Virginia.'[24] In *Dombey and Son*, almost as richly peopled with the master figures of empire, the shadowy and speechless 'Native' again serves as an embodiment of imperial domination. At the same time, as surely as Dombey's collection of plate in a society where power is expressed through the possession of objects, Bagstock's 'delicate exotic' registers his possessor's rating on the scale of economic value (ch. 29).

A second indicator of value on the same scale is female beauty. Introduced to the aristocratic Edith by Bagstock, Dombey hastily acquires her, then loses no time in displaying his bargain to a guestlist of 'sundry eastern magnates' (ch. 36). His first signs of dissatisfaction with his wife appear when she is not sufficiently enthusiastic in her reception of an East India Company director. In refusing to perform for the assembled bankers and magnates, Edith rejects her chief function in the contract between the couple – a contract openly alluded to in the unfortunate anecdote told at their first dinner party: '*She* is regularly bought, and you may take your oath *he* is as regularly sold!' (ch. 36). Edith's beauty has always been recognized as a commodity by her mother, the ancient Cleopatra, who has devoted her 'pains and labour' to developing it for a future consumer (ch. 30). In this she is most fundamentally connected to 'good Mrs. Brown,' who makes 'a sort of property' of her own daughter, Alice, then trades her on less advantageous terms to the villainous Carker (ch. 53). Alice bitterly appraises the cost to herself of her own good looks: 'There was a girl called Alice Marwood. She was handsome . . . She was too well cared for, too well trained . . . What came to that girl comes to thousands every year. It was only ruin and she was born to it . . . There was a criminal called Alice Marwood . . . And lord, how the gentlemen in court talked about it! and how grave the judge was . . . on her having perverted the gifts of nature – as if he didn't know better than anybody there, that they had been made curses to her!' (ch. 34).

Alice and Edith are fatally linked by the unnatural transformation of personal gifts into saleable goods, a link underscored by their hidden blood relationship and by their common seducer. Here, as elsewhere in Dickens, the location of a range of vices in the same character works to identify a deeper connection. The licentious Carker, agent of public 'ruin' for both Alice and Edith, is simultaneously Dombey's trusted agent, speculating in women even as he directs the firm's 'prodigious ventures' through 'the great labyrinth' of empire (ch. 53). Similarly, if Edith must be 'sold as infamously as any woman with a halter round her neck is sold,' her logical purchaser is that 'Colossus of Commerce,' Dombey, in person (chs 54, 26). Dombey's grand desire to 'swell the reputation of the House . . . and to exhibit it in magnificent contrast to other merchant's Houses . . . in most parts of the world' is complemented by an imperious insistence on Edith's public recognition of his power: 'I must have a positive show and confession of deference before the world, Madam' (chs 53, 40).[25]

Trade and sex operate as the medium of exchange between master and man: Dombey uses Carker as a menial go-between to deliver lordly reprimands to Edith; while Carker successfully manipulates the inordinate expansion of Dombey's pride to bring about both a financial and a sexual downfall. The mid-section of the novel is a lengthy scuffle for turf between employer and assistant as Dombey's overweening self-assertion (what Auerbach terms his 'inveterate phallicism') is countered by Carker's public embezzlement of the House's funds and subsequent elopement with Dombey's wife (ch. 5).

In the complex interplay of class, sex, and trade, Florence's status is defined by her position as Dombey's daughter. Dombey's fatal error is his early miscalculation of Florence's worth: 'But what was a girl to Dombey and Son! In the capital of the House's name and dignity, such a child was merely a piece of base coin that couldn't be invested – a bad Boy – nothing more' (ch. 1). This error in reckoning marks not only a personal but a business failure. Dombey's mistaken assessment of Florence is recalled again in the last pages of the novel:

'And so Dombey and Son . . . ' said Miss Tox, winding up a host of recollections, 'is indeed a daughter, Polly, after all.'
'And a good one!" exclaimed Polly.

(ch. 59)

The process of Dombey and Son's conversion, its movement from rejecting 'a bad Boy' to accepting a good daughter, involves a recognition and incorporation of gender as a distinct function in the mercantile economy.[26] When Dombey writes Florence off as a bad investment prospect he misses a factor equally well understood both by the designing Carker and by the romantic Captain Cuttle. Both the Captain and Uncle Sol allude to the economic opportunity manifested in Florence on the very first day of Walter's employment by Dombey and Son: 'We'll finish the bottle to the House . . . Walter's House. Why it may be his House one of these days, in part. Who knows? Sir Richard Whittington married his master's daughter' (ch. 4).

Dombey's refusal to accommodate Florence within the economy of the family business denies her a role in the domestic economy. As several critics have pointed out, Dombey's angry rejection of that comforting Victorian construct, a de-sexed, nurturing daughter or 'little mother,' brings the dangerous possibilities of the father-daughter connection into full focus.[27] These possibilities include not only forbidden sexuality, but domestic rebellion. Left unmanaged or uninvested by paternal authority, womanly influence threatens the patriarchal household. Dombey's resentful suspicion of Florence's influence on her dying mother, on Paul, and finally and most decisively on Edith (all figures who resist his greatness), turns Florence into Dombey's domestic rival, appropriating the devotion due to the husband and father-figure: 'Who was it who could win his wife as she had won his boy? . . . Who was it whose least word did what his utmost means could not? Who was it who, unaided by his love, regard or notice, thrived and grew beautiful when those so aided died?' (ch. 40).

It seems to go unnoticed that Dombey's jealousy of the bond between Florence and Edith is markedly sexual: 'He knew now that she was beautiful . . . and that in the bright dawn of her womanhood she had come upon him, a surprise. But he turned even this against her . . . Did she grace his life – or Edith's? Had her attractions been manifest first to him – or Edith? . . . Her very beauty softened natures that were obdurate to him, and insulted him with an unnatural triumph' (ch. 40). The obdurate Edith's 'softness' towards Florence accounts for Dombey's use of his daughter in the tangled negotiations between himself, Edith, and Carker: 'You will . . . tell [Edith] that her show of devotion for my daughter is disagreeable to me . . . It is likely to induce people to contrast Mrs Dombey in her relation to my daughter, with Mrs Dombey in her relation towards myself' (ch. 42).

Set in opposition to one another, Dombey and Florence become mutually destructive; his hate blighting her life, her love blighting the objects of his life. The two are reconciled only after the overthrow of Dombey's unsound economic principles; his bankruptcy, not the blow to his sexual pride, finally undermines him to Florence's softening influence. Simultaneously, Florence's dangerously unregulated emotion is defused as she is reabsorbed, through marriage and motherhood, into the domestic order. The original family is reconstituted through Florence's union with her childhood 'brother,' Walter, and by the birth of her son, another little Paul. (The Blimbers, the family responsible for Paul's fatally harsh schooling, are a significant variation on this pattern. Dr. Blimber educates his daughter, the short-haired and spectacled Comelia, as an asexual duplicate of himself, then marries her to his assistant, Mr. Feeder, who will inherit the family business. The wistful and maternal Mrs. Blimber is the disposable factor in this successful family romance.)

Florence's containment in marriage signals the regeneration of the family business, a regeneration all the more significant in the economy of the novel for beginning with a trading voyage. Williams describes Dickens's evasion of a tragic ending for *Dombey and Son* as an act of 'willed . . . intervention,' a 'personal change' in Dombey rectifying the pride of the system: 'Kindness and capitalism – a small firm, humbly remembering its origins – are made compatible after all' (Williams, Introduction, p. 30). The system is certainly amended in the last chapters of the novel, but less by a personal redemption than by a forced realignment of the mercantile ideal with marriage and adventure. It is no coincidence that Florence, probably the first Victorian heroine to sail on a trading venture to China for her honeymoon, gives birth at sea to a son who will be the means by which 'from his daughter, after all, another Dombey and Son will . . . rise . . . triumphant' (ch. 62). The system is finally sanctioned in *Dombey and Son*, not through a penitential myth of humble origins, but by the triumphal myth of mercantilism frequently invoked by Walter's friends: that of the legendary Mayor of London, Dick Whittington, who grew rich by venturing his sole possession, his cat, on a trading voyage to Barbary, and ended by marrying his master's daughter. The revivification of this patron saint of London merchants, who united the avocations of apprentice, trader/adventurer and prosperous city father in a single career, manifests Dickens's willed reversion to the traditional partnership of commerce and adventure.[28] The return of Florence and Walter from their successful venture precedes a general restoration of trade and prosperity: 'some of our lost ships, freighted with gold . . . come home, truly,' bringing in, like Whittington's cat, foundation for future riches, and reconciling the traditional adventurousness of imperial trade with the new scientific practices (ch. 62). The reconstituted family in turn forms the base from which a new 'edifice . . . perhaps to equal, perhaps excel' the old House of Dombey is to rise, presided over, in time, by Florence's son. In the revised scheme of things, the benign incorporation of 'woman's influence' ensures that the functions of love, marriage, and family are firmly regulated by the exigencies of sound business. But even as the principle of masculine preeminence is temporarily overset, the system is maintained by the continued division of labour by gender . . . The ultimate restitution of the restored patriarch, Dombey, is neither communal nor public: enfolded in a loving family, he learns to value the second 'little Florence' only by 'hoard[ing] her in his heart' (ch. 62).

4

GEORGE ELIOT, *MIDDLEMARCH*

Sally Shuttleworth's essay, '*Middlemarch*: An Experiment in Time', extracted from *George Eliot and Nineteenth-Century Science*, looks at the complex narrative organisation of the novel in terms of contemporary methods of scientific research. It claims that *Middlemarch* is not just a novel in which science is treated as an explicit theme, but a novel which is, itself, a kind of scientific experiment. The medical research of Lydgate provides a paradigm for the methods and beliefs that George Eliot wishes to pursue in fiction writing. Drawing on the findings of experimental biology, she develops a style of writing that not only records what is already known, but pursues and reveals the hidden connections in life. The essay is particularly valuable in demonstrating how Eliot's interests in scientific methodology affect her conception of realism and her understanding of literary form.

Gillian Beer's essay, '*Middlemarch*: The Web of Affinities', from *Darwin's Plots*, is also concerned with the extent to which *Middlemarch* draws on the scientific discourse of its time, but the focus here is very much on the impact of ideas and images to do with evolution. George Eliot is seen to be concerned with 'relations' and 'origins', two closely related ideas that are prompted by Darwin's striking metaphor of 'the inextricable web of affinities' in *The Origin of Species* (1859). The essay pursues the image of the web in all its possible manifestations – the spider's web, the weaving of fabric, the composition of human tissue – and it shows how, at every opportunity, the novel emulates the image of the web, promoting 'a sense of inclusiveness and extension'.

In '*Middlemarch*: Empiricist Fables', David Carroll looks at the shaping influence of diagnostic medicine and anatomical research on George Eliot's prose. His emphasis, however, is on the wide gap that opens up between different, conflicting models of interpretation, both in scientific experiment and in the reading of fiction. Just as nineteenth-century scientific knowledge is riven with conflict and controversy, so the novel enacts its own interpretative crises. The presentation of Lydgate typifies this process; on one level he is applauded as a bold reformer and discoverer; on another he is deeply mistrusted for his progressive ideals. *Middlemarch* pushes towards a final 'unresolvable interpretative crux'. How we come to assess Lydgate depends on the values and assumptions with which we approach 'the cluster of signs' by which he is known.

The interests of Elizabeth Deeds Ermarth in 'George Eliot and the World as Language' overlap considerably with those of the preceding article. Her essay explores the complexity of viewpoint in *Middlemarch*: the way in which 'shifting constellations of viewpoint gather, and dissolve', reminding us continually that 'nothing is final'. This essay, however, is strongly marked by post-structuralist theories of language and representation, in particular the idea that language constructs what we come to know as 'reality', rather than passively reflecting it. Ermarth claims that George Eliot's novels are alert to the ways in which discourses (systems of belief and value that operate through language) provide differing points of perspective. Whereas modern linguistic theory tends to regard these discursive systems as perpetually in dispute and lacking any possibility of resolution, George Eliot insists on the need and possibility of common denominators: her novels 'characteristically cruise the boundaries between different systems of intelligibility, but her narrative style always maintains a common horizon'.

Sally Shuttleworth, *Middlemarch*: An Experiment in Time (1984)

. . . *Middlemarch* is a work of experimental science: an examination of the 'history of man' under the 'varying experiments of Time' (Prelude).[1] In *Adam Bede*, the scientific methodology of natural history had sustained the novel's static vision of social order. George Eliot brings to *Middlemarch*, however, a more questioning social vision; the Middlemarch of the Prelude is neither a static nor a harmoniously integrated society. The role of natural historian, passively transcribing a given order, will no longer suffice. George Eliot turns instead to the more dynamic methodology of experimental biology, a stance which receives paradigmatic expression in the novel in the research of Lydgate.[2] *Middlemarch* is the first novel in which science is treated as an explicit theme, and in the long discussions of Lydgate's methods and beliefs one can discern George Eliot's reflections on her own assumptions and procedures.[3]

Speaking as an experimental scientist, Lydgate summarily dismisses Farebrother's practice of natural history. He was, he declares, 'early bitten with an interest in structure' (ch. 17). This interest in structure is expressed in his belief that living bodies 'are not associations of organs which can be understood by studying them first apart, and then as it were federally' (ch. 15). Though offered only as a biological observation, Lydgate's statement in fact holds the key to George Eliot's social theory and narrative practice in

Middlemarch. The natural historian looks at society as a collection of individuals that can be viewed first separately, and then federally, but the experimental scientist challenges this conception of individual autonomy. The characters in *Middlemarch* cannot be abstracted out from the life-processes of the town. As George Eliot tries to suggest through the complex narrative organisation of her novel, each part of Middlemarch life is related to every other part; individual identity is not only influenced by the larger social organism, it is actively defined by it.

On a more fundamental level, Lydgate's theory of organic interdependence also affects George Eliot's conception of realism. The natural historian's function is to label and classify the individual components of a fixed reality; conceptions of dynamic interdependence, however, undermine that possibility.

The function of the scientist is no longer simply to transcribe the 'real.' Following the theory of organic interdependence, observations only possess meaning when placed in an ideally constructed framework. George Eliot's narrative practice in *Middlemarch* accords with these principles. She no longer adheres to the naive realism of *Adam Bede* with its apologetic image of the defective mirror, but actively accepts the creative role of author. Dexterously interweaving many strands of material, she uses the resources of both myth and symbol to create the 'ideal experiment' of her novel. The image of the historian untangling the pre-existent web is complemented by that of the creative scientist; and the realism of the Garths' presentation is balanced by the mythological resonances of the story of Dorothea, Casaubon, and Will.

For Claude Bernard, the experimental physiologist, the scientist was 'a real foreman of creation'; in creating the conditions of his experiments, he actively engineered the appearance of phenomena.[4] His methodology, moreover, was firmly based, as Lewes also believed, on the processes of ideal construction and imaginative pre-vision[5] for, as Bernard observes, 'Ideas, given form by facts, embody science.'[6] Bernard held adamantly to the conviction that 'We must give free rein to our imagination; the idea is the essence of all reasoning and all invention.'[7] This conception of scientific method, which underpins George Eliot's 'experiment in time,' is articulated in the novel by Lydgate who adheres, somewhat in advance of his time, to a belief in the scientific imagination. Lydgate disdains the form of imagination present in cheap narration which he regards as

> rather vulgar and vinous compared with the imagination that reveals subtle actions inaccessible by any sort of lens, but tracked in that outer darkness through long pathways of necessary sequence by the inward light which is the last refinement of Energy, capable of bathing even the ethereal atoms in its ideally illuminated space. (ch. 16)

Like his creator, Lydgate conceives science not simply as a process of observation and classification, but rather as the pursuit of ideas and hypotheses. The object of science is not to record the already known, but to reveal hidden connections, through the creation of an 'ideally illuminated space' – Lewes' 'manifold ideal constructions of the Possible' that help to reveal the Actual.

In creating the experimental conditions through which to explore the possible outcome of the life of a 'later-born Theresa' placed in the uncongenial social medium of Middlemarch, George Eliot follows Lydgate's scientific methodology. Her labour of imagination is not 'mere arbitrariness, but the exercise of disciplined power.' She combines and constructs all the multitudinous elements of Middlemarch life 'with the clearest eye for probabilities and the fullest obedience to knowledge' (ch. 16). The purpose behind her labour also corresponds to that of scientific practice, for the aim of science, Lewes suggests, is to link together, through imaginative construction, the fragments of the phenomenal world so as to reveal an underlying order. While 'Perception gives the naked fact of Sense, isolated, unconnected, merely juxtaposed with other facts, and without far-reaching significance,' science reveals connections and confers significance: 'The facts of Feeling which sensation differentiates, Theory integrates.'[8] George Eliot tries, through the structural organisation of her work, to reveal underlying organic unity beneath apparent surface disorder. The pursuit of significant order constitutes, indeed, both the major theme and methodology of the novel, for George Eliot's characters share her goal. Thus Lydgate searches for the one primitive tissue, and Casaubon for the 'Key to all Mythologies.' Dorothea, in similar fashion, yearns for 'a binding theory which would bring her own life and doctrine into strict connection with that amazing past' (ch. 10). On a more humorous level, Mr Brooke seeks, in his usual rambling way, for a means of ordering his documents other than by the arbitrary system of A to Z. Author and characters alike quest for an organising principle or theory which would bind together disparate parts and reveal unity beneath apparent chaos.

In their search, the characters often fall into the stance of natural historians, holding, mistakenly, that meaning actually inheres in external form. Thus Lydgate believes that Rosamond's physical appearance expresses her virtue 'with a force of demonstration that excluded the need for other evidence' (ch. 16) while Dorothea is similarly misled by Casaubon: 'Everything I see in him,' she responds rather haughtily to Celia, 'corresponds to his pamphlet on Biblical Cosmology' (ch. 2). Casaubon is similarly guilty of treating the world as a system of signs to be decoded. His Key is to make 'the vast field of mythical constructions . . . intelligible, nay, luminous with the reflected light of correspondences' (ch. 3). He wishes to reveal the underlying order of history through the external correspondences of myths, though, as the narrator observes, this approach had been discredited in both mythological studies, and the related science of philology: Mr Casaubon's theory 'floated among flexible conjectures no more solid than those etymologies which seemed strong because of likeness in sound until it was shown that likeness in sound made them impossible' (ch. 48). External correspondences can be actively misleading. Thus Lewes, in *Sea-side Studies*, confirmed Bernard's warning against 'attempting to deduce a function from mere inspection of the organ' for the external resemblance of organs cannot be taken as evidence of their similar functions.[9] The same principle of organic interdependence applies to physiological life, language, social relations, or historical development. One must look beyond the details of external form to the underlying dynamic process, for, as in Bernard's linguistic analogy, each part only derives meaning from its position within the whole.

The structure of *Middlemarch* reflects this principle of interdependence. The unity of the novel is not based, as in that earlier study of provincial life, Mrs Gaskell's *Cranford*, on spatial continuity or community of life style.[10] The life portrayed is both geographically and socially dispersed, moving from Tipton to Frick, from the gentry to labourers, and from the measured cadences of Casaubon's speech to the trenchant assertions of Mrs Dollop. Unlike the earlier *Felix Holt*, or Dickens' *Bleak House*, the plot does not revolve around the gradual revelation of hidden connections between socially disparate groups, or a cumbersome legal machinery. Indeed the sole links that emerge from the past – those of Bulstrode, Raffles, and Will – seem rather to disturb than affirm our sense of the unity of Middlemarch life. Though the Bulstrode and Casaubon plots are connected by Will, in his capacity as twice disinherited heir, George Eliot actively eschews, in general, the technique of linking all her characters through relations of direct personal contact. No links, for example, are drawn between. Dorothea and Farebrother or Caleb until after Casaubon's death, while the sole direct connection between Dorothea and Featherstone occurs with Dorothea's distant glance at Featherstone's funeral. The structure of *Middlemarch* conforms to Lewes' definition of organic life: 'The part exists only as part of a whole; the whole exists only as a whole of its parts.'[11]

The unity of *Middlemarch* is based, primarily, not on relations of direct effect, but on the shared community of language. In constructing her 'Study of Provincial Life' George Eliot adhered to the same social interpretation of organicist premises as Lewes. Her representation of Middlemarch life accords with the theory of the social medium Lewes was concurrently defining in *The Foundations of a Creed*. Lewes differentiates his approach from that of psychologists; his was the first survey, he believed, to take fully into account the role of the social medium in determining individual psychology. Thus, 'The psychologist, accustomed to consider the Mind as something apart from the Organism, individual and collective, is peculiarly liable to this error of overlooking the fact that all mental manifestations are simply the resultants of the conditions external and internal.'[12] These external conditions are not simply the material or economic conditions of society but 'the collective accumulations of centuries, condensed in knowledge, beliefs, prejudices, institutions, and tendencies,' and transmitted primarily through language.[13] The individual and social life of Middlemarch conforms to this model. Though characters are linked in material relations of dependency, the primary connecting bond is the shared linguistic medium. Through language characters articulate both their individual and communal identity: gossip, or the exchange of opinion, functions as the fundamental linking force. The structure of the individual chapters reflects this principle. Chapters move either linearly, connecting various strands of plot through an extended chain of characters' opinions about each other, or laterally, from a larger social issue to its effects upon the thoughts and reflections of a single life.[14]

A linear structure is manifest, for example, in chapter 71 which traces the revelation, through gossip, of Bulstrode's story, and the indignant responses in each social stratum. In keeping with George Eliot's commitment to organic heterogeneity, the chapter concludes, not with Bulstrode, but with Dorothea, fervently asserting her faith in Lydgate. Though the majority of characters in this chapter scarcely know of each other's existence, they are all linked together by the connecting chain of opinion.

An example of the principles of lateral construction is furnished by Chapter 56 which moves from a general discussion of the coming of the railway to trace its effects on individual lives. George Eliot enumerates in this chapter the three social issues she employs to unite the disparate elements of Middlemarch existence: 'In the hundred to which Middlemarch belonged,' she observes, 'railways were as exciting a topic as the Reform Bill or the imminent horrors of Cholera, and those who held the most decided views on the subject were women and landholders' (ch. 56). Though the three issues of railways, Reform, and Cholera engross the social organism, their unifying force lies less in their material effects than in their mobilisation of public opinion. Individual psychology is defined, in accordance with Lewes' theories, both by the accumulated beliefs and prejudices stored within language, and the contemporary functions of gossip. Indeed, the processes of gossip constitute both the dominant principles of chapter construction, and one of the novel's major themes. As George Eliot demands, in reference to Bulstrode, 'Who can know how much of his inward life is made up of the thoughts he believes other men to have about him, until that fabric of opinion is threatened with ruin?' (ch. 68). Public opinion cannot be ignored; it actively enters into the creation of both mind and self-identity. George Eliot explores through the plot and formal structure of her novel the implications of this principle of organic interdependence.

The constant shifts in perspective within the chapters, from the social whole to the individual parts, accord with George Eliot's conception of organic form which she outlined in her notebook essay 'Notes on Form in Art' (1868). Form, she argued, 'must first depend on the discrimination of wholes & then on the discrimination of parts.'[15] Lydgate, translating this premise into biological practice, believed that 'there must be a systole and diastole in all inquiry.' Unlike Lydgate, George Eliot actually follows this method; her novel is 'continually expanding and shrinking between the whole human horizon and the horizon of an object glass' (ch. 63). Both the chapter construction and larger structure of the work reinforce this process. Book titles, like 'Old and Young' or 'Waiting for Death,' draw attention away from the continuity of plot to suggest a wider unity of theme, while the epigraphs, which often hold an enigmatic relation to the following material, similarly disrupt linear narration to establish a framework of expectations for the ensuing chapter. The jumps in perspective reflect the heterogeneous structure of the social organism itself, for, as George Eliot argued in her essay, 'The highest Form . . . is the highest organism, that is to say, the most varied group of relations bound together in a wholeness which again has the most varied relations with all other phenomena.'[16] Her definition follows Spencer's theory that the highest form of art will be 'not a series of like parts simply placed in juxtaposition, but one whole made up of unlike parts that are mutually dependent.'[17] The universal principle of development from homogeneity to heterogeneity to which Spencer refers here is one, George Eliot suggests in the essay, that governs equally the development of organic life, or poetic form, and the growth of mind, both in the individual and in the race.[18] Within the form of her novel she attempts to capture the organic principles that govern both historical growth and social interdependence . . .

At every level, the interdependence of Middlemarch life seems to be based not on harmony, but on conflict. Thus Mr Brooke learns, during his lamentable experience as a political candidate, that Middlemarch is not the cosy paternalist society of his imaginings: 'the weavers and tanners of Middlemarch . . . had never thought of Mr. Brooke as a neighbour' (ch. 51). Economically, indeed, Middlemarch society reveals the worst vices of capitalism. We discover, for instance, from Mr Vincy that Bulstrode is associated with Plymdale's house which employs dyes liable to rot the silk, while Mr Vincy himself is identified by Mrs Cadwallader as 'one of those who suck the life out of the wretched handloom weavers in Tipton and Freshitt' (ch. 34). Though the narrator refers at one stage to the 'stealthy convergence of human lots,' thus seeming to offer a moral rebuke to Lydgate and Dorothea for their 'mutual indifference,' the description of social interaction which follows is scarcely suggestive of harmonious integration:

> Old provincial society had its share of this subtle movement: had not only its striking downfalls, its brilliant young professional dandies who ended by living up an entry with a drab and six children for their establishment, but also those less marked vicissitudes which are constantly shifting the boundaries of social intercourse, and begetting new consciousness of interdependence. (ch. 11)

Social interdependence is defined primarily by vicissitudes, while the actual process of change is marked by Darwinian elements of competition. The inhabitants of Middlemarch are displaced by successful settlers who 'came from distant counties, some with an alarming novelty of skill, others with an offensive advantage in cunning.' In the Darwinian battle for survival, success belongs to those with the highest powers of adaptation. Middlemarch life exhibits all the characteristics of a vital organism, for movement of each part affects the whole. Thus, even those who stand 'with rocky firmness amid all this fluctuation' are by the surrounding changes themselves transformed, 'altering with the double change of self and beholder.' Yet despite this evident interdependence, town life displays none of the peaceful unity of the organic social ideal.

George Eliot adheres, in *Middlemarch*, to the moral ideal of organic unity while simultaneously demonstrating the social impossibility of attaining this goal. Such an internal contradiction does not lead her, however, to deconstruct notions of historical unity and continuity. Though innovatory in form, *Middlemarch* is a solidly nineteenth-century text, constructed in the light of contemporary social and scientific debates concerning historical growth. In true realist fashion, the novel poses a social and moral problem which the narrative seeks to resolve. George Eliot is committed, ultimately, not to openness and discontinuity but to narrative closure. The difficulties she encounters in moving towards the desired resolution are clearly exacerbated, however, by her recognition of the social conflict which the myth of social heterogeneity actually conceals.

On a more fundamental level, her difficulties are also increased by the model of individual development to which she subscribes. Though the function of her 'experiment in time' is to assess the relative claims of the individual and the social organism, she actually adheres to a dynamic theory of organic process which undermines conceptions of individual autonomy upon which such judgements must necessarily be based. Thus, Lewes, outlining the psychological implications of Lydgate's theory of organic interdependence, argued that the division between self and not-self is false; it is analytic rather than real. The individual cannot be isolated out and defined apart from the organic process, for the individual, he concludes, is its relations.[19] This model suggests a fluidity and openness incompatible with the traditional realist demand for moral closure. If character is treated as flux, or process, there can be no fixed points of value, no grounds for assessing individual moral responsibility for action. Nor can the narrative draw to a defined close. The dynamic theory of organic order in fact undercuts the terms of the original organic problematic. George Eliot strives in *Middlemarch* to resolve this contradiction: to reconcile the idea of individual fluidity with the need for fixed moral judgement.

The opening chapter of *Middlemarch* clearly reveals George Eliot's organicist premises. Characters are introduced not in terms of fixed personal attributes, but in terms of their social effects. Dorothea, we learn in the opening paragraph, 'was usually spoken of as being remarkably clever.' Public opinion defines each character: thus Mr Brooke 'was held in this part of the county to have contracted a too rambling habit of mind,' while 'The rural opinion about the new young ladies, even among the cottagers, was generally in favour of Celia.' We discover, furthermore, that Mr Brooke, though blamed by neighbouring families for not securing a companion for Dorothea, was yet 'brave enough to defy the world – that is to say, Mrs. Cadwallader the Rector's wife, and the small group of gentry with whom he visited in the north-east corner of Loamshire' (ch. 1). The increased particularisation draws attention to the specificity of their environment. To comprehend Dorothea or Mr Brooke, one must bring knowledge, not of the world, but rather of that particular 'north-east corner of Loamshire' which determines their lives.

Our understanding of each character is formed through the medium of his neighbours' eyes. The narrator's protest against the reader's possible response to Casaubon draws attention to her own technique:

> I protest against any absolute conclusion, any prejudice derived from Mrs Cadwallader's contempt for a neighbouring clergyman's alleged greatness of soul, or Sir James Chettam's poor opinion of his rival's legs, – from Mr Brooke's failure to elicit a companion's ideas, or from Celia's criticism of a middle-aged scholar's personal appearance. (ch. 10)

Character cannot be defined apart from social opinion, for each individual is only the sum of his, constantly changing, relations with the social organism. Such relativism, however, is more apparent than real; it is clearly undercut by the text's claim to offer authoritative judgement. We rest in little doubt concerning the 'absolute conclusion' we should draw about each character. Through analysis of the three histories of Lydgate, Bulstrode, and Dorothea I will try to suggest the different ways in which George Eliot actually used the premises of organicist theory to achieve this moral closure. Drawing on the assumption, which she outlined in 'Notes on Form in Art,' that the same principles of organic life govern physiological, psychological, and social development, she mediates constantly between these different levels of analysis in *Middlemarch* in an attempt to impose structural and moral order on the text.

Introducing Lydgate, George Eliot observes that 'character too is a process and an unfolding' (ch. 15). This admission of fluidity is not borne out, however, by the narrative. The statement is immediately followed by a detailed account of Lydgate's history which functions to define his character independently of his life within the social organism of Middlemarch. In the case of Lydgate, plot, or the patterning of social events, does not trace a process of dynamic interaction between the individual and the social whole. It functions, rather, as a structural analogue of the predefined composition of his mind. The history of Lydgate's association with Laure illustrates his 'two selves'; his relations with Middlemarch are but an external enactment of this fixed internal contradiction. The 'spots of commonness' in his nature find their reflection in the petty judgements of the Middlemarch mind, while his other, idealistic, self finds its social correlative in Dorothea's willing faith. But as the 'spots of commonness' predominate in his nature, so the judgement of Middlemarch ultimately prevails. The social drama is merely that of his psychological constitution writ large. Reflecting on Lydgate's failure, George Eliot observes that 'It always remains true that if we had been greater, circumstance would have been less strong against us' (ch. 58). Sympathy is linked to firm moral judgement, thus suggesting a strong sense of order in the world. This stance is possible, however, only because George Eliot did not adhere firmly to a fluid model of character. It is, in the final instance, Lydgate's intrinsic moral flaws, his lack of innate greatness, and not the circumstances of his interaction with Middlemarch, that create his downfall.

The need to offer moral judgement also determines the representation of Bulstrode. At its simplest level, George Eliot wants to suggest that crime does not pay. If organic social harmony is to be preserved, wrong-doing must be shown to have undesired consequences for the perpetrator. In order to enforce this moral George Eliot departs once more from the fluid model of character. Bulstrode is the only other character apart from Lydgate who is given a detailed history outside his incorporation within Middlemarch life; his relations with Middlemarch can similarly be defined as the gradual unfolding or revelation of the prior structure of his mind. The history of Bulstrode is the only one in which coincidence strains credibility; Will's presence in Middlemarch, and Raffles' re-emergence conform more to a desired moral configuration than to the laws of realistic probability. In order to naturalise these occurrences George Eliot turns once more to physiology, to the idea of a physical basis for memory:

> The terror of being judged sharpens the memory: it sends an inevitable glare over that long-unvisited past which has been habitually recalled

> only in general phrases. Even without memory, the life is bound into one by a zone of dependence in growth and decay; but intense memory forces a man to own his blameworthy past. With memory set smarting like a reopened wound, a man's past is not simply a dead history, an outworn preparation of the present: it is not a repented error shaken loose from the life: it is a still quivering part of himself, bringing shudders and bitter flavours and the tinglings of a merited shame. (ch. 61)

The final term 'merited' reveals the moral bias of the whole description. George Eliot uses physiology to suggest that for the individual, as much as for the society or culture, there is a vital interdependence in history. Past history can never be 'dead,' never be discarded; shame must inevitably occur. All the terms employed reinforce the idea of a physical basis of memory; whether the 'shudders' and 'tinglings' of the sensations aroused, or the quivering vibrations which constitute the physiological response. The zone of dependence in growth and decay recalls de Blainville's theory upon which Lewes based his theory of mind: that organic life is a process of composition and decomposition in interaction with the environment.[20] George Eliot employs this physical theory to suggest a moral conclusion which is by no means sure: that a man will always be called to account for his past actions. The apparent transitory nature of social experience is referred to the constancy of physiological composition.

Raffles' social ostracism mirrors his status in Bulstrode's mind. George Eliot employs the operations of the unconscious as a model for the plot and social events, thus proposing a form of homology between the social and psychic realms that appears to offer a grounding within nature for the moral patterning of the narrative. She draws, however, on contemporary theories of unconscious life which do not simply reinforce ideas of a linear, cumulative history. Thus Bulstrode:

> felt the scenes of his earlier life coming between him and everything else, as obstinately as when we look through the window from a lighted room, the objects we turn our backs on are still before us, instead of the grass and the trees. The successive events inward and outward were there in one view: though each might be dwelt on in turn, the rest still kept their hold in the consciousness. (ch. 61)

This superb image presents a model of the mind which, departing from the linear model of associationist theory, admits the simultaneity of different levels of consciousness. The analysis of Bulstrode's mental processes focuses strongly on duality, whether of past and present, or the simultaneous existence of the 'theoretic phrases' he had used to justify his actions, and his actual experience of egoistic terror (ch. 53). Both modes are captured in Lewes' theory of the psychological subject:

> He lives a double life and has a double world – the world of Feeling and the world of Thought, that of sensations and images and that of abstract ideas. The Present is to him a complex web, with threads of the Past and threads of the Future inextricably interwoven.[21]

The web image recalls Bulstrode's inability to 'unravel' his confused promptings (ch. 70), while the distinction between thought and image is that which occurs when he attempts to pray: 'through all this effort to condense words into a solid mental state, there pierced and spread with irresistible vividness the images of the events he desired' (ch. 70). Although Bulstrode has interpreted history as one unified Providential order, his psychological experience of duality and contradiction exposes the falsity of this model.

Gillian Beer, *Middlemarch*: The Web of Affinities (1983)

The two major and interconnected problems on which Darwin wrote which fascinated George Eliot were those of *relations* and of *origins*. These preoccupations control her late novels both as theme and structure. The interdependence of the two ideas is expressed in *The Origin of Species* in the metaphor of 'the inextricable web of affinities'.[1] In his discussion of descent and morphology Darwin writes:

> We can clearly see how it is that all living and extinct forms can be grouped together in one great system; and how the several members of each class are connected together by the most complex and radiating lines of affinities. We shall never, probably, disentangle the inextricable web of affinities between the members of any one class; but when we have a distinct object in view, and do not look to some unknown plan of creation, we may hope to make sure but slow progress. (415)

Darwin's metaphor is striking, not for its novelty, but because it combines in a peculiarly Victorian manner two models of 'the web' and adds a third, which further complicates the explanatory and imaginative possibilities of the image. 'The several members of each class are connected together by the most complex and radiating lines of affinities' – the spatial pattern suggests a spider's web. 'We shall never, probably, disentangle the inextricable web of affinities between the members of any one class' – the suggestion is now of woven fabric. There is also the further space-free suggestion of chemical affinities, unsettling the space-bound order of the web. But the degrees of relatedness suggest, further, the 'table of affinities' by which sexual relations between kin are tabooed and this introduction of the family connections needs further discussion.

For us now, the spider's web is probably the predominant association of the word 'web'. But for Victorian people, woven fabric seems to have been the predominant reference. Web imagery is to be found everywhere in Victorian writing. It is as common among scientists and philosophers as it is among poets and novelists. Mill wrote in the *System of Logic* that 'the regularity which exists in nature is a web composed of distinct threads,' and G. H. Lewes in *Foundations of a Creed*:

> Out of the general web of Existence certain threads may be detached and rewoven into a special group – the Subject – and this sentient group will in so far be different from the larger group, the Object; but whatever different arrangement the threads may take on, they are always threads of the original web, they are not different threads.[2]

The absence of transformation is important in both these citations. Threads remain themselves, though part of a total fabric. When Tyndall seeks expression for endless movement he achieves it through an implicit metaphor which draws simultaneously on the concepts of wave and web – the process of weaving is foregrounded here, rather than the achieved fabric.

> Darkness might then be defined as ether at rest; light as ether in motion. But in reality the ether is never at rest, for in the absence of light-waves we have heat waves always speeding through it. In the spaces of the universe both classes of undulations incessantly commingle. Here the waves issuing from uncounted centres cross, coincide, oppose and pass through each other, without confusion or ultimate extinction. The waves from the zenith do not jostle out of existence those from the horizon, and every star is seen across the entanglement of wave motions produced by all other stars. [The waves of interstellar ether] mingle in space without disorder, each being endowed with an individuality as indestructible as if it alone had disturbed the universal repose.[3]

Spider, fabric, human tissue: Alexander Bain in *Mind and Body* describes the nerves thus: 'They are a set of silvery threads, or cords of various sizes, ramifying from centres to all parts of the body, including both sense surfaces and muscles.'[4] The webs of bodily order – veins, nerves, tissues – allow the metaphor of the web to move into the intimate ordering of life. Tissue and cloth are contiguous images. So are web and tree: 'threads . . . ramifying'. The web could intimate the 'milieu intrieur' – the relations within bodily and mental experience as much as the interconnections of society.

Hardy, for example, wrote in his diary on 4 March, 1886: 'The human race to be shown as one great network or tissue which quivers in every part when one point is shaken, like a spider's web if touched.'

The web as woven cloth expressed also the process of coming to knowledge. Descartes had already used it as an image of heurism.[5] Tennyson's Lady of Shalott works on the reverse side of her weaving and sees the pattern gradually emerging only through the mirror, through which she also sees the world beyond. This narrative element in the image had a particular usefulness for George Eliot. The web exists not only as interconnection in space but as succession in time. This was the aspect of the image emphasised by Darwin in his genealogical ordering.

Several connections implicit in the Victorian apprehension of the image do not seem self-evident to us now. One is family and kin; the other is the idea of origins.

Robert Chambers quotes Herschel on bodies in space. Again 'true affinities' are distinguished from mere analogies by means of the web image (as in the Darwin passage already quoted.) Herschel writes:

> When we contemplate the constituents of the planetary system from the point of view which this relation affords us, it is no longer mere analogy which strikes us, no longer a general resemblance among them, as individuals independent of each other, and circulating about the sun, each according to its own peculiar nature, and connected with it by its own peculiar tie. The resemblance is now perceived to be a true *family likeness*; they are bound up in one chain – interwoven in one web of mutual relation and harmonious agreement.[6]

'One web of mutual relation': Herschel's space-ordered family becomes Darwin's sequences of descent. The suggestion of family harmony in Herschel's description is given a genetic actuality by Darwin. In his most developed and climactic discussion of classification the 'web of affinities' expresses equally the interconnections of kinship and the energies of descent. In the immediately preceding passage Darwin has called on the image of the tree: 'In a tree we can specify this or that branch', and on the image of family descent: 'the many descendants from one dominant parent-species'. 'I believe,' he writes, 'this element of descent is the hidden bond of connexion which naturalists have sought under the term of the Natural System.'

The web is a different shape from the chain, and this formal property of the image has great importance for Darwin: 'The several subordinate groups in any class *cannot be ranked in a single file*, but seem rather to be clustered round points' (171) [my italics]. Sequence is so ramified and diversified, so devious, that it presents itself in the form of web or cycle rather than pure onward procedure.

Darwin twice elsewhere develops the image of 'entanglement' in relation to the web: 'Plants and animals, most remote in the scale of nature, are bound together by a web of complex relations.' In the next paragraph he writes: 'When we look at the plants and bushes clothing an entangled bank, we are tempted to attribute their proportional numbers and kinds to what we call chance.' But: 'What a struggle between the different kinds of trees' . . . 'what war between insect and insect' has brought about this proportioning? (125–6). In Darwin's first passage on the 'entangled bank' confusion and struggle are emphasised, the claustrophobic interconnections of like and of unlike. When he takes up the image again in the Conclusion, profusion and harmonious contiguity replace conflict:

> It is interesting to contemplate an entangled bank, clothed with many plants of many kinds, with birds singing on the bushes, with various insects flitting about, and with worms crawling through the damp earth, and to reflect that these elaborately constructed forms, so different from each other, and dependent on each other in so complex a manner, have all been produced by laws acting around us. (459)

The emphasis in these final affirmative pages is on the delicate richness and variety of life, on complex interdependency, ecological interpretation, weaving together an aesthetic fullness.

The cluster of common contiguous metaphors (tree, family, web, labyrinth) was given a new meaning by his theory. No single one of the metaphors was peculiar to Darwin. But in his argument the gap between metaphor and actuality was closed up, the fictive became substantive. Fictional insights were confirmed as physical event. The web is not a hierarchical model. It can express horizontality and extension, but it does not fix places, as on the rungs of a ladder or 'in single file'. Yet an important emphasis in the idea of the web is fixed patterns and achieved limits.[7] That tendency of the image is taken up by Darwin immediately after his description of 'the inextricable web of affinities' in his discussion of morphology:

> What can be more curious than that the hand of a man, formed for grasping, that of a mole for digging, the leg of the horse, the paddle of the porpoise, and the wing of the bat, should all be constructed on the

same pattern, and should include the same bones, in the same relative positions? (415)

Undeviating patterns and their diverse uses raise problems which are the novelist's province. George Eliot's awareness of the varying powers of the web image are expressed in the successive, and very diverse, references in chapter 15 of *Middlemarch*. In the well-known passage that opens the chapter she compares her own practice with that of Fielding, the 'great historian, as he insisted on calling himself':

> We belated historians must not linger after his example, I at least have so much to do in unravelling certain human lots, and seeing how they were woven and interwoven, that all the light I can command must be concentrated on this particular web, and not dispersed over that tempting range of relevancies called the universe. (ch. 15)

The web is not co-extensive with the universe. The weaver poring over the fabric needs a concentrated light. Indeed, (as in the round eye of the microscope) it is the light which concentrates and which creates an effect of wholeness.

Next the narrative alludes to the web of the human body and its contiguous image, the labyrinth, which will become of such importance later in *Middlemarch*. The connection of evolutionary theory and labyrinth was already established for example, in an article by Julia Wedgwood (Darwin's niece)[8] in *Macmillan's Magazine* in 1861. We read:

> The infinitude of small deviations from the parent type . . . may be regarded as a labyrinth laid out by the hands of the Creator, through which he furnishes a clue to a higher state of being, in the principle which rewards every step in the right direction.

The *Middlemarch* passage describes the awakening of Lydgate's scientific interests:

> The page he opened on was under the heading of Anatomy, and the first passage that drew his eyes was on the valves of the heart. He was not much acquainted with valves of any sort, but he knew that *valvae* were folding doors, and through this crevice came a sudden light startling him with his first vivid notion of finely-adjusted mechanism in the human frame. A liberal education had of course left him free to read the indecent passages in the school classics, but beyond a general sense of secrecy and obscenity in connection with his internal structure, had left

> his imagination quite unbiassed, so that for anything he knew his brains lay in small bags at his temples, and he had no more thought of representing to himself how his blood circulated than how paper served instead of gold. But the moment of vocation had come, and before he got down from his chair, the world was made new to him by a presentiment of endless processes filling the vast spaces planked out of his sight by that wordy ignorance which he had supposed to be knowledge. From that hour Lydgate felt the growth of an intellectual passion. (ch. 15)

The 'presentiment of endless processes filling the vast spaces', the circulation of the blood, the *valvae* through which 'a sudden light comes', all these interpenetrating metaphors express the process of coming to knowledge. And the imagery reaches its issue in the concept of 'primary webs or tissues' which Bichat has established. Lydgate's speculation adds to the consideration of tissues the question, again, of origins: 'some common basis' of 'the raw cocoon'.

> Of this sequence to Bichat's work, already vibrating along many currents of the European mind, Lydgate was enamoured; he longed to demonstrate the more intimate relations of living structure and help to define men's thought more accurately after the true order . . . What was the primitive tissue? In that way Lydgate put the question – not quite in the way required by the awaiting answer; but such missing of the right word befalls many seekers. (ch. 15)

The various threads from which are woven 'sarsnet, gauze, net, satin, and velvet' have one basis. The image of the spider's web stirs again in 'the vibration along many currents'. Lydgate's work is to demonstrate 'the more intimate relations of living structure'. Relations, and origins, are both implicit in the one metaphor. This organisation is taken over into that of the book itself, so that its enterprise is preoccupied both with morphological likeness and with variation.

In *Middlemarch* George Eliot seeks out ways beyond the single consciousness. She creates a sense of inclusiveness and extension. Nothing is end-stopped. Multiplicity is developed through the open relation created between narrator and reader, through participation in the immanent worlds of others and through the unlimited worlds of ideas. When she uses the image of the microscope in *Middlemarch* there is no suggestion of condescension to ways of being more minute in scale: rather there is a recognition of the multiple unseen worlds by which we are surrounded and which new methods of perception may reveal without reducing the mystery inherent in the fact of multiplicity. Simultaneity of experiences is the equivalent in the novelist's art, and *Middlemarch* is enriched by a sense of multiple latent relations which are permitted to remain latent.

Significant repetition and variation is an essential principle in the structure of *Middlemarch*. Science and mythology create within the work ways beyond the single into a shared, anonymous, and therefore more deeply creative knowledge. Myth, in particular, offers the continuity of collective insight against the anomie of the solitary perceiver. It is with the uses of myth as a means of enriching the concept of 'relations' that I shall be chiefly concerned in the argument that follows.

Middlemarch the book is something different from Middlemarch the town. It's worth emphasising this simple primary distinction because the inhabitants of Middlemarch within the book are so confident that Middlemarch is not only in the Midlands but in the Middle of the world; the book's expansiveness creates an effect of size for the town, so that Paris, Rome, and London look thin and small by comparison. But we as readers are made also to recognise its mediocrity. George Eliot, or Marian Evans, after all, escaped from Middlemarch. The narrator's business in the novel is to remind us of worlds intellectual, aesthetic, spiritual, which do not naturally flourish in the provinces. Not only the individual selves but the collective social self of Middlemarch is framed and placed. She creates a double time within the novel – the 'now' of herself and her first readers and the 'now-then' of the late 1820s. The intellectual concerns of the people and period within the novel are carefully dated and set in relation to her own time. This relation is often ironic, as in her treatment of the Reform Bill, sometimes prophetic, as in the imagery drawn from the development of the microscope, and occasionally a fusing of the values of several times, as in the opening sentence of chapter 1 which makes of Dorothea a genuinely pre-Raphaelite Madonna.

The typical concern of the intellectual characters in the book is with visions of unity, but a unity which seeks to resolve the extraordinary diversities of the world back into a single answer: the key to all mythologies, the primitive tissue, allegorical painting (Ladislaw mocks Naumann: 'I do *not* think that all the universe is straining towards the obscure significance of your pictures' (ch. 19). Casaubon and Dorothea, for different reasons, are distressed by the miscellaneity of Rome, where the remains of different cultures are all topographically jostling each other, apparently without hierarchy of meaning:

> She had been led through the best galleries, had been taken to the chief points of view, had been shown the grandest ruins and the most glorious churches, and she had ended by oftenest choosing to drive out to the Campagna where she could feel alone with the earth and sky, away from

> the oppressive masquerade of ages, in which her own life too seemed to become a masque with enigmatical costumes. (ch. 20)

Much later in the book, at the great crisis of her life, that earth and sky are peopled in the dawn with impersonal permanent figures, characteristic of human destiny in their ordinariness and their mystery: 'On the road there was a man with a bundle on his back and a woman carrying her baby; in the field she could see figures moving – perhaps the shepherd with his dog' (ch. 80). In that image of the family (though we are not certain that it is a family) and of the possible shepherd there are echoes of Christian mythology – but it is here diffused and brought down to earth. These are valuable figures because, simply, they are human figures each pursuing their own concerns: 'she felt the largeness of the world and the manifold wakings of men to labour and endurance'. The numinous must express itself in this book solely through the human.

Myths – the religious and proto-scientific perceptions of differing cultures – survive because they tell stories about human or quasi-human figures which satisfy the need for recurrence. Cultures are defined by their myths but myths outlive the culture which produced them. Casaubon's dry collation of myth, arranged according to the authenticity of their 'period', is set against George Eliot's own rich, manifold, free-ranging invocation of diverse mythologies within the book. Casaubon cannot accept the protean nature of myth because renewal and embodiment are beyond his imaginative grasp. Dorothea may be a poem to Ladislaw; she is never, in any sense, myth to Casaubon.

Casaubon is in a sense judged by myth. (The original bearer of his name, the seventeenth-century Casaubon, had written a treatise *against* John Dee, the Elizabethan necromantic scientist who believed he had discovered the key to the universe.) The acquisitive sensibility tabulates, collects, and reduces; the creative sensibility has the responsibility not only of perceiving but of making connections. In Dorothea knowledge and feeling actively generate each other. So she can learn; he must withdraw from learning. We see this particularly clearly in their attitude to art and Christian legend.

Instead of the desolate privacy of the Romantic ego, or the moral types of neo-classicism, George Eliot is seeking communal insights. In *Middlemarch* the narrator weaves into commentary, dialogue, and metaphor, allusions to a great number of mythological systems: classical myth, folk-tale and theatre, Troubadour romance and courtly love, the Arabian Nights, hagiography, mythography, the Brothers Grimm's collections, Christian legend and martyrology. Most of them are unemphatically placed, not seeming to demand a contextual alertness from the reader. But if we explore the context the allusions always yield insights into the accord between any individual's experience and the lived world of remote others.

So, for example, a little earlier in the scene between Ladislaw and Dorothea where he tells her that she is a poem, he has accused her of wanting to be a martyr:

> I suspect that you have some false belief in the virtues of misery, and want to make your life a martyrdom . . . You talk as if you had never known any youth. It is monstrous – as if you had had a vision of Hades in your childhood, like the boy in the legend. You have been brought up in some of those horrible notions that choose the sweetest woman to devour – like Minotaurs. (ch. 22)

Ladislaw's verbal energy readily shifts dead metaphor into myth: (monstrous becomes Minotaur). The labyrinth of ideas and beliefs harbours monsters. Before pursuing the Minotaur, however, that other, less familiar, allusion is worth pondering. Who was the boy in the legend? and how does he relate to the idea of martyrdom? The answer seems to be that he was Anskar, a ninth-century missionary to Scandinavia, whose boyhood vision was a promise of his own eventual martyrdom. In the event, he died in his bed, finally full of faith in God's purpose: his martyrdom was *not to be a martyr.*[9] This curiously Jamesian tale lies buried beneath that allusion of Ladislaw's. Its beautiful appropriateness to Dorothea's problems and fate is complete but latent. It is an extraordinary example of the 'inextricable web of affinities' recorded in *Middlemarch* and of the labyrinthine sub-text of allusions which are never brought to the surface.

George Eliot uses diverse mythological structures simultaneously; in particular the lives of the saints and classical myth. She was indebted particularly to Anna Jameson for her full realisation of the value of 'Christian legends or fairy tales'. George Eliot knew Mrs Jameson personally. She used her *Legends of the Monastic Orders* (1850) and *Legends of the Madonna* (1852) while she was writing *Romola*. And *Sacred and Legendary Art* (1848) has particular significance for *Middlemarch*. Anna Jameson's main contention in that book is that in the mythology of the saints we have a visual and symbolic system equivalent in complexity and in intensity to classical myth. She contrasts the knowledge of classical myth with the general ignorance of the symbolism of medieval Christian legend in a way likely to discomfit the modern reader:

> Who ever confounds Venus with a Minerva, or a Vestal with an Amazon; or would endure an undraped Juno, or a beardless Jupiter? . . . but . . . We learn to know St Francis by his brown habit and shaven crown and wasted ardent features: but how do we distinguish him from St Anthony, or St Dominick?[10]

George Eliot takes up Mrs Jameson's point quite directly at the beginning of chapter 19 where she is discussing the coming of Romanticism and the deliberately religious, symbolic art of the Nazarenes (whom many art-historians see as the precursors of the Pre-Raphaelite movement).

> Travellers did not often carry full information on Christian art either in their heads or their pockets; and even the most brilliant English critic of the day [Hazlitt] mistook the flower-flushed tomb of the ascended Virgin for an ornamental vase due to the painter's fancy. (ch. 19)

She expects her readers of the 1870s to register the start of a movement which opened a system of symbolism vital to the sensibility of their own time. What seems decorative and discrete to the ignorant eye is part of a far-ranging, implicit system of meaning: that had been Mrs Jameson's central point too.

In the very next paragraph George Eliot presents 'a young man whose hair . . . was abundant and curly . . . who had just turned his back on the Belvedere Torso in the Vatican'. The Apollonian figure is, of course, Will Ladislaw. Then, beside 'the reclining Ariadne, then called the Cleopatra,' the two men see 'a breathing, blooming girl whose form, not shamed by the Ariadne, was clad in Quakerish grey drapery . . . ' (ch. 19). In the description of Dorothea the double-time system enters: the knowledge that the figure is Ariadne, who can offer a means of disentangling the labyrinth, is historically beyond the reach of the characters, but is invoked by George Eliot as part of the shared world-knowledge of herself and her reader. Ladislaw, the bringer of cultural tidings, as so often, is given a midway status; it is he who two chapters later brings into the open the idea of Dorothea 'brought up in some of the horrible notions that choose the sweetest women to devour – like Minotaurs'. To Naumann she is 'antique form animated by Christian sentiment – a sort of Christian Antigone – sensuous force controlled by spiritual passion' (ch. 19). But if she is related in terms of classical myth to Ariadne she is also Dorothea. She cannot become a St Theresa. Who then was St Dorothea? The answer is to be found in the second volume of Mrs Jameson's work. St Dorothea was both a martyr and a spiritual bride.

> She was then led forth to death; and, as she went, a young man, a lawyer of the city named Theophilus, who had been present when she was first brought before the governor, called to her mockingly: 'Ha! fair maiden, goest thou to join thy bridegroom? Send me, I pray thee, of the fruits and flowers of that same garden of which thou hast spoken: I would fain taste of them!' And Dorothea looking on him inclined her head with a gentle smile, and said: 'Thy request. O Theophilus, is granted!' Whereat

> he laughed aloud with his companions; but she went on cheerfully to death. When she came to the place of execution, she knelt down and prayed: and suddenly appeared at her side a beautiful boy, with hair bright as sunbeams:
>
> A smooth-faced glorious thing,
> With thousand blessings dancing in his eyes.
>
> In his hand he held a basket containing three apples, and three fresh-gathered and fragrant roses. She said to him: 'Carry these to Theophilus; say that Dorothea hath sent them, and that I go before him to the garden whence they came, and await him there.' With these words she bent her neck and received the death-stroke.
>
> Meantime the angel (for it was an angel) went to seek Theophilus; and found him still laughing in merry mood over the idea of the promised gift. The angel placed before him the basket of celestial fruit and flowers, saying: 'Dorothea sends thee this,' and vanished. What words can express the wonder of Theophilus?[11]

The 'beautiful boy, with hair bright as sunbeams,' bringer of fruit and flowers, seems a familiar figure. Within the novel Ladislaw fitfully appropriates images of sunlight, issuing perhaps not only from Apollo but from St Dorothea's 'smooth-faced glorious' angel. Müller's solar myth and Jameson's saint's tale reinforce Ladislaw's sunny brightness, the little ripple in his nose which is a preparation for metamorphosis. The way his hair seems to shake out light is set in contrast (perhaps too easy contrast) with the Saturnian presence of Mr Casaubon, even with Casaubon's own idealised description of himself at the beginning of the book: 'My mind is something like the ghost of an ancient, wandering about the world and trying mentally to construct it as it used to be, in spite of ruin and confusing changes' (ch. 2).

These fugitive references give no guarantees of human perfection, but they do enlarge the scale of reference for the fallible present-day which Ladislaw represents. Casaubon cannot grasp the ongoing nature of experience, or of knowledge. Imprisoned in his tractate on the Egyptian mysteries, he is incapable of perceiving any relation between the present world and his work. Not only is he ignorant of German scholarship on mythology (which would include the Brothers Grimm's work on folk myth as well as on linguistics), but he is ignorant of the significance of Christian iconography:

> Dorothea felt that she was getting quite new notions as to the significance of Madonnas seated under inexplicable canopied thrones with the simple country as a background, and of saints with architectural models in their hands, or knives accidentally wedged in their skulls. Some

> things which had seemed monstrous to her were gathering intelligibility and even a natural meaning; but all this was apparently a branch of knowledge in which Mr Casaubon had not interested himself. (ch. 22)

The suggestion is that he thinks it beneath his attention, just as, in a poignant passage, he dismisses the Cupid and Psyche myth as a 'fable . . . probably the romantic invention of a literary period,' which 'cannot, I think, be reckoned as a genuine mythical product' (ch. 20). The beating of wings, the castle of Amor, night flesh, the travails of Psyche to come again to Love – all these lie outside his imaginative experience. He tabulates; he does not inhabit myth. His method is acquisitive, not radiating. He sees 'the world's ages as a set of box-like partitions without vital connection' (ch. 22). He is disquieted by the multiplicity of myth: the ways in which differing systems refract meaning at diverse angles, the sense of revelation and yet of incomplete relevance which George Eliot herself explores in her suffusing of experience with mythical analogues, analogues which emphasise variability while accepting the morphological 'Soul' of common patterns.

In contrast to the scientific or artistic imagination which is capable ultimately of 'bathing even the ethereal atoms in its ideally illuminated space' Mr Casaubon has lost the sense of mystery which for George Eliot lies in connections and relations. 'Lost among small closets and winding stairs' he cannot recognise the Ariadne who could deliver him out into sunlight. In his 'bitter manuscript remarks on other men's notions about the solar deities, he had become indifferent to the sunlight' (ch. 20).

At the beginning of the 1870s Max Müller's interpretation of myth in terms of solar symbolism was the dominant intellectual reading. George Eliot invokes the system herself within the novel in her treatment of Ladislaw and in the hindsight knowledge with which she judges Casaubon, but she does not allow it to dominate her created world. The scientific imagery ranges far forward beyond any research that Lydgate succeeds in accomplishing. The variety of myth and legend within the book embraces a free-ranging lateral world of meaning beyond Mr Casaubon's awareness. Most important of all, she uses these immanent worlds to indicate that any single interpretation of experience will mislead. The self, to be valid, must stand as pars pro toto. The single focus contains; the one candle makes for introspective vision.

> Your pier-glass or extensive surface of polished steel made to be rubbed by a house-maid, will be minutely and multitudinously scratched in all directions; but place now against it a lighted candle as a centre of illumination, and lo! the scratches will seem to arrange themselves in a fine series of concentric circles round that little sun. It is demonstrable that the scratches are going everywhere impartially, and it is only

> your candle which produces the flattering illusion of a concentric arrangement, its light falling with an exclusive optical selection. These things are a parable. (ch. 27)

The maze is what matters. The recurrent imagery of the web suggests simultaneously entanglement and creative order – and beyond them both, the web of human veins and tissues: human being.

The labyrinth, the web, the tree, the microscope: the contiguity of these concepts is significant for *Middlemarch*. But George Eliot needs also a sense of disparity and unrelatedness which cannot be expressed by any of these means. Much earlier, in a letter, she had used the web as an image of impassive uniformity and unvarying process from which she needed to escape: 'If one is to have the freedom to write out of one's own varying unfolding self, and not to be a machine always grinding out the same material or spinning the same sort of web, one cannot always write for the same public.'[12] In the Finale to *Middlemarch* the writing repudiates the evenness of spun fabric as a sufficient image of the potentialities of human life: 'the fragment of a life, however typical, is not the sample of an even web'.

The web is not co-terminous with life: it is not, either, identical with organicism. The shears as well as the spinning haunt the metaphor from its oldest use. In this final section of her book the imagery of the web is hauntingly suggested but never reconstituted. At the beginning of the final paragraph its powers are fugitively recollected and then given up:

> Her finely-touched spirit had still its fine issues, though they were not widely visible. Her full nature, like that river of which Cyrus broke the strength, spent itself in channels which had no great name on the earth. (Finale)

'Finely-touched' suggests the tremor of a spider's web as well as of musical instrument, and that parallelism of 'finely-touched', 'fine issues', with the four insistent preceding 't's just stirs the suggestion of 'tissues' to extend the parallelism. Then the image changes to that of the nameless river, spent in many channels: the irrigating version of the labyrinth.

David Carroll, *Middlemarch*: Empiricist Fables (1992)

Lydgate's provincial martyrdom is the most painful of the frequent tragedies which 'have not yet wrought [themselves] into the coarse emotion of mankind' (ch. 20). This is because his career originates in a moment of 'intellectual passion', an epiphany in which 'the world was made new to him' (ch. 15), and contains, as we have seen, glimpses of possible sublimity through his scientific research which seem far more realisable than, say, those of Dorothea. But this puts him more at risk when 'the gradual action of ordinary causes' which begins to impinge on his life is ignored, and then it is simply a matter of time before he becomes 'shapen after the average and fit to be packed by the gross' (ch. 15).

In one sense, Lydgate represents a new type coming into prominence in the 1820s with the growth and increasing specialisation of the professions. He aims to combine his various roles – family doctor, medical scientist, and provincial citizen – in order ultimately to make a link in the chain of discovery. And Lydgate maps out his future career like a research proposal. His scientific and professional work 'would illuminate each other: the careful observation and inference which was his daily work, the use of the lens to further his judgment in special cases, would further his thought as an instrument of larger inquiry'. Middlemarch is to fit into these plans as the suitable location which 'could hold no rivalry' (ch. 15) with this projected inquiry. In another sense, however, Lydgate is like the saint and the justified sinner – a recognisably traditional type, the scientific discoverer. This is an ambivalent role. In his own private topology he identifies himself with the sixteenth-century anatomist, Vesalius, in the tradition of 'the great originators', the 'Shining Ones', as he builds upon the work of Bichat and strives 'towards final companionship with the immortals' (ch. 15). But there is another image of the scientist in competition with that of the heroic reformer and discoverer. Surfacing from the depths of Middlemarch prejudice and primitivism is the mistrust of scientific knowledge of any kind, 'the world-old association of cleverness with the evil principle being still potent in the minds even of lady-patients who had the strictest ideas of frilling and sentiment' (ch. 18). The 'pride of intellect' (ch. 30), as Mrs Bulstrode describes it at one social level, is quickly translated at another into Mrs Dollop's conviction that Lydgate's main aim in the New Hospital is to acquire, by whatever means, dead bodies for his experiments. And when to this are added growing rumours of his power of resuscitating 'persons as good as dead' (ch. 45), his research into 'the homogeneous origin of all the tissues' (ch. 45) becomes increasingly Frankenstein-like.

The question the plot initially frames is, which of these two models or stereotypes interprets his career most adequately? Which provides the more plausible interpretation of that 'cluster of signs for his neighbours' false suppositions' (ch. 15)? In the home epic the answer must, of course, be neither. But, as with the other protagonists, such typologies enter the social medium and prove decisive when the climactic crisis of interpretation occurs. The danger signal in all cases is the wide gap which opens up between the conflicting interpretative models, a gap which Lydgate cheerfully acknowledges to Rosamond as he discourses on his hero Vesalius: 'They called him a liar and a poisonous monster. But the facts of the human frame were on his side, and so he got the better of them.' In his enthusiasm he fails to register Rosamond's disapproving reaction ('I do *not* think it is a nice profession, dear') nor the end of his hero's career ('He died rather miserably') which she elicits from him (ch. 45). The gap is exacerbated by the division between his intellectual activity and the rest of his life, the one rigorously scrutinised, the other led by habit and convention with 'that *naïveté* which belonged to preoccupation with favourite ideas' (ch. 36). It is a more subtle, psychological version of the kind of arrangement Dr Frankenstein makes as he is about to begin his sacrilegious quest for the secret of life: 'I wished, as it were, to procrastinate all that related to my feelings of affection until the great object, which swallowed up every habit of my nature, should be completed.' If this is the price, then the notorious doctor acknowledges in retrospect – and in line with the empiricist fable – 'that study is certainly unlawful, that is to say, not befitting the human mind'.[1]

The representation of Lydgate's career provides George Eliot with the opportunity to exploit the fictional possibilities of two other hermeneutic disciplines – diagnostic medicine and anatomical research. She employs them with the searching irony of her own double hermeneutic: as Lydgate practices these disciplines they are practiced upon him by the narrator and the community. This dramatises the true nature of the *hubris* of his life in Middlemarch: he thinks that he, uniquely, is the observer, the experimenter, the interpreter who, despite everything, 'may work for a special end with others whose motives and general course are equivocal, if he is quite sure of his personal independence' (ch. 46). His martyrdom is to discover otherwise, as the different elements in his life, far from supporting, checkmate each other. Each of his initiatives – the New Hospital and its chaplaincy, the non-dispensing of drugs, his advanced practices – becomes enmeshed in the 'petty medium of Middlemarch' (ch. 18) and so progressively misinterpreted. A wonderfully subtle contrast is provided by Farebrother, that true denizen of the home epic, who manages to accommodate his various activities – pastoral duties, scientific hobby, and family responsibilities – to the provincial world in a low-key, dispirited, occasionally heroic way.

It was clear as early as *Scenes of Clerical Life* that George Eliot was fascinated by the role of the family doctor in the community. He serves as a focus for the hermeneutics of everyday life, a professional deliverer of opinions on whom everyone has an opinion. First of all, there are the practitioners themselves with their outdated medical theories: 'For the heroic times of copious bleeding and blistering had not yet departed, still less the times of thoroughgoing theory, when disease was called by some bad name, and treated accordingly without shilly-shally.' But the patients upon whom they practise their theories respond by diagnosing the diagnosticians, with everyone swearing by his own doctor: 'each lady who saw medical truth in Wrench and "the strengthening system" regarding Toller and "the lowering system" as medical perdition'. The evidence for their cleverness 'was of a higher intuitive order' (ch. 15), as the citizens decide who to follow. When in a more serious crisis the physicians have to be called in, the choice is easier as each man becomes a metaphor for his mode of treatment. Dr Minehin is 'soft-handed, pale-complexioned', while Dr Sprague is 'superfluously tall' and noisy: 'In short, he had weight, and might be expected to grapple with a disease and throw it; while Dr Minchin might be better able to detect it lurking and to circumvent it.' The complex situation of patients interpreting doctors who interpret patients becomes a kind of caricature of the double hermeneutic. And it is into this traditional symbiotic relationship, 'the mysterious privilege of medical reputation' (ch. 18) as the narrator calls it, that Lydgate briskly and ingenuously intrudes, as a new type of family doctor with the latest modern methods. Then they all, doctors and patients alike, bring their interpretative skills to bear upon him. Keen to see how this interloper 'might be wrought into their purposes', they misunderstand both his successes and his limitations, as Lydgate gradually comes to realise: 'it was as useless to fight against the interpretations of ignorance as to whip the fog' (ch. 45). There is a remorselessness in the complacency with which Middlemarch 'counted on swallowing Lydgate and assimilating him very comfortably' (ch. 15).

The narrator, too, switches into the medical mode in interpreting the 'cluster of signs' by which Lydgate is known. To begin with, prognosis points out 'all the niceties of inward balance' upon which his future depends and 'which makes many a man's career a fine subject for betting'. For character like disease 'is a process and an unfolding' which requires careful observation, as Borthrop Trumbull's symptoms demonstrate when subjected to Lydgate's 'expectant theory'. Then from the general diagnosis of both faults and virtues the narrator passes, like a discreet physician, to 'the particular faults from which these delicate generalities are distilled [which] have distinguishable physiognomies, diction, accents, and grimaces'. This requires an examination of 'the minutiae of mental make in which one of us differs from another', and leads to that definitive diagnosis which combines succinctly the language of character analysis with that of the medical practitioner: 'Lydgate's spots of commonness lay in the complexion of his prejudices' (ch. 15). The whole of chapter fifteen is a deservedly famous piece of extensive character analysis, and it vividly demonstrates the extraordinary facility with which the novelist adopts in her narrative commentary the hermeneutic language and perspective of the character under discussion. Interpretation and representation again become one in this refinement of the double hermeneutic. Just as the narrator scrutinises Bulstrode's life for the true evidences of salvation, so he diagnoses

Lydgate's spots of commonness as the doctor begins his own career of medical practitioner.

Lydgate's other activity, his scientific research, is used in a similarly ironic manner to reveal the *naïveté* of his relationship with women. 'Plain women he regarded as he did the other severe facts of life, to be faced with philosophy and investigated by science. But Rosamond Vincy seemed to have the true melodic charm'[2] (ch. 11). Then he puts aside his science and becomes himself the bewildered object to be experimented on. In the earlier episode with the actress, for example, he 'left his frogs and rabbits to some repose under their trying and mysterious dispensation of unexplained shocks', while he himself is subjected to 'some galvanic experiments' (ch. 15) at the hands of Laure. He is saved from 'hardening effects' (ch. 15) by his good nature but he has learned very little. And the experimental language is continued into his relationship with Rosamond as he persists in 'bringing a much more testing vision of details and relations into [his] pathological study than he had ever thought it necessary to apply to the complexities of love and marriage' (ch. 16). Unwittingly subjected to the 'shaping activity' of Rosamond's idea of marriage while his own 'lay blind and unconcerned as a jelly-fish which gets melted without knowing it', he returns home to his own experiments in maceration and other scientific reveries: 'the primitive tissue was still his fair unknown' (ch. 27). Much later in the novel, after their marriage, the double experimenting continues with Lydgate preoccupied with 'the construction of a new controlling experiment' (ch. 64), but he is forced soon after to accept the results of Rosamond's research: 'Nevertheless she had mastered him' (ch. 65).

Rosamond is able to turn the experimental tables in this way because her world-view is coherent and her life undivided. She embodies 'that combination of correct sentiments, music, dancing, drawing, elegant note-writing, private album for extracted verse, and perfect blond loveliness, which made the irresistible woman for the doomed man of that date' (ch. 27). She never questions this model on which her life is constructed – it is the pier-glass analogy which ironically confirms that 'Rosamond had a Providence of her own' (ch. 27) and, crucially, it is accepted by the community from which it draws its strength. As with the other protagonists, George Eliot subjects this mode of interpreting the world to hermeneutic scrutiny in various ways, but especially in the way Rosamond deploys and realises her own idea of what is called her 'social romance' (ch. 12). It is an idea which requires intense observation of social niceties and assumes, in competition with the novelist, its own form of narrative: 'Rosamond had registered every look and word, and estimated them as the opening incidents of a preconceived romance – incidents which gather value from the foreseen development and climax' (ch. 16). In one sense she is the most persistent idealist in the novel, as she insists on shaping, interpreting, subduing everything to this romantic idea.

More specifically, her power consists in not allowing the double hermeneutic of interpreting and being interpreted, of self and beholder, to escape from her control. Her 'eyes of heavenly blue', for example, are 'deep enough to hold the most exquisite meanings an ingenious beholder could put into them, and deep enough to hide the meanings of the owner if these should happen to be less exquisite' (ch. 12). This is the power of the stereotype she embodies. There is no gap, no discrepancy possible between what she projects and the recognised image. 'She was by nature an actress of parts that entered into her *physique*: she even acted her own character, and so well, that she did not know it to be precisely her own' (ch. 12). And to stress the formidable nature of such characters in which there is no slippage, as it were, between role and identity, George Eliot feels it necessary to introduce the episode of Laure. That actress utilises her role in the melodrama in which she is supposed to stab her lover in error, actually to murder her husband. The appalled Lydgate finally begins to grasp what has happened ('And you planned to murder him?'), but her reply closes the gap between intention and role: 'I did not plan; it came to me in the play – *I meant to do it*' (ch. 15). This could well have been Rosamond's comment when her rare 'moment of naturalness' becomes the 'crystallizing feather-touch' (ch. 31) which successfully completes the first part of her preconceived romance with Lydgate. 'What she liked to do was to her the right thing' (ch. 58). Both women spontaneously act their roles to achieve their desired ends. The roles, of course, have been established and tested by others, but each time they are assumed they are subtly adapted and modified, as Rosamond's piano-playing from which 'a hidden soul seemed to be flowing forth' demonstrates: 'and so indeed it was, since souls live on in perpetual echoes, and to all fine expression there goes somewhere an originating activity, if it be only that of an interpreter' (ch. 16). As J. Hillis Miller points out, interpretation is recognised paradoxically as a foundational activity.[3] But this is an *imitatio* of a different kind from Dorothea's.

Lydgate is vulnerable to these stereotypes, not only because of his emotional callowness, but also by reason of his intellectual acuity from which, as we have seen, it is inseparable. Unlike Farebrother he is not interested in the traditional taxonomies of natural history but in origins, the homogeneous origin of the tissue, the morphology beneath appearances, so that when his emotional commonness mistakes Rosamond for something special, his science is ready to hand to justify his perception. 'After all, he thought, one need not be surprised to find the rare conjunctions of nature under circumstances apparently unfavourable: come where they may, they always depend on conditions that are not obvious' (ch. 16). It takes them both some time to realise their mutual misinterpretation, that powerful shaping activity of which human, especially marital, relationships are shown to consist. Lydgate eventually links together his two actresses 'in a sudden speculation about this new form of feminine impassibility revealing itself in the sylph-like frame which he had once interpreted as the sign of a ready intelligent sensitiveness'. 'Would *she* kill me because I wearied her?' he asks (ch. 58). Form and function are finally discriminated, as the motto to the next chapter confirms in its juxtaposition of the soul and its 'fleshy self': 'And see! beside her cherub-face there floats/A pale-lipped form aerial whispering/Its promptings in that little shell her ear' (ch. 59). By then Lydgate's scientific work has been sabotaged. But Rosamond is thoroughly disappointed, too, in that the 'group of airy conditions' with which she had fallen in love and had tried to turn into her aristocratic dreams have proved insubstantial. If she is the 'anencephalous monster' that Lydgate acquires from Farebrother, then he displays 'a morbid vampire's taste' in his obsession with his scientific research. She begins to extend her ideas of romance to include the making of 'captives from the throne of marriage with a husband as crown-prince by your side' (ch. 43); but the 'thin romance' (ch. 75) with Ladislaw collapses at the climax of the novel when all the romantic conventions are shattered. Her chevalier turns viciously on her so that she almost loses 'the sense of her identity'; and with 'her little world in ruins' (ch. 78), she is further bewildered to find the preferred woman coming to plead heroically on behalf of her (Rosamond's) disgraced husband.

It is with the death of Raffles that the three strands of Lydgate's life finally compromise and checkmate each other. Was Raffles murdered? Did Lydgate's advanced treatment make possible Bulstrode's equivocation? Lydgate's open, experimental mind is aware of the complexity of the situation and so reacts against any simple conspiracy theory: 'What we call the "just possible" is sometimes true', he acknowledges to himself, 'and the thing we find easier to believe is grossly false' (ch. 73). But this scientific open-mindedness prevents Lydgate himself acting decisively so that there remains an 'uneasy corner of [his] consciousness while he was reviewing the facts and resisting all reproach' (ch. 73). Had he allowed his indebtedness to Bulstrode to influence his interpretation of the symptoms? Suddenly, scientific niceties about the nature of the experimental hypothesis take on a very different significance.[4] Had he colluded in murder? This is where George Eliot locates, characteristically, her crisis of interpretation. Both of the obvious explanations – bribed accomplice or victimised healer – are shown to be inadequate the more they have become enmeshed in the details of provincial life. Lydgate, however, knows he has slipped from his own earlier high standards when 'he had denounced the perversion of pathological doubt into moral doubt' under the conviction that 'the very breath of science is a contest with mistake, and must keep the conscience alive' (ch. 73). This is the nature of his indeterminate crime and, though it is beyond a court of law, it is punished, as with Bulstrode's, by the community. Self-exculpation is self-defeating, as Lydgate's knows. 'The circumstances would always be stronger than his assertion' (ch. 73) because 'it is always possible for those who like it to interpret them into a crime', says Farebrother cautiously: 'there is no proof in favour of the man outside his own consciousness and assertion' (ch. 72).

This is the unresolvable interpretative crux of Lydgate's career in the town. To what extent was he influenced by Bulstrode's loan? Middlemarch gossip is in no doubt, and even his friend Farebrother, 'with a keen perception of human weakness', can understand his falling from his own high standards (ch. 71). But George Eliot creates these ambiguous situations in order to show that the final analysis really depends on one's premises – and these are breathed in like air from the social medium in which we live. On this occasion, Dorothea initiates a countervailing interpretation by offering to her friends the proof of 'a man's character beforehand'. But Farebrother ('smiling gently at her ardour') counters with his statement that 'character is not cut in marble . . . It is something living and changing, and may become diseased as our bodies do'. Picking up the medical metaphor, Dorothea leaps over the question of guilt or innocence in her reply: 'Then it may be rescued and healed' (ch. 72). It all depends on one's hypothesis, the act of faith (or suspicion) which – and this is where *Middlemarch* points ahead to *Daniel Deronda* – brings into existence what it believes to be true. This is the necessary response to that interpretation of the evidence which imputes guilt which cannot be refuted, 'the public belief', as Lydgate describes it, 'that [a man] has committed a crime in some undefined way, because he had the motive for doing it' (ch. 76). It is left to Dorothea to initiate this alternative interpretation based on different premises which will also create what it hypothesises. With Lydgate himself at the point of uncertainty between the two hypotheses, Dorothea decisively tips the balance by providing him with, in terms of his own scientific research, an 'illuminated space' in which confused things can be seen clearly. 'The presence of a noble nature . . . changes the lights for us: we begin to see things again in their larger, quieter masses, and to believe that we too can be seen and judged in the wholeness of our character' (ch. 76). The various fissures and divisions in Lydgate's character are briefly overcome at this point when he simply describes to Dorothea what happened: it is George Eliot's secularised version of the moment when we shall see as we are seen. Lydgate undergoes no miraculous cure but the healing begins as he makes his confession – the confession denied to Bulstrode – narrating his version of events without equivocation, and 'recovering his old self in the consciousness that he was with one who believed in it' (ch. 76). Within this illuminated space, as in the account of his research, the hypothesis and the reality it explains become inseparable as each creates the other; or, in religious terms, Dorothea imputes righteousness to Lydgate and so imparts it. His future martyrdom spent between London and a Continental bathing-place – 'he always regarded himself as a failure' (Finale) – is made more bearable.

Elizabeth Deeds Ermarth, George Eliot and the World as Language (1997)

The particular topical issue that my title suggests is the role of language in our lives, and the extent to which language constructs rather than passively reflects reality, if we can still use such a word as 'reality'.

This issue is not a particularly new one; it goes back well through the nineteenth century. George Eliot certainly knew as well as anyone that, like languages, cultural values deeply differ. She emphasizes the fact that cultural values are just that, cultural, *not* natural, and that much unhappiness is caused by the naturalization of those constructs. 'Construct' is a word that would not have surprised her or sent her scurrying for cover. Her novels prepare us to understand how languages, and the systems of belief and value that act like languages, provide differing habitations in the world. To inhabit a language, as Cortázar says, is to inhabit a world: a world of systemic differences that shape and limit and enable all kinds of function.

But there *is* a point of emphasis at which the problem of language becomes controversial: the point of distinguishing between relativism on the one hand and relativity on the other. What is at stake in this distinction is whether the constructed world is one or many: whether the grammatical differences between systems can be mediated according to some common denominator, perhaps even a common grammar of some kind, or whether their differences are absolute and unmediateable. I shall come back to this problem later.

But first, I would like to begin considering how the world is language by reflecting on my experience of writing about George Eliot – an experience that I know is not limited to me. For me, then, writing on George Eliot usually is a particularly mixed experience consisting of both pleasure and frustration. On the one hand, she says complex things with such wit and generosity, that I feel delighted, and compelled to assent. There is always an extra margin for amusement in the narrative language, a kind of chronic risibility in the text. Taking *Middlemarch* as perhaps the most familiar example, there are those continuous small turns of vocabulary that open new vistas, like the description of Lydgate's situation in terms of 'the hampering threadlike pressure of small social conditions' – a quiet, literary joke linking Middlemarchers with Lilliputians. There are the little dramas of indirection, like that immortal breakfast conversation between Rosamond and Fred Vincy on various matters of accompaniment: her piano to his flute, in return for his accompaniment on her expedition to encounter Lydgate; and with the implicit extension of their musical duo playing in the background (ch. 11). The little dramas and new vistas sometimes even include me, the reader, as for example when her narrator speaks of 'the grins of suppressed bitterness or other conversational flavours which make half of us an affliction to our friends' (ch. 18).

To take a final example, here is a little commentary from *Middlemarch* on the subject of French influence and English tradition:

> 'Lydgate has lots of ideas, quite new, about ventilation and diet, that sort of thing,' resumed Mr Brooke, after he had handed out Lady Chettam, and had returned to be civil to a group of Middlemarchers.
> 'Hang it, do you think that is quite sound? – upsetting the old treatment, which has made Englishmen what they are?' said Mr Standish. (ch. 10)

There is some continuing topicality in this conversation on the subject of French influence; similar ones still do take place, here and there, in British universities. But the best fun here is in the way perspectives multiply and balance. Lydgate's ideas receive a certain transfiguration in Mr Brooke's way of putting things; thus transfigured these ideas receive decided opposition from Mr Standish, whose own interest itself requires such deconstruction. Throughout such passages I especially enjoy the extra edge that belongs to the narrative voice, that margin of wider perspective that implicates much that is not explicit in these speeches.

The pleasure I find in such narrative moments has to do with the complexity of the viewpoint and the clarity concerning differences between one and another. Taken in series moments such as this constitute George Eliot's narrative sequence. Around one centre of interest and attention, and then the next, and the next, shifting constellations of viewpoint gather, and dissolve. This complex treatment of perspective is a mystery of realist narration that we have only begun to recognize. In these constellations are embodied the collective awareness of a culture, perhaps even the self-consciousness of the species, but in any case an invisible community of awareness in each novel, that transcends the particular moment at the same time as it finds expression there. George Eliot has few equals – perhaps no equals – when it comes to presenting this complex of awareness. Elsewhere I have called this representation the 'Nobody' narrator in order to distinguish if from anything so limited as a particular individual viewpoint.[1] This blend of consciousness, time, and language does not belong exclusively to any character or even to the historical George Eliot; the entire range of narrative awareness constitutes it; its narrative expression is precisely Nobody. George Eliot's management of this complex perspectival system constitutes one of her great achievements and accounts for much of the fun of reading her. That narrative slide from one view to another engages readers in a kind of suspense that has little to do with plot, and it reminds us continually that nothing is final.

Such are the pleasures of writing on George Eliot. They are also the basis of the frustration I mentioned. The frustration lies in the fact that all but the most carefully formulated conclusions about George Eliot are reversible. No sooner do you say something definitive about her novels than you confront a counterbalancing consideration, a qualifying remark, that inevitable 'on the other hand'. Perhaps the archetype of such moments is that one in chapter 29 of *Middlemarch*, when the narrator says: 'One morning, some weeks after her arrival at Lowick, Dorothea – but why always Dorothea? Was her point of view the only possible one with regard to this marriage?'. The narrative then gives us the counterbalancing viewpoint. There is never a single way of looking at things in George Eliot. There is always that 'on the other hand' that makes conclusions difficult.

Just to confirm this for any remaining skeptics, consider those commonplaces of George Eliot criticism, the subject of egoism and her particular treatment of it in the pier-glass description. There are many examples in George Eliot's novels of egoism working its destructiveness. Arthur Donnithorne, Tito Melema, Edward Casaubon, Henleigh Grandcourt – the destructiveness of such egoists might seem rather unproblematically to recommend altruism. If thinking of oneself is worst, then thinking of others must be best. It seems an obvious conclusion, and has often been stated in George Eliot criticism. The pier-glass has often been taken as a comment at the expense of egoism. But no sooner does one think of this, than something whispers, 'on the other hand'. Let me refresh memory briefly with this familiar passage:

> Your pier-glass or extensive surface of polished steel made to be rubbed by a housemaid, will be minutely and multitudinously scratched in all directions; but place now against it a lighted candle as a centre of illumination, and lo! the scratches will seem to arrange themselves in a fine series of concentric circles round that little sun. It is demonstrable that the scratches are going everywhere impartially, and it is only your candle which produces the flattering illusion of concentric arrangement, its light falling with an exclusive optical selection. These things are a parable. The scratches are events, and the candle is the egoism of any person now absent – of Miss Vincy, for example. (ch. 27)

That little reduction at the end – the remark about someone who is absent – might sound the warning that all is not quite as it seems here. The curious thing about this pier-glass metaphor is its double message about egoism. On the one hand I can think of several examples of egoism in *Middlemarch* to which this passage might apply – Casaubon, Raffles, Bulstrode, and of course poor Miss Vincy. Clearly egoism cannot be a good thing. But no sooner do these applications appear than, 'on the other hand', I recognize in Dorothea Brooke an important exception. She is always thinking of others; she considers Sir James from Celia's point of view. She *likes* giving up things as her carnally minded sister complains. In fact Dorothea is far too good at the selflessness business and it gets her into trouble. She is so badly inexperienced at acting on, or even knowing her own personal feelings that she very nearly leaves her chance for happiness pointlessly in the dust. She is the altruist whose example recommends egoism. George Eliot explicitly comments in an essay, 'We should distrust a man who sets up shop purely for the good of the community'.[2] Altruism in George Eliot has little to do with selflessness or lack of ego; instead, it has to do with balancing the conflicting claims of ego and of community. Pure egoism may be destructive on the one hand; but (and here it is again) 'on the other hand', a developed ego is necessary to independent and adult life. Dorothea's example simply stands in the way of what might otherwise have been an easy generalization about the pier-glass and about egoism. The metaphor asserts the powerfully narcissistic potential of ego, but it also asserts the *importance* of ego as a condition of light and order.

George Eliot often causes such havoc with interpretive generalizations. At least one reason for this is that she undermines the dualisms that such generalizations depend upon. She pushes readers beyond the dualism between egoism and altruism, and beyond the implicit hierarchies that always underlie such a dualism. Her narratives engage us in a different kind of problematic, where the important questions are matters of scope and emphasis, and not at all of deciding which side wins in a dualistic competition. When we come across that inevitable 'on the other hand', hang it (as Mr Standish would say), we are probably being required to deconstruct a dual opposition. This commitment in George Eliot's work is, I think, one reason why she favours metaphors of webs or networks: because they are headless and footless systems of relationship without a common centre. There are many centres in George Eliot, not one. In any case, the dual experience of interpretive enjoyment and frustration amounts to a reader's version of that 'antagonism of valid claims' that is a familiar moral problem to most of the characters in George Eliot's novels.

This 'on the other hand' brings me around again to language because, with each such shift of viewpoint, George Eliot invokes a difference, and a difference that depends upon deep structures, not superficial accidents alone. In her novels a 'valid claim' is never *solely* an individual matter; it is always cultural and systemic as well. Rosamond Vincy is, after all, the flower of Mrs Lemon's school, and Lydgate chooses her for that reason; it is no good then complaining of narcissistic performances that are put on in the first place at the request of the community and with their entire approval. Where was Rosamond to learn otherwise? She meets *her* first 'on the other hand' from Will Ladislaw, a man who is not interested in female flowers. And her husband Lydgate also depends on systems much larger than he is, both for his strengths and his weaknesses; his intellectual independence has been fostered by science; his carelessness is gender-specific. Just as Antigone's claims rest on a religion and Creon's on a political system, so the conflicting claims of Rosamond and Lydgate, and every other George Eliot character, rest on something larger and more grammatical in the sense already hinted at.

It is precisely because of what we can call their grammatical properties that actions and events are intelligible or perhaps even possible at all. George Eliot's genius appears in the way she makes visible the difficult, complex fact that each individual act specifies anew some traditional arrangement, some systemic order, modifying in some minuscule way a broadly interconnected balance of things. It is precisely thus that unheroic acts become powerful: in their specification and possible modification of a grammar of belief and value.

Such grammars become evident at crucial moments in her novels. The effort to understand a strange book, the refusal to burn a will, the silence about injustice that breeds guilt and violence. These moments have to do with more than an individual or a single event; they carry the traces of systemic organization. The religious tradition that brings Thomas à Kempis to Maggie Tulliver combines fatally with the tribal narrowness that prompts her to heed him. Mary Garth's family life gives her a set of principles, a grammar of independence, that prepares her to refuse Featherstone's request to burn his will. Gwendolen Harleth grows up in a culture and a family riddled with prejudice against women and obsequiousness before money and rank; these are powerful preparations for her fatal choices.

So the conflict of valid claims is never an individual matter only but always a discursive one having to do with a cultural grammar. Because this is true, the conflict can *not* be settled easily, or perhaps at all. The conflicts between systems, between languages, between discursive formations in George Eliot admit of no absolute distinction between right and wrong. What solution is easy or 'right' to the conflict in *Adam Bede* between feudalism and modernity; to the conflict in *The Mill on the Floss* between clan law and more modern rules; to the conflict in *Daniel Deronda* between national and ethnic cultures? What is right for one is wrong for another, what invigorates a strong mind may derange a weak one. There is always that 'on the other hand'. Even Rosamond Vincy has her excellent reasons. Even Rosamond Vincy has her chance to differ from herself.

This uniquely sophisticated emphasis on the balance between systemic claims has much to do with George Eliot's knowledge of language: knowledge that she deliberately cultivated early in her career. She was close to forty when she published her first stories. She was in her thirties when she published those brilliant essays and reviews. She was still in her formative twenties when she worked on her translations, and when, on top of the French she had learned at school, she added not one, not two, not even three or four, but *five* new languages: Italian, German, Latin, Greek, and Hebrew. Very few English novelists, for that matter very few novelists have had anything like this grasp of the fundamental differences between languages. More than anything else, I think, George Eliot's knowledge of language accounts for her happy grasp of systemic limitation. Her chronic 'on the other hand' belongs to this deep knowledge.

To reflect a minute on this claim, it seems obvious that knowledge of languages teaches the limits of all systems as nothing else can do. To learn a second language is to discover a second system for formulating everything. The gain in perspective is powerful. A second or third language, even if one rarely uses it, always presents a limit to any way of formulating or perceiving. One's native language is no longer *the* language, but instead only *a* language among others: one way, and only one way, of mapping the world and managing practical affairs. As a thoroughly modern philologist, George Eliot knew that language determines possible perception.

Even more to the point, linguistic differences demonstrate that language is not a matter of vocabulary. It is not a collection of little stickers to put on things, as Garcia-Marquez's characters do in *One Hundred Years of Solitude* when the great forgetfulness plague falls on them and they run around putting little signs on things so that they will remember what they are called. Language is more than a collection of tags; it is a system of relationship and value that must make sense internally, grammatically. But while the speech act, the *parole*, even the unspoken gesture are all tangible, a linguistic system *itself* never appears explicitly, except in grammar books or other secondary derivations from usage. We do not go about actually saying 'subject, verb, object'. We speak, using the implicit structure, the common *langue* that supports the *parole* invisibly. Various overlapping systems of value and expression at once hamper Rosamond Vincy and support her: systems that are not unique to her but that nevertheless do not at all foreclose on the unique and unrepealable poetry of an individual life.

If I were to carry this line of inquiry only one step further – over the hedge, in fact – I might ask, Where does the grammar of English exist? Not in textbooks, certainly, which are merely partial records of speech acts; not in some permanent world of Platonic Forms above and beyond speech acts; no, English, as a living and changing language, exists distributed, and very broadly distributed, in all, and only, the particular expressions of native speakers. Its grammar – that is, its *langue* – though never itself spoken, nevertheless remains a powerful condition of intelligibility for what *is* spoken, for the *parole*. The difference between English and another language, say Chinese, lies not merely in different words for things but in entirely different systemic *preparations* for expression. For example, English separates agent and action; Chinese does not. How much of cultural practice, I wonder, must follow from such deep linguistic preparations of discourse? George Eliot's writing has done much to prepare us for our current interest in language as a model for all systems, for all economies of belief and value. As she so brilliantly shows, to know a language, to know a discourse, is to inhabit a world.

Moments when such grammatically separate worlds intersect constitute the cruxes of all George Eliot's novels. The fistfight between Adam Bede and Arthur Donnithorne brings two systems into conflict: one where men are equals and one where they are not. When Arthur Donnithorne gallops in with the last minute pardon, he reenacts an gesture of ancient privilege, but he does so under constraint of a new world where law, not privilege, prevails. In Renaissance Florence various worlds collide that inform individual lives. In the confrontation between Romola and Tito we find writ small certain cultural differences that are also writ large in the reactionary religious teaching of Savonarola and in the garden of humanist scholars. Dorothea's world and that of the Vincys revolve side by side, encountering each other occasionally but remaining pointedly separate. When Lydgate leaves Miss Vincy in the lane to go and attend Casaubon, or when Dorothea goes to Rosamond about Lydgate's disgrace, two individuals meet but so do two different ways of constructing the world; the meeting is informed not only by the sympathy that Dorothea attempts, more successfully in their second meeting than in their first, but also by the powerful disparity between these two women's conditions of intelligibility, the difference in their grammars of experience. And those differences are nothing to the differences between the planetary systems of her next novel, *Daniel Deronda*, that brilliant, massive, and completely unified epic. Gwendolen's tight little, right little world comes into contact with inescapable, intractable cultural difference; and she, at least, begins to encompass it.

The growing points of the novels – the moments of opportunity for individuals and plot – are almost always such moments of encounter between one system of intelligibility and another. Throughout the Nobody narrator hovers, always maintaining its promise of relatedness between systems.

Such an encounter dramatically redirects many a character. Gwendolen Harleth has such an encounter most strikingly when she realizes that the man she has mentally wrapped and delivered as a husband is not only an English aristocrat but also ('on the other hand') a Jew, and a Zionist to boot. Suddenly an entire order of things, a grammar of belief and value that 'had lain aloof in newspapers and other neglected reading' enters her life 'like an earthquake' and dislodges her for the first time 'from her supremacy in her own world' so that she is reduced in her own mind 'to a mere speck' (ch. 69, 875–6).[3] When

Deronda tries to reassure her that, though they are parted, their 'minds may get nearer', it could seem a bit lame, except for the fact that it has the authority of George Eliot's whole narrative style behind it: the authority of that invisible community maintained by the Nobody narrator, that formality which includes all individuals and is congruent with none. The invisible bridge Deronda mentions is the thing that really counts in realism because it is the potential of the future – the more-than-this that makes not for righteousness but for experiment, adventure, generosity, even play.

George Eliot does not leave Gwendolen a mere speck in her encounter with the wide ranging 'purposes of others'. That encounter is precisely a beginning, as well as an end. Not for nothing does George Eliot dramatize this young woman's determination as well as her disadvantages, her wit and intelligence as well as her thoroughly-cultivated mercenary selfishness. Just as Deronda is more than an English gentleman, Gwendolen is more than an individual girl; she is one of those girls with 'their blind visions' who are the 'delicate vessels' bearing onward the treasure of human affections (ch. 11, 160). Whatever we make of this claim, it is clear enough that Gwendolen manages to accomplish something that few others do: she begins actually to change her vision, her grammar, her expectations, her acts of attention. By the end of the novel she is back where she must be in order to survive: renegotiating her relationship with her mother and, notably, through that act renegotiating her relationship with the plurality of worlds. *Daniel Deronda*, even more than her other novels, asserts the radical relativism of cultural value. From one side of London to the other, as from West to East, grammars differ.

In this discussion you will have heard echoes of contemporary theoretical debate about language as a model of systemic order. Since Saussure, it has become increasingly useful – we may even say profitable – for those interested in language to consider the extent to which *everything* operates like language. Politics. Music. Fashion. These operate as English and Hebrew do, according to invisible grammars or discursive rules that govern what it is possible to do, and not do: that govern what it is possible to say and what it is possible to hear; that govern who may speak. Awareness of this power of discourse to form perception and to limit it comes directly from the nineteenth century, and is not at all the recent brainchild of what Lionel Robbins once called 'the stunt anti-rationalism' of certain French intellectuals.[4] With post-structuralist theory we are still working on this problem of plural systems, and the difficult problem of negotiating between them where there seem to be *no* common denominators, and no possibility of a common world. Even though temporal and spatial horizons may seem to be continuous, language and discourse may not be. This is precisely the problem that post-structuralist theory presents to us. It is precisely the intractable, perhaps absolute differences between one language, one discourse, and another, that Jean-Francois

Lyotard has christened 'the differend': 'a case of conflict, between (at least) two parties, that cannot be equitably resolved for lack of a rule of judgement applicable to both arguments. One side's legitimacy does not imply the other's lack of legitimacy' and 'applying a single rule of judgement to both in order to settle their differend as though it were merely a litigation would wrong (at least) one of them (and both of them if neither side admits this rule)'.[5]

This description may claim only what George Eliot claims, that what is right for one is wrong for another; that what stimulates a strong mind only deranges a weak one; that what applies in the one system simply does not apply in the other. What then? Lyotard asks, what do we do when there seems to be no way to establish privilege between systems, even between moral systems: no common denominator, but only 'phrases in dispute'? Whatever the outcome of the complex debate on this point, Lyotard's discussion provides an example of that situation beyond relativism – of that condition of relativity – where the conflict of claims must be negotiated *without* the possibility of resolution or even of mediation. In various forms, most fundamentally in our scientific description of nature since 1900, relativity has already challenged the common denominators with which nineteenth-century writers unified the world, especially the common denominators of time and space.

The cultural implications of this step beyond relativism are profound – none more so for a democratic society. Truthfully, and even while our tastes in narrative may run to the objectivity of realists like George Eliot, we know that our political world is fractured by tribal warfare in ways that make a joke of mediation. What resolution, what translation, what mediation is possible between the grammar of awareness in Palé, Bosnia, on the one hand and in Paris or Geneva on the other?

Still, intractable as these discursive differences seem, they are fundamentally the same differences the nineteenth century faced. The difference between Lyotard and George Eliot is that he pushes relativism to relativity, and here I return to my opening remark about the point at which language becomes controversial. To Lyotard all systems are finite and self-contained so that negotiations between them *can* find no common denominator. The problem of relationship must be deeply reconceived. The relativism we find in George Eliot, on the other hand, insists on the possibility of common denominators. In contradistinction with Mr Dagley's darkness, or Rosamond's or Casaubon's or even Dorothea's, the novel presents us with the ripple and amplification of language and of the narrative perspective system that contains so much, much more than these limited cases. George Eliot acknowledges that every language has its limit, but in her work crucially all limited languages coexist in a common world. Communication between them may be difficult; it may be hampered by traditional usage and prejudice; but communication remains possible. Communication may require separateness, but as Deronda tells Gwendolen, across that gap minds may get nearer.

George Eliot's novels characteristically cruise the boundaries between different systems of intelligibility, but her narrative style always maintains a common horizon. It is the same world for everyone, even Henleigh Grandcourt; he practically mutates into a sub-human species, but he, too, was once young and impressionable.

The real beneficiaries of George Eliot's narrative style are of course not her characters but her readers. We are the ones, unlike Maggie or Tito, who are continually forced to move from one private centre of interest to another, one place to another, one discourse or system of values to another. Some readers report feeling positively harried by the shifting in perspective at all levels: from the microscopic level of sentences and brief dialogue to the macroscopic level of the whole narration, itself implicated by continuous extension in a yet wider world. This highly achieved narrative medium provides an outside to every inside, a margin to every system. It is a trial for those who, like old Mrs Farebrother, have determined never to change; but it is a welcome opportunity for those interested in a plurality of worlds, for those interested in languages.

5

THOMAS HARDY, *FAR FROM THE MADDING CROWD*

Richard C. Carpenter's essay, 'The Mirror and the Sword: Imagery in *Far from the Madding Crowd*', offers a potent Freudian reading of Hardy's novel, and one that demonstrates the characteristic strengths and weaknesses of psychoanalytical criticism. The opening pages of Carpenter's essays are largely formalist, in that they concentrate on the patterns of imagery that help to structure Hardy's novel; for instance, the colour red, associated with the scarlet of Bathsheba's jacket and Sergeant Troy's uniform, is a familiar motif that appears repeatedly in different situations and settings, giving the narrative a structure that is 'fundamentally musical'. The later part of the essay, however, concentrates specifically on sexual imagery, especially in those chapters of the novel involving the shearing of sheep and Troy's sword exercise. While the essay offers an illuminating account of phallic symbolism in *Far from the Madding Crowd*, its more general analysis of sexual relations is highly questionable, especially the assertion that in her meetings with Troy, 'Bathsheba courts aggression, a kind of symbolic rape'.

Judith Bryant Wittenberg also concentrates on the Freudian dimensions of Hardy's novel in 'Angles of Vision and Questions of Gender in *Far from the Madding Crowd*'. Her concern is with the extent to which 'seeing' is an essential part of the awakening desire for love in sexual development, and with Hardy's abiding interest in shifting perspectives and different vantage points. Wittenberg's view of Bathsheba is markedly different from that of Carpenter: she claims that Bathsheba is 'controlled' by the male gaze and that her struggles with various male 'looks' are instances of a larger struggle with patriarchal society. Bathsheba's story depicts the possibilities, and also the constraints, facing 'a spirited woman' who tries to affirm her individuality in a society not prepared to condone the unconventional behaviour of such a woman. Wittenberg nevertheless sees the novel ending with a 'harmonious equilibrium' established between the competing views of Bathsheba and Gabriel.

John Lucas draws attention very valuably to 'Bathsheba's radical uncertainties about herself' and argues persuasively that these anxieties have as much to do with social class as with gender. He points, for instance, to the episode in chapter 3 in which Bathsheba saves Gabriel from suffocation in his hut, and shows how the dialogue conveys her sense of unease about her social standing and even her own name. The essay proceeds to argue that the three relationships – with Oak, Boldwood and Troy – constitute a kind of testing of Bathsheba's identity. The conclusion puts the emphasis on the attainment of social and economic equality between Bathsheba and Gabriel, as well as on their 'unvisionary' apprehension of each other. Lucas is less sanguine about the ending of the novel than Wittenberg, drawing attention to the way in which the narrative emphasis on separation heavily qualifies the final coming together of the two characters. In his recognition of the 'solidly bourgeois' relationship between Bathsheba and Gabriel, he provides an exemplary instance of historicist or 'materialist' criticism of Hardy's novel.

The essay by Raymond Williams is adapted from *The English Novel from Dickens to Lawrence* (1970), which explores the shifting meanings and representations of 'community' in a range of nineteenth- and early twentieth-century novels. Williams offers a tradition and a way of thinking about fiction consciously opposed to the highly selective and limiting ideas of F.R. Leavis in *The Great Tradition* (1948), a book that deliberately excludes from consideration the novels of Dickens, Hardy and the Brontës. The essay begins with a searching account of Hardy's critical reputation: it deflects attention away from the familiar constructions of Hardy the regional novelist and Hardy the chronicler of an old rural civilisation, and places the emphasis very firmly on the novelist who speaks to us *now*, 'from the heart of a still active experience'. What Williams acknowledges and values in Hardy's fiction is its unflinching recognition of the making and breaking of relationships within a social process that produces isolation and separation. Class division and economic insecurity are sources of tragedy and frustration in the fiction, and Williams shows this process at work in a wide range of novels, including *Far from the Madding Crowd* and *Jude the Obscure*. The critical method is an early instance of what became known as 'cultural materialism' (the term is Williams's own). Dismissing those views of Hardy's work that idealise a 'timeless' rural order, Williams argues that the novels are deeply enmeshed in the harsh economic processes and chronic insecurity of nineteenth-century rural life. The novels confront the social pressures of division and rejection, but they also show the strength and perseverance of people living together, in work and in love.

Richard C. Carpenter, The Mirror and the Sword: Imagery in *Far from the Madding Crowd* (1964)

Thomas Hardy's early novels show in embryo many of the characteristics to be found in the later masterpieces. *Desperate Remedies* has a Mephistophelian villain and a disastrous fire; *A Pair of Blue Eyes*, a heroine who cannot make up her mind between two lovers; *Under the Greenwood Tree*, a rustic chorus both humorous and wise in their simplicity. Flashes of the familiar Hardy imagery also appear from time to time to intensify the reader's perception and enrich his response: the Mellstock choir gathered around Mr. Penny's cobbler shop; Fancy Day framed by the window architrave; Manston peering into the rain-barrel to see 'minute living creatures' tumbling about in its greenish depths; Knight clinging to the Cliff-Without-a-Name while 'time closed up like a fan before him.' All these and more are indicative of the kinds of images Hardy was to employ throughout his novels: the intertwined relationship of man and Nature; mutability as seen in the change in manners and customs; the contrast between light and shadow, illusion and reality.

These are, however, only flashes. Not until *Far from the Madding Crowd*, the first of the major novels, was Hardy to achieve an integrated design such as we find in *Tess of the d'Urbervilles* or *The Mayor of Casterbridge*. One of the reasons these novels are 'major' is precisely that in them Hardy managed to create a fabric of images, repeated and 'concatenated' to deepen and make complex the emotional and conceptual significance. The structure of images in *The Return of the Native* is as much superior to that of *Two on a Tower* as are the plot and theme.

To see how this is applicable to *Far from the Madding Crowd*, I wish to take a passage from the early part of the novel and trace out some of the ways in which its images are used as the story moves on. The passage I have in mind comes directly after our introduction to Gabriel Oak, the representative of rural stability and firmness. As he glances casually over the hedge at the side of a road, he sees 'an ornamental spring waggon, painted yellow and gaily marked, drawn by two horses, a waggoner walking alongside bearing a whip perpendicularly' (ch. 1). The 'waggon' is piled high with household furniture and plants, while a 'young and attractive woman' sits on the 'apex' of the load. The wagoner leaves her for a few minutes, while he goes back to retrieve the tailboard, which has fallen off. She waits 'for some time idly in her place' until she looks attentively down at a package wrapped in paper, which she unwraps to reveal a 'small swing looking-glass.' She gazes at herself in this mirror, then parts her lips and smiles:

> It was a fine morning, and the sun lighted up to a scarlet glow the crimson jacket she wore, and painted a soft lustre upon her bright face

> and dark hair. The myrtles, geraniums, and cactuses packed around her were fresh and green, and at such a leafless season they invested the whole concern of horses, waggon, furniture, and girl with a peculiar vernal charm. What possessed her to indulge in such a performance in the sight of the sparrows, blackbirds, and unperceived farmer who were alone its spectators, – whether the smile began as a factitious one, to test her capacity in that art, – nobody knows; it ended certainly in a real smile. She blushed at herself, and seeing her reflection blush, blushed the more. (ch. 1)

Hardy cannot resist, at this stage of his career, commenting wrily on 'woman's prescriptive infirmity,' but he does not succeed in spoiling the effect of this vivid bit of characterization.

Although this scene is memorable because of its presentational quality – its vivid colors of scarlet, green, and yellow; its visual composition; the contrasts of bright face and dark hair, crimson jacket and green plants, vernal freshness and leafless season, it is also part of a larger context with which it interacts, and individual images are lifted out of it to be employed in many different ways throughout the novel. The imagistic design of *Far from the Madding Crowd*, unlike the straightforward structure of its narrative, is fundamentally musical. A motif, announced in an early scene, reappears time after time, sometimes as a leitmotiv attached to similar situations or characters and gaining in significance because of repetition in an expanding milieu, but more often transposed, inverted, taken up by a different character or situation.

For example, when Bathsheba Everdene meets Gabriel Oak in a later scene – also a crucial one – several images of this first episode are evident, now transposed and varied. Oak has fallen in love with Bathsheba, been refused, and lost his entire flock of sheep in an accident; while she, without his knowing it, has inherited a prosperous farm from her uncle and is now the owner of a thousand acres. It is night and one of her straw ricks has caught fire. The flames reflect on Gabriel's face as he passes by, with a "rich orange glow." Not a living soul seems to be about, and he watches as an interested spectator only, until the smoke swirling aside shows that a number of grain-ricks are in danger, whereupon he starts to work to quell the fire, several of Bathsheba's workmen coming up to help. When Bathsheba finally arrives, Gabriel is on top of the rick fighting the fire.

Here again we have a meeting in which neither character is aware of the other's identity. But the encounter takes on more meaning because of what has happened in the interval: Gabriel's love of Bathsheba, her refusal of his suit, his poverty and her inheritance. Their positions in society are inverted: he is the wanderer, she the established landowner and farmer. Similarly, their position in this scene as contrasted to the first has been inverted. He is now, ironically, above her on the rick though below her in station; the plants are now straw and grain, dried from their 'vernal' freshness; the yellow and scarlet of the wagon and jacket are the orange and ruddy glow of the fire; instead of in bright winter sunshine the scene takes place at night.

Perhaps this is mere coincidence, a trifle stretched at that, but there are further indications of this technique of picking up images for use in later scenes. When Bathsheba meets Sergeant Troy, we see once again a chance encounter which will become of supreme importance in the course of Bathsheba's life. Each is unaware of the other's identity; the meeting takes place at night in a dense plantation of young firs on Bathsheba's farm. Troy's spur becomes hooked in her gown as they pass each other on the path, and they cannot manage to disentangle themselves. He asks her permission to open the slide of her dark lantern, and reveals himself in the process as a soldier 'brilliant in brass and scarlet' (ch. 24). The chiaroscuro which typified the encounter with Oak is evident in this scene too, although the light is more concentrated and the darkness more intense; the glow of the fire has been transformed into the scarlet and brass of a soldier's uniform. The colors of sex and passion which were connected with Bathsheba in the first scene are now associated with the man, while the green of the plants has become the predominant hue of Bathsheba's apparel. He is the tempter and charmer rather than she, his sudden revelation out of the dark equivalent to her appearance to Gabriel as he looked over the hedge. As in the earlier scenes, the characters are embosomed in nature, which has provided the conditions under which they meet and which also provides an oblique commentary on their situation. As the plants invested the first encounter with their 'peculiar vernal charm' at odds with the season, and the burning ricks endangered the newfound prosperity of Bathsheba, so does the dense growth of evergreens contrast with the cultivation of the farm and makes necessary a narrow and tortuous path which foreshadows the road Bathsheba and Troy are to tread together.

To force these parallels further would be obtuse, although the fondness for symmetry apparent in his plots may be typical of Hardy's imagery as well. It does seem clear that he tends to employ certain clusters and pursue certain patterns as he goes on. The scarlet which has appeared in the three scenes already mentioned is thus a familiar motif in the novel. Oak gazes fixedly at the red berries of a holly bush when Bathsheba refuses him; the seal of the Valentine sent to Boldwood becomes 'as a blot of blood on the retina of his eye'; Troy's scarlet uniform is constantly in evidence and becomes especially significant when we see him presiding, a Lord of Misrule, over the drunken debauch in the barn: 'The candles suspended among the evergreens had burnt down to their sockets, and in some cases the leaves tied about them were scorched . . . Here, under the table, and leaning against forms and chairs in every conceivable attitude except the perpendicular, were the wretched persons of the work-folk . . . In the midst of these shone red and distinct the figure of Sergeant Troy, leaning back in a chair' (ch. 36). The fertility images, the innocence and gaiety of the first scene have been here transposed with a vengeance.

Later, when the evil implicit in Troy's carelessness and Bathsheba's wilfulness has been brought to a head, the scarlet motif is used even more ironically. Bathsheba, having gone to the sheep fair, a presumed widow, takes a reserved seat: 'one raised bench in a very conspicuous part of the circle, covered with red cloth, and floored with a piece of carpet.' To her dismay she finds that she is the only 'reserved individual' in the tent. 'Hence as many eyes were turned upon her, enthroned alone in this place of honor, against a scarlet background, as upon the ponies and clown . . . ' (ch. 50). It takes no subtle analysis to see that the wheel has come full around. Bathsheba no longer has to gaze in a mirror to be the cynosure of all eyes; now she is raised above the common level indeed, with the scarlet which has come to symbolize the source of her bitter unhappiness sardonically forming the setting instead of trees and a country road.

In a similar fashion Hardy employs throughout his novel other images of the initial scene: later we see the green of Bathsheba's riding habit echoing the green plants in the wagon; the yellow of the wagon itself is echoed in Troy's uniform buttons; the constant chiaroscuro used as the plot unfolds is reminiscent of the contrasts observed by Oak. But these are only details. The pervasive image-patterns are those related to the looking-glass and the uprooted furniture. Natural as these things are, and explicable enough from the dramatic and thematic import of the scene, they are also significantly symbolic.

The mirror is an ambivalent symbol. As we see it in Hawthorne, for example, it shows the inner truth of character or situation; but it may also be an instrument for illusion. Though in one way a mirror presents us with the truth, cruelly or satisfyingly, it also shows shadow, not substance. We are aware of this fact in the carnival 'fun-house'; too often, however, we are apt to equate a mere reflection, a play of light and shadow, with reality itself. Like Alice we believe that there must be a world correspondent to the one we call real, on the other side of the looking-glass.

What Bathsheba sees in her mirror is a handsome girl on a bright winter morning, but that this is her substantive nature, that her beauty and youth are her only reality, is an illusion. She later sees herself as the competent mistress of a large farm because those around her find it convenient to fall in with this notion, yet events show that she is no more mature as a landlord than as a farm-girl. She thinks she can indulge in such ill-advised pranks as sending Boldwood a Valentine, without serious consequences because she is deceived by his appearance of stability, not realizing that his nature is in a delicate state of equilibrium, like a bomb that is safe until one more atom is added beyond its critical mass. Despite everyone's contrary opinion and advice she thinks Troy a worthy man; and even after he has been proved otherwise she persists in believing in his love for her. Troy himself is illusioned – his attempt to right the wrong he has done Fanny by planting flowers on her grave is as patent a self-deception as Hardy can make it. The gargoyle which spouts its rainwater on the grave, washing the flowers away, is a clear enough indication of this. Boldwood is perhaps the most illusioned of all the characters in his infatuation for Bathsheba. Interestingly enough he also sees himself in a mirror, his square features transformed into something 'wan in expression and insubstantial in form' (ch. 14).

Complementary to this motif is that of instability, which is signified by the homely business of the house furnishings with their legs pointing upward into the air. In this novel for the first time Hardy strikes a chord which sounds through all his major works of fiction; the pathos, even tragedy, of lives warped out of their orbit and thrown into chaos and confusion, the incursion of change into situations where change can produce nothing but disaster. As Lionel Johnson pointed out in Hardy's own lifetime and as Douglas Brown has demonstrated recently, one of Hardy's major preoccupations is with this dissolution of the old, stable, rural and provincial life under the pressure of urban encroachment and technological change.[1] It might even be true that the very specification of country detail for which he has been so much praised, the attempt to crystallize in words an age which was rapidly passing, or had even passed, was Hardy's compensatory endeavor to present something undeniably *there*, in contrast to the phantasmagoric transformations that overtake the lives of his characters.

These transformations are scattered liberally throughout *Far from the Madding Crowd*. Like the furniture which typifies an unstable way of life, many of them are trivial, yet they have a cumulative effect. Cain Ball is so named because his mother made a mistake, 'thinking 'twas Abel killed Cain, and called en Cain, meaning Abel all the time' (ch. 10). The moon, shining into Boldwood's room, has a 'reversed direction' because of its reflection from the snow, 'coming upward and lighting up his ceiling in an unnatural way, casting shadows in strange places, and putting lights where shadows had used to be . . . a preternatural inversion of light and shade . . . ' (ch. 14). The lambing is 'very queer' this year, with too many twins; and when Joseph Poorgrass prints the name *James*, the *J* and the *e* are backwards. Of more significance perhaps are changes in costume: Troy's uniform has to Bathsheba the 'effect of a fairy transformation'; her crimson jacket becomes a green habit; Troy dresses in her bee-keeper's costume at one point; and later he appears disguised as Turpin, the highwayman.

Such transvestisms are the emblems of more profound mutations in character: Bathsheba from farm-girl to landowner; Oak from sheepherder to farm-hand to bailiff; Fanny from farm-girl to homeless wanderer to death in the workhouse; Troy from soldier to squire to wandering actor to death at the hands of Boldwood. And Boldwood's transformation is the most violent and significant of all, because through it Hardy makes clear the illusory nature of man's apparent security and stability:

> His square-framed perpendicularity showed more fully now than in the crowd and bustle of the market-house. In this meditative walk his foot met the floor with heel and toe simultaneously, and his fine reddish-fleshed face was bent downwards just enough to render obscure the still mouth and the well-rounded though rather prominent and broad chin . . . The phases of Boldwood's life were ordinary enough, but his was not an ordinary nature. That stillness, which struck casual observers more than anything else in his character and habit, and seemed so precisely like the rest of inanition, may have been the perfect balance of enormous antagonistic forces – positives and negatives in fine adjustment. His equilibrium disturbed, he was in extremity at once. (ch. 18)

Boldwood is transmuted from this picture of firmness into a tremulous fool of love because he does not have adequate defense against change. Although he is in many respects an unusual character for Hardy's fiction, he does represent a basic and typical problem. Man achieves security in a world of violent change only through a delicate balance of contraries, or a resolution and resignation like that of Gabriel Oak or Giles Winterborne, or the tradition-bound simplicity of the folk. Boldwood presents as his bastion only a façade behind which lie heaps of rubbish. Ultimately declared insane after his murder of Troy, he demonstrates the vulnerability of such a man against the slings and arrows of what seem to him an outrageous fortune. No matter how square and solid he may *look*, his soul is an easy prey to the assault of change, and in this way he is a representative Hardy figure.

Counterpointed against the vicissitudes of men's lives are Hardy's images for the permanent, some merely exacerbations of the feeling of human finitude and ephemerality, others implying a means of warding it off. The gargoyle which we have already mentioned as destroying Troy's illusions by washing the flowers from Fanny's grave is a prime example of the former (although the grotesque automaton that strikes the hours while Troy waits for Fanny at the wrong church is a close rival); while the great shearing-barn is an instance of the latter. The gargoyle perches hideously in the church tower above the cemetery, symbolizing Time and its inexorability: 'too human to be called like a dragon, too impish to be like a man, too animal to be like a fiend, and not enough like a bird to be called a griffin,' it has 'for four hundred years laughed at the surrounding landscape, voicelessly in dry weather, and in wet with a gurgling and snorting sound' (ch. 46). After Troy has finished his gardening and the rain begins, a stream from the gargoyle's mouth becomes a 'persistent torrent' that directs 'all its vengeance into the grave,' washing the flowers out of the ground and leaving a pool of mud in their place. Its vengeance is, of course, the vengeance of Time, which impersonally decrees that man's illusion of turning the clock back on his errors be as impersonally destroyed. Troy, like Bathsheba and Boldwood, labors under the common misapprehension that things are the way we want them to be rather than the way they are. Like Boldwood he suffers the most drastic consequences as a result.

In such images of Time there is something of the feeling found in the existentialists – a sense of human finitude and helplessness in a world of alien forces. The automaton and the gargoyle have through the course of years lost their relation with humanity and now mock the hands that made them, quite like natural features of the environment which mock man's finitude – Egdon Heath for a prime example, or Norcombe Hill where Oak kept his sheep, 'a featureless convexity of chalk and soil' suggesting to the passer-by that he is observing 'a shape approaching the indestructible as nearly as any to be found on earth.' Such a natural phenomenon seems to represent to Hardy the blank face of a Nature indifferent to man, and brings the same chill and numbing sense of horror that overtakes Henry Knight on the Cliff-Without-a-Name as he sees the fossilized trilobites before his face and becomes existentially aware of the span of time and the ephemerality of human life.

In contrast to these images which emphasize finitude are those which illustrate the stability associated with the recurrent rhythms of agricultural life where man has constructed forms of action seemingly immune to vicissitude. While the lives of the principals undergo violent transmutations, those of the folk remain the same; though Fanny dies of neglect and Bathsheba suffers the pangs of self-knowledge, though Boldwood is driven to murder and Troy dies for his sins, the sheep-washing and the sheep-shearing go on as they always have. The scene of the shearing-barn, especially, besides being one of Hardy's finest architectural descriptions, emphasizes the stability and antiquity of the building, and, by extension, the stability of the occupation which has been carried on in it for centuries:

> The dusky, filmed, chestnut roof, braced and tied in by huge collars, curves, and diagonals, was far nobler in design, because more wealthy in material, than nine-tenths of those in our modern churches. Along each side wall was a range of striding buttresses, throwing deep shadows on the spaces between them, which were perforated by lancet openings,

> combining in their proportions the precise requirements both of beauty and ventilation . . . The old barn embodied practices which had suffered no mutilation at the hands of time. Here at least the spirit of the builders was at one with the spirit of the modern beholder. Standing before this abraded pile, the eye regarded its present usage, the mind dwelt upon its past history, with a satisfied sense of functional continuity throughout – a feeling almost of gratitude, and quite of pride, at the permanence of the idea which had heaped it up. (ch. 22)

Hardy continues by describing the sun streaming in on the shearing floor, thick oak polished by the beating of flails for generations, the shearers kneeling at their work, 'the sun slanting in upon their bleached shirts, tanned arms, and the polished shears they flourished . . . ' (ch. 22). Truly a bucolic scene, saying in essence: 'Here is something that endures, something in which you can put your trust,' a defense against the mutability of the world of flux.

The actuality of the shearing itself, however, injects another factor into the human equation and brings us back to some implications of the first scene which I have intentionally withheld discussing until this point. Although Hardy himself and most of his critics and readers would most certainly deny it, there seems to be a strong Freudian thread running through *Far from the Madding Crowd* which should be unraveled if we are to appreciate the force of the novel's imagery. In fact, it is almost axiomatic that there should be such a thread: a writer in Hardy's position, writing of sex and passion in the accents of a most exquisite prudery, must, if there is anything to Freud at all, have compensated for his inhibition symbolically. Victorian restrictions resulted not in the abolition of sex but only in displacement, like trying to compress an incompressible substance such as water; push it down here and it seeps (or floods) up there.

In all his novels, I think it may safely be said, Hardy illustrates this axiom; and in *Far from the Madding Crowd* the appearance of sexual imagery is particularly instructive because it explains the problems of Bathsheba and her lovers, which remain curiously inexplicable otherwise. Oak, for example, has strength of character but seems impotent in love, easily fobbed off by Bathsheba. He is more the spectator than the lover, and his relation to Bathsheba is fundamentally that of the voyeur we see in the first scene. The sheep-shearing episode bears this out, because both Oak and Bathsheba are looking rather than loving when he 'drags a frightened ewe to his shear-station, flinging it upon its back with a dexterous twist of the arm.' He lops 'off the tresses about its head, and opens up the neck and collar, his mistress quietly looking on' (ch. 22). Oak, who is Hardy's ideal hero, chivalrous, courageous, altruistic, long-suffering, loyal, is shown by the imagery in a rather different light. '"She blushes at the insult," murmured Bathsheba, watching the pink flush which arose and overspread the neck and shoulders of the ewe where they were left bare by the clicking shears – a flush which was enviable, for its delicacy, by many queens of coteries, and would have been creditable, for its promptness, to any woman in the world' (ch. 22). The ewe seems to be a surrogate for Bathsheba herself, a feminine creature who can be assaulted with impunity while the woman watches the violation with interest and approval. Oak is, significantly, in a state of bliss, his 'soul . . . content by having her over him, her eyes critically regarding his skillful shears, which apparently were going to gather up a piece of the flesh at every close, and yet never did so.' When he finishes the task:

> The clean, sleek creature arose from its fleece – how perfectly like Aphrodite rising from the foam should have been seen to be realized – looking startled and shy at the loss of its garment, which lay on the floor in one soft cloud, united throughout, the portion visible being the inner surface only, which, never before exposed, was white as snow, and without flaw or blemish of the minutest kind. (ch. 22)

This voluptuous picture, with all its sexual overtones, including the allusions to the goddess of erotic love and to Botticelli's painting, quite certainly means more than an exposition of a commonplace agrarian event should. The denuded sheep is, through the metaphorical structure, assimilated to woman, becomes a beautiful woman, and creates in the reader's sensibility, I suspect, more the visual image of Aphrodite than of a sheared sheep.

When Boldwood, Oak's rival, appears on the scene and Bathsheba converses with him, blushing in a way reminiscent of the ewe, Gabriel watches from the barn. She goes into the house, then reappears in a few moments in her new green riding-habit that fits 'her to the waist as a rind fits its fruit.' Oak, trying to watch her and continue to shear, nips one of the sheep in the groin. The animal plunges; Bathsheba seeing the blood reproaches Oak; but the reader is told that both of them know she herself was 'the cause of the poor ewe's wound, because she had wounded the ewe's shearer in a still more vital part' (ch. 22).

As Freud would point out, this is no accident at all, but a displacement of Oak's jealousy. The language skirts very close to explicit explanation of the sexual elements involved; it seems to me most likely that Hardy was aware – even though intuitively aware – of the implications both of the symbolism of the scene and the effect of the diction. It would also seem that he did not choose the site of the ewe's wound entirely by chance. Oak, in short, is taking his revenge symbolically and on a surrogate for the fair Bathsheba. The imagery shows what the events themselves only hint at: that Bathsheba longs to be dominated and violated by an aggressive male, that Gabriel lacks the recklessness to do this directly and must employ a symbolic substitute, that Bathsheba recognizes this displaced aggression and is affected by it emotionally but not to the point of acceptance. Gabriel is altogether too passive, too much the father-image also represented by Boldwood. Bathsheba, on the other hand, is sexually desirable and arouses desire in men from the moment they see her. Despite her wealth there is never any hint that the men want to marry her for a good match, as they undoubtedly would in Jane Austen. Instead they all react in fundamentally the same way though they show it differently – they 'want' Bathsheba.

Two scenes with Troy underline the idea that Bathsheba courts aggression, a kind of symbolic rape. The first is that meeting with Troy we have already glanced at, where his spur becomes hooked into her gown, so thoroughly that they cannot disentangle themselves. For a moment Bathsheba thinks of leaving her skirt behind in order to free herself – in a Victorian context a titillating idea in itself – but Troy's continuing flattery of her beauty, though embarrassing, is also intriguing, and she allows herself to be drawn into conversation with him, a first premonition of the mingled fascination and distress which will typify her later connection with the dashing sergeant. From a contemporary perspective, however, there is patent phallic symbolism also involved in this scene in the cruel potency of the spur and the soft, enveloping tissues of the gown. Bathsheba is not only caught by her dress (and it might be noted that Hardy often emphasizes that a woman's clothing is an extension of her self), but she is also caught by the dominant male whom she subconsciously desires.

Such an implication seems equally valid, and more apparent, in the remarkable scene of the 'sword-exercise,' usually interpreted as a bit of the bizarre which has as its purpose to demonstrate Troy's and Bathsheba's reckless character, but which also seems to indicate the deep sexual current swirling beneath the surface of the novel. At the outset of this scene the setting is rich in erotic imagery. The sun, a 'bristling ball of gold in the west' sweeps the 'tips of the ferns with its long, luxuriant rays'; the 'soft, feathery arms' of the ferns in turn caress Bathsheba 'up to her shoulders'; the hollow in which the sword-exercise is to take place is a lush concavity in the land, lined on its sides with 'plump and diaphanous' ferns and in its center with a 'thick flossy carpet of moss and grass intermingled, so yielding that the foot was half-buried within it' (ch. 28). Bathsheba is so excited at the prospect of Troy's demonstration with the broad-sword that she is 'literally trembling and panting at her temerity,' while her breath comes and goes quickly, and her eyes shine 'with an infrequent light.' These images are obviously couched in a diction quite as suitable to preparation for a scene of passion as for a description of a military demonstration; while the sword-exercise itself, once the possibility of Freudian interpretation has been admitted, is embarrassingly explicit. The sword, raised into the sunlight, 'gleams like a living thing'; and swishes through the air with demonic speed and brilliance. Troy shows his skill by using Bathsheba as a mock-victim, darting the blade 'towards her left side, just above her hip . . . emerging as it were from between her ribs, having apparently passed through her body.' And then:

> In an instant the atmosphere was transformed to Bathsheba's eyes. Beams of light caught from the low sun's rays, above, around, in front of her, well-nigh shut out earth and heaven – all emitted in the marvelous evolutions of Troy's reflecting blade, which seemed everywhere at once, and yet nowhere especially. These circling gleams were accompanied by a keen rush that was almost a whistling – also springing from all sides of her at once. In short, she was enclosed in a firmament of light, and of sharp hisses, resembling a sky-full of meteors close at hand. (ch. 28)

As a final gesture, Troy cuts a lock of hair from Bathsheba's head and then splits a caterpillar which has fallen from the fern on to the bodice of her dress: she sees the point 'glisten toward her bosom, and seemingly enter it,' but opens her eyes to find herself unharmed.

We have here a description of phallic aggression both marvelously vivid and acutely aware of the subjective impressions on a woman's mind of a substitute sex experience. One wonders if Hardy, freed from the inhibitions of his age, might not have rivalled Lawrence in the intensity of his artistic perception of the feelings of sexual relationships. While on the overt level there is the most sensitive prudery in his novels (largely the fault of his prudish audience), he partly compensates for this by portraying the quintessence of the passional life in symbolic terms. Whether consciously (and this is just barely possible because he does mention phallicism in *Tess*), or intuitively, Hardy seems to have recognized the power of sexual images and their usefulness in getting across to the reader the *emotion*, if not the explicit content, of erotic situations. And of course *Far from the Madding Crowd* is not the only novel where he employs images and symbols which would have horrified his readers but which may well appear to us as among the most effective of his meanings. *Tess*, especially, and much of *Jude the Obscure* are rich in such imagery, while *The Return of the Native* and *The Woodlanders* can also be profitably interpreted in a Freudian way. This is an aspect of Hardy's fiction which has been too long overlooked.

But the point of this imagery in *Far from the Madding Crowd* is not confined to a general intuitive attitude, for it forms a powerful cross-current in the thematic intent of the novel. From the very beginning we know that Bathsheba is a wilful and vain young woman for whom life lies in wait to bring her *hubris* down to earth. We are told this quite plainly by the first scene where we realize that pride and beauty and youth go before a fall. The fundamental mainspring of her character, however, seems to be a bit of a mystery. Just *why* does she persist in coquetting Gabriel, whom she recognizes as a worthy man, and Boldwood, who worships the ground she walks on, only to fall into the toils of the raffish Troy? Why cannot she listen to the advice everyone is glad to give her? What feminine perversity accounts for this blind spot in an otherwise intelligent woman?

While the ultimate solution to such human frailty may not easily be found, if indeed it is ever found, at least part of the answer seems to lie in sexual attitudes. What Bathsheba wants on a conscious and rational level is denied by the subconscious desire to be dominated, perhaps to be raped. The two aspects of her character – the respectable Victorian girl on the surface and the amoral Dionysiac beneath are reflected throughout the female characters of Hardy's novels until we see the final development in *Jude*. Eustacia Vye, Grace Melbury, Lucetta Templeman, Felice Charmond, Elizabeth-Jane Henchard represent either the type of character we see in Bathsheba or one of the extremes; and in Arabella and Sue Bridehead we can discern the culmination of this strain in the unregenerate animality of the one and the epicene frigidity of the other. Bathsheba, the first of Hardy's fascinating women, is a long way from the polarities represented by Arabella and Sue, and lacks the intensity of Eustacia; nevertheless it appears that her capriciousness is rooted in the tensions between her overt and covert nature as symbolized by the scenes we have briefly scrutinized. Most certainly the sword-exercise cannot be dismissed in toto as a mere bizarre once the possibility of hidden erotic symbolism is admitted at all. The powerful emotions generated in this scene, and others as well, cannot be summed up in the simple context of the narrative. Somewhat in the fashion of Eliot's criticism of *Hamlet*, the feelings are in excess of the situation; and the solution to this disproportion quite possibly lies in the machinations of subconscious desires too disreputable to be shown the light of day.

Thus it may be argued that Hardy's imagery constitutes a secondary dimension to his ostensible narrative and theme, a kind of oblique commentary sometimes at odds with the manifest content, sometimes complementary, but always supplying an enriching affective aspect to the developing novel. While common sense and the sheer bulk of direct narrative and dialogue in his fiction are deterrents to the proposition that Hardy should be reassessed as a writer whose real value lies in his use of imagery, one might reasonably maintain that this secondary dimension is too vital to have been so long neglected. Without such imagery, *Far from the Madding Crowd* would be merely a kind of melodramatic folk tale about the fair charmer who overplayed her capriciousness and came to insight and repentance almost too late. With this imagery, the novel becomes, formally, a tight-woven texture of symbolic and structural meaning. Without the affective communication of such images, the novel would be an inconsequential tale of foolish people rather than the powerful probing into the human significance of vanity, desire, and despair which it assuredly is. As central to Hardy's fable as the death of Fanny Robin or the infatuation of poor Boldwood are Bathsheba's looking-glass and Troy's broadsword.

Judith Bryant Wittenberg, Angles of Vision and Questions of Gender in *Far from the Madding Crowd* (1986)

One of the more controversial issues in recent Hardy criticism concerns his attitudes toward and fictional treatments of women. For example, in a 1975 article, Katharine Rogers says that, although 'Thomas Hardy repeatedly shaped his characters and plots to show his sympathy with women and his awareness of the disadvantages society laid upon them, . . . if we look beyond Hardy's conscious intentions to such things as repeated themes, incidental comments, and subtle differences in the presentation of analogous male and female characters, we find evidence that he could not altogether overcome the sexual stereotypes of his culture.'[1] Despite the fact that critics are unlikely to reach any consensus on this topic in the near future, it remains a fruitful one. Readerly awareness of Hardy's ambivalence on this particular subject provides a useful avenue to understanding the sort of larger dialectic that gives his best fiction much of its tension and power. This essay will examine one aspect of Hardy's method – his preoccupation with sight-centered matters and their relationship to his depiction of women and their problems in *Far from the Madding Crowd* – and the way in which it embodies a dialogue having both philosophical and psychoanalytic implications that places Hardy's work in a larger context.

I

Perception and its role in both intellectual and emotional development has been important to thinkers other than aesthetic theoreticians such as E. H. Gombrich and Rudolph Arnheim.[2] Several English philosophers, most notably John Locke, George Berkeley, and David Hume, all of whose works Hardy was familiar with, had, by the end of the eighteenth century, elaborated upon the compelling problems of epistemological definition in a Cartesian universe and collectively posited a world in which the seeing 'eye' was the point of origin for the knowing 'I.' Later psychoanalytic theorists, some of whose work Hardy anticipates in intriguing ways,[3] such as Freud, regarded the drive to see as fundamental to the instinct for knowledge and as basic to the process of awakening desire for the love-object during later sexual development.[4] Thus the eye becomes throughout life, particularly for males, one of the important erotogenic zones.[5] Seeing can also, of course, lead to trauma and thence to neurosis or perversion.[6]

While much of Hardy's fiction is informed by post-Lockean and psychoanalytic theories of seeing, *Far from the Madding Crowd* (1874), his fourth published novel and the first great work of his career, represents a culmination of his treatment of the various visual preoccupations that are evident in all the work of his early period. Persistently and complexly present in the text are several thematic and technical elements arising from Hardy's concepts of the individual eye as the inlet of sense knowledge and as a sexual force, of the way in which one's sense of self is essentially created in perceptual moments, and of the collective eye as the locus of moral judgment: moreover, Hardy relates such issues in intriguing ways to questions of gender and control. Though these elements are clearly subordinated to the story, they underlie both its basic assumptions and its presentation.

The early pages of the novel serve in this respect as a paradigm both of the entire work and of all Hardy's fiction of this period, compressing an extraordinary number of sight-centered components into our introduction to Gabriel Oak and Oak's meeting with Bathsheba Everdene and linking them to crucial aspects of male and female roles. They constitute a rich exemplification of Hardy's conception of the complex role which vision plays in life and in the fiction-making process. Several physical points of station (i.e., the distance of the spectator from the nearest point of the 'picture' he sees), each with significant implications, are juxtaposed in these opening pages, the first of them, that of the narrator, being the most important to this and all of Hardy's ficion. The spectatorial narrator begins by offering a Halsian portrait of a ruddy, smiling Oak that obviously applies to the general as well as the specific instance, going on, in a confident, somewhat amused tone, to describe Oak's behavior, character, and religious views, contrasting the limited 'mental picture formed by his neighbours' with the things available to the notice of 'thoughtful persons' (ch. 1), among whom the narrator obviously belongs.[7]

Oak's point of view is the second one offered and the second in importance. Hardy shifts us to him, 'glancing over the hedge' in a typical voyeuristic moment of the benign variety. He sees Bathsheba preening on her wagon and judges her as vain, remaining himself seemingly unaroused, but the more libidinal moments of peeping which immediately follow are portended by the cat who 'affectionately survey[s] the small birds around.' Women are often identified with birds in Hardy's fiction (as in much earlier writing in English), and the cat's gaze, though idle, is unquestionably predatory, like the male gaze.

Although there is no overt sexual component in Oak's second instance of peeping at Bathsheba, its basic nature is implied by the narrator's comment that 'he saw her in a bird's eye view, as Milton's Satan first saw Paradise' (ch. 2). The invocation of one of the most sexually destructive voyeurs in English literature suggests what sort of unconscious motives underlie Oak's voyeuristic impulses. Although when he next peeps through the loophole of his hut at Bathsheba behaving in a strikingly unconventional manner on her horse, he is described as merely amused and astonished, he has obviously been aroused, for shortly afterward he looks at her 'proportions,' Hardy's euphemism for her figure, 'with a long consciousness of pleasure'. Hardy's narrator comments on the sexuality involved – 'Rays of male vision seem to have a tickling effect upon virgin faces in rural districts' – while Oak himself seems to become aware of the violating penetration of his gaze, guiltily withdrawing his eyes from Bathsheba 'as suddenly as if he had been caught in a theft' (ch. 3).

In a moment with similar implications, Farmer Boldwood's sexual awakening from long years of celibacy is revealed in a phrase about his using his gaze in a penetrating way: '[He] had never before inspected a woman with the very centre and force of his glance' (ch. 17). Here, as in the depiction of Aeneas Manston's forceful eye in *Desperate Remedies*, Hardy is quite explicit in his treatment of the eye as a substitute sexual organ and of seeing as not only a prologue to but also a displaced form of sexual possession of the female. That Hardy was far more candid in his treatment of sexual matters than his Victorian contemporaries has long been acknowledged; by examining Hardy's recurrent depiction of the male gaze, we can see that that candor was of an extraordinary range.

How deeply disconcerting Oak's gaze is to Bathsheba is made clear by her response. She blushes deeply, her blush signifying embarrassment and possibly some unwitting form of tumescence, and she later refuses to look at him, apparently feeling 'that Gabriel's espial had made her an indecorous woman.' Her sense of vulnerability manifestly has a social as well as a sexual component, for, as Hardy's narrator points out, 'as without law there is no sin, without eyes there is no indecorum' (ch. 3). Here, as throughout the novel, we are shown how the awareness of being seen by some form of the collective eye, the location of moral-social judgments, engenders anxiety and prompts action that ranges from efforts at self-control to rash alterations of plans. So Sergeant Troy's fury at being publicly kept waiting at the altar by Fanny Robin leads him to cancel their wedding and, in effect, to destroy her life.

Though Troy's anger at being seen in a humiliating moment precipitates the central tragedy of the novel, it is usually Bathsheba who, like many of Hardy's heroines, evinces the sensitivity to being seen, and subsequently to being judged, that is a direct consequence of the sense of vulnerability. During her first appearance in the cornmarket, she is appalled by her awareness of 'eyes everywhere!' (ch. 12). Then in one of her early intimate conversations with Boldwood (it occurs, perhaps significantly, shortly after he loses his ocular 'virginity' and turns his gaze upon her), she becomes 'afraid they will notice us' (ch. 19). In a similar moment of intimacy with Troy, she says to him anxiously, 'My workfolk see me following you about the field – and are wondering – O this is dreadful!' (ch. 26). Later, her increased isolation and status as an object on which the collective eye is focused is symbolized by her moment alone in the circus tent when 'many eyes were turned upon her.' She 'make[s] the best of it' (ch. 50), however, in a manner that signifies her growing maturity and portends her protectiveness of another person exposed to the social gaze, when she removes her husband's corpse from Boldwood's parlor, unwilling to leave it 'neglected for folks to stare at' (ch. 54). Thus throughout the novel characters implicitly face the judgments of the community as they explicitly confront its eyes, for 'they see' is, as always in the fictive Hardyan world, an inevitable prologue to 'they say.'

II

There is, of course, along with a felt sense of social and sexual vulnerability, an element of paranoia in this hypersensitivity to being seen. Hardy may have been anticipating (and articulating) some of the linkages between paranoia and the constitution of the ego made by Jacques Lacan decades later, when his formulation of the theory of the *stade du miroir* grew out of his early studies of paranoia, and by Jean-Paul Sartre, who pointed out that 'the Other is not only the one whom I see but the one who sees me.'[8] Certainly there are some suggestive mirror scenes in *Far from the Madding Crowd* that seem, if not pre-Lacanian, at least evocative of his concept of the self awakening to consciousness in awareness of the alienated non-self, the mirrored Other. When Oak first sees Bathsheba in the opening pages of the novel, she is gazing into a looking-glass, where she 'survey[s] herself attentively' (ch. 1), smiling and then blushing. 'Seeing her reflection blush, [she] blushed the more' (ch. 1). Oak adjudges her action as motivated by simple vanity arising from narcissism of a sort that also made George Eliot's vain heroines gaze into mirrors, as in *Adam Bede*; but Hardy's narrator reminds us that Oak's assessment may be inadequate, for it is based on 'conjecture,' and, in fact, 'nobody knows' why she smiled (ch. 1).

What is also important is that Bathsheba comes into being, as it were, in that mirrored moment, comes alive for herself, for Oak, the narrator, and for us. The most vivid female character of Hardy's early fiction springs into existence in the instant she gazes at herself in a looking-glass. In like fashion, one of Hardy's most memorable male characters, William Boldwood, discovers himself, so to speak, as he looks into a mirror. Bathsheba begins the awakening process by sending him the valentine with a red seal that appears 'as a blot of blood on the retina of his eye,' portending its ultimate passional and murderous effect (ch. 14). Boldwood places it in the frame of a mirror, and in looking at it again also really looks at himself, perhaps for the first time. His 'nervous excitability' is disclosed to Boldwood in the form of his 'reflected features' (ch. 14) and though this excitability will finally have ruinous effects on himself and others, it signifies the inception of his efforts to participate emotionally in the life around him. Boldwood's physical awareness of himself in the glass mirrors his momentous awareness of another person. In both instances, Hardy strikingly presents central characters beginning the complex interaction of self and world that is signalled by the interaction of self and reflected self. Hardy's mirrors are more than symbols of simple vanity; they are tools for intensifying characters' awareness of themselves and heralding the intense way in which they will 'live' for us.

Thus in these brief opening scenes, Hardy manages technically and thematically to posit a series of points of station, each subordinate – and psychologically related – to the previous one as he moves from the narrator to Oak to Bathsheba, simultaneously presenting in complex fashion his essential concept of the eye as it functions in the epistemological, sexual, and sociomoral processes. The pages which follow variously reiterate these techniques and concepts in a series of highly visual scenes of great power as we watch the pastoral melodrama being enacted. These characters may in some sense be archetypal figures out of ballad or the French *pastourelle*, but aspects of both their psyches and their situations derive from Hardy's own ongoing preoccupations and from his efforts to explore the problems inevitably faced by individuals who might find themselves at variance with dominant forces in nineteenth-century English society.

The way in which Bathsheba is introduced, admired, and controlled by the male point of view is entirely relevant to her characterization in the largest sense. Her complex struggles with the various male 'looks' she confronts are mirrored by her difficulties with the patriarchal society. Her story depicts both the possibilities open to, and the limitations imposed upon, a spirited woman who tries to affirm her individuality in a society unready to accept unconventional behavior, particularly on the part of a woman. From the very outset, Bathsheba reveals her ambivalence about becoming, like most women, a visual and sexual possession; she wishes to live by her own rules and to take charge of her life. She early asserts that she has no sweetheart because 'I *hate* to be thought men's property in that way' and that she is interested in 'being a bride at a wedding [only] if I could be one without having a husband' (ch. 4). She possesses articulateness, almost always an emblem of superiority in Hardy's fiction, glibly teasing and criticizing Oak in their early encounters, and she is, says Hardy's narrator, a 'novelty among women – one who finished a thought before beginning the sentence which was to convey it' (ch. 3).

Not only is she intellectually in charge, she is physically assertive, as in the scenes in which she runs after Oak to clear up a misunderstanding and in which she rescues him from near death, dashing milk on his face, holding him in her lap, and unbuttoning his collar in a tableau that intriguingly suggests both a *pietà* and a seduction scene with Bathsheba as the sexual aggressor. Oak ironically seems far more 'female' than she in these early scenes, passively falling asleep like Tess Durbeyfield at crucial moments, struggling with the language he cannot use effectively, and then appearing as a visual 'object' at the Casterbridge hiring fair; the role reversal is striking.

Bathsheba soon progresses from emotional and intellectual control to economic control when her uncle leaves her his farm in recognition of her capabilities. The 'unpractised girl' develops into a 'supervising and cool woman' (ch. 7). When we see her framed in her bedroom window in a visual moment typical of Hardy's heroines, the scene has a crucial difference, for she is there giving orders to her male employees. When she makes the speech announcing her decision to be her own bailiff, thus augmenting her already considerable responsibility, she performs with great confidence, vowing to 'do my best' and to 'astonish you all' (ch. 10). Women farmers were not unknown in Hardy's day – there were quite a few in the Dorset area, most of them widows – but they were certainly uncommon in fiction; strong, unmarried females running their own farming operations would not appear in works by major writers until the creation of Willa Cather's Alexandra Bergson and Ellen Glasgow's Dorinda Oakley in the early twentieth century.

Both Bathsheba's competence and her desire to succeed are impressive, but she soon encounters a series of difficulties that reveal the dangers for a woman of being alone, being different, and being a cynosure. The first of these is criticism from the denizens of the malthouse who serve as a rustic chorus. They call her 'proud as a lucifer,' a 'very vain feymell' (ch. 6), denigrate her as a 'tom boy' and a 'headstrong maid' and doubt that 'she can carr' on alone' (chs 8; 15). Much of this is petty or jealous, and Oak often attempts to defend her, but even he irrationally blames Bathsheba for the threat posed to the year's crops by the harvest supper debacle, attributing it to 'the instability of a woman' (ch. 36). Even when the rustics are not being overtly critical, they subtly deprecate with their praise, as when they call her 'a handsome body' (ch. 8). Despite her strengths, Bathsheba cannot escape the reductive situation of being a 'sight,' a physical object to the male eyes around her.

Though Bathsheba is more fortunate than many of Hardy's heroines in having confidantes and being an integral member of a closely knit community, she often feels 'friendless' and 'unprotected' (chs 30; 31), with 'nobody in the world to fight my battles for me' (ch. 31). She also, in spite of her desire for independence, feels some pressure to accept a worthwhile offer of marriage, because 'in every point of view, ranging from politic to passionate, it was desirable that she, a lonely girl, should marry' (ch. 20). About a decade before Hardy began work on *Far from the Madding Crowd*, an article in the *National Review* had lamented the 'redundancy' of the single women in England, 'who, in place of completing, sweetening, and embellishing the existence of others, are compelled to lead an independent and incomplete existence of their own.' The writer called women of strength and intelligence 'abnormal' and suggested that no woman should hold a responsible job because 'the cerebral organisation of the female is far more delicate than that of man.'[9]

Certainly Bathsheba's behavior in much of the novel suggests that she is open to arguments such as these, for she seriously entertains proposals from three men who are not of her calibre in some respects, and ends up marrying two of them. While marriage may improve her social status, the first one imperils her economic well-being, because Troy begins to squander her money on betting, after using some of it to purchase his discharge from the military. There is some evidence that Hardy intended this portion of the novel to be set after 1870, because that year saw the passage of the Married Women's Protective Act, which no longer made the acquisition of a woman's property by her husband a foregone conclusion; Troy says, 'I have [no money] but what my wife gives me' (ch. 39). Nevertheless, Bathsheba apparently feels powerless to prevent her husband's improvident use of her modest wealth.

III

While various degrees of community hostility to her independent life and her sensitivity to the social pressure to marry affect Bathsheba to some degree, direct coercion by men who are representative members of the patriarchal society have the most powerful influence on her. Boldwood, with his burning eyes and coercive speeches, is a man of some substance and community standing, so the pressure she receives from him is simultaneously sexual, linguistic, and socio-economic. Sergeant Troy, whose power over Bathsheba seems almost exclusively sexual and rhetorical, is also in certain respects an emblem of the English patriarchy, for his father was a nobleman, his step-father a physician, and he himself is a non-commissioned military officer.

Bathsheba's extreme ambivalence toward what these suitors represent is revealed by her varying responses, many of them originating in her reactions to being seen, like those in her early encounter with Oak mentioned above. Although she has moments of feeling burdened by her femaleness, she also expresses a desire to be 'tamed' and a fear of being too 'mannish' that make her receptive to visual-sexual advances. Thus she initially seeks to elicit Boldwood's invasive gaze, finding it 'depressing that the most dignified and valuable man in the parish should withhold his eyes' (ch. 13) and feeling triumphant once his eyes are 'following her everywhere' (ch. 17); however, she later finds his stares – and him – too intense and is repelled. In her first encounter with Troy, as his emblematic spurs become entangled with the fragile stuff of her gown in a symbolic moment, she feels assailed by his gaze, which is 'too strong to be received point-blank with her own' (ch. 24). Yet because the strength of Troy's ardent eyes is reinforced by his prowess at rhetoric and sword-play, Bathsheba's defenses are rapidly breached; Troy's linguistic and physical adroitness, coupled with his sexual aggressiveness, make him an almost irresistible emblem of male power.

In the famous sword scene, with its highly charged sexual elements on which critics have commented,[10] Troy deftly wields his phallic and dangerous weapon, controlling it with his keen eyes; in the process he reduces Bathsheba to a mass of sexually quivering femininity and captures a fitting trophy, a lock of her hair. Aside from the sword, however, there are other visual and auditory elements of the scene with sexual associations whose presence would, even in the absence of the sword, portend the process taking place. The sun, that recurrent symbol of masculine power often visible in Hardy's fiction at traumatic moments, is here a 'bristling ball of gold' with 'long, luxuriant rays' sweeping the feathery ferns that in turn caress Bathsheba (ch. 28). In this scene, the sun's bristling signifies its potency, as it did earlier in the novel, where its reflection in the sheepmen's shears is 'strong enough to blind a weak-eyed man' (ch. 22), and as it appeared in Hardy's personal memorandum of 1873 about the 'brazen sun, bristling with a thousand spines, which struck into & tormented my eyes.'[11] The sun makes of Troy's sword 'a living thing.' Bathsheba's arrival has been heralded by her 'rustling' amid the ferns, just as her first meeting with Troy was signalled by a 'rustle of footsteps' (ch. 24); rustling was obviously for Hardy a sexually evocative sound, associated in the *Life* with Julia Martin's silken dresses and often a factor in scenes in his fiction with emotional and erotic overtones.

The confluence of strong sun, redness, and the sound of rustling in the opening paragraphs of the chapter depicting the sword exercise all portend what is to come, even before Troy unsheathes his weapon. In the scene which follows, the point of station is Bathsheba's, as she watches and experiences her 'ravishing' by Troy's impressive strength and dexterity. Significantly, his eye is connected to and necessary for his control of the sword; she can see it 'always keenly measuring her breadth and outline' (ch. 28). The uniting of eye and sword in a dazzling display of masculine power creates in Bathsheba a response that seems virtually orgasmic. She is 'enclosed in a firmament of light, and of sharp hisses,' aroused and overwhelmed, after which 'she felt like one who has sinned a great sin' (ch. 28). Interestingly, Hardy's narrator intervenes at the most intense moment in the scene, generalizing and explaining and thus asserting himself both as a physical presence and as one capable of having the 'last word,' revealing in the process that he is another of the male forces inhibiting Bathsheba's freedom.

Yet the novel is balanced, and Hardy depicts two other characters whose difficulties parallel or illuminate Bathsheba's – one male, the other female. Boldwood is the male, at the outset much like her in his self-sufficiency and independence, subsequently succumbing with great rapidity, as did she, to the suggestive presence of a sprightly and attractive member of the opposite sex. Both are punished quite severely for their sudden sexual responsiveness; Bathsheba is consigned to will-lessness and bitter disillusionment, Boldwood to mounting frustration that culminates in murderous anger.

Fanny Robin is the female character whose situation both parallels and contrasts with that of Bathsheba. When the novel was first published, reviewers suggested that Hardy had drawn his material from *Adam Bede*; if so, he divided Hetty Sorrel into two characters, both seduced and in some sense abandoned by the dashing soldier, eliminating the Dinah Morris figure. What is also interesting is that Fanny, a servant impregnated by the man she hopes to marry, faces a plight in which Hardy's mother and grandmother found themselves. Yet they married, while Fanny becomes the archetypal fallen woman of Victorian melodrama and visual art, a wandering outcast pictured most often in the dark and snow, like Eppie's mother in *Silas Marner* or the women in paintings such as Frederick Walker's *The Lost Path*, Richard Redgrave's *The Outcast*, and the last panel of Augustus Egg's *Past and Present*. As so often in Hardy's novels, he uses visuals as indices of a psychological condition; in Fanny's case, her vulnerability is indicated by the depiction of her seen from a distance as 'small,' a 'spot' on the landscape (ch. 11).

Appropriately, since both Fanny and Bathsheba are victims of the predatory Troy, Hardy suggests similarities between the two. In moments when Bathsheba confronts romantic predicaments, she is described as a 'robin' (chs 4; 29), and both women are shown in moments of desperation 'unfemininely' running after a man in order to clear up a misunderstanding. At the same time, significant differences between the two reveal that, as the narrator points out, 'their fates might be supposed to stand in some respects as contrasts to each other' (ch. 43). While Fanny is weakened by having no socio-economic power and little self-confidence, Bathsheba has a good deal of both; Fanny often seems hyper-feminine in her helplessness, while Bathsheba frequently stands her ground 'manfully.' Hardy tacitly underscores the contrasts between the two by showing them in alternating scenes. Bathsheba's confident speech to her workers is followed by the chapter depicting Fanny in the snow outside the barracks, even as the chapter describing Fanny's agonizing trip into Casterbridge is bracketed by two scenes of Bathsheba with her husband, both times in emblems of prosperity, her gig and her house. The women may be 'sisters' in their susceptibility to male sexual power, but

Bathsheba has other qualities that make survival possible. Some of these could be called masculine, so Hardy may be implying something about the merits of an androgynous model, because he also kills off, by the end of the novel, the highly feminine Fanny and the hyper-masculine Troy, concluding the work with the union of a strong woman and a man who has displayed a number of traits that might be described as 'feminine.'

At one point Bathsheba expresses her admiration for the goddess Diana, and even in times of great difficulty she exhibits strength and resolution that could identify her with that mythological figure, as in the moments when she staunchly helps Oak in his battle to save the hayricks from the thunderstorm and when she advises Liddy about coping with marriage, 'stand your ground, and be cut to pieces' (ch. 44). Yet she is more than a female warrior, for she has significant moral strengths, showing remorse for her capricious treatment of Boldwood, revealing a sense of responsibility, on more than one occasion, for the hapless Fanny, and evincing compassion even for the husband who mistreated and then abandoned her. Here, as elsewhere in the novel, the changing nature of her interior situation is indicated in visual ways. She bravely confronts the 'worrying perceptions' engendered by her traumatic discoveries of the lock of blond hair in Troy's watch and the corpse of Fanny's baby and reveals a protective and forgiving decency when she cradles Troy's body to rescue it from the stares of onlookers. By the end of the novel, she has grown in moral stature and been rewarded, not only with what promises to be a serene and comradely marriage but also with tributes from those crochety male voices, the rustics and the narrator. The former praise her bravery and honesty and the latter, in a memorable back-handed compliment, calls her 'the stuff of which great men's mothers are made' (ch. 54).

IV

If Bathsheba passes from an early phase marked by stubborn independence to a second one where she exhibits, as the narrator says, 'too much womanliness to use her understanding to the best advantage' (ch. 29), falling into a state of listless dependency, she emerges finally as an individual capable of meshing both sorts of impulses. Her arrival at this final stage is signalled by her visit to Oak, a courageous and rather aggressive act, during which she coyly cajoles him into acknowledging his feelings for her, even as she has fully acknowledged to herself her emotional dependency on him; she thus evinces a harmonious blend of the masculine and the feminine. Oak, too, arrives at a point where he effectively meshes disparate tendencies. Early in the work he had seemed both to be somewhat 'feminine' and to reveal qualities that would later prove problematic for Jude Fawley – a wish to improve his lot in life, a sympathetic concern for animals, and a moment of contemplating suicide by water; Oak's vulnerability is evinced by moments of being, like most of Hardy's women and like Jude, a visual 'object' exposed to the investigative and occasionally dismissive stares of others. Yet he has strengths not shown by Jude – persistence and perceptiveness among them – and he also assumes an increasingly 'masculine' socio-economic role, when his evident competence is rewarded by jobs as bailiff for Bathsheba and as the manager of Boldwood's property. At the same time, he never loses the tenderness that makes him so responsive to the plights of others and we come to view some of his passivity as an almost aggressive tenacity.

Thus the marriage of Oak and Bathsheba seems highly appropriate as an outgrowth of their separate arrivals at a point where the masculine and feminine in each of them are nicely integrated, for it represents the merging of those balanced individuals in a larger whole. Each has undergone, at differing times, the experiences of being both helpless and in control, of being both seen and seer, object and subject. Their angles of vision, so suggestively presented in the opening pages of the novel, have not only been juxtaposed but have attained a harmonious equilibrium. Hardy celebrates their union with the narrator's disquisition in the penultimate chapter, on the merits of camaraderie between men and women which 'is unfortunately seldom superadded to love between the sexes, because men and women associate, not in their labours, but in their pleasures merely' (ch. 56). It is a moment, to be sure, calculated to remind us that if the consummate 'eye' in the novel is that of the narrator, the dominant 'I' is also, but the attainment of an equilibrated state between the male and female protagonists is singular in a Hardy novel.

John Lucas, Bathsheba's Uncertainty of Self (1977)

When we come to *Far from the Madding Crowd* we encounter a heroine who is a good deal more difficult to place than is either Fancy or Elfride [*Under the Greenwood Tree* and *A Pair of Blue Eyes*]. For one thing Bathsheba has no living parents, and this is important because it means that she can have an independence of behaviour and action which is new among Hardy's women. For another, Hardy seems to me to be trying to do something far more ambitious with her than anything he had attempted with the earlier heroines. We can perhaps get some clue to what he has in mind if we ask what kind of a woman Bathsheba Everdene is (which includes asking what kind of a woman she thinks she is). What are her origins, where are her roots, what is her present social situation? Take the scene where she saves Gabriel from suffocating in his hut. He tells her:

> 'I believe you saved my life, Miss – I don't know your name. I know your aunt's, but not yours.'

> 'I would just as soon not tell it – rather not. There is no reason why I should, as you probably will never have much to do with me.'
> 'Still, I should like to know.'
> 'You can enquire at my aunt's – she will tell you.'
> 'My name is Gabriel Oak.'
> 'And mine isn't. You seem fond of yours in speaking it so decisively, Gabriel Oak.'
> 'You see it's the only one I shall ever have, and I must make the best of it.'
> 'I always think mine sounds odd and disagreeable.'
> 'I should think you might soon get a new one.'
> 'Mercy! – how many opinions you keep about you concerning other people, Gabriel Oak.' (ch. 3)

It may remind us of the great scene in *Our Mutual Friend*, where Eugene Wrayburn doesn't want to know Bradley Headstone's name, and reduces him to 'Schoolmaster'. Names suggest identity, so that to know the name is in some measure to know the person. Eugene doesn't want to know who Bradley is (his chosen ignorance produces, of course, disastrous consequences); and Bathsheba doesn't want to be known by Gabriel. 'You will probably never have much to do with me.' The voice of class speaks there as clearly as it does in Eugene's acceptance that Bradley's name doesn't 'concern' him. But the difference is that whereas Eugene chooses to have no doubts about his own identity, Bathsheba obviously has doubts about hers. It is hardly necessary to analyse in any detail that fragment of dialogue with Gabriel to recognise that she isn't entirely sure of herself or of her name. She thinks herself above him, wants to put him down, is warmed by his unshakeable self-reliance and composure to reveal something of herself and is then sufficiently discomposed by his familiarity to retreat into conventional flightiness and would-be acerbity. ('Mercy!' sounds to my ear slightly vulgar – as though Bathsheba isn't at all secure in the identity which she puts on when she tells Gabriel he will probably not have much to do with her.)

The point is that the impulsiveness and changes in manner of speaking that we can find in that dialogue point forward to such matters as the sending of the valentine to Boldwood and the elopement with Troy: they hint at Bathsheba's radical uncertainties about herself, which she tries to resolve by sudden action. To act is to discover herself. Or so she hopes. In short, Bathsheba offers Hardy a way of dramatising the nature of social movement, and of how it works through individuals. Jacob Smallbury says that her parents 'were townsfolk, and didn't live here . . . I knowed the man and woman both well. Levi Everdene – that was the man's name, sure. "Man" said I in my hurry, but he were of a higher circle in life than that – 'a was a gentleman-tailor really, worth scores of pounds. And he became a very celebrated bankrupt two or three times' (ch. 8). And a little later, commenting on the coolness of her manner to Oak, Hardy remarks that 'perhaps her air was the inevitable result of that social rise that had advanced her from a cottage to a large house and fields'. But Bathsheba herself doesn't find it easy to cope with that advancement, and although she can adopt the air of Mrs Charmond (shall we say), it never becomes natural to her. When, much later, she learns of Troy's affair with Fanny Robin, we are told: 'Her simple country nature, fed on old-fashioned principles, was troubled by that which would have troubled a woman of the world very little . . . ' (ch. 43). 'Simple country nature' is perhaps overdoing it, but one sees what Hardy means.

It is in Bathsheba's relationship with the three men, however, that Hardy's meaning emerges at its richest. Risking oversimplification for the moment we might say that Oak appeals to Bathsheba's 'simple country nature', Boldwood to that air that accompanies her social rise 'from a cottage to a large house and fields', and Troy to the improbable romanticism of town-bred bankrupt gentlemen-tailors. Oak and Boldwood both have visions of Bathsheba, and she nurtures a vision of Troy. All three visions have to be shattered before Bathsheba can achieve anything like a firm sense of self.

Gabriel's first sight of her is when, imagining herself alone on a wagon, she takes out a looking-glass and studies her reflection. It is a device which Hardy has already used with Elfride and Knight and here as there the question is how to 'read' the incident.

> The picture was a delicate one. Woman's prescriptive infirmity had stalked into the sunlight, which had clothed it in the freshness of an originality. A cynical inference was irresistible by Gabriel Oak, as he regarded the scene, generous though he fain would have been. There was no necessity whatever for her looking in the glass. She did not adjust her hat, or pat her hair, or press a dimple into shape, or do one thing to signify that any such intention had been her motive in taking up the glass. She simply observed herself as a fair product of Nature in the feminine kind, her thoughts seeming to glide into far-off though likely dramas in which men would play a part – vistas of probable triumphs – the smiles being of a phase suggesting that hearts were imagined as lost or won. Still, this was but conjecture, and the whole series of actions was so idly put forth as to make it rash to assert that intention had any part in them at all. (ch. 1)

It is inevitable that Gabriel should interpret her actions as dictated by vanity, and right that Hardy should separate himself from that interpretation, and that we should therefore be left with an impression of Bathsheba that makes her something of a mystery: is she vain, shallow, coquettish; or is she trying to recognise, account for herself?

Gabriel creates her in his own image. His first vision of her is followed by another, at night, as she and her aunt tend a cow that has just given birth. He doesn't know it's her because of the 'hooding effect' of her cloak, and so, wanting

> . . . to observe her features . . . he felt himself drawing upon his fancy for their details. In making even horizontal and clear inspections we colour and mould according to the wants within us whatever our eyes bring in. Had Gabriel been able from the first to get a distinct view of her countenance, his estimate of it as very handsome or slightly so would have been as his soul required a divinity at the moment or was readily supplied with one. Having for some time known the want of a satisfactory form to fill an increasing void within him, his position moreover affording the widest scope for his fancy, he painted her a beauty.

The prose is pretty clumsy, but the reference to painting and the acceptance of the romantic credo about what we half-perceive and half-create make it clear that Hardy is drawing our attention to the inventiveness of Gabriel's vision. Immediately after this he recognises who she is, and then she and her aunt 'took up the lantern, and went out, the light sinking down the hill till it was no more than a nebula' (ch. 2). That the word should make its appearance here is, I think, a clear indication of Hardy's interest in Oak's mental processes, and the fact that he has now his fixed vision of the girl. As with Dick's vision of Fancy and Stephen's of Elfride, it has to be decreated. Gabriel has to become an ignorant man again, in the sense in which Wallace Stevens meant the phrase.

It is Bathsheba, of course, who does most to shatter his vision. There is a brilliant moment – it comes after a very clumsy description of her – when we are told of Gabriel's staring at her: 'Rays of male vision seem to have a tickling effect upon virgin faces in rural districts; she brushed hers with her hand, as if Gabriel had been irritating its pink surface by actual touch, and the free air of her previous movements was reduced at the same time to a chastened phase of itself' (ch. 3). An acutely imagined incident, and one that tells us much about the aggressive, possessive nature of Gabriel's vision of Bathsheba, and against which she fights back. Gabriel tells her he loves her and wants to marry her.

> 'Mr Oak', she said, with luminous distinctness and common sense, 'you are better off than I. I have hardly a penny in the world – I am staying

> with my aunt for a bare sustenance. I am better educated than you – and I don't love you a bit: that's my side of the case. Now yours: you are a farmer just beginning, and you ought in common prudence, if you marry at all (which you should certainly not think of doing at the moment), to marry a woman with money, who would stock a larger farm for you than you have now.' (ch. 4)

The direct practicality of this speech, and the toughness of Bathsheba's spoken thoughts, effectively destroy Gabriel's vision of her. She has broken free of him. And as a result he can now deal with her at a practical level. There is a telling scene where Gabriel rebukes her for sending the valentine to Boldwood. 'Bathsheba would have submitted to an indignant chastisement for her levity had Gabriel protested that he was loving her at the same time . . . This was what she had been expecting, and what she had not got. To be lectured because the lecturer saw her in the cold morning light of open-shuttered disillusion was exasperating' (ch. 20). The camera has replaced the artist's eye. Vision cancelled by the truthful clarity of the photograph: 'faithful as no art is'. Understandable, therefore, that Bathsheba should feel pique at being exposed to an eye 'that will not censor blemishes'. And of course she knows she has behaved badly to Boldwood. Self-reproach has much to do with her exasperation.

But why send the valentine? It's part of her restlessness, her impulsiveness, and of her desire for a full – equal – relationship. Education and station prevent such a relationship with Gabriel, whereas she learns that Boldwood is a squire and a man of learning. And, as she tells Gabriel when she rejects him, she also wants to be tamed, is almost frightened of her independence. The problem of finding herself, deciding who and what she is, tugs her in different directions. And is the cause of the valentine.

Unfortunately for her, Boldwood is very like Henry Knight in his romantic vision of women. Indeed, in many respects he is a rewriting of Knight. He doesn't like to think of Bathsheba in the market place: 'it was debasing loveliness to ask it to buy and sell and jarred upon his conceptions of her' (ch. 17). It is only when she is away from work that she becomes a vision to him: 'Boldwood, looking into the distant meadows, saw there three figures. They were those of Miss Everdene, Shepherd Oak, and Cainy Hall. When Bathsheba's figure shone upon the farmer's eyes it lighted him up as the moon lights up a great tower' (ch. 18). It is an extraordinary image, and a considered one. Radiance positively flows from Bathsheba, bringing Boldwood into light. She has the power to illumine him and yet at the same time he creates the light, for in the market place she has no such effect on him.

When Boldwood proposes marriage, the decency and limitations of his view of her become obvious.

> I fear I am too old for you, but believe me I will take more care of you than would many a man of your own age. I will protect and cherish you with all my strength – I will indeed! You shall have no cares – be worried by no household affairs, and live quite at ease, Miss Everdene. The dairy superintendence shall be done by a man – I can afford it well – you shall never have so much as to look out of doors at haymaking time, or to think of weather in the harvest . . . I cannot say how far above every other idea and object on earth you seem to me – nobody knows – God only knows – how much you are to me! (ch. 19)

And there is the offer which will lead to her taming. Bathsheba is struck by it and entirely sympathetic to the 'deep-natured man who spoke so simply'. Left to herself, she muses that 'he is so disinterested and kind to offer me all that I can desire'. Yet she doesn't truly desire it. Though she may countenance this male vision of a woman's life she instinctively rebels against it, as Elfride had done. But where Hardy had occasionally cheapened Elfride in the interest of retaining our sympathy for Knight, he can now dramatise the tensions between Bathsheba and Boldwood without offending against the complexity of either. Both are treated with sympathy, and in the study of Bathsheba's agonised indecision over whether to accept or reject Boldwood's offer Hardy adroitly manages to reveal her struggle to keep free from a coercive vision of her that will separate her from herself. For the fact is that for her not to work amounts to self-separation. And indeed Boldwood's vision is of a woman parted from herself: 'you shall never have so much as to look out of doors at haymaking time, or to think of the weather in the harvest'.

Something of this comes out in the very beautiful chapter of the sheep-shearing supper, where the labourers are seated outside the house at a long table and 'an unusually excited' Bathsheba is inside the parlour window, facing down the table. The bottom place is left empty, until after the meal begins.

> She then asked Gabriel to take the place and the duties appertaining to that end, which he did with great readiness.
> At this moment Mr Boldwood came in at the gate, and crossed the green to Bathsheba at the window. He apologised for his lateness: his arrival was evidently by arrangement.
> 'Gabriel', said she, 'will you move again, please, and let Mr Boldwood come there?'

It is an image of contained harmony and order such as one associates with a whole tradition of English literature going at least as far back as 'To Penshurst'. On a lower scale, it is true, but identical in its feeling of achieved repose. Except, of course, for the moving of Gabriel. And that tiny moment neatly emblematises Hardy's refusal to be taken in by the myth of agreed order. Gabriel is shifted about at Bathsheba's whim; and is displaced by Boldwood, though he has a fuller understanding of her than the gentleman-farmer does. But she is the lady of the house, and her social position is one that makes it possible for her to deny him the right to be opposite her – to be her equal in love.

The twilight expands and, 'Liddy brought candles into the back part of the room overlooking the shearers, and their lively new flames shone down the table and over the men, and dispersed among the green shadows behind. Bathsheba's form, still in its original position, was now again distinct between their eyes and the light, which revealed that Boldwood had gone inside the room, and was sitting near her' (ch. 23). The candle light shining out of the house and over Bathsheba's employees is like that of the lares and Penates: 'thy fires/Shine bright on every harth as the desires/Of the Penates had been set on flame,/To entertayne . . . ' And the singing of Coggan, Poorgrass and of Bathsheba herself remind us of that notion of social harmony and order implicit in the music which flows from the great house of Belmont: 'It is your music, Madam, of the house.' Hardy pays his tribute to the idea of achieved harmony, stability.

And at the same time he knows that it won't do. It is not merely the moving of Gabriel that reminds us that order depends on ordering; nor that Boldwood's going into the house can be seen as a dangerous invasion. There is also the threat implicit in the song Bathsheba sings. 'For his bride a soldier sought her,/And a winning tongue had he . . . ' It hints at Bathsheba's dissatisfaction with herself. As madam of the house she is separated from Gabriel; as madam she equally doesn't want Boldwood's appropriation of her.

What does she want, then? Well, what she thinks she wants turns up soon enough. The shearing-supper over, she walks round her estate and in the darkness collides with a man.

> The man to whom she was hooked was brilliant in brass and scarlet. He was a soldier. His sudden appearance was to darkness what the sound of a trumpet is to silence. Gloom, the *genius loci* at all times hitherto, was now totally overthrown, less by the lantern-light than by what the lantern lighted. The contrast of this revelation with her anticipations of some sinister figure in sombre garb was so great that it had upon her the effect of a fairy transformation. (ch. 24)

This is her vision of Troy, a romantic one, of course, and one that she has painfully to undo. For Troy is as utterly conventional in his attitude to women as is Boldwood. This is revealed in the famous sword-exercise display, in which Bathsheba is quite passive, 'enclosed in a firmament of light, and of sharp hisses'; and it is also revealed in Troy's relationship with Fanny Robin, sentimental and brutal as that is by turns.

What Bathsheba thinks to find in Troy is a certain excitement which has to do with sexual abandonment: he is her folly, 'lymph on the dart of Eros'. It may seem that Hardy intends a reproof to Bathsheba's sexuality: 'though she had too much understanding to be entirely governed by her womanliness, [she] had too much womanliness to use her understanding to the best advantage'. Yet I think that by womanliness Hardy means conventional 'romantic' femininity, which doesn't permit her to see that, like Isabel Archer, her choice of apparent unconventionality will lead her to be ground in the very mill of the conventional. We are told that after one meeting with Troy 'there burst upon [Bathsheba's] face when she met the light of the candles the flush and excitement which were little less than chronic with her now' (ch. 30), and we need to recall that by the time Hardy came to use the word 'chronic' it meant not only constant, but bad, and was customarily applied to the condition of a disease (the word can be linked to the 'lymph on the dart of Eros' which Troy is for her). Troy's presence is an infection, a kind of sexual illness. It leads her to abandoning the affairs of her house, just as Boldwood's romantic love for her leads to the ruin of his harvests: between romantic love and the concerns of social life is another separation. What is apparently unconventional – the sexual excitement – is actually deeply conventional, and potentially disastrous to Bathsheba's full self-awareness.

Besides, it seems clear that she and Troy have no sexual life together. Later on we are told that Troy thought of how 'the proud girl . . . had always looked down upon him even whilst it was to love him . . . ' and I detect there a hint that Troy feels himself incapable of sexual relationships unless he is the aggressor (as he certainly is with Fanny Robin).

Troy also threatens Bathsheba's social well-being, her being the madam of the house. And so we have the famous scene of the wedding-night drunkenness, and later we hear of Troy's gambling, which all but ruins her. Bathsheba's vision of him fades, and when that happens he disappears – for he is *only* vision, he himself recognises that he can't survive once he can no longer be a vision to her. He takes off, and when he belatedly returns to Boldwood's house and Boldwood tells Bathsheba she must go to her husband, 'she did not move. The truth was that Bathsheba was beyond the pale of activity – and yet not in a swoon. She was in a state of mental *gutta serena*; her mind was for the minute totally deprived of light at the same time that no obscuration was apparent from without' (ch. 54).

I think that such a moment shows beyond all reasonable doubt how seriously Hardy took the psychological implications of vision and its loss. For I do not think that he is playing with words here. Bathsheba literally cannot see Troy because since he is no longer a vision to her he is nothing. He has ceased to have an identity which she can acknowledge.

By contrast, her relationship with Gabriel becomes anti-visionary because it is anti-romantic. Each comes to accept the other's social position, and their ripening friendship is dependent on the fact that Gabriel is once more a rising man, and has money. The relationship is solidly bourgeois.

> He accompanied her up the hill, explaining to her the details of his forthcoming tenure of the other farm. They spoke very little of their mutual feelings; pretty phrases and warm expressions being probably unnecessary between such tried friends. Theirs was that substantial affection which arises (if any arises at all) when the two who are thrown together begin first by knowing the rougher side of each other's character and not the best till further on, the romance growing up in the interstices of hard prosaic reality. This good-fellowship – *camaraderie* – usually occurring through similarity of pursuits, is unfortunately seldom superadded to love between the sexes, because men and women associate, not in their labours, but in their pleasures merely. Where, however, happy circumstance permits its development, the compounded feeling proves itself to be the only love which is strong as death – that love which many waters cannot quench, nor the floods drown, beside which the passion usually called by the name is evanescent as steam. (ch. 57)

Substantial: 'having a real existence'. Not a vision, not steam. But such affection depends on 'happy circumstance' which, as Hardy's fiction shows, is very rare indeed. Class differences, expectation, change, the rise and fall of families and of individuals: all these matters typically forestall the circumstance which allows for the growth of substantial affection between Bathsheba and Oak. *Far from the Madding Crowd* is the last of the novels to deal with a centrally successful relationship, one in which both man and woman can allow for the substantiality of the other's identity – simply because 'the mass of hard prosaic reality' which largely forms their knowledge of one another has to do with an attained, and a rare, balance of social and economic quality as well as an unvisionary forbearance towards one another. (In the famous scene where they work side by side to save the harvest, Gabriel is still Bathsheba's 'hand', their togetherness no more than an interlude.)

In implying, through a narrative which elaborates on their separations, how unlikely is their coming together, Hardy seems to me finely to recognise and explore a subject that is crucial to nineteenth-century experience, and in no way to be thought of as exotic, pastoral or escapist.

Raymond Williams, Thomas Hardy (1970)

The more I read Hardy the surer I am that he is a major novelist, but also that the problem of describing his work is central to the problem of understanding the whole development of the English novel. It is good that so many people still read him, and also that English students are reading him increasingly and with increasing respect. Yet some influential critical accounts have tried to push him aside, and even some of those who have praised him have done so in ways that reduce him. Thus he can very easily be praised as what we now call a regional novelist: the incomparable chronicler of his Wessex. Or he can be taken as the last voice of an old rural civilisation. The acknowledgement, even the warm tribute, comes with the sense that the substance of his work is getting further and further away from us: that he is not a man of our world but the last representative of old rural England or of the peasantry.

Actually, the very complicated feelings and ideas in Hardy's novels, including the complicated feelings and ideas about country life and people, belong very much, I think, in a continuing world. He writes more consistently and more deeply than any of our novelists about something that is still very close to us wherever we may be living: something that can be put, in abstraction, as the problem of the relation between customary and educated life; between customary and educated feeling and thought. This is the problem we already saw in George Eliot and that we shall see again in Lawrence. It is the ground of their significant connection.

Most of us, before we get any kind of literary education, get to know and to value – also to feel the tensions of – a customary life. We see and learn from the ways our families live and get their living; a world of work and of place, and of beliefs so deeply dissolved into everyday actions that we don't at first even know they are beliefs, subject to change and challenge. Our education, quite often, gives us a way of looking at that life which can see other values beyond it: as Jude saw them when he looked across the land to the towers of Christminster. Often we know in ourselves, very deeply, how much those educated values, those intellectual pursuits, are needed urgently where custom is stagnation or where old illusions are still repeated as timeless truths. We know especially how much they are needed to understand *change* – change in the heart of the places where we have lived and worked and grown up.

The ideas, the values, the educated methods are of course made available to us if we get to a place like Christminster: if we are let in as Jude was not. But with the offer, again and again, comes another idea: that the world of everyday work and of ordinary families is inferior, distant; that now we know this world of the mind we can have no respect – and of course no affection – for that other and still familiar world. If we retain an affection Christminster has a name for it: nostalgia. If we retain respect Christminster has another name: politics or the even more dreaded sociology.

But it is more than a matter of picking up terms and tones. It is what happens to us, really happens to us, as we try to mediate those contrasted worlds: as we stand with Jude but a Jude who has been let in; or as we go back to our own places, our own families, and know what is meant, in idea and in feeling, by the return of the native.

The Hardy country is of course Wessex: that is to say mainly Dorset and its neighbouring counties. But the real Hardy country, I feel more and more, is that border country so many of us have been living in: between custom and education, between work and ideas, between love of place and an experience of change. This has a special importance to a particular generation, who have gone to the university from ordinary families and have to discover, through a life, what that experience means. But it has also a much more general importance; for in Britain generally this is what has been happening: a moving out from old ways and places and ideas and feelings; a discovery in the new of certain unlooked-for problems, unexpected and very sharp crises, conflicts of desire and possibility.

In this characteristic world, rooted and mobile, familiar yet newly conscious and self-conscious, the figure of Hardy stands like a landmark. It is not from an old rural world or from a remote region that Hardy now speaks to us; but from the heart of a still active experience, of the familiar and the changing, which we can know as an idea but which is important finally in what seem the personal pressures – the making and failing of relationships, the crises of physical and mental personality – which Hardy as a novelist at once describes and enacts.

But of course we miss all this, or finding it we do not know how to speak of it and value it, if we have picked up, here and there, the tone of belittling Hardy.

I want to bring this into the open. Imagine if you will the appearance and the character of the man who wrote this:

> When the ladies retired to the drawing-room I found myself sitting next to Thomas Hardy. I remember a little man with an earthy face. In his evening clothes, with his boiled shirt and high collar, he had still a strange look of the soil.

Not the appearance and the character of Thomas Hardy; but of the man who could write that about him, that confidently, that sure of his readers, in just those words.

It is of course Somerset Maugham, with one of his characteristic tales after dinner. It is a world, one may think, Hardy should never have got near; never have let himself be exposed to. But it is characteristic and important, all the way from that dinner-table and that drawing-room to the 'look of the soil', in that rural distance. All the way to the land, the work, that comes up in silver as vegetables, or to the labour that enters that company – that customary civilised company – with what is seen as an earthy face.

In fact I remember Maugham, remember his tone, when I read Henry James on

> the good little Thomas Hardy

or F. R. Leavis saying that *Jude the Obscure* is impressive 'in its clumsy way'. For in several ways, some of them unexpected, we have arrived at that place where custom and education, one way of life and another, are in the most direct and interesting and I'd say necessary conflict.

The tone of social patronage, that is to say, supported by crude and direct suppositions about origin, connects interestingly with a tone of literary patronage and in ways meant to be damaging with a strong and directing supposition about the substance of Hardy's fiction. If he was a countryman, a peasant, a man with the look of the soil, then this is the point of view, the essential literary standpoint, of the novels. That is to say the fiction is not only about Wessex peasants, it is by one of them, who of course had managed to get a little (though hardly enough) education. Some discriminations of tone and fact have then to be made.

First, we had better drop 'peasant' altogether. Where Hardy lived and worked, as in most other parts of England, there were virtually no peasants, although 'peasantry' as a generic word for country people was still used by writers. The actual country people were landowners, tenant farmers, dealers, craftsmen and labourers, and that social structure – the actual material, in a social sense, of the novels – is radically different, in its variety, its shading, and many of its basic human attitudes from the structure of a peasantry. Secondly, Hardy is none of these people. Outside his writing he was one of the many professional men who worked within this structure, often with uncertainty about where they really belonged in it. A slow gradation of classes is characteristic of capitalism anywhere, and of rural capitalism very clearly. Hardy's father was a builder who employed six or seven workmen. Hardy did not like to hear their house referred to as a cottage, because he was aware of this employing situation. The house is indeed quite small but there is a little window at the back through which the men were paid, and the cottages down the lane are certainly smaller. At the same time, on his walk to school, he would see the mansion of Kingston Maurward (now happily an agricultural college) on which his father did some of the estate work, and this showed a sudden difference of degree which made the other distinction comparatively small though still not unimportant. In becoming an architect and a friend of the family of a vicar (the kind of family, also, from which his wife came) Hardy moved to a different point in the social structure, with connections to the educated but not the owning class, and yet also with connections through his family to that shifting body of small employers, dealers, craftsmen and cottages who were themselves never wholly distinct, in family, from the labourers. Within his writing his position is similar. He is neither owner nor tenant, dealer nor labourer, but an observer and chronicler, often again with uncertainty about his actual relation. Moreover he was not writing for them, but about them, to a mainly metropolitan and unconnected literary public. The effect of these two points is to return attention to where it properly belongs, which is Hardy's attempt to describe and value a way of life with which he was closely yet uncertainly connected, and the literary methods which follow from the nature of this attempt. As so often when the current social stereotypes are removed the critical problem becomes clear in a new way . . .

It is the critical problem of so much of English fiction, since the actual yet incomplete and ambiguous social mobility of the nineteenth century. And it is a question of substance as much as of method. It is common to reduce Hardy's fiction to the impact of an urban alien on the 'timeless pattern' of English rural life. Yet though this is sometimes there the more common pattern is the relation between the changing nature of country living, determined as much by its own pressures as by pressures from 'outside', and one or more characters who have become in some degree separated from it yet who remain by some tie of family inescapably involved. It is here that the social values are dramatised in a very complex way and it is here that most of the problems of Hardy's actual writing seem to arise . . .

We have to get beyond the stereotypes of the autodidact and the countryman and see Hardy in his real identity: both the educated observer and the passionate participant, in a period of general and radical change.

Hardy's writing, or what in abstraction can be called his style, is obviously affected by the crisis . . . which I have been describing. His complex position as an author, writing about country living to people who almost inevitably saw the country as empty nature or as the working-place of their inferiors, was in any case critical in this matter of language. What have been seen as his strengths – the ballad form of narrative, the prolonged literary imitation of traditional forms of speech – seem to me mainly weaknesses. This sort of thing is what his readers were ready for: a 'tradition' rather than human beings. The devices could not in any case serve his major fiction where it was precisely disturbance rather than continuity which had to be communicated. It would be easy to relate Hardy's problem of style to the two languages of Tess: the consciously educated and the unconsciously customary. But this comparison, though suggestive, is inadequate, for the truth is that to communicate Hardy's experience neither language would serve, since neither in the end was sufficiently articulate: the educated dumb in intensity and limited in humanity; the customary thwarted by ignorance and complacent in habit. The marks of a surrender to each mode are certainly present in Hardy but the main body of his mature writing is a more difficult and complicated experiment . . .

Hardy's mature style is threatened in one direction by a willed 'Latinism' of diction or construction, of which very many particular instances can be collected (and we have all done it, having taken our education hard), but in the other direction by this much less noticed element of artifice which is too easily accepted, within the patronage we have discussed, as the countryman speaking (sometimes indeed it is literally the countryman speaking, in a contrived picturesqueness which is now the novelist's patronage of his rural characters). The mature style itself is unambiguously an educated style, in which the extension of vocabulary and the complication of construction are necessary to the intensity and precision of the observation which is Hardy's essential position and attribute.

> The gray tones of daybreak are not the gray half-tones of the day's close, though the degree of their shade may be the same. In the twilight of the morning, light seems active, darkness passive; in the twilight of evening, it is the darkness which is active and crescent, and the light which is the drowsy reverse.

This is the educated observer, still deeply involved with the world he is watching, and the local quality of this writing is the decisive tone of the major fiction.

The complication is that this is a very difficult and exposed position for Hardy to maintain. Without the insights of consciously learned history and of the educated understanding of nature and behaviour he cannot really observe at all, at a level of extended human respect. Even the sense of what is now called the 'timeless' – in fact the sense of history, of the barrows, the Roman remains, the rise and fall of families, the tablets and monuments in the churches – is a function of education. That real perception of tradition is available only to the man who has read about it, though what he then sees through it is his native country, to which he is already deeply bound by memory and experience of another kind: a family and a childhood; an intense association of people and places, which has been his own history. To see tradition in both ways is indeed Hardy's special gift: the native place and experience but also the education, the conscious inquiry. Yet then to see living people, within this complicated sense of past and present, is another problem again. He sees as a participant who is also an observer; this is the source of the strain. For the process which allows him to observe is very clearly in Hardy's time one which includes, in its attachment to class feelings and class separations, a decisive alienation . . . This is what is sometimes called Hardy's bitterness, but in fact it is only sober and just observation. What Hardy sees and feels about the educated world of his day, locked in its deep social prejudices and in its consequent human alienation, is so clearly true that the only surprise is why critics now should still feel sufficiently identified with that world – the world which coarsely and coldly dismissed Jude and millions of other men – to be willing to perform the literary equivalent of that stalest of political tactics: the transfer of bitterness, of a merely class way of thinking, from those who exclude to those who protest. We did not after all have to wait for Lawrence to be shown the human nullity of that apparently articulate world. Hardy shows it convincingly again and again. But the isolation which then follows, while the observer holds to educated procedures but is unable to feel with the existing educated class, is severe. It is not the countryman awkward in his town clothes but the more significant tension – of course with its awkwardness and its spurts of bitterness and nostalgia – of the man caught by his personal history in the general structure and crisis of the relations between education and class, relations which in practice are between intelligence and fellow-feeling. Hardy could not take the James way out, telling his story in a 'spirit of intellectual superiority' to the 'elementary passions' . . . It is in this sense finally that we must consider Hardy's fundamental attitudes to the country world he was writing about. The tension is not between rural and urban, in the ordinary senses, nor between an abstracted intuition and an abstracted intelligence. The tension, rather, is in his own position, his own lived history, within a general process of change which could come clear and alive in him because it was not only general but in every detail of his feeling observation and writing immediate and particular.

Every attempt has of course been made to reduce the social crisis in which Hardy lived to the more negotiable and detachable forms of the disturbance of a 'timeless order'. But there was nothing timeless about nineteenth-century rural England. It was changing constantly in Hardy's lifetime and before it. It is not only that the next village to Puddletown is Tolpuddle, where you can look from the Martyrs' Tree back to what we know through Hardy as Egdon Heath. It is also that in the 1860s and 1870s, when Hardy was starting to write, it was what he himself described as

> a modern Wessex of railways, the penny post, mowing and reaping machines, union workhouses, lucifer matches, labourers who could read and write, and National school children.

Virtually every feature of this modernity preceded Hardy's own life (the railway came to Dorchester when he was a child of seven). The effects of the changes of course continued. The country was not timeless but it was not static either; indeed, it is because the change was long (and Hardy knew it was long) that the crisis took its particular forms.

We then miss most of what Hardy has to show us if we impose on the actual relationships he describes a pastoral convention of the countryman as an age-old figure, or a vision of a prospering countryside being disintegrated by Corn Law repeal or the railways or agricultural machinery. It is not only that Corn Law repeal and the cheap imports of grain made less difference to Dorset: a country mainly of grazing and mixed farming in which the coming of the railway gave a direct commercial advantage in the supply of milk to London: the economic process described with Hardy's characteristic accuracy in *Tess*:

> They reached the feeble light, which came from the smoky lamp of a little railway station; a poor enough terrestrial star, yet in one sense of more importance to Talbothays Dairy and mankind than the celestial ones to which it stood in such humiliating contrast. The cans of new milk were unladen in the rain, Tess getting a little shelter from a neighbouring holly tree . . .
>
> . . . 'Londoners will drink it at their breakfasts tomorrow, won't they?', she asked. 'Strange people that we have never seen? . . . who don't know anything of us, and where it comes from; or think how we two drove miles across the moor tonight in the rain that it might reach 'em in time?'

It is also that the social forces within his fiction are deeply based in the rural economy itself: in a system of rent and trade; in the hazards of ownership and tenancy; in the differing conditions of labour on good and bad land and in socially different villages (as in the contrast between Talbothays and Flintcomb Ash); in what happens to people and to families in the interaction between general forces and personal histories – that complex area of ruin or survival, exposure or continuity. This is his actual society, and we cannot suppress it in favour of an external view of a seamless abstracted country 'way of life'.

It is true that there are continuities beyond a dominant social situation in the lives of a particular community (though two or three generations, in a still partly oral culture, can often sustain an illusion of timelessness). It is also obvious that in most rural landscapes there are very old and often unaltered physical features, which sustain a quite different time-scale. Hardy gives great importance to these, and this is not really surprising when we consider his whole structure of feeling. But all these elements are overridden, as for a novelist they must be, by the immediate and actual relationships between people, which occur within existing contemporary pressures and are at most modulated and interpreted by the available continuities.

The pressures to which Hardy's characters are subjected are then pressures from within the system of living, not from outside it. It is not urbanism but the hazard of small-capital farming that changes Gabriel Oak from an independent farmer to a hired labourer and then a bailiff. Henchard is not destroyed by a new and alien kind of dealing but by a development of his own trade which he has himself invited. It is Henchard in Casterbridge who speculates in grain as he had speculated in people; who is in every sense, within an observed way of life, a dealer and a destructive one; his strength compromised by that. Grace Melbury is not a country girl 'lured' by the fashionable world but the daughter of a successful timber merchant whose own social expectations, at this point of his success, include a fashionable education for his daughter. Tess is not a peasant girl seduced by the squire; she is the daughter of a lifeholder and small dealer who is seduced by the son of a retired manufacturer. The latter buys his way into a country house and an old name. Tess's father and, under pressure, Tess herself, are damaged by a similar process, in which an old name and pride are one side of the coin and the exposure of those subject to them the other. That one family fell and one rose is the common and damaging history of what had been happening, for centuries, to ownership and to its consequences in those subject to it. The Lady Day migrations, the hiring fairs, the intellectually arrogant parson, the casual gentleman farmer, the landowner spending her substance elsewhere: all these are as much parts of the country 'way of life' as the dedicated craftsman, the group of labourers and the dances on the green. It is not only that Hardy sees the realities of labouring work, as in Marty South's hands on the spars and Tess in the swede field. It is also that he sees the harshness of economic processes, in inheritance, capital, rent and trade, within the continuity of the natural processes and persistently cutting across them. The social process created in this interaction is one of class and separation, as well as of chronic insecurity, as this capitalist farming and dealing takes its course. The profound disturbances that Hardy records cannot then be seen in the sentimental terms of a pastoral: the contrast between country and town. The exposed and separated individuals, whom Hardy puts at the centre of his fiction, are only the most developed cases of a general exposure and separation. Yet they are never merely illustrations of this change in a way of life. Each has a dominant personal history, which in psychological terms bears a direct relation to the social character of the change.

One of the most immediate effects of mobility, within a structure itself changing, is the difficult nature of the marriage choice. This situation keeps recurring in terms which are at once personal and social: Bathsheba choosing between Boldwood and Oak; Grace between Giles and Fitzpiers; Jude between Arabella and Sue. The specific class element, and the effects upon this of an insecure economy, are parts of the personal choice which is after all a choice primarily of a way to live, of an identity *in* the identification with this or that other person. And here significantly the false marriage (with which Hardy is so regularly and deeply concerned) can take place either way: to the educated coldness of Fitzpiers or the coarseness of Arabella. Here most dramatically the condition of the internal migrant is profoundly known. The social alienation enters the personality and destroys its capacity for any loving fulfilment. The marriage of Oak and Bathsheba is a case of eventual stability, after so much disturbance, but even that has an air of inevitable resignation and lateness. It is true that Hardy sometimes, under pressure, came to generalise and project these very specific failures into a fatalism for which in the decadent thought of his time the phrases were all too ready. In the same way, seeing the closeness of man and the land being broken by the problems of working the land, he sometimes projected his insistence on closeness and continuity into the finally negative images of an empty nature and the tribal past of Stonehenge and the barrows, where the single observer, at least, could feel a direct flow of knowledge. Even these, however, in their deliberate hardness – the uncultivable heath, the bare stone relics – confirm the human negatives, in what looks like a deliberate reversal of pastoral. In them the general alienation has its characteristic monuments, though very distant in time and space from the controlling immediate disturbance.

But the most significant thing about Hardy, in and through these difficulties, is that more than any other major novelist since this difficult mobility began he succeeded, against every pressure, in centring his major novels in the ordinary process of life and work. For all his position as an educated observer, he still took his actions from where the majority of his fellow-countrymen were living. Work enters his novels more decisively than in any English novelist of comparable importance. And it is not merely illustrative; it is seen as it is, as a central kind of learning. Feeling very acutely the long crisis of separation, and in the end coming to more tragically isolated catastrophes than any others within this tradition, he yet created continually the strength and the warmth of people living together: in work and in love; in the physical reality of a place.

> To stand working slowly in a field, and feel the creep of rain-water, first in legs and shoulders, then on hips and head, then at back, front, and sides, and yet to work on till the leaden light diminishes and marks that the sun is down, demands a distinct modicum of stoicism, even of

> valour. Yet they did not feel the wetness so much as might be supposed. They were both young, and they were talking of the time when they lived and loved together at Talbothays Dairy, that happy green tract of land where summer had been liberal in her gifts: in substance to all, emotionally to these.

The general structure of feeling in Hardy would be much less convincing if there were only the alienation, the frustration, the separation and isolation, the final catastrophes. What is defeated but not destroyed at the end of *The Woodlanders* or the end of *Tess* or the end of *Jude* is a warmth, a seriousness, an endurance in love and work that are the necessary definition of what Hardy knows and mourns as loss. Vitally – and it is his difference from Lawrence, as we shall see; a difference of generation and of history but also of character – Hardy does not celebrate isolation and separation. He mourns them, and yet always with the courage to look them steadily in the face. The losses are real and heartbreaking because the desires were real, the shared work was real, the unsatisfied impulses were real. Work and desire are very deeply connected in his whole imagination. That the critical emotional decisions by Tess are taken while she is working – as in the ache and dust of the threshing-machine where she sees Alec again – is no accident of plot; it is how this kind of living connects. The passion of Marty or of Tess or of Jude is a positive force coming out of a working and relating world; seeking in different ways its living fulfilment. That all are frustrated is the essential action: frustrated by very complicated processes of division, separation and rejection. People choose wrongly but under terrible pressures: under the confusions of class, under its misunderstandings, under the calculated rejections of a divided separating world.

It is important enough that Hardy keeps to an ordinary world, as the basis of his major fiction. The pressures to move away from it, to enter a more negotiable because less struggling and less divided life, were of course very strong. And it is even more important, as an act of pure affirmation, that he stays, centrally, with his central figures; indeed moves closer to them in his actual development, so that the affirmation of Tess and of Jude – an affirmation in and through the defeats he traces and mourns – is the strongest in all his work.

Beginning with a work in which he declared his hand – *The Poor Man and the Lady, by the Poor Man*; finding that rejected as mischievous, and getting advice, from Meredith, to retreat into conventional plots; letting the impulse run underground where it was continually disturbing but also always active; gaining a growing certainty which was a strengthening as well as a darkening of vision: Hardy ran his course to an exceptional fidelity.

'Slighted and enduring': not the story of man as he was, distant, limited, picturesque; but slighted in a struggle to grow – to love, to work with meaning, to learn and to teach; enduring in the community of this impulse, which pushes through and beyond particular separations and defeats. It is not only the continuity of a country but of a history that makes me now affirm, with his own certainty and irony: Hardy is our flesh and our grass.

6

ÉMILE ZOLA, *GERMINAL*

Georg Lukács (1885–1971) was one of the leading Marxist intellectuals of his time, a member of the Hungarian Communist Party from 1918 onwards, and a formidable critic of European philosophy, art and culture. A staunch defender of social realism, Lukács was wary of artistic developments, including modernism, that veered too far from the critical insights that realism afforded. In the first of two pieces printed here, 'Narrate or Describe?', he contemplates the difference between narration and description (in essence, the difference between an older realist method and the new method of naturalism). Zola's meticulous observation is contrasted with the more commodious and experiential narrative of writers like Balzac and Tolstoy. What Zola is seen to omit in his scientific exactitude is the element of chance or fortuitousness on which so much action can turn in life and in fiction, and therefore the basic ingredient of drama. Characteristic of Lukács's criticism, however, is his determination to see both methods or styles as products of their own social and historical circumstances. Zola, like Flaubert, is seen to be constrained by the forces of bourgeois retrenchment after the revolutionary impulse of 1848 had been lost: 'For them, the only solution to the tragic contradiction in their situation was to stand aloof as observers and critics of capitalist society'.

In 'The Zola Centenary', Lukács elaborates and refines the arguments of his earlier essay, but also develops them into a much more incisive and acerbic critique of naturalism. Again, he sees the events of 1848 standing between Balzac and Zola: the social evolution of the bourgeoisie has changed the way of life of writers: 'The writer no longer participates in the great struggles of his time, but is reduced to a mere spectator and chronicler of public life'. Zola's method, he claims, prevents any profoundly realistic representation of life. The 'scientific' technique of naturalism always seeks the average, blunting distinctions between the noble and the base, the beautiful and the ugly, and this 'grey statistical mean', as Lukács sees it, 'spells the doom of great literature'.

Irving Howe, in 'The Genius of *Germinal*', takes issue with Lukács's suggestion that Zola's writing is mechanistic and passive, lacking revolutionary dynamism. He makes a careful distinction between Zola's theories of the experimental novel and the actual practice of his writing, and he claims that what is vital in naturalist novels is the patience with which they record the suffering of their time. Howe acknowledges the extent to which *Germinal* embodies insights about class struggle that are fundamentally Marxist, but he tempers this realisation with his own cautious American liberalism. What gives the novel its stature, he insists, is its universal, mythic quality: '*Germinal* releases one of the central myths of the modern era: the story of how the dumb acquire speech'. Similarly, the scene in which Etienne and Catherine are trapped in the mine is seen as a version of the classical story of Orpheus and Eurydice. Howe goes so far as to claim that, more than any other European novelist before him, Zola shows the emergence of a new historical force in the working class, but he argues that 'its outcome remains uncertain, shadowy, ambiguous'.

Henri Mitterand's essay, 'Ideology and Myth: *Germinal* and the Fantasies of Revolt', marks a decisive shift in literary analysis, away from an assessment and appreciation of the novel's 'accurate' depiction of events towards an understanding of the structural principles and systems of signification through which meanings are generated. Mitterand shows that, despite the theoretical claims of naturalism, *Germinal* makes extensive use of mythical elements: the mine, for instance, has an extensive connotative range that includes ideas of being buried alive, eaten to death, lost in a labyrinth or transformed into a beast. In this respect, Mitterand would seem to be on common ground with Howe. His method, however, is to seek out the deep structure of Zola's novel, and he does so in the peculiarly diagrammatic way characteristic of the French structuralist methodology popularised by Roland Barthes in the 1970s and 1980s. He offers us a series of binary oppositions which are seen to underpin the novel: surface/pit, bourgeoisie/proletariat, light/night, and so on. Mitterand is not oblivious to the politics of the novel. He finds in *Germinal* 'a mythified version of social history' in which the miners are depicted as a primitive society, but he also acknowledges the extent to which the novel exposes the shameful conditions of northern Industrial France at the end of the nineteenth century. In this respect Mitterand shows how a Marxist structuralist analysis of culture might be applied to specific literary works.

Georg Lukács, Narrate or Describe? (1936)

. . . Compare the description of the theatre in [Zola's *Nana*] with that in Balzac's *Lost Illusions*. Superficially there is much similarity. The opening night, with which Zola's novel begins, decides Nana's career. The première in Balzac signifies a turning point in Lucien de Rubempré's life, his transition from unrecognized poet to successful but unscrupulous journalist.

In this chapter Zola, with characteristic and deliberate thoroughness, describes the theatre only from the point of view of the audience. Whatever happens in the auditorium, in the foyer or in the loges, as well as the appearance of the stage as seen from the hall, is described with impressive artistry. But Zola's obsession with monographic detail is not satisfied. He devotes another chapter to the description of the theatre as seen from the stage. With no less descriptive power he depicts the scene changes, the dressing-rooms, etc., both during the performance and the intermissions. And to complete this picture, he describes in yet a third chapter a rehearsal, again with equal conscientiousness and virtuosity.

This meticulous detail is lacking in Balzac. For him the theatre and the performance serve as the setting for an inner drama of his characters: Lucien's success, Coralie's theatrical career, the passionate love between Lucien and Coralie, Lucien's subsequent conflict with his former friends in the D'Arthèz circle and his current protector Lousteau, and the beginning of his campaign of revenge against Mme de Bargeton, etc.

But what is represented in these battles and conflicts – all directly or indirectly related to the theatre? The state of the theatre under capitalism: the absolute dependence of the theatre upon capital and upon the press (itself dependent upon capital); the relationship of the theatre to literature and of journalism to literature; the capitalistic basis for the connection between the life of an actress and open and covert prostitution.

These social problems are posed by Zola, too. But they are simply described as social facts, as results, as *caput mortuum* of a social process. Zola's theatre director continually repeats: 'Don't say theatre, say bordello.' Balzac, however, depicts *how* the theatre *becomes* prostituted under capitalism. The drama of his protagonists is simultaneously the drama of the institution in which they work, of the things with which they live, of the setting in which they fight their battles, of the objects through which they express themselves and through which their interrelationships are determined.

This is admittedly an extreme case. The objective factors in a man's environment are not always and inevitably so intimately linked to his fate. They can provide instruments for his activity and for his career and even, as in Balzac, turning points in his fortunes. But they may also simply provide the setting for his activity and for his career.

Does the contrast in approach we have just noted arise where there is a simple literary representation of a setting?

In the introductory chapter to his novel *Old Mortality*, Walter Scott depicts a marksmanship contest during some national holiday in Scotland after the Restoration, organized as part of a campaign to revive feudal institutions, as a review of the military power of the Stuart supporters and as a provocation for unmasking disaffection. The parade takes place on the eve of the revolt of the oppressed Puritans. With extraordinary epic artistry Walter Scott assembles on the parade ground all the opposing elements about to explode in bloody conflict. In a series of grotesque scenes during the military review, he exposes the hopeless anachronism of the feudal institutions and the stubborn resistance of the population to their revival. In the subsequent contest he exposes the contradictions within each of the two hostile parties; only the moderates on both sides take part in the sport. In the inn we see the brutal outrages of the royal mercenaries and encounter Burley, later to become the leader of the Puritan uprising, in all his gloomy magnificence. In effect, in narrating the events of this military review and describing the entire setting, Walter Scott introduces the factions and protagonists of a great historical drama. In a single stroke he sets us in the midst of a decisive action.

The description of the agricultural fair and of the awarding of prizes to the farmers in Flaubert's *Madame Bovary* is among the most celebrated achievements of description in modern realism. But Flaubert presents only a 'setting'. For him the fair is merely background for the decisive love scene between Rudolf and Emma Bovary. The setting is incidental, merely 'setting'. Flaubert underscores its incidental character; by interweaving and counterposing official speeches with fragments of love dialogue, he offers an ironic juxtaposition of the public and private banality of the petty bourgeoisie, accomplishing this parallel with consistency and artistry.

But there remains an unresolved contradiction: this incidental setting, this accidental occasion for a love scene, is simultaneously an important event in the world of the novel; the minute description of this setting is absolutely essential to Flaubert's purpose, that is, to the comprehensive exposition of the social milieu. The ironic juxtaposition does not exhaust the significance of the description. The 'setting' has an independent existence as an element in the representation of the environment. The characters, however, are nothing but observers of this setting. To the reader they seem undifferentiated, additional elements of the environment Flaubert is describing. They become dabs of colour in a painting which rises above a lifeless level only insofar as it is elevated to an ironic symbol of philistinism. The painting assumes an importance which does not arise out of the subjective importance of the events, to which it is scarcely related, but from the artifice in the formal stylization.

Flaubert achieves his symbolic content through irony and consequently on a considerable level of artistry and to some extent with genuine artistic means. But when, as in the case of Zola, the symbol is supposed to embody social monumentality and is supposed to imbue episodes otherwise meaningless, with great social significance, true art is abandoned. The metaphor is over-inflated in the attempt to encompass reality. An arbitrary detail, a chance similarity, a fortuitous attitude, an accidental meeting – all are supposed to provide direct expression of important social relationships. There are innumerable possible examples in Zola's work, like the comparison of Nana with the golden fleece, which is supposed to symbolize her disastrous effect on the Paris of before 1870. Zola himself confessed to such intentions, declaring: 'In my work there is a hypertrophy of real detail. From the springboard of exact observation it leaps to the stars. With a single beat of the wings, the truth is exalted to the symbol.'

In Scott, Balzac or Tolstoy we experience events which are inherently significant because of the direct development of the characters in the events and because of the general social significance emerging in the unfolding of the characters' lives. We are the audience to events in which the characters take active part. We ourselves experience these events.

In Flaubert and Zola the characters are merely spectators, more or less interested in the events. As a result, the events themselves become only a tableau for the reader, or, at best, a series of tableaux. We are merely observers.

II

The opposition between experiencing and observing is not accidental. It arises out of divergent basic positions about life and about the major problems of society and not just out of divergent artistic methods of handling content or one specific aspect of content.

Only after making this assertion can we attempt a concrete investigation of our problem. As in other areas of life, in literature there are no 'pure' phenomena. Engels once noted ironically that 'pure' feudalism had existed only in the constitution of the ephemeral Kingdom of Jerusalem. Yet feudalism obviously was an historical reality and as such is a valid subject for scientific investigation. There are no writers who renounce description absolutely. Nor, on the other hand, can one claim that the outstanding representatives of realism after 1848, Flaubert and Zola, renounced narration absolutely. What is important here are philosophies of composition, not any illusory 'pure' phenomenon of narration or description. What is important is knowing how and why description, originally one of the many modes of epic art (undoubtedly a subordinate mode), became the principal mode. In this development the character and function of description underwent a fundamental transformation from what it had been in the epic.

In his critique of Stendhal's *Charterhouse of Parma*, Balzac had emphasized the importance of description as a mode of modern fiction. In the novel of the eighteenth century (Le Sage, Voltaire, etc.) there had scarcely been any description, or at most it had played a minimal, scarcely even a subordinate, role. Only with romanticism did the situation change. Balzac pointed out that the literary direction he followed, of which he considered Walter Scott the founder, assigned great importance to description.

But after emphasizing the contrast with the 'aridity' of the seventeenth and eighteenth centuries and associating himself with the modern method, he adduced a whole series of stylistic criteria for defining the new literary direction. According to Balzac, description was only one stylistic mode among several. He particularly emphasized the new significance of the dramatic element in fiction.

The new style developed out of the need to adapt fiction to provide an adequate representation of new social phenomena. The relationship of the individual to his class had become more complicated than it had been in the seventeenth and eighteenth centuries. Formerly a summary indication of the background, external appearance and personal habits of an individual (as in Le Sage) had sufficed for a clear and comprehensive social characterization. Individualization was accomplished almost exclusively through action, through the reactions of characters to events.

Balzac recognized that this method could no longer suffice. Rastignac is an adventurer of quite another sort to Gil Blas. The precise description of the filth, smells, meals and service in the Vauquier pension is essential to render Rastignac's particular kind of adventurism comprehensible and real. Similarly, Grandet's house and Gobseck's apartment must be described accurately and in precise detail in order to represent two contrasting usurers, differing as individuals and as social types.

But apart from the fact that the description of the environment is never 'pure' description but is almost always transformed into action (as when old Grandet repairs his decayed staircase himself), description for Balzac provides nothing more than a base for the new, decisive element in the composition of the novel: the dramatic element. Balzac's extraordinarily multifaceted, complicated characterizations could not possibly emerge with such impressive dramatic effectiveness if the environmental conditions in their lives were not depicted in such breadth. In Flaubert and Zola description has an entirely different function.

Balzac, Stendhal, Dickens and Tolstoy depict a bourgeois society consolidating itself after severe crises, the complicated laws of development operating in its formation, and the tortuous transitions from the old society in decay to the new society in birth . . .

Georg Lukács, The Zola Centenary (1946)

Émile Zola the novelist is the 'historian of private life' under the Second Empire in France in the same way as Balzac was the historian of private life under the restoration and the July monarchy. Zola himself never disclaimed this heritage. He always protested against the assumption that he had invented a new art form and always regarded himself as the heir and follower of Balzac and Stendhal, the two great realists of the beginning of the nineteenth century. Of the two, he regarded Stendhal as the connecting link with the literature of the eighteenth century. Of course so remarkable and original a writer as Zola could not regard his literary predecessors as mere models to copy: he admired Balzac and Stendhal but vigorously criticized them none the less; he tried to eliminate what he considered dead and antiquated in them and to work out the principles of a creative method which could have a fertilizing influence on the further evolution of realism. (It should be said here that Zola never speaks of realism, but always of naturalism.)

But the further development of realism in Zola's hands took a far more intricate course than Zola himself imagined. Between Balzac and Zola lies the year 1848 and the bloody days of June, the first independent action of the working class, which left so indelible an impression on the ideology of the French *bourgeoisie*, that after it *bourgeois* ideology ceased to play a progressive part in France for a long time. Ideology grew adaptable and developed into more apologetics on behalf of the *bourgeoisie*.

Zola himself, however, never stooped to be an apologist of the *bourgeois* social order. On the contrary, he fought a courageous battle against the reactionary evolution of French capitalism, first in the literary sphere and later openly in the political. In the course of his life he gradually came ever closer to socialism, although he never got beyond a paler version of Fourier's Utopianism, a version lacking, however, Fourier's brilliantly dialectical social criticism. But the ideology of his own class was too deeply ingrained in his thinking, his principles and his creative method, although the conscious sharpness of his criticism of society was never dulled; on the contrary, it was much more vigorous and progressive than that of the Catholic Royalist Balzac.

Balzac and Stendhal, who had described the ghastly transformation of bourgeois France from the heroic period of the revolution and Napoleon to the romantically hypocritical corruption of the restoration and the no longer even hypocritical philistine filth of the July monarchy, had lived in a society in which the antagonism of bourgeoisie and working-class was not as yet the plainly visible hub around which social evolution moved forward. Hence Balzac and Stendhal could dig down to the very roots of the sharpest contradictions inherent in bourgeois society while the writers who lived after 1848 could not do so: such merciless candour, such sharp criticism would have necessarily driven them to break the link with their own class.

Even the sincerely progressive Zola was incapable of such a rupture.

It is this attitude which is reflected in his methodological conception, in his rejection, as romantic and 'unscientific,' of Balzac's bred-in-the-bone dialectic and prophetic fervour in the exposure of the contradictions of capitalism, for which he, Zola, substitutes a 'scientific' method in which society is conceived as a harmonious entity and the criticism applied to society formulated as a struggle against the diseases attacking its organic unity, a struggle against the 'undesirable features' of capitalism.

Zola says: 'The social cycle is identical with the life-cycle: in society as in the human body, there is a solidarity linking the various organs with each other in such a way that if one organ putrefies, the rot spreads to the other organs and results in a very complicated disease.'

This 'scientific' conception led Zola to identify mechanically the human body and human society, and he is quite consistent when he criticizes Balzac's great preface to *The Human Comedy* from this angle. In this preface Balzac, as a true dialectician, raises the same question: he asks to what extent the dialectic of race evolution as developed by Geoffroy de Saint Hilaire applies to human society; but at the same time he sharply stresses the new categories created by the specific dialectic of society. Zola thinks that such a conception destroys the 'scientific unity' of the method and that the conception itself is due to the 'romantic confusion' of Balzac's mind. What he then puts in the place of Balzac's ideas, as a 'scientific' result, is the undialectic conception of the organic unity of nature and society; the elimination of antagonisms is regarded as the motive power of social movement and the principle of 'harmony' as the essence of social being. Thus Zola's subjectively most sincere and courageous criticism of society is locked into the magic circle of progressive *bourgeois* narrow-mindedness. On this basis of principle, Zola carries on the tradition established by the creative methods of Balzac and Stendhal with great consistency. It is not by accident nor a result of some personal bias in favour of his older friend and comrade-in-arms Flaubert that Zola found in the latter the true realization of all that in Balzac was merely a beginning or an intent.

Zola wrote about *Madame Bovary*: 'It seems that the formula of the modern novel, scattered all over Balzac's colossal *oeuvre*, is here clearly worked out in a book of 400 pages. And with it the code of the modern novel has now been written.'

Zola stresses as the elements of Flaubert's greatness: above all the elimination of romantic traits. 'The composition of the novel lies only in the way in which incidents are chosen and made to follow each other in a certain harmonic order of evolution. The incidents themselves are absolutely average . . . All out-of-the-ordinary inventions have been excluded . . . The story is unfolded by relating all that happens from day to day without ever springing any surprises.' According to Zola, Balzac, too, had in his greatest works sometimes achieved this realistic presentation of everyday life. 'But before he could reach the point of concerning himself only with accurate description, he revelled for a long time in inventions and lost himself in the search for false thrills and false magnificence.'

He continues: 'The novelist, if he accepts the basic principle of showing the ordinary course of average lives, must kill the "hero." By "hero" I mean inordinately magnified characters, puppets inflated into giants. Inflated "heroes" of this sort drag down Balzac's novels, because he always believes that he has not made them gigantic enough.' In the naturalist method 'this exaggeration by the artist and this whimsicality of composition are done away with' and 'all heads are brought down to the same level, for the opportunities permitting us to depict a truly superior human being are very rare.'

Here we already see quite clearly the principles on the basis of which Zola criticizes the heritage left by the great realists. Zola repeatedly discusses the great realists, particularly Balzac and Stendhal, and constantly reiterates the same basic idea that Balzac and Stendhal were great because, in many details and episodes of their works, they described human passions faithfully and contributed very interesting documents to our knowledge of human passions. But according to Zola both of them, and particularly Stendhal, suffered from a mistaken romanticism . . .

According to Zola, Balzac's greatness and his claim to immortality lay in the fact that he was one of the first who 'possessed a sense of reality.' But Zola arrived at this 'sense of reality' by first cutting out of Balzac's life-work the great contradictions of capitalist society and accepting only the presentation of everyday life which was for Balzac merely a means of throwing the contradictions into bolder relief and giving a total picture of society in motion, complete with all its determinants and antagonisms.

It is most characteristic that Zola (and with him Hippolyte Taine) should speak with the greatest admiration of General Hulot, a character in the novel *La Cousine Bette*. But both of them see in him only a masterly portrait of an oversexed man. Neither Zola nor Taine says a word about the artistry with which Balzac traces Hulot's passions to the conditions of life in the Napoleonic era: and yet it would not have been difficult to notice this for Balzac uses Grével, a character also painted with no less consummate mastery, as a counterfoil to show up the difference between the eroticism of the Napoleonic era and that of the reign of Louis Philippe. Neither Zola nor Taine mentions the doubtful operations with which Hulot tries to make money, although in describing them, Balzac gives an admirable picture of the infamies and horrors of incipient French colonial policy.

In other words both Zola and Taine insulate Hulot's erotic passion from its social basis and thus turn a socially pathological figure into a psychopathological one. It is natural that looking at it from this angle he could see only 'exaggeration' (i.e. romanticism) in the great, socially typical characters created by Balzac and Stendhal.

'Life is simpler than that,' Zola says at the end of one of his criticisms of

Stendhal. He thus completes the transition from the old realism to the new, *from realism proper to naturalism*. The decisive social basis of this change is to be found in the fact that the social evolution of the *bourgeoisie* has changed the way of life of writers. The writer no longer participates in the great struggles of his time, but is reduced to a mere spectator and chronicler of public life. Zola understood clearly enough that Balzac himself had to go bankrupt in order to be able to depict Cesar Birotteau; that he had to know from his own experience the whole underworld of Paris in order to create such characters as Rastignac and old Goriot.

In contrast, Zola and to an even greater extent Flaubert, the true founder of the new realism, – were solitary observers and critical commentators of the social life of their own day. (The courageous public fight put up by Zola in connection with the Dreyfus affair came too late and was too much a mere episode in Zola's life to effect any radical change in his creative method.) Zola's naturalist 'experimental' novels were therefore merely attempts to find a method by which the writer, now reduced to a mere spectator, could again realistically master reality. Naturally Zola never became conscious of this social degradation of the writer: his theory and practice grew out of this social existence without his ever becoming aware of it. On the contrary, inasmuch as he had some inkling of the change in the writer's position in capitalist society, he, as the liberal positivist that he was, regarded it as an advantage, as a step forward, and therefore praised Flaubert's impartiality (which in reality did not exist) as a new trait in the writer's make-up. Lafargue who, in accordance with the traditions of Marx and Engels, severely criticized Zola's creative method and contrasted it with that of Balzac, saw very clearly that Zola was isolated from the social life of his time. Lafargue described Zola's attitude to reality as similar to that of a newspaper reporter and this is perfectly in accordance with Zola's own programmatic statements about the correct creative method in literature.

Of these statements we quote only one, in which he gives his opinion on the proper conception of a good novel: 'A naturalist writer wants to write a novel about the stage. Starting from this point without characters or data, his first concern will be to collect material, to find out what he can about this world he wishes to describe. He may have known a few actors and seen a few performances. Then he will talk to the people best informed on the subject, will collect statements, anecdotes, portraits. But this is not all. He will also read the written documents available. *Finally* he will visit the locations, *spend a few days* in a theatre in order to acquaint himself with the smallest details, pass an evening in an actress' dressing-room and absorb the atmosphere as much as possible. When all this material has been gathered, the novel will take shape of its own accord. All the novelist has to do is to group the facts in a logical sequence . . . *Interest will no longer be focussed on the* peculiarities of the story – on the contrary, the more general and commonplace the story is, the more typical it will be.'

Here we have the new realism, *recte* naturalism, in concentrated essence and in sharp opposition to the traditions of the old realism; a mechanical average takes the place of the dialectic unity of type and individual: description and analysis is substituted for epic situations and epic plots. The tension of the old-type story, the co-operation and clashing of human beings who are both individuals and at the same time representatives of important class tendencies: all these are eliminated and their place is taken by 'average' characters whose individual traits are accidents from the artistic point of view (or in other words have no decisive influence on what happens in the story) and these 'average' characters act without a pattern, either merely side by side or else in completely chaotic fashion.

It was only because he could not always consistently adhere to his own programme that Zola could ever come to be a great writer . . .

Zola's method, which hampered not only Zola himself but his whole generation, because it was the result of the writer's position as solitary observer, prevents any profoundly realistic representation of life. Zola's scientific method always seeks the average, and this grey statistical mean, the point at which all internal contradictions are blunted, where the great and the petty, the noble and the base, the beautiful and the ugly are all mediocre 'products' together, spells the doom of great literature.

Zola was a far too naive liberal all his life, far too ardent a believer in *bourgeois* progress, ever to harbour any doubts regarding his own very questionable, positivist 'scientific' method.

Nevertheless the artistic implementation of his method was not achieved without a struggle. Zola the writer was far too conscious of the greatness of modern life (even though the greatness was inhuman) for him to resign himself without a struggle to the grey tedium which would have been the result of a method such as his, if consistently carried through. Zola hated and despised far too much the evil, base, reactionary forces which permeate capitalist society, for him to remain a cold, unsympathetic 'experimenter' such as the positivist-naturalist doctrine required him to be.

As we have seen, the struggle resulting from this was fought out within the framework of Zola's own creative method. In Balzac it was reality and political bias that were at war with each other, in Zola it was the creative method and the 'material' presented. Hence in Zola there is no such universal break-through as the 'triumph of realism' in Balzac, there are only isolated moments, details, in which the author breaks the chains of his own positivist, 'scientific', naturalist dogmas in order to give free scope to his temperament in truly realist fashion.

We can find such a break-through in almost every one of Zola's novels and hence there are admirably life-like *single episodes* in every one of his major books. But they can not permeate the entire work, for the doctrine still triumphs in the general lay-out of each of them. Thus the strange situation is created that Zola, although his life-work is very extensive, has never created a single character who grew to be a type, a by-word, almost a living being such as for instance the Bovary couple or Homais the apothecary in Flaubert, not to mention the immortal figures given us by such creators of men as Balzac or Dickens.

But there was an urge in Zola, to go beyond the grey average of naturalism in his composition. Thus it is that he created many extraordinarily effective pictures. No reader can fail to be deeply impressed by his admirable descriptions of pits and markets, the stock exchange, a racecourse, a battlefield or a theatre. Perhaps no one has painted more colourfully and suggestively the outer trappings of modern life.

But only the *outer* trappings.

They form a gigantic backdrop in front of which tiny, haphazard people move to and fro and live their haphazard lives. Zola could never achieve what the truly great realists Balzac, Tolstoy or Dickens accomplished: to present social institutions as human relationships and social objects as the vehicles of such relationships. Man and his surroundings are always sharply divided in all Zola's works.

Hence, as soon as he departs from the monotony of naturalism, he is immediately transmuted into a decorative picturesque romanticist, who treads in the footsteps of Victor Hugo with his bombastic monumentalism.

There is a strange element of tragedy here.

Zola, who as we have seen, criticized Balzac and Stendhal so vehemently for their alleged romanticism, was compelled to have recourse to a romanticism of the Victor Hugo stamp in order to escape, in part at least, from the counter-artistic consequences of his own naturalism.

Sometimes Zola himself seemed to realise this discrepancy. The romantic, rhetoric and picturesque artificiality of style produced by the triumph of French naturalism was at variance with Zola's sincere love of truth. As a decent man and honest writer he felt that he himself was much to blame for this. 'I am too much a son of my time. I am too deeply immersed in romanticism for me to dream of emancipating myself from certain rhetorical prejudices . . . Less artificiality and more solidity. I should like us to be less brilliant and to have more real content . . .'

But he could find no way out of this dilemma in the sphere of art. On the contrary, the more vigorously he participated in the struggle of opinions, the more rhetorical his style became.

For there are only two roads leading out of the monotonous, commonplace of naturalism, which results from the direct, mechanical mirroring of the humdrum reality of capitalism. Either the writer succeeds in revealing the human and social significance of the struggle for life and lifting it to a higher plane by artistic means (as Balzac did) or else he has to overstress the mere outward scenery of life, rhetorically and picturesquely, and quite independently of the human import of the events depicted (like Victor Hugo).

Such was the romantic dilemma which faced French naturalism. Zola (as before him Flaubert) took the second road because he was in sincere opposition to the ideology of the post-revolutionary *bourgeoisie*; because he hated and despised that glorification of false ideals and false 'great men' which was the fashion of his time and because he was quite determined to expose all this without mercy. But the most honest and sincere determination to fight for such things could not make up for the artistic falsity of the method and the inorganic nature of the presentation resulting from it . . .

Zola depicts with naturalist fidelity the biological and 'psychological' entity of the average human being and this preserves him from treating his characters as arbitrarily as Victor Hugo. But on the one hand this method sets his characterization very narrow limits and on the other hand the combination of two contradictory principles. i.e. of naturalism and romantically rhetorical monumentality again produce a Hugoan discrepancy between characters and environment which he cannot overcome.

Hence Zola's fate is one of the literary tragedies of the nineteenth century. Zola is one of those outstanding personalities whose talents and human qualities destined them for the greatest things, but who have been prevented by capitalism from accomplishing their destiny and finding themselves in a truly realistic art.

This tragic conflict is obvious in Zola's life-work, all the more as capitalism was unable to conquer Zola the man. He trod his path to the end, honourably, indomitably, uncompromisingly. In his youth he fought with courage for the new literature and art (he was a supporter of Manet and the impressionists) and in his riper years he again played the man in the battle against the conspiracy of the French clericals and the French general staff in the Dreyfus affair.

Zola's resolute struggle for the cause of progress will survive many of his one-time fashionable novels, and will place his name in history side by side with that of Voltaire, who defended Calas as Zola defended Dreyfus. Surrounded by the fake democracy and corruption of the Third Republic, by the false so-called democrats who let no day pass without betraying the traditions of the great French revolution. Zola stands head and shoulders above them as the model of the courageous and high-principled *bourgeois* who even if he failed to understand the essence of socialism did not abandon democracy even when behind it the Socialist demands of the working class were already being voiced.

We should remember this today when the Republic has become a mere cover for a conquest-hungry colonial imperialism and a brutal oppression of the metropolitan working class.

The mere memory of Zola's courageous and upright figure is an indictment of the so-called 'democracy' represented by the men who rule France today.

Irving Howe, The Genius of *Germinal* (1970)

Each literary generation fashions its own blinkers, and then insists that they allow unimpeded vision. My generation grew up with a mild scorn for the writers of naturalistic fiction who flourished in the late 19th and early 20th centuries. Some of them we took to be estimable and others talented: we did not mean to be unfair. Many naturalists had a strong feeling for social justice, and if irrelevant to their stature as writers, this seemed to their credit as men. Zola's great cry during the Dreyfus Affair could still rouse us to admiration. His great cry could stir even those of us who had reached the peak of sophistication where Flaubert was judged superior to Balzac, Stendhal to Flaubert, and all three, it need hardly be said, to Zola. For Zola was tendentious, Zola was rhetorical, Zola was coarse, Zola knew little about the new psychology. With such wisdom, we entered the world.

Everyone had of course read Zola earlier, in those years of adolescence when all that matters in our encounter with a novel is eagerly to soak up its experience. Then *Germinal* had stirred us to the bone. But later we learned that literary judgment must not be defiled by political ideas, and Zola, that damp and clumsy bear of a novelist, became an object of condescension.

It was wrong, hopelessly wrong – like those literary fashions of our own moment which two or three decades from now will also seem all wrong. Reading *Germinal* again, and reading it with that emotional readiness which middle age can sometimes grant, I have been overwhelmed by its magnitude of structure, its fertility of imagination, its re-enactment of a central experience in modern life.

Still, it should be admitted that if we have been unjust to Zola these last few decades, some of the blame must fall on his own shoulders. He talked too much, he pontificated too much about Literature and Science, he advertised himself too much. We are accustomed in America to bemoaning the redskin dumbness that overcomes so many of our writers when confronted with a need to theorise about their craft, and behind this complaint of ours there is often a naïve assumption that European writers have commonly possessed the range of culture we associate with, say, a Thomas Mann. It is not true, of course. What had Dickens or Balzac to say about the art of the novel? As for Zola, there can hardly have been a modern writer so repeatedly confused about the work he was doing.

Consider the mechanical scientism to which he clung with the credulousness of a peasant in a cathedral; the ill-conceived effort to show forces of heredity determining the lives of his characters (so that a reader of *Germinal* unaware of the other volumes in the Rougon-Macquart series could hardly understand why Etienne Lantier should suddenly, without preparation or consequence, be called 'a final degenerate offshoot of a wretched race'); the wilful absurdity of such declarations as 'the same determinism should regulate paving-stones and human brains'; the turgid mimicry with which Zola transposed the physiological theories of Dr. Claude Bernard into his *Le Roman expérimental* . . .

Yet we ought not to be too hasty in dismissing Zola's intellectual claims. If his physiological determinism now seems crude, his sense of the crushing weight which the world can lower upon men remains only too faithful to modern experience, perhaps to all experience. If his theories about the naturalistic novel now seem mainly of historical interest, this does not mean that the naturalistic novel itself can simply be brushed aside. What remains vital in the naturalistic novel as Zola wrote it in France and Dreiser in America is not the theoretic groupings towards an assured causality; what remains vital is the massed detail of the fictional worlds they establish, the patience – itself a form of artistic scruple – with which they record the suffering of their time.

In looking back upon the philosophical improvisations of those late 19th-century writers who were driven by conscience to surrender their Christian faith and then to improvise versions of rigid mechanism and spiritualised secularism, we like to suppose that their 'ideas,' once so earnestly studied by literary scholars, were little more than impediments they had to put aside, dead weight on the tissue of their work . . . There is of course something to be said for this view of the matter, but less than we commonly suppose. For the announced ideas behind a novel, even those thrust forward by the author as direct statement, ought not to be confused with the actual play of his intelligence. We may judge these announced ideas as tiresome or inert or a mere reflex of fashion; we may be irritated by their occasional appearance, like a mound of fossil, along the path of the narrative; yet in the novel itself the writer may be engaged in a play of intelligence far more supple than his formal claims lead us to suppose. A reductive determinism is what Zola flaunts, as when he places Taine's not very brilliant remark, 'vice and virtue are products like sugar and vitriol,' on the title page of *Thérèse Raquin*; but a reductive determinism is by no means what controls *Germinal* and *L'Assomoir*. When we say that a work of literature 'takes on a life of its own,' we mean in part that the process of composition has brought textural surprises, perhaps fundamental shifts in perspective, which could not have been foreseen by studying the author's original intention.

Even among ideas we regard as mistaken, sharp discriminations must be made when trying to judge their literary consequences. A writer infatuated with one or another kind of psychic charlatanism is hard to take seriously. A writer drawn to the brutalities of fascism rouses a hostility that no creed of aesthetic detachment can keep from spilling over into our feeling about his work. But when writers like Zola and Hardy and Dreiser were attracted to the thought of Darwin and Huxley, or to popular versions of their thought, they were struggling with serious and urgent problems . . .

Zola went still further than those writers who transferred the dynamic of faith into a fixity of law. Like Balzac before him, he yielded to the brilliant impiety of transforming himself into a kind of god, a god of tireless fecundity creating his universe over and over again. The 19th-century novelist – Dickens or Balzac, Hardy or Zola – enacts in his own career the vitalism about which the thought of his age drives him to a growing scepticism.

Zola's three or four great novels are anything but inert or foredoomed. He may start with notions of inevitability, but the current of his narrative boils with energy and novelty. *Germinal* ends with the gloom of defeat, but not a gloom predestined. There is simply too much appetite for experience in Zola, too much sympathy and solidarity with the struggles by which men try to declare themselves, too much hope for the generations always on the horizon and always promising to undo the wrongs of the past, for *Germinal* to become a mere reflex of a system of causality. Somehow – we have every reason to believe – Zola's groupings into the philosophy of determinism freed him to become a writer of energy, rebellion, and creation.

Germinal releases one of the central myths of the modern era: the story of how the dumb acquire speech. All those at the bottom of history, for centuries objects of manipulation and control, begin to transform themselves into active subjects, determined to create their own history.

Now we cannot say that this myth has gained universal acceptance in our culture, nor that those of us who register its moral claims can do so with the unquestioning credence and mounting awe we suppose characteristic of men in ancient cultures. Still, we might remember that in so far as we know Greek myth through Greek drama, we know it mediated by individual artists, and with the passage of time, mediated in directions increasingly sceptical. The myth in *Germinal* – if we agree, however hesitantly, to call it a myth – is one that may have some parallels in earlier cultures, but it takes its formative energies from the French Revolution. It is the myth of the People and more particularly, of the Proletariat. They who had merely suffered and at times erupted into blind rebellion; they who had been prey to but not part of society; they who had found no voice in the cultures of the past – they now emerge from the sleep of history and begin the task of a collective self-formation. This, of course, is a schematised version of historical reality, or at least a perspective on historical reality – which may indeed be the distinctiveness of whatever modern myths we have. Where traditional myth appears to us as trans-historical, a frieze of symbolic representation, our own take their very substance from the materials of history, magnifying and rendering heroic the actions of men in time. Some idea of this kind may have led Thomas Mann to write that 'in Zola's epic,' made up as it is of events taken from everyday life, 'the characters themselves are raised up to a plane above that of everyday life.'

The myth of *Germinal* as I have been sketching it is close to the Marxist view of the dynamics of capitalism, but to yield ourselves to Zola's story is not necessarily to accept the Marxist system. Zola himself does not accept it. At crucial points he remains a sceptic, as we may imagine Euripides to have been, about the myth that forms the soul of his action. His scepticism concerns not so much the recuperative powers of the miners, for it is his instinctive way of looking at things that he should see the generations crowding one another, pushing for life space, thrusting their clamour on to the world. His scepticism runs deeper. Zola sees the possibility that in the very emergence of solidarity – that great and terrible word for which so many have gone smiling to their death! – there would be formed, by a ghastly dialectic of history, new rulers and oppressors: the Rasseneurs, the Plucharts, and even the Lantiers of tomorrow, raised to the status of leaders and bureaucrats, who would impose their will on the proletariat. Zola does not insist that this must happen for he is a novelist, not a political theoretician. What he does is to show in the experience of the Montsou workers the germ of such a possibility. As it celebrates the greatest event of modern history, the myth of emergence contains within itself the negation of that greatness.

At the centre of the novel is the mine. Dramatic embodiment of exploitation, the mine nevertheless makes possible the discipline through which to overcome exploitation. But for the moment, man's nature still bows to his history, personal need to the workings of the market. The mine has a 'natural' awesomeness, with its crevices and alleys, depths and darkness: its symbolic power arises organically, spontaneously, and not as a willed imposition of the writer. And then, in a stroke that does bear the mark of will, Zola creates an astonishing parallel to the miners. The mine-horses share the misery of the men, but without the potential for motivated rebellion; the mine-horses represent, as a gruesome foreshadowing and with an expressionist grossness that defeats critical scruples, what the men may yet accept or sink to.

The mine is voracious and unappeasable, a physical emblem of the impersonality of commodity production. It 'seemed evil-looking, a hungry beast crouched and ready to devour the world.' It 'kept devouring men . . . always ravenous, its giant bowels capable of digesting an entire nation.' But this suggestion of a force bursting out of the control of its creators gains its strength not merely from the intrinsic properties of the mine. Here Zola does come close to the Marxist notion that men must beware of fetishising their predicaments, they must recognise that not in mines or factories lie the sources of their misery but in the historically determined relations between contending classes. And here surely historical associations come into play which even the least literate reader is likely to have with mining – a major industry of early industrialism, notorious for its high rate of exhaustion and accident. As always in *Germinal*, the mythic and symbolic are of the very substance of the historical. And thereby Zola can fill out his myth with the evidence of circumstantiality. The more he piles up descriptions of the mine's tunnels, shafts, timbering, airlessness and dampness, the more are we prepared to see it as the setting for the apocalypse with which the book reaches its climax . . .

Zola controls his narrative with one overriding end in mind, and that is to show not the way men are swallowed by their work (surely not new) nor how a hero can emerge healed from the depths (also not new) but the gradual formation of a collective consciousness. When Maheu, that superbly drawn worker, begins to speak to the manager, 'the words were coming of themselves, and at moments he listened to himself in surprise, as though some stranger within him were speaking.' The stranger is his long-buried self, and this transfiguration of Maheu is at least as morally significant as that of the individual protagonist gaining access to self-knowledge in the earlier 19th-century novel.

Etienne reads, Maheu speaks, La Maheude cries out: everything is changed. Gathering their strength and for a time delirious with fantasies of freedom, almost child-like in the pleasures of their assertiveness, the workers become what Marx called a class for themselves. And then, with his uncanny gift for achieving mass effects through individual strokes, Zola begins to individualise his characters. He does this not to approximate that fragmented psychology we associate with 19th-century fiction but towards the end of preparing the characters for their new roles: Etienne in the pride and exposure of leadership, Maheu in the conquest of manhood, La Maheude as the voice of ancient grievance, and even the children, led by the devilish Jeanlin, who in their debauchery release the spontaneous zest that the overdisciplined life of the miners has suppressed.

The strike becomes the central action: thereby the myth of emergence takes on the sharp edge of conflict. The workers are shown in their rise to a noble solidarity and their fall to a brutal mob – better yet, in the ways the two, under intolerable stress, become all but indistinguishable. ('Do not flatter the working class nor blacken it,' Zola told himself in notes for *L'Assomoir*.) And nothing is more brilliant than Zola's intuition – it speaks for his powers of insinuating himself beneath the skin of the miners – that after the horrible riot with which Book V closes, he sees the men continuing their strike, digging in with a mute fatalism, 'a great sombre peacefulness,' which rests far less on expectations of victory than a common yielding to the pathos of standing and starving together. Defeat comes, and demoralisation too, but only after Zola has charted with a precise objectivity the rhythms of struggle, rhythms as intrinsically absorbing for the novelist (and at least as difficult to apprehend) as those of the individual psyche in turmoil.

Again, it should be stressed that the myth Zola employs is not the vulgar-Marxist notion of an inevitable victory or of a victory-in-defeat ending with noble resolves for the future. True, he shows as no other European novelist before him, the emergence of a new historical force and he reveals the conflict that must follow; but its outcome remains uncertain, shadowy, ambiguous. The more serious versions of Marxism speak of historical choice: freedom or barbarism. It is a choice allowing for and perhaps forming the substance of tragedy. *Germinal* shares that view . . .

Again we reach an interpenetration of commanding myth and historical material, what I take to be Zola's great achievement in *Germinal.* A stranger arrives, slightly removed from the workers because of his superior intellect, yet required to enter their lives and ready to share their troubles. So far, the pattern of the story is not very different from that of much fiction composed earlier in the 19th century. But then comes a radical shift: the stranger, now on the way to being a leader, remains at the centre of the book but his desires and reflections do not constitute its central matter. What engages us primarily is the collective experience of the miners, the myth of their emergence. In Book V of *Germinal*, both the most original and exciting portion of the novel, this entry into consciousness is shown in its two-sidedness, and with a complexity of tone that unites passionate involvement and dispassionate removal. In his notes for the book Zola understood that he must remain faithful to his story as archetype:

> To get a broad effect I must have my two sides as clearly contrasted as possible and carried to the very extreme of intensity. So that I must start with all the woes and fatalities which weigh down the miners. Facts, not emotional pleas. The miner must be shown crushed, starving, a victim of ignorance, suffering with his children in a hell on earth – but not persecuted, for the bosses are not deliberately vindictive – *he is simply overwhelmed by the social situation as it exists*. On the contrary I must make the bosses humane so long as their direct interests are not threatened; no point in foolish tub-thumping. The worker is the victim of the facts of existence – capital, competition, industrial crises.

For this perception to be transformed into a dramatic action, Zola relies mainly on the narrative increment that follows from his myth of the speechless and the symbolic suggestiveness of the mine.

In saying this I don't mean to imply that everything which occurs in the novel is necessary or appropriate. The narrative is frequently flawed by cheap and lurid effects. Zola, as a critic has remarked, had an overwhelming imagination but only an uncertain – and sometimes a corrupted – taste. That the riot of the miners should be a terrifying event seems entirely right; that it should end with the ghastly *frisson* invented by Zola is a sign of his weakness for sensationalism. Zola tries hard to present his middle-class characters, the Hennebeaus and Gregoires, with some objectivity and even sympathy, but he usually fails . . . Zola fails because in this novel he is not interested in such people at all. They are there because his overall scheme demands it, because he feels an obligation to 'fill out the picture.' Sensing as much, we read these inferior portions with a certain tolerance, assuaged by the likelihood that further great scenes with the miners lie ahead. The mediocre intervals come to serve as 'rests' helping Zola create or re-gather suspense. M. Hennebeau, the mine manager, is a partial exception, if only because he is a figure of power and power is always fascinating for Zola. Still, the sub-plot of Hennebeau's personal unhappiness and his envy of what he takes to be the miners' unsoiled virility is obviously weak – just how weak one can see by comparing it to D. H. Lawrence's treatment of similar material. And again, the immersion of Etienne and Catherine in the mine, once the strike has been lost, is a scene of considerable power but also marred by Zola's lack of discipline in having the body of Chaval, the girl's former lover, float horribly up to them in the darkness. Zola does not know when to stop.

To notice such flaws can be damaging, and to write as if *Germinal* were no more than the sum of local incidents could be a strategy for dismissing the book entirely. But this seems a poor way of dealing with a novel. *Germinal*, like many works of fiction, depends upon effects that are larger, more gross, and less open to isolated inspection than picking out scenes of weakness would suggest; it depends upon the large-muscled rhythms of the narrative as a whole . . .

If what I have been saying has validity, it follows that there will also be frequent episodes of brilliance – else, how could the novelist achieve his large rhythms of narration? And there are, of course, such episodes. Two kinds may be distinguished: those persuading us of Zola's authority as imaginative historian (substantiating detail) and those persuading us of his psychological penetration into a given moment of the action (illuminating detail).

The first kind is to be found mainly in his treatment of the miners at the peak of crisis. Etienne, reading a Belgian socialist weekly, hastily and poorly absorbing its contents, seeking to make up for years of waste as he is 'gripped by the uneducated man's methodless passion for study' and then overcome by 'the dull dread that he had shown himself unequal to the task' – all this bears the thick circumstantiality of the actual. Zola knew the kind of men who were drawn to socialist politics, not merely learned bourgeois intellectuals like Marx and Kautsky, but self-educated workers like Bebel, straining with ambition and stumbling into knowledge. This command of his material is shown even more subtly in the portrayal of the inner relationships among his three radicals: Rasseneur, the most cautious and experienced, clearly on the way to becoming a classical Social Democrat; Souvarine, also a classical figure, though of the anarchist-terrorist kind who declares the need 'to destroy everything . . . no more nations, no more governments, no more property, no more God or religion' and then to return to 'the primitive and formless community'; and Etienne, the sincere unformed worker, open to a wide range of possibilities but determined – his aspiring intellectuality prods his ambition – to make a place for himself on the stage of history.

The second and more striking kind of detail shows Zola's imagination at work somewhat more freely, releasing incidents which do not depend directly on the overall design of the novel. On the simplest level there is the pathos of the mine girl Mouquette, hopelessly generous with all she has (her body to the men, her affection to almost anyone, her bared bottom to the strike-breakers), who offers Etienne a dozen cold potatoes to still the hunger of the Maheu household. It is a trifle, but from such trifles affecting novels are made. On a level hard to apprehend in strictly rational terms, there is Etienne finding himself a place to hide, after the riot, in one of the hated mines. (A little bitterly, one remember's Fabrice's chestnut tree, emblem of innocence, in *The Charterhouse of Parma.*) But the greatest of such imaginative strokes concerns the strange old Bonnemort, introduced at the outset as a ghost of a man embodying the exhaustion of the workers' lives. He has nothing to say, he is barely alive, until at the strike meeting, amid the predictably rousing speeches,

> everybody was surprised to see Bonnemort standing on the tree trunk and trying to make himself heard . . . No doubt he was giving way to one of those sudden fits of babbling that would sometimes stir up the past so violently that old memories would rise from his depths and flow from his lips for hours. It had become very quiet, and everybody listened to the old man, so ghostly pale in the moonlight; as he was talking about things that had no obvious connection with the discussion, long stories that nobody could understand, their astonishment increased. He spoke of his youth, told of his two uncles who had been crushed to death at Le Voreaux, then went on to the pneumonia

that had carried off his wife. Through it all, however, he never lost hold of his one idea: things had never been right and they never would be right.

Without rhetorical strain, this passage summons the losses of the past, the whole unreckoned waste that forms our history. The mode is grotesque, but for readers with a measure of historical imagination, Zola achieves something far beyond the limits of what that description usually suggests.

Zola is not a fine writer. His style aspires towards a rich and heavy impasto rather than a lucid line-drawing, and often it is marred by excess. In *Germinal* the writing is nevertheless effective at two points: first, the passages describing the mine with that wary respect for the power of the actual a novelist must have, and second, the episodes in which he evokes the surge of conflict and the passions of enraged men. In these episodes the prose can be extremely effective, combining mass and speed – effective as long as Zola stays with his central purpose, which is to depict the sensations of men who have thrown off the discipline of society but not yet discovered the discipline of self. Nor need we succumb to any version of 'the imitative fallacy' – that in its internal qualities a style must reflect the matter it is trying to convey – in order to recognise at least some correspondences as proper to the relation between style and subject. One does not write about the collapse of a mine in the style of Henry James analysing an exquisite heroine . . . His effort to create an action of extreme objectivity, a plot of collective behaviour, leads the novelist to a style of extreme subjectivity in which he finds himself driven to 'impersonate' the group. At its worst, this kind of writing can seem willed, an effort to do for the action through rhetoric what film-makers try to do for their stories through music. At its best, the writing has a coarse strength and even splendour, what might be called the poetry of naturalism.

Still, it would be foolish to claim for Zola that his prose can yield the kind of sentence-by-sentence pleasure that can be had from the prose of a writer like James or Flaubert. Zola is often careless as a stylist, sometimes wanton, occasionally cheap. His trouble, however, is not that his prose lacks nicety of phrasing or epigrammatic neatness; it is that he does not content himself with a utilitarian plainness but must reach out for the ornamental and exalted, seeking through rhetorical fancy-work to establish his credentials as a literary man. Like other half-educated novelists and journalists of the 19th century, Zola was painfully susceptible to those charms of the 'literary' which he claimed to dismiss.

His style, like almost everything else in *Germinal*, is interesting mainly when considered in the large. One then encounters a phenomenon I do not pretend to understand, and which seems to be an essential mystery of literature. For long portions of the novel Zola yields himself entirely to the passions of the miners, and his prose becomes strongly, even exorbitantly, passionate. We are swept along, as we are meant to be, by the surge of men in revolt; we are with them, the starving and the hunted, and the language heaves and breaks, sweeping across us with torrents of rhetoric. But let us not be frightened by that word 'rhetoric': it bears the strength, not only the weakness, of Zola's novel. Here is a passage in which Zola describes (he is always strong in parallel effects, grotesque doublings) the behaviour of the miners' children during the strike:

> The scamps had become the terror of the countryside, which they had invaded, little by little, like a savage horde. At first they had been satisfied with the yard at Le Voreux, where they rolled around in the piles of coal, becoming black as Negroes, and played hide-and-seek through the stacks of timber among which they wandered as though in a virgin forest. Then they had taken over the slag heap, where they would slide on their behinds down the bare parts, still hot with interior fires, and dart among the brambles of the older parts – hidden all day and as busy as mischievous mice with their quiet little games. Enlarging their territory still further, they fought among the piles of bricks until blood flowed; raced through the fields, eating all sorts of juicy herbs without bothering about bread, searched the banks of the canal for mudfish, which they swallowed raw, and roamed ever further afield, travelling as far as the forest of Vandame, where they would stuff themselves with strawberries in the spring and hazelnuts and huckleberries in the summer. Soon the whole immense plain belonged to them.

Rhetoric, yes; but a rhetoric which accompanies and sustains a remarkably strong evocation. The passion Zola pours out finds its match, its justification, in the incident he imagines. Yet, as we read into the depths of the book, we grow aware that there is another side of Zola, one who draws back a little, seeing the whole tragedy as part of an eternal rhythm of struggle and decision. This Zola is finally dispassionate, withdrawn from his own commitments, as if writing from some timeless perch, and capable of a measure of irony towards the whole human enterprise. Zola the partisan and Zola the artist: for those who like their 'commitment' straight, in the duped formulas of 'socialist realism' such ambivalence is detestable. But I take it to be a sign of Zola's achievement. If there has ever been a novel concerning which one might forgive a writer his unmodulated passions it is *Germinal*; yet precisely here Zola's 'scientism' proves to be an unexpected advantage, enabling him to achieve an aesthetic distance that gives the book its ultimate austerity.

There is still another doubleness of response in *Germinal*. Hardly a Zola critic has failed to note the frequency with which images of fecundity occur in the book, repeated scenes in which, along and beyond the margin of his central narrative, Zola displays the unplanned and purposeless creativity of existence. Henry James, in his essay on Zola, remarks:

> To make his characters swarm, and to make the great central thing they swarm about 'as large as life,' portentously, heroically big, that was the task he set himself very nearly from the first, that was the secret he triumphantly mastered.[1]

Now this 'swarming,' for many 19th-century novelists, can be a source not merely of narrative energy but also of a mindless and pseudo-religious sentimentalism. Everyone has encountered it as a special kind of fictional cant: the generations come, the generations go, etc. Asserted without irony, such declamations often constitute a kind of psychic swindle, convenient enough for novelists who fear the depressing logic of their own work or who need some unearned lilt in their final pages. That Zola does approach this kind of sentimentalism seems beyond doubt, but again and again he draws back into a baffled stoicism, evading the trap his romantic heritage has set for him. 'A black avenging army' is 'germinating in the furrows; soon this germination would . . . sunder the earth.' But even as such sentiments fill Zola's final pages there is no simple assurance, indeed, no assurance of any kind. Despite the sense of a swarming procreation which keeps the race alive, Zola ends on a note of anguish; he does not propose an easy harmony between the replenishments of nature and the desires of men. Etienne, clumsily balancing his idealism and ambition, goes out into the world.

To one reader at least, he enters neither upon personal triumph nor the 'final conflict' promised by the dialectic of history, but upon a journey into those treacherous regions of the unknown where sooner or later all men find themselves.

Henri Mitterand, Ideology and Myth: *Germinal* and the Fantasies of Revolt (1986)

Knowledge and denotation

I would like, first of all . . . to point out that the text of *Germinal* conveys and transmits a *body of knowledge* ['un savoir'] that is historical in nature, specific, and determines a field of investigation (the workers movement), an area of observation (the mining industry), a period of time (the end of the Second Empire). This information produces the entire denotated world of the book: technical descriptions, the analysis of social stratification, observations concerning the emergence of class consciousness, the exposition of political factors, etc.

The text depicts for instance a *décor*, a landscape, with all its indispensable technical denotations, so that its pertinent traits, and most especially those of a technological nature, clearly stand out. Thus the mine appears, at a first level of analysis (that is first in the order of the texts, and first in the order of the meanings that they convey to the reader), as a space hollowed out by man, organised by man, marked by his own work.

Mythical investment

But each denotated detail is, so to speak, impure, weighed down by the connotated correspondences invested in it. In the mine, *the rain, the fog, the smell of old metals*, are precise terms destined to define, to particularize this *décor*. But they also function equally well as impressive elements, destined to emphasize the inhuman, uncomfortable nature of these places, the contradiction created between basic human needs and human presence in such a place. The text is laden therefore with correspondences between the inanimate world and the human world: ' . . . the air became more poisoned and heated with the smoke of the lamps, with the pestilence of their breaths, with the asphyxia of the fire-damp . . . At the bottom of their molehill, beneath the weight of the earth, with no more breath in their inflamed lungs, they went on hammering.'[1] Several metaphors, mixed together, can be discerned here: metaphors of asphyxiation, of immurement, of the mole or the damned. A code of analogies is gradually established whereby every denotated element (the narrowness of the galleries, the rarefaction of the air, the heat) becomes the signifier of an entire system of connotations which describe less an aspect of the modern industrial and social landscape as some of the forms of the curse that afflicts humanity.

The components of mythical structure are also present: on the one hand we have a description which tends constantly to blend into the narrative sequence: 'They went on hammering'; a pictorial form of description (a 'tableau') which is perpetually being integrated into the narrative, at the same time as the narrative itself seems to come to a halt in a highly synthetic image; on the other hand, the text itself is built around an exemplar. Here a man is all but lost in the dark, crushed beneath the rock, his breath like fire, hammering away without respite (and the verb *hammer* itself has intransitive connotations). The character is frozen in a gesture which is presented as an eternal one and he becomes an allegory of misery. Concrete reality and rational analysis gradually give way to the fantastic and the fabulous.

If one were to extend this line of research beyond a brief example to include all of the passages which describe the subterranean world, a complex and correlative system of explicit connotations would be revealed:

– The mine, as a subterranean space, refers to the concept of burrowing and burying (the miners are insects, they are also buried alive, prisoners of the grave), to the concept of suffocation (the galleries become narrower and narrower, poisonous gases are given off), to the concept of devouring (Le Voreux devours, wolfs down its daily ration of miners, is an insatiable belly).

– The organisation of this subterranean space calls to mind buried cities: its labyrinth refers to the concept of wandering, of disorientation, of deliberately concealed exits.

– The mine, as an area of shadows, is the place where instinctive impulses – hunger, sex, murder – which daylight normally censures or controls, break loose freely and violently. This is the place where man reverts to beast.

Thus, the constituent elements of this space lose their inertia and become mythical elements, since this set of correspondences is the result of the system of correlations established between these elements and man, between the inanimate and the animate. Earth, rock, water, fire are the natural instruments of persecution against man, and the coordinates of what in *Germinal* is called 'that horizon of misery, sealed like a tomb.'

A multitude of myths spring forth within this profusion of analogies. It is not at all surprising that several of these are created by the discourse of the miners themselves: the myth of the Torrent (a water-dream), the myth of the Tartaret (fire), of the Black Man (night, sexual and homicidal violence), etc. As for Zola himself, he makes myths out of myth. The miners' labor, in its various stages, tells the tale of a myth of immurement.

But things are not quite that simple.

Two parallel worlds

The mine is but one of the two poles of a structure which establishes equivalent relationships between the two societies above- and below-ground, between the surface and the pit, day and night, bosses and workers, the haves and the have-nots, etc.

The structure of the entire novel is based on this relationship between the 'superior-tive' and the 'inferior-tive,' which may be presented on a chain of substitutions in the following way:

$$\frac{\text{Surface}}{\text{Pit}} \sim \frac{\text{Bourgeoisie}}{\text{Proletariat}} \sim \frac{\text{Haves}}{\text{Have-nots}} \sim \frac{\text{Light}}{\text{Night}} \quad \text{etc.}$$

This chain of relationships can take on multiple forms, the complete inventory of which remains to be drawn up. But the system appears to be totally coherent. A categorical, paradigmatic opposition between the Bourgeoisie and the Workers, the Haves and the Have-nots exists. And each one of the terms of this opposition is linked to the other terms of the same level by a syntagmatic correlation. A vertical reading defines the core of the code of meaning and the kernel of the myth, a horizontal reading defines the narrative text. Here are two examples: the relationship between the wealthy and the starving is the same as that between the devouring god and the devoured population, as it is between the feast and fornication. If the bourgeois eat, the miners go hungry, and if the miners indulge everywhere and at any time in the pleasures of copulation, Hennebeau is constantly in despair because of his own frustrations. Scenes with the Grégoires or the Hennebeaus at the table occur with the same frequency as sexual scenes with the miners in their habitual haunts. On the vertical axis, a relationship of equivalence is thereby established (Lévi-Strauss has pointed out that in many myths an analogy between *eating* and *copulating* is evident; this is one of the outstanding characteristics of *Germinal*): on the horizontal axis, one finds a relationship of contiguity. Connotation circulates along both of these vectors. Each element is determined by its relationships with the others.

Thus the articulation of the novel appears to resemble closely that of the myths by which the 'savage mind' organises its interpretation of the world.

And it is here that ideology breaks through. The social structure is thus correlated organically, in the textual universe, to natural structures (light and darkness, the surface world and the subterranean one) and to biological structures. The division into two classes is a natural and eternal phenomenon, not a social and transitory one. It is a fact of nature, not of culture. There is, in the nature of things, no antagonism inherent in such a division. If such an antagonism does appear, the system, on the contrary, will absorb it and neutralize it.

Structure and narration

For myth is dynamic, just as it appears to be in the original titles that Zola considered for the novel. Of course, the opposition between two of these titles, *L'Assiette au beurre* [*The Soft Life*] and *Les Affamés* [*The Hunger-Stricken*], reflects the static nature of this structure. But others introduce the idea of a dynamic transformation: *La Maison qui craque* [*The Break-up*], *Le Sol qui brûle* [*Eruption*]. Here, the chain of substitutions is transformed into a chain of transformations. From the depths of the underground world there bursts forth the explosion which destroys the home, the tabernacle for which it was the foundation. The hungry come out of their holes and destroy the universe of the rich. From the purifying destruction of the old world, a new world will spring forth.

In this way the basic principle on which the previous structure is founded, one of homological parallelism, is undermined by the narration itself. The rebels invade the territory of the wealthy, in order to destroy it, and in so doing they substitute a relationship of contiguity for a relationship of equivalence and attempt to upset the order of the world.

But the remarkable fact is that this attempted overthrow is dealt with in a mythical mode, and in several different manners, all of them forms of travesty. I shall give but two examples:

The Simulacrum. – We must now turn to three scenes in the novel: the castration of Maigrat, the murder of the little soldier, the strangulation of Cécile Grégoire by Old Bonnemort. Three scenes of sacrifice, of magical and not practical action. In each of these cases the working class does not attack the real power of the bourgeoisie, but believes it can modify the order of the universe by means of a ritual sacrifice, which moreover is carried out by marginal officiants (women, children, old men). In each case, the victim is an intermediate being who, by nature, represents the possible connecting link between the two worlds. The grocer, the soldier, Cécile, are *ambiguous*. They are the ones designated by the narrative to serve at the same time as expiatory and propitiatory victims. When Bonnemort raises his hand against Cécile a connection between the two worlds is established. Once Cécile is dead, the gods must fill in the empty space by establishing social justice, a reward on which the miners secretly, unconsciously, have been counting. But all of this is mere dream, magic, sham . . . The revolution fades into fantasies. The metonymical journey has failed.

The *Metaphorisation of Revolt.* – The narrative of the strike makes use of all the images accumulated in previous passages of the text:

> It was the red vision of the revolution, which would one day inevitably carry them all away, on some bloody evening at the end of the century. Yes, some evening the people, unbridled at last, would thus gallop along the roads, making the blood of the middle class flow, parading severed heads and sprinkling gold from disembowelled coffers. The women would yell, the men would have those wolf-like jaws open to

> bite. Yes, the same rags, the same thunder of great sabots, the same terrible troop, with dirty skins and tainted breath, sweeping away the old world beneath an overflowing flood of barbarians. Fire would flame; they would not leave standing one stone of the towns: they would return to the savage life of the woods, after the great rut, the great feast-day, when the poor in one night would emaciate the wives and empty the cellars of the rich. There would be nothing left, not a sou of the great fortunes, not a title-deed of properties acquired: until the day dawned when a new earth would perhaps spring up once more. Yes, it was these things which were passing along the road: it was the force of nature herself, and they were receiving the terrible wind of it in their faces.
>
> A great cry arose, dominating the *Marseillaise:*
>
> 'Bread! Bread! Bread!'[2]

In this passage, the proletarian uprising is likened to the unleashing of a troop of brutish creatures, a pack of ferocious beasts, the over-flowing of a mighty stream, the reappearance of characters from the Reign of Terror, the resurgence of ancient *jacqueries*. In all of these comparisons, the author makes use of a-historical and non-rational concepts which are borrowed sometimes from the order of natural catastrophes (floods, earthquakes, fires), sometimes from the order of instinctual behaviour (passionate anger, violence, the thirst for rape, fire and blood).

A type of magical transformation occurs here as well, but it is the author's doing: human actions are naturalised, treated as if they formed an integral part of physical determinism. Historical and social denotation is overwhelmed, submerged by biological and natural connotation. The narrative leaves history behind to inject social tragedy into the series of cataclysms which periodically affect the order of the world and are constituent elements of this order.

Ideological significance

So it is up to the reader to work out his own method of deciphering this decipherment, his own interpretation of this interpretation. The author's interpretation of the event is a mythifying travesty. But this interpretation points directly to the ideology which underlies it and which it denotes. The mythical structure is deeper than the superficial structure of the events related. But the ideological structure is even deeper than the mythical structure(s). It is at this level that we must seek the minimal sentence of the narrative. As Hjemlslev put it, denotative semiology subsumes connotative semiotics.

On all levels, we have isolated the process of naturalisation and immobilisation in the eternal. This process is also one of reversal and of idealisation. Marx wrote in *The German Ideology:* 'Social power appears as an outside force, a force in itself, independent of will and of human development.' History vanishes and gives way to nature. Elaborating on one of Marx's ideas, Barthes wrote in his *Mythologies*: 'The status of the bourgeoisie is particular and historical: the man it represents will be universal, eternal.' One can easily apply this statement to *Germinal*, a novel which, seen as the union of historical fact and of a mythified version of social history, refracts the middle class ideology of the end of the 19th century, a mixture of lucidity and of the inability to take a rational view of social evolution. By depicting the society of miners as a primitive society, as a world of nature, and not a world of culture and of history, Zola helps us to understand what Althusser somewhere calls 'the discourse of the unspoken desire of the bourgeoisie.'

But, without knowing it, he also applies a precept of Marx, who, in his *Critique of Hegel's Philosophy of Law* exclaimed: 'We must represent each sector of German society as the shameful part of German society. We must shake up these fossilized conditions by singing their own tunes back to them. We must teach the people self-horror, in order to instill courage in them.' This explains the ambiguity of the lessons offered by this work and the availability of meanings that it has maintained, well outside the social structures which gave rise to the author's reflections and dreams.

7

GUSTAVE FLAUBERT, *MADAME BOVARY*

Tony Tanner's essay is extracted from his chapter on *Madame Bovary* in *Adultery in the Novel*, where it appears with the more elaborate title, 'Fetishism – Castles of Cake, Pellets from the Seraglio, the Damascened Rifle'. Tanner offers a highly illuminating and suggestive account of the 'fetishistic displacement' that pervades the society depicted in Flaubert's novel. Drawing on Freud's 1927 essay on fetishism, Tanner describes the phenomenon as the displacement of libidinal feeling from a person to an ancillary object, or to some portion of the body, as a way of accommodating what might seem threatening or dangerous about full sexual identity. He argues that the sentimental songs and romantic stories fed to Emma in her early 'education' induce a certain kind of fetishism; she begins to experience an erotic thrill simply in handling books and turning the tissue paper that floats over the illustrations. As part of the wider 'degenerative transformation' in Emma's society, he cites three main examples: the wedding cake (in which a detailed social setting has been transformed into confectionery); the pellets from the seraglio (which show the exotic from all realms being transported to a bourgeois domestic setting); and the damascened rifle (an object of violence incongruously decorated). Tanner very deftly shifts from Freud to Marx, drawing attention to Marx's ideas on 'The Fetishism of Commodities' in *Capital*. A mystified relation to sex and a mystified relation to the products of labour are seen as complementary aspects of the same degenerative capitalist society.

Elisabeth Bronfen's essay, from her provocatively titled book, *Over Her Dead Body*, argues that the pervasive imagery of death in the nineteenth century is a cultural indication that death was 'neither successfully repressed nor worked through'. Instead, death was displaced on to the feminine body. Bronfen reads *Madame Bovary* as a suicidal autobiography. The heroine's life, which in effect is a lengthy process of dying, begins with her entrance into the imaginary world of romantic and religious fiction. Like Tanner, Bronfen argues that reading initiates a process of desire, but her claim that Emma longs for an imaginary wholeness that precedes her acquisition of language and literacy owes more to the

French psychoanalyst Jacques Lacan than it does to Sigmund Freud. At a more mundane level, the essay suggests that Emma is dissatisfied in marriage because it does not fulfil the expectations and desires raised by literature. Paradoxically, Emma lives romance by dying a romantic death.

Tony Tanner, Fetishism in *Madame Bovary* (1979)

In connection with the phenomenon of fetishistic displacement that pervades the society depicted by the book as well as the book itself, I want to give three examples. The cake at Emma's wedding that so impresses the guests is made up of three tiers. It has as a base a blue cardboard imitation of a temple complete with porticoes, colonnades, and stucco statuettes; on top of that is a 'castle-keep in Savoy cake' ('un donjon en gâteau de Savoie') (pt. 1, ch. 4), with fortifications of almonds and raisins and so on; the top layer is a green meadow with lakes of jam and a Cupid ('un Amour') on a chocolate swing. One could say that this object is an implicit comment on the degeneration of society from the religious age, through the heroic age, finally evolving into the placid age of the pastoral-bourgeois. But of course the main feature of this object is that everything has been turned into cake. Just as all the varied signs and fragments that went into the making of Charles Bovary's cap were equalized and rendered meaningless by their transposition into the material and context of the cap, so the temple and the castle and even Amour itself are all reduced to the level of a rich dessert, a confectionery translation or displacement that robs them of their real significance by reconstituting them as a series of devourable references. (In the same way we find in the book napkins like bishop's miters and loaves like turbans reminiscent of the Gothic crusades – history, heroism, and religion have all been moved into the bourgeois kitchen and dining room, for cooking, serving, and decoration.) This is an example of what I mean by degenerative displacements or transformations. It is this process that underlies the whole description of Emma's early 'education' in part 1, chapter 6, where Flaubert describes all the debased metaphors and images fed into Emma from a religious upbringing without any notion of real belief: bad novels, romantic stories, exaggerated painted plates, sentimental songs, and all the books and pictures that poured their stereotypes into Emma's head – not filling gaps, but causing them. This of course is part of the fog in Emma's head and has been often noted (as by Girard). What we should also note is that it serves inevitably to induce in Emma herself a certain kind of fetishism. Thus she starts to experience what amounts to an erotic thrill just by handling the books and watching the tissue paper float over the plates. 'She thrilled as she blew back the tissue paper over the prints. It rose in a half-fold and sank gently down on the opposite page'. ('Elle frémissait, en soulevant de son haleine le papier de soie des gravures, qui se levait à demi plié et retombait deoucement contre la page' [pt. 1, ch. 6].) This sensuous rising and falling of the soft white paper seems like a morphological prefiguration of the more overtly erotic risings and fallings of clothes, sheets, bodies implied or described in Emma's later sexual life (the smell of 'damp sheets' is detectable in the setting of Emma's first appearance); it even suggests the kind of sensual inhaling and exhaling of breath of which she often becomes conscious both in herself and others. One could see that one triggering stimulus in her later life might be traced to a fetishistic attachment to the childhood excitement at blowing back the tissue paper over pictures. Not exactly that she is trying to love by the book, but rather that she is trying to recapture an experience in the flesh that originated as a sensation caused by paper, and thus to rediscover in 'love' the texture (even more than the text) of the book.

My second example occurs quite near the end, when Emma's disintegration is well advanced. We are told that she spends her days in her room, mentally benumbed and physically scarcely clothed, 'occasionally burning some aromatic pellets that she had bought at an Algerian shop in Rouen' ('faisant fumer des pastilles du sérail qu'elle avait achetées à Rouen dans la boutique d'un Algérien' [pt. 3, ch. 6]). Literally these are pellets of the seraglio, as though the essence of an oriental harem had been transformed (or 'decanted') into a pill that can then be sold as a commodity in a shop that is itself an anomalous displacement (an Algerian shop in Rouen). The power behind this alchemical feat lies in the verb *acheter* of course, for money turns everything to transportable goods, so that there is seemingly no limit to the process by which the exotic from all realms and at all levels can be transplaced into the bourgeois domestic setting (witness the piece of coral in Emma's house).[1] I have alluded to this phenomenon of fragmenting the world, and moving it around as sample and spectacle, in connection with Goethe's novel. Flaubert reveals a society in which the process seems to permeate almost every area of activity. In this case these 'pellets' also serve to contribute to the fog in Emma's head: indeed it would seem that she bought them for that purpose, as if seeking to confound one sort of fog with another, or perhaps to compound all the fogs and fumes that seem subtly, then more obviously, to swarm upon her.

A rather different but related kind of displacement is in evidence when Emma goes to make her final appeal to Rodolphe, who turns her down with the explanation that he is a 'bit short' ('gêné') himself. She says sarcastically how sorry she is for him and then looks around the room. 'She let her gaze rest on a damascened rifle that glittered in a rack on the wall' ('une carabine damasquinée' [pt. 3, ch. 8]) and starts to remark on the opulent objects that Rodolphe still retains in his 'poverty.' 'When people are poor, they don't put silver on the butts of their guns! Or buy a clock inlaid with tortoise-shell! . . .

or silver-plated whistles for their whips . . . or trinkets for their watches' (p. 323). Manifest in these objects are inappropriate and incongruous and totally pointless mergings of items and materials – a damascened rifle? What conceivable reason could there be for such an alogical collocation? Except that the rifle has ceased to be a genuine instrument to be used and has shifted into a fetish that can be decorated; and why put tortoiseshell on a clock ('une pendule avec des incrustations d'écailles' [pt. 3, ch. 8]): and what on earth is a silver-plated whistle doing on a whip ('des sifflets de vermeil pour ses fouets' [pt. 3, ch. 8])? Such questions could be answered in terms of the history of decoration, but in the terms of this book they seem to have the same origin in that incoherent assemblage of signs and materials that was manifest in that cap of 'enculturation' that Charles Bovary holds onto so awkwardly during his initiation into the school and language of his society. The answer to Emma's protest is that it is precisely when people are 'poor' that they indulge in the multiplying absurdities of displacement of materials and decorations and functions such as are exemplified in the objects in Rodolphe's room. This bespeaks a far-reaching impoverishment of feeling, emotion, spirit – whatever we might still mean by human and humane response to other human beings. It is the ultimate poverty, and Rodolphe is quite right in intimating that he is deep into it, much deeper than he thinks or could ever know. And the manifestation of this kind of poverty is, I suggest, visible in the fetishism implied by such as object as *une carabine damasquinée*.

I have been using *fetishism* in a general sense to denote that displacement of libidinal feeling from the complete sexual identity of the other (let us say the woman), to an ancillary object, some adjunct or appurtenance, or to some *portion* of the body (which being isolated from the living body, by drawing attention *away from* the whole to the part, takes on the status of a thing). The full sexual identity of the other is threatening, dangerous, unpredictable, and alive, and requires a commitment and engagement (and thus a risk) on the part of the one whose feelings are aroused. By contrast the 'fetishized' objects are relatively safe, easily available, undemanding of reciprocity or commitment and thus allowing the person whose feelings have been aroused to remain in a passive, spectator/consumer relationship to the other (again, let us say the women – and here we should differentiate between transitional objects, which help to wean the child away from complete identification with the mother, and fetish objects, by which what is termed mature genital relationships are avoided so that the mutuality of love is never attempted). This kind of displacement of feeling onto decontextualized objects or fragments (the context would be the whole living woman) as substitutes or replacements, once it has been engendered, may take over increasingly large areas of the person's approach to life in general, and thus it can permeate an entire society's modes of feeling and dealing (thus misplaced emotion may lavish its loving attentions on a rifle instead of a person and produce the *carabine damasquinée*). At a certain indefinite point the fetish need not be in any way related to a woman or indeed women in general, so that the libidinal feeling does not, as it were, slide or veer away from, or stop short of, confronting the full sexuality of the woman to arrest itself in the security of an accessory object or an unsexual part, but can attach itself directly to objects. Thus I have called Binet's ecstatic devotion to his napkin rings a kind of extreme fetishism though there is no instance of his having transferred that feeling from any female object or femininity in general. However, in addition to this rather all-embracing use of the word, we do have Freud's essay, 'Fetischism' (1927), and it is worth restating some of his ideas and insights here, since I think they are very relevant to Flaubert's depiction of what has happened to modes of sexual feelings and libidinal attachment in the society he describes. In the Standard Edition, the editor's note points out that in his earliest discussion of fetishism (*Three Essays*), Freud wrote that 'no other variation of the sexual instinct that borders on the pathological can lay so much claim to our interest as this one,' but did not go beyond maintaining that 'the choice of a fetish is an after-effect of some sexual impression, received as a rule in early childhood.' There are some intervening references to foot fetishism, but it is not until this famous essay that Freud introduces what the editors call a 'fresh metapsychological development.' It is this aspect of the essay that I wish to summarize here.

Freud starts by citing the case of a young man who 'had exalted a certain sort of "shine on the nose" into a fetishistic precondition.' The explanation turned out to be that the boy had been brought up in an English nursery but had later come to Germany, where he forgot his mother tongue. 'The fetish, which originated from his earliest childhood, had to be understood in English, not German. The "shine on the nose" (in German "*Glanz auf der Nase*") – was in reality a "*glance* at the nose." The nose was thus the fetish, which, incidentally, he endowed at will with the luminous shine which was not perceptible to others.' Freud goes on to maintain that 'the meaning and the purpose of the fetish' in every instance he studied turned out to be the same. 'When now I announce that the fetish is a substitute for the penis, I shall certainly create disappointment; so I hasten to add that it is not a substitute for any chance penis, but for a particular and quite special penis that had been extremely important in early childhood but had later been lost. That is to say, it should normally have been given up, but the fetish is precisely designed to preserve it from extinction. To put it more plainly: the fetish is a substitute for the woman's (the mother's) penis that the little boy *once believed in and* – for reasons familiar to us – *does not want to give up*.' (My italics.) Freud maintains that 'the boy *refused to take cognizance of the fact of his having perceived* that a woman does not possess a penis' (my italics) – a refusal based on the ensuing fear of his own castration. What this amounts to in more general terms is no less than a strategy whereby new and threatening *knowledge* is overlaid by an earlier and comforting *belief*. In a crucial passage Freud differentiates this process from pathological repression. 'If we wanted to differentiate more sharply between the vicissitude of the *idea* as distinct from that of the *affect*, and reserve the word "*Verdrängung*" ("repression") for the affect, then the correct German word for the vicissitude of the idea would be "*Verleugnung*" ("disavowal").' Freud explains further, 'It is not true that, after the child has made his observation of the woman, he has preserved unaltered his belief that women have a phallus. *He has retained that belief, but he has also given it up*. In the conflict between the weight of the unwelcome perception and the force of his counter-wish, a compromise has been reached . . . Yes, in his mind the woman *has* got a penis, in spite of everything: but this penis is no longer the same as it was before. *Something else has taken its place, has been appointed its substitute, as it were, and now inherits the interest which was formerly directed to its predecessor*.' (All my italics.) And while interest in the fetish increases 'because the horror of castration has set up a memorial to itself in the creation of this substitute,' so 'aversion' [the German word *der Abscheu* implies even stronger feelings of both disgust and awe], 'which is never absent in any fetishist, to the real female genitals remains a *stigma indelible* of the repression that has taken place.' One could thus conceive of how the two processes are mutually reinforcing, and an increased attachment to the fetishistic object(s) would both intensify and be intensified by a growing aversion to the actual genital identity of the woman. Irrespective of what a reader may think of Freud's unitary explanation of the source of all fetishism, we can, I think recognize that this process is ubiquitous in Flaubert's novel.

In his further comments on the choice of fetish objects (or 'substitutes for the absent female phallus'), Freud maintains that it often seems that 'when the fetish is instituted some process occurs which reminds one of the stopping of memory in traumatic amnesia. As in this latter case, the subject's interest comes to a halt half-way, as it were; it is as though the last impression before the uncanny and traumatic one is retained as a fetish.' Thus fixing emotional regard on an object may be a deliberate way of *not* seeing the woman or the person; perception may in this way blockade its own processes with things. This too obtains in Flaubert's world.

Freud extends his discussion by describing the case of two boys who seem to have 'failed to take cognizance' of the death of the 'beloved father.' It turned out that this was not so any more than the fetishist fails to take cognizance of the fact that women are 'castrated.' 'It was only one current in their mental life that had not recognized their father's death; there was another current which took full account of that fact. The attitude which fitted in with the wish and the attitude which fitted in with reality existed side by side.' This idea of the coexistence of two currents of thought avowing different and contradictory things and aims – one geared to 'wishes' (*wunschgerechte*) and the other doing justice to 'reality' (*realitätsgerechte*) – becomes increasingly common in later nineteenth-century thought and may be found, for example, in late Dickens, or William James. (*Dr. Jekyll and Mr. Hyde* is a well-known popular version of this particular condition). The importance of Freud's formulation lies in the identification of a possible 'splitting of the ego' involved in this process of acknowledgment/disavowal. 'In very subtle instances both the disavowal and the affirmation of the castration have found their way into the construction of the fetish itself . . . Affection and hostility in the treatment of the fetish – which run parallel with the disavowal and the acknowledgment of castration – are mixed in unequal proportions in different cases, so that the one or the other is more clearly recognizable.' This uneasy combination of both acknowledgment (*der Anerkennung*) and affirmation (*die Behauptung*) with disavowal and denial (*die Verleugnung*) – whether or not we want to accept that it always ultimately involves the question of the female penis/castration – produces a fetishistic attitude to reality in general in which there is a constant attempt to substitute belief for knowledge. This may take many forms, including the substitution of a damascened rifle safely fastened on the wall – for Emma Bovary – sexual, dangerous, and mobile. 'In later life, the fetishist feels that he enjoys yet another advantage from his substitute for a genital. The meaning of the fetish is not known to other people, so the fetish is not withheld from him: it is easily accessible and he can readily obtain the sexual satisfaction attached to it. What other men have to woo and make exertions for can be had by the fetishist with no trouble at all.' Freud uses the word for traditional courtship, *werben* ('to woo'), and we may note how very little genuine wooing of that kind there is in Madame Bovary. Indeed is there any at all? Clothes and costumes woo each other more than people, another perverse displacement of the kind I have mentioned. And how much real 'exertion' (*sich mühen* suggests travail, effort, and strain) is there in Flaubert's somnolent and idle world? Thus Charles Bovary's 'wooing' of Emma is almost completely inarticulate. They are reported as having a conversation in which they each recall various childhood memories, but their most significant contacts as adults are restricted to a drink and a chance physical contact of chest and back while Emma is bending down to pick up Charles's whip, which, in a gesture that needs no further comment, she hands over to him. The actual proposal is avoided by Charles, and it is Emma's father who has to conduct whatever exchanges with Emma are necessary. The courtship in fact is reduced to an arbitrary sign that the father arranges and Charles can translate – i.e., instead of the man pleading his cause to the woman and winning her with his presence, his gestures, his words, we have Charles timidly waiting for forty-nine minutes outside the house while the father talks to the daughter, until the window shutter is pushed open and flat against the wall (the sexual implications of this sign are crudely and degradingly obvious) – 'the shutter had been folded back, the hook was still rattling' ('l'auvent s'était rabattu, la cliquette tremblait encore' [pt. 1, Ch. 3]. The difficult and delicate persuasions traditionally involved in the language of love have been replaced by *l'auvent*; and the 'work' of the suitor is conducted in summary form by the father: two more deteriorative displacements that fall within the 'fetishised' atmosphere of the world of the book. It is indeed a society of fetishists.[2]

Elisabeth Bronfen, Over Her Dead Body: *Madame Bovary* (1992)

My discussion of Flaubert's *Madame Bovary* will focus on the relation between imagination, its materialization in writing, and death, for here a woman's authorship is shown as the act of voluntary fading before the text she writes, and serves self-reflexively to comment on the function and status of novel reading and writing in general. As Emma writes herself out of existence to become the romantic heroines she has been so possessed by in her reading, she does so almost exclusively in the order of the body, supplemented by very few pieces of writing in the order of the text.[1] Her self-textualisation engenders a form of self-obliteration while at the same time suicide generates texts and constructs the dead self as author.

Flaubert presents his heroine's life as that of a lengthy process of dying, which begins with her entrance into the imaginary world of romantic and religious fiction.[2] Reading is shown to be the source of a figural suicide, because it places the reader into the liminality between living reality and the dead figures of the imaginary; because it consumes the life of the reader, who reads instead of living, and whose living is killed by these books. Reading is also a form of suicide in the sense that it offers images of plenitude and unbroken identification, a repetition of the jubilation the child experiences in relation to the phallic mother, but which life disillusions. Reading initiates a process of desire that points to a lack in the reality of social existence, to the split from wholeness inherent to this existence, and to the presence of death's ubiquitous 'castrative' threat to life. The conjunction of death with the image resides in the fact not only that death is the radical opposite of the stability and wholeness an image evokes but that the image itself produces an ambiguous division in its spectator and is itself also the location of death. The texts Emma uses to construct herself and her world mark the double presence of death. They serve as the 'inanimate' words and images outside of which reality remains inconceivable, the inanimate shield on the basis of which reality is constructed. Yet they are also clichés, commonplace conventions, a 'corpse of a metaphor', killed through overuse.[3] . . .

In Emma's case, marriage as an experience of wounded narcissism and the ensuing desire for romantic fulfilment in adultery only supplements the much earlier loss of the imaginary sense of wholeness produced through fiction . . . A longing for death comes to assuage the gap between . . . ideal self-image and . . . existence in social reality, a courtship with death serving as substitution for an inadequate lover or death as the first realisation of love . . . Death emerges as that entity only imperfectly veiled by beauty and love, as that which was in fact always the aim and object displaced in the search for the beauty and love transmitted by the imagination.

Emma, who slips and changes, and has difficulty locating herself in one name and one role, can be diagnosed as a hysteric, owing to her histrionic simulation and her *belle indifférence* for each one of her roles. Her narrative exemplifies . . . the proximity between writing with the body and hysteria. In Emma's story the issue is once more the notion that a fatal perfection occurs when a copy resembles the model to such an extent that the space between the two has been obliterated. Flaubert, however, gives his narrative two crucial alterations, so as to set himself up as an iconoclastic commentator on the convention I have been tracing. Firstly, in his narrative the model is the corpus of novels Emma reads while the copy is her body-corpse . . . Not only does Emma partake of a confusion between the figural and the literal, not only is her hysteria such that she can't distinguish between the reality of the body and a fictionality of the sign. She subverts the conventional relation between the two, making the body a supplement to the sign. The notion that an imaginary wholeness is always constructed in response to a cut induced by the presence of language and of death is repeated in her autobiographical suicide. For in this act the imaginary wholeness constructed with her body against the double wound of language and death collapses with these two when she conjoins death and textuality at her deanimated body. Secondly, though his heroine's detextualisation seeks to fulfil a self-disintegration as re-integration of the self into narratives she has read, Flaubert depicts the failure of this process, as death emerges not only as the fulfilment but also as the destruction of the beauty and integrity of the image.

From the very beginning Emma's imagination connects unfulfilled romantic desires with death. She is dissatisfied early on in her marriage, because it does not fulfil expectations and desires raised by literature, does not seem to materialise 'the words of *felicity*, *of passion* and *drunkenness*, which had appeared to be so beautiful in the books she read' (pt. 1, ch. 5). The token of this marriage lets thoughts about death arise. As she sees the marriage bouquet of Charles's first, now dead, wife, she thinks of her own bouquet 'and asked herself, dreaming, what they would do with it, if by chance she were to die' (pt. 1, ch. 5).[4]

At stake is less an identification with the dead first wife than a fascination for the dead heroines in the novels she read while she was being educated at a convent, and this fascination for beautiful images of death serves as a way to eclipse the reality of death, to cap its unremitting wound. This is shown in her response to her mother's death, which is one of aesthetisation, the first instance of her self-authorship against death and under its auspices. She has a sombre painting made of the hair of the deceased, writes a letter to her father in which she designs her own death in the same tomb as her mother's. She finds narcissistic satisfaction in imagining for herself 'that rare ideal of pale creatures . . . she let herself glide along Lamartinien meanders . . . pure virgins who ascended to heaven' (pt. 1, ch. 6). Her hysteria is characterised by volatility ('ungraspable illness, which changed its manner like clouds') and lets her endlessly seek new roles to express her dissatisfaction with life. Yet the death of the mother serves as a quintessential cornerstone in a dialectic of death and imagination which Emma will endlessly repeat. It provokes satisfying images that triumph over her absence, yet the paradigm Emma chooses for her texts is one connected with absence.

In Emma's imaginary register there is a rivalry between nature (or domestic love) and art. On the one hand she places the 'bad' natural dyad of marriage with her husband Charles, which leads to states of death-like boredom and melancholy and functions as the Other whose existence can cancel her own, while on the other she places the 'good' artifical dyad with the objects of her fantasy, interchangeably money and material objects of luxury, lovers as romances she lives, romances she reads and images of the self. All of these are metonymies for the Otherness she lacks and as such aspects of the Other that reassure and reinforce her identity. She constructs the image of the other man long before any concrete lover enters her life and preserves it beyond each lover's exit. Only when she can no longer hold on to these good images of the other (whether of romance or of luxury), when she can not sustain her hysterical *belle indifférence*, does real death, kept at bay though always also the source of the imaginary images, break into her existence.

Yet her ambivalent gesture of desiring fiction as a simultaneous disavowal and acknowledgment of death surfaces in the semantic encoding of her self-image. In the first of several mirror scenes it becomes clear that reading, writing and death merge as the three faces which an escape from her limitations can assume: 'She bought herself a blotter, stationary, a penholder and envelopes, although she had no one to write to; she looked at herself in the mirror, taking a book, then, dreaming between the lines, she let the book fall to her knees. She wanted to voyage or to return to the convent. In one and the same moment she wanted to die and to live in Paris' (pt. 1, ch. 9). The purchase of writing implements is meant to satisfy the lack her desire expresses, yet to do so in a self-reflexive way, since she has no addressee. The message remains within a closed circuit. Equally self-reflexive is her reading activity, since it returns her to herself – she watches her self in the mirror, she reads herself 'between the lines,' foreclosing the book's alterity. Finally two of the sites she desires are connected with mortality, the liminality of the convent, the site of her first seduction by literature and death itself. In the same manner, imaging catastrophes and dangers that would let her first imagined lover suspect her desire for him while at the same time celebrating her position of loss, Emma tells herself with pride and joy, '"I am virtuous," and she looked at herself in the mirror, assuming poses of resignation' (pt. 2, ch. 5). Staging her wound becomes part of the self-construction.

The crucial mirror scene occurs after her first embrace with Rudolfe: 'noticing herself in the mirror, she was astounded to see her face . . . She would enter into a marvellous state where all would be passion, ecstasy, delirium . . . she remembered the heroines in novels . . . these adulterous women . . . she would herself become like a veritable part of these imaginations and realise the long dream of her youth, by conceiving herself as that type of lover which she had so strongly desired . . . now she triumphed' (pt. 2, ch. 9). For the first time she can successfully merge her bodily sensations with the desires aroused by her imagination as she finds in her illicit love the passion so long expected. Her triumph consists in two gestures. She experiences with her body the passion she has up to that point known only imaginatively, as she realises her youthful imaginations at her body. She embodies the texts she has read, becomes a sister to the adulterous heroines, by textualising her body into 'a veritable part of these imaginations'. She finds a sense of wholeness in Rudolphe because he fills her romantic lack, but also because he allows her to construct herself as part of the texts she has read, filling a lack in her desire to write herself into these texts.

The important omission in this mirror-reverie is that the fate of her sister adulteresses is usually death, and it is this occulted event that she will need to write with her body to perfect her triumph and be like them completely. Death is implicitly present in this self-reflection on two scores. Emma identifies herself with fictional heroines whose adulterous love, in the cultural conventions they support, is inextricably connected with suicide or execution. At the same time she identifies herself with inanimate figures or dead letters in texts, metaphorically killing herself into an inanimate art work. Again the duplicity of the mirror as device supports Emma's ambivalent position between integration and disintegration. For even as the mirror allows Emma to triumph over the experience of lack by eternalising and unifying her image as one with other, textual images, this is a form of seeing oneself that confirms the split between self and unified image of self, that shows wholeness as being a misrecognition.

Two forms of death are invoked in the imaginary gaze into the mirror – a good dying, which supports Emma's narcissistic illusion of entering into a self-stability by virtue of writing herself into a text, and a bad dying, where the non-semiotic real of death disrupts the self-affirming images of a beautiful death. That the good death is inextricably connected with writing shows itself by virtue of the fact that Emma begins to write the letters she had up to that point only intended. Rudolphe embodies her privileged addressee, even though on some level the closed circuit of her epistolary activity is kept upright, since his status is that of imaginary other.

Emma's psychic changes are registered in her somatic changes, so that she not only collides her body with deanimated textual feminine bodies but writes with her body so it can be read as a text of her emotions. Three times a psychic wound to her imaginary wholeness occurs after the loss of a lover, and each episode induces in her the wish to write this woundedness in the order of her body. After the first loss of Léon she poses as an old maid with facial folds that signify 'disappointed ambitions', she grows 'completely pale, white like linen'; she stares 'in a vague manner', speaks of 'her old age', and has a spasm of spitting blood (pt. 2, ch. 7). She materialises with her body the last of the four sites of escape she had imagined before her mirror – the escape 'or die'.

Far more elaborate is her body's staging of the wound to her imaginary wholeness after the loss of Rudolphe. In this second instance an important dimension is added to her displaced courtship of death, namely the question of reciprocity between Emma and her lover. For both Rudolphe and Emma the other as object of desire has been killed before a consummation of their passion ever occurs. In Emma's case Rudolphe is one of a series of metonymies in the chain of desired objects meant to fill the lack she experiences, along with the waltzing vicomte at whose ball her vainglory had found its first realisation, as well as with Léon. In the same manner that she loses her particularity before the other adulteresses of fiction, merging with them, Rudolphe is also deanimated into a cipher for that Otherness which will complete her. In Rudolphe's case, his fascination for Emma was from the start coupled with a disposal of her, 'but how to get rid of her after the affair' (pt. 2, ch. 7). Flaubert highlights the reciprocity in their gestures, so as to emphasize that because these objects of love were always also imaginary, their relationship was always grounded on deanimation.

When Rudolphe decides to abandon Emma after she has proposed a mutual flight, she becomes for him a sign of death, a phantom, fading into the shadows and then a dead letter, no longer of any real practical consequence; the story of a beautiful romance, 'she had been a pretty mistress . . . and soon Emma's beauty reappeared in his mind' (pt. 2, ch. 12). While he can not endure her constant presence, a designation of her absence, 'she had been' allows him to re-invoke her in her beauty, as one re-invokes a dead person. This gesture implies both that she is now a dead person for him, an object of memory, and that her fascination in part resided in her imaginary, non-real quality – he recalls her beauty as that of an absent body.

The conjunction of imagination and deanimation which Emma stages with her image before the mirror is analogous to Rudolphe's form of disposing of her. He merges first her body with her image and then Emma as an image with the images of other past lovers until in this process of integration all distinctions are effaced: 'he had close by . . . the miniature given by Emma and in an effort to study this image and evoke a memory of the model, Emma's traits became confused in his memory, as though the living face and the painted face rubbed one against the other; and fusing, reciprocally effaced each other' (pt. 2, ch. 13). Rummaging in the box containing her other letters he finds strands of the hair of other lovers, their letters – dead body parts that converge into the monster of his romantic memory: 'In fact, these women, all rushing into his thoughts at the same time, disturbed each other, reduced each other in size, as though the same level of love made them all equal.' To demonstrate the levelling of individual identity, and the killing into sameness his memory undertakes, he merges all the letters into one pile, before he writes Emma his farewell. This series of lovers correlates with Emma's serialisation of adulteresses and of her own lovers, though here again the question of who is the agent of semantic encoding is crucial. While Emma fades out of existence in Rudolphe's series of letters, she intends to fade into existence when she perfectly enters her series of adulteresses and dead heroines through her literal death. Though it is the repetition of earlier texts, her deanimation is the way she intends to leave a distinctive mark.

Yet before she chooses death directly, Emma reciprocates Rudolphe's killing in a lengthy detextualising procedure that emphasises precisely the sheer materiality of the body and its presence, even as its message is the threat of bodily disintegration. Flaubert disrupts the possibility of a conventional beautiful suicide by defenestration to let his heroine descend not to death but rather to the domestic banality of soup already served. Emma, responding to Rudolphe's wounding rejection in the form of a brain fever, becomes the dead letter to which he has reduced her, by living a despondency in which no tension exists, 'as though her body and her soul had come together, taking leave of all their agitations' (pt. 2, ch. 13). This staging of death as stasis is followed by another version of death, the deathbed ecstasy. As she awaits her last sacrament she experiences a self-annihilation before the love of God, the 'splendid vision' of seraphic harps, azure sky, God the father on a golden throne amidst saints holding green palms and angels with flaming wings descending to fetch her. This vision is a copy of the texts she has read in the convent as well as an alteration of her privileged image of adulteress, exchanging the social transgression of illicit love for the etherealisation of the earthly body as it transcends into an ecstatic enjoyment of divinity.

In the final part of the novel, Emma's writing activity continues to be directed at the three paradigms of desired objects – romance, luxury and self-textualisation – while the connection to death is made ever more explicit. Having refound in her adulterous relation with Léon all the 'platitudes of marriage', Emma nevertheless holds on to the idea that a woman must always write to her lover. Yet her writing becomes a way of dematerialising her lover, turning the addressee and object of her desire once again into a dead letter, a figure of her imagination: 'as she wrote, she perceived another man, a phantom made up of her most ardent memories, of her most beautiful reading experiences . . . and in the end he seemed to become true and accessible' (pt. 3, ch. 6). Existing as long as she is able to imagine him, this phantom lover becomes the proof of the textual superseding bodily existence. Once again the self-reflexivity, as obliteration of the referential validity and emphasis on sheer textuality is shown in conjunction with death. To avoid the gap reopening once again, Emma resorts to a form of writing that obliterates her addresses, returns to the semiotic situation of a closed circuit. While her last romance ends in a superfluity of texts without a recipient or a reference point in reality, her desire for luxury commodities results in another form of textual production, a surplus of bills of debt, carrying her signature. Here too, the response, in this case by her creditors, is to read materiality as dematerialised signs. As they examine her possessions, her clothes, her linens, 'her existence, down to the innermost intimate recess was like a corpse at an autopsy, spread out before the gaze of these three men' (pt. 3, ch. 7).

With her object of romantic desire and addressee of her epistolary activity a phantom, her possessions the dead body parts of a corpse-existence, Emma can have recourse only to her body as the last tie at which to preserve the wholeness she has longed to construct. Yet this means writing herself out of existence, turning herself into a phantom as well. Though Flaubert leaves the exact reason for Emma's suicide unspecified, one could speculate that Rudolphe's refusal to lend her money is the final shattering of her narcissistically informed self-fashioning, leaving not a wound but a real and irrevocable abyss. All reminiscences, all assuring images diminish, leaving her with the feeling that her existence is disappearing from her. As she displaces the nominal reason for her distress, money, on to the more ambivalent term, 'she suffered only from love' (pt. 3, ch. 8), Rudolphe's refusal forces her to face the lack she has tried to cover with the various versions of her imaginary fictions. Her debt is the last of many signs for the failure of her ambitions, and Rudolphe's refusal to support the fiction of their romance enables death to emerge as that which she has ambivalently tried to conceal and to court with her multifarious shades of self-fashioning by dint of romance or luxury. Death was the signifier displaced by her series of fictions, yet once these images of desire fail, she is forced to recognise that the effacement or patching of an originary gap was always based on the illusion of misrecognition, so that the signifier or image of death translates into a real state.

Admittedly ambivalence remains till the end, since Emma preserves an image of death even as she enters death as the shattering of her imaginary register. Death is both the fulfilment of her desire to transform her life, modelled on literary principles into a text; a last effort to live romance by dying a romantic death. It is the radical disruption of the imaginary, effecting the recognition that all romances are illusory. Her final death scene is significantly doubled, recalling medieval tombstone sculpture, where the intact body of the deceased, the *gisant*, is doubled with a figuration of the decayed body, the *transi*.[5] The first death performs the beautiful, good death induced by romantic fiction. It comes as a painless death that allows her to write one last letter for posthumous reading (the complete fulfilment of writing as death staged earlier before her mirror) and glide out of life. She thinks, 'Oh, it is very little, death . . . I will fall asleep, and all will be finished!' (pt. 3, ch. 8).

Along the lines of Benjamin's definition of the death of the maternal force giving birth to the author as the first progeny of his (or her) text, the death of Emma's mother initiated a trajectory that culminates in a suicidal autobiography. This body-text is informed by a wish to completely possess oneself by becoming author of one's existence as dead body/letter, which will generate commemorative texts and render the body analogous to heroines in texts. Emma intends her self to emerge after death as a work of art, an image of the romantic notion of a *belle morte*, and presenting a hermeneutic task to her survivors, so that her corpse poses as part of and repetition of the romantic corpus.

Yet the second ugly phase of her death subverts this first beautiful image. Equally functioning as representation (because always implying the spectatorship of her husband and friends), what it signifies is the realistic detail of the dying process. It is a horrible spectacle of pain, agony and physical decomposition. Though both phases are representations, their contradictory conjunction implies that the reality of death recedes from both depictions. Ironically Emma's death, as the moment that radically shatters all images and puts the assurance which images lend to the narcissistically informed process of self-fashioning into question, engenders only another phase of images on the part of her survivors, who use her dying and her dead body as an image of re-stabilisation. Homais brings his two sons to her deathbed so that her dying can serve as 'a lesson, an example, a solemn picture which will remain in their mind' (pt. 3, ch. 8).

In her dying moments Emma returns to aspects of the death imaginarily staged before. She experiences again the visions of external beatitude, the voluptuousness of her first mystic thrust. With an expression of serenity she seems to awake as from a dream and desires, as last object of her gaze, a mirror, 'and she remained leaning over it for some time, until the moment when large tears rolled from her eyes' (pt. 3, ch. 8). Though Flaubert denies his readers a semantic encoding of this last pose, Emma dies confirming the control over her self, in the detour of her reflected image.

After her death she becomes an object of sight for her survivors, and though this hovers between the romantic image of the beautiful corpse, serene and intact, as if in slumber, and the realistic image of the ugly corpse, with black liquid coming out of its nose and putrefaction beneath its veil, the crucial point is that Emma's suicide spurs on her husband's imagination, so that, over her dead body, she passes on to him the dialectic of imagination as response to and resulting in death. He adopts her predilections, her ideas, preserves her room, designs an elaborate grave. While the living Emma found no sympathetic response to her fancies in her husband, the dead Emma corrupts his imagination 'from beyond the tomb'. Once again the insecurity of the image is stressed, for the more Charles seeks to retain Emma's image, the more it escapes his memory, and the beauty of the absent woman he preserves by dint of commemorative objects is counteracted by his nightmare vision, where as he approaches Emma 'she decomposes in his arms' (pt. 3. ch. 11).

Charles repeats her desire to transform herself into a text, though in his case it is the text his wife has written with her body, until he too dies, holding a braid of her black hair in his hand. The equation between Emma's suicide and her writing falls into two parts. It is a moment of supreme authorship because it offers her her first authentic reader in Charles, who empathises with and imitates her text to perfection, while her love letters never produced a real response. Her corpse is the result of a series of previously read texts, subverting the opposition between model and copy, authenticity and secondary appropriation. The corpse is shown both as a unified body, assuring the stability of the author's self-conception, and as an image of decay, and both representations have the function of reassuring her surviving spectators in their process of self-construction. As an uncanny movement, death hovers between stability and castration, thematically and, on the level of language itself, articulating a disruption of the process of imaging, a falling out of an economy of representation, even as it returns to confirm it.

The paradox that repeatedly emerges in all these representations of feminine death is the visibility and presence of the dead body. Though representation is used to repress or deny both femininity and death, it does so by virtue of fetishism – by acknowledging precisely those values to be negated – so that the veiling of death comes also to be its articulation. If one considers Freud's definition of the symptom as failed repression, the ubiquity of images of death in the nineteenth century as cultural symptom indicates that death was neither successfully repressed nor worked through.

Woman, constructed by culture as man's symptom, marks the site where repressed material resurfaces, materialises, returns. The feminine body is used to figure death as the repressed *par excellence* and the displacement of death on to the feminine allows a mitigated articulation of that value otherwise threatening to the stability of the system. Because it is bound to a signifier encoded as radically Other, non-masculine, the material inadequately repressed finds a conscious articulation, but in a way that allows it to be exteriorised, and in the form of a representation as symptom, the subject community compulsively repeats what it tries to repress in the displacement on to another. This strategy is a way of removing any immediate threat but does so by constructing a permanent memorial to precisely the threat it wishes to occlude. Like a symptom, these representations deny death in the sense of suspending it – an arrestation of/by death. By finding a signifier for that which threatens, they can provisionally discharge it, yet the partiality of a repression that articulates denial and acknowledgement suggests that any representational symptom effecting the closure of a disruption, as it is posed by death, is less stable than meets the eye.

8

WILKIE COLLINS, *THE WOMAN IN WHITE*

Jenny Bourne Taylor's essay argues that the rise of the sensation novel coincided with anxieties about the effects of certain kinds of literature on a rapidly growing readership and about the disintegration of class boundaries within that readership. In this respect she provides a social and moral context for thinking about generic conventions and cultural codes in the 1850s. The essay is particularly interesting on the evolution of narrative forms in that decade and raises pertinent questions about the extent to which the sensation novel is a modern adaptation of earlier Gothic and romance forms or a degenerated subspecies of them. The crucial insight that emerges here is that the supernaturalism of such fiction is not necessarily incompatible with or distantly removed from contemporary scientific knowledge. Arguing that 'terror' in the sensation novel grows out of realistic psychological and physiological devices, Taylor proposes that the sensation novel might be regarded as 'naturalistic fantasy'.

D.A. Miller explores the social significance of nervousness and claims that the experience of reading *The Woman in White* might be said to induce a nervous condition. The meanings we find in the novel are intricately bound up with the ways in which it operates on our nerves. Miller goes on to claim that nervousness in the nineteenth century was regarded as an essentially feminine malady, and that every reader of the novel, to some extent becomes an extension or a version of 'The Woman in White'. The text, however, seems to assume a male reader. The readerly sensation that the novel affords invites reflections on male homosexuality, on what mid-Victorian readers might have considered as 'the woman in the man'. As well as harbouring fantasies about male homosexuality, however, the text also raises disturbing questions about 'enclosing and secluding the woman in male "bodies", among them institutions like marriage and madhouses'.

Elisabeth Bronfen, in a second extract from *Over Her Dead Body*, looks at the strange ambiguities and indeterminacies at work in *The Woman in White*. The novel presents us with a woman bearing a secret; this woman both fascinates and terrifies her onlookers; she is both angelic (from beyond) and demonic (from below); and her whiteness is reminiscent of both the bridal gown and the shroud. Collins's tale of sensation and mystery is propelled by secrets, but the narrative itself remains undecided, even after the various plots and conspiracies have been resolved. One question that lingers is whether death is eroticised as a way of displacing anxiety and fear, or as a way of concealing some forbidden desire for annihilation.

Jenny Bourne Taylor, Collins as a Sensation Novelist (1988)

The panic generated by the sensation novel as much as the mode itself provided a focus for a range of distinct, though interrelated, tensions about wider and longer-term transformations that were taking place in middle-range middle-class publishing and literary culture. As with responses to the Minerva Press, the establishment and expansion of the circulating libraries, and the rise of Gothic romance in the eighteenth century, worries about the effects on the public's nervous systems, particularly those of 'vulnerable' women readers, were connected with anxieties that class-based cultural boundaries were breaking down with the expansion of new methods of production and circulation: 'She may boast without fear of contradiction, of having temporally succeeded in making the literature of the kitchen the favourite reading of the Drawing Room', the *North British Review* remarked of Mary Braddon.[1] But this anxiety was now specifically connected with worries about the longer-term *evolution* of generic conventions and cultural forms, and here the most important question was whether the sensation novel represented a modern adaptation of earlier Gothic or romance forms or a degenerated sub-species of them – and thus a morbid deviation from a dominant mode. 'Sensation' was now posed against 'sensibility', retrospectively elevating the latter; unlike the quivering reaction generated by the very fantastic and exotic intensity of Gothic romance in which the finely tuned nerves operated as delicate moral mediators, the immediate nervous reaction elicited by sensation fiction apparently short-circuited morality, and thus became morbid by becoming more directly sensualized. 'The faults of the French school are creeping into our literature and threaten to flourish there', maintained *Fraser's Magazine*. 'The morbid analysation of feeling, which we have already reprobated, bids fair to be succeeded by an equally morbid analysation of mere sensation.'[2] 'The progress of fiction as an art', the *Westminster Review*'s article on the evolution of narrative forms, had begun to discuss this process in 1853, arguing firstly that fictional forms became more complex as they came to correspond more closely with the conceptual and scientific models of their culture; secondly, that cultural progress itself was marked by an increasingly hierarchic division between 'higher' and 'lower' forms – divisions that were thus its inevitable concomitant. In this analysis there was a class of novel (represented here by Collins's *Basil*) which occupied an uneasy liminal, or threshold, realm as a form of naturalistic fantasy. This new type was based in recognizable everyday reality rather than the purely marvellous setting of romance proper; it drew on subjective sense experience in a way that correspond with contemporary scientific models, but as it attempted to achieve the intensity of supernatural terror by these means, the stress on subjectivity now meant that the real itself was pathologized. 'It was the fashion then to construct a story out of strange and unnatural *circumstances*, it is the fashion now to elaborate it out of morbid *feelings* and overwrought *sensibilities*.'[3]

Yet this shift towards a materialist supernaturalism, in which 'terror' grew out of realistic psychological and physiological devices and processes used to achieve 'Gothic' effects, was not new either. Actually it had taken place many years before, and in both *Basil* and his early short stories Collins was accentuating a shift in fictional conventions that had begun at the end of the eighteenth century and was developed in the work of Godwin, of Mary Shelley, of Hogg, of the writers of the 'Tales' whose tensions were based primarily in physiological sensation published in *Blackwood's Edinburgh Magazine* and above all in Edgar Allan Poe's intricate, obsessive exploration of the interconnections between physiological and psychological states.[4] George Eliot had approvingly noted the influence of Poe in her review of the collection of stories *After Dark* in the *Westminster Review* in 1856:

> The great interest lies in the excitement either of curiosity or of terror . . . Instead of turning pale at a ghost we knit our brows and construct hypotheses to account for it. Edgar Poe's tales were an effort of genius to reconcile the two tendencies – to appal the imagination yet satisfy the intellect, and Mr Wilkie Collins in this respect often follows in Poe's tracks.[5]

And while the fictional assimilation of 'sensationist' psychological references only culminated fully with the sensation novel of the 1860s, it contributed to the mode's morbid cultural status primarily in becoming a link in a new chain of cultural and psychological associations, creating meanings which were linked in turn with the other characteristics of the form – above all, though not exclusively, its fascination with various forms of transgressive sexuality. Sensation fiction certainly shared a common pool of narrative tropes, but these were not stable; they drew on and broke down distinct methods of generating strangeness within familiarity, of creating the sense of a weird and different world within the ordinary, everyday one: the tale of terror, high melodrama, the 'Newgate' novel, the domestic story. And it was through these intricate interactions that its appeal to sensation, to 'nerves', had both such psychological resonance and social complexity, providing it with the means that enabled it to explore 'those most mysterious of mysteries, the mysteries that are at our own doors' by bringing into play the possibilities offered by its central narrative features – *secrecy* and *disguise*.

These features were brought into play above all by narrative intricacy, by the plotting itself, the vital characteristic by which sensation fiction was at once distinguished and condemned. The *Spectator* identified 'a host of cleverly complicated stories, the whole interest of which consists in the gradual unraveling of some carefully prepared enigma'.[6] That enigma often involved the disclosure of transgression or villainy – the tearing off of a mask, the lifting of a veil. But what was particularly exciting was that the pleasurable process of unravelling itself involved revealing a secret identity which in turn disclosed not a truth, but another set of questions and dissemblances which hinged on the transgressor's position within the family. In Mary Braddon's *Lady Audley's Secret*, Lady Audley's ostensible secret – that she is a bigamist – both conceals and reveals a further one – that she is mad. As with melodrama, tension hinges on things not being what they seem, but here identity is not simply dissembled through a masquerade. People assume false selves in order to steal a position and a property or to retrieve a place that they had lost: the fallen, outcast heroine of Mrs Henry Wood's *East Lynne*, her face rendered unrecognizable by a railway accident, steals back to her lost home, disguised as the governess to her own children, playing a role that is essentially a lower pitch of her earlier one. In sensation fiction masks are rarely stripped off to reveal an inner truth, for the mask is both the transformed expression of the 'true' self and the means of disclosing its incoherence. In the process identity itself emerges as a set of elements that are actively constructed within a dominant framework of social interests, perceptions, and values. These novels thus focused on the ambiguity of social and psychological codes to insinuate that seeming, too, is not always what it seems to be.

D.A. Miller, *Cage aux Folles*: Sensation and Gender in Wilkie Collins's *The Woman in White* (1986)

To be sure, the silence that falls over the question of sensation seems first enjoined by the sensation novel itself, which is obsessed with the project of finding meaning – of staging the suspense of its appearance – in everything except the sensations that the project excites in us. Yet in principle the sensation novel must always at least imply a reading of these sensations, for the simple reason that it can mobilize the sympathetic nervous system only by giving it something to sympathize with. In order to make us nervous, nervousness must first be represented: in situations of character and plot which, both in themselves and in the larger cultural allusions they carry, make the operation of our own nerves significant in particular ways. The fiction elaborates a fantasmatics of sensation in which our reading bodies take their place from the start, and of which our physiological responses thus become the hysterical acting out. To speak of hysteria here, of course, is also to recall the assumption that always camouflages it – that what the body suffers, the mind needn't think. 'So far as my own sensations were concerned, I can hardly say that I thought at all.' The efficacy of psychosomatisms as 'defences' presupposes a rigorously enforced separation in the subject between *psyche* and *soma*, and hysteria successfully breaches the body's autonomy only on the condition that this autonomy will be felt to remain intact. Reading the sensation novel, our hystericized bodies 'naturalize' the meanings in which the narrative implicates them, but in doing so, they also nullify these meanings as such. Incarnate in the body, the latter no longer seem part of a cultural, historical process of signification, but instead dissolve into an inarticulable, merely palpable self-evidence. Thus, if every sensation novel necessarily provides an interpretation of the sensations to which it gives rise in its readers, the immediacy of these sensations can always be counted on to *disown* such an interpretation. It may even be that the non-recognition that thus obtains between our sensations and their narrative thematization allows the sensation novel to 'say' certain things for which our culture – at least at its popular levels – has yet to develop another language.

Wilkie Collins's *The Woman in White* (1860) – of all sensation novels the best-known and considered the best – seems at any rate an exemplary text for making this case. For what 'happens' in this novel becomes fully clear and coherent only, I think, when one takes into account the novel's implicit reading of its own (still quite 'effective') performative dimension and thus restores sensation to its textual and cultural mediations. For the reason given above, the attempt to do so must be prepared to seem rather 'forced' – as unprovable as a connotation and as improbable as a latency – but it is worth undertaking for more than a better understanding of this particular text. The ideological valences with which sensation characteristically combines in the novel do not of course absolutely transcend the second half of the Victorian period in which they are elaborated – as though the social significance of nervousness (itself an historical construct) were fixed once and for all; but neither are they restricted to this period. Collins's novel continues to be not just thoroughly readable, but eminently 'writable' as well. If it is still capable of moving readers to the edge of their seats (and how sharp a sense of this edge may be is suggested when one character starts from his own seat 'as if a spike had grown up from the ground through the bottom of [his] chair', 13)[1], this is because its particular staging of nervousness remains cognate with that of many of our own thrillers, printed or filmed. It thus offers a pertinent, if not exhaustive, demonstration of the value, meaning, and use that modern culture – which in this respect has by no means broken radically with Victorian culture – finds in the nervous state.

Without exception, such a state affects all the novel's principal characters, who are variously startled, affrighted, unsettled, chilled, agitated, flurried. All sooner or later inhabit the 'sensationalized' body where the blood curdles, the heart beats violently, the breath comes short and thick, the flesh creeps, the cheeks lose their colour. No one knows what is the matter with Mr Fairlie, but 'we all say it's on the nerves' (34), and in widely different ways, his niece Laura is 'rather nervous and sensitive' (36). The 'nervous sensitiveness' (104) of her double and half-sister Anne Catherick, the 'woman in white', issues in the aneurism that causes her death. Characters who are not constitutionally nervous become circumstantially so, in the unnerving course of events. Unsettled by the mystery surrounding Anne, fearful that Laura may be implicated in it, suspecting that he is himself being watched, Walter Hartright develops a 'nervous contraction' about his lips and eyes (157), which he appears to have caught from Laura herself, whose 'sweet, sensitive lips are subject to a slight nervous contraction' (49). At first 'perfect self-possession' (190), Sir Percival Glyde degenerates after his marriage to Laura into 'an unsettled, excitable manner . . . a kind of panic or frenzy of mind' (405). And Marian Halcombe, Laura's other half-sister, has already lost the 'easy inborn confidence in herself and her position' (33) that initially characterized her by the time of the first anxious and 'sadly distrustful' extract (164) from her diary. In the course of keeping that diary, of gathering the increasingly less equivocal evidence of a 'plot' against Laura, she literally writes herself into a fever. It is a measure of Count Fosco's control over these characters that he is said to be 'born without nerves' (361), though his 'eternal cigarettes' (232) attest that even here nervousness is not so much missing as mastered, and mastered only in so far as its symptoms are masked in the banal practices of civilized society.

Nervousness seems the necessary 'condition' in the novel for perceiving its real plot and for participating in it as more than a pawn. The condition is not quite sufficient, as the case of the wilfully ignorant Mr Fairlie shows, but otherwise those without the capacity to become nervous also lack the capacity to interpret events, or even to see that events require interpreting. The servants, for instance, also called (more accurately) 'persons born without nerves' (43), are uniformly oblivious to what is or might be going on: the 'unutterably tranquil' governess Mrs Vesey (46), the maid who 'in a state of cheerful stupidity' grins at the sight of Mrs Catherick's wounded dog (208), the housekeeper Mrs Michelson, whose Christian piety prevents her from advancing 'opinions' (367). It is not exactly that the novel uses nervousness to mark middle-class status, since the trait fails to characterize the 'sanguine constitution' of Mr Gilmore, the family lawyer, who 'philosophically' walks off his 'uneasiness' about Laura's marriage (137). Rather the novel makes nervousness a metonymy for reading, its cause or effect. No reader can identify with unruffled characters like Gilmore or Mrs Michelson, even when they narrate parts of the story, because every reader is by definition committed to a hermeneutic project that neither of these characters finds necessary or desirable. Instead we identify with nerve-racked figures like Walter and Marian who carry forward the activity of our own deciphering. We identify even with Anne Catherick in her 'nervous dread' (111), though she is never capable of articulating its object, because that dread holds at least the promise of the story we will read. Nervousness is our justification in the novel, as Mrs Michelson's faith is hers, in so far as it validates the attempt to read, to uncover the grounds for *being* nervous.

The association of nervousness with reading is complicated – not to say troubled – by its coincident, no less insistent or regular association with femininity. However general a phenomenon, nervousness is always gendered in the novel as, like Laura's headache symptom, an 'essentially feminine malady' (33). Of the novel's three characters who seem 'born' nervous, two are women (Anne and Laura), and the third, Mr Fairlie, an effeminate. 'I am nothing', the latter pronounces himself, 'but a bundle of nerves dressed up to look like a man' (356). No one, however, is much convinced by the drag, and Walter's first impression – 'he had a frail, languid-fretful, over-refined look – something singularly and unpleasantly delicate in its association with a man' (39) – never stands in need of correction. Even in the less fey male characters, nervousness remains a signifier of femininity. At best it declares Walter still 'unformed', and Sir Percival's imposture – that he is not, so to speak, the man he is pretending to be – is already in a manner disclosed when Mrs Michelson observes that 'he seemed to be almost as nervous and fluttered . . . as his lady herself' (390). Fosco himself, Marian informs us, 'is as nervously sensitive as the weakest of us [women]. He starts at chance noises as inveterately as Laura herself' (222).

The novel's 'primal scene', which it obsessively repeats and remembers ('Anne Catherick again!') as though this were the trauma it needed to work through, rehearses the 'origins' of male nervousness in female contagion – strictly, in the woman's touch. When Anne Catherick, in flight from the asylum where she has been shut away, 'lightly and suddenly' lays her hand on Walter Hattright's shoulder, it brings 'every drop of blood in [his] body . . . to a stop' (20). Released from – and with – the Woman, nervousness touches and enters the Man: Anne's nervous gesture is at once sympathetically 'caught' in Walter's nervous response to it. Attempting to recover himself, Walter tightens his fingers round 'the handle of [his] stick,' as though the touch – 'from behind [him]' (20) – were a violation requiring violent counteraction, and what was violated were a gender-identification that needed to be reaffirmed. Yet Anne Catherick impinges on him again: 'the loneliness and helplessness of the woman touched me' (22). His formulation hopefully denies what is happening to him – Anne's weak femininity is supposed to evince *a contrario* his strong masculinity – but the denial seems only to produce further evidence of the gender slippage it means to arrest. Even in his classic gallantry, Walter somehow feels insufficiently manly, 'immature': 'The natural impulse to assist her and spare her got the better of the judgement, the caution, the worldly tact, which an older, wiser, and colder man might have summoned to help him in this strange emergency' (22). He is even 'distressed by an uneasy sense of having done wrong' (27), of having betrayed his sex: 'What had I done? Assisted the victim of the most horrible of all false imprisonments to escape; or cast loose on the wide world of London an unfortunate creature, whose actions it was my duty, and every man's duty, mercifully to control?' (29). Walter's protection has in fact suspended the control that is 'every man's duty' to exercise over the activity of the neuropathic woman. Thanks to his help, Anne eludes a manifold of male guardians: the turnpike man at the entry-gate of the city; the two men from the asylum including its director; the policeman who, significantly, is assumed to be at their disposal; and even Walter himself, who puts her into a cab, destination unknown. 'A dangerous woman to be at large' (156): the female trouble first transmitted to Walter will extend throughout the thick ramifications of plot to excite sympathetic vibrations in Laura and Marian, and in Sir Percival and even Fosco as well. And not just in them. 'The reader's nerves are affected like the hero's', writes Mrs Oliphant in a contemporary review of the novel; in what I have called the novel's primal scene, this means that 'the silent woman lays her hand upon our shoulder as well as upon that of Mr Walter Hartright'.[2] As the first of the novel's sensation effects *on us*, the scene thus fictionalizes the beginning of our physiological experience of the sensation novel as such. Our first sensation concides with – is positively triggered by – the novel's originary account of sensation. Fantasmatically, then, we 'catch' sensation from the neuropathic body of the woman who, no longer confined or controlled in an asylum, is free to make our bodies resonate with – like – hers.

Every reader is consequently implied to be a version or extension of the woman in white, a fact which entails particularly interesting consequences when the reader is – as the text explicitly assumes he is – male.[3] This reader willy-nilly falls victim to an hysteria in which what is acted out (desired, repressed) is an essentially female 'sensation'. His excitements come from – become – her nervous excitability; his ribcage, arithmetically Adam's, houses a woman's quickened respiration and his heart beats to her skittish rhythm;

even his pallor (which of course he cannot see) is mirrored back to him only as hers, the woman in white's. This reader thus lends himself to elaborating a fantasy of *anima muliebris in corpore virili inclusa* – or as we might appropriately translate here, 'a woman's breath caught in a man's body'. The usual translation, of course, is 'a woman's soul trapped . . . ', and it will be recognized as nineteenth-century sexology's classic formulation (coined by Karl Ulrichs in the 1860s) for male homosexuality.[4] I cite it, not just to anticipate the homosexual component given to readerly sensation by the novel, but also, letting the phrase resonate beyond Ulrichs's intentions, to situate this component among the others that determine its context. For if what essentially characterizes male homosexuality in this way of putting it is the woman-in-the-man, and if this 'woman' is *inclusa*, incarcerated or shut up, her freedoms abridged accordingly, then homosexuality would be by its very nature homophobic: imprisoned in a carceral problematic that does little more than channel into the homosexual's 'ontology' the social and legal sanctions that might otherwise be imposed on him. Meant to win a certain intermediate space for homosexuals, Ulrichs's formulation in fact ultimately colludes with the prison or closet drama – of keeping the 'woman' well put away – that it would relegate to the unenlightened past. And homosexuals' are not the only souls to be imprisoned in male bodies; Ulrichs's phrase does perhaps far better as a general description of the condition of nineteenth-century women, whose 'spirit' (whether understood as intellect, integrity, or sexuality) is massively interned in male corporations, constitutions, contexts. His metaphor thus may be seen to link or condense together (1) a particular fantasy about male homosexuality; (2) a homophobic defence against that fantasy; and (3) the male oppression of women that, among other things, extends that defence. All three meanings bear pointedly on Collins's novel, which is profoundly about enclosing and secluding the woman in male 'bodies', among them institutions like marriage and madhouses. And the sequestration of the woman takes for its object not just women, who need to be put away in safe places or asylums, but men as well, who must monitor and master what is fantasized as the 'woman inside' them.

Elisabeth Bronfen, Over Her Dead Body: *The Woman in White* (1992)

The exposition of *The Woman in White* presents a woman bearing a secret, socially dead because buried alive in an insane asylum to procure her silence, literally dying of a heart disease, as she escapes her confinement and returns to the world of the living. As Walter Hartright walks home along the lonely road to London at the 'dead of the night', about to embark for Cumberland to begin work as a drawing master for the daughters of Mr Fairlie, the 'touch of a hand laid lightly and suddenly' on his shoulder from behind petrifies him 'from head to foot' (20).[1] What he sees as he turns instantly, 'with my fingers tightening round the handle of my stick', is an apparition which 'seriously startled' him because of the suddenness of its appearance, 'as if it had sprung out of the earth or dropped from the heaven' and because of its extraordinary guise – 'a solitary Woman, dressed from head to foot in white garments'. Like Medusa, she fascinates and terrifies, because her femininity is not only doubly encoded but also resonates death. She is thought to emerge from the beyond (angel) or beneath (demon), while the whiteness of her clothes refers simultaneously to a bridal gown or a shroud. The touch of her hand laid with 'a sudden gentle stealthiness' elicits a sexual response. He notes it was a 'cold hand' when he 'removed it with mine', and excuses himself by claiming 'I was young . . . the hand which touched me was a woman's' (23). The woman's touch, however, also effects a death-like experience in the touched masculine body – 'in one moment every drop of blood in my body was brought to a stop'.[2]

The feminine figure appears at precisely the moment when Walter wonders 'what the Cumberland young ladies would look like.' Her uncanny touch initiates a first enigma, which in turn generates a plethora of secrets and detections that propel this tale of sensation and mystery but which itself remains undecided even after the diverse plots and conspiracies have been resolved. This nocturnal walk towards London with a woman 'whose name, whose character, whose story, whose objects in life, whose very presence by my side, at that moment, were fathomless mysteries to me', arouses a sensation in Walter which is so perturbing because strangely undefined. An erotic desire is displaced on to a curiosity to penetrate her social identity, 'to lift the veil that hung between this woman and me' (25). Yet the eroticised form of detective desire further displaces the fact that the initial sensation was one of death. What is left open is whether the plot of detection arising from this uncanny encounter is erotically encoded merely to displace the anxiety of death her touch produced or precisely to occlude a forbidden desire for the death this woman seemingly incarnates.

A second indeterminacy is maintained throughout Collins's text, namely the fact that along with Walter's motivation, the feminine object of his desire is not entirely clear. The entire narrative is constructed around the seeming coincidence that one of the Cumberland ladies, Laura Fairlie, looks like the mysterious woman in white, who withholds her identity, who preserves her secret – Anne Catherick. Even before Walter has seen the woman he will eventually marry and for whose sake he undertakes the dangerous and cumbersome task of detection, the other woman has inscribed herself in his imaginary register. She disturbs his drawing and his reading and is the object of his first conversation with Laura's companion Marion. Given the extraordinary physical and psychic similarity between Anne and Laura (who herself is 'rather nervous and sensitive' (36), the question Collins raises is whether Walter doesn't in fact love Anne in Laura. Within such a scenario, his wife serves as the repetition and displacement of the startling woman, and the domestic happiness repeatedly invoked as the context from which he writes veils the fact that his initial object of desire was the death-like Anne not the bride Laura. Walter desires Laura precisely because she recalls the other woman who, insane and dying, is an impossible choice, with his choice of Laura denying even as it affirms that what initiated desire in him was this impossible woman on the edge of death. That the ambivalent desire for Laura veils the desire for Anne as she represents the trauma of a death sensation finds implicit articulation in the first description Walter gives of Laura. He argues that the 'mystery which underlies the beauty of women', of which Laura's is the paragon, is such that it touches sympathies other than the charm the senses feel, that it is the 'visionary nurseling' of the viewer's 'fancy'. Yet his first sight of Laura is mingled with a sensation that 'troubled and perplexed' him, with the impression of 'something wanting'. Significantly the source of this lack is undetermined – 'At one time it seemed like something wanting in *her*: at another, like something wanting in myself.' Like Georgiana's birth-mark it articulates itself in a contradictory manner, a sense of incompleteness troubling the harmony and charm of her face, eluding his discovery (50).

Only when Marion reads the part of Mrs Fairlie's letter pertaining to the accidental resemblance between Anne and her daughter can Walter affix a signifier to the 'something wanting', namely that of 'ominous likeness'. More importantly, only when looking down at Laura from a window, while she, dressed in white, walks in the moonlight, when he sees her *as* 'the living image . . . of the woman in white' (the word living implying he fancied the original as a dead image), is Walter chilled again by a 'thrill of the same feeling which ran through me when the touch was laid upon my shoulder on the lonely high-road' (60). While Laura's type of beauty can claim kin with the 'deeper mystery in our souls' (50), in her function as Anne's double she induces those other charms which Walter feels with the senses.

Solving the uncanny relation of ominous likeness between these two women by cleanly severing the one from the other may as much involve a foreclosure of the necrophilic thrill of the senses that the one feminine figure of death evokes, as it involves the social restitution of the other. While Walter can allow himself to want woman as the visionary nurseling of his fancy, he must repress his desire for woman as an uncanny apparition, who thrills him even as she must be forbidden precisely because she evokes the presence of death in life, because she represents what lies beneath the veil of Laura's bright, innocent beauty, because she enacts the decaying body not the beautiful body masking its mortality. As Walter calls out 'let me lose the impression again as soon as possible. Call her in', he refers to the twofold threat this instance of uncanny doubling poses. He literally sees that Laura is divided, is more and other than her fair, sweet and simple appearance, and he figurally sees her as a double of Anne. If to see one's double is a harbinger of death, the twist Collins gives to this folklore motif is that Laura does indeed herald Anne's death. She will herself experience a form of death due to this duplicity, even as she will also be the living image that death has not taken place.

From the moment of her escape from the asylum Anne traces the figure of death in more than one sense. Given that she appears only to disappear and reappear again elsewhere, as the material bearer of a secret, as elusive in body as the truth she can not tell, incessantly receding from the grasp of those who seek her until death fixes her in place, she enacts the figure of *aphanisis*; a paragon of the rhetoric of death. She is also the image Walter compulsively returns to in his fantasies, whereby compulsive repetition functions as another sign of the death drive. She causes difference to emerge in Walter's imaginary relation with Laura because speaking of Miss Fairlie repeatedly raises the memory of Anne Catherick, 'setting her between us like a fatality that it was hopeless to avoid' (73). When Marion trusts Walter she does so because of his conduct towards 'that unhappy woman'; when she asks him to leave because Laura is engaged she appeals to the same honest, manly consideration for his pupil which he had once showed to 'the stranger and the outcast'. The mention of Sir Percival Glyde as Laura's betrothed reinvokes 'again, and yet again, the woman in white. There *was* fatality in it' (75). His farewell from his mother and sister are irrevocably connected with 'that other memory of the moonlight walk', and even as he leaves England with the image of Laura Fairlie 'a memory of the past', the name of Anne Catherick remains present, 'pronounced behind him as he got into the boat' (185).

In a less rhetorical and a more literal sense, Anne appears and fades in Laura's proximity as an overdetermined figure of death. She is literally dying and shows Laura what she will look like when death sets in. Her letter warning her of Sir Percival's fiendish nature beneath his fair appearance implies that Laura's 'beautiful white silk dress' and bridal veil could by virtue of marriage turn into a shroud, and in so doing confirms the bride's own nervous premonitions. Her proclivity toward Mrs Fairlie's grave and her choice to wear only white lets her appearance be interpreted by spectators such as the schoolboy Jacob Postlewaite as that not merely of a ghost but 't'ghaist of Mistress Fairlie'. The brilliant turn on which the other villain Count Fosco's masterful death plot hinges is that by turning the bride Laura into the dead girl Anne, the former will become her own ghost, will literally repeat at her own body what the schoolboy saw. As Laura's double, then, Anne is a figure of death in life on several scores – she literally signifies a dying body, her repeated appearance is a trope for fatality and, though she means to warn against danger, she will be the concrete instrument by which Laura's figural burial succeeds, by which the trope becomes materialised reality.

Significantly this image of the 'ghost of Miss Fairlie' standing beside the marble cross over Mrs Fairlie's grave repeatedly draws Walter to the graveyard, first to meet Anne a second and last time and then, upon his return to England, to see her double, the 'dead' Laura. At the grave Walter himself consciously reverses the relation between the two half-sisters, sees not Anne in Laura, but 'Miss Fairlie's likeness in Anne Catherick'. Even more startling, analogous to the thrill he felt standing at the window, is the dissimilarity this likeness articulates, because it imposes the hateful thought that if 'ever sorrow and suffering set their profaning mark on the youth and beauty' of Laura, the two would be 'the living reflections of one another' (96). Given that he never fancies what Anne would look like in health, his interest is clearly in the common denominator he finds in the process of dying. What startles him is not merely the issue of likeness but the way likeness points to the figure of death. The effect of this body double is contrary to that of the gravestone. Rather than indicating the presence of the dead in the beyond she represents uncanny difference, as a figure of death, in the realm of the living.[3]

Anne's own desire for death articulates itself in her longing to clean Mrs Fairlie's grave, to whose memory she clings as the one kind person in her youth. Kissing the gravestone, she expresses the wish to die so as to 'be hidden and at rest with *you*' (103), with death understood as a closure of the gap, as the release from tension. It is precisely this desire which Fosco, having overheard Anne repeat it to Laura, will fulfil as he exchanges the identities of the two women, so that his plot merely materialises what the mentally unbalanced Anne enacts and fancies. Walter's and later Laura's attraction to Anne, nominally because she harbours the secret of Glyde's past which could destroy him, draws both towards the realm of the dead. Walter meets this woman a second time at an equally lonely, nocturnal site, 'a grave between us, the dead about us' (95). When Laura is faced with her double, with the 'sight of her own face in the glass after a long illness', she too experiences a death-like shock, incapable of speaking for the moment. What she elicits from Anne is, however, not the secret that would empower her against Glyde but rather the madwoman's fantasies about being buried with her mother, to 'wake at her side, when the angel's trumpet sounds, and the graves give up their dead at the resurrection' (285). Like Walter, Laura is startled not only at the likeness between herself and a dying woman but also because this sight is duplicated by a spoken representation of death and its encroachment on life – 'I trembled from head to foot – it was so horrible to hear her.'

As Walter's later investigation shows, Anne serves as the embodiment of two enigmas – of dying and of Sir Percival's secret. Yet while she has a true knowledge of dying the truth of Glyde's illegitimacy is only in her mother's possession and inaccessible to her. In a manner fatal to her, she mimicks possessing the truth of his past, has the signifier (her mother's threat to expose Sir Percival's secret) but not the signified. Given that the answers Walter and Laura receive from her only pertain to her fantasies of death and resurrection, Collins's narrative implies that the search for a truth to the mystery of a man's past as it relates to a woman's future materialises another desire – the search for a contact with those on the edge of death, with the fantasy of Christian resurrection as a counter-image to that of the socially-dead returned, the revenant. Under the influence of Walter and Laura's contact with Anne even the reasonable Marion, supposedly beyond superstition, repeatedly dreams of death in the form of the representation of Walter 'kneeling by a tomb of white marble', and the shadow of a veiled woman, or 'the veiled woman rising out of the grave and waiting by his side' (279, 293). This dream representation connects the schoolboy's fanciful vision with Anne's fantasies of resurrection and will, owing to Fosco's brilliant creation of death and resurrection, find a materialised representative in Laura's body. In the figure of the woman in white, haunting the fantasies of all those involved with her, death is given a representation before its occurrence and preserved even after the event, because the revenant remains in a double guise – in the body of the living-dead Laura and in the survivors' memory of Anne.

Though the narrative privileges Walter's relation to this revenant, Anne continues to appear and disappear even after he has left England. By dissimulating that she could disclose a powerful secret she poses as a threat to Glyde and Fosco while figuring the sign of hope for the two sisters. By simulating a form of living death, she serves as a source of inspiration for the villains and a source of anxiety for Laura and Marion. For the two sisters, catching Anne's incessantly eluding body means disclosing the secret it bears, while for the two villains tracing Anne means preserving the secret. While she haunts in the double guise of a harbinger of death and a bearer of a secret, her detection offers Fosco the possiblity of yet another form of double plot, in which mourning hides an economic speculation. Because Laura's sole heir is her husband, the conspiracy he devises is such that Glyde can pay his bills with his wife's fictional death.

For the three detectives in the narrative, Marion, Walter and Fosco, disclosure is meant either to ward off death, to distance death from life or to create it in life. Marion writes in her diary, spurred on by 'a fear beyond all other fears', the fear of impending death. Walter collects written narratives from all those involved owing to the desire to put closure on the event of death that has occurred. Fosco traces Anne in order to create a death artificially, to give a fatal fixture to the doubleness her body staged. Having been tricked into entering his London home, Anne dies of a heart attack under the false name Laura Glyde and is buried ironically where she wished, in the grave with Mrs Fairlie, while Laura, passed off as Anne Catterick, is returned to the asylum. Although the enigma she falsely signified, Glyde's past, seems to be buried with her body, the other, death, is precisely what does not remain under ground, for in the body of Laura, Anne continues to haunt until the headstone inscription has been undone, fixing the ghost of Anne in place and separating a living from a dead woman.

There are, then, two sets of doubles. Firstly, the somatic double of one woman by another resulting in a fatal exchange which leaves Laura socially dead, psychically numb and without a will of her own. Secondly, two semiotic doubles, the gravestone inscribed 'Sacred to the memory of Laura, Lady Glyde', which restitutes her in the beyond as well as Walter's collection of narratives meant to undo the false inscription and give Laura a second symbolic birth. While the first leaves death present in life, the second marks an effort to sever death from life cleanly . . .

While Anne as Laura's double served as a harbinger of death, signified what Laura would look like dying, Laura as Anne's double signifies that death has only taken place in an uncanny sense, with a body beneath connected to its double before rather than beyond. By virtue of death exchangeable with Anne, Laura is forced to retrace the social and psychic death of her double, must duplicate the socially hidden, mad and dying Anne in the guise of the symbolically dead Laura, with a confused and weakened memory, without strength, without any will of her own, her mental faculties shaken and weakened. The fatal resemblance that had thrilled Walter earlier, as an idea only, is now by virtue of death realised – now 'a real and living resemblance which asserted itself before my own eyes' (443) – the subject become object.

Because Laura is symbolically designated as dead, none of her community will recognise her. Because she wears Anne's clothes, the director of the asylum accepts her back. Once she has, like her double, escaped, she strikes all others as a mad impostress who is dissimulating 'the living personality of the dead Lady Glyde' (421); an excessive figure of duplicity in that she dissimulates herself as dead and living alike. Though Walter claims that, unlike all the others who refuse to recognise Laura, no suspicion crossed his mind from the moment she lifed her veil, the scene of recognition can be interpreted in a more complex manner. If to lift the veil is understood as a cultural sign for the disclosure of truth, the truth Walter sees is not only that Laura is alive, in contradiction to the headstone, but that the beloved he invoked, with his head on the grave, and that means in relation to death, is precisely the uncanny merger of the two – the figure of fatality that had initially thrilled him; the feminine body which merges object (thrown before) and subject (thrown beneath) in its relation to death; the revenant. For significantly he affixes his claim of possession 'mine at last' to the description of a woman more like Anne than Miss Fairlie, 'Forlorn and disowned, sorely tried and sadly changed – her beauty faded, her mind clouded – robbed of her station in the world, of her place among living creatures' (422).

The mourning and the detection plot merge in such a way that the object of mourning must be exchanged, Anne's death acknowledged and Laura's life reconfirmed. Death is in this case literally solved when it is proved that it did not occur. The trajectory of the investigation is twofold. Firstly, there is the investigation of the conspiracy, discovering and convicting the guilty. Secondly, there is the denial that death has occurred by healing Laura's psychic physical feebleness and by symbolically healing her social loss of place produced by the false headstone inscription. The veil Laura lifts to expose an uncanny figure, the 'dead-alive', the Laura-Anne now united at one and the same body, must fall again. The dead girl once again becomes a bride, Mrs Hartright socially reaggregated. In the course of a dual social ritual, a second burial/birth and second marriage, the revenant is undone, the doubled body cleanly split into two separate beings. Until this solution has been found, however, the twofold revenant remains in the form of Laura impersonating Anne, and Anne mentally reanimated as the woman in white through whose mystery the way to the secret lies (465). The urgency to restore the one to the living is coterminous with restoring the other to death and both acts hinge on solving the secret that her first appearance in their midst heralded. The doubled bride/dead girl engenders two plots. The one an economic speculation of a husband fulfilled by virtue dissimulating death, the other the spectacle of an uncanny resemblance transformed into a living trope for fatality. Both plots, however, use the likeness achieved by the double to articulate death in a manner where the literal and the rhetorical merge. The literal death of Anne evokes a conspiracy of dissimulation where the dead body serves as instrument to victimise a second body into living death, while the rhetoric of the double as harbinger of death finds a 'living resemblance' when Laura equals the dead Anne.

In that sense Fosco's conspiracy is the acme of the chain of uncanny double events, a masterful creation of death in life, with the gravestone precisely not dividing the two. Indeed his plot uncannily blurs another opposition, that between life and art, when he compares his grand scheme to 'the modern Rembrandt' and suggests in his narrative testimony that the situation he created in life – the resurrection of the woman who was dead in the person of the woman who was living – might serve as model for the 'rising romance writers of England' (626). He takes particular pride in his function as the resurrectionist of the dead Anne in Laura and privileges this part of the conspiracy over the production, even if accidental, of Anne's real death. Solving Laura's fictional death also means resolving what was intertwined with her by Fosco's plot and by Walter's eroticised fancy, the ghostly figure of Anne, which, in Walter's words, 'has haunted these pages, as it haunted my life' (569). If Fosco turns death into an artwork, Anne even before her entanglement with Laura's story, served as a living emblem of death, so that her second burial implicitly buries the body that thrills as a figure of death in life.

The final opposition, then, is between two forms of creating signs out of death, between Fosco's creation of death in life and life out of death, with women's bodies his instruments, and Walter's retracing of events in the form of collecting and combining documents that are meant to double the absent like the headstone, and to restitute the absent not here but beyond. Both men represent themselves in relation to death with women's bodies as the site of this exchange. Fosco, the creator of a fatal conspiracy plot, employs the indexic, iconic mode of semiosis when he uses two women's bodies as his material, and turns his written confession of the crime into a remarkable creation meant to represent 'my own ingenuity, my own humanity' (628). Walter represents himself in the collection of testimonies as the one who resuscitated Laura, as the one who repeats and surpasses the maternal by giving a symbolic rebirth to his wife.

Installing the ritual of second burial, Walter calls together Laura's community before which he leads her back into the home from which she had left as bride and was later expelled as a madwoman. Before the collected audience he presents a public disclosure of the funereal conspiracy, outlines its course and the motives behind it, only to close the proceeding by informing those present of Sir Percival's death and his own marriage. Once the symbolic recognition has occurred, Laura is socially reaggregated. Raised by her husband's arm 'so that she was plainly visible to everyone in the room' the community responds by declaring her regained identity – 'there she is, alive and hearty'. Though the grave is not reopened, the disjunction it signified is obliterated, the false inscription erased and replaced with Anne Catherick's name and date of death. This socially sanctioned burial of Anne resolves the uncanny likeness between the two half-sisters, and with it one aspect of death's rhetoric in life. It also fixes the ghost which had haunted Walter independently of Fosco's conspiracy plot, and resolves the uncanny desire for anxiety about death, puts closure on his compulsive return to Anne as the figure whose sudden appearance had initially brought every drop of blood in his body to a stop. In the end he has successfully decathected Anne, by symbolically severing the woman whose appearance thrills from the innocent beauty of his restored wife. Second burial puts an end to the bad corpse of Anne's ghostly haunting figure and Laura's simulation of a revenant, by disjoining the bride's name from the tombstone and inscribing it so that it truly doubles a woman restituted in the beyond. In an analogous manner, Fosco's bad art, using women's bodies to materialise death and resurrection, to produce uncanny representations is exchanged for the stable art of narrative documentation that results in a recuperation of canny division.

9

HENRY JAMES, *THE PORTRAIT OF A LADY*

Eugenia C. DeLamotte's essay on *The Portrait of a Lady* has much in common with Robert B. Heilman's essay on *Jane Eyre* (above). Both critics look at the ways in which Gothic conventions are adopted and modified within predominantly realist texts. DeLamotte's essay considers *The Portrait of a Lady* in terms of its exploration of conscious virtue as a defence against Gothic villainy. The Gothic literary tradition presents the terror-stricken woman fleeing from her pursuer in darkness, but James's novel renounces the idea of escape. Instead, it shows us Isabel Archer waking to the Gothic horrors that have surrounded her in a process of self-discovery and self-knowledge. If *The Portrait of a Lady* draws on well-established Gothic tropes, it also modifies these in the light of a specifically American Romantic tradition that fostered ideals of self-reliance.

Barbara Hardy argues that Henry James was 'the founder of modern criticism of fiction'. She claims that James was responsible for turning critics away from the Victorian novel towards a modernist understanding of form and technique. Her essay shows that James's critical writings were unusually theoretical for their time, and that they encouraged a reflexive, self-conscious artistry in the writing of fiction. It also reveals the extent to which James used his own fiction for critical analysis, and it marks important shifts of emphasis between 'The Art of Fiction' (1884) and the prefaces written for the New York edition of the novels (1907–9). One of the important points of clarification in this essay concerns the way in which James promoted ideas of unity and organic form in fiction, but also made it his business to create spaces, ask questions, present enigmas and leave endings open.

The following abbreviations are used in the text:

AS *The American Scene*, intro. W. H. Auden (New York: Scribner's, 1946)

CM *Henry James: The Critical Muse: Selected Literary Criticism*, ed. Roger Gard (Harmondsworth: Penguin, 1987)

Life Leon Edel, *The Life of Henry James*, 2 vols (Harmondsworth: Penguin, 1977)

NSB *Notes of a Son and Brother* (London: Macmillan, 1914)

SBO *A Small Boy and Others* (London: Macmillan, 1913)

Eugenia C. DeLamotte, Gothic Conventions in *The Portrait of a Lady* (1990)

. . . It was Henry James who gave American literature its richest exploration of conscious virtue as a defense against Gothic villainy. *The American* and *The Portrait of a Lady* are meditations on the previously unexploited potential of that theme. Both novels raise the issue by means of a catastrophe undreamt of in Radcliffe's philosophy but perhaps prepared for by Richardson's. What would happen, James asks, if the hero renounced his opportunity to rescue the victim or the victim renounced her opportunity to escape? Might not the Gothic villain still be defeated in some way? Might not the renunciation itself be a victory for conscious worth?

The American contains quite a collection of Gothic conventions: a gloomy old house, decayed aristocratic villains, a mysterious crime, ruins, imprisonment in a convent, a manuscript revealing its author's murder, an atmosphere of suspense. On the surface, these conventions are no better than they should be. But one anomaly makes them new. The imprisoned heroine is disposed of in none of the usual ways. No crazed monk kills her to complete the tragedy;[1] she is not rescued from the convent at the last minute;[2] the villains do not solve her problems by doing away with themselves and/or one another;[3] no accomplice leads her through an underground labyrinth to freedom.[4] The hero could rescue her by using blackmail and thus forfeiting the goodness that makes him the hero in the first place; so he does not. Claire could escape by rebelling against her wicked relatives, but like the ancestor to whom she presumably owes her name, she regards filial obedience as a categorical imperative. Indeed, her voluntary immurement might have shamed even Ellena di Rosalba, who merely considered refusing an indecorous rescue from a convent (*The Italian*).

It could be argued that Claire and her suitor win anyway, by refusing to compromise their virtue. They transgress none of their principles in the struggle with those who have transgressed all of them, and thus maintain the boundary between themselves and what is evil. The walls of Claire's convent are a symbol of those boundaries; they ensure a safe separation from the evil in her family as well as protection against the internal evil that might tempt her, against her conscience, to a union with Christopher Newman. By resisting the temptation to do evil in order to fight evil, Claire and Newman defend themselves against it, even though those who are themselves evil seem outwardly to triumph.

In many ways the novel invites such an interpretation; on the other hand, James is never so unsubtle a moralist or even so unsubtle a story-teller. Encrusted as it is with the easily definable clichés of old romance, the plot of *The American* still somehow slips through one's fingers, recalling William James's comment that among the conventions his brother defied in another of his novels was the convention of telling the story.[5] Did Claire choose the convent, or did her relatives force her into it? Was she in love with Newman? Did she regard immurement in a convent with the same loathing as did her Protestant lover, or the Protestant readers of Gothic romance? Were the relatives really wicked, and is Newman really a hero?[6] The image of Christopher, belated discoverer of the Old World and its fabulous wealth, staring in bewilderment at the convent walls, has after all its comic side. The New World millionaire is baffled of his purchase by shockingly old-fashioned villainy and incomprehensibly Catholic piety – together the quintessence of the Europe from which he will always be shut out. Paradoxically, its very inaccessibility affirms his own worth, but even that may be a dubious prize – the weapon his enemies relied on for his defeat.

James suggests that perhaps Claire either chose or did not resist the convent in order to protect herself against an inclination of her own to which she felt it would be wrong to yield. The focus, however, is not on the victim but on her potential rescuer, Newman. *The Portrait of a Lady* makes richer the ambiguities surrounding the Gothic theme of conscious worth, by focusing on a heroine's renunciation of escape rather than the hero's renunciation of a plan to rescue her and by developing more fully the suggestion in the earlier work that defense of oneself may rest ironically on a defense against oneself.

In *The Portrait of a Lady* James introduces Gothic conventions more subtly than in *The American*; they belong, for the most part, to the metaphorical rather than the physical level of action.[7] For that reason they are also in the eye of the beholder . . . Unlike other heroines, Isabel does not see a ghost the first night she sleeps in a strange house, but only at the end of the novel. Italy is filled with ruins, but Isabel is not conscious of them as *ruined* until her vision has been educated by suffering. Rosier recognized Osmond's palace as 'a kind of domestic fortress, which bore a stern old Roman name, which smelt of . . . crime and craft and violence . . . ' (ch. 36). But the fact that she is imprisoned by a Gothic villain comes to Isabel's consciousness only gradually:

> [W]hen, as the months elapsed, she followed him further and he led her into the mansion of his own habitation, then, then she had seen where she really was. She could live it over again, the incredulous terror with which she had taken the measure of her dwelling . . . It was the house of

> darkness, the house of dumbness, the house of suffocation. Osmond's beautiful mind gave it neither light nor air; Osmond's beautiful mind, indeed, seemed to peer down from a small high window and mock at her. (ch. 42)

This metaphor of Osmond's personality as a suffocating mansion turned prison reveals James's perception of the symbolic content latent in much Gothic romance. Isabel is surrounded by an alien personality who crushes in upon her, mocks her, suffocates her, and is all the while trying to erase the boundaries between her and him, to remake her in his image.

In the long series of 'lurid flashes' (ch. 52) at the climax of the novel, Isabel wakes to the Gothic horrors that have so long surrounded her. She sees herself in a dark prison with Osmond as jailer; she sees that Rome is filled with ruins; she sees the 'ghost' of Gardencourt. Heiress of an Emersonian faith in self-reliance, Isabel has never doubted her reality as a distinct individual. Now she finds that her very feelings have not been her own; the boundaries of her self were violated before she recognized a threat. 'What have you to do with me?' she asks Osmond's accomplice Madame Merle, who answers, 'Everything!' (ch. 49).

Isabel discovers too late the assassin hid in her apartment, but that is not the worst horror. 'Ourself behind ourself, concealed – Should startle most—.' Caspar Goodwood's kiss, 'like a flash of lightning,' provides that final revelation. The additions James made in the New York edition at this point make clearer that the 'lightning' illuminates Isabel's own hitherto-unacknowledged sexuality. Discovering the force of Caspar's offer, she also discovers what she must do: renounce the temptation he represents. By doing so, she is, like Christopher Newman, resisting the temptation of yielding to evil in order to fight it. The encounter with Caspar, presented in such erotic imagery, establishes that Isabel is fully conscious of what she is rejecting. She runs in terror, not from her own sexuality, as is sometimes suggested, but from what it might have led her to do. Her flight therefore reveals her strength by announcing her refusal to stoop to Osmond's level in order to escape him. She has been shocked at Osmond's cavalier attitude toward marital infidelity; now she is shocked that she herself almost yielded to it. Osmond's power has been manifested in his slow transformation of Isabel into someone more and more like himself. When Isabel refuses what would in her eyes have been an illicit sexual relationship, she is holding herself back from the center of Osmond's own life, warding off the insidious encroachment of his personality on hers, evading the last transformation.

Appropriately, the image of Isabel at her final moment of illumination is the image of a woman with her hand on the latch of a door. Behind her is the darkness; inside the house she is about to enter is light; she stands at the threshold. This final portrait recalls other images of doors: Osmond's sinister comparison of himself to a rusty key turning in the lock of Isabel's intellect; the grim image of Isabel 'framed' in his gilded doorway, 'the picture of a gracious lady' (chs 24; 37). It also recalls a particularly evocative image from the days of Isabel's earliest acquaintance with Pansy. In that earlier scene, before Isabel's marriage, Pansy stood in Osmond's doorway looking wistfully out as Isabel took leave of her. 'I am only a little girl,' she said, 'but I shall always expect you.' Then from the darkness of the house her father had forbidden her to leave, Pansy watched Isabel go out: '[A]nd the small figure stood in the high, dark doorway, watching Isabel cross the clear, grey court, and disappear into the brightness beyond the big *portone*, which gave a wider gleam as it opened.' 'I have promised papa not to go out of this door,' Pansy had explained (ch. 30).

The Gothic novelist always pauses at the threshold of the villain's dim domain, allowing the heroine and the reader to shudder with sudden, intuitive horror. In this pause at the *portone* of Osmond's villa, the reader shudders but the heroine misses her chance. Only from Pansy's vantage point is the meaning of the threshold clear. It is perhaps this vantage point that Isabel has in mind in the last scene when she chooses to return; she did, after all, promise Pansy to come back. The final image of Isabel thus reverses the earlier one and yet repeats it in one significant detail. Once again the freedom to cross the threshold is hers . . .

James . . . unites the theme of conscious worth with that of self-knowledge, presenting self-discovery as the basis of a new, stronger self-defense. By renouncing rescue, Isabel achieves it, because her renunciation is based on James's version of conscious worth: the virtue of those who are 'finely aware and richly responsible.' The final scene between Isabel and Caspar belongs to an old Gothic tradition. Terror stricken, a woman flees through the darkness from her pursuer. But this time it is the rescue she flees, and the possibility arises that the woman in flight may at last have the power to defend herself.

In exploiting the potential of the Gothic theme of conscious worth, however, James also exploited its ambiguities. The doubt that the last image of Isabel evokes in the reader's mind is in part the doubt evoked in all those Radcliffean scenes in which the very splendor of the heroine's spiritual power raises the question of its practical efficacy in the real world. It is easy to imagine that a new, stronger Isabel will go back to Rome and, as the Countess Gemini once imagined, draw herself up 'the taller spirit of the two' (ch. 44). It is more difficult to imagine how. In addition, the question arises of where the ultimate power lies. Did Isabel, after all, have a choice? Or is the final image of her just one more image of a frightened woman at a door that represents her vulnerability?

Isabel has promised Pansy to come back, but she has also implied to Henrietta that she needed an excuse (ch. 53). As in the case of many a Gothic heroine before her, Isabel's final consciousness of her virtue is wedded to her consciousness of the proprieties. To do, at the crucial moment, what is conventional is an act loaded with significance in a novel in which the conventions of European society have a force like fate. Perhaps the final scene with Caspar represents Isabel's definitive demarcation from Osmond; it could, on the other hand, represent the collapse of her last fortification against the man who is, in his own words, 'convention itself' (ch. 29). Or perhaps it is just that, like Clarissa's triumph, Isabel's final victory is rooted in her final defeat: her defeat by life or experience or fate or simply, as Godwin would have said, 'things as they are.'

Barbara Hardy, Henry James: The Literary Critic (1996)

James wrote literary criticism from the beginning. He began reviewing in his early twenties, concentrating on novels. He deplored the absence of 'any critical treatise upon fiction' in his first piece for the *North American Review* in 1864, after drifting away from his study of law at Harvard (*Life*, i. 175). The reviews were quickly joined by short stories and eventually, in the next decade, by the novels, but he remained a stylish and knowledgeable critic, sought after by editors. Literary journalism, like travel-writing, was an important source of his earnings. He was a reviewer of painting and drama, rarely of poetry, and most influentially of novels, doing for his art what Aristotle did for tragedy and Coleridge for Shakespeare and Wordsworth.

Like many English novelists from Defoe onwards, James began as a journalist, and his reviewing was intimately related to his creative writing in a way which continued throughout his life. He learnt to write as a journalist, needing to shape and enliven his prose in the business of attracting readers. Though his style grew less concise and more mannered, he remains one of the few entertaining literary critics. When he read his lecture on Browning, 'The Novel in *The Ring and the Book*', the audience murmured with pleasure at his language. He followed a standard of excellence set in America by such editors as Charles Eliot Norton, Edwin Lawrence Godkin, W.D. Howells, and James Russell Lowell, and in England by such critics as E.S. Dallas, G.H. Lewes and Marian Evans, who offered knowledge, intelligent judgement, and style. The Victorian novelists – Thackeray, Dickens, George Eliot – learnt their trade in brief pieces intended to amuse, often sheltering under an absence of signature. As Roger Gard says, introducing *Henry James: The Critical Muse: Selected Literary Criticism*, James's 'literary criticism is so vivacious, informative, and elegant that few readers will find it other than a pleasure to read'.

Gard contrasts two main responses to James's criticism: an exaggerated attention to the theoretical implications and influences of the Preface to the New York Edition, and Leavis's view of James as a pragmatic, impressionistic, and occasional critic, whose work, 'was determined by his own creative preoccupations'. (You could turn this round and say that his novels were determined by his grasp of structural principle but I don't think we can distinguish cause and effect in James's case.) Leavis was criticized by Vivien Jones in *James the Critic*, as appropriating James for an 'aggressively untheoretical criticism of moral evaluation by rejecting the Prefaces'. Rebuking Jones for simplifying Leavis and overrating the Prefaces, Gard regrets that Leavis's essay on James was used as a preface for Moriss Shapira's collection *Henry James: Selected Literary Criticism*, which, reprinted 'disproportionately much of James's dismissals of various types of aestheticism'. He believes the debate represents extremes of response and judgement likely to be felt 'at different but quickly succeeding times, by any alert reader', concluding that James reconciled a life-based and an art-defending view of fiction, steering a 'middle way . . . not . . . of timid mediocrity but of reconcilling critical genius'. Gard's is a valuable reminder that James the formalist is concerned with 'the art of rendering life'. But questionings of mimesis in the second half of this century make it possible to see James's views on fiction, stated in critical essays and revealed in novels, in a way which avoids this polarity of formalism and realism.

Though not even appearing to be a mimetic novelist – as George Eliot, for instance, does – James is passionately concerned with what he carefully calls not realism but 'the air of reality' ('The Art of Fiction', *CM*, no. 26). He insists on it in the early reviews, 'The New Novel', the lectures on Balzac and Browning, and the Prefaces. His discovery of refraction through a centre of consciousness allows him to be realistic or mimetic while admitting into the novel a principle of conspicuous fiction-making, though he does not formulate it in these terms. But he was a theorist, always deploring critics' neglect of the art of fiction. His criticism was unusually theoretical for its time, concerned with form as well as mimesis, and one of his great attractions as a theorist is the detached and intimate use of his own writing for structural analysis. This gives his analysis a special tone, an unabstract, vivid, terminology. Gard stresses the inseparability of James's metaphorical wit from his thinking, in examples chiefly drawn from the occasional pieces, but it is also the great brightener and lightener of his discussions of form.

Seeing character as functional, for instance, is an abstract formulation, but James turns it into the animated figure of a carriage, with some figures seated as privileged passengers, others only wheels that run and roll. Looking, in 'The New Novel' (1914) (*CM*, no. 76), at Conrad's narrators and listeners, as they compound narrative speculation, he calls them the 'tell-tale little dogs', and I have already mentioned the startling comparison of refracted narrative to the shadow of a plane's wings in the same article. He thinks in pictures. His criticism is a creator's criticism, sensuous as well as intellectual, like Coleridge's. He is as amusing a critic as he is a novelist, using the same individual voice, not using the language of abstraction. Making up his language as he goes along, he articulates the trajectory of a response, in words conveying affection and pleasure, or dismay and hostility, moved but sufficiently detached to categorize. These qualities are present from the beginning, but it is in the discussions of form that they are most unusual and valuable.

James was a brilliant reviewer, judicial and personal, harsh and generous, but never too harsh or too generous. All his criticism is the work of someone who cares intensely about the novel. The voice and feeling are less rapturous and private than his astonishingly excited and intimate addresses to a Muse – *mon bon* – in the notebooks, but are stirred by passion. His early work is not just pragmatic: the 'Art of Fiction', written in response to Walter Besant's *Art of Fiction*, in 1884, is the beginning of a fervent effort to treat the novel with the seriousness directed to poetry and drama. But many of its famous utterances about the indissolubility of character, plot, and incident, and the relationship of art to life, are made excitingly specific in the detailed, patient, detached examinations of his own work in the Prefaces, and it is that discussion which is central to James's originality as the founder of modern criticism of fiction – perhaps of other genres too.

In the later writing there are important shifts in emphasis. For example, 'The Art of Fiction' asserts an organic unity in which character, incident, picture, narrative, and description are all inextricably joined. 'A novel', he says, 'is a living thing, all one and continuous, like any other organism, and in proportion as it lives will it be found, I think that in each of the parts will be found something of each of the other parts'. This is a valuable restatement of Coleridge's formulation of the relation of part to whole in Shakespeare or Wordsworth, and its application to fiction treats the Cinderella genre analytically and judiciously.

He later comes to look closely at the texts he knows most intimately, after a gap in time which makes him reader as well as writer, of context as well as text, past as well as present. In the Prefaces he makes distinctions not dreamt of in the reply to Besant, between elements of fiction which are means and others that are ends. Instead of saying that everything in a novel is illustrative, he says some things are more illustrative than others. In 'The Art of Fiction' he says, 'I cannot imagine composition existing in a series of blocks', but in the Prefaces that is precisely how he does see composition. The Preface to *The Wings of the Dove* (*CM*, no. 69) says:

> There was all the 'fun', to begin with, of establishing one's successive centres – of fixing them so exactly that the portions of the subject commanded by them as by happy points of view, and accordingly treated from them, would constitute, so to speak, sufficiently solid *blocks* of wrought material, squared to the sharp edge, as to have weight and mass and carrying power . . . Such a block . . . is the whole preliminary presentation of Kate Croy.

This building imagery is frequent here and in the Prefaces to *The Portrait of a Lady* and *The Awkward Age*, with related images of architecture, theatre, and painting. He has not rejected organicism, but he has refined and redefined his concept of artistic unity, analysing components with a practitioner's sense of composition.

It is as a critic of his own fiction that his influence is established. The Prefaces he wrote for the New York Edition of his novels and stories, published between 1907 and 1909, have been reprinted in several selections, those by Shapira and Gard, the collection edited by R.P. Blackmur as *The Art of the Novel*, and reprints of the novels. The Prefaces, essays like 'The New Novel', revaluations of French novelists, a few reviews, and the notebooks, offer the most important analysis of narrative form in the first half of the twentieth century. James's preoccupations turn up in later theoretical and textual criticism, and when we look back at Victorian and Edwardian criticism of fiction, before and during James's time, it is plain that he is the novel's first analytic critic. His work was used and popularized by his editor and friend Percy Lubbock, whose *Craft of Fiction* (1921) was one of the few 'treatises on fiction' available in the pre-war and war years, Jamesian in analytic method and judgement, and elegantly retelling the great stories. When I read it as an undergraduate, it took me at once to James.

James contemplates his own work in a way which is probably unique, as he rereads and rewrites it. Always an imagistic critic, he recycles the imagery of his fiction in his Prefaces and later essays in a remarkable way. Rereading *The Portrait of a Lady*, he transfer the poetics of architecture from novel to Preface, then in later novels he revises it again: the house, the room, the corridor, and the window are spatial symbols invented by Isabel Archer and Maggie Verver, in collaboration with their narrator, and they become terms in James's narratives of composition, his analysis and judgement of form and genre, his criticism of Wells and Conrad, and his defence of the novel's elastic art. His rhetoric is functional, persuasive, and illuminating, as he thinks out his theory of form. A common imagery bonds criticism with fiction. His work is all of a piece. Those who want to see the novel as scientific, and criticism as narrative and imagistic, will find support in James's generic fluidities of discourse.

James began as a young reviewer sounding like an old judge, praising Scott and deprecating Dickens with an air of authority, scrupulously weighing words, speaking out of literary and historical knowledge. I don't suggest that the magisterial voice is spurious, far from it: the grand manner of this very young man is amusing, but he gets away with it because of fresh perception and example, far-ranging fact and sheer intelligence. He writes as someone who knows the books backwards. I often disagree with him, but he always says something sharp and deep. He judges his own work with stunning detachment, writing from a deep inwardness with its history, and a care for the craft.

Of course, like any artist, he is publicizing and promoting his own art and methods. He does this less conspicuously in the early reviews, but it is present, because he is reviewing as an ambitious artist, writing reviews and stories at the same time. Shrewdly criticizing Dickens's representation of society in *Our Mutual Friend* as a 'community of eccentrics', when the whole point of 'society' is conformity to rule (*CM*, no. 6), he speaks for the sociological imagination which was to create the seedy rich parties in *The Wings of the Dove, The Ambassadors*, and *The Sacred Fount*, where the society is as greedy, self-indulgent, hypocritical, and snobbish as the Veneerings, but disguised and distinguished by elegant conformity, superior to eccentricity. That is his point. Dickens gets an unfair review as James studies social representation. When in the shrewd witty lines of '"Daniel Deronda": A Conversation' Constantius objects that the novel shows 'views' on life instead of life, he speaks for a writer whose gift for abstraction never shows in dialogue, and not often in narrative (*CM*, no. 18). (The Wildean views and manner of Gabriel Nash in *The Tragic Muse* form an exception which proves a rule, as the novel does itself, in theme and form.) Interestingly, Edward L. Burlingame in the *North American Review* (Sept. 1877) and an anonymous writer in the *Eclectic Review* (Aug. 1877) say almost the same about James's *The American*.

What James says about Balzac, Zola, Tolstoy, Edith Wharton, Wells, Bennett, and Hugh Walpole is consistent with his values and practice. When he writes to Wharton and Walpole, trying to be nice to his friends, critical sternness gets the upper hand. If his critical response seems surprising, in his admiration of *Kipps*, Gissing, Stevenson, Zola, there is a reason in his fiction. The affinities or links are not always explicit, but they are there to be discovered. He does not lack empathy, but his overriding concern is with his ideal of artistic conscience. He is a thoroughly consistent critic and artist, always on duty.

Self-analysis develops in the Prefaces. From the accumulated particulars of the novels that he rereads, with pleasure, surprise, chagrin, and admiration, and rewrites, emerge generalizations, then definitions of form and genre. His insistence on visible shape and unity, economy of form and total relevance, is also a reaction against contemporary fiction. In his self-critique and his criticism of other novelists he voices grievances against the Victorians, though he loves and admires the writers who delighted his youth, and nourished his art too. He is saturated in Dickens, Thackeray, and George Eliot. Even Trollope, whom he dislikes, he knows thoroughly. Never was there such a devoted anti-Victorian.

His Isabel Archer owes much to Gwendolen Harleth, as Leavis showed, though also much to Maggie Tulliver and Dorothea Brooke. Some of his best comic, grotesque, and pathetic characters, Henrietta Stackpole, Millicent Hemming, Madame Grandoni, would not exist without Dickens – though other comic characters are more Thackerayan, comic without being grotesque, like Bob Assingham, the Pococks, and the nameless narrator of *The Sacred Fount*. In *The Wings of the Dove*, crammed with the conspicuous consumption Thackeray loved to catalogue, price, and judge, James unsurprisingly links Kate Croy with the Thackerayan heroine, thinking of Ethel Newcome, and also Becky Sharp and Blanche Amory, for whom, he lamented, Thackeray lacked the love Balzac felt for *sa Valérie*. The great Victorians mark a valuable negative for James, act as stop-signals of life without art, wasteful manner, loose form, terrible fluidity, a leak in the interest. He makes such rejections explicitly, but implicitly too, in his concision, economy, total relevance, symmetry, and asserted rhetoric.

He gave modernism a language as it was beginning to develop. For half a century, with the brilliant help of Lubbock, who wrote about him and for him, he turned critics and students away from the Victorian novel, persuading them by example and argument that such 'large loose baggy monsters' (*CM*, no. 60) as Thackeray, Dumas, Tolstoy, George Eliot, and Dickens, whom he admired with reservations, were story-tellers not artists, leading them to judge the multiple plot as rambling and disordered, the omniscient narrator as 'intrusive', dismissible as an element of matter not manner. Until the late 1950s this was the assumption in George Eliot criticism, and still occasionally crops up. Other novelist-critics, D. H. Lawrence and Virginia Woolf, for instance, have written a subjective and self-promoting critique of their genre but they have not strongly influenced critical opinion. Only James Joyce's influence on ideas of impersonality and multivocalism has made a critical impact as radical as James's. He helped to make critics look at the novel's form, but his singleminded promotion of that form as he saw and made it was bad news for the study of his Victorian ancestors, though if it proceeds from an anxiety about influence, it is well disguised as superiority.

James introduced new structural concepts into the criticism of fiction. They have formed the basis of much of our theory and analytic practice: point of view, voice, functional character, foreshortening, anticipation, and unity are all concepts explicitly developed in the critical analysis and theory of prose narrative which James formed or helped to form. They were developed in the solvent of performance. When he formulates points of view, as 'centre' and 'consciousness', it is with Roderick Mallett's, through whom Roderick Hudson and other characters are imagined, as example (*CM*, no. 56). When he discusses characters belonging to form rather than subject, the subject comes up as he judges Henrietta Stackpole and Maria Gostrey to have been overtreated (*CM*, no. 70). When he speaks of major and minor characters (as in *CM*, no. 56), there is the sense of character as construct, aesthetically adjusted as part of the whole unified work of art: it is not enough for Mary Garland to be a realistic character, but necessary for her and her habitat to balance the presence and background of Christina Light. James joins the theatrical and poetic reactions against Bradleyan character-criticism to make us see character as rhetoric not reality. Whatever he says about the air of reality, he makes it clear that mimesis is an inadequate concept.

When *Middlemarch* is judged 'a treasure-house of details, but . . . an indifferent whole' (*CM*, no. 11), I hope we disagree, but we know what he means. He is comparing it with the streamlined and symmetrical elegance of his novels. Their symmetries and antithesis are as plain as in a lyric, their scenes contrast like those in a well-made play, their narrators are subdued and disguised, to promote scene and dialogue, their scheme of total relevance charges every object and act so that characters cannot put on the light or eat fruit without symbolic meaning. Criticism has taken its time to shed his insistence on norms of concentration and unity. Wayne Booth's *The Rhetoric of Fiction*, W.J. Harvey's *The Art of George Eliot*, and my *Novels of George Eliot* and *The Appropriate Form* all argued a case against this insistence, analysing a variety of voice and form, defending the loose, fluid, and episodic three-volume novel against James's charge of redundancy, waste, and looseness, proposing a more flexible concept of novelistic structure. Since those critiques of the late 1950s and early 1960s, structuralist theories have classified and standardized the concepts of form, and post-structuralism eroded ideas of closure, unity, and organicism. James needed to pursue his own ideal of 'a deep-breathing economy and an organic form' (Preface to *The Tragic Muse*, *CM*, no. 60), and the old New Critical ideas and methods created a climate in which he won admiration for his novels and his criticism, as Blackmur's edition of the Prefaces makes especially clear. Once we have placed that criticism and shown its limits, it can be appreciated for what it is, an idea of form which applies to some artists not to all, but an idea which can be expanded and modified.

James is the promoter of conspicuous form, a displayed mannerism and flourish which Auden calls Gongorist (in his 1946 introduction to *The American Scene*), a visible unity and symmetry which his symbolic titles announce and his dynamic symbols help to create. James's concentration had many origins. There were the living examples of Flaubert and Turgenev, whom he knew, and whose pursuit of the art of fiction was an inspiration and a counter-model for a reader brought up on Dickens and Scott. There was the devotion to painting and architecture which we can see in his travel writings and reviews of exhibitions, developing his taste for conspicuous unity. Most ironic, in view of his failure in the genre, is his passion for theatre, rooted in his experience of the stage as a young child, first in New York, then in Paris. James cultivated the right word, like Flaubert, and the right construction. He chose to concentrate, in the genre in which such concentration is optional, as the painter and dramatist are forced to concentrate by the compulsions of their genre.

He gave – or helped to give – modern criticism its method and techniques. The New Criticism's interpretation of dominant themes and analysis of symmetry, balance, antithesis, imagery, and symbolism are all present in the New York Prefaces, as James sets new readings against old ones, in an unprecedentedly sustained retrospect. Of course James was not the first novelist to make images dominate and draw attention to prevailing themes. Dickens and George Eliot did so before him, and, though influenced by Ibsen, as Michael Egan shows, James had earlier models before him too. His last novels remind us of Ibsen's symbolic phenomena, but the sprawling Victorians were also symbolists, though Ibsen's economy and fantasy made him especially attractive to James, despite an uncongenial didacticism.

James's critical ideas get into his stories as well as his Prefaces. 'The Figure in the Carpet' is a tease and a temptation for critics, who cannot resist trying to guess what they cannot possibly guess, the undisclosed key figure of an invented and imaginary *œuvre*. The idea of such a key figure, its image taken from the spatial art of oriental carpet-making, may have helped to develop that interest in image-patterns which started with Shakespeare criticism. Joseph Frank's idea of spatial form clearly derived from James's practice, perhaps from this famous story whose novelist and whose critic take so readily to the idea of a key figure. James anticipates the critic's enthusiasm for staking a claim to hermeneutic discovery, in playful but baleful putting-down of critical hubris. James knew that a search for a key to a work, or all the works, turns students of fiction into critical Casaubons.

The story turns on that fashionable item, the absence. James is probably the first novelist to encourage the idea of absences, though Meredith is a rival. James puts absences in conspicuous places – the figure in the carpet, Amerigo and Charlotte in Italy, the scandalous behaviour of Lionel Croy, the object manufactured in Woollett, the name of Milly's illness – aren't these the first significant gaps in American and European fiction? As we ponder those essays claiming to discover the carpet's figure and Woollett's object – R.W. Stallman knows it is a watch – we should recall James's case in 'The Figure in the Carpet' against the avidity of critics. There are many motives for making holes in the fabric of art, and the contrivance of elegant revenge is not James's only one. James is, of course, interested in avoiding omniscience, so cuts down information severely, anticipating the *scriptible* novel of Roland Barthes. He also sees the funny side of refusing to tell, and the joke, like his other jokes, is good because it is ingenious, serious and ambiguous, sometimes refusing to disclose that it is a joke. Jamesian uncertainty is nothing to do with Heisenberg, whose name is sometimes taken in vain by critics avid for structural subversions, but it is subversive.

One way or another, he was ripening modern theory. While he explicitly insists on unity and organic form, what he does as a novelist is to make spaces, ask questions, present enigmas, and leave endings open. He encourages the reader to construct as well as receive, in Barthean terms, to write as well as read. Most graceful of formalists, he can delight in breaking a line, forcing a discord, opening an ending, ruffling a smoothness. We are beginning to catch up with him, and since the author of his supersubtle ghost-stories must be a ghost on whom nothing is lost, a recognition of that irony may compensate for the obtuseness of his contemporaries.

Those critics grumbled at his obscurity, and it was with James – unless it was with Browning or Meredith – that the obscurity of modern literature arrived. Obscurity is relative: perhaps a better word is difficulty. The difficulty of James is the product of his closely observed and pondered enquiry into imagination, in and outside art.

It is a function of a complex analysis of method, medium, form, and mind, which anticipates the central reflexiveness of modern art, articulated by Barthes and other theorists. Reflexiveness is present in Victorian fiction too, and is, I think, only quantitatively a sign of twentieth-century art, in modernist or, more conspicuously, post-modernist self-consciousness. James's reflexive art is complex and various. As I have said, his novels and stories are never thinly concerned with the special subject of art and the artist. Though the subject of art is prominent, and the concern with imagination central, James insisted that the novelist should write as a historian, not an inventor. He disliked extremes of authorial self-consciousness, criticizing Trollope (in *Century Magazine*, in July 1883 (*CM*, no. 23) for insisting on his fiction-making within the fiction: 'He took a suicidal satisfaction in reminding the reader that the story he was telling, was only, after all, a make-believe.' In the next year, he repeated the criticism in 'The Art of Fiction': 'He admits that the events he narrates have not really happened, and that he can give his narrative any turn the reader may like best. Such a betrayal of a sacred office seems to me, I confess, a terrible crime . . . '.

James wrote a number of stories dealing with the novelist's art, mostly in his earlier period. 'The Lesson of the Master', 'The Death of the Lion', and 'The Figure in the Carpet' are subtly amusing self-analysing stories about acts and arts of writing, reading, and interpreting. The figure of the artist, however, is always dramatized indirectly, with a double advantage, from James's point of view. The subject of narration is put at a distance from the reader, making no claims to verisimilitude or flexible artifice; and the making of the fiction is the subject of the story. The narrator sometimes speaks in a first person, but is kept on a tight rein by scope and selection, never constituting what James in the Preface to *The Tragic Muse* called 'a leak in the interest'. Such narrators are never omniscient, but struggle to carry out difficult or impossible enquiries into the nature of art and the artist. They allow James to assume the most interesting of his absences, the absence of the author-surrogate, the dominant teller.

James loved to fuse event and character, and these stories are frequently about making out a story. In 'The New Novel' James praised Conrad for the refracted narrative in *Chance*, which created the 'fusion between what we are to know and that prodigy of our knowing which is ever half the beauty of the atmosphere of authenticity'. Not for James Conrad's 'reciter', that 'definite responsible intervening first-person singular, possessed of infinite sources of reference, who immediately proceeds to set up another, to the end that this other may conform again to the practice', but his admiration for the 'reciting' construction of *Chance* springs from his own affection for structures of enquiry and speculation. In the short fiction the reciters are sometimes definite and developed, sometimes even a literary voice, but in the novels his structures are very different from Conrad's, though they, too, are designed to fuse subject and object of knowing. In James as in Conrad the characters try to find each other's secrets and understand each other's mysteries. These are true epistemological narratives. The story in them, usually of more magnitude than in 'The Story in It', may be a story of ordinary life. In the quiet delicacy of 'The Story in It', James is like Wordsworth in 'Goody Blake', trying to make his reader see 'a tale in everything'. His minimal narrative may be a paradigm for art, but also brings out the telling and listening in every life.

He wrote with fine enthusiasm about 'Ivan Turgenev' (*CM*, no. 40), whom he called 'the novelists' novelist': 'His vision is of the world of character and feeling, the world of relations life throws up at every hour and on every spot . . . his air is that of the great central region of passion and motive, of the usual, the inevitable, the intimate – the intimate for weal or woe.'

James's social range is much more restricted than Turgenev's but he wrote warmly about his friend's influential social sympathies, and if the creator of Miss Pynsent, Hyacinth's foster-mother, the clerk 'In the Cage', and the cheeky couple in 'The Papers' draws fewer humble characters like Turgenev's, his occasional humble people and some of the grander ones are images of 'the usual, the inevitable, the intimate'. Lacking the astonishing naturalness of Turgenev's attachment 'to the misery, the simplicity, the piety, the patience, of the unemancipated peasant', James loved Turgenev – who never responded to his admirer's work – in a response to political feeling as well as artistry.

James's late criticism refined and qualified his utterances about organic form. His development of influential critical concepts took his lifetime, and crowned his achievement. But for him, life and form go hand in hand, and this is seen in the development of his historical sense. 'The Jolly Corner', the three great novels, and the unfinished fiction show a clear sense of the making of character by circumstance, and there is a parallel insight in his literary criticism. It is not prominent in the Prefaces, where the emphasis is placed on form and technique, but it is present in several essays on other novelists. Like Thackeray, James was a member of the Reform Club, and, like Thackeray's, his attitude to reform cannot be judged by his hob-nobbing with *le beau monde*. Sidney Waterlow, one of his Rye friends, reports him wondering 'how so complete and cumbrous a thing as the British Empire managed to go on at all . . . perhaps it was simply easier for it to go on than to stop . . . He felt tempted to call himself a rapid Socialist' (*Life*, 96). As a radical declaration, this echoes Thackeray's prediction that the scaffolding of society must be torn down, and Gerard Hopkins's famous 'red letter' to Robert Bridges.

James wrote an admiring review of Edith Wharton's *The Reef* (1912) (*CM*, no. 74), but criticizes it for locating an American story in a French habitat, 'the whole thing, unrelated and unreferred save in the most superficial way to its milieu and background, and to any determining or qualifying *entourage*'. He concludes that the social isolation works for her 'Racinian' characterization, but the comment on milieu is significant. The historic sense is central in a review of Emile Faguet's *Balzac* which appeared in the *Times Literary Supplement* in 1913 (*CM*, no. 75), in which he judges Balzac – for James, always the great novelist – to have been happy to have been born in his time, a time of historical visibilities, the 'later part of the eighteenth century, with the Revolution, the Empire, and the Restoration' showing with distinctness 'their separate marks and stigmas, their separate trails of character and physiognomic hits', less clearly differentiated to later generations confronted by 'fatal fusions and uniformities . . . the running together of . . . differences of form and tone . . . the ruinous liquefying wash of the great industrial brush'. Balzac's strength is in the grasp of creature in circumstance:

> What makes Balzac so pre-eminent and exemplary that he was to leave the novel a far other and a vastly more capacious and significant affair than he found it, is his having felt his fellow-creatures (almost altogether for him his contemporaries) as quite failing of reality, as swimming in the vague and the void and the abstract, unless their social

> conditions, to the last particular, their generative and contributive circumstances, of every discernible sort, enter for all these are 'worth' into his representative attempt. This great compound of the total looked into and starting up in its element, as it always does, to meet the eye of genius and patience half way, bristled for him with all its branching connections.

This passage is over-elaborate in style, teasing out shades of meaning, scrupulously but fussily, and muffling the main point: 'unless their social conditions . . . enter . . . into his representative attempt'. The word *representation* is an exact term in James, meaning solid specification. In the earlier 'Lesson of Balzac', published in the *Atlantic Monthly* in 1905 (*CM*, no. 56), he contrasts Balzacian realism with Zola's researched historicism, which he calls 'representation imitated', and in his 1903 tribute, 'Emile Zola' (*CM*, no. 50), 'the most extraordinary *imitation* of observation'.

James loved Balzac even more than he loved Turgenev, master of grace and economy, and his meditations on Balzac continue and mutate. His writings on Turgenev are not just about form, and the essay of 1896 (*CM*, no. 40) shows his insistence on the novelist's social circumstance: he translates it into American terms, comparing the Russian nobleman to a 'Virginian or Carolinian slaveholder during the first half of the century', inclining to 'Northern views'. Compared with the comments on Balzac, Zola, and Wharton, the essay underplays history, admiring concision, 'the unity . . . of material and form', and the tender and ironic creation of an 'innermost' world. But history comes in, with the praised vision of the 'individual figure . . . in the general flood of life, steeped in all its relations and contacts, struggling or submerged, a hurried particle in the stream'. The historical sense was not new in James's criticism, any more than in his fiction, but in both it is more apparent in the later years, and directly, rather than indirectly, articulated.

Although Balzac is the master, 'pre-eminent and exemplary', James's deep affinity was with Turgenev, the visible model in the early work. The Preface to *The Portrait of a Lady* (*CM*, no. 58) shows how James meditated on Turgenev's tale of a novel's genesis and growth, from soliciting figure to peopled context. But one of his finest creations, Lewis Lambert Strether, was named after Balzac's *Louis Lambert*, and is the centre of one of James's most socially questioning novels. James is engaged in a perpetual dialogue with Turgenev the formalist and Balzac the historian, offering grateful homage to his two markedly different teachers.

It is a reticent homage, stated in his critical essays but understated in the late fiction. James's literary references are always thoroughly assimilated, part of the form and fabric of his art; they seem to have slowly reduced from the early ironic imitations of Tennysonian themes in 'A Landscape Painter' and 'A

Day of Days', and the naming of George Eliot as an influence on Isabel Archer, to subdued echoes like the references to Thackeray and Maeterlinck in *The Wings of the Dove*, Blake's poem in *The Golden Bowl*, and the quiet naming in *The Ambassadors*. Strether was not to be a novelist, as James once intended, but he was to be tenderly and ironically named, in an Americanized version, after Balzac's eponymous hero, in one of many small links between James's criticism and his fiction. Like Turgenev, and unlike the artists – serious or just fashionable – whose self-reference is abstract, clever, imitative, and amoral, James is self-analytic and also amusing, individual, and moral. This is true of his criticism as well as his fiction, though as a critic he is capable of being absorbed in a response to other people's art. While we regret his failures to admire Jane Austen, much of Conrad, and *Sons and Lovers*, we must appreciate the sensibility which placed Balzac so high, knew Flaubert thoroughly, warmed to Stevenson and Zola, 'clung' to Gissing, and loved Turgenev.

There are many artists who are perceptive critics of their own work and other people's, less than a handful whose criticism matches their art. In criticism and fiction, James transforms the language and structures in which art contemplates society, history, and the personal life.

10

BRAM STOKER, *DRACULA*

Stephen D. Arata argues that *Dracula* makes a decisive break with Gothic tradition by setting part of the narrative in Transylvania, which for readers in 1897 was part of the vexed 'Eastern Question'. In the minds of those contemporary readers, Transylvania was not so much a site of Gothic romance and superstition as a place of political turbulence and racial strife. Bram Stoker's peculiar achievement was to transform the materials of the vampire myth in a way that would tap nineteenth-century concerns about the politics of Empire. In allowing the narrative to shift from the Carpathians to London, Stoker controversially places the central disturbance of the novel at the heart of modern Europe's largest empire and induces a 'late Victorian nightmare of reverse colonization'. Dracula's journey from Transylvania to England can then be read in terms of invasion or a reversal of imperial exploitation. Arata makes the further point that Stoker was a displaced Irishman, whose national allegiances were conspicuously divided, and whose writing engages with the history of conquest and domination in Anglo-Irish relations.

Phyllis A. Roth's essay draws on the insights of psychoanalysis as a way of understanding the nature of fantasy in *Dracula*. Refining and extending some earlier Freudian readings of the novel based on the Oedipus complex, the essay argues that *Dracula* harbours a deep hostility towards female sexuality. The 'suddenly sexual woman' in the title of the essay is a reference to the so-called 'new woman' of the late nineteenth century, castigated for being sexually aggressive and sexually problematic. In Roth's estimation, vampirism is a manifestation of repressed sexual wishes, which are the source of both morbid dread and lustful anticipation. This tension between fear and desire also characterises the kind of reader response that *Dracula* elicits. The essay suggests that readers of the novel are caught between identifying with those who are fighting Dracula and identifying with Dracula himself, which is also to identify with his victimization of women.

Stephen D. Arata, The Occidental Tourist: *Dracula* and the Anxiety of Reverse Colonization (1990)

In many respects, *Dracula* represents a break from the Gothic tradition of vampires. It is easy, for instance, to forget that the 'natural' association of vampires with Transylvania begins with, rather than predates, *Dracula*. The site of Castle Dracula was in fact not determined until well after Stoker had begun to write. As Joseph Bierman points out, Stoker originally signalled his debt to his countryman Le Fanu's *Carmilla* (1872) by locating the castle in 'Styria,' the scene of the earlier Gothic novella.[1] In rewriting the novel's opening chapters, however, Stoker moved *his* Gothic story to a place that, for readers in 1897, resonated in ways Styria did not. Transylvania was known primarily as part of the vexed "Eastern Question" that so obsessed British foreign policy in the 1880s and '90s. The region was first and foremost the site, not of superstition and Gothic romance, but of political turbulence and racial strife. Victorian readers knew the Carpathians largely for its endemic cultural upheaval and its fostering of a dizzying succession of empires. By moving Castle Dracula there, Stoker gives distinctly political overtones to his Gothic narrative. In Stoker's version of the myth, vampires are intimately linked to military conquest and to the rise and fall of empires. According to Dr. Van Helsing, the vampire is the unavoidable consequence of any invasion: 'He have follow the wake of the berserker Icelander, the devil-begotten Hun, the Slav, the Saxon, the Magyar' (ch. 18).

Nowhere else in the Europe of 1897 could provide a more fertile breeding ground for the undead than the Count's homeland. The Western accounts of the region that Stoker consulted invariably stress the ceaseless clash of antagonistic cultures in the Carpathians.[2] The cycle of empire – rise, decay, collapse, displacement – was there displayed in a particularly compressed and vivid manner. 'Greeks, Romans, Huns, Avars, Magyars, Turks, Slavs, French and Germans, all have come and seen and gone, seeking conquest one over the other,' opens one late-century account (Bates, p. 3). The Count himself confirms that his homeland has been the scene of perpetual invasion: 'there is hardly a foot of soil in all this region that has not been enriched by the blood of men, patriots or invaders,' he tells Harker (ch. 2). His subsequent question is thus largely rhetorical: 'Is it a wonder that we were a conquering race?' (ch. 3).

The 'race' in which Dracula claims membership is left ambiguous here. He refers at once to his Szekely warrior past and to his vampiric present. The ambiguity underscores the impossibility of untangling the two aspects of Dracula's essential nature, since his vampirism is interwoven with his status as a conqueror and invader. Here Stoker departs significantly from his literary predecessors. Unlike Polidori and Le Fanu, for instance, who depict their vampires as wan and enervated, Stoker makes Dracula vigorous and energetic. Polidori's Count Ruthven and Le Fanu's Carmilla represent the aristocrat as decadent aesthete; their vampirism is an extension of the traditional aristocratic vices of sensualism and conspicuous consumption. Dracula represents the nobleman as warrior.[3] His activities after death carry on his activities in life; in both cases he has successfully engaged in forms of conquest and domination.

Racial conquest and domination, we should immediately add. Stoker continues a Western tradition of seeing unrest in Eastern Europe primarily in terms of racial strife. For Stoker, the vampire 'race' is simply the most virulent and threatening of the numerous warrior races – Berserker, Hun, Turk, Saxon, Slovak, Magvar, Szekely – inhabiting their area. Nineteenth-century accounts of the Carpathians repeatedly stress its polyracial character. The standard Victorian work on the region, Charles Boner's *Transylvania* (1865), begins by marvelling at this spectacle of variety:

> The diversity of character which the various physiognomies present that meet you at every step, also tell of the many nations which are here brought together . . . The slim, little Hungarian . . . the more oriental Wallachian, with softer, sensuous air, – in her style of dress and even in her carriage unlike a dweller in the West; a Moldavian princess, wrapped in a Turkish shawl . . . And now a Serb marches proudly past, his countenance calm as a Turk's; or a Constantinople merchant sweeps along in his loose robes and snowy turban. There are, too, Greeks, Dalmatians, and Croats, all different in feature: there is no end to the variety. (pp. 1–2)

Transylvania is what Dracula calls the 'whirlpool of European races' (ch. 3), but within that whirlpool racial interaction usually involved conflict, not accommodation. Racial violence could in fact reach appalling proportions, as in the wholesale massacres, widely reported by the British press, of Armenians by Turks in 1894 and 1896, the years in which *Dracula* was being written. For Western writers and readers, these characteristics – racial heterogeneity combined with racial intolerance considered barbaric in its intensity – defined the area east and south of the Danube, with the Carpathians at the imaginative center of the turmoil.

By situating Dracula in the Carpathians, and by continually blurring the lines between the Court's vampiric and warrior activities, Stoker forges seemingly 'natural' links among three of his principal concerns: racial strife, the collapse of empire, and vampirism. It is important too to note the sequences of events. As Van Helsing says, vampires follow 'in [the] wake' of imperial decay (ch. 18). Vampires are generated by racial enervation and the decline of empire, not vice versa. They are produced, in other words, by the very conditions characterizing late-Victorian Britain.

Stoker thus transforms the materials of the vampire myth, making them bear the weight of the culture's fears over its declining status. The appearance of vampires becomes the sign of profound trouble. With vampirism marking the intersection of racial strife, political upheaval, and the fall of empire, Dracula's move to London indicates that Great Britain, rather than the Carpathians, is now the scene of these connected struggles. The Count has penetrated to the heart of modern Europe's largest empire, and his very presence seems to presage its doom:

> This was the being I was helping to transfer to London [Harker writes in anguish] where, perhaps for centuries to come, he might, amongst its teeming millions, satiate his lust for blood, and create a new and ever widening circle of semi-demons to batten on the helpless. (ch. 4)

The late-Victorian nightmare of reverse colonization is expressed succinctly here: Harker envisions semi-demons spreading through the realm, colonizing bodies and land indiscriminately. The Count's 'lust for blood' points in both directions: to the vampire's need for its special food, and also to the warrior's desire for conquest. The Count endangers Britain's integrity as a nation at the same time that he imperils the personal integrity of individual citizens.

Harker's lament highlights the double thrust – political and biological – of Dracula's invasion, while at the same time conflating the two into a single threat. Dracula's twin status as vampire and Szekely warrior suggests that for Stoker the Count's aggressions against the body are also aggressions against the body politic. Indeed, the Count can threaten the integrity of the nation precisely because of the nature of his threat to personal integrity. His attacks involve more than an assault on the isolated self, the subversion and loss of one's individual identity. Again, unlike Polidori's Count Ruthven or Le Fanu's Carmilla (or even Thomas Prest's Sir Francis Varney), Dracula imperils not simply his victims' personal identities, but also their cultural, political, and racial selves. In *Dracula* vampirism designates a kind of colonization of the body. Horror arises not because Dracula destroys bodies, but because he appropriates and transforms them. Having yielded to his assault, one literally 'goes native' by becoming a vampire oneself. As John Allen Stevenson argues, if 'blood' is a sign of racial identity, then Dracula effectively deracinates his victims (p. 144). In turn, they receive a new racial identity, one that marks them as literally, 'Other.' Miscegenation leads, not to the mixing of races, but to the biological and political annihilation of the weaker race by the stronger.

Through the vampire myth, Stoker Gothicizes the political threats to Britain caused by the enervation of the Anglo-Saxon 'race.' These threats also operate independently of the Count's vampirism, however, for the vampire was not considered alone in its ability to deracinate. Stoker learned from Emily Gerard that the Roumanians were themselves notable for the way they could 'dissolve' the identities of those they came in contact with:

> The Hungarian woman who weds a Roumanian husband will necessarily adopt the dress and manners of his people, and her children will be as good Roumanians as though they had no drop of Magyar blood in their veins; while the Magyar who takes a Roumanian girl for his wife will not only fail to convert her to his ideas, but himself, subdued by her influence, will imperceptibly begin to lose his nationality. This is a fact well known and much lamented by the Hungarians themselves, who live in anticipated apprehension of seeing their people ultimately dissolving into Roumanians.[4]

Gerard's account of the 'imperceptible' but inevitable loss of identity – national, cultural, racial – sounds remarkably like the transformations that Lucy and Mina suffer under Dracula's 'influence.' In life Dracula was a Roumanian (Gerard designates the Szekelys as a branch of the Roumanian race); his ability to deracinate could thus derive as easily from his Roumanian as from his vampire nature.

The 'anticipated apprehension' of deracination – of seeing Britons 'ultimately dissolving into Roumanians' or vampires or savages – is at the heart of the reverse colonization narrative. For both Gerard and Stoker, the Roumanians' dominance can be traced to a kind of racial puissance that overwhelms its weaker victims. This racial context helps account for what critics routinely note about Dracula: that he is by his very nature vigorous, masterful, energetic, robust. Such attributes are conspicuously absent among the novel's British characters, particularly the men. All the novel's vampires are distinguished by their robust health and their equally robust fertility. The vampire serves, then, to highlight the alarming decline among the British, since the undead are, paradoxically, both 'healthier' and more 'fertile' than the living. Perversely, a vampiric attack can serve to invigorate its victim. 'The adventure of the night does not seem to have harmed her,' Mina notes after Lucy's first encounter with Dracula; 'on the contrary, it has benefited her, for she looks better this morning than she has done in weeks' (ch. 8). Indeed, after his attack, Lucy's body initially appears stronger, her eyes brighter, her cheeks rosier. The corresponding enervation that marks the British men is most clearly visible in Harker (he is 'pale,' 'weak-looking,' 'exhausted,' 'nervous,' 'a wreck'), but it can be seen in the other male British characters as well. Harker and Dracula in fact switch places during the novel; Harker becomes tired and white-haired as the action proceeds, while Dracula, whose white hair grows progressively darker, becomes more vigorous.

The vampire's vigor is in turn closely connected with its virility, its ability to produce literally endless numbers of offspring. Van Helsing's concern that the earth in Dracula's boxes be 'sterilized' (chs 18; 19) underlines the connection between the Count's threat and his fecundity. In marked contrast, the nonvampires in the novel seem unable to reproduce themselves. Fathers in particular are in short supply: most are either dead (Mr. Westenra, Mr. Harker, Mr. Murray, Mr. Canon), dying (Mr. Hawkins, Lord Godalming, Mr. Swales), or missing (Mr. Seward, Mr. Morris), while the younger men, being unmarried, cannot father legitimately. Even Harker, the novel's only married man, is prohibited from touching Mina after she has been made 'unclean.' In *Dracula*'s lexicon, uncleanliness is closely related to fertility, but it is the wrong kind of fertility; Mina, the men fear, is perfectly capable of producing 'offspring,' but not with Jonathan. The prohibition regarding Mina is linked to the fear of vampiric fecundity, a fecundity that threatens to overwhelm the far less prolific British men. Thus, as many critics have pointed out, the arrival of the little Quincey Harker at the story's close signals the final triumph over Dracula, since the Harkers' ability to secure an heir – an heir whose racial credentials are seemingly impeccable – is the surest indication that the vampire's threat has been mastered. Even this triumph is precarious, however. Harker proudly notes that his son is named after each of the men in the novel, making them all figurative fathers (ch. 27), yet Quincey's multiple parentage only underscores the original problem. How secure is any racial line when five fathers are needed to produce one son?

Such racial anxieties are clearest in the case of Lucy Westenra. If Dracula's kiss serves to deracinate Lucy, and by doing so to unleash what the male characters consider her incipiently monstrous sexual appetite, then the only way to counter this process is to 're-racinate' her by reinfusing her with the 'proper' blood. But Stoker is careful to establish a strict hierarchy among the potential donors. The men give blood in this order: Holmwood, Seward, Van Helsing, Morris. Arthur Holmwood is first choice ostensibly because he is engaged to Lucy, but also, and perhaps more importantly, because his blood is, in Van Helsing's words, 'more good than' Seward's (ch. 10). As the only English aristocrat in the novel, Holmwood possesses a 'blood so pure' (ch. 10) that it can restore Lucy's compromised racial identity. Dr. Seward, whose blood though bourgeois is English nonetheless, comes next in line, followed by the two foreigners, Van Helsing and Morris. We should note that Van Helsing's old, Teutonic blood is still preferred over Morris's young, American blood, for reasons I will take up in a moment. Even foreign blood is better than lower-class blood, however. After Lucy suffers what proves to be the fatal attack by Dracula, Van Helsing, looking for blood donors, rejects the four apparently healthy female servants as unsafe: 'I fear to trust those women' (ch. 12).

More precisely, Van Helsing's distrust of 'those women' marks a point of intersection between his usually covert class prejudices and his often overt misogyny.[5] That Dracula propagates his race solely through the bodies of women suggests an affinity, or even an identity, between vampiric sexuality and female sexuality. Both are represented as primitive and voracious, and both threaten patriarchal hegemony. In the novel's (and Victorian Britain's) sexual economy, female sexuality has only one legitimate function, propagation within the bounds of marriage. Once separated from that function, as Lucy's desire is, female sexuality becomes monstrous. The violence of Lucy's demise is grisly enough, but we should not miss the fact that her subjection and Mina's final fate parallel one another. They differ in degree, not kind. By the novel's close, Mina's sexual energy has been harnessed for purely domestic use. In the end, women serve identical purposes for both Dracula and the Western characters. If in this novel blood stands for race, then women quite literally become the vehicles of racial propagation. The struggle between the two camps is thus on one level a struggle over access to women's bodies, and Dracula's biological colonization of women becomes a horrific parody of the sanctioned exploitation practiced by the Western male characters.

By considering the parallel fates of Lucy and Mina, moreover, we can see how the fear and guilt characteristic of reverse colonization narratives begin to overlap. The fear generated by the Count's colonizations of his victims' bodies – a colonization appropriately designated monstrous – modulates into guilt that his practices simply repeat those of the 'good' characters. Dracula's invasion and appropriation of female bodies does not distinguish him from his Western antagonists as much as at first appears. Instead of being uncannily Other, the vampire is here revealed as disquietingly familiar. And since the colonizations of bodies and territory are closely linked, the same blurring of distinctions occurs when we consider more closely the nature of the Count's invasion of Britain. Just as Dracula's vampirism mirrors the domestic practices of Victorian patriarchs, so his invasion of London in order to 'batten on the helpless' natives there mirrors British imperial activities abroad.

As a transplanted Irishman, one whose national allegiances were conspicuously split, Stoker was particularly sensitive to the issues raised by British imperial conquest and domination. Britain's subjugation of Ireland was marked by a brutality often exceeding what occurred in the colonies, while the stereotype of the 'primitive . . . dirty, vengeful, and violent' Irishman was in most respects identical to that of the most despised 'savage.'[6] The ill will characterizing Anglo-Irish relations in the late-nineteenth century, exacerbated by the rise of Fenianism and the debate over Home Rule, far surpassed the tensions that arose as a result of British rule elsewhere. When that ill will erupted into violence, as it did in the 1882 Phoenix Park murders, Victorian readers could see, up close and in sharp focus, the potential consequences of imperial domination. For Stoker's audience, Dracula's invasion of Britain would conceivably have aroused seldom dormant fears of an Irish uprising.

The lack of autobiographical materials makes it difficult to determine the extent, if any, to which Stoker consciously felt himself in solidarity with his Irish brethren. On the one hand, his few published essays, particularly one advocating censorship, reveal a deeply conservative outlook in which 'duty to the [British] state' outweighs all other considerations, even those of a dubious freedom or self-determination. On the other hand, through Stoker's very adherence to what he calls 'forms of restraint' runs a deeply anarchic streak. The attraction of forbidden, outlawed, disruptive action is evident enough in *Dracula* as well as in Stoker's other fictions; the same tension between restraint and rebellion may have characterized his relation to the ruling state. It probably also characterized his professional life. Certainly, his status as glorified manservant to the autocratic Henry Irving almost uncannily reenacted, on the personal level, the larger cultural pattern of English domination and Irish subservience. Stoker's lifelong passion for Irving had its dark underside: the rumors, persistent in Stoker's lifetime, that Count Dracula was modelled on Irving suggests the deep ambivalence with which the transplanted Irishman regarded his professional benefactor. Like Quincey Morris, Stoker seems finally to stand in alliance with his English companions without ever being entirely of their camp.

Dracula suggests two equations in relation to English-Irish politics: not just, Dracula is to England as Ireland is to England, but, Dracula is to England as England is to Ireland. In Count Dracula, Victorian readers could recognize their culture's imperial ideology mirrored back as a kind of monstrosity. Dracula's journey from Transylvania to England could be read as a reversal of Britain's imperial exploitations of 'weaker' races, including the Irish. This mirroring extends not just to the imperial practices themselves, but to their epistemological underpinnings. Before Dracula successfully invades the spaces of his victims' bodies or land, he first invades the spaces of their knowledge. The Count operates in several distinct registers in the novel. He is both the warrior nobleman, whose prowess dwarfs that of the novel's enfeebled English aristocrat, Lord Godalming, and the primitive savage, whose bestiality, fecundity, and vigor alternately repel and attract. But he is also what we might call an incipient 'Occidentalist' scholar. Dracula's physical mastery of his British victims begins with an intellectual appropriation of their culture, which allows him to delve the workings of the 'native mind.' As Harker discovers, the Count's expertise in 'English life and customs and manners' (ch. 2) provides the groundwork for his exploitative invasion of Britain. Thus, in Dracula the British characters see their own ideology reflected back as a form of bad faith, since the Count's Occidentalism both mimics and reverses the more familiar Orientalism underwriting Western imperial practices.[7]

Phyllis A. Roth, Suddenly Sexual Women in Bram Stoker's *Dracula* (1977)

Criticism of Bram Stoker's *Dracula*, though not extensive, yet not insubstantial, points primarily in a single direction: the few articles published perceive *Dracula* as the consistent success it has been because, in the words of Royce MacGillwray, 'Such a myth lives not merely because it has been skillfully marketed by entrepreneurs [primarily the movie industry] but because it expresses something that large numbers of readers feel to be true about their own lives.'[1] In other words, *Dracula* successfully manages a fantasy which is congruent with a fundamental fantasy shared by many others. Several of the interpretations of *Dracula* either explicitly or implicitly indicate that this 'core fantasy'[2] derives from the Oedipus complex – indeed, Maurice Richardson calls *Dracula* 'a quite blatant demonstration of the Oedipus complex . . . a kind of incestuous, necrophilous, oral-anal-sadistic all-in-wrestling match'[3] and this reading would seem to be valid.

Nevertheless, the Oedipus complex and the critics' use of it does not go far enough in explaining the novel: in explaining what I see to be the primary focus of the fantasy content and in explaining what allows Stoker and, vicariously, his readers, to act out what are essentially threatening, even horrifying wishes which must engage the most polarized of ambivalences. I propose, in the following, to summarize the interpretations to date, to indicate the pre-Oedipal focus of the fantasies, specifically the child's relation with and hostility toward the mother, and to indicate how the novel's fantasies are managed in such a way as to transform horror into pleasure. Moreover, I would emphasize that for both the Victorians and twentieth century readers, much of the novel's great appeal derives from its hostility toward female sexuality. In 'Fictional Convention and Sex in *Dracula*,' Carrol Fry observes that the female vampires are equivalent to the fallen women of eighteenth and nineteenth century fiction.[4]

The facile and stereotypical dichotomy between the dark woman and the fair, the fallen and the idealized, is obvious in *Dracula*. Indeed, among the more gratuitous passages in the novel are those in which the 'New Woman' who is sexually aggressive is verbally assaulted. Mina Harker remarks that such a woman, whom she holds in contempt, 'will do the proposing herself.'[5] Additionally, we must compare Van Helsing's hope 'that there are good women still left to make life happy' (ch. 14) with Mina's assertion that 'the world seems full of good men – even if there *are* monsters in it' (ch. 17). A remarkable contrast![6]

Perhaps nowhere is the dichotomy of sensual and sexless woman more dramatic than it is in *Dracula* and nowhere is the suddenly sexual woman more violently and self-righteously persecuted than in Stoker's 'thriller.'

The equation of vampirism with sexuality is well established in the criticism. Richardson refers to Freud's observation that 'morbid dread always signifies repressed sexual wishes.'[7] We must agree that *Dracula* is permeated by 'morbid dread'. However, another tone interrupts the dread of impending doom throughout the novel; that note is one of lustful anticipation, certainly anticipation of catching and destroying forever the master vampire, Count Dracula, but additionally, lustful anticipation of a consummation one can only describe as sexual. One thinks, for example, of the candle's 'sperm which "dropped in white patches" on Lucy's coffin as Van Helsing opens it for the first time' (ch. 15). Together the critics have enumerated the most striking instances of this tone and its attendant imagery, but to recall: first, the scene in which Jonathan Harker searches the Castle Dracula, in a state of fascinated and morbid dread, for proof of his host's nature. Harker meets with three vampire women (whose relation to Dracula is incestuous[8]) whose appeal is described almost pornographically:

> All three had brilliant white teeth that shone like pearls against the ruby of their voluptuous lips. There was something about them that made me uneasy, some longing and at the same time deadly fear. I felt in my heart a wicked, burning desire that they would kiss me with those red lips. (ch. 3)

The three debate who has the right to feast on Jonathan first, but they conclude, 'He is young and strong; there are kisses for us all' (ch. 3). While this discussion takes place, Jonathan is 'in an agony of delightful anticipation' (ch. 3). At the very end of the novel, Van Helsing falls prey to the same attempted seduction by, and the same ambivalence toward, the three vampires.

Two more scenes of relatively explicit and uninhibited sexuality mark the novel about one-half, then two-thirds, through. First the scene in which Lucy Westenra is laid to her final rest by her fiance, Arthur Holmwood, later Lord Godalming, which is worth quoting from at length:

> Arthur placed the point [of the stake] over the heart, and as I looked I could see its dint in the white flesh. Then he struck with all his might.

> The thing in the coffin writhed; and a hideous, blood-curdling screech came from the opened red lips. The body shook and quivered and twisted in wild contortions; the sharp white teeth champed together till the lips were cut, and the mouth was smeared with a crimson foam. But Arthur never faltered. He looked like a figure of Thor as his untrembling arm rose and fell, driving deeper and deeper the mercy-bearing stake, whilst the blood from the pierced heart welled and spurted up around it. (ch. 16)

Such a description needs no comment here, though we will return to it in another context. Finally, the scene which Joseph Bierman has described quite correctly as a 'primal scene in oral terms,'[9] the scene in which Dracula slits open his breast and forces Mina Harker to drink his blood:

> With his left hand he held both Mrs. Harker's hands, keeping them away with her arms at full tension; his right hand gripped her by the back of the neck, forcing her face down on his bosom. Her white nightdress was smeared with blood, and a thin stream trickled down the man's bare chest which was shown by his torn-open dress. The attitude of the two had a terrible resemblance to a child forcing a kitten's nose into a saucer of milk to compel it to drink. (ch. 21)

Two major points are to be made here, in addition to marking the clearly erotic nature of the descriptions. These are, in the main, the only sexual scenes and descriptions in the novel; and, not only are the scenes heterosexual,[10] they are incestuous, especially when taken together, as we shall see.

To consider the first point, only relations with vampires are sexualized in this novel; indeed, a deliberate attempt is made to make sexuality seem unthinkable in 'normal relations' between the sexes. All the close relationships, including those between Lucy and her three suitors and Mina and her husband, are spiritualized beyond credibility. Only when Lucy becomes a vampire is she allowed to be 'voluptuous,' yet she must have been so long before, judging from her effect on men and from Mina's descriptions of her (Mina, herself, never suffers the fate of voluptuousness before or after being bitten, for reasons which will become apparent later.) Clearly, then, vampirism is associated not only with death, immortality and orality; it is equivalent to sexuality.[11]

Moreover, in psychoanalytic terms, the vampirism is a disguise for greatly desired and equally strongly feared fantasies. These fantasies, as stated, have encouraged critics to point to the Oedipus complex at the center of the novel. Dracula, for example, is seen, as the 'father-figure of huge potency.'[12] Royce MacGillwray remarks that:

> Dracula even aspires to be, in a sense, the father of the band that is pursuing him. Because he intends, as he tells them, to turn them all into vampires, he will be their creator and therefore 'father.'[13]

The major focus of the novel, in this analysis, is the battle of the sons against the father to release the desired woman, the mother, she whom it is felt originally belonged to the son till the father seduced her away. Richardson comments:

> the set-up reminds one rather of the primal horde as pictured somewhat fantastically perhaps by Freud in *Totem and Taboo*, with the brothers banding together against the father who has tried to keep all the females to himself.[14]

The Oedipal rivalry is not, however, merely a matter of the Van Helsing group, in which, as Richardson says, 'Van Helsing represents the good father figure,'[15] pitted against the Big Daddy, Dracula. Rather, from the novel's beginning, a marked rivalry among the men is evident. This rivalry is defended against by the constant, almost obsessive, assertion of the value of friendship and *agape* among members of the Van Helsing group. Specifically, the defense of overcompensation is employed, most often by Van Helsing in his assertions of esteem for Dr. Seward and his friends. The others, too, repeat expressions of mutual affection *ad nauseum*: they clearly protest too much. Perhaps this is most obviously symbolized, and unintentionally exposed, by the blood transfusions from Arthur, Seward, Quincey, Morris, and Van Helsing to Lucy Westenra. The great friendship among rivals for Lucy's hand lacks credibility and is especially strained when Van Helsing makes it clear that the transfusions (merely the reverse of the vampire's blood-letting) are in their nature sexual; others have recognized, too, that Van Helsing's warning to Seward not to tell Arthur that anyone else has given Lucy blood, indicates the sexual nature of the operation.[16] Furthermore, Arthur himself feels that, as a result of having given Lucy his blood, they are in effect married. Thus, the friendships of the novel mask a deep-seated rivalry and hostility.

Dracula does then appear to enact the Oedipal rivalry among sons and between the son and the father for the affections of the mother. The fantasy of parricide and its acting out is obviously satisfying. According to Holland, such a threatening wish-fulfillment can be rewarding when properly defended against or associated with other pleasurable fantasies. Among the other fantasies are those of life after death, the triumph of 'good over evil,' mere man over super-human forces, and the rational West over the mysterious East.[17] Most likely not frightening and certainly intellectualized, these simplistic abstractions provide a diversion from more threatening material and assure the fantasist that God's in his heaven; all's right with the world. On the surface, this is the moral of the end of the novel: Dracula is safely reduced to ashes, Mina is cleansed, the 'boys' are triumphant. Were this all the theme of interest the novel presented, however, it would be neither so popular with Victorians and their successors nor worthy of scholarly concern.

Up to now my discussion has been taken from the point of view of reader identification with those who are doing battle against the evil in this world, against Count Dracula. On the surface of it, this is where one's sympathies lie in reading the novel and it is this level of analysis which has been explored by previous critics. However, what is far more significant in the interrelation of fantasy and defense is the duplication of characters and structure which betrays an identification with Dracula and a fantasy of matricide underlying the more obvious parricidal wishes.

As observed, the split between the sexual vampire family and the asexual Van Helsing group is not at all clear-cut: Jonathan, Van Helsing, Seward and Holmwood are all overwhelmingly attracted to the vampires, to sexuality. Fearing this, they employ two defenses, projection[18] and denial: it is not we who want the vampires, it is they who want us (to eat us, to seduce us, to kill us). Despite the projections, we should recall that almost all the on-stage killing is done by the 'good guys': that of Lucy, the vampire women, and Dracula. The projection of the wish to kill onto the vampires wears thinnest perhaps when Dr. Seward, contemplating the condition of Lucy, asserts that 'had she then to be killed I could have done it with savage delight' (ch. 16). Even earlier, when Dr. Seward is rejected by Lucy, he longs for a cause with which to distract himself from the pain of rejection: 'Oh, Lucy, Lucy, I cannot be angry with you . . . If I only could have as strong a cause as my poor mad friend there [significantly, he refers to Renfield] – a good, unselfish cause to make me work – that would be indeed happiness' (ch. 6). Seward's wish is immediately fulfilled by Lucy's vampirism and the subsequent need to destroy her. Obviously, the acting out of such murderous impulses is threatening: in addition to the defenses mentioned above, the use of religion not only to exorcise the evil but to justify the murders is striking. In other words, Christianity is on our side, *we must* be right. In this connection, it is helpful to mention Wasson's observation[19] of the significance of the name 'Lord Godalming' (the point is repeated). Additional justification is provided by the murdered themselves: the peace into which they subside is to be read as a thank you note. Correlated with the religious defense is one described by Freud in *Totem and Taboo* in which the violator of the taboo can avert disaster by Lady Macbeth-like compulsive rituals and renunciations.[20] The repeated use of the Host, the complicated ritual of the slaying of the vampires, and the ostensible, though not necessarily conscious, renunciation of sexuality are the penance paid by those in *Dracula* who violate the taboos against incest and the murder of parents.

Since we now see that Dracula acts out the repressed fantasies of the others, since those others wish to do what he can do, we have no difficulty in recognizing an identification with the aggressor on the part of characters and reader alike. It is important, then, to see what it is that Dracula is after.

The novel tells of two major episodes, the seduction of Lucy and of Mina, to which the experience of Harker at Castle Dracula provides a preface, a hero, one whose narrative encloses the others and with whom, therefore, one might readily identify. This, however, is a defense against the central identification of the novel with Dracula and his attacks on the women. It is relevant in this context to observe how spontaneous and ultimately trivial Dracula's interest in Harker is. When Harker arrives at Castle Dracula, his host makes a lunge for him, but only after Harker has cut his finger and is bleeding. Dracula manages to control himself and we hear no more about his interest in Harker's blood until the scene with the vampire women when he says. 'This man belongs to me!' (ch. 3) and, again a little later, 'have patience. Tonight is mine. To-morrow night is yours!' (ch. 4). After this we hear no more of Dracula's interest in Jonathan; indeed, when Dracula arrives in England, he never again goes after Jonathan. For his part, Jonathan appears far more concerned about the vampire women than about Dracula – they are more horrible and fascinating to him. Indeed, Harker is relieved to be saved from the women by Dracula. Moreover, the novel focusses on the Lucy and Mina episodes from which, at first, the Jonathan episodes may seem disconnected; actually, they are not, but we can only see why after we understand what is going on in the rest of the novel.

In accepting the notion of identification with the aggressor in *Dracula*, as I believe we must, what we accept is an understanding of the reader's identification with the *aggressor's* victimization of women. Dracula's desire is for the destruction of Lucy and Mina and what this means is obvious when we recall that his attacks on these two closest of friends seem incredibly coincidental on the narrative level. Only on a deeper level is there no coincidence at all: the level on which one recognizes that Lucy and Mina are essentially the same figure: the mother. Dracula is, in fact, the same story told twice with different outcomes. In the former, the mother is more desirable, more sexual, more threatening and must be destroyed. And the physical descriptions of Lucy reflect this greater ambivalence: early in the story, when Lucy is not yet completely vampirized, Dr. Seward describes her hair 'in its usual sunny ripples' (ch. 12); later, when the men watch her return to her tomb, Lucy is described as 'a dark-haired woman' (ch. 16). The conventional fair/dark split, symbolic of respective moral casts, seems to be unconscious here, reflecting the ambivalence aroused by the sexualized female. Not only is Lucy the more sexualized figure, she is the more rejecting figure, rejecting two of the three 'sons' in the novel. This section of the book ends with her destruction, not by Dracula but by the man whom she was to marry. The novel could not end here, though; the story had to be told again to assuage the anxiety occasioned by matricide. This time, the mother is much less sexually threatening and is ultimately saved. Moreover, Mina is never described physically and is the opposite of rejecting: all the men become her sons, symbolized by the naming of her actual son after them all. What remains constant is the attempt to destroy the mother. What changes is the way the fantasies are managed. To speak of the novel in terms of the child's ambivalence toward the mother is not just to speak psychoanalytically. We need only recall that Lucy, as 'bloofer lady', as well as the other vampire women, prey on children. In the case of Lucy, the children are as attracted to her as threatened by her.

I have already described the evidence that the Van Helsing men themselves desire to do away with Lucy. Perhaps the story needed to be retold because the desire was too close to the surface to be satisfying; certainly, the reader would not be satisfied had the novel ended with Arthur's murder of Lucy. What is perhaps not so clear is that the desire to destroy Mina is equally strong. Let us look first at the defenses against this desire. I have already mentioned the great professions of affection for Mina made by most of the male characters. Mina indeed acts and is treated as both the saint and the mother (ironically, this is particularly clear when she comforts Arthur for the loss of Lucy). She is all good, all pure, all true. When, however, she is seduced away from the straight and narrow by Dracula, she is 'unclean,' tainted and stained with a mark on her forehead immediately occasioned by Van Helsing's touching her forehead with the Host. Van Helsing's hostility toward Mina is further revealed when he cruelly reminds her of her 'intercourse' with Dracula: '"Do you forget," he said, with actually a smile, "that last night he banqueted heavily and will sleep late?"' (ch. 22). This hostility is so obvious that the other men are shocked. Nevertheless, the 'sons,' moreover, and the reader as well, identify with Dracula's attack on Mina; indeed, the men cause it, as indicated by the events which transpire when all the characters are at Seward's hospital-asylum. The members of the brotherhood go out at night to seek out Dracula's lairs, and they leave Mina undefended at the hospital. They claim that this insures her safety; in fact, it insures the reverse. Furthermore, this is the real purpose in leaving Mina out of the plans and in the hospital. They have clear indications in Renfield's warnings of what is to happen to her and they all, especially her husband, observe that she is not well and seems to be getting weaker. That they could rationalize these signs away while looking for and finding them everywhere else further indicates that they are avoiding seeing what they want to ignore; in other words, they want Dracula to get her. This is not to deny that they also want to save Mina; it is simply to claim that the ambivalence toward the mother is fully realized in the novel.

We can now return to that ambivalence and, I believe, with the understanding of the significance of the mother figure, comprehend, the precise perspective of the novel. Several critics have correctly emphasized the regression to both orality and anality[21] in *Dracula*. Certainly, the sexuality is perceived in oral terms. The primal scene already discussed makes abundantly clear that intercourse is perceived in terms of nursing. As C. F. Bentley sees it:

> Stoker is describing a symbolic act of enforced fellation, where blood is again a substitute for semen, and where a chaste female suffers a violation that is essentially sexual. Of particular interest in the . . . passage is the striking image of 'a child forcing a kitten's nose into a saucer of milk to compel it to drink,' suggesting an element of regressive infantilism in the vampire superstition.[22]

The scene referred to is, in several senses, the climax of the novel; it is the most explicit view of the act of vampirism and is, therefore, all the more significant as an expression of the nature of sexual intercourse as the novel depicts it. In it, the woman is doing the sucking. Bierman comments that 'The reader by this point in the novel has become used to Dracula doing the sucking, but not to Dracula being sucked and specifically at the breast.'[23] While it is true that the reader may most often think of Dracula as the active partner, the fact is that the scenes of vampire sexuality are described from the male perspective, with the females as the active assailants.[24] Only the acts of phallic aggression, the killings, involve the males in active roles. *Dracula*, then, dramatizes the child's view of intercourse insofar as it is seen as a wounding and a killing. But the primary preoccupation, as attested to by the primal scene, is with the role of the female in the act. Thus, it is not surprising that the central anxiety of the novel is the fear of the devouring woman and, in documenting this, we will find that all the pieces of the novel fall into place, most especially the Jonathan Harker prologue.

As mentioned, Harker's desire and primary anxiety is not with Dracula but with the female vampires. In his initial and aborted seduction by them, he describes his ambivalence. Interestingly, Harker seeks out this episode by violating the Count's (father's) injunction to remain in his room; 'let me warn you with all seriousness, that should you leave these rooms you will not by any chance go to sleep in any other part of the castle' (ch. 3). This, of course, is what Harker promptly does. When Dracula breaks in and discovers Harker with the vampire women, he acts like both a jealous husband and an irate father: 'His eyes were positively blazing. The red light in them was lurid . . . "How dare you touch him, any of you?"' (ch. 3). Jonathan's role as child here is reinforced by the fact that, when Dracula takes him away from the women, he gives them a child as substitute. But most interesting is Jonathan's perspective as he awaits, in a state of erotic arousal, the embraces of the vampire women, especially the fair one: 'The other was fair as fair can be, with great wavy masses of golden hair and eyes like pale sapphires. I seemed somehow to know her face and to know it in connection with some dreamy fear, but I could not recollect at the moment how or where' (ch. 3). As far as we know, Jonathan never recollects, but we should be able to understand that the face is that of the mother (almost archetypally presented), she whom he desires yet fears, the temptress-seductress, Medusa. Moreover, this golden girl reappears in the early description of Lucy.

At the end of the following chapter, Jonathan exclaims, 'I am alone in the castle with those awful women. Faugh! Mina is a woman, and there is nought in common.' Clearly, however, there is. Mina at the breast of Count Dracula is identical to the vampire women whose desire is to draw out of the male the fluid necessary for life. That this is viewed as an act of castration is clear from Jonathan's conclusion: 'At least God's mercy is better than that of these monsters, and the precipice is steep and high. At its foot a man may sleep – *as a man*. Goodbye, all! Mina!' (ch. 4, emphasis mine).

The threatening Oedipal fantasy, the regression to a primary oral obsession, the attraction and destruction of the vampires of *Dracula* are, then, interrelated and interdependent. What they spell out is a fusion of the memory of nursing at the mother's breast with a primal scene fantasy which results in the conviction that the sexually desirable woman will annihilate if she is not first destroyed. The fantasy of incest and matricide evokes the mythic image of the *vagina dentata* evident in so many folk tales[25] in which the mouth and the vagina are identified with one another by the primitive mind and pose the threat of castration to all men until the teeth are extracted by the hero. The conclusion of *Dracula*, the 'salvation' of Mina, is equivalent to such an 'extraction': Mina will not remain the *vagina dentata* to threaten them all.

Central to the structure and unconscious theme of *Dracula* is, then, primarily the desire to destroy the threatening mother, she who threatens by being desirable. Otto Rank best explains why it is Dracula whom the novel seems to portray as the threat when he says, in a study which is pertinent to ours:

> through the displacement of anxiety on to the father, the renunciation of the mother, necessary for the sake of life is assured. For this feared father prevents the return to the mother and thereby the releasing of the much more painful primary anxiety, which is related to the mother's genitals as the place of birth and later transferred to objects taking the place of the genitals [such as the mouth].[26]

Finally, the novel has it both ways: Dracula is destroyed,[27] and Van Helsing saved; Lucy is destroyed and Mina saved. The novel ends on a rather ironic note, given our understanding here, as Harker concludes with a quote from the good father, Van Helsing:

> 'We want no proofs; we ask none to believe us! This boy will some day know what a brave and gallant woman his mother is. Already he knows her sweetness and loving care; later on he will understand how some men so loved her, that they did dare so much for her sake.' (ch. 27)

11

KATE CHOPIN, *THE AWAKENING*

Helen Taylor's essay briefly surveys the work of three women writers who lived in the American South (Louisiana) during the turbulent years of the Civil War and Reconstruction. Grace King (1852–1932) and Ruth McEnery Stuart (1849–1917) lived in New Orleans throughout the war and the period of Reconstruction (roughly 1862–77 in Louisiana), while Kate Chopin was resident in New Orleans for the final seven years of Reconstruction. All three women began to write in 1883–4, and all witnessed dramatic transformations in the social and political life of Louisiana. The essay provides a valuable insight into the ethnic complexity and diversity of New Orleans in the 1870s and 1880s.

Anne Goodwyn Jones looks at the ways in which the slave-owning South fostered ideals of womanhood that differed significantly from models of female conduct in the rest of America, as well as in Europe. Her purpose, however, is to challenge the stereotypes of the Southern woman by showing how familiar images failed to correspond to the reality of women's lives. She strongly contests the idea that Southern women were uniformly constrained by social ideals of leisure and sexual purity, and she also claims that white women's attitudes to slavery were often ambiguous and complicated.

Elizabeth Ammons draws attention to the 'repressed African American context' of *The Awakening*, and she argues that Edna Pontellier's 'liberation' is achieved at the expense of women of other races and other social groups, who have suffered a much more profound oppression. Kate Chopin's novel exposes racist abuse, but remains at a fundamental distance from the lives of those outside its own well-to-do domain. In this respect. *The Awakening* is not a universal story of emancipation, but a privileged white female fantasy.

Bert Bender's essay reads *The Awakening* as a meditation on modern civilisation, profoundly influenced by Kate Chopin's reading of Charles Darwin's *Descent of Man* (1871). To begin with, Darwin's work confirmed the celebration of life that Chopin had encountered in her reading of Walt Whitman's *Leaves of Grass*, and it seemed to offer encouragement to Victorian women living repressed, secluded lives. Chopin's response, however, seems to have darkened as she continued to ponder the implications of Darwin's theories of natural selection and sexual desire. In her writings, she adopts some basic Darwinian ideas, but remains ambivalent about the notion of sexual selection and the passive role allotted to women. The essay concentrates on *The Awakening*, but also makes reference to an earlier novel, *At Fault*, and several short stories.

Helen Taylor, Gender, Race and Region in the Writings of Grace King, Ruth McEnery Stuart and Kate Chopin (1989)

The women who are the subject of this study were all old enough to understand the disruptions and suffering caused by the Civil War. Grace King (1852–1932) and Ruth McEnery Stuart (1849–1917) lived in New Orleans through the war and Reconstruction (which lasted in Louisiana from approximately 1862 to 1877), while Kate Chopin (1850–1904), who was part of a pro-Confederate family living in St. Louis, a major Union stronghold, moved to New Orleans for the last seven years of Reconstruction. As with other southern writers, the three women's experiences of this turbulent and politically charged period of Louisiana's history stirred their imaginations and to some extent structured the political and racial ideological positions that their fiction was to explore. It is significant that they all began to write between 1883 and 1884, some half-dozen years after Republican carpetbag governments had been permanently driven from the state by Louisiana's traditional white ruling class, and also at the time of the state's greatest popularity in the nation's cultural life. I will discuss later the way the writers were influenced by Louisiana's mythic construction as romantic paradise. Of significance here is the fact that these women were strongly influenced by the contemporary definitions of the causes and effects of the war: Reconstruction, Counter-Reconstruction, and Redemption.[1]

All three writers lived in Louisiana during a period of crisis and dramatic transformations of political, economic, and social life. Louisiana was much affected by the Civil War.[2] One-fifth of all her Confederate troops were killed in battle, and many more wounded or crippled for life. Most families lost at least one member. Around six hundred military engagements took place in the state, leaving considerable destruction of property and land. With freed slaves counted as lost property, the banking system shattered, and Confederate paper money and bonds worthless, Louisiana lost one-third of its wealth. In 1860, in terms of (white) per capita wealth, the state ranked first in the South, second in the nation. By the first census after Reconstruction, Louisiana was thirty-seventh among all American states and territories. Plantations and farms were badly damaged and pillaged: crumbling levees, rusting equipment, and neglected, scattered farm animals meant that the mainstays of Louisiana's antebellum prosperity, its sugar and cotton plantations, were badly hit. Before the war, Louisiana had produced 95 percent of the South's sugar crop; by 1877, it was producing a mere one-third of that output. Furthermore, after Radical Republican and then Bourbon misrule throughout the 1870s, the state's reputation for fraud, corruption, lawlessness, and violence was unparalleled. By the 1880s, northern businessmen who had formerly invested heavily in Louisiana were wary of its political corruption, fraudulent ballot box practices, and high crime rate – especially in New Orleans. In the 1880s and 1890s, the state had the dubious distinction of boasting the highest rate of illiteracy in the South, and the worst national record for public institutions – schools, asylums, and prisons.

The New Orleans in which the three women lived – and of which King and Stuart were natives – had long been an important world port and commercial, cultural, and social center. From 1800 to 1861, a large proportion of the world's goods in transit had gone through New Orleans, and (while the rest of Louisiana was rural and unsophisticated) the city in which Grace King and Ruth McEnery grew up had a large population with a cosmopolitan atmosphere because of its many ethnic groups, including the largest community of free blacks in the South. It was occupied by Union troops as early as 1862, and during the course of the war lost most of its wealth and commercial functions. Although its postbellum fortunes revived, especially when it resumed its functions as an exporting depot, by 1870 the city's financial crisis (begun by the war) had increased. It was deeply in debt, and for decades continued in economic chaos, due largely to the activities of corrupt businessmen, politicians, and companies (notably the Louisiana Lottery Company). A mecca for the hungry, vagrant, and sick (including thousands of freed blacks fleeing from plantations), the city became a center of violent crime, social problems, and disease. Yellow fever epidemics, unwholesome sanitation, and frequent floodings, which all went untreated until the late 1890s, meant that in economic, social, and racial terms New Orleans was a tense, difficult, and dangerous city in which to live – hardly the "Paradise Regained" Edward King hoped it would be by the 1890s, nor the "place so full of romantic sentiment" that William Dean Howells imagined it to be in the late 1880s.[3]

But in some ways, in the years following the Civil War, it was business-as-usual. The image that white Democrats perpetuated of the carpetbag southern governments was grossly exaggerated. Not only was most confiscated land restored to its former owners within a few years after the war – on condition the loyalty oath was signed or a presidential pardon given – but the temporary advantages conferred on freed blacks (suffrage, public education, minimal land ownership, or sharecropping) were soon brutally removed. As John Hope

Franklin points out, 'effective political power therefore remained where it had been before the war – with an oligarchy, a small ruling clique, which wielded power far out of proportion to its numerical strength . . . Contrary to the widely held view, there was no significant breakup of the plantation system during and after reconstruction.'[4] When the Constitution of 1868 was written by the state conventions of 1867–68, Louisiana agreed that blacks were to constitute 50 percent of the delegates, hardly a clear majority as some whites implied. Indeed, political participation by blacks in the South during Reconstruction was 'never more than a thin veneer of integration.' Though they had unusually high rates of literacy and status within the community, black politicians in Louisiana had little capital, few contacts, minimal patronage, and therefore derisory power. The lot of the southern black man (and to a lesser extent and in different ways, black woman) can be summarized by the new regulations and events of Reconstruction: black codes regulating black vagrancy, labor, and legal rights (modeled on slave codes); the unenforced Civil Rights Act of 1865; the lack of federal support given the few scattered Freedmen's Bureaus: the convict-leasing and contract labor systems that returned freed blacks to the conditions of slavery; the failure of black trade unions and free integrated public education; intimidation and violence at the ballot box; extreme rural poverty because of a lack of capital and land, resulting in badly paid labor on the land or shabby sharecropping agreements; unemployment in towns and cities; and the constant harassment, victimization, and murder of individual blacks in all parts of the southern states.

In terms of race, Louisiana had long been a far more relaxed and mixed state than any other. In New Orleans, for decades there had been an unusually large community of free blacks with a sophisticated and economically and culturally varied lifestyle. Both in the city and throughout the state, the integration of public places and interracial sexual contacts were fairly common before and after the war. The population of Louisiana in general, and of New Orleans in particular, had the highest percentage of mixed-race ancestry of any American city or state.[5] Since New Orleans had a heterogeneous citizenry comprising Italians, Spaniards, and French as well as blacks and people of mixed race, it was impossible to differentiate people simply by color or language – free mulattoes, for instance, were usually French-speaking. The practice of 'passing for white' was common, and as racial tensions increased during Reconstruction this practice accelerated considerably. Also, miscegenation (usually between white men and black or mulatto women) had been a tolerated feature of city life before the war – through *placage* (the common-law alliances formulated mainly at quadroon balls, a practice popular in the 1820s and 1830s, though in bad repute by the 1850s), and the many casual alliances between whites and free blacks. By 1860, New Orleans had adopted a fairly liberal attitude toward black-white relations, which was soon to be eroded.

Soon after the war began, especially with the Emancipation Proclamation and the Federal occupation of New Orleans, whites began to turn on blacks, blaming them for the humiliation and devastation that the fighting and occupation were causing. The increasing riots, tensions, and diseases caused by black migration into New Orleans from the plantations, and the subsequent imposition of the black codes between 1865 and 1866, caused much interracial hatred and suspicion. That very tolerance between the races in antebellum New Orleans was seized on by the old white ruling class as one of the main cards that had played into the carpetbaggers' hands, and as a major threat to the reestablishment of white supremacy and (in eugenicist terms) the maintenance of a 'pure' race. This new suspicion and tension turned even more uncompromisingly to violence as soon as the Reconstruction period began.

After the notorious New Orleans riot of July, 1866, when thirty-four blacks were shot dead by white citizens furious at the reconvening of a black suffrage convention, armed bands of whites roamed Louisiana. In the 1860s, over three thousand people, mostly black, were killed or wounded in massacres, and the process of 'whitecapping' (terrorizing blacks at random) continued long after the end of Reconstruction.[6] When the disputed state governorship election of 1872 was settled by presidential fiat in favor of the Republican candidate William Pitt Kellogg, Democratic fury ran high. Kellogg's authority was challenged by the newly organized White Leagues – paramilitary groups dedicated to the restoration of white supremacy. Their numbers rose rapidly to approximately 25,000, with many large property-holders and respected citizens in their ranks – including Grace King's brother and Kate Chopin's husband. The White Leagues were crucial both in helping destroy Louisiana's Reconstruction government and also in preventing plans, laboriously worked out in the early postwar governments, to desegregate schools, churches, and other public places. Whites had opposed school integration as soon as it began in 1869, but only in 1874 did the leagues' concerted attacks on schools in the form of parental boycotts and the forcible removal of black children from classrooms persuade the school boards to close schools and drop plans for full integration. Although the Catholic Church officially opposed segregation, many priests supported the White Leagues. In 1875 priests in New Orleans' Saint Louis Cathedral tried to segregate their parishioners. The league was also very vocal in defending the purity of white women. John Blassingame argues that the rage that interracial marriage aroused in white supremacists 'lay at the foundation of almost all white opposition to the Negro's acquisition of civil and political rights.'[7]

In 1874, at the Battle of Liberty Place, the White League staged a violent, bloody confrontation in Canal Street against Kellogg's militia and police, which was quelled only when Federal troops were called in. Reconstruction was already collapsing, and two years later the federal government refused to support Louisiana's Radical Republicans against such militant Democratic insurrection. 'Redemption' had begun. From being one of the most racially harmonious cities in the Union the New Orleans of the 1870s and 1880s became one of the most racially violent and explosive. In addition to the clashes provoked by the leagues and new proscriptions on interracial contacts in public meeting places there were many labor strikes with blacks used often as 'scabs' and angry fights between white and black workers (especially in the docks). White newspapers encouraged bitterness and whipped up angry feelings toward blacks and against integration. Free blacks, regarded for the first time with considerable suspicion, turned angrily on the many homeless, penniless freedmen coming into the city from rural plantations and tried to maintain a difference of status.

It is important to emphasize that Grace King, Ruth McEnery, and Kate Chopin were all living in New Orleans at the time of these disturbances. King's correspondence in particular discussed many of these tensions, and when she began to correspond with northern editors and friends in the late 1880s and early 1890s she often attacked carpetbag governments and New Orleans' black community. King's brother was a sergeant in the city's White League, and he and Oscar Chopin, who was also prominent in league activities, fought in the Battle of Liberty Place. The Chopins later moved to Red River Parish in northwest Louisiana, site of the other most violent white supremacy demonstration of Reconstruction, the Coushatta Massacre, where Oscar Chopin's New Orleans activities found considerable approval.

Anne Goodwyn Jones, The Woman Writer in the South (1981)

Let us focus on image and reality, southern womanhood and southern women. In the South, the conflict between image and reality took its purest form in the years before the Civil War. During that period the southern lady became a walking oxymoron, gentle steel, living marble. Although the ideology depicted them as passive, submissive, and dependent symbols of leisure, these women found that actual experience involved long days of hard active work making administrative decisions that determined how the household ran. 'The popular delusion is that the ante-bellum Southern woman, like Christ's lilies, "toiled not,"' remembered Belle Kearney. 'Though surrounded by the conditions for idleness she was not indolent after she became the head of her own household. Every woman sewed, often making her own dresses: the clothing of all the slaves on a plantation was cut and made by negro seamstresses under her direct supervision, even the heavy coats of the men; she ministered personally to them in cases of sickness, frequently maintaining a well managed hospital under her sole care. She was a most skillful housekeeper, though she did none of the work with her own hands, and her children grew up around her knees; however, the black "mammy" relieved her of the actual drudgery of child-worry.'[1]

Where the image had her needing the economic protection of her husband, reality found her chafing, as did Mary Boykin Chesnut, at her economic dependence. 'Why feel like a beggar, utterly humiliated and degraded, when I am forced to say I need money? I cannot tell, but I do and the worst of it is, this thing grows worse as one grows older. Money ought not to be asked for, or given to a man's wife as a gift. Something must be due her, and that she should have, and with no growling as to the need of economy, nor amazement that the last supply has given out already.'[2]

Where the ideal southern woman was chaste as that cake of ice, many women felt a natural physical attraction to their husbands and even possessed a 'humor so earthy as to contradict the romantic tradition of universal refinement among Southern ladies,' says Bell Wiley.[3] When such feelings were suppressed it may often have been because southern women knew the consequences of sexual passion: almost yearly pregnancies for them and, for some, their husbands philandering with black women. The fertility rate of southern women consistently exceeded that of women in New England and the Middle Atlantic states. Childbirth and diseases of reproductive organs accounted for 10 percent of the southern female deaths in the 1860 census.[4] An affectionate husband, General William Dorsey Pender, wrote to his pregnant wife in 1863 that he 'did sincerely hope that you escaped this time, but darling it must be the positive and direct will of God that it should be so.' He nevertheless enclosed pills that were purported to cause abortion.[5] Yet, Scott points out, 'in the face of the idealization of the family and the aura of sanctity surrounding the word "mother," only in private could women give voice to the misery of endless pregnancies, with attendant illness, and the dreadful fear of childbirth, a fear based on fact.'[6]

Where the ideal woman lived in presumed ignorance of it, miscegenation aroused this commentary from Mary Chesnut:

> I wonder if it be a sin to think slavery a curse to any land. Men and women are punished when their masters and mistresses are brutes, not when they do wrong. Under slavery, we live surrounded by prostitutes, yet an abandoned woman is sent out of any decent house. Who thinks any worse of a Negro or mulatto woman for being a thing we can't name? God forgive us, but ours is a monstrous system, a wrong and an iniquity! Like the patriarchs of old, our men live all in one house with their wives and their concubines: and the mulattoes one sees in every family partly resemble the white children. Any lady is ready to tell you

who is the father of all the mulatto children in everybody's household but her own. Those, she seems to think, drop from the clouds. My disgust sometimes is boiling over. Thank God for my country women, but alas for the men! They are probably no worse than men everywhere, but the lower their mistresses, the more degraded they must be.[7]

Where the ideal woman was a repository of culture and the arts, her actual ignorance of worldly reality (which the image called innocence) was maintained by the low quality of education available for women in the South. Though he wrote after the Civil War, A. D. Mayo here describes the prewar 'miseducation' of southern girls: 'Trifled with at school, [she] goes out into a hotbed of perilous flattery. From the hour when she receives her lying diploma, in a cloud of "illusion," . . . lifted on the tide of inflated masculine rhetoric . . . her life wavers in a mirage of self-delusion. Out of that realm of falsehood she emerges, often too late, at thirty, with broken health, bowed under the cares of a family she is incompetent to rear . . . and the most melancholy feature of the case is that the girl is not to blame for all this, but is the victim of a system of miseducation.'[8] Sarah Grimké wrote in 1852 that 'the powers of my mind have never been allowed expansion: in childhood they were repressed by the false idea that a girl need not have the education I coveted.'[9] Indeed she *could* not have it: even after a few female institutions tried to shape their offerings to match the men's colleges, 'the greater number of southern educational institutions for women were directed at making young girls into ladies.'[10] Men and women consistently supported men's institutions at the cost of women's; although the first women's colleges in the nation were founded in the South, endowments were low, and women faculty there worked longer hours for less pay and at lower rank than their male colleagues.[11]

Nevertheless, women did read – in private and at home. They read Darwin, Emerson, Margaret Fuller, Madame de Staël; they even passed copies of *Uncle Tom's Cabin* from woman to woman. Caroline Merrick, born in 1825, called Margaret Fuller D'Ossoli a 'large-souled woman.'[12] And they read the novels that southern women wrote: one Georgian 'announced her resolution to resume the study of Latin under the inspiration of Augusta Evans' *St. Elmo*.'[13] Moreover, running their households required women (like the fictional Ellen O'Hara in *Gone With the Wind*) to learn bookkeeping, healing, biology, and numerous other semi-academic skills.

The ideal woman remained a pious Protestant. And in fact evidence of any widespread (if private) religious skepticism is rare. Bell Wiley notes that, after an early resurgence of interest in the church, 'during the last two years of the war ministers often complained about shrinking congregations and the waning of interest in spiritual activities.' Wiley attributes this decline in women's zeal to lack of clothing, transportation, and hope for military victory.[14] Though it seems that analysis of the culture would have revealed the connection between patriarchal society and patriarchal religions (black literature consistently shows this perception) and though women clearly disliked Pauline theology, few women went so far as to leave the church. Perhaps, as Scott suggests, they needed the consolation of religion more than they wanted to see what it did to them; perhaps the perfect mesh between what God and man said about woman made religious questions taboo; perhaps the lack of education prevented the development of the habit of intellectual analysis; perhaps they believed in spite of their awareness. In any case, Scott found that 'Elizabeth Avery Meriwether stood practically alone among the diary-keepers and memoirists when she asserted . . . that at an early age she had rejected immortality on her own initiative.'[15]

Thus each element of the image – leisure, passivity, dependence, sexual purity, submission, ignorance (with the possible exception of piety) – failed to correspond to the reality of women's lives, and for women to undertake to match the ideal must have required creativity and persistence.

In their relations to the peculiar institution of the South, however, women were less eager to conform to the official ideology. The relations between white women and slaves were significantly different from other white-black relationships. White women took on a nurturing role, clothing and nursing the slaves as well as supervising their work. They in turn had been raised by slave women who served as mother surrogates and role-models. Irving H. Bartlett and C. Glenn Cambor have argued that the two-mother system may have perpetuated idealized southern womanhood by producing white women who are 'dependent on and locked into perpetuating an authoritarian system' and hence are willing to accept the paradoxical combination of overvaluation and devaluation that characterizes the treatment of southern women. Such a system reveres the white mother yet deprives her of her sexual and maternal identity, leaving her a child-wife, and forces the black woman into a paradoxical position, strong and dependent, responsible and subservient. 'Each image was paradoxical and something far less than that of a mature, autonomous, and well integrated woman,' they argue; this 'perpetuated the underdeveloped personality structure which we associate with the stereotyped feminine ideal,' and which, in turn, responds well to external authority. It is an ideal, they note, 'significantly different from the national [feminine] norm.'[16]

In any case, between white woman and black there was a good deal of love and not a little hostility. The white woman's love was in part for those with whose lives she was intimately and daily connected: the hostility was in part for the fearful responsibility entailed on her by the slave relation and its attendant anxieties. Ultimately this led many southern white women privately to oppose slavery itself, a conviction far more widely spread in diaries and letters than one might expect. And, further, many white women began – also privately – to make connections between the condition of slavery and the requirements of southern womanhood.

Elizabeth Ammons, Women of Color in *The Awakening* (1991)

The background of *The Awakening* is filled with nameless, faceless black women carefully categorized as black, mulatto, quadroon, and Griffe.[1] Also, Mexican American and Mexican women play crucial subordinate roles in *The Awakening*. Taken together, all of these women of color make Edna Pontellier's 'liberation' possible. As menials they free her from work, from cooking to childcare. As prostitutes they service/educate the men in her world. Chopin is both in and out of control of this political story.

Compared to a Thomas Nelson Page or Thomas Dixon, Kate Chopin had liberal, enlightened views on the subject of race.[2] One of the ways that she shows how despicable Victor Lebrun is, for example, is by providing glimpses of his racism – his contempt for black people in general, his verbal abuse of the black woman who insists on doing her job of opening the door when Edna knocks, his arrogant assumption of credit for the silver and gold cake which he orders two black women to create in his kitchen. It is also possible to argue that, as Edna awakens, black characters change from nameless parts of the scenery to individuals with names and voices. On Grand Isle the blacks who tend white women's children, carry messages, sweep porches, and crouch on the floor to work the treadle of Madame Lebrun's sewing machine (a child does this) so that Madame's health is not imperiled move through the narrative speechless and nameless. As the book progresses, however, individuals emerge: the 'boy' Joe who works for the Pontelliers in the city, the 'mulatresse' Catiche to whose tiny garden restaurant in the suburbs Edna repairs, the capable 'Griffe' nurse who sees Madame Ratignolle through the birth of her baby. Yet as even these mentions betray, the individual people of color who do emerge from the background, as the book traces Edna's increasing distance from the rigid class- and gender-bound world of her marriage, are finally no more than types, human categories – unexamined representatives of the novel's repressed African American context. Minor white characters are not identified by the cups of Irish or French or German blood in them. In other words, even an argument that claims progression in the individualization of black characters has to face the fact that images of black people in *The Awakening*, a book about a woman trying to escape a limiting, caging assignment of gender that stunts her humanity and robs her of choices, are stereotypic and demeaning.

Deeper is the problem that the very liberation about which the book fantasizes is purchased on the backs of black women. If Edna's children did not have a hired 'quadroon' to care for them night and day, it is extremely unlikely that she would swim off into the sunset at the end of *The Awakening* in a glorious burst of Emersonian free will. Edna's story is not universal, although most feminist literary criticism has failed to acknowledge the fact. It is the story of a woman of one race and class who is able to dream of total personal freedom because an important piece of that highly individualistic ideal (itself the product of the very capitalism that Edna in some ways gropes to shed) has already been bought for her. Though she does not see it, her freedom comes at the expense of women of other races and a lower class, whose namelessness, facelessness, and voicelessness record a much more profound oppression in *The Awakening* than does the surface story of Edna Pontellier. The great examined story of *The Awakening* is its heroine's break for freedom. The great unexamined story, one far more disturbing than the fiction privileged in the text, is the narrative of sororal oppression across race and class.

Toni Morrison argues in her groundbreaking essay 'Unspeakable Things Unspoken: The Afro-American Presence in American Literature' that it is not the why but the how of racial erasure that constitutes the truly important question: 'What intellectual feats had to be performed by the author or his critic to erase me from a society seething with my presence, and what effect has that performance had on the work?'[3] The answer to this question in *The Awakening* is in one way quite simple. The repression of black women's stories – and with them Edna's identity as oppressor as well as oppressed – plunges not just Edna but also Chopin into a killing silence from which neither returns. It is widely agreed that Kate Chopin did not write much after *The Awakening* because the hostile reviews of the novel devastated her. I am sure that is true. One might ask, however, after *The Awakening*, unless Chopin was willing to confront race, what was there to say? The book brilliantly spins the privileged white female fantasy of utter and complete personal freedom out to its end, which is oblivion – the sea, death. The fantasy itself deadends. (Willa Cather's irritation with the novel, which she criticized for its 'over-idealization of love' and its shallowly 'expecting an individual and self-limited passion to yield infinite variety, pleasure, and distraction,' does not seem so cranky when viewed from this perspective.[4] Cut off from the large, urgent, ubiquitous struggle for freedom of African Americans in Chopin's America, a struggle hinted at but repeatedly repressed in the text, the utterly individualistic and solipsistic white female fantasy of freedom that *The Awakening* indulges in can only end in silence – in death.

Bert Bender, The Teeth of Desire: *The Awakening* and *The Descent of Man* (1991)

Kate Chopin's fiction is an extended and darkening meditation on the meaning of human life and love in the light of Darwinian thought. Like many other serious writers of her time, she was struck by *The Descent of Man and Selection in Relation to Sex* (1871). But she read Darwin more closely than did most of her contemporaries, and much more closely than her many interpreters have realized.[1] She did not find Darwin's 'main conclusion . . . distasteful' (as he 'regret[ted] to think' many readers would).[2] Rather, in his main idea (that 'man is descended from some lowly-organised form') and especially in his theory of sexual selection she found scientific support for the celebration of life that she knew and loved in Whitman's song of the 'body electric.' As she first viewed it, the theory of sexual selection offered a profoundly liberating sense of animal innocence in the realm of human courtship, especially for the Victorian woman.

In her first optimistic, if artless, presentation of the courtship drama, she created a heroine in *At Fault* (1890) who finally recognizes her 'fault' of self-sacrifice for 'what [had] seemed the only right.'[3] Because of her commitment to conventional morality, she had denied the natural 'electric' attraction she had felt for a divorced man (2, 762). But Chopin's announced purpose in the novel is to console the reader who she imagines is 'driven by earthly needs to drag the pinioned spirit of your days through rut and mire' (II, 858). Thus she arranges for nature to intervene and provide a happy ending: the former wife drowns in a flood-swollen river, clearing the way for the lovers' 'natural adjustment' to their predicament (2, 792). Chopin ended *At Fault* by bringing in a 'highly gifted' new woman named Mrs. Griesmann to articulate the sense of reality that would support this first novel's happy ending. Mrs. Griesmann is a robust student of 'Natural History' who collects 'specimens' out west and promises that by 'studying certain fundamental truths,' we can attain a 'restful' view 'of life as it is' (2, 875).

Mrs. Griesmann also indicates the direction Chopin would take in her subsequent stories, and had she allowed us a closer view of Mrs. Griesmann, we might have seen her with a copy of *The Descent of Man*; for all of Chopin's courtship plots during the next ten years are studies in natural history according to the logic of sexual selection – the primary mechanism in 'the whole process of that most important function, the reproduction of the species' (*Descent*, 1, 13). Apparently rather simple in its general outlines, sexual selection 'depends,' as Darwin explains,

> on the success of certain individuals over others of the same sex in relation to the propagation of the species; whilst natural selection

> depends on the success of both sexes, at all ages, in relation to the general conditions of life. The sexual struggle is of two kinds; in the one it is between the individuals of the same sex, generally the male sex, in order to drive away or kill their rivals, the females remaining passive; whilst in the other, the struggle is likewise between the individuals of the same sex, in order to excite or charm those of the opposite sex, generally the females, which no longer remain passive, but select the more agreeable partners. (2, 398)

Despite the apparent simplicity of sexual selection, however, it took Darwin many pages to explain how it is actually 'an extremely complex affair' (1, 296). And as Chopin pursued her own studies in the natural history of sex, she read *The Descent of Man* more and more closely until her references to it became most extensive and explicit in *The Awakening*. But her response to Darwin is complicated in this way: although she accepted his basic premises that evolution proceeds through the agencies of natural selection and sexual selection, she quarreled with his analysis of the female's role in sexual selection. And – throughout the 1890s – as she continued her meditations on sexual selection and its implications for the meaning of love, her initial optimism developed into ambivalence and finally into a sense of despair that Darwin had not expressed in *The Descent of Man*.

Many of her stories dramatize the 'law of battle' that dictates 'a struggle between the males for the possession of the female,' but she also resisted its corollaries concerning the female's passive and modest role in sexual relations and the male's physical and mental superiority to the female.[4] Chopin's women often manage in various ways to deny Darwin's definitions of the female's inferiority. And Chopin was particularly interested in Darwin's interpretation of the evolutionary development among 'savage' human beings, whereby the male had 'gained the power of selection' by having kept the female in an 'abject state of bondage.'[5] Although Darwin wrote that 'the civilized nations' were vastly improved in this regard (women now having 'free or almost free choice' [2, 356]), Chopin still felt the bind. And – increasingly throughout the middle and late nineties – her women characters not only reclaim the power to select, but select for their own reasons. Eventually, especially in the case of Edna Pontellier in *The Awakening*, Chopin's women select on the basis of their own sexual desires rather than for the reasons Darwin attributed to civilized women, who 'are largely influenced by the social position and wealth of the men' (2, 356).

Chopin's ambivalence toward the idea of sexual selection is apparent in two stories she wrote in 1894, five years after she had completed *At Fault* and four years before she began *The Awakening*. On one hand, Mrs. Baroda (in 'A

Respectable Woman') recognizes the sexual desire she feels for her husband's visiting friend and is at first repulsed by these feelings. She is a 'respectable woman.' But Mrs. Baroda will soon become one of the most daring women in American fiction during these years. For when she asks her husband to invite their friend for another visit, declaring that 'I have overcome everything!' and promising that 'this time I shall be very nice to him,' it is clear that she is now determined to select the lover she desires. In creating this woman who not only threatens the institution of marriage but whose motive in sexual selection (her desire) is independent of the drive to propagate the species, Chopin modified Darwin's theory of sexual selection in a way that would have offended his Victorian sensibility. But Chopin did not at this stage in her development dare to depict a mother's desire (as she would in Edna Pontellier).

In Darwin's theory, civilization had evolved largely because woman's modesty curbs the male's eagerness to couple; and in this theory of the sexual reality, the male's eagerness is not only biologically innocent or red-blooded, but necessary. 'In order that [the males] should become efficient seekers,' Darwin concluded, 'they would have to be endowed with strong passions. The acquirement of such passions would naturally follow from the more eager males leaving a larger number of off-spring' (1, 274). The woman's role is of course different. As Ruth Bernard Yeazell has recently explained, in Darwin's description of 'Nature's courtship,' 'females are at once less lustful and more discriminating' than males: 'Like a respectable Victorian novel, *The Descent of Man, and Selection in Relation to Sex* implicitly defers the representation of sex in order to focus on the story of selection.'[6] As Yeazell remarks, the 'satisfying conclusion' to Darwin's story preserves the ideals of motherhood and the modest woman who knows nothing of appetite or sexual desire (p. 37). Clearly, Chopin had freed the 'respectable' Mrs. Baroda from the restrictive definitions of womanhood provided by both *The Descent of Man* and the respectable Victorian novel.

In 'The Story of an Hour,' on the other hand, Mrs. Mallard feels the ecstasy of being liberated from what seems an agreeable marriage after the apparent accidental death of her husband. But then she comes to question the meaning of love. At first she realizes that there would no longer be a 'powerful will bending hers in that blind persistence with which men *and* women believe they have a right to impose a private will upon a fellow-creature' (my emphasis). Then, thinking that 'she had loved him – sometimes,' she wonders, 'what could love, the unsolved mystery, count for in the face of this possession of self-assertion which she suddenly recognized as the strongest impulse of her being!' A few years later, Edna Pontellier's conflict will develop from feelings like these in Mrs. Baroda and Mrs. Mallard. Like Mrs. Baroda, Edna will be determined to select the lover she desires; and like

Mrs. Baroda, her desire will develop to the accompaniment of an explicitly Whitmanesque celebration of sexual innocence.[7] But also, after she has acted in response to her desire, Edna will realize that 'it was not love which had held this cup of life to her lips' (ch. 28). She will become depressed by what had only puzzled Mrs. Mallard: the meaninglessness of love in natural history. Realizing by 1897 that love has no claim to constancy, that it beats in self-assertion to the evolutionary time of sexual selection, Chopin had come to feel that the human spirit had been denied its place not only in a Christian universe but also in the more limited sphere of human courtship and love.

Chopin's darkening response to *The Descent of Man* is reflected in her translations of Maupassant. In 'A Divorce Case,' for example, a young man with 'a noble and exalted soul' falls 'in love.' But his love turns to despair, his 'dream' to 'miserable dust,' when he becomes obsessed with the inescapable 'bestial instinct' to 'couple': 'Two beasts, two dogs, two wolves, two foxes, roaming the woods, encounter each other. One is male, the other female,' and they couple because the 'bestial instinct . . . forces them to continue the race.' He realizes that 'all beasts are the same, without knowing why . . . We also.'[8] And in 'It,' another of Maupassant's maddened narrators confesses that he cannot stop himself from marrying repeatedly, even though he considers 'legal mating a folly.' He is 'incapable of confining [his] love to one woman' and marries again and again only 'in order not to be alone!' (p. 189).

The solitude of Maupassant's characters – like that of Chopin's 'solitary soul,' Edna Pontellier – follows their shattering realizations that human sexuality as presented in *The Descent of Man* denies the myth of constant love. This is not to suggest that Chopin merely rewrote Maupassant; rather, that writing from the female point of view, she addressed the same troubling question that she saw in Darwin and Maupassant. When Edna finally realizes 'that the day would come when [Robert], too, and the thought of him would melt out of her existence, leaving her alone,' she enters the 'abysses of solitude' (ch. 39); and Maupassant's narrator in 'Solitude' (again, as translated by Chopin), feels that he is 'sinking . . . into some boundless subterranean depths.' Sexual intercourse merely intensifies his solitude, for then he is momentarily 'deceived . . . with the illusion that [he is] not alone'; 'the rapturous union which must, it would seem, blend two souls into one being' ends in 'hideous solitude' (pp. 196–97).

Edna Pontellier is a 'solitary soul' in this modern sense. We cannot appreciate Chopin's understanding of life if we imagine Edna as the goddess of love reincarnated. For the sea with which Edna is repeatedly associated and in which she dies is millions of years older than that which had given birth to Venus in classic mythology: Edna is a post-Darwinian woman-animal who had evolved from the sea in a world without gods. Nor can we justly evaluate

Chopin's work if we fail to see that beyond her unquestionable exploration of the female 'self and society' – an exploration which has been so profoundly resonant in the feminist movement of the last quarter century – she explored the larger question of the female (and male) self in *life*.[9]

As a meditation on the Darwinian reality of Edna's life, *The Awakening* begins and ends with the essential fact of motherhood. Edna is of course a mother, but she cannot be like the 'mother-women' she sees at Grand Isle, whose 'wings as ministering angels' identify them as 'the bygone heroine[s] of romance' (ch. 4). By the end of the novel Dr. Mandelet will refer to this 'illusion' of angelic love as 'Nature['s] . . . decoy to secure mothers for the race,' but this cannot console Edna (ch. 38). Attending the birth of her friend's child, she had seen this 'little new life' as merely another in the grotesque 'multitude of souls that come and go'; thus she revolts 'against the ways of nature' and finally sees her own children as 'antagonists' (chs 37; 39).

Twenty-eight years old at the beginning of the novel, Edna was ready to become a woman like the one Chopin knew in Whitman's 'Song of Myself' – whose 'Twenty-eight years of womanly life and all so lonesome' end in the vision of her bathing with the twenty-eight young men (section 11). In her twenty-eighth year, Edna, too, will discover the watery, erotic innocence that Whitman had dreamt for his woman. She will soon be ready to love 'young men,' to let her hand 'descend tremblingly from their temples and ribs' (section 11). And she will know 'the first-felt throbbings of desire' on August twenty-eighth, after her midnight swim with Robert (ch. 10). Chopin's emphasis on Edna's twenty-eight years is only one of her many references to Whitman; but Chopin's critics have never grasped the relevance of these references in *The Awakening*. Harold Bloom, for example, has recently concluded that 'Chopin's representation of Edna's psychic self-gratification is not essentially altered from Whitman's solitary bliss'; Emerson is her 'literary grandfather.'[10] But Chopin could scarcely indicate her rejection of Emersonian thought more emphatically than she does in noting that Edna cannot read Emerson without growing 'sleepy' (ch. 24). Edna awakens to a new reality. True, she begins her career as a conventional Victorian woman and then awakens in her twenty-eighth year to the joy of Whitman's transcendental eroticism. But as Chopin frees Edna to satisfy her desire for a lover, she will cause her to awaken more fully (in the pivotal twenty-eighth chapter of her story) to realize that desire had not brought her 'love.' And in the ritual celebration of her twenty-ninth birthday, Edna will know the strife and struggle for self-assertion that Darwin had uncovered in *The Descent of Man*: she will confront the 'graven image of Desire' in the face of Victor, with his smile and gleaming 'white teeth' – Victor, Robert's brother and antagonist in sexual competition first for Mariequita and now for Edna.[11]

In tracing the story of Edna's development from her twenty-eighth to her twenty-ninth year, Chopin begins where she must – 'by the shore,' as Whitman did in section 11 of 'Song of Myself.' But her logic in choosing this setting is not to affirm but to revise Whitman's view of the self in life. Beginning where she knew that life itself had begun according to *On the Origin of Species*, Chopin first presents Edna 'advancing at snail's pace from the beach' with Robert. We will last see these creatures of evolution together in chapter 36, which opens in a scarcely Edenic 'garden' (where they have met as though 'destined to see [each other] only by accident') and which ends in Edna's 'pigeon house.' Here Chopin will describe the lovers' relationship with explicit references to *The Descent of Man*.

Chopin's first pointed reference to the role of sexual selection in Edna's life occurs in chapter 9. She has already responded to 'the seductive odor of the sea,' but now she will know the 'wonderful power' of music as Darwin described it in both *The Descent of Man* and *The Expression of Emotions in Man and Animals*. Edna's response to Mademoiselle Reisz's piano performance of a piece by Frederic Chopin is clearly based on a passage from Darwin, the point of which is that music was originally the means by which our 'half-human ancestors aroused each other's ardent passions' (*Descent*, 2, 337).

Edna had responded to music before, but never as she will during this performance. Before, music had sometimes evoked in her a picture of 'solitude' that is again a measure of Chopin's passage beyond Whitman's mid-nineteenth-century view of life. She had imagined 'the figure of a man standing beside a desolate rock on the seashore. He was naked. His attitude was one of hopeless resignation as he looked toward a distant bird winging its flight away from him' (ch. 9). Even in this echo from 'Out of the Cradle Endlessly Rocking,' the 'hopeless resignation' of Chopin's man presents a considerably darker view of life and solitude than that projected by Whitman. Still, in this image of a 'distant bird winging its flight away,' there is a suggestion of the consoling thought which Whitman had imagined in the surviving he-bird's song, or in the solitary thrush's in 'When Lilacs Last in the Dooryard Bloom'd.' But this image had come to Whitman's 'awaken[ed]' imagination in 'Out of the Cradle' (in 1859), and when Edna fully awakens to Chopin's view of the Darwinian reality by the end of the novel, the bird will reappear as the image of the spirit defeated – 'with a broken wing . . . beating the air above, reeling, fluttering, circling disabled down, down to the water' (ch. 39).

The musical performance on August twenty-eighth is crucial in propelling Edna toward her final bleak awakening, for here her response to the music is as Darwin explained in *The Expression of Emotions*: music can cause a person to 'tremble,' to feel 'the thrill or slight shiver which runs down the backbone and limbs,' or to experience 'a slight suffusion of tears' that resembles 'weeping' caused by other emotions.[12] Thus, during this musical performance in *The Awakening*, 'the very first chords which Mademoiselle Reisz struck upon the piano sent a keen tremor down Mrs. Pontellier's spinal column.' And because 'her being was tempered to take an impress of the abiding truth,' she finds that 'the very passions themselves were aroused within her soul, swaying it, lashing it, as the waves daily beat upon her splendid body. She trembled, she was choking, and the tears blinded her' (ch. 9). The musical performance moves others, too: 'What passion!' one exclaims – 'It shakes a man!' Immediately following the performance the group decides to take a midnight swim; and now, like a joyful child taking her first steps, Edna realizes that she can swim. Feeling that 'some power of significant import had been given her to control the workings of her body and her soul,' she wants to 'swim far out, where no woman had swum before' (ch. 10). Later, alone with Robert, she tells him of the 'thousand emotions' that had swept through her as a result of Mademoiselle Reisz's playing, and before they part she is 'pregnant with the first-felt throbbings of desire.'

Chopin indicates at once that Edna's developing desire will eventually lead her into the 'abysses of solitude.' When she enters the water on this night, she gathers 'in an impression of space and solitude' from 'the vast expanse of water'; and in her solitary swim she realizes that she might perish 'out there alone.' Moreover, the simultaneous development of her desire and her sense of solitude will eventually lead her to a clearer understanding of her 'position in the universe' as an animal and therefore as a creature empowered to participate fully in the sexual reality as a self-conscious selector (ch. 6). Her development toward claiming the power to select is gradual, but she takes a first crucial step immediately after her swim by refusing to yield to Mr. Pontellier's 'desire.' And a few days later she awakens more fully to her animal nature after fleeing from an oppressive church service to Madame Antoine's seaside home. Here, awakened from a nap, 'very hungry,' she 'bit a piece' from a loaf of brown bread, 'tearing it with her strong, white teeth' (ch. 13).

In his remarks on the canine tooth in human beings, Darwin notes that it 'no longer serves man as a special weapon for tearing his enemies or prey.' But he sharpens his main point here by adding: 'He who rejects with scorn the belief that the shape of his own canines, and their occasional great development in other men, are due to our early forefathers having been provided with these formidable weapons, will probably reveal, by sneering, the line of his descent. For though he no longer intends, nor has the power to use these teeth as weapons, he will unconsciously retract his "snarling muscles" . . .'[13] Clearly, Edna's strong teeth indicate her kinship with our 'half-human ancestors' in *The Descent of Man*, for she tells Robert that the 'whole island seems changed' now: 'a new race of beings must have sprung up, leaving only you and me as past relics' (ch. 13).

But now Chopin will force the awakening Edna to endure the frustrations of civilized life, first by having to contend with Robert's sudden departure and the jealousy she feels when Robert writes only to others; and then when she suffers more consciously from the restrictions in her marriage. She rebels against her husband's and society's covenants, refuses to be one of his 'valued . . . possessions,' and stamps on her wedding ring (ch. 17). And when she obstinately withdraws her normal 'tacit submissiveness' in her marriage (ch. 19), she takes another of her crucial steps toward claiming her place in the arena of sexual selection. Before she selects a lover, she rejects her husband's sexual advances, leaving him 'nervously' to explain to Dr. Mandelet that her 'notion. . . . concerning the eternal rights of women' means that 'we meet in the morning at the breakfast table' (ch. 22).

Dr. Mandelet counsels Mr. Pontellier to be patient with Edna, for 'woman . . . is a very peculiar and delicate organism.' But it would seem that even the doctor does not understand the 'new set of sensations' Edna experiences in response to her father's visit (chs 22; 23). That is, he knows 'the inner life' of his 'fellow creatures' better than most men; and, seeing the subtle change in Edna after her father's visit ('palpitant with the forces of life . . . she reminded him of some beautiful, sleek animal waking up in the sun'), he guesses that she has taken Arobin as her lover (ch. 23). But he does not theorize, as Chopin does, on how the 'laws of inheritance' (as Darwin understood them before Mendel) might have enabled Edna to acquire some of her father's masculine authority and passion. Her father has the essential male qualities that are 'accumulated by sexual selection' – 'ardour in love' and 'courage' (*Descent*, 1, 296). An aging Confederate colonel, he still has the power to arouse Madame Ratignolle at a *soirée musicale* (here again Chopin indicates her understanding of the sexual meaning of music): she 'coquetted with him in the most captivating and naïve manner,' and she invites him to dinner with her on 'any day . . . he might select' (ch. 23). The Colonel plays an essential role in Chopin's effort to validate Edna's developing power to select, and in this scene at the *soirée musicale* 'her fancy selected' one or two men.

This is perhaps the most intricate part of Chopin's quarrel with Darwin, for in referring to his theory on the laws of inheritance, she exploits a possibility that he allows the female but does not himself develop: to do so would have contradicted his image of the modest woman with 'powers of perception' and 'taste' (*Descent*, 1, 296). In this way, Chopin used Darwin's own theory in order to modify his definition of the sexual reality among humans: building on his 'hypothesis of pangenesis,' whereby 'gemmules . . . are transmitted to the offspring of both sexes,' she suggests that Edna is an example of how 'both sexes' can be 'modified in the same manner' (1. 280, 299). Chopin's point seems clear when she has the Colonel imagine that 'he had bequeathed to all of his daughters the germs of a masterful capability' (ch. 23). And, in arranging for Edna's lover, Arobin, to toast the Colonel for having 'invented' Edna (ch. 30), Chopin underscores the irony of her quarrel with Darwin. After the Colonel's visit, Edna will attend the horse races; and there, her 'blood' and 'brain' inflamed, she talks 'like her father,' causing nearby people to turn 'their heads' and Arobin to feel her magnetic force (ch. 25). Later that evening, when Arobin is moved by an impulse to show her the scar on his wrist which he had received – according to Darwin's law of battle for possession of the female – 'from a saber cut . . . in a duel . . . when he was nineteen,' Edna is agitated and sickened; but Arobin 'drew all her awakening sensuousness' (ch. 23). Within days, she will respond to his effrontery not with a 'crimson' blush of modesty, as Darwin might have imagined,[14] but with pleasure because it 'appeal[ed] to the animalism that stirred impatiently within her' (ch. 26).

By now Edna has awakened enough to her own sexual reality to articulate the main point in Chopin's quarrel with Darwin. In a discussion with Mademoiselle Reisz about the meaning of love, Edna exhibits a wisdom that Chopin will not grant Mademoiselle Reisz, whose 'avoidance of the water' is not only amusing (some of the bathers imagined that 'it was on account of her false hair') but indicative of her essential sexlessness (ch. 16). Accusing Mademoiselle Reisz of either lying or having 'never been in love,' Edna proclaims, 'do you suppose a woman knows why she loves? Does she select? Does she say to herself: "Go to! Here is a distinguished statesman with presidential possibilities. I shall proceed to fall in love with him . . . [or with] this financier?"' She admits that she loves Robert when she 'ought not to,' but Chopin's 'ought' refers more to Darwin's theory about why civilized women select (modestly and discriminately, for wealth, etc.) than to the more obvious social prohibition against extramarital love. Edna loves Robert for the same reason that Whitman's imagined woman let her hand descend 'tremblingly from [the young men's] temples': 'Because his hair is brown and grows away from his temples, because he opens and shuts his eyes,' because she likes his 'nose,' 'two lips,' and 'square chin' – in short, because she is 'happy to be alive' (ch. 26).

In her next meeting with Arobin, then, Edna's 'nature' responds fully and for the first time to a kiss – 'a flaming torch that kindled [her] desire' (ch. 27). And she will awaken next morning – in the pivotal twenty-eighth chapter – to her post-Whitmanian sense of the 'significance of life, that monster made up of beauty and brutality.' Comprehending life in this new way – 'as if a mist had been lifted from her eyes' – she feels neither shame nor remorse, only 'regret' that 'it was not the kiss of love which had inflamed her, because it was not love which had held this cup of life to her lips' (ch. 28).

But far from denying this regrettable reality, Edna enters bravely and immediately into her new sexual independence by moving out of the family home into her own 'pigeon house.' In creating Edna's pigeon house, Chopin refers to Darwin's theories of sexual selection as explicitly as she had in her earlier references to the law of battle, the role of music in sexual selection, the relevance of our canine teeth, or the laws of inheritance. Scarcely a merely eccentric name for Edna's new dwelling after the *coup d'état*, 'pigeon house' is an emphatic reference to the triumphant female pigeons Darwin describes in *The Descent of Man* – creatures who, like Edna, 'occasionally feel a strong antipathy towards certain males [and preference *for* certain other males] without any assignable cause' (2, 118). Quoting a French study, Darwin tells how, when a female pigeon experiences an antipathy for a male, nothing can cause her to submit to him – neither the male's flaming desire nor any inducements a breeder might give her. She constantly refuses his caresses, even if confined with him for a year, sulking in a corner of her 'prison,' and coming out only to eat or drink; and if he forces his affections, she will repel him in a rage.[15] 'On the other hand,' Darwin notes, some females will desert their mates if they take 'a strong fancy' for another; and some are even so 'profligate' that they 'prefer almost any stranger to their own mate' (2, 119).

Edna's birthday party is a ritual celebration of her entry into the modern sexual reality that Whitman's woman could not have known when he created her in 1855. Edna 'selected [her guests] with discrimination,' and Victor, 'a graven image of Desire,' is among them. When she tries to stop him from singing Robert's love song ('*Ah! si tu savais!*'), placing her hand over his mouth, 'the touch of his lips was like a pleasing sting' (ch. 30). Thus, when Robert returns unexpectedly, she will quickly see that the love she had imagined is now impossibly complicated with all the strife even pigeons know in the arena of sexual selection. Robert is jealous of Arobin; she is jealous of the Mexican woman who gave Robert his embroidered tobacco pouch. And when she sleeps with Arobin again – to satisfy 'her nature's requirements' – she enters into the hopelessness that will lead her back to the sea (ch. 35). After her accidental meeting with Robert (in a garden), they return to her 'pigeon house' and define their irreconcilable differences as would-be lovers: he explains that he had left her because she belonged to Mr. Pontellier and that it was impossible to imagine him setting Edna 'free.' For Edna, of course, this would be absurdly 'impossible,' for she is 'no longer one of Mr. Pontellier's possessions . . . I give myself where I choose' (ch. 36). Although Robert is shocked by Edna's assertion of her absolute liberation, his only impulse at last is still 'to hold her and keep her.' Then – even after Edna revolts against nature when she helps her friend give birth, and even after she hears Dr. Mandelet's explanation about nature's 'decoy' for securing 'mothers for the race' – she returns to Robert, imagining 'no greater bliss on earth than possession of the beloved one' (ch. 38). Even now she, too, would, impose her 'private will upon a fellow creature' and call it love, as Mrs. Mallard had imagined. And she will follow the illusion of love, nature's decoy, until she returns to her empty 'pigeon house' and finds Robert's note.

Edna is now fully awake to her new reality: 'Today it is Arobin,' she tells herself, and 'tomorrow it will be someone else' (ch. 39). Her desire (like the passion she had felt at the musical performance that night when she was twenty-eight) will rise and fall, 'lashing' her soul 'as the waves daily beat upon her splendid body' (ch. 9). She knows that the sense of her absolute isolation as a solitary soul will descend inevitably when she forgets even Robert. She will find no peace until she feels the 'soft, close embrace' of the sea, her true element. And in this despair she sees her children as 'antagonists,' for *they* are nature's cause in natural and sexual selection – the force within herself by which love's wing was broken.

12

JOSEPH CONRAD, *HEART OF DARKNESS*

In 'Conrad and the Idea of Empire', Robert Hampson argues convincingly that the political significance of *Heart of Darkness* cannot be assessed without consideration of its initial publication circumstances and its immediate readership. The essay is particularly valuable for its discerning account of Conrad's involvement with *Blackwood's Magazine*, in which *Heart of Darkness* was serialised in 1899. It claims that Conrad's narrative strategies were directed on one level towards a specific group of readers ('conservative and imperialist in politics, and predominantly male'). At another level, however, Conrad is able to occupy a space within which a subversive response to imperialist discourse becomes possible. The essay proceeds to show how Conrad's narrative exists in dialogue with other *Blackwood's* publications, including an anonymous article, 'Life and Death in the Niger Delta', which appeared in April 1898. The similarities and differences between this article and *Heart of Darkness* confirm the suggestion that Conrad's writing both emulates and dissents from prevailing imperialist and nationalist rhetoric. Similarly, comparisons of *Heart of Darkness* with Henry Stanley's *In Darkest Africa* and William Booth's *In Darkest England* (both published in 1890) reveal the extent to which Conrad's narrative is part of a simultaneous mapping of two strange and unknown places. The civilising mission in Africa, as in working-class London, brings light to darkness, but Conrad's text finds darkness at the very heart of the mission itself.

Edward Said's essay on *Heart of Darkness* is adapted from an early section of *Culture and Imperialism*. His anguish as a Palestinian exile in the United States undoubtedly informs his astute account of Conrad's 'persistent residual sense of his own exilic marginality'. Conrad's self-conscious 'provisionality' is seen to emerge from the experience of living between two worlds, and the resulting ironic distance from any secure sense of location enables a form of narrative in which two arguments, two visions, become possible. The formal devices in *Heart of Darkness* repeatedly draw attention to the way in which ideas and values are constructed (and deconstructed) through dislocations in the narrator's language: 'Marlow unsettles the reader's sense not only of the very idea of empire but of something more basic, reality itself. What appears stable and secure can suddenly appear less so'. Despite the critique of imperialism that *Heart of Darkness* affords, Said concludes that Conrad's double vision was tragically limited: he was unable to see all the way beyond the immediate abuses of imperialism to the necessary freedom of those 'natives' whose lives it enslaved.

Robert Hampson, Conrad and the Idea of Empire (1989)[1]

'The civilising work in Africa'

Marlow begins the story of his own experience of imperialism (or, rather, of his collusion with imperialism) after some general remarks on the subject:

> The conquest of the earth, which mostly means the taking it away from those who have a different complexion or slightly flatter noses than ourselves, is not a pretty thing when you look into it too much. What redeems it is the idea only. An idea at the back of it; not a sentimental pretence but an idea; and an unselfish belief in the idea – something you can set up, and bow down before, and offer a sacrifice to . . .[2]

These words constitute what Joyce critics call a 'reader trap' (see Hart 1974:181–216). On a first reading of *Heart of Darkness*, the emphasis upon the redeeming 'idea' behind imperialism in these remarks can easily lead the reader to assume that the story that follows is to be an exploration and enunciation of that 'idea'. It is only on subsequent readings that proper weight is given to the image with which Marlow concludes ('something you can set up, and bow down before, and offer a sacrifice to'), and that the reader begins to appreciate the psychological dynamics implicitly underlying both the aposiopesis with which the speech ends and Marlow's impulse to narrate the tale that follows. Marlow's assertion of the redeeming 'idea' behind imperialism leads him into figurative language which subverts the idea he has been asserting. Marlow's speech breaks off – it does not trail away – and it breaks off because he realises the implications of the image he has just used: Marlow, after all, (according to the logic of realism) knows the end of the story he is about to tell, and the story concerns not (as the first-time reader might assume) the redeeming 'idea' behind imperialism but rather someone who sets himself up as something for others to 'bow down before, and offer a sacrifice to'. Indeed, it might be argued that it is this image that prompts the story that follows rather than any search to express the redeeming 'idea'. In other words, right at the end of Marlow's speech, the relative weighting of 'vehicle' and 'tenor' suddenly shifts (Richards 1936:96). As in those *gestalt* drawings which can be read as either a vase or two profiles, foreground and background change places: language which is offered as figurative suddenly asserts its literal meaning, and this kind of unsettling of language proves to be a characteristic feature of Marlow's narration.

Since he was writing *Heart of Darkness* for *Blackwood's Magazine*, Conrad had a fairly clear conceptualisation of the nature of his immediate readership: conservative and imperialist in politics, and predominantly male. He wrote to his agent, J.B. Pinker, on 12 or 19 November 1911: 'There isn't a single club and messroom and man-of-war in the British Seas and Dominions which hasn't its copy of *Maga*' (Karl & Davies, Volume 4, 1990:506). Thus we find Conrad reassuring William Blackwood, the publisher, in advance: 'The title I am thinking of is "The Heart of Darkness" – but the narrative is not gloomy. The criminality of inefficiency and pure selfishness when tackling the civilizing work in Africa is a justifiable idea' (Karl & Davies, Volume 2, 1986:139–140).[3] The first sentence suggests something of the reliability of Conrad's statements in this letter. The second sentence, with its criticism of 'inefficiency' and its apparent endorsement of 'the civilising work in Africa', is the counterpart of that speech by Marlow from which I have already quoted. Marlow describes the Roman colonisation of Britain in terms which suggest an obvious parallel with later British imperialism, but he then offers the disclaimer: 'Mind, none of us would feel exactly like this. What saves us is efficiency' (HD 50). Marlow, like Conrad in his letter to Blackwood, apparently remains within the frame of reference of imperialist discourse, but the Company's chief accountant, whom Marlow encounters at the Central Station, offers the definitive placing of the moral inadequacy of 'efficiency' in this context. After the ironic praise of the chief accountant for 'keeping up his appearance' (his 'starched collars and got-up shirt-fronts were achievements of character', HD 68), Marlow reveals the dissociation of sensibility that lies behind the accountant's efficient book-keeping:

> When a truckle-bed with a sick man (some invalid agent from up-country) was put in there, he exhibited a gentle annoyance. 'The groans of this sick person', he said, 'distract my attention. And without that it is extremely difficult to guard against clerical errors in this climate.' (HD 69)

In the opening section of *Heart of Darkness*, then, Conrad deploys a series of strategies in relation to the implied reader, who, in the first instance, was the conservative reader of *Blackwood's Magazine*. To begin with, there is the evocation of 'the great spirit of the past' (HD 47) by the unnamed first narrator. This celebration of British trade and exploration 'from Sir Francis Drake to

Sir John Franklin' is another form of reader-trap: Conrad offers, through this anonymous narrator, the kind of nationalist history and imperialist rhetoric with which his first readers would have been familiar in order to lull them into a false sense of security at the outset. But, again, for the careful or experienced reader, hints of a different vision are suggested at the end: 'Hunters of gold or pursuers of fame, they had all gone out on that stream, bearing the sword, and *often* the torch, messengers of the *might* within the land' (HD 47, my italics). The narrator's earlier reference to 'the men of whom the nation is proud, from Sir Francis Drake to Sir John Franklin' might also have reminded some of the story's first readers of a less than flattering article on Sir Francis Drake by David Hannay that had appeared in *Blackwood's* six months earlier (1898:796–808). In this article, Hannay had characterized Drake as violent and self-seeking – and, probably, a murderer. Hannay had also offered an unromantic, anti-heroic classification of Elizabethan adventurers:

> The men who went on these ventures staked their necks. . . . Prudent men would not go on such enterprises. The adventurers would be of three classes. There would be bold ambitious men of the stamp of Drake . . . and with them sailors who had probably had a share in the piracy then rampant on the coasts of England and Ireland. . . . Then there were the 'gentlemen adventurers' – gamblers who held with Sir Walter Raleigh that the greatest of misfortunes is to be poor, and who, like him, were not overscrupulous as to how they became rich. (1898:807)

It is quite possible that Conrad himself had read this article and was making conscious use of it.[4] A letter from Conrad to William Blackwood (4 September 1897) contains his detailed response to an issue of *Blackwood's Magazine*, which he had just received (Karl & Davies, Volume 1, 1983: 378–380). Over a year later, in a letter of 13 December 1898, he writes again to Blackwood: 'I owe you a great many thanks for the *Maga*, which reaches me with a most charming regularity. In truth it is the only monthly I care to read, and each number is very welcome' (Karl & Davies, Volume 2, 1986: 129–130). Indeed, there is evidence that Conrad was reading *Blackwood's Magazine* throughout this period.[5] In addition, Hannay's approach to Drake suggests that we should be wary of creating too crude an image of the nationalism of *Blackwood's Magazine* and its readers: there is space for a certain, limited, critical play within the overall framework of its imperialist discourse.

Blackwood's Magazine for April 1898 included an anonymous article which provides an interesting comparison with *Heart of Darkness*. 'Life and Death in the Niger Delta' is the account of a journey by steamer up the Niger. The description of the journey itself has certain immediate similarities with some aspects of Marlow's account of his journey up the Congo:

> The steamer panted softly past many a mile of oozy swamp . . . On either hand the leather-leaved mangroves rose up on their high-arched roots . . . sickening emanations rose up into the steamy air, and the whole place reeked with putrefaction. . . . At times we slid through the heart of a shadowy forest . . . (1898:455–457)

The similarities are, perhaps, less significant than the differences. 'Life and Death in the Niger Delta' is written in a simple, empirical, documentary style. Even the passages of Marlow's narration which most resemble this documentary style are differentiated by a play of speculative intelligence or by a verbal self-consciousness and wit quite absent from the documentary:

> Trees, trees, millions of trees, massive, immense, running up high: and at their foot, hugging the bank against the stream, crept the little begrimed steam-boat, like a sluggish beetle crawling on the floor of a lofty portico. . . . The reaches opened before us and closed behind, as if the forest had stepped leisurely across the water to bar the way for our return. We penetrated deeper and deeper into the heart of darkness. (HD 95)

In addition, 'Life and Death in the Niger Delta' has only this one voice, whereas *Heart of Darkness* is multivocal. In the first place, the novella has literally more than one voice: there are the two narrators (the first, anonymous narrator and Marlow), and there is the interaction between Marlow and his audience. Its narrative is layered: Marlow's utterances are provided with a context, and those of the anonymous narrator are as much the product of a specific viewpoint as Marlow's. There is a displacement between Conrad and the anonymous narrator, thus Marlow is doubly displaced from Conrad. In the second place, the narrative of *Heart of Darkness* deploys a range of registers or types of discourse: the documentary element is fractured, disrupted, overwritten with a variety of literary and mythical patterns.[6]

There are, nevertheless, certain interesting points of resemblance between 'Life and Death in the Niger Delta' and *Heart of Darkness*. For example, as we might perhaps expect from such a traveller's tale, the author repeats stories of alleged cannibalism and rumours of human sacrifices: 'Within ten miles the tribesmen still offer up human sacrifice in honour of their Ju-Ju gods, – so at least the Irish traders say, – and inaugurate various devilish feasts' (1898:459).[7] He even alludes to an exceptional white man, who goes safely through areas where 'few Europeans dare set foot' (1898:459). More striking is the tone of some of the details of this narration. For example, at one point the author writes: 'Climbing the verandah stairway, which on that memorable morning was piled high with corpses drilled through and through by Lee-Metford bullets, we entered the European quarters' (1898:453). These 'corpses' are never identified or explained. It is not even clear whether the morning was 'memorable' because of the pile of corpses or for some other reason. And there is a curious discrepancy between the careful identification of the bullets and the absence of any other interest in the bodies. The effect on the modern reader is not unlike the effect Marlow experiences when he watches the French man-of-war shelling the bush – or when he describes his progress down the coast:

> We pounded along, stopped, landed soldiers; went on, landed custom-house clerks to levy toll in what looked like a God-forsaken wilderness . . . landed more soldiers – to take care of the custom-house clerks, presumably. Some, I heard, got drowned in the surf; but whether they did or not, nobody seemed particularly to care (HD 60–61).

The difference, of course, is that Marlow himself registers and draws our attention to the sense of pointless and brutal activity, to the absence of affect, which 'Life and Death in the Niger Delta' merely displays.

The treatment of another incident, however, is much closer to Marlovian narrative. This is the account of the funeral of a European clerk at one of the settlements visited by the steamer:

> Four naked Krooboys were busy bailing the water out of a 3-foot trench, while a white trader stood above them mumbling something from the book held in a shaking hand. . . . A rough deal box, such as 'long-Dane' guns are shipped in, lay sinking in the ooze, and a few dripping men stood bareheaded in the rain. Then at a signal the naked aliens tumbled the case into the trench – and it refused to sink. Clods were flung upon it: but the buoyant deal rose stubbornly to the surface, until two Krooboys stood upon it to hold it down, and the mould was shovelled about their knees. (1898:456–457)

In this passage, the anonymous writer has a certain literary self-awareness: he refers in advance to the mixture of the 'pathetic and grotesque' in this incident, but it is noticeably the grotesque that is most in evidence in his account. The affectless style is unable to create any sense of pathos. (Marlow's account of Kurtz's funeral offers an extreme example of such absence of affect – 'I am of course aware that next day the pilgrims buried something in a muddy hole', HD 150 – but this absence of affect is functional and motivated within the narrative.) Apparently the narrator of 'Life and Death in the Niger Delta' is unaware of the implications of some of the details of his own narrative. For example, where Marlow's account of the landing of soldiers and custom-house clerks signals both the installation of the machinery of colonial exploitation and, as the narrative proceeds, the simultaneous exploitation of the agents of imperialism, this *Blackwood's* writer produces the telling symbol of the clerk buried in a disused rifle-box, but, in this univocal, unreflective narrative, such detail is never raised to the level of symbol: the reader is never prompted to such a reading. In the same way, the *Blackwood's* writer, who is presumably a visiting European, refers unselfconsciously to the Africans as 'aliens'. Marlow, by contrast, is very conscious of the problematic relationship between language and reality, and he is particularly conscious of colonial linguistic impositions upon the African reality: 'These men could by no stretch of the imagination be called enemies. They were called criminals' (HD 64).[8] The Blackwood's writer does leave unacknowledged what Marlow calls 'the merry dance of death and trade' (HD 62), as his account of the funeral suggests. He observes: 'In even the newest settlements there are far more crosses in the cemetery than living white men in the factories; and it is hard to consider the conditions of life in any settlement without the thought arising, Is it worth the price?' (1898:454). His concern, however, is only for 'white men'. *Heart of Darkness*, by contrast, gives equal, if not more, weight to the sufferings of the Africans – as, for example, in the descriptions of the chain-gang and the 'grove of death'.[9] In addition, the question that is asked ('Is it worth the price?'), in effect, supplies its own answer. It is on a par with the manager's criticism of Kurtz's activities as an 'unsound method' of trade (HD 137). In both cases, the language remains within a commercial frame of reference. And the *Blackwood's* writer indeed concludes by asserting that the 'sacrifice' is not wasted: 'Humble trader, fearless teacher, and highly trained official, though they stumble many times . . . are little by little preparing a way in the face of many perils for the development, which is bound to come some day, of that last and largest empire, whose map is but half-unrolled' (1898:460).

If the article acknowledges the sufferings of the agents of imperialism, even that perception is firmly held within the frame of 'material interests'. The observation 'we pay for our hold on Western Africa with blood' (1898:454) refers, of course, to the blood of the white men (not the Africans), and, if it seems to signal some element of caring or compassion for this loss of life, this idea is quickly elided with what Deasy, in *Ullyses*, refers to as the Englishman's proudest boast – 'I paid my way' (Joyce 1986: 25). 'Life and Death in the Niger Delta' remains within and asserts the discourse of imperialism. *Heart of Darkness*, by contrast, subverts that discourse. If we consider just the conclusion of Marlow's narrative: far from unequivocally reasserting the imperial mission, this reinstates the discourse of imperialism but reinstates it as a lie. Marlow protects the faith of the Intended in that world of illusions, which she and Marlow's aunt are represented as inhabiting. In addition, Marlow's narrative is itself framed within a return to the Thames, but it is now a Thames that 'flowed sombre under an overcast sky', that 'seemed to lead into the heart of an immense darkness' (HD 162). This equation of the Congo and the Thames takes us back to Marlow's first words in *Heart of Darkness*. After the first narrator had evoked 'the great spirit of the past upon the lower reaches of the Thames' (HD 47), an utterance represented in the text as indirect speech, Marlow had responded to his images of light and darkness ('jewels flashing in the night of time', 'the torch', 'the sacred fire') by observing 'And this also has been one of the dark places of the earth' (HD 48).[10] Marlow had then explained this statement by reference to the Roman colonisation of Britain. But, by the end of his narrative, we can see that 'darkness' is not something safely in the past ('nineteen hundred years ago'). Nor is it something 'other'. Instead of an opposition of darkness and light – corresponding to the opposition of 'savage' and 'civilised' – Marlow's narrative locates darkness at the heart of the 'civilising' mission, and the frame narrative reaffirms that by its final linking of 'darkness' with the Thames.[11]

'The dark places of the earth'

In 1890 Henry Stanley published a book called *In Darkest Africa*, which was his account of the expedition which he led to rescue Emin Pasha, the Governor of the Equatorial Provinces, from the Mahdi's troops. The first stage of the expedition took Stanley and his forces up the Congo from its mouth to Matadi – the journey that Conrad and Marlow were to make a few years later. As Norman Sherry has pointed out, when Conrad went up the Congo in May 1890, it would have been difficult for him not to have been aware of Stanley. Stanley's expedition had left England in January 1887, and it was in January 1889 that Stanley's message, that he had found Emin Pasha, reached London. Furthermore, 'throughout that summer further news of his expedition continued to be published in the press' (Sherry 1971:14). That is, in the summer before Conrad's own journey into Africa, the press was full of Stanley's latest exploits, and, in the November of that year, Conrad went to Brussels to be interviewed for a job in the Congo. The narrative of *In Darkest Africa* begins with a tension between the urgent need to reach Emin Pasha ('Emin will be lost unless immediate aid be given him', Stanley 1893:50) and the delays occasioned by the absence of river-worthy steamers for the Upper Congo.

Stanley observes: 'The whole of the naval stock promised did not exist at all except in the imagination of the gentleman of the Bureau at Brussels' (1893:50).[12] The steamers were 'wrecked, rotten, or without boilers or engines' (1893:50), and Stanley describes the repairs, the replacement of plates and so on, that was necessary before the expedition could get under way again. Both these motifs – the urgent need to reach someone up-river and delays occasioned by the need to repair a steamer – were also part of Marlow's experience, though not of Conrad's. (Indeed, far from being delayed at Kinshasa, Conrad was annoyed because he was immediately rushed up-river.) It is worth nothing that Emin Pasha was a rank not a name: the man Stanley's expedition was seeking to reach was a German called Edward Schnitzler, whom Stanley described as 'a great linguist, Turkish, Arabic, German, French, Italian and English being familiar to him' (1893:40). We might also notice that the expedition was organised not just to rescue Emin Pasha. Stanley remarked that 'Emin Pasha possessed about seventy-five tons of ivory. So much ivory would amount to £60,000' (1893:42), and he made arrangements not only to bring back the ivory but also to distribute the £60,000.

Norman Sherry has suggested that Conrad drew upon *In Darkest Africa* for certain details in *Heart of Darkness*. Marlow's use of the steam-whistle, for example, to disperse the armed crowd of Africans attacking the steamer probably derives from Stanley's account of similar incidents, given that the whole episode of the attack upon the steamer had no counterpart in Conrad's own experience (1971:53). Sherry has also suggested that another of Stanley's books, *The Congo*, provided material for Conrad's sardonic, anti-imperialist short story 'An Outpost of Progress', and that a speech by Stanley, reported in *The Times* of 4 October 1892 (i.e. after Conrad's return from the Congo) might also have contributed to *Heart of Darkness* (1971:130–131, 119–121). In this speech, Stanley made the equation of the Roman colonisation of Britain and British colonisation of Africa with which Marlow begins, and he made use of the recurrent figure of imperialist discourse – the metaphorical contrast of darkness and light. Thus Stanley concludes: 'God forbid that we should any longer subject Africa to the same dreadful scourge and preclude the light of knowledge which has reached every other quarter of the globe from having access into her coasts' (quoted in Sherry 1971:121). As Eric Woods has argued, darkness/light imagery in imperialist discourse contained an ambivalence which proved ideologically useful: on the one hand, as Stanley's speech illustrates, it implies a moral imperative (to bring light into areas of darkness) and thus justified missions and settlements: on the other hand, it also served to consolidate fixed categories, a perception of 'them' and 'us' (1989). Thus it simultaneously suggested a desire for change and fixed an opposition. By contrast, Conrad's handling of this imagery breaks down that sense of fixed opposition, while it simultaneously problematises the idea of change – in the sense that the 'civilising' mission is shown to be driven by a will-to-power and is vitiated by the 'savagery' within itself.

In subverting this discourse of darkness/light, Conrad could draw upon another discourse, another kind of power-knowledge,[13] well-established in Victorian Britain. Perhaps the quickest way to approach this is through William Booth's *In Darkest England*, published in 1890. As the title suggests, and as the first chapter makes clear, Booth was consciously responding to Stanley's *In Darkest Africa* in order to draw attention to the plight of the poor in England:

> As there is a darkest Africa is there not also a darkest England? Civilisation which can breed its own barbarism, does it not also breed its own pygmies? May we not find a parallel at our own doors, and discover within a stone's throw of our cathedrals and palaces similar horrors to those which Stanley has found existing in the great Equatorial forests? (1890:9).[14]

On one level, Booth's criticism is similar to that embodied by Dickens in the figure of Mrs Jellyby in *Bleak House*: the criticism of a kind of long-sightedness, which sees poverty and suffering in Africa, but not on its own doorstep. On another level, Booth is engaged in an interesting transfer of the discourse of imperialism to the English working-class. As with Marlow's observation that 'this also has been one of the dark places of the earth', Booth's oxymoronic title aims to shock: it is conscious of the scandal implicit in the transference of this metaphor from imperialist discourse to the metropolis.

The transferred use of this metaphor, however, is not original to Booth. As Woods notes, 'Darkest England' and 'Terra Incognita' already existed as tropes in the discourse of Victorian social reform (1989).[15] Thackeray, for example, wrote in *Fraser's Magazine*: 'The English gentleman knows as much about the people of Lapland or California as he does of the aborigines of The Seven Dials or the natives of Wapping'. George Sims proposed, in *How the Poor Live* (1883), to describe 'a journey into a region which lies at our own door into a dark continent that is within easy walking distance of the General Post Office'. Woods cites other examples, but I want to consider in detail *The Heart of the Empire* (Masterman 1901), in which both images occur, and which also offers an explanation for the situation it describes.[16] In his first chapter, 'Realities at Home', Masterman observes: 'You find yourself at Cambridge Heath or Dalston Junction or Walworth Road – in the heart of the mysterious *terra incognita*' (1901:15). The 'Preface' had referred to 'the stupendous growth of cities' and the unequal distribution of the 'enormous increase in wealth' which had produced 'the contrast between the lives of the rich and the poor' and 'their complete separation not only in sympathy and feeling but in actual geographical aggregation'. Masterman's chapter takes this further: he argues that 'the squalid inequality of unchecked private enterprise . . . has bound an almost insupportable burden upon the shoulders of the succeeding generations'. As a counter to the depredations of 'unchecked private enterprise', Masterman welcomes the work of local councils (and, in doing so, produces what seems to be an echo of *Heart of Darkness*): 'Public bodies, the London County Council and similar authorities in the great provincial cities have been pushing their activities into *the dark places of the earth*, slum areas are broken up, sanitary regulations enforced, *the policeman and the inspector at every corner*'. The ease with which this metaphorical transfer takes place is itself easily explained. In the passage by Thackeray quoted above, there is an ambivalence, a double-edgedness, about the references to 'the aborigines of The Seven Dials' and 'the natives of Wapping': while ostensibly criticising the 'English gentleman' for his ignorance of the working-class 'other', these phrases also register and fix a sense of the 'otherness' of that other. There is precisely the same kind of ambivalence as in the use of darkness/light imagery in imperialist discourse. 'Darkest Africa' and 'Darkest England' have different referents but embody the same relation of power-knowledge. The metaphor produces 'Africa' or the working class as an object for investigation and manipulation. At the same time, it positions the subject as not available to such examination and control. By contrast, Conrad's narrative method in *Heart of Darkness* carefully positions Marlow's narration as an object for examination: Marlow's representations are objectified and made available for scrutiny.

One manifestation of this power-knowledge is suggested in the concluding words of 'Life and Death in the Niger Delta', when the author refers to 'that last and largest empire, whose map is but half-unrolled'. In the late-Victorian period, there was a simultaneous mapping of two *terrae incognitae*: one as part of the extension of empire, the other at the heart of empire itself. In 1886, Charles Booth, a Liverpool ship-owner, merchant and positivist, set on foot an investigation into the 'condition and occupations of the inhabitants of London' (Volume 1, 1902:3). This investigation was to take up the next seventeen years and to produce seventeen volumes, but the most impressive part of this achievement was what Beatrice Webb called 'The Map of Poverty':

> The economic and social circumstances of all the families of London were graphically displayed in a series of maps, carefully coloured, street by street, according to the actual data obtained for each street . . . it was possible . . . to display graphically on these wonderful maps, by an eightfold colouration, the extent, the local distribution and even the

exact location of the misery, the poverty, the comfort and the luxury of the whole Metropolis (1926: 140–141).

A map also figures briefly in *Heart of Darkness*: Marlow observes that, when he was a boy, 'there were many blank spaces on the earth' (HD 52), and the biggest was in Africa.[17] He continues: 'True, by this time it was not a blank space any more. It had got filled since my boyhood with rivers and lakes and names. It had ceased to be a blank space of delightful mystery . . . It had become a place of darkness' (HD 52). Where William Booth's project replaced the *terra incognita* of working-class London with a house by house, street-by street mapping, colour-coded in eight different shades with seventeen volumes of commentary, *Heart of Darkness* replaces a blank with a darkness. Where Booth's positivist project sought to replace the unknown by the known, *Heart of Darkness* replaces the unknown with the unspeakable – instead of bringing light into darkness, it uncovers darkness at the heart of the 'civilising' mission.

Edward Said, Two Visions in *Heart of Darkness* (1993)

Domination and inequities of power and wealth are perennial facts of human society. But in today's global setting they are also interpretable as having something to do with imperialism, its history, its new forms. The nations of contemporary Asia, Latin America, and Africa are politically independent but in many ways are as dominated and dependent as they were when ruled directly by European powers. On the one hand, this is the consequence of self-inflicted wounds, critics like V. S. Naipaul are wont to say: *they* (everyone knows that 'they' means coloureds, wogs, niggers) are to blame for what 'they' are, and it's no use droning on about the legacy of imperialism. On the other hand, blaming the Europeans sweepingly for the misfortunes of the present is not much of an alternative. What we need to do is to look at these matters as a network of interdependent histories that it would be inaccurate and senseless to repress, useful and interesting to understand.

The point here is not complicated. If while sitting in Oxford, Paris, or New York you tell Arabs or Africans that they belong to a basically sick or unregenerate culture, you are unlikely to convince them. Even if you prevail over them, they are not going to concede to you your essential superiority or your right to rule them despite your evident wealth and power. The history of this stand-off is manifest throughout colonies where white masters were once unchallenged but finally driven out. Conversely, the triumphant natives soon enough found that they needed the West and that the idea of *total* independence was a nationalist fiction designed mainly for what Fanon calls the 'nationalist bourgeoisie', who in turn often ran the new countries with a callous, exploitative tyranny reminiscent of the departed masters.

And so in the late twentieth century the imperial cycle of the last century in some way replicates itself, although today there are really no big empty spaces, no expanding frontiers, no exciting new settlements to establish. We live in one global environment with a huge number of ecological, economic, social, and political pressures tearing at its only dimly perceived, basically uninterpreted and uncomprehended fabric. Anyone with even a vague consciousness of this whole is alarmed at how such remorselessly selfish and narrow interests – patriotism, chauvinism, ethnic, religious, and racial hatreds – can in fact lead to mass destructiveness. The world simply cannot afford this many more times.

One should not pretend that models for a harmonious world order are ready at hand, and it would be equally disingenuous to suppose that ideas of peace and community have much of a chance when power is moved to action by aggressive perceptions of 'vital national interests' or unlimited sovereignty. The United States' clash with Iraq and Iraq's aggression against Kuwait concerning oil are obvious examples. The wonder of it is that the schooling for such relatively provincial thought and action is still prevalent, unchecked, uncritically accepted, recurringly replicated in the education of generation after generation. We are all taught to venerate our nations and admire our traditions: we are taught to pursue their interests with toughness and in disregard for other societies. A new and in my opinion appalling tribalism is fracturing societies, separating peoples, promoting greed, bloody conflict, and uninteresting assertions of minor ethnic or group particularity. Little time is spent not so much in 'learning about other cultures' – the phrase has an inane vagueness to it – but in studying the map of interactions, the actual and often productive traffic occurring on a day-by-day, and even minute-by-minute basis among states, societies, groups, identities.

No one can hold this entire map in his or her head, which is why the geography of empire and the many-sided imperial experience that created its fundamental texture should be considered first in terms of a few salient configurations. Primarily, as we look back at the nineteenth century, we see that the drive toward empire in effect brought most of the earth under the domination of a handful of powers. To get hold of part of what this means, I propose to look at a specific set of rich cultural documents in which the interaction between Europe or America on the one hand and the imperialized world on the other is animated, informed, made explicit as an experience for both sides of the encounter. Yet before I do this, historically and systematically, it is a useful preparation to look at what still remains of imperialism in recent cultural discussion. This is the residuum of a dense, interesting history that is paradoxically global and local at the same time, and it is also a sign of how the imperial past lives on, arousing argument and counter-argument with surprising intensity. Because they are contemporary and easy at hand, these traces of the past in the present point the way to a study of the histories – the plural is used advisedly – created by empire, not just the stories of the white man and woman but also those of the non-whites whose lands and very being were at issue, even as their claims were denied or ignored.

One significant contemporary debate about the residue of imperialism – the matter of how 'natives' are represented in the Western media – illustrates the persistence of such interdependence and overlapping, not only in the debate's content but in its form, not only in what is said but also in how it is said, by whom, where, and for whom. This bears looking into, although it requires a self-discipline not easily come by, so well-developed, tempting, and ready at hand are the confrontational strategies. In 1984, well before *The Satanic Verses* appeared, Salman Rushdie diagnosed the spate of films and articles about the British Raj, including the television series *The Jewel in the Crown* and David Lean's film of *A Passage to India*. Rushdie noted that the nostalgia pressed into service by these affectionate recollections of British rule in India coincided with the Falklands War, and that 'the rise of Raj revisionism, exemplified by the huge success of these fictions, is the artistic counterpart to the rise of conservative ideologies in modern Britain'. Commentators responded to what they considered Rushdie's wailing and whining in public and seemed to disregard his principal point. Rushdie was trying to make a larger argument, which presumably should have appealed to intellectuals for whom George Orwell's well-known description of the intellectual's place in society as being inside and outside the whale no longer applied; modern reality in Rushdie's terms was actually 'whaleless, this world without quiet corners [in which] there can be no easy escapes from history, from hullabaloo, from terrible, unquiet fuss'.[1] But Rushdie's main point was *not* the point considered worth taking up and debating. Instead the main issue for contention was whether things in the Third World hadn't in fact declined after the colonies had been emancipated, and whether it might not be better on the whole to listen to the rare – luckily, I might add, extremely rare – Third World intellectuals who manfully ascribed most of their present barbarities, tyrannies, and degradations to their own native histories, histories that were pretty bad before colonialism and that reverted to that state after colonialism. Hence, ran *this* argument, better a ruthlessly honest V. S. Naipaul than an absurdly posturing Rushdie.

One could conclude from the emotions stirred up by Rushdie's own case, then and later, that many people in the West came to feel that enough was enough. After Vietnam and Iran – and note here that these labels are usually employed equally to evoke American domestic traumas (the student insurrections of the 1960s, the public anguish about the hostages in the 1970s) as much as international conflict and the 'loss' of Vietnam and Iran to radical nationalisms – after Vietnam and Iran, lines had to be defended. Western democracy had taken a beating, and even if the physical damage had been done abroad, there was a sense, as Jimmy Carter once rather oddly put it, of 'mutual destruction'. This feeling in turn led to Westerners rethinking the whole process of decolonization. Was it not true, ran their new evaluation, that 'we' had given 'them' progress and modernization? Hadn't we provided them with order and a kind of stability that they haven't been able since to provide for themselves? Wasn't it an atrocious misplaced trust to believe in their capacity for independence, for it had led to Bokassas and Amins, whose intellectual correlates were people like Rushdie? Shouldn't we have held on to the colonies, kept the subject or inferior races in check, remained true to our civilizational responsibilities?

I realize that what I have just reproduced is not entirely the thing itself, but perhaps a caricature. Nevertheless it bears an uncomfortable resemblance to what many people who imagined themselves speaking for the West said. There seemed little scepticism that a monolithic 'West' in fact existed, any more than an entire ex-colonial world described in one sweeping generalization after another. The leap to essences and generalizations was accompanied by appeals to an imagined history of Western endowments and free handouts, followed by a reprehensible sequence of ungrateful bitings of that grandly giving 'Western' hand. 'Why don't they appreciate us, after what we did for them?'[2]

How easily so much could be compressed into that simple formula of unappreciated magnanimity! Dismissed or forgotten were the ravaged colonial people who for centuries endured summary justice, unending economic oppression, distortion of their social and intimate lives, and a recourseless submission that was the function of unchanging European superiority. Only to keep in mind the millions of Africans who were supplied to the slave trade is to acknowledge the unimaginable cost of maintaining that superiority. Yet dismissed most often are precisely the infinite number of traces in the immensely detailed, violent history of colonial intervention – minute by minute, hour by hour – in the lives of individuals and collectivities, on both sides of the colonial divide.

The thing to be noticed about this kind of contemporary discourse, which assumes the primacy and even the complete centrality of the West, is how totalizing is its form, how all-enveloping its attitudes and gestures, how much it shuts out even as it includes, compresses, and consolidates. We suddenly find ourselves transported backward in time to the late nineteenth century.

This imperial attitude is, I believe, beautifully captured in the complicated and rich narrative form of Conrad's great novella *Heart of Darkness*, written between 1898 and 1899. On the one hand, the narrator Marlow acknowledges the tragic predicament of all speech – that 'it is impossible to convey the life-sensation of any given epoch on one's existence – that which makes its truth, its meaning – its subtle and penetrating essence . . . We live, as we dream – alone' (part 1) – yet still manages to convey the enormous power of Kurtz's African experience through his own overmastering narrative of his voyage into the African interior towards Kurtz. This narrative in turn is connected directly with the redemptive force, as well as the waste and horror, of Europe's mission in the dark world. Whatever is lost or elided or even simply made up in Marlow's immensely compelling recitation is compensated for in the narrative's sheer historical momentum, the temporal forward movement – with digressions, descriptions, exciting encounters, and all. Within the narrative of how he journeyed to Kurtz's Inner Station, whose source and authority he now becomes, Marlow moves backward and forward materially in small and large spirals, very much the way episodes in the course of his journey up-river are then incorporated by the principal forward trajectory into what he renders as 'the heart of Africa'.

Thus Marlow's encounter with the improbably white-suited clerk in the middle of the jungle furnishes him with several digressive paragraphs, as does his meeting later with the semi-crazed, harlequin-like Russian who has been so affected by Kurtz's gifts. Yet underlying Marlow's inconclusiveness, his evasions, his arabesque meditations on his feelings and ideas, is the unrelenting course of the journey itself, which, despite all the many obstacles, is sustained through the jungle, through time, through hardship, to the heart of it all, Kurtz's ivory-trading empire. Conrad wants us to see how Kurtz's great looting adventure, Marlow's journey up the river, and the narrative itself all share a common theme: Europeans performing acts of imperial mastery and will in (or about) Africa.

What makes Conrad different from the other colonial writers who were his contemporaries is that, for reasons having partly to do with the colonialism that turned him, a Polish expatriate, into an employee of the imperial system, he was so self-conscious about what he did. Like most of his other tales, therefore, *Heart of Darkness* cannot just be a straightforward recital of Marlow's adventures: it is also a dramatization of Marlow himself, the former wanderer in colonial regions, telling his story to a group of British listeners at a particular time and in a specific place. That this group of people is drawn largely from the business world is Conrad's way of emphasizing the fact that during the 1890s the business of empire, once an adventurous and often individualistic enterprise, had become the empire of business. (Coincidentally we should note that at about the same time Halford Mackinder, an explorer, geographer, and Liberal Imperialist, gave a series of lectures on imperialism at the London Institute of Bankers:[3] perhaps Conrad knew about this.) Although the almost oppressive force of Marlow's narrative leaves us with a quite accurate sense that there is no way out of the sovereign historical force of imperialism, and that it has the power of a system representing as well as speaking for everything within its dominion, Conrad shows us that what Marlow does is contingent, acted out for a set of like-minded British hearers, and limited to that situation.

Yet neither Conrad nor Marlow gives us a full view of what is *outside* the world-conquering attitudes embodied by Kurtz, Marlow, the circle of listeners on the deck of the *Nellie*, and Conrad. By that I mean that *Heart of Darkness* works so effectively because its politics and aesthetics are, so to speak, imperialist, which in the closing years of the nineteenth century seemed to be at the same time an aesthetic, politics, and even epistemology inevitable and unavoidable. For if we cannot truly understand someone else's experience and if we must therefore depend upon the assertive authority of the sort of power that Kurtz wields as a white man in the jungle or that Marlow, another white man, wields as narrator, there is no use looking for other, non-imperialist alternatives; the system has simply eliminated them and made them unthinkable. The circularity, the perfect closure of the whole thing is not only aesthetically but also mentally unassailable.

Conrad is so self-conscious about situating Marlow's tale in a narrative moment that he allows us simultaneously to realize after all that imperialism, far from swallowing up its own history, was taking place in and was circumscribed by a larger history, one just outside the tightly inclusive circle of Europeans on the deck of the *Nellie*. As yet, however, no one seemed to inhabit that region, and so Conrad left it empty.

Conrad could probably never have used Marlow to present anything other than an imperialist world-view, given what was available for either Conrad or Marlow to see of the non-European at the time. Independence was for whites and Europeans; the lesser or subject peoples were to be ruled; science, learning, history emanated from the West. True, Conrad scrupulously recorded the differences between the disgraces of Belgian and British colonial attitudes, but he could only imagine the world carved up into one or another Western sphere of dominion. But because Conrad also had an extraordinarily persistent residual sense of his own exilic marginality, he quite carefully (some would say maddeningly) qualified Marlow's narrative with the provisionality that came from standing at the very juncture of this world with another, unspecified but different. Conrad was certainly not a great imperialist entrepreneur like Cecil Rhodes or Frederick Lugard, even though he understood perfectly how for each of them, in Hannah Arendt's words, to enter 'the maelstrom of an unending process of expansion, he will, as it were, cease to be what he was and obey the laws of the process, identify himself with anonymous forces that he is supposed to serve in order to keep the whole process in motion, he will think of himself as mere function, and eventually consider such functionality, such an incarnation of the dynamic trend, his highest possible achievement'.[4] Conrad's realization is that if, like narrative, imperialism has monopolized the entire system of representation – which in the case of *Heart of Darkness* allowed it to speak for Africans as well as for Kurtz and the other adventurers, including Marlow and his audience – your self-consciousness as an outsider can allow you actively to comprehend how the machine works, given that you and it are fundamentally not in perfect synchrony or correspondence. Never the wholly incorporated and fully acculturated Englishman, Conrad therefore preserved an ironic distance in each of his works.

The form of Conrad's narrative has thus made it possible to derive two possible arguments, two visions, in the post-colonial world that succeeded his. One argument allows the old imperial enterprise full scope to play itself out conventionally, to render the world as official European or Western imperialism saw it, and to consolidate itself after World War Two. Westerners may have physically left their old colonies in Africa and Asia, but they retained them not only as markets but as locales on the ideological map over which they continued to rule morally and intellectually. 'Show me the Zulu Tolstoy', as one American intellectual has recently put it. The assertive sovereign inclusiveness of this argument courses through the words of those who speak today for the West and for what the West did, as well as for what the rest of the world is, was, and may be. The assertions of this discourse exclude what has been represented as 'lost' by arguing that the colonial world was in some ways ontologically speaking lost to begin with, irredeemable, irrecusably inferior. Moreover, it focuses not on what was shared in the colonial experience, but on what must never be shared, namely the authority and rectitude that come with greater power and development. Rhetorically, its terms are the organization of political passions, to borrow from Julien Benda's critique of modern intellectuals, terms which, he was sensible enough to know, lead inevitably to mass slaughter, and if not to literal mass slaughter then certainly to rhetorical slaughter.

The second argument is considerably less objectionable. It sees itself as Conrad saw his own narratives, local to a time and place, neither unconditionally true nor unqualifiedly certain. As I have said, Conrad does not give us the sense that he could imagine a fully realized alternative to imperialism: the natives he wrote about in Africa, Asia, or America were incapable of independence, and because he seemed to imagine that European tutelage was a given, he could not foresee what would take place when it came to an end. But come to an end it would, if only because – like all human effort, like speech itself – it would have its moment, then it would have to pass. Since Conrad *dates* imperialism, shows its contingency, records its illusions and tremendous violence and waste (as in *Nostromo*), he permits his later readers to imagine something other than an Africa carved up into dozens of European colonies, even if, for his own part, he had little notion of what that Africa might be.

Recall once again that Conrad sets the story on the deck of a boat anchored in the Thames; as Marlow tells his story the sun sets, and by the end of the narrative the heart of darkness has reappeared in England; outside the group of Marlow's listeners lies an undefined and unclear world. Conrad sometimes seems to want to fold that world into the imperial metropolitan discourse represented by Marlow, but by virtue of his own dislocated subjectivity he resists the effort and succeeds in so doing, I have always believed, largely through formal devices. Conrad's self-consciously circular narrative forms draw attention to themselves as artificial constructions, encouraging us to sense the potential of a reality that seemed inaccessible to imperialism, just beyond its control, and that only well after Conrad's death in 1924 acquired a substantial presence.

This needs more explanation. Despite their European names and mannerisms, Conrad's narrators are not average unreflecting witnesses of European imperialism. They do not simply accept what goes on in the name of the imperial idea: they think about it a lot, they worry about it, they are actually quite anxious about whether they can make it seem like a routine thing. But it never is. Conrad's way of demonstrating this discrepancy between the orthodox and his own views of empire is to keep drawing attention to how ideas and values are constructed (and deconstructed) through dislocations in the narrator's language. In addition, the recitations are meticulously staged: the narrator is a speaker whose audience and the reason for their being together, the quality of whose voice, the effect of what he says – are all important and even insistent aspects of the story he tells. Marlow, for example, is never straightforward. He alternates between garrulity and stunning eloquence, and rarely resists making peculiar things seem more peculiar by surprisingly misstating them, or rendering them vague and contradictory. Thus, he says, a French warship fires 'into a continent'; Kurtz's eloquence is enlightening as well as fraudulent; and so on – his speech so full of these odd discrepancies (well discussed by Ian Watt as 'delayed decoding') that the net effect is to leave his immediate audience as well as the reader with the acute sense that what he is presenting is not quite as it should be or appears to be.

Yet the whole point of what Kurtz and Marlow talk about is in fact imperial mastery, white Europeans *over* black Africans and their ivory, civilization *over* the primitive dark continent. By accentuating the discrepancy between the official 'idea' of empire and the remarkably disorienting actuality of Africa, Marlow unsettles the reader's sense not only of the very idea of empire but of something more basic, reality itself. For if Conrad can show that all human activity depends on controlling a radically unstable reality to which words approximate only by will or convention, the same is true of empire, of venerating the idea, and so forth. With Conrad, then, we are in a world being made and unmade more or less all the time. What appears stable and secure – the policeman at the corner, for instance – is only slightly more secure than the white men in the jungle, and requires the same continuous (but precarious) triumph over an all-pervading darkness, which by the end of the tale is shown to be the same in London and in Africa.

Conrad's genius allowed him to realize that the ever-present darkness could be colonized or illuminated – *Heart of Darkness* is full of references to the *mission civilisatrice*, to benevolent as well as cruel schemes to bring light to the dark places and peoples of this world by acts of will and deployments of power – but that it also had to be acknowledged as independent. Kurtz and Marlow acknowledge the darkness, the former as he is dying, the latter as he reflects retrospectively on the meaning of Kurtz's final words. They (and of course Conrad) are ahead of their time in understanding that what they call 'the darkness' has an autonomy of its own, and can reinvade and reclaim what imperialism had taken for *its* own. But Marlow and Kurtz are also creatures of their time and cannot take the next step, which would be to recognize that what they saw, disablingly and disparagingly, as a non-European 'darkness' was in fact a non-European world *resisting* imperialism so as one day to regain sovereignty and independence, and not, as Conrad reductively says, to re-establish the darkness. Conrad's tragic limitation is that even though he could see clearly that on one level imperialism was essentially pure dominance and land-grabbing, he could not then conclude that imperialism had to end so that 'natives' could lead lives free from European domination. As a creature of his time, Conrad could not grant the natives their freedom, despite his severe critique of the imperialism that enslaved them.

The cultural and ideological evidence that Conrad was wrong in his Eurocentric way is both impressive and rich. A whole movement, literature, and theory of resistance and response to empire exists . . . and in greatly disparate post-colonial regions one sees tremendously energetic efforts to engage with the metropolitan world in equal debate so as to testify to the diversity and differences of the non-European world and to its own agendas, priorities, and history. The purpose of this testimony is to inscribe, reinterpret, and expand the areas of engagement as well as the terrain contested with Europe. Some of this activity – for example, the work of two important and active Iranian intellectuals, Ali Shariati and Jalal Ali i-Ahmed, who by means of speeches, books, tapes, and pamphlets prepared the way for the Islamic Revolution – interprets colonialism by asserting the absolute opposition of the native culture: the West is an enemy, a disease, an evil. In other instances, novelists like the Kenyan Ngugi and the Sudanese Tayib Salih appropriate for their fiction such great *topoi* of colonial culture as the quest and the voyage into the unknown, claiming them for their own, post-colonial purposes. Salih's hero in *Season of Migration to the North* does (and is) the reverse of what Kurtz does (and is): the Black man journeys north into white territory.

Between classical nineteenth-century imperialism and what it gave rise to in resistant native cultures, there is thus both a stubborn confrontation and a crossing over in discussion, borrowing back and forth, debate. Many of the most interesting post-colonial writers bear their past within them – as scars of humiliating wounds, as instigation for different practices, as potentially revised visions of the past tending towards a new future, as urgently reinterpretable and redeployable experiences, in which the formerly silent native speaks and acts on territory taken back from the empire. One sees these aspects in Rushdie, Derek Walcott, Aimé Césaire, Chinua Achebe, Pablo Neruda, and Brian Friel. And now these writers can truly read the great colonial masterpieces, which not only misrepresented them but assumed they were unable to read and respond directly to what had been written about them, just as European ethnography presumed the natives' incapacity to intervene in scientific discourse about them.

NOTES

George Eliot, The Natural History of German Life

1 Throughout this article, in our statement of Riehl's opinions, we must be understood not as quoting Riehl, but as interpreting and illustrating him.

George Henry Lewes, Realism in Art: Recent German Fiction

1 Gott bewahre: God preserve!

2 This is only true of the original. No copy or engraving that we have ever seen has even a tolerable accuracy in these finer, subtler beauties. (Lewes's footnote.)

Henry Mansel, Sensation Novels

1 'Les nerfs, voilà tout l'homme': 'the nerves – there is the whole man', George Cabanis (1757–1808) [. . .].

2 *Si possis, recte; si non, quocumque modo*: 'by right means if you can, but, if not, by any means' [. . . Horace, *Epistles* I.i.66].

3 ' . . . But one halfpennyworth of bread to this intolerable deal of sack!' *Henry IV, Part One*, II.iv.524–6.

4 The Minerva Press, famous at the turn of the previous century for publishing sentimental novels.

5 John Dryden, 'Alexander's Feast', ll.106–7:

> Lovely Thais sits beside thee,
> Take the good the gods provide thee.

Émile Zola, The Experimental Novel

1 Zola uses empiricism in this essay in the sense of 'haphazard observation' in contrast with a scientific experiment undertaken to prove a certain truth. [Translator.]

Sigmund Freud, The Interpretation of Dreams

1 Another great creation of tragic poetry is rooted in the same soil as *Oedipus the King*: Shakespeare's *Hamlet*. But the change in treatment of the same material reveals the difference in the inner life of these two cultural periods so remote from each other: the advance of repression over the centuries in mankind's emotional life. In *Oedipus* the child's wishful fantasy on which it is based is out in the open and realized – as it is in dreams; in *Hamlet* it remains repressed, and we learn of its existence – as we learn of a neurosis – only through the inhibiting effects it produces. Curiously, *Hamlet* has shown that the overwhelming power of modern drama is compatible with the fact that we can remain quite unclear about the hero's character. The play is based on Hamlet's hesitation in fulfilling the task of revenge laid upon him; what the reasons or motives are for this hesitation the text does not say; the most various attempts at interpretation have not been able to identify them. According to the view argued by Goethe and still dominant today, Hamlet represents the type of human being whose power of action is paralysed by the over-development of the activity of thought ('sicklied o'er with the pale cast of thought'). According to others, the poet has attempted to portray a pathological, irresolute character close to neurasthenia. However, the drama's plot tells us that Hamlet should certainly not appear to be entirely incapable of action. We see him in action twice, once in sudden passion, when he stabs the eavesdropper behind the arras, the second time purposefully, indeed cunningly, when with all the insouciance of a Renaissance prince he dispatches the two courtiers to the death intended for himself. So what inhibits him from fulfilling the task laid upon him by his father's ghost? Here again we have at our disposal the knowledge that it is the particular nature of this task. Hamlet can do anything – except take revenge on the man who removed his father and took the latter's place beside his mother, the man who shows him his own repressed infant wishes realized. The revulsion that should urge him to revenge is thus replaced by self-recrimination, by the scruples of conscience which accuse him of being, quite literally, no better than the sinner he has to punish. I have translated into conscious terms what is bound to remain unconscious in the hero's psyche; if anyone wants to call Hamlet a hysteric, I can only acknowledge that it is an inference my interpretation

admits. The sexual revulsion which Hamlet expresses in the dialogue with Ophelia is congruent with it – the same sexual revulsion which was to take increasing hold of the poet's psyche in the following years, reaching its extreme in *Timon of Athens*. Of course it can only have been the poet's own inner life that confronts us in *Hamlet*: I note from the work on Shakespeare by Georg Brandes (1896) that the drama was written immediately after his father's death (1601), that is, when Shakespeare's mourning for his father was still fresh, and when presumably his childhood feelings towards him were revived. It is also known that Shakespeare had a son called Hamnet (identical with Hamlet) who died young. Just as *Hamlet* deals with the relationship of the son to his parents, so *Macbeth*, written in much the same period, deals with the theme of childlessness incidentally, just as every neurotic symptom, even the dream, is capable of over-interpretation, indeed demands it, if we are to understand it fully, so every truly poetic creation will have arisen from more than one motive and more than one impulse in the poet's psyche, and will admit of more than one interpretation. What I have attempted here is only an interpretation of the deepest layer of the impulses in the psyche of the creative poet.

Marilyn Butler, The Juvenilia and *Northanger Abbey*

1 *Northanger Abbey*, which was accepted for publication by Cadell under its title of *Susan* in 1803, was probably ready by then in substantially its present form.

2 It was Adeline, heroine of that novel, who stayed at a ruined abbey and found a secret chamber behind the arras, containing a rusty dagger and a roll of paper which told the story of the man kept prisoner there.

3 One of the commonest misconceptions about *Northanger Abbey* is that Isabella leads Catherine astray by introducing her to a world of horror and make-believe. But Catherine's worst error, to be taken in by Isabella, occurs before she has begun to read popular novels. Cf. Kenneth L. Moler, *Jane Austen's Art of Allusion*, Nebraska, 1969, pp. 19–20.

4 Professor Wright is one of the most influential critics to hold that Catherine's view of the General is not altogether illusory (*Jane Austen's Novels: A Study in Structure*, London, 1954, pp. 100–7).

5 The General's behaviour was so out of line with gentlemanly standards in the period that early readers found it incredible. Maria Edgeworth called it 'out of drawing and out of nature' (letter to Mrs. Ruxton, 21 Feb. 1818: Mrs. Edgeworth, *Memoir of Maria Edgeworth*, privately published, 1807, ii. 6). Hitherto we have thought of him as over-formal, and there is no room to modify his character sufficiently.

Marilyn Butler, Introduction to *Northanger Abbey*

1 In their *Life and Letters of Jane Austen* (London, 1913), p. 96, R. A. and W. Austen-Leigh changed these dates to 1797 and 1798. That error is still often found, though B.C. Southam drew attention to it in *TLS*, 12 October 1962. Cassandra Austen's Memorandum, probably written late 1817, is reproduced in R.W. Chapman, *Jane Austen's Minor Works* (Oxford, OUP, 1954), facing p. 242.

2 *Life and Letters*, op. cit., pp. 229–33.

3 Brian Southam, 'The Seventh Novel: *Sanditon*', ed. Juliet McMaster, *Jane Austen's Achievement* (London, Macmillan, 1976), p. 9.

4 For the variety, self-consciousness and formal experimentation typical of Romantic-age novels, see Gary Kelly, *English Fiction of the Romantic Period, 1789–1830* (London, Longman, 1989).

5 *Rambler*, no.4, 31 March 1730 (in *Works of Samuel Johnson*, ed. W.J. Bate and Albrecht B. Strauss, New Haven, Conn., Yale University Press, III, p. 21). Cf. Katrin Ristkok Burlin, 'The pen of the contriver: the four fictions of *Northanger Abbey*', ed. John Halperin, *Jane Austen: Bicentenary Essays* (Cambridge, CUP, 1975), p. 95.

6 [Richardson], *Rambler*, no. 97 (*Works of Samuel Johnson*, op. cit., IV, pp. 153–9) A rout was a large fashionable assembly, especially an evening party or reception (*OED*, from 1742). A drum, sometimes kettledrum, was more typically a large tea-party.

7 Godwin's essay belatedly achieved publication as an Appendix to Godwin's *Caleb Williams*, ed. M. Hindle (London, Penguin Books, 1988), pp. 359–74, especially 370, 372. Baillie claims the superiority of the modern novelist over the historian in individual psychology, pp. 12–17, and over the tragedian, romance-writer and poet in the accurate delineation of middle- and lower-class life, pp. 18–23. 'Introductory Discourse', *A Series of Plays . . . [on] the Stronger Passions of the Mind* (London, 1798).

8 See n.24 below.

9 See p. 33.

10 Camilla's character is much debated during the parts of the novel dealing with her girlhood, especially Books I and II. She too falls in love with her future husband before he with her. Mostly in the care of inattentive or treacherous mentors, she is watched over from the sidelines by wise (clerical) parents. A leading theme to emerge is that her happy, artless, naturally virtuous nature deserves to win through.

11 For an account of the romance revival, 1790–1810, see Stuart Curran, *Poetic Form and British Romanticism* (New York and Oxford, OUP, 1986), pp. 128–57. The scholarly interest in narratives transmitted across the ages in ballad, folk-tale and romance, from culture to culture, impacts on

the plotting of poems and novels. Godwin for example remarked in 1832 (*Caleb Williams*, ed. Hindle, op. cit., p.352) that the plot of his novel *Caleb Williams* (1794) was essentially that of the story of Bluebeard's Wife, which he knew from Perrault's volume of fairy-tales, *Contes et fées*, 1698.

12 For the currently burgeoning topic of the rhetorical and social use of goods as 'incarnated signs', see, e.g., Arjun Appadurai, *The Social Life of Things: Commodities in Cultural Perspective* (Cambridge, CUP, 1985); Jean Baudrillard, 'The System of Objects', *Selected Writings*, ed. M. Poster (Cambridge, Polity Press, 1989); Pierre Bourdieu, *Distinction: A Social Critique of the Judgment of Taste*, trans. R. Nice (London, Routledge & Kegan Paul, 1984); Colin Campbell, *The Romantic Ethic and the Spirit of Modern Consumerism* (Oxford, Blackwell, 1987). Among the best considerations of Austen's novels from this viewpoint are Barbara Hardy, 'Properties and Possessions in Austen's Novels', ed. J. McMaster, *Jane Austen's Achievement* (London, Macmillan, 1976); and Edward Copeland, who advances the argument that Austen and her contemporaries shape a new domestic ideology, foregrounding the economic significance of the role of the wife and mother, in 'Austen and the Consumer Revolution', *Jane Austen Companion*, ed. David Gray (New York, Macmillan, 1986) and *Women Writing about Money* (Cambridge, CUP, 1995).

13 John Booth, publisher, advertised an anonymous novel named *Susan* (2 vols., 8 shillings) in Bent's *Monthly Advertiser*, 10 June 1809.

14 See Michael Sadleir, 'The Northanger Novels: a Footnote to Jane Austen', *English Association Pamphlet*, no. 60 (Nov. 1927); Dorothy Blakey, *The Minerva Press, 1790–1820* (London, OUP, for the Bibliographical Society, 1939); Emma Clery, *The Rise of Supernatural Fiction* (Cambridge, CUP, 1995), pp. 135–8.

15 Ann Radcliffe, *Romance of the Forest* [1791], ed. Chloe Chard (Oxford, OUP, World's Classics, 1986), p. 165.

16 Cf. Margaret Ann Doody, 'Deserts, Ruins and Troubled Waters', *Genre* 10 (1977), 529–72, Tanya Modleski, *Loving with a Vengeance* (New York, Methuen, 1984) and Patricia Yaegar, 'Toward a Female Sublime', *Gender and Theory: Dialogues on Feminist Criticism*, ed. Linda Kauffman (Oxford, OUP, 1989), 191–212.

17 For the case of Lord Milton at Milton Abbas, and its aptness to the strictures on proprietor-led change in Blackstone's *Commentaries*, this discussion is indebted to Nigel Everett's book on the Tory idea of landscape (New Haven, Yale University Press, 1994), pp. 53–60.

18 E.P. Thompson, *Customs in Common* (London, Merlin Press, 1991), especially pp. 185–351.

19 Kenyon's 'Charge to the Grand Jury at Shropshire Assizes' appeared in the *Annals of Agriculture* 25 (1795), pp. 110–11. The 1800 case is discussed

in Douglas Hay's unpublished paper, 'The State and the Market: Lord Kenyon and Mr Waddington', cited Thompson, op. cit., p. 270.

20 Gilpin, *Remarks on Forest Scenery* (1791), II, pp. 9–10.

21 Uvedale Price, *Essay on the Picturesque*, 1794, *Letter to Humphry Repton, Esq.*, 1794, and *Thoughts on the Defence of Property Addressed to the County of Hereford*, 1797; Richard Payne Knight, *The Landscape, A Didactic Poem*, 1794, and *Progress of Civil Society, A Didactic Poem*, 1796. Stephen Daniels and Charles Watkins have shown that Price especially was indebted to the writings of the land agent Nathaniel Kent, currently the leading English exponent of a socially conscious style of agrarian improvement, in *Hints to Gentlemen of Landed Property*, 1775, and *General View of the Agriculture of the County of Norfolk*, 1794.

22 *Historic and Local New Bath Guide*, n.d. [1802], p. 94.

23 Lane devised one of the most advanced entrepreneurial sales campaigns of the 1790s, using techniques calculated to teach brand recognition and loyalty. His firm's name or in effect logo was both woman-catching and eye-catching, in that it was printed in dominant black-letter script on each title-page, and often on the lists of his forthcoming novels, which frequently appeared in the press, or on the back flysheets of the novels themselves. All three of Minerva's English authors on Isabella's list are women, demonstrating the same tendency as a Minerva prospectus of 1798, which lists ten 'particular and favourite' women authors; the translations from the German are of men's books, by men.

24 Beddoes first serialized, then issued in volume form a 1000-page study of social health and sickness, *Hygeia* (Bristol, 1802–3).

25 *Historic and Local New Bath Guide*, n.d. [1802]

26 Claudia L. Johnson, *Jane Austen: Women, Politics and the Novel* (Chicago, Chicago University Press, 1988), p. 48.

27 Cf. T. Day, *Sandford and Merton* (1783–9); A.L. Barbauld, *Little Lessons for Children Two and Three Years Old* (1778); Edgeworth, *Early Lessons* (1801–25).

Claudia L. Johnson, Women, Politics and the Novel: *Northanger Abbey*

1 The compositional history of *Northanger Abbey* is still widely debated. For a clear summary of hypotheses see A. W. Litz, *Jane Austen: A Study of Her Artistic Development* (New York: Oxford University Press, 1965), pp. 175–6, and B. C. Southam *Jane Austen's Literary Manuscripts* (London: Oxford University Press, 1964), pp. 60–62. While Cassandra Austen's Memorandum dates the novel at 'about the years 98 & 99,' C. S. Emden has argued that *Northanger Abbey* evolved as early as 1794, a conjecture which would anchor the novel even more firmly to political controversies;

see '*Northanger Abbey* Re-Dated?,' *Notes & Queries* 105 (September 1950), 407–10.

2 R. Paulson, *Representations of Revolution* (New Haven and London: Yale University Press, 1983), p. 221.

3 Charlotte Smith, *Desmond* (London, 1792), vol. 2, p. 174. For a discussion of the radical character of Smith's novel, see Diana Bowstead, 'Charlotte Smith's *Desmond*: The Epistolary Novel as Ideological Argument,' in Schofield and Macheski, *Fetter'd or Free*, pp. 237–63. For a general essay on the relation of Smith to Austen – which does not, however, make an issue of the former's radical sympathies – see William H. Magee, 'The Happy Marriage: The Influence of Charlotte Smith on Jane Austen,' *SNNTS*, 7 (1975), 120–32.

4 See Paulson, *Representations of Revolution*, pp. 225–27, and Poovey, 'Ideology and *The Mysteries of Udolpho*,' *Criticism* 21 (1971), 307–30.

5 Marc Girouard, *Life in the English Country House: A Social and Architectural History* (New Haven: Yale University Press, 1978), p. 242.

6 Critics who have argued that *Northanger Abbey* shows 'ordinary' life to be safe and fundamentally 'a-Gothic' include Butler, *War of Ideas*, pp. 178–79; Moler, *Art of Allusion*, pp. 38–40; and most recently P. J. M. Scott, who contends that much of this neither 'profound' nor 'even fairly interesting' novel is devoted to exposing a gap between 'the worlds of art and the life outside them' which is doomed to triviality because the heroine 'is simply not intelligent enough' to make her adventures interesting; in *Jane Austen: A Reassessment* (New York: Barnes & Noble, 1982), pp. 37–39. Most other readers feel that while *Northanger Abbey* does discredit the Gothic, it nevertheless prohibits us from trusting too unsuspiciously in 'common life,' as represented by General Tilney. Such critics include Lionel Trilling, *Opposing Self* (New York: Viking Press, 1955), p. 207; A. W. Litz, *Artistic Development*, p. 63; Barbara Hardy, *A Reading of Jane Austen* (New York: New York University Press, 1976), pp. 130–31.

7 Olivia Smith, *The Politics of Language 1791–1819* (Oxford: Clarendon Press, 1984), p. 19. I am much indebted to this important study.

8 Judith Wilt, *Ghosts of the Gothic* (Princeton: Princeton University Press, 1980), p. 138. My views on the gothic have also been greatly influenced by George Levine, '*Northanger Abbey*: from Parody to Novel and the Translated Monster' in *The Realistic Imagination: English Fiction from Frankenstein to Lady Chatterley* (Chicago: University of Chicago Press, 1981), pp. 61–80; and by William Patrick Day, *In the Circles of Fear and Desire: A Study of Gothic Fantasy* (University of Chicago Press, 1985), pp. 22–67.

9 Eaton Stannard Barrett, *The Heroine* (London, 1813), 3 vols., vol. 3, pp. 288–89. Austen reports that she was 'very much amused' by this novel, and that it 'diverted' her 'exceedingly.' See *Letters*, p. 376 (2 March 1814).

10 My discussion owes much to Robert Hopkins, 'General Tilney and Affairs of State: The Political Gothic of *Northanger Abbey*,' *Philological Quarterly* 57 (1978), 213–25, and B. C. Southam, 'General Tilney's Hot-Houses,' *Ariel* 2 (1971), 52–62.

Mary Poovey, The Anathematized Race: The Governess and *Jane Eyre*

1 For discussions of nineteenth-century governess novels, see Wanda F. Neff, *Victorian Working Women: An Historical and Literary Study of Women in British Industries and Professions, 1832–1850* (1929; reprint, New York: Humanities Press, 1966), pp. 153–74; Jerome Beaty, '*Jane Eyre* and Genre,' *Genre* 10 (Winter 1977): 619–54; and Robert A. Colby, *Fiction with a Purpose: Major and Minor Nineteenth-Century Novels* (Bloomington: Indiana University Press, 1967), pp. 178–212. More theoretical discussions of the governess include: Shoshana Felman, 'Turning the Screw of Interpretation,' *Yale French Studies 55/56* (1977): 94–207; and Jane Gallop, *The Daughter's Seduction: Feminism and Psychoanalysis* (Ithaca: Cornell University Press, 1982), pp. 141–48.

2 For the history of the Governesses' Benevolent Institution, see *The Story of the Governesses' Benevolent Institution* (Southwick, Sussex, England: Grange Press, 1962). The GBI (which was still in existence in 1962) was the second institution to address the governesses' plight. The first, the Governesses' Mutual Assurance Society, founded in 1829 to help governesses save for sickness, unemployment, and old age, did not fare well and dissolved in 1838. The GBI also got off to an uncertain start, and, largely because it had managed to save only about £100 in its first two years, was substantially reorganized in 1843 under the Rev. David Laing, chaplain of Middlesex Hospital and pastor of the Holy Trinity Church of Saint Pancras. The stated goals of the GBI were 'to raise the character of governesses as a class, and thus improve the tone of Female Education; to assist Governesses in making provision for their old age; and to assist in distress and age those Governesses whose exertions for their parents, or families have prevented such a provision' (*Story of the GBI*, p. 14). What is interesting about these goals is the way they combine provisions that encourage professional identification and co-operation with more explicitly moral (and implicitly class-specific) aims ('raise the character'). The GBI gave its first annuity in May 1844, and by 1860, ninety-nine governesses were receiving annuities from the GBI, although the annual reports made it clear how dramatically the need exceeded the monies the GBI had at its disposal. See [Jessie Boucherette], 'The Profession of the Teacher: The Annual Reports of the Governesses' Benevolent Institution, from 1843 to 1856,' *English Woman's Journal* 1 (March 1858), 1–13. Other activities of the

GBI included the opening in 1845 of a home in Harley Street to provide cheap, respectable lodgings for governesses who were temporarily unemployed; the establishment at about the same time of a free employment register; and, in 1849, the establishment of a permanent home for aged governesses in the Prince of Wales Road.

3 Boucherette, 'Profession of the Teacher,' p. 1.

4 Leonore Davidoff and Catherine Hall, *Family Fortunes: Men and Women of the English Middle Class, 1780–1850* (Chicago: University of Chicago Press, 1987), pp. 312–13.

5 See M. Jeanne Peterson, 'The Victorian Governess: Status Incongruence in Family and Society,' in Martha Vicinus, ed., *Suffer and Be Still: Women in the Victorian Age* (Bloomington: Indiana University Press, 1972), p. 4; and Martha Vicinus, *Independent Women: Work and Community for Single Women, 1850–1920* (Chicago: University of Chicago Press, 1985), pp. 23, 26.

6 Peterson, 'Victorian Governess,' pp. 3–19.

7 For a discussion of the increasingly problematized conceptualization of Victorian children, see Mark Spilka, 'On the Enrichment of Poor Monkeys by Myth and Dream; or, How Dickens Rousseauisticized and Pre-Freudianized Victorian Views of Childhood,' in Don Richard Cox, ed., *Sexuality and Victorian Literature* (Knoxville: University of Tennessee Press, 1984), pp. 161–79.

8 The phrase 'tabooed woman' comes from Lady Eastlake (Elizabeth Rigby), '*Vanity Fair* – and *Jane Eyre*,' *Quarterly Review* 84 (1848), 177, hereafter cited as *QR*. See ibid.; and 'Hints on the Modern Governess System,' *Fraser's Magazine* 30 (November 1844), 573, hereafter cited as *FM*.

9 *The Governess: Or, Politics in Private Life* (London: Smith, Elder, 1836), p. 310. One of the few departures from the conceptualization of the governess as 'genteel' appears in an article entitled 'The Governess Question,' *English Woman's Journal* 4 (1860). In this essay, the author argues that the governess's position is not considered genteel and is never likely to be elevated in status. 'Whatever *gentility* may once have attached to the profession of the governess has long since vanished, and it is impossible to name any occupation, not positively disreputable, which confers so little respectability, – respectability in the worldly sense . . . The governess, however well-conducted, remains a governess; may starve *genteely*, and sink into her grave friendless and alone' (pp. 163, 170). This is explicitly a polemical article, however, 'addressed to parents, who, not having the means of giving their daughters any fortune, seem seized with an epidemic madness to make them governesses' (p. 163). It is, in other words, designed to discourage lower-middle-class women from entering the governesses' ranks by disparaging the social status of this work.

10 The phrase about 'degradation' appears in [Sarah Lewis], 'On the Social Position of Governesses,' *Fraser's Magazine* 34 (April 1848), 414. See also *FM* 581.

11 See *QR* 180; *FM* 173, 580; 'Social Position,' pp. 413–14.

12 Peterson also makes this point. See 'Victorian Governess,' p. 17.

13 For an autobiographical report of a governess's sexual vulnerability, see Ellen Weeton, *Miss Weeton's Journal of a Governess*, ed. J. J. Bagley (New York: Augustus M. Kelley, 1969), 1, 209–327. The sexual exploitation to which the governess was potentially exposed surfaces obliquely at the end of an 1858 essay in the *English Woman's Journal*. 'Depths of horror,' the author (Jessie Boucherette) warns, 'into which men cannot fall' await the unemployed governess ('Profession of the Teacher' p. 13).

14 See *QR* 177; and *FM* 573.

15 *FM* 574.

16 The phrase 'white slavery' is the title of a letter about governesses published in the *London Times* and cited by Barbara Leigh Smith Bodichon, *Women and Work* (London: Bosworth and Harrison, 1857), p. 17. The phrase 'needlewomen forced to take to the streets' was used by Henry Mayhew in his 1849–50 *Morning Chronicle* series on London, 'Labour and the Poor.' See *The Unknown Mayhew: Selections from the 'Morning Chronicle,' 1849–50*, ed. E. P. Thompson and Eileen Yeo (Harmondsworth: Penguin Books, 1973), p. 200.

17 See Elizabeth K. Helsinger, Robin Lauterbach Sheets, and William Veeder, eds., *The Woman Question: Social Issues, 1837–1883*, vol. 2 of *The Woman Question: Society and Literature in Britain and America, 1837–1883* (New York: Garland Publishing, 1983), p. 115.

18 Henry Mayhew, 'Second Test – Meeting of Needlewomen Forced to Take to the Streets,' in *Unknown Mayhew*, pp. 200–16; and Anthony Ashley Cooper (Lord Ashley, later the seventh Earl of Shaftesbury), in *Hansard's Parliamentary Debates*, 3rd series, March 15, 1844, cc. 1088–89, 1091–96, 1099–1100.

19 *QR* 181.

20 Other early reviews of *Jane Eyre* include: George Henry Lewes's review in *Fraser's Magazine*, December 1847, pp. 690–93; John Eagles' essay in *Blackwood's Magazine*, October 1848, pp. 473–74; [H. R. Bagshawe], '*Jane Eyre, Shirley*,' *Dublin Review* 28 (March 1850): 209–33; [G. H. Lewes], 'The Lady Novelists,' *Fraser's Magazine*, o.s., 58 (July 1852): 129–41; and [E. S. Dallas], 'Currer Bell,' *Blackwood's Magazine* 82 (July 1857), 77–94.

21 Charlotte Brontë, *Jane Eyre*, ed. Q. D. Leavis (Harmondsworth: Penguin Books, 1966), p. 344. All future references will be cited in the text by page numbers. *Jane Eyre* was initially published by the firm of Smith, Elder.

22 Other essays on these dreams include Margaret Homans, 'Dreaming of Children: Literalization in *Jane Eyre* and *Wuthering Heights*,' in Juliann E. Fleenor, ed., *The Female Gothic* (Montreal: Eden Press, 1983), pp. 257–79; and Maurianne Adams, 'Family Disintegration and Creative Reintegration: The Case of Charlotte Brontë and *Jane Eyre*,' in Anthony S. Wohl, ed., *The Victorian Family: Structure and Stresses* (London: Croom Helm, 1978), pp. 148–79.

23 See Sandra M. Gilbert and Susan Gubar, *The Madwoman in the Attic: The Woman Writer and the Nineteenth-Century Literary Imagination* (New Haven: Yale University Press, 1979), pp. 336–71.

24 Nancy Armstrong, in *Desire and Domestic Fiction: A Political History of the Novel* (New York: Oxford University Press, 1987), p. 79, discusses the problematic position the governess occupied. The unstable boundary between the governess and the mother was explicitly explored by Mrs. Henry Wood in *East Lynne*, when the (disfigured) mother returns home as the governess for her own children.

25 The only reference to Jane's child is this sentence: 'When his firstborn was put into his arms, he could see that the body had inherited his own eyes, as they once were – large, brilliant, and black' (*Jane Eyre*, p. 476).

26 Jane's father is only obliquely held responsible for her situation – but her maternal grandfather is more directly to blame. Jane's father, a poor clergyman, wooed her mother into marriage against her father's wishes, and it was the old man's inexorable anger that caused him to leave all his money to Jane's uncle, thus leaving her penniless and dependent when her parents died.

Gayatri Chakravorty Spivak, *Jane Eyre*: A Critique of Imperialism

1 My notion of the 'worlding of a world' upon what must be assumed to be uninscribed earth is a vulgarization of Martin Heidegger's idea; see 'The Origin of the Work of Art,' *Poetry, Language, Thought*, trans. Albert Hofstadter, (New York, 1977), pp. 17–87.

2 I have tried to do this in my essay 'Unmaking and Making in *To the Lighthouse*,' in *Women and Language in Literature and Society*, ed. Sally McConnell-Ginet, Ruth Borker, and Nelly Furman (New York, 1980), pp. 310–27.

3 As always, I take my formula from Louis Althusser, 'Ideology and Ideological State Apparatuses (Notes towards an Investigation),' '*Lenin and Philosophy' and Other Essays*, trans. Ben Brewster (New York, 1971), pp. 127–86. For an acute differentiation between the individual and individualism, see V. N. Vološinov, *Marxism and the Philosophy of Language*, trans. Ladislav Matejka and I. R. Titunik, *Studies in Language*, vol. 1 (New York, 1973),

pp. 93–94 and 152–53. For a 'straight' analysis of the roots and ramifications of English 'individualism,' see C. B. MacPherson, *The Political Theory of Possessive Individualism: Hobbes to Locke* (Oxford, 1962). I am grateful to Jonathan Rée for bringing this book to my attention and for giving a careful reading of all but the very end of the present essay.

4 I am constructing an analogy with Homi Bhabha's powerful notion of 'not-quite/not-white' in his 'Of Mimicry and Man: The Ambiguity of Colonial Discourse,' *October* 28 (Spring 1984), 132. I should also add that I use the word 'native' here in reaction to the term 'Third World Woman.' It cannot, of course, apply with equal historical justice to both the West Indian and the Indian contexts nor to contexts of imperialism by transportation.

5 See Elizabeth Fox-Genovese, 'Placing Women's History in History,' *New Left Review* 133 (May–June 1982), 5–29.

6 Rudolph Ackerman, *The Repository of Arts, Literature, Commerce, Manufactures, Fashions, and Politics* (London, 1823), p. 310.

7 See Terry Eagleton, *Myths of Power: A Marxist Study of the Brontës* (London, 1975); this is one of the general presuppositions of his book.

8 See Sandra M. Gilbert and Susan Gubar, *The Madwoman in the Attic: The Woman Writer and the Nineteenth-Century Literary Imagination* (New Haven, Conn., 1979), pp. 360–62.

9 Immanuel Kant, *Critique of Practical Reason, The 'Critique of Pure Reason,' the 'Critique of Practical Reason' and Other Ethical Treatises, the 'Critique of Judgement,'* trans. J. M. D. Meiklejohn et al. (Chicago, 1952), pp. 328, 326.

10 I have tried to justify the reduction of sociohistorical problems to formulas or propositions in my essay 'Can the Subaltern Speak?' The 'travesty' I speak of does not befall the Kantian ethic in its purity as an accident but rather exists within its lineaments as a possible supplement. On the register of the human being as child rather than heathen, my formula can be found, for example, in 'What Is Enlightenment?' in Kant, *'Foundations of the Metaphysics of Morals,' 'What Is Enlightenment?' and a Passage from 'The Metaphysics of Morals,'* trans. and ed. Lewis White Beck (Chicago, 1950). I have profited from discussing Kant with Jonathan Rée.

11 Jean Rhys, in an interview with Elizabeth Vreeland, quoted in Nancy Harrison, *Jean Rhys and The Novel as Women's Text* (Chapel Hill: University of North Carolina Press, 1988). This is an excellent, detailed study of Rhys. References are to the 1966 Penguin edition of *WSS*.

12 See Louise Vinge, *The Narcissus Theme in Western European Literature Up to the Early Nineteenth Century*, trans. Robert Dewsnap et al. (Lund, 1967), chap. 5.

13 For a detailed study of this text, see John Brenkman, 'Narcissus in the Text,' *Georgia Review* 30 (Summer 1976), 293–327.

14 See, e.g., Thomas F. Staley, *Jean Rhys: A Critical Study* (Austin, Tex, 1979), pp. 108–16; it is interesting to note Staley's discomfort with this and his consequent dissatisfaction with Rhys' novel.

15 I have tried to relate castration and suppressed letters in my 'The Letter As Cutting Edge,' in *Literature and Psychoanalysis; The Question of Reading: Otherwise*, ed. Shoshana Felman (New Haven, Conn., 1981), pp. 208–26.

Susan L. Meyer, Colonialism and the Figurative Strategy of *Jane Eyre*

1 Christine Alexander, *The Early Writings of Charlotte Brontë* (Oxford: Basil Blackwell, 1983), p. 30. This work provides a detailed summary of the plots of Charlotte Brontë's juvenile writings as well as an analysis of Charlotte Brontë's development as a writer as manifested in this early fiction. Alexander is currently working on an authoritative edition of the Charlotte Brontë juvenilia, the first volume of which has now been published as *An Edition of the Early Writings of Charlotte Brontë 1826–1832* (New York: Basil Blackwell, 1987).

2 Charlotte Brontë, *Shirley* (1849; rpt. New York: Oxford University Press, 1981), p. 613.

3 Charlotte Brontë, *The Professor*, ed. Margaret Smith and Herbert Rosengarten (Oxford: Charendon Press, 1987), p. 14.

4 Gayatri Chakravorty Spivak, 'Three Women's Texts and a Critique of Imperialism,' *Critical Inquiry* 12 (1985), 243–61, reprinted here, pp. 215–24.

5 Anthony Trollope, 'Miss Sarah Jack of Spanish Town, Jamaica,' in his *Tourists and Colonials*, ed. Betty Jane Slemp Breyer (Fort Worth, Texas: Texas Christian University Press, 1981), p. 8.

6 See, for example, Adrienne Rich's reference to Bertha's 'dark sensual beauty,' 'Jane Eyre: The Temptations of a Motherless Woman' (1973), reprinted in her *On Lies, Secrets, and Silence: Selected Prose 1966–1978* (New York: Norton, 1979), p. 99, or Sandra Gilbert and Susan Gubar's description of Bertha as 'a Creole – swarthy, "livid," etc.' (*The Madwoman in the Attic* [New Haven: Yale University Press, 1979], p. 680n).

7 For discussions of the practices of and attitudes toward interracial sex and manumission in the English colonies, see Winthrop Jordan, *The White Man's Burden: Historical Origins of Racism in the United States* (New York: Oxford University Press, 1974), pp. 70–3 and Craton, pp. 176, 181–6, 223–6.

8 J.M. Ludlow, *History of the United States* (1862), quoted in *The Compact Edition of the Oxford English Dictionary* (New York: Oxford University Press, 1981), 1, 601.

9 For the association of the racial 'other' with madness, see Sander Gilman,

Difference and Pathology: Stereotypes of Sexuality, Race, and Madness (Ithaca: Cornell University Press, 1985), esp. pp. 131–49.

10 Only excerpts from this journal entry, which begins 'Well here I am at Roe Head,' have been published. One excerpt appears in Alexander, *Early Writings*, p. 148. A different, but partially overlapping, excerpt appears in Fannie Elizabeth Ratchford, *The Brontës' Web of Childhood* (1941; rpt. New York: Russell and Russell, 1964), p. 114.

11 'The West India Controversy,' *Blackwood's Edinburgh Magazine* 14 (1823), 442.

12 Q. D. Leavis, 'Notes,' in *Jane Eyre*, pp. 487–9.

13 Terry Eagleton, *Myths of Power: A Marxist Study of the Brontës* (New York: Barnes and Noble, 1975), pp. 4, 16.

14 Carol Ohmann, 'Historical Reality and "Divine Appointment" in Charlotte Brontë's Fiction,' *Signs* 2 (1977), pp. 757–78 and Igor Webb, *From Custom to Capital: The English Novel and the Industrial Revolution* (Ithaca: Cornell University Press, 1981), esp. pp. 70–86.

15 See Patricia Meyer Spacks, *The Female Imagination* (New York: Knopf, 1972), pp. 64–5; Rich, pp. 97–9; and Gilbert and Gubar, pp. 336–71, esp. 359–62.

16 For an excellent discussion of the European fear of 'going native' in the colonies, which includes a discussion of Kurtz in Conrad's *Heart of Darkness*, see Patrick Brantlinger, 'Victorians and Africans: The Genealogy of the Myth of the Dark Continent,' *Critical Inquiry* 12 (1985), 166–203, esp. 193–198. Brantlinger argues that 'the potential for being "defiled" – for "going native" or becoming "tropenkollered" – led Europeans again and again to displace their own "savage" impulses onto Africans' (p. 196).

17 For two very interesting discussions of the Victorian bourgeoisie's equation of dirt with the 'lower orders,' see Leonore Davidoff's analysis of the relationship between the upper-middle-class A. J. Munby and his servant Hannah Cullwick in 'Class and Gender in Victorian England,' in *Sex and Class in Women's History*, ed. Judith L. Newton, Mary P. Ryan, and Judith R. Walkowitz (Boston: Routledge and Kegan Paul, 1983), pp. 17–71, and Peter Stallybrass and Allon White, *The Politics and Poetics of Transgression* (Ithaca: Cornell University Press, 1986), pp. 125–48.

18 Patricia Beer also notes that 'the fresh air and the open countryside remain for [Jane] symbols of personal freedom and independence' which she opposes to the thought of suffocation as Rochester's 'slave' (p. 126).

19 Ironically, the name 'Indian ink' or 'India ink' is a misnomer: the black pigment was actually made in China and Japan.

Catherine Waters, Ambiguous Intimacy: Brother and Sister Relationships in *Dombey and Son*

1 Michael Slater, *Dickens and Women* (London, 1983), p. 32.

2 Lydia Zwinger, 'The Fear of the Father: Dombey and Daughter', *NCF*, Vol. 39 (1985), pp. 420–40.

3 Charles Dickens, *Dombey and Son*, ed. Alan Horsman (Oxford, 1974), p. 5. All subsequent references are to this edition.

4 The Manuscript and First Proof emphasise this by repetition: 'I know it's very weak and silly of me,' she repeated, 'to be so tremble and shakey from head to foot, and to allow my feelings so completely to get the better of me, but I cannot help it' (*Dombey and Son*, ed. Horsman, p. 6, n. 1).

5 Louise Yelin, 'Strategies for Survival: Florence and Edith in *Dombey and Son*', *Victorian Studies*, Vol. 22 (1979), p. 305.

6 Quoted in Patricia Branca, *Silent Sisterhood* (London, 1975), pp. 25–6.

7 'On Female Education', quoted in Janet Murray, *Strong-Minded Women and Other Lost Voices from Nineteenth-Century England* (Harmondsworth, 1984), p. 217.

8 Sarah Stickney Ellis, *The Wives of England*, quoted in Murray, op.cit., p. 125.

9 See Roselee Robison, 'Victorians, Children and Play', *English Studies*, Vol. 64 (1983), p. 318.

10 Quoted in John Butt and Kathleen Tillotson, *Dickens at Work* (London, 1982), p. 95.

11 Mark Spilka, *Dickens and Kafka* (Bloomington, 1963), p. 53.

12 Russell M. Goldfarb, *Sexual Repression and Victorian Literature* (Lewisburg, 1970), p. 119.

13 Judith Schelly, 'A Like Unlike: Brother and Sister in the Works of Wordsworth, Byron, George Eliot, Emily Brontë and Dickens', Diss. Univ. of California 1980 (Ann Arbor: Univ. Microfilms International, 1980), p. 207.

14 Spilka, op. cit., p. 51.

15 This description comes from one of the many passages deleted in the proof stage of the novel (correction in Forster's hand) due to the space restrictions imposed by serial publication. See *Dombey and Son* ed. Horsman, Introduction, p. xx. The passage is restored in a number of modern editions, such as the Penguin English Library edition, ed. Peter Fairclough (Harmondsworth, 1970), as follows: 'Dreaming, perhaps, of loving tones for ever silent, of loving eyes for every closed, of loving arms again wound round her, and relaxing in that dream within which no tongue can relate. Seeking, perhaps – in dreams – some natural comfort for a heart, deeply and sorely wounded, though so young a child's; and finding it, perhaps, in dreams, if not in waking, cold, substantial truth' (*Dombey and Son*, ed. Horsman, p. 52, n. 1).

16 Schelly, op.cit., p. 208.

17 Deborah Gorham, *The Victorian Girl and the Feminine Ideal* (Bloomington, 1982), p. 4.

18 Nancy F. Anderson, 'The "Marriage with a Deceased Wife's Sister Bill" Controversy: Incest Anxiety and the Defence of Family Purity in Victorian England', *Journal of British Studies*, Vol. 21 (1982), p. 77.

19 Anderson, op.cit., p. 83.

Suvendrini Perera, Wholesale, Retail and for Exportation: Empire and the Family Business in *Dombey and Son*

1 *Narrative of the Expedition sent by her Majesty's Government to the River Niger in 1841, under the command of Captain H. D. Trotter, R. N., by Captain William Allen, R. N. and T. R. H. Thompson M.D., 'Published with the sanction of the Colonial Office and the Admiralty.' Quotations are from Dickens's review, 'The Niger Expedition,' (hereafter cited as 'Niger'), which appeared in The Examiner* on 19 August 1848, reprinted in *Miscellaneous Papers*, 2 vols. (London: MacDonald, 1913), 1, 50.

2 See Eric Williams, *From Columbus to Castro: The History of the Caribbean 1492–1969* (London: Andre Deutsch, 1970), and Patrick Brantlinger, *Rule of Darkness: British Literature and Imperialism 1830–1914* (Ithaca, NY: Comell University Press, 1988), pp. 174–179.

3 See Judith Newton, 'Making – and Remaking – History: Another Look at "Patriarchy," ' in Shari Benstock, ed., *Feminist Issues in Literary Scholarship* (Bloomington: Indiana University Press, 1987), pp. 124–140, and Nancy Armstrong, *Desire and Domestic Fiction* (New York: Oxford University Press, 1987), pp. 72–74.

4 Bernard Semmel, *The Rise of Free Trade Imperialism* (Cambridge: Cambridge University Press, 1970), p. 5.

5 P. 45. Exeter Hall, the centre of abolitionist and missionary activity, is a favourite literary target throughout the mid-Victorian period. Godfrey Ablewhite, the hypocritical villain of Collins's *The Moonstone* (1868), is one of its most eloquent members. Carlyle dubbed Exeter Hall politics 'rose-pink sentimentalism' in his 'Occasional Discourses on the Negro Question' (1849); Disraeli attacked it in both *Sybil* (1845) and *Tancred* (1847).

6 See Nina Auerbach, *Romantic Imprisonment* (New York: Columbia University Press, 1985), p. 116, and David Musselwhite, 'The Novel as Narcotic,' in Francis Barker and others, eds., 1848: *The Sociology of Literature* (Colchester: University of Essex, 1978), p. 208.

7 Compare Marx's linkage, in 1867, of the three key elements in Dickens's passage: 'The colonial system ripened trade and navigation as in a hothouse. The "Companies called Monopolia" . . . were powerful levers for the

concentration of capital. The colonies provided a market for the budding manufactures, and a vast increase in accumulation which was guaranteed by the mother country's monopoly of the market. The treasures captured outside Europe by undisguised looting, enslavement and murder flowed back to the mother-country and were turned into capital there' (*Capital*, 3 vols. [1867–94; rpt. New York: Vintage, 1981]), 1, 918.

8 Michael Nerlich, *Ideology of Adventure*, trans. Ruth Crowley, 2 vols. (1977; rpt. Minneapolis: University of Minnesota Press, 1987), 1, 129.

9 Nerlich, I, 128. 'The magic word in which the different classes and strata seemed to converge was "adventure." The knightly adventure, the cooperative trade enterprise, the manly deed, the life of employees, of entrepreneurs who no longer went on trade journeys themselves, even the dangerous enterprise and the goods themselves – all went by the same name . . . But it would be a mistake to see only this magic key word and to overlook the ideological differences contained in the various ideological systems which seem to be united at this one point: the class antagonisms are only superficially concealed (if at all) in this word' (I, 133).

10 Ramkrishna Mukherjee's classic study of mercantilism, *The Rise and Fall of the East India Company* (1957; rpt. New York: Monthly Review Press, 1974), traces the career of the Company from its aggressive militarist phase (which was 'not an accidental phenomenon but the consummation of the governing desire of merchant capital') to its overthrow by the more cautious, overtly pacifist, proponents of free-trade capitalism (p. 39).

11 Compare Musslewhite: 'the structural description of the polarities of the book . . . is no more than a practice of collusion with the very ambition the text sets itself – that of distracting attention away from its real conditions of existence . . . and promoting a "critical" discourse ever pre-empted by its object' (p. 211).

12 On the domestic upheaval wrought by the railway, electric telegraph, and other products of Victorian industrialization, see Raymond Williams's 1970 Introduction to the Penguin edition of *Dombey and Son* [reprinted here, pp. 244–60].

13 Auerbach's reading follows from her contention that 'unlike other overweening institutions in Dickens' novels – Chancery in *Bleak House*, or the Circumlocution Office in *Little Dorrit* – Dombey and Son is defined in terms that are sexual and metaphysical rather than social. It exists as a gigantic end, the source and destination of all motion, all order, the center not so much of its society as of its universe' (p. 112). I suggest that Auerbach's exclusion of empire as a social reality in the novel accounts for her perception of the House of Dombey as a primarily 'sexual and metaphysical' concern.

14 For two critics who also comment on the stifling, unhealthy nature of

Florence's overwhelming love, but assign different values to it, see Julian Moynahan, 'Dealings with the Firm of *Dombey and Son*: Firmness versus Wetness,' in John Gross and Gabriel Pearson, eds., *Dickens and the Twentieth Century* (Toronto: University of Toronto Press, 1962), pp. 121–131, and Alexander Welsh, *The City of Dickens* (Cambridge: Harvard University Press, 1986), pp. 185–191.

15 Harriet Martineau, 'Cinnamon and Pearls, A Tale,' in *Illustrations of Political Economy* (London: Charles Fox, 1833), VII, 77.

16 Chapter 14. Robert Clark has commented on the impact of the various free trade struggles of the 1840s, including the repeal of the Navigation and the Corn Laws, in 'Riddling the Family Firm: The Sexual Economy in *Dombey and Son*,' *English Literary History* 51 (Spring 1984), pp. 75–76. Dickens's early enthusiasm for the repeal of the Corn Laws has been noted also by Michael Sheldon in 'Dickens, "The Chimes," and the Anti-Corn Law League,' *Victorian Studies* 25 (Spring 1982), pp. 229–353. But it is difficult to infer support for the entire platform of free trade from early sympathy for the Anti-Corn-Law Leaguers alone. By mid-century, a pro-industrialist and generally pacifist approach was among the most prominent characteristics of free trade 'radicals.'

17 For more on free trade and the Opium Wars, see Semmel, pp. 152–154. For the view that mid-Victorian free-trade *ideology* was pacifist and anti-imperialist, even though English armies and administrators throughout the empire continued to follow an expansionist and militaristic course – idiosyncratically or by reflex – *see* Ronald Robinson, John Gallagher, and Alice Denny, *Africa and the Victorians* (New York: St. Martin's Press, 1961).

18 Compare Esther's description of Mr. Jellyby in *Bleak House*: 'As he never spoke a word, he might have been a native, but for his complexion' (1852–53; rpt. New York: Norton, 1977), p. 41.

19 Disraeli, *Sybil* (1845; rpt. Harmondsworth: Penguin, 1980), p. 107.

20 Mineke Schipper, *Unheard Words*, trans. Barbara Potter Fasting (London: Allison and Busby, 1985), p. 15.

21 Chapter 26. In a probable allusion to Dickens's character, Thackeray's Anglo-Indian magnate Mr. Binnie, in *The Newcomes*, has 'a perfect appetite . . . and not the shadow of a black servant' (1, 99–100). Thackeray features the Bagstock type most famously in Jos Sedley, the unfortunate collector of Bogley Wollah in *Vanity Fair*, a novel set in the early years of the century; his Munchausen-like Major Gahagan, however, suggests that the Anglo-Indian soldier was already an old literary joke by 1838. *The Tremendous Adventures of Major Gahagan* is an extended parody of Anglo-Indian clichés, uncannily foreshadowing Kipling's *Plain Tales from the Hills*.

22 Raymond Williams, *The Country and The City* (New York: Oxford University Press, 1973), p. 115.

23 Peter Fryer quotes Charles Dunster's 1790 poem, *St. James's Street*, which describes dark servants as the 'Index of Rank or Opulence Supreme', in *Staying Power* (London: Pluto Press, 1984), p. 73. See also Fryer, pp. 29–30, and John Berger, *Ways of Seeing* (London: BBC, 1972), pp. 83–95, for a general discussion of the colonial relationship as produced in art.

24 David Dabydeen, *Hogarth's Blacks* (Athens: University of Georgia Press, 1987), p. 21.

25 Here the novel contradicts Robert Clark, who suggests that Dombey 'seems improbably disinclined to invest or speculate' and claims that 'the text is so opaque about what Dombey actually does that we can only conjecture about his business dealings, but his mode of confronting the world is essentially ungiving and unadventurous. Apart from the . . . occasional soirée of conspicuous consumption . . . Dombey's austerity provides an upper class version of Scrooge's miserliness' (p. 76). But Dombey's 'prodigious ventures' in the empire are invisible only to critics who seek the key to his operation in strictly metropolitan manifestations.

26 Dombey's obliviousness to gender as a distinct factor is already apparent in his assumption that Polly Toodles's maternal breast can be bought and replaced on the same principles as any other merchandise.

27 For instance, Lynda Zwinger writes: 'A daughter is anomalous in the patriarchal nuclear family. Virtually every other daughter-heroine in the canon occupies a place Dickens fudged for her by literally or figuratively removing her mother . . . or by de-sexualizing the father figure . . . In either case the sexuality inherent in her separate desirable qualities is repressed beneath the sanctity and asexuality of the maternal role . . . In *Dombey and Son* Dickens comes as close as he ever does to revealing the hollowness of his fictional, and his culture's ideological, daughter alibis' ('The Fear of the Father: Dombey and Daughter,' *Nineteenth-Century Fiction* 39 [March 1985], 429–430).

28 The Whittington figure also reappears in *The Newcomes*, but as the founder of the banking dynasty (1, 15). Unlike *Dombey and Son*, *The Newcomes* ends with the Colonel an actual penitent, a charity pensioner at his old school. The same fate – 'refuge in one of them genteel almshouses of the better kind' – is actually suggested for Dombey by one of his servants (*DS*, ch. 59).

Sally Shuttleworth, *Middlemarch*: An Experiment in Time

1 In Lewes' *The Study of Psychology* (London, 1879), which George Eliot prepared for publication, there occurs the observation that we may 'term History an experiment instituted by Society, since it presents conspicuous variations of mental reactions under varying social conditions' (p. 152). In

writing the history of *Middlemarch*, George Eliot was instituting her own experiment, creating her own experimental conditions.

2 My interpretation of George Eliot's fictional methodology differs from that of Bernard J. Paris (*Experiments in Life* [Detroit, 1965]) who views her as a 'militant empiricist' throughout her career (p. 73). I would argue that the theory of realism which she defined in her review of Ruskin's *Modern Painters* (see Paris, p. 26 and ch. 4) only applies to her earlier work. Although Paris views all George Eliot's novels as 'experiments', I would suggest that the term should perhaps be more narrowly applied to *Middlemarch* and *Daniel Deronda* in order to distinguish the radical changes which occur in her methodology in these works.

3 For discussion of this point see Michael York Mason, '*Middlemarch* and Science: Problems of Life and Mind', *Review of English Studies*, 22 (1971) 151, 162; Gillian Beer, 'Plot and the Analogy with Science in Later Nineteenth-Century Novelists', *Comparative Criticism: A Yearbook*, ed. E. S. Shaffer, 2 (1980), pp. 138, 144–5; George Levine, 'George Eliot's Hypothesis of Reality', *Nineteenth-Century Fiction*, 35 (1980), 12–13.

4 Claude Bernard, *An Introduction to the Study of Experimental Medicine*, trans. Henry C. Green (New York, 1949), p. 18.

5 G. H. Lewes, *The Foundations of a Creed*, vol. 1 (London, 1874), p. 26.

6 Claude Bernard, *An Introduction to the Study of Experimental Medicine*, trans. Henry C. Green (New York, 1949), p. 26.

7 Ibid., p. 34.

8 G. H. Lewes, *The Foundations of a Creed*, vol. 1 (London, 1874), p. 296; vol. 2 (London, 1875), p. 28.

9 G. H. Lewes, *Sea-side Studies* (Edinburgh, 1858), p. 153.

10 George Eliot observes, in a letter to Mrs Gaskell written in 1859, that, 'I was conscious, while the question of my power was still undecided for me, that my feeling towards Life and Art had some affinity with the feeling which had inspired *Cranford* and the earlier chapters of *Mary Barton*' (G. S. Haight, *The George Eliot Letters*, vol. 3 [New Haven and London, 1954–5], p. 198). The spirit of *Cranford*, which George Eliot read for the first time in 1857, lies behind *Scenes of Clerical Life* and *Adam Bede*.

11 G. H. Lewes, *The Foundations of a Creed*, vol. 2 (London, 1875), p. 18.

12 G. H. Lewes, *The Foundations of a Creed*, vol. 1 (London, 1874), p. 128.

13 G. H. Lewes, *The Foundations of a Creed*, vol. 1 (London, 1874), p. 124.

14 For an extended analysis of chapter construction in *Middlemarch* see John Holloway, 'Narrative Process in *Middlemarch*', in *Narrative and Structure: Exploratory Essays* (Cambridge, 1979), pp. 38–52.

15 George Eliot, 'Notes on Form in Art (1868)', in Thomas Pinney (ed.), *Essays of George Eliot* (London, 1963), pp. 431–6 (p. 432).

16 Thomas Pinney (ed.), *Essays of George Eliot* (London, 1963), p. 433.

17 This theory was first outlined in 'The Philosophy of Style', published in the *Westminster Review*, 58 (October, 1852), 234–47, whilst George Eliot was editor. Herbert Spencer, *Essays: Scientific, Political and Speculative, First Series* (London, 1858), p. 261.

18 Thomas Pinney (ed.), *Essays of George Eliot* (London, 1963), pp. 435–6.

19 G. H. Lewes, *The Foundations of a Creed*, vol. 2 (London, 1875), p. 27.

20 Lewes had adopted de Blainville's definition from Comte. See G. H. Lewes, *Comte's Philosophy of the Sciences* (London, 1852–3), pp. 171–3.

21 G. H. Lewes, *The Foundations of a Creed*, vol. 2 (London, 1875), pp. 122–3.

Gillian Beer, *Middlemarch*: The Web of Affinities

1 Page references in the text are to the first edition of *The Origin of Species*, reprinted in the Pelican Classics Volume edited by John Burrow (Harmondsworth: Penguin, 1968).

2 *The Foundations of a Creed* (London, 1873–5), vol 1, p. 26. Huxley's review of *The Origin* in *The Westminster Review*, 73 (1860), 541–70 uses a rose-coloured version of the metaphor: 'Harmonious order governing eternally continuous progress – the web and woof of matter and force interweaving by slow degrees, without a broken thread, that veil which lies between us and the Infinite.' (Reprinted in *Darwiniana* (London 1893), p. 59.)

3 John Tyndall, *On Radiation* (London, 1865), pp. 9–10.

4 Alexander Bain, *Mind and Body: the Theories of their Relation* (London, 1873), p. 27.

5 I. J. Beck, *The Method of Descartes* (Oxford, 1952), especially ch. 11. Compare Willard van Quine and Joseph Ullian in *The Web of Belief* (New York, 1970).

6 Cited by Robert Chambers, *Vestiges of the Natural History of Creation* (London, 1844), pp. 11–12.

7 See Terry Eagleton, *Criticism and Ideology* (London, 1977) for an interesting discussion of some ideological functions of the web. He links it more closely to organicism than I do. For a witty and provocative discussion of spinning, weaving and yarning in George Eliot, see Sandra H. Gilbert and Susan Gubar, *The Madwoman in the Attic: The Woman Writer and the Nineteenth Century Literary Imagination* (New Haven and London, 1979), especially pp. 519–28.

8 Darwin said that Julia Wedgwood was one of the few who perfectly understood his work. 'The Boundaries of Science: a Second Dialogue', *Macmillan's Magazine*, 4 (1861), 241.

9 Anskar's thousandth anniversary fell in 1865 and an account of his life was prepared for the occasion by L. Dreves, *Leben des heiligen Ansgar* (Paderborn, 1864).

10 *Sacred and Legendary Art* (London 1848), p. xxii.

11 *Sacred and Legendary Art*, vol. 2, pp. 184–9.

12 *Letters*, vol. 4, p. 49.

David Carroll, *Middlemarch*: Empiricist Fables

1 Mary Shelley, *Frankenstein; or, The Modern Prometheus*, ed. M. K. Joseph (Oxford University Press, 1969), pp. 55–6.

2 Alan Mintz, *George Eliot and the Novel of Vocation* (Cambridge, Mass.: Harvard University Press), p. 95, refers to this as an example of Lydgate's 'fatal taxonomic carelessness'.

3 J. Hillis Miller, "Narrative and History", *English Literary History* 41 (1974), 468.

4 The best account of this scientific dispute between John Stuart Mill and William Whewell and its relevance to the novel is Michael York Mason, '*Middlemarch* and Science: Problems of Life and Mind', *Review of English Studies*, 22 (1971), 151–69.

Elizabeth Deeds Ermarth, George Eliot and the World as Language

1 Elizabeth Deeds Ermarth, *Realism and Consensus in the English Novel* (Princeton: Princeton University Press, 1983).

2 *Essays of George Eliot*, ed. by Thomas Pinney (New York: Columbia University Press, 1963), p. 156.

3 George Eliot, *Daniel Deronda* (1876), ed. by Barbara Hardy (Harmondsworth: Penguin Books, 1967). All references are to this edition.

4 Lionel Robbins, *The Economic Basis of Class Conflict and other Essays in Political Economy* (London: Macmillan, 1939), p. viii.

5 Jean-François Lyotard, *The Differend: Phrases in Dispute*, trans. by George Van den Abbecle (Minneapolis: University of Minnesota Press, 1983), p. xi.

Richard C. Carpenter, The Mirror and the Sword: Imagery in *Far from the Madding Crowd*

1 Lionel Johnson, *The Art of Thomas Hardy* (London, 1894); Douglas Brown, *Thomas Hardy* (London, 1954).

Judith Bryant Wittenberg, Angles of Vision and Questions of Gender in *Far from the Madding Crowd*

1 Katharine Rogers, 'Women in Thomas Hardy,' *Centennial Review*, 19 (1975), 249–58.

2 In E. H. Gombrich, *Art and Illusion* (New York: Bollingen, 1965), and Rudolph Arnheim, *Art and Visual Perception* (Berkeley: University of California Press, 1954).

3 See Rosemary Sumner, *Thomas Hardy: Psychological Novelist* (New York: St. Martin's, 1981).

4 *The Standard Edition of the Complete Works of Sigmund Freud*, trans. James Strachey (London: Hogarth, 1953), VII. p. 156.

5 See, for example, Sandor Ferenczi, 'On Eye Symbolism,' in *First Contributions to Psychoanalysis*, trans. Ernest Jones (London: Hogarth, 1952), pp. 270–6.

6 See Otto Fenichel, *The Psychoanalytic Theory of Neurosis* (New York: Norton, 1945), pp. 71–2, 92, 345–9; Otto Fenichel, 'The Scoptophilic Instinct and Identification,' *Collected Papers*, First Series (New York: Norton, 1953); David W. Allen, *The Fear of Looking* (Charlottesville: University of Virginia Press, 1974).

7 The spectatorial quality of Hardy's narrator has been commented on by, for example, J. Hillis Miller, *Thomas Hardy: Distance and Desire* (Cambridge: Belknap Press of Harvard University Press, 1970), pp. xii, 7; and David Lodge, 'Thomas Hardy and Cinematographic Form,' *Novel, 7* (1974), 250.

8 Jacques Lacan, 'The Mirror Stage as Formative of the Function of the I as Revealed in Psychoanalytic Experience,' *Écrits*, trans. Alan Sheridan (New York: Norton, 1977), pp. 1–7; Jean-Paul Sartre, *Being and Nothingness*, trans. Hazel Barnes (New York: Washington Square Press, 1966), p. 310.

9 W. R. Greg, 'Why Are Women Redundant?', *National Review*. (14 April 1862), 434–60.

10 See Richard Carpenter. 'The Mirror and the Sword: Imagery in *Far from the Madding Crowd*,' *Nineteenth Century Fiction*, 18 (1964), 331–45.

11 *The Personal Notebooks of Thomas Hardy*, ed. Richard H. Taylor (London: Macmillan, 1978), p. 14.

Irving Howe, The Genius of *Germinal*

1 Henry James, 'Zola' (1903), in *Selected Literary Criticism* (ed. Shapira, 1964).

Henri Mitterand, Ideology and Myth: *Germinal* and the Fantasies of Revolt

1 [Editor's note: Émile Zole, *Germinal*, trans. Havelock Ellis (New York: Dutton, 1951), 50–51: original date of this translation: 1894.]

2 [*Ibid.*, p. 368.]

Tony Tanner, Fetishism in Flaubert's *Madame Bovary*

1 Money also can *transform* anything and everything, as Marx noted: thus, to give only one quotation:

> Money is the universal means and power, exterior to man, not issuing from man as man or from human society as society, to turn imagination into reality and reality into mere imagination. Similarly it turns real human and natural faculties into mere abstract representations and thus imperfections and painful imaginings, while on the other hand it turns the real imperfections and imaginings, the really powerless faculties that exist only in the imagination of the individual, into real faculties and powers. This description alone suffices to make money the universal inversion of individualities that turns them into their opposites and gives them qualities at variance with their own. As this perverting power, money then appears as the enemy of man and social bonds that pretend to self-subsistence. It changes fidelity into infidelity, love into hate, hate into love, virtue into vice, vice into virtue, slave into master, master into slave, stupidity into intelligence, and intelligence into stupidity.
>
> Since money is the existing and self-affirming concept of value and confounds and exchanges all things, it is the universal confusion and exchange of all things, the inverted world, the confusion and exchange of all natural and human qualities.
>
> ('On Money': *The Early Texts* in Karl Marx, *Selected Writings*, ed. David McLellan [Oxford: Oxford University Press, 1977] pp. 110–11)

This whole description of the 'confusion and exchange of all natural and human qualities' is very appropriate to the world of Flaubert's novel, for as Emma experiences it, it is indeed an 'inverted world,' and the perverse power of money is made terribly clear.

2 It is also appropriate here to refer to Marx's writing on 'The Fetishism of Commodities' (in *Capital*, volume one); indeed, it could be argued that there are possible and plausible relations between the fetishism described by Freud (concentrating on man's mystified 'relation' to women) and that described by Marx (concentrating on man's mystified relation to his products), both emerging from the bourgeois-capitalist society that both men studied. I will quote one passage from Marx, noting that the mysteriousness of commodities was also clearly visible to Flaubert, who could see things relating to each other more purposefully than – and instead of – people.

> A commodity is therefore a mysterious thing, simply because in it the social character of men's labour appears to them as an objective character stamped upon the product of that labour; because the

relation of the producers to the sum total of their own labour is presented to them as a social relation, existing not between themselves, but between the products of their labour. This is the reason why the products of labour become commodities, social things whose qualities are at the same time perceptible and imperceptible by the senses . . . There is a physical relation between physical things. But it is different with commodities. There, the existence of the things *qua* commodities, and the value relation between the products of labour which stamps them as commodities, have absolutely no connection with their physical properties and with the material relations arising therefrom. There is a definite social relation between men, that assumes, in their eyes, the fantastic form of a relation between things. In order, therefore, to find an analogy, we must have recourse to the mist-enveloped regions of the religious world. In that world the productions of the human brain appear as independent beings endowed with life, and entering into relation both with one another and the human race. So it is in the world of commodities with the products of men's hands. This I call the Fetishism which attaches itself to the products of labour, so soon as they are produced as commodities, and which is therefore inseparable from the production of commodities.

From Marx, *Selected Writings*, ed. David McLellan (Oxford: Oxford University Press, 1977), p. 436.

Elisabeth Bronfen, Over Her Dead Body: *Madame Bovary*

1 See also N. Shor, "For a Restricted Thematics", in *Breaking the Chain*, New York, Columbia University Press, 1985, pp. 3–28, who argues that Emma's ambitions to be a writer focus on her desire to transform the texts she has read into lived experience as well as in her choice of a lover as initiator and receiver of those letters that will make her the author of an epistolary novel. She argues that Emma's suicide is a form of authorship because writing comes to be equated with becoming the inanimate shadow of the text itself, writing as absence of the self even as suicide generates texts. Like Clarissa, Emma's fatal passion is for reading and scribbling letters, forbidden by her mother-in-law as the source of all misfortune.

2 See T. Tanner, *Adultery and the Novel*, Baltimore, Johns Hopkins University Press, 1979, who argues that Emma's story can be read as a long process of disintegration based on the loss of an ability to distinguish image and model, a confusion of the literal and the figural, of reality and literature.

3 See H. Michie's discussion of cliché as dead metaphor, following the

language philosopher Donald Davidson, *The Flesh Made Word*, Oxford, Oxford University Press 1986.

4 Having pricked her finger on one of the wires, she burns this bouquet just before leaving Tostes for Rouen, a gesture in which she destroys the object at which her first conjunction of death and marriage took place, as a triumph over the mortification this marriage has come to mean.

5 See M. Vovelle, *La Mort et l'Occident, de 1300 à nos jours*, Paris, Gullimard, 1983.

Jenny Bourne Taylor, Collins as a Sensation Novelist

1 (1865) 'Sensation novelists: Miss Braddon', *North British Review* 4, p. 204. For a discussion of the Minerva Press, see J.M.S. Tomkins (1932) *The Popular Novel in England 1770–1800*, London, pp. 243–95.

2 (1860) 'Novels of the day: their writers and readers', *Fraser's Magazine* 62 (August 1860), p. 210.

3 (1853) 'The progress of fiction as an art', *Westminster Review* 60 (October 1853), p. 358.

4 For a full analysis of the development of this mode, and the argument that it should be clearly distinguished from Gothic romance as it uses different techniques and has distinct epistemological origins, see Peter Denman (1981) 'The supernatural referent: the presence and effect of supernatural terror in English fiction in the mid nineteenth century' (unpublished Ph.D. dissertation, University of Keele), especially pp. 142–60 on the *Blackwood*'s stories. In contrast, in 'The demon in the house, or the domestication of gothic in the novels of Wilkie Collins' Reierstad develops the argument that Collins's fiction transforms and adapts Gothic conventions to explore sexual and modal ambiguity; his study includes an interesting discussion of Collins's early novella, *Mr Wray's Cash Box, or The Mask and the Mystery* (1852). On the formal links between different forms of 'Gothic' writing, see Eve Kosofsky Sedgwick (1986) *The Coherence of Gothic Conventions*, 2nd edn, London.

5 George Eliot (unsigned, 1856) 'Arts and belles lettres', *Westminster Review* 9 (April 1856), p. 640.

6 (1861) 'The enigma novel', *Spectator*, 28 December 1861, p. 1428.

D. A. Miller, *Cage aux Folles*: Sensation and Gender in Wilkie Collins's *The Woman in White*

1 Page numbers refer to the World's Classics edition of *The Woman in White* (Oxford: Oxford University Press, 1996).

2 Mrs [Margaret] Oliphant, 'Sensation Novels,' *Blackwood's Magazine* (May

1862, xci), reprinted in Norman Page, ed., *Wilkie Collins: The Critical Heritage*, (London, Routledge and Kegan Paul, 1974), pp. 119 and 118.

3 For example, Walter, the master narrator who solicits the others' narratives and organizes them into a whole, speaks of Laura to the reader: 'Think of her as you thought of the first woman who quickened the pulses within you' (50). The same identification is also sustained implicitly, as in the equation between the reader and a judge (5).

4 See Jeffrey Weeks, *Coming Out: Homosexual Politics in Britain, from the Nineteenth Century to the Present* (London, Quartet Books, 1977), pp. 26–7.

Elisabeth Bronfen, Over Her Dead Body: *The Woman in White*

1 Page numbers refer to the World's Classics edition of *The Woman in White* (Oxford: Oxford University Press, 1996).

2 D. A. Miller, *The Novel and the Police*, Berkeley, University of California Press, 1988, argues that this scene is the novel's 'primal scene which it obsessively repeats and remembers . . . as though this were the trauma it needed to work through,' p. 152. He emphasizes that the protagonist is nervous about the possibility of being contaminated by virtue of the unknown woman's touch, whereas I will argue that this touch elicits an uncanny desire for and anxiety about death.

3 J.-P. Vernant, *La mont dans les yeux*, Paris, Hachette, 1988, argues that the gravestone holds the place of the deceased as a double, incarnating its life in the beyond. It marks a clear opposition between the world of the living and the world of the dead. As sign of an absence, it signifies that death reveals itself precisely as something which is not of this world. Though this double marks the site where the dead are present in the world of the living or the living project themselves on to the universe of the dead, it makes the invisible visible even as it reveals that death belongs to an inaccessible mysterious realm beyond, fundamentally Other.

Eugenia C. DeLamotte, Gothic Conventions in *The Portrait of a Lady*

1 As is Antonia's case in *The Monk*.

2 As in the case of Agnes (*The Monk*), Ellena (*The Italian*), and numerous others.

3 As in *A Sicilian Romance*, in which the villainness poisons the villain and stabs herself; or in *The Italian*, in which Schedoni poisons both Nicola and himself.

4 As in *The Italian* and *A Sicilian Romance*.

5 About *The Wings of the Dove*, William wrote, 'You've reversed every

traditional canon of story-telling (especially the fundamental one of "telling" the story, which you carefully avoid) . . . ' (William James to Henry James, October 25, 1902).

6 An ingenious attempt to attribute the villainy to Mrs. Bread reveals little about Mrs. Bread but much about James's elusiveness even on the simplest level of plot. Compare the opportunities James gives us for wondering whether Milly Theale was really ill.

7 For two other perspectives on the Gothicism of *The Portrait of a Lady*, see Nettels and Banta, both of whom read the whole plot as in some sense Gothic and discuss the Gothic metaphors in the scene of the midnight vigil: Martha Banta, Henry James and the Occult (Bloomington: Indiana University Press, 1972); Elsa Nettels, James and Conrad (Athens: University of Georgia Press, 1977).

Stephen D. Arata, The Occidental Tourist: *Dracula* and the Anxiety of Reverse Colonization

1 Joseph Bierman, 'The Genesis and Dating of *Dracula* from Bram Stoker's Working Notes,' *Notes and Queries* 24 (1977), 39–41. For a brief description of Stoker's manuscripts and notes for *Dracula*, including a 'List of Sources' that Stoker drew up, see Phyllis Roth, *Bram Stoker* (Boston: Twayne, 1982), pp. 145–146. Stoker gleaned his version of Carpathian history and culture entirely from travel narratives, guidebooks, and various works on Eastern European superstitions, legends, and folktales. Daniel Farson, one of Stoker's biographers, mentions his 'genius for research' (*The Man Who Wrote Dracula: A Biography of Bram Stoker* [London: Michael Joseph, 1975], p. 148). Stoker's debt to Le Fanu is most immediately evident in a chapter deleted from *Dracula*, in which Harker, travelling to Castle Dracula, discovers the mausoleum of a 'Countess Dolingen of Gratz in Styria.' The chapter was later reprinted separately as 'Dracula's Guest.' See *The Bram Stoker Bedside Companion: Ten Stories by the Author of 'Dracula,'* ed. Charles Osborne (New York: Taplinger, 1973).

2 I have based my observations on the standard Victorian and Edwardian works in English on the region, which include John Paget, *Hungary and Transylvania* (London: Murray, 1855); James O. Noyes, *Roumania* (New York: Rudd & Carlton, 1857); Charles Boner, *Transylvania: its Products and Its People* (London: Longmans, 1865); Andrew W. Crosse, *Round About the Carpathians* (Edinburgh and London: William Blackwood and Sons, 1878); C. Johnson, *On the Track of the Crescent* (London: Hurst & Blackelt, 1885); M. Edith Durham, *The Burden of the Balkans* (London: Edward Arnold, 1905); Jean Victor Bales, *Our Allies and Enemies in the Near East* (New York: E. P. Dutton & Co., n.d.); and especially Emily Gerard, *The Land Beyond*

the Forest: Facts, Figures, and Fancies from Transylvania, 2 vols. (Edinburgh and London: William Blackwood and Sons, 1888).

3 Several critics have, correctly I think, placed Dracula in the tradition of aristocratic rakes like Richardson's Lovelace, who in turn have their roots in the medieval lord with his demands for the *droit de seigneur*. This view can obscure Stoker's emphasis on Dracula's military, rather than just his sexual, prowess. In addition to Bentley, Fry, and Hatlen, *see* Judith Weissman, 'Women as Vampires: *Dracula* as a Victorian Novel,' *Midwest Quarterly* 18 (1977), 392–405. It is also possible to read *Dracula* as a bourgeois fantasy of aristocratic power and privilege; like the hereditary nobleman, Dracula is associated most closely with land (he must stay in contact with his native soil to survive), wealth (which he literally digs out of the land on the night of Harker's arrival in Transylvania), family (this name is transmitted through generations without the line being interrupted), and of course blood (which in turn is connected with the other three; remember, for instance, that when Harker cuts Dracula with his knife, he 'bleeds' a 'stream of gold' coins (ch. 23)). For the middle-class Victorian audience, the vision of aristocratic puissance embodied by Dracula would have been deeply attractive, especially given the ineffectuality of the novel's only English aristocrat, Lord Godalming.

4 Gerard, I. 304–305. Scholars have long recognized Stoker's reliance on Gerard. See Roth, *Bram Stoker*, pp. 13–14, and Leonard Wolf, *The Annotated Dracula* (New York; Clark & Potter, 1975), pp. xiii–xiv and references in his annotations throughout.

5 A full discussion of the gender issues raised by *Dracula* is outside the scope of this. Many critics have discussed the thinly disguised fear of women evident in the novel. In addition to Craft, Demetrakapoulous, Fry, Griffin, Roth, and Weissman, see Alan Johnson, ' "Dual Life": The Status of Women in Stoker's *Dracula*,' *Tennessee Studies in Literature* (1984), 20–39.

6 See L. P. Curtis, *Anglo-Saxons and Cells: A Study of Anti-Irish Prejudice in Victorian England* (Bridgeport, CT: Bridgeport University Press, 1968).

7 See Edward Said, *Orientalism* (New York: Vintage, 1979).

Phyllis A. Roth, Suddenly Sexual Women in Bram Stoker's *Dracula*

1 Royce MacGillwray, '*Dracula*: Bram Stoker's Spoiled Masterpiece,' *Queen's Quarterly*, LXXIX, 518.

2 See Norman N. Holland, *The Dynamics of Literary Response* (New York: W. W. Norton & Co., 1975).

3 Maurice Richardson, 'The Psychoanalysis of Ghost Stories,' *Twentieth Century*, CLXVT (December 1959), 427.

4 *Victorian Newsletter*, XLII.

5 See Sally Ledger, *The New Woman: Fiction and Feminism at the Fin De Siècle* (Manchester: Manchester University Press, 1997).

6 While it is not my concern in this paper to deal biographically with *Dracula*, Harry Ludlam's biography (a book which is admittedly anti-psychological in orientation despite its provocative title, A *Biography of Dracula: The Life Story of Bram Stoker*) includes some suggestive comments about Bram Stoker's relationship with his mother. Ludlam remarks on an ambivalence toward women on the part of Charlotte Stoker, who, on the one hand, decried the situation of poor Irish girls in the workhouse which was 'the very hot-bed of vice' and advocated respectability through emigration for the girls and, on the other, 'declared often that she "did not care tuppence" for her daughters.' Charlotte told her son Irish folk tales of banshee horrors and a true story of 'the horrors she had suffered as a child in Sligo during the great cholera outbreak that claimed many thousands of victims in Ireland alone and which provoked the most dreadful cruelties' (New York: The Fireside Press, 1962, p. 14). I cannot help but wonder how old Stoker was when his mother discussed these matter with him. Certainly, they made a vivid impression, for later, Charlotte wrote her story down and Bram based his own 'The Invisible Giant' on his mother's tale of the cholera epidemic in Sligo.

7 Richardson, p. 419.

8 C. F. Bentley, 'The Monster in the Bedroom: Sexual Symbolism in Bram Stoker's *Dracula*,' *Literature and Psychology*, XXII (1972), 29.

9 Joseph S. Bierman, '*Dracula*: Prolonged Childhood Illness and the Oral Triad,' *American Image*, XXIX, 194.

10 Bentley, p. 27.

11 See Tsvetan Todorov, *The Fantastic*, trans. Richard Howard (Cleveland: Case Western Reserve, 1973), pp. 136–39.

12 Richardson, p. 427.

13 MacGillwray, p. 522.

14 Richardson, p. 428. The Oedipal fantasy of the destruction of the father is reinforced by a number of additional, and actually gratuitous, paternal deaths in the novel. See also MacGillwray, p. 523.

15 Richardson, p. 428.

16 See, for instance, Richardson, p. 12.

17 Richard Wasson, 'The Politics of *Dracula*,' *English Literature in Translation*, IX, pp. 24–27.

18 Freud, *Totem and Taboo*, trans. James Strachey, in *The Standard Edition of the Complete Psychological Works of Sigmund Freud*, Vol XIII (1913–1914) (London Hogarth Press, 1962), 60–63.

19 Wasson, p. 26.

20 Freud, pp. 37ff.

21 Bentley, pp. 29–30; MacGillwray, p. 522.

22 Bentley, p. 30.

23 Bierman, p. 194. Bierman's analysis is concerned to demonstrate that '*Dracula* mirrors Stoker's early childhood . . . ,' and is a highly speculative but fascinating study. The emphasis is on Stoker's rivalry with his brothers but it provides, albeit indirectly, further evidence of hostility toward the rejecting mother.

24 Ludlam cites one of the actors in the original stage production of *Dracula* as indicating that the adaptation was so successful that 'Disturbances in the circle or stalls as people felt faint and had to be taken out were not uncommon – and they were perfectly genuine, not a publicity stunt. Strangely enough, they were generally men.' (Ludlam, 1.165.).

25 See, for instance, Wolfgang Lederer, M.D., *The Fear of Women* (New York: Harcourt Brace Jovanovich Inc., 1968), especially the chapter entitled, 'A Snapping of Teeth.'

26 Otto Rank, *The Trauma of Birth* (New York: Harper & Row, 1973), p. 73.

27 When discussing this paper with a class, two of my students argued that Dracula is not, in fact, destroyed at the novel's conclusion. They maintained that his last look is one of triumph and that his heart is not staked but pierced by a mere bowie knife. Their suggestion that, at least, the men do not follow the elaborate procedures to insure the destruction of Dracula that they religiously observe with regard to that of the women is certainly of value here, whether or not one agrees that Dracula still stalks the land. My thanks to Lucinda Donnelly and Barbara Kotacka for these observations.

Helen Taylor, Gender, Race and Region in the Writings of Grace King, Ruth McEnery Stuart and Kate Chopin

1 The history of southern women is not the only lacuna in southern historiography. Although there have been historiographical controversies centering on the quarter-century following the Civil War, as late as 1980 the Reconstruction scholar John Hope Franklin deplored the absence of a considered overview of the period and the lack of new scholarship that would fill the many gaps. He argues that, of all periods in American history, Reconstruction arouses most passionate feelings, and that the 'objective' scholarship he seems to believe possible has been hampered by a legacy of sectional bitterness, racial animosity, and bigotry, together with conflicting political analyses of a number of issues, especially abolition. See John Hope Franklin, 'Mirror for Americans: A Century of Reconstruction History,' *American Historical Review*, LXXXV (February, 1980), 1–14. The absence of authoritative accounts of the period makes a literary scholar's work doubly difficult.

2 The following information is summarized from C. Vann Woodward, *Origins of the New South, 1877–1913* (Baton Rouge, 1951); John D. Winters, *The Civil War in Louisiana* (Baton Rouge, 1963); William Ivy Hair, *Bourbonism and Agrarian Protest: Louisiana Politics, 1877–1900* (Baton Rouge, 1969): Joe Gray Taylor, *Louisiana Reconstructed, 1863–1877* (Baton Rouge, 1974); Mark T. Carleton, Perry H. Howard, and Joseph B. Parker (eds.), *Readings in Louisiana Politics* (Baton Rouge, 1975), Bennett H. Wall (ed.), *Louisiana: A History* (Arlington Heights, Ill., 1984).

3 Edward King, *The Great South*, ed. W. Magruder Drake and Robert R. Jones (Baton Rouge, 1972), 17; Grace King, *Memories of a Southern Woman of Letters* (New York, 1932), 85.

4 John Hope Franklin, *Reconstruction After the Civil War* (Chicago, 1961), 219.

5 John W. Blassingame, *Black New Orleans, 1860–1880* (Chicago, 1973), 201.

6 Ruth McEnery Stuart's story, *Napoleon Jackson* features this group's activities.

7 See H. Oscar Lestage. Jr., 'The White League in Louisiana and Its Participation in Reconstruction Riots,' *Louisiana Historical Quarterly*, XVIII (July, 1935); Walter Prichard (ed.), 'The Origin and Activities of the "White League" in New Orleans (Reminiscences of a Participant in the Movement),' *Louisiana Historical Quarterly*, XXIII (April, 1940). Both articles were read in reprinted monographs, so pagination was different from the originals. Also, see Richard Hodstadter and Michael Wallace (eds.), *American Violence: A Documentary History* (New York, 1971), 101–105; Blassingame, *Black New Orleans*, 204.

Anne Goodwyn Jones, The Woman Writer in the South

1 Belle Kearney, *A Slaveholder's Daughter* (1900; Reprint. New York: Negro Universities Press, 1969), p. 3.

2 Mary Boykin Chesnut, *A Diary from Dixie*, ed. Ben Ames Williams (Boston: Houghton Mifflin, 1949), 186.

3 Bell Irvin Wiley, *Confederate Women* (Westport, Conn.: Greenwood Press, 1975), 174.

4 John Carl Ruoff, 'Southern Womanhood, 1865–1920: An Intellectual and Cultural Study', Ph. D. Dissertation, University of Illinois, 1976, pp. 26–7.

5 Anne Firor Scott, The Southern Lady: from Pedestal to Politics, 1830–1930 (Chicago: University of Chicago Press, 1970), p. 38.

6 *Ibid.*, 37.

7 Chesnut, *Diary from Dixie*, 21–22. Chesnut's passionate writing here apparently evoked the following intriguing image of woman writing, *i.e.*, creating rather than absorbing: 'I think this journal will be disadvantageous

for me, for I spend my time now like a spider spinning my own entrails, instead of reading as my habit was in all spare moments' (p. 22).

8 Amory Dwight Mayo, *Southern Women in the Recent Educational Movement in the South*, ed. Dan T. Carter and Amy Friedlander (1892; reprint ed., Baton Rouge: Louisiana State University Press, 1978), 65.

9 Quoted in Scott, *The Southern Lady*, 64.

10 Ruoff, 'Southern Womanhood,' 29.

11 Eudora Ramsay Richardson, 'The Case of the Women's Colleges in the South,' *South Atlantic Quarterly*, XXIX (April, 1930), 126–39.

12 Caroline E. Merrick, *Old Times in Dixie Land: A Southern Matron's Memories* (New York: Grafton Press, 1901), 16.

13 Anne Firor Scott, 'Women's Perspective on the Patriarchy in the 1850s,' *Journal of American History*, LXI (June, 1974), 59.

14 Wiley, *Confederate Women*, 156.

15 Scott, 'Women, Religion, and Social Change in the South, 1830–1930.' In Religion and the Solid South, ed. Samuel S. Hill, Jr (Nashville: Abingdon Press, 1972), p. 100.

16 Irving H. Bartlett and C. Glenn Cambor, 'The History and Psychodynamics of Southern Womanhood,' *Women's Studies*, II (1974), 20, 19, 11.

Elizabeth Ammons, Women of Color in *The Awakening*

1 In her 'People of Color in Louisiana', *Journal of Negro History 1* (October 1916), Alice Dunbar-Nelson writes: The *gens de couleur*, colored people, were always a class apart, separated from and superior to the Negroes, ennobled were it only by one drop of white blood in their veins. The caste seems to have existed from the first introduction of slaves. To the whites, all Africans who were not of pure blood were *gens de couleur*. Among themselves, however, there were jealous and fiercely-guarded distinctions: 'griffes, briques, mulattoes, quadroons, octorooms, each term meaning one degree's further transfiguration toward the Caucasian standard of physical perfection' (Grace King, *New Orleans, the Place and the People During the Ancien Regime* [New York, 1895] 333).

2 Discussion of the treatment of race in Chopin's work can be found in P. Seyersted, *Kate Chopin* (Baton Rouge: Louisiana State University Press, 1969), and in Anne Goodwyn Jones's excellent chapter on Chopin in *Tomorrow is Another Day: The Woman Writer in the South*, 1859–1936 (Baton Rouge: Louisiana State University Press, 1981), pp. 135–54.

3 Toni Morrison, 'Unspeakable Things Unspoken: The Afro-American Presence in American Literature,' *Michigan Quarterly Review*, 28 (Winter 1989), 12.

4 *Pittsburgh Leader* (8July 1899), 6.

Bert Bender, The Teeth of Desire: *The Awakening* and *The Descent of Man*

1 In his 1894 portrait of Chopin, William Schuyler reported that 'the subjects which . . . attracted her were almost entirely scientific, the departments of Biology and Anthropology having a special interest for her. The works of Darwin, Huxley, and Spencer were her daily companions; for the study of the human species . . . has always been her constant delight' (in *A Kate Chopin Miscellany*, ed. Per Seyersted [Natchitoches, La.: Northwestern State Univ. Press, 1979], p. 117). But no critic to date has looked closely at Chopin's response to Darwin.

2 *The Descent of Man and Selection in Relation to Sex*, 2 vols. (1871; rpt. Princeton: Princeton Univ. Press, 1981), II, 404. Unless otherwise noted, further references to *The Descent* are from this edition and this text, and are cited parenthetically by volume and page.

3 *The Complete Works of Kate Chopin*, 2 vols (Baton Rouge: Louisiana State University Press, 1969) II, 872. Subsequent references to *At Fault* will be to this text, cited parenthetically by page. In subsequent references to *The Awakening*, however – because there are now so many reliable editions of that book – I cite chapter numbers only. Also, since the two stories I discuss here ('A Respectable Woman,' and 'The Story of an Hour') are so short and so widely collected, I have not cited page numbers.

4 *The Descent of Man*, I, 259; for Darwin's understanding of the female's inferiority, see, for example, his remark that 'man is more powerful in body and mind than woman' (II, 371). Cynthia Eagle Russett's *Sexual Science: The Victorian Construction of Womanhood* (Cambridge: Harvard Univ. Press, 1989) is an indispensable guide to the implications of Darwinian thought for the Victorian woman.

5 *The Descent of Man*, II, 371. Among most animals (birds, especially), in Darwin's analysis, the female selects the victorious male or the most attractive one – i.e., the most colorful or highly ornamented one.

6 'Nature's Courtship Plot in Darwin and Ellis,' *Yale Journal of Criticism*, 2 (1989), 36–37.

7 Sitting under a live oak alone with Mrs. Baroda, the Barodas' friend, Gouvernail, murmurs these lines from 'Song of Myself': 'Night of south winds – night of the large few stars! Still nodding night': these lines are contained in Whitman's sentence, 'Press close bare bosom'd night . . . mad naked summer night,' in section 21, which ends, 'O unspeakable passionate love.'

8 Thomas Bonner, Jr., *The Kate Chopin Companion, with Chopin's Translations from French Fiction* (New York: Greenwood, 1988), pp. 179, 181. Further references to Chopin's translations of Maupassant are cited parenthetically by page from this text.

9 The distinctions I suggest here in my remarks about Aphrodite and the 'self and society' refer to two of the very best essays on *The Awakening* – Sandra M. Gilbert's 'The Second Coming of Aphrodite: Kate Chopin's Fantasy of Desire,' *Kenyon Review*, 5 (1983), 42–56; and Nina Baym's 'Introduction' to *The Awakening and Selected Stories* (New York: Random House, 1981), p. xxxiv.

10 *Kate Chopin*, ed. Harold Bloom (New York: Chelsea House, 1987), pp. 3, 2, 1.

11 Ch. 30; in ch. 16 Edna hears that Robert had once 'thrashed' Victor for thinking 'he had some sort of claim upon' Mariequita. In ch. 39 Mariequita senses that Victor is 'in love with Mrs. Pontellier'; and Victor, jealous of one of Mariequita's lovers, threatens 'to hammer his head into a jelly.'

12 *The Expression of Emotions in Man and Animals* (1872; rpt. New York: Appleton, 1924), p. 217.

13 *The Descent of Man and Selection in Relation to Sex*, 2nd ed. (New York: Wheeler, n.d.), pp. 40–41. In the second edition, Darwin added this new ch. 2; and Chopin's apparent reference to it is one of several suggestions in her work that her text was the second edition.

14 See, for example, Darwin's discussion of blushing in *The Expression of Emotions* (p. 334). Many of Chopin's characters blush or flush in ways that indicate their animal emotions.

15 The quoted passage (from Boitard and Corbié, 'Les Pigeons' [1824]) reads: 'Quand une femelle éprouve de l'antipathie pour un mâle avec lequel on veut l'accoupler, malgré tous les feux de l'amour, malgré l'alpiste et le chènevis dont on la nourrit pour augmenter son ardeur, malgré un emprisonnement de six mois et méme d'un an, elle refuse constamment ses caresses; les avances empressées, les agaceries, les tournoiemens, les tendres roucoulemens, rien ne peut lui plaire ni l'émouvoir; gonflée, boudeuse, blottie dans un coin de sa prison, elle n'en sort que pour boire et manger, ou pour repousser avec une espèce de rage des caresses devenues trop pressantes' (II, 118–119).

Robert Hampson, Conrad and the Idea of Empire

1 This article originally appeared in *L'Epoque Conradienne* (Limoges, 1989), 9–22.

2 Joseph Conrad, *Heart of Darkness*, in *Youth – A Narrative, and Two Other Stories*, 50–51. All references are to the Uniform Edition (London: J.M. Dent & Sons, 1923), which will be cited in the text as HD.

3 Conrad to William Blackwood, 31 December 1898. 'The Heart of Darkness' was serialised in *Blackwood's Magazine* from February to April 1899.

4 In the same issue, there appeared an article by Robert C. Witt, 'An

Experiment in Colonisation', which described a visit to the German colony in East Africa and recorded how, before disembarking, German beer 'flowed as it flows in the Hofbrau at Munich on a hot summer's day' (1898:789). Was this perhaps the source for Marlow's reference to the East Coast colony 'where the jolly pioneers of progress drink the jolly lager beer' (HD 55)?

5 For example, on 30 July 1898, Conrad wrote to R.B. Conninghame Graham about the contents of the August issue of *Blackwood's Magazine*. His comments on *Blackwood's* treatment of the Spanish-American war imply attentive reading of the magazine (Karl & Davies, Volume 2, 1986:80–81).

6 See Lillian Feder, 'Marlow's Descent into Hell' (1955:280, 292); W.B. Stein, 'The Heart of Darkness: A Bodhisattva Scenario' (1969–1970:39, 52); Peter Caracciolo, 'Buddhist Typologies in *Heart of Darkness* and *Victory*' (1989:67–91).

7 Cf. Benita Parry's account of the European fantasy of Africa: 'the sensational world of promiscuity, idolatry, satanic rites and human sacrifices unveiled in nineteenth-century travellers' tales' (1983:29).

8 See Hawthorn 1979:7–36.

9 This does not negate Parry's point that 'the blacks are not functional protagonists but figures in a landscape' (1983:33). The Africans are objects, never subjects, of European discourses. As Chinua Achebe observed: 'it is set in Africa and teems with Africans whose humanity is admitted in theory but totally undermined' by other aspects of the text (1980:113). One response to Achebe's criticism would be that *Heart of Darkness* engages with European representations of Africa rather than with Africa (as Benita Parry's analysis demonstrates). See also my '*Heart of Darkness* and "The Speech that Cannot be Silenced" ' (1990:15–32).

10 Marlow's words 'Light came out of the river since – you say Knights?' (HD: 49) clearly pick up the narrator's reference to Sir Francis Drake and Sir John Franklin and 'the great knights-errant of the sea' (HD 47) and, by doing so, reveal retrospectively that the passage was spoken aloud by the narrator to the company on board the *Nellie*.

11 As Parry observes, 'the antinomian categories are subjected to a radical rearrangement subverting Europe's customary imagery' (1983:22). But, where Parry sees Conrad in *Heart of Darkness* finally reinstating 'the view of two incompatible orders within a manichean universe' (1983:23), I will argue that the 'categories' are not merely subjected to 'a radical rearrangement' but are effectively undermined.

12 Bentley, in *Pioneering on the Congo* (1900), gives the missionaries' version of Stanley's subsequent requisitioning of their steamer, the *Peace*.

13 For 'power-knowledge', see Michel Foucault, *Discipline and Punish* (1982): 'there is no power relation without the correlative constitution of a

field of knowledge, nor any knowledge that does not presuppose and constitute at the same time power relations' (27).

14 Edward Jay followed Booth's lead by calling his description of one of London's worst slums ('the Old Nicholl' in Bethnal Green) *Life in Darkest London* (1891).

15 See also F.S. Schwarzbach, '"Terra Incognita" – An Image of the City in English Literature, 1820–1855', in Dodd (1983); and Patrick Brantlinger, 'Victorians and Africans: The Genealogy of the Myth of the Dark Continent' (1985).

16 Masterman was also a close friend of Ford Madox Ford.

17 See Philip & Juliana Muchricke, 'Maps in Literature,' (1974:320–328); and J.B. Harley, 'Maps, Knowledge and Power,' in Cosgrove & Daniels (1988:277–312).

Edward Said, Two Visions in *Heart of Darkness*

1 Salman Rushdie, 'Outside the Whale,' in *Imaginary Homelands: Essays and Criticism*, 1981–1991 (London: Viking/Granta, 1991), pp. 92, 101.

2 This is the message of Conor Cruise O'Brien's 'Why the Wailing Ought to Stop,' *The Observer*, June 3, 1984.

3 For Mackinder, see Neil Smith, *Uneven Development: Nature, Capital and the Production of Space* (Oxford: Blackwell, 1984), pp. 102–3. Conrad and triumphalist geography are at the heart of Felix Driver, 'Geography's Empire: Histories of Geographical Knowledge,' *Society and Space*, 1991.

4 Hannah Arendt, *The Origins of Totalitarianism* (1951; new ed., New York: Harcourt Brace Jovanovich, 1973), p. 215. See also Fredric Jameson, *The Political Unconscious: Narrative as a Socially Symbolic Act* (Ithaca: Cornell University Press, 1981), pp. 206–81.

References: Robert Hampson, Conrad and the Idea of Empire

Achebe, C. 1980. 'Viewpoint'. *Times Literary Supplement* 4010: 1 February.

Anon. 1898. 'Life and Death in the Niger Delta' *Blackwood's Magazine*. April, 451–60.

Bentley, W.H. 1900. *Pioneering on the Cango*. London: Religious Tract Society.

Booth, C. 1902. *Life and Labour of the People in London*. Volume I. First Series, London: Macmillan.

Booth, W. 1890. *In Darkest England and the Way Out*. Reprinted USA: Salvation Army Supplies and Purchasing Department.

Brantlinger, P. 1985. 'Victorians and Africans: The Genealogy of the Myth of the Dark Continent'. *Critical Inquiry* 12(1), 166–203.

Caracciolo, P. 1989. 'Buddhist Typologies in *Heart of Darkness* and *Victory*'. *The Conradian* 14(1/2), 67–91.

Conrad, J. 1923. *Heart of Darkness*, in *Youth – A Narrative, and Two Other Stories*. London: Dent.

Cosgrove, D. & Daniels, S. (eds) 1988. *The Iconography of Landscape*. Cambridge: Cambridge University Press.
Dodd, P. (ed) 1983. *The Art of Travel*. London: Frank Cass and Co.
Feder, I. 1955. 'Marlow's Descent into Hell'. *Nineteenth-Century Fiction* 9, 280–292.
Foucault, M. (1975) 1982. *Discipline and Punish*. Harmondsworth: Penguin.
Hampson, R. 1990. "*Heart of Darkness* and 'The Speech that Cannot be Silenced'". *English* 163. 15–32.
Hannay, D. 1898. 'The Case of Mr Doughty'. *Blackwood's Magazine*. June, 796–808.
Harley, J.B. 1988. 'Maps, Knowledge and Power'. In Cosgrove & Daniels 1988:277–312.
Hart, C. 1974. 'Wandering Rocks', in Hart & Hayman 1974:181–216.
Hart, C. & Hayman, D. (eds) 1974. *James Joyce's 'Ulysses'*. Berkeley & Los Angeles: University of California Press.
Hawthorn, J. 1979. *Joseph Conrad: Language and Fictional Self-Consciousness*. London: Edward Arnold.
Joyce, J. 1986. *Ulysses*. London: The Bodley Head.
Karl, F.R. & Davies, I. (eds) 1983–1990. *The Collected Letters of Joseph Conrad*, Volumes 1–4. Cambridge: Cambridge University Press.
Masterman, C.F.G. (ed) 1901. *The Heart of the Empire*. London: T. Fisher Unwin.
Muehricke, P. & J. 1974. 'Maps in Literature'. *The Geographical Review* 44(3), 320–338.
Parry, B. 1983. *Conrad and Imperialism*. London: Macmillan.
Richards, I.A. 1936. *The Philosophy of Rhetoric*. New York & London.
Schwarzbach, F.S. 1983. '"Terra Incognita": An Image of the City in English Literature, 1820 1855', in Dodd 1983.
Sherry, N. 1971. *Conrad's Western World*. Cambridge: Cambridge University Press.
Stanley, H.M. (1890) 1893. *In Darkest Africa*. London: Sampson, Low & Marston.
Stein, W.B. 1969, 1970. 'The Heart of Darkness: A Bodhisattva Scenario'. *Conradiana* II, 39–52.
Watts, C. 1977. *Conrad's* Heart of Darkness: *A Critical and Contextual Discussion*. Mursia: Milan International.
Webb, B. 1926. *My Apprenticeship*. London: Longmans, Green & Co.
Witt, R.C. 1898. 'An Experiment in Colonisation'. *Blackwood's Magazine*. June.
Woods, E. 1989. 'A Darkness Visible: Gissing, Masterman, and the Metaphors of Class, 1880–1914'. Unpublished D.Phil. Thesis. University of Sussex.

INDEX

Note: **emboldened** page numbers indicate quoted passages.